The Spaces of the Modern City

The Spaces
of the Modern City

*IMAGINARIES, POLITICS,
AND EVERYDAY LIFE*

EDITED BY
GYAN PRAKASH AND KEVIN M. KRUSE

PRINCETON UNIVERSITY PRESS

PRINCETON AND OXFORD

Published by Princeton University Press, 41 William Street,
Princeton, New Jersey 08540

In the United Kingdom: Princeton University Press, 3 Market Place,
Woodstock, Oxfordshire OX20 1SY

Library of Congress Cataloging-in-Publication Data

The spaces of the modern city : imaginaries, politics, and everyday life /
edited by Gyan Prakash and Kevin M. Kruse
p.   cm.
Includes bibliographical references and index.

ISBN 978-0-691-13339-3 (hardcover : alk. paper)
ISBN 978-0-691-13343-0 (pbk. : alk. paper)
1. Cities and towns—Case studies. 2. Sociology, Urban—Case studies.
I. Prakash, Gyan, 1952–. II. Kruse Kevin Michael, 1972–.
HT119.S653   2008
307.76 dc—22   2007021223

British Library Cataloging-in-Publication Data is available

This book has been composed in Aldus

Printed on acid-free paper. ∞

press.princeton.edu

Printed in the United States of America

1   3   5   7   9   10   8   6   4   2

❊ Contents ❊

CONTENTS

❋ *Illustrations* ❋

✳ *Preface* ✳

THIS VOLUME grew out of seminars and colloquia organized by the Shelby Cullom Davis Center for Historical Studies, Princeton University, under its program from 2003 to 2005 on "Cities: Space, Society, and History." The Center's interest in the theme was a response to new challenges in the historical understanding of the modern city posed by globalization and spatial transformations across the world effected under neoliberal capitalism. Instead of seeing the city as a bounded space, some urban theorists now speak about vast urban systems and the "placeless" spaces of shopping malls, airports, and global lifestyles. Others cite the fact that much of the current urban expansion concerns the developing world and involves a massive flow of rural migrants into the city to conjure up the specter of the "planet of slums," a world overrun by the teeming and undifferentiated multitude of the urban poor. Such representations require critical scrutiny, but they also suggest that we rethink the paradigmatic model of the modern city based on western Europe's culture of industrialization. We need to develop a global understanding of the historical experience of urban modernity even as we reexamine and learn from the writings of the European modernists of the early twentieth century.

Fortunately, such rethinking and reexamination can be witnessed in the literature of urban studies. Vibrant scholarship has transformed the field into an interdisciplinary venture with a global perspective. With a view to advance this scholarship, the Center conducted this two-year program to consider the history of the city as a physical and social space—not as an inert container for social, political, and economic processes, but as a historically produced space that shapes, and is shaped by, power, economy, culture, and society. The Center appointed visiting fellows and invited speakers from a range of disciplines and specialists in different areas. Papers and lectures encompassed analyses of social and political history; political economy; literature, art, and cinema; and urban planning and architecture. The discussions were always interdisciplinary and stimulating, and they spilled over from weekly seminars and lectures on Thursday afternoons into dinners and weekends and the following weeks' seminars.

We were lucky to have a fabulous group of visiting fellows who provided continuity from week to week and sustained a lively intellectual and social atmosphere. Unfortunately, we could not include all the fellows' papers because they either were already committed elsewhere or fell outside the thematic focus of this volume. In any case, even those whose papers are not included helped to sharpen and deepen the discussion that has gone into the conception of this book. We owe them gratitude. Thanks are also due to the regular participants in the seminar from history and other departments. These include our colleagues Michael Gordin and Helen Tilley, who heroically attended every seminar, every lecture, and added a great deal to the discussion. We would like to extend our appreciation as well to the Davis Center manager, Jennifer Houle, who cheerfully and efficiently handled the logistics of the program and this volume. We were fortunate to have Peter Dougherty's support in establishing the Davis Center's publication arrangements with Princeton University Press, and Brigitta van Rheinberg's enthusiastic editorial stewardship. We deeply appreciate the helpful and critical comments of the three anonymous reviewers of the manuscript. Sara Lerner dealt with the complications of multiple authors and images with humor and patience. Beth Gianfagna's expert and sensible approach made copyediting smooth and pleasant. We are thankful to our contributors who responded promptly and fully to editorial instructions and to suggestions for revisions. Ultimately, it is their contribution that has helped make this collection an important intervention in the debate over the city.

The volume is dedicated to Natalie Zemon Davis, who set a brilliant example of intellectual and human stewardship of the Davis Center.

Gyan Prakash
Kevin Kruse

The Spaces of the Modern City

* *Introduction* *

GYAN PRAKASH

IF MODERNITY IS A Faustian bargain to unleash human potential and subdue
nature to culture, then modern cities are its most forceful and enduring
expressions.[1] The breathless intensity and the awesome power of modern
life have made and remade cities across the world: London and Paris, Shanghai and Hong Kong, Tokyo and Mumbai, New York and Mexico City. The
great dramas of recent centuries—the triumph of industrialization and capitalism, the erection of powerful state apparatuses and the outbreaks of political insurrections, the exercise of colonial control and eruptions of anticolonial movements—were enacted on the stage of the modern cities. These
urban spaces have shaped, and were shaped by, race, class, and gender relations and exclusions. Modern urban life, lived on streets and in apartments
and slums, has produced new subjects, solidarities, and meanings. The cityscape—its streets and sidewalks, its public space, the ebb and flow of its
crowd, its infrastructure of transportation—has served as the setting for
dynamic encounters and experiences. A great deal of modern literature, art,
and cinema would be unthinkable without the modern city. In an important
sense, cities are the principal landscapes of modernity.

Nearly as old as the modern city is the critical attention from writers and
social commentators. One has to only think of the brilliant reflections of
the European urbanists of the early twentieth century: Georg Simmel on
the psychic space of the metropolis; Siegfried Kracauer on the mass forms
of everyday life, taste, and entertainment; and Walter Benjamin on the
dreamscape of commodities.[2] These writings continue to inform our understanding of the contemporary urban experience. But the recent spurt of urbanization questions the idea of the European metropolis, defined as a
bounded unit by modernist theory, as the paradigmatic modern city. As
globalization increasingly extends urban forms across the world and inte-
grates the existing cities into vast urbanized systems of communication,
transnational flows of finance, commodities, labor, images, and ideas, the
idea of the city as an organism, defined by an internally coherent civic life
and structured by clear relationships to the region, nation, and wider world,
appears obsolete. Urban theorists tell us that the city is dead. They suggest

that, in place of the clearly defined unity called *the city*, we live increasingly in the amorphous and expanding spaces of urban networks.

Even as recent change forces us to rethink the urban form, it is undeniable that we continue to speak of cities as specific spatial formations: London, New York, Mumbai, Hong Kong. Urban sprawl and the rise of vast urban networks connected by rapid transportation systems do not erase the idea of cities as particular places, each defined by its distinctive constellation of social space, history, and memory. It may be the case that the production of space—binding center and periphery, city and the countryside—has superseded the city, as Lefebvre suggests, but lived experience, as he himself also argues, is not subsumed by spatial practices.[3] Urban dwellers experience their globally situated and connected urban space as decidedly local lifeworlds, thick with specific experiences, practices, imaginations, and memories.

Written against the background of these two opposed representations, this volume represents an effort to rethink the history of urban modernity and urban change. This means, first, expanding the focus beyond Europe and North America to include the experiences of urban modernity in Asia, Africa, and Latin America. It entails approaching the historical experiences of modern urban forms and transformations as ineluctably global, specific, diverse, and divergent. Second, what unites the essays dealing with cities ranging across the world and discrepant historical moments is the concentrated focus on the city *as* a spatial form of social life and power relations, not just a site of society and politics. The contributors identify historical processes in the urban form itself. This does not only mean the structure and design of the built environment but also the entire architecture of urban life and representations; they regard urban forms *as* society, economy, culture, and politics. Third, its approach is interdisciplinary. The contributions range across several disciplines—sociology, history, art history, cinema, and cultural studies—and each essay treats different fields of knowledge. This is as it should be, for cities are composed of many fragments, each one requiring the examination of several dimensions of knowledge. Any attempt to provide a singular and totalizing map of the city can only impoverish the richness and multiplicity of the urban experience.

THE CITY AND THE URBAN

Urban studies is not a new field, but the past two decades have witnessed a noticeable "urban turn" in scholarship.[4] In disciplines ranging from anthropology to history, sociology to literature, and architecture to film and cultural studies, there is renewed interest in urbanism. This spurt of academic attention has occurred against the background of the rapidly quickening pace of urbanization. As early as 1970, Henri Lefebvre wrote about urbanization superseding industrialization as the global dynamic of capitalism.[5] Whatever one may think of his view about the supplanting of industrialization, there is no doubt that urbanization is a central force in the contemporary world. According to UN estimates, whereas 30 percent of the world population was urban in 1950, this proportion rose to 47 percent in 2000 and is expected to reach 60 percent by 2030.[6] Much of the developed world has been predominantly urban at least since the early twentieth century as a result of capitalist industrialization and colonial and imperial expansion. The recent spurt in urbanization, therefore, is concentrated in the developing regions of the world. Mexico City, Sao Paolo, and Mumbai are experiencing explosive growth, outstripping the populations of old cities such as London, Paris, and even New York. Breakneck expansion of manufacturing and striking economic growth animate rapid urbanization in some cases, as in China. But, in other cases, as in sub-Saharan Africa, the runaway growth of cities occurs in the context of economic stagnation, growing debt, and economic crisis, producing specters of political and social convulsions.

The spurt in urbanization is a matter not just of numbers but also of change in the urban form. Suburbanization and the proliferation of "edge" cities at highway interchanges encapsulate the transformation in the urban landscape in North America.[7] Paris no longer consists only of the city built by Baron Haussmann but also includes the towns connected to it through roadways, airports, and metro lines.[8] The megacities of the developing world, swollen with rural immigrants, are burgeoning with slums and squatter settlements, pointing to the increasing urbanization of poverty.[9] As the urban network extends to fill the spaces between the city and the countryside, one can no longer speak of a strict divide between the two. Increasingly, regional urban complexes and huge urban corridors have blurred the earlier city-hinterland distinctions. China, for example, now contains two immense urban networks, one extending from Hong Kong to Guangzhou on the Pearl River Delta, and the other spreading outward from Shanghai on the Yangtze River Delta. The emergence of such regional constellations has also meant a massive urbanization of the countryside.[10] These urban processes cannot be situated exclusively within national borders, for global movements of finance capital, people, ideas, and images traverse the cities. These movements across territories are not qualitatively equal—the migration of Mexi-

3

can laborers across the border to the United States and the circulation of Hollywood films across the globe are not the same—but globalization confounds the earlier center-periphery dichotomy.

Urban theorists contend that capitalist globalization has also overwhelmed the modernist city of the nineteenth and early twentieth centuries.[11] Classic political movements and ideologies nursed in the heyday of modernist cities have lost their appeal, and new informational networks and "pirate modernity" have marginalized old urban solidarities.[12] As globalization produces different kinds of legal regimes and citizens, and new hierarchies of cities and urban dwellers, it poses a new set of questions for citizenship, identity, and politics.[13] The nonlegal basis of urban existence and politics in the slums and squatter settlements of the global South mocks the classic ideal of the city as the space of civil society and political discourse.[14] Never realized in practice even in European cities, this ideal lies in ruins. The global processes and representations of contemporary urbanization have destroyed the halo of this modernist urbanism. Today, it is difficult to sustain the paradigmatic notion of modern cities as unified formations, securely located within their national borders, with clearly legible politics and society.

Paul Virilio had predicted the dissolution of the city by media and communication.[15] But it was left to Rem Koolhaas, the architect and urban theorist, to celebrate the death of the modernist city and hail the emergent urban form: the "Generic City." Writing in 1988 about the emergent urban forms, he emphasized a shift from the center to the periphery, fragmentation, and spontaneous processes, and described his research on the contemporary city as "a retro-active manifesto for the yet to be recognized beauty of the twentieth-century urban landscape."[16] He followed this up by directing a research program at the Harvard School of Design, called the "Project on the City," that aimed to understand the "the maelstrom of modernization" that was creating a "completely new urban substance."[17] The project has produced three jumbo volumes of text, photographs, maps, graphics, and statistics that chart the mutations of urban culture, the explosive urbanization in China's Pearl River Delta, and the global expansion of consumption.[18] Assemblages of different materials rather than conventional books, these volumes embody in their form the fragmented, patched-together, runaway urbanism that they seek to represent. There is no prior theory that drives this investigation, only the premise that the paradigmatic European city of the nineteenth and early twentieth centuries provides little understanding for the emergent form. Consisting of the endless repetition of certain simple structural modules, the Generic City, according to Koolhaas, has spread across continents.[19] "The definitive move away from the countryside, from agriculture, to the city is not a move to the city as we knew it: it is a move to the Generic City, the city so pervasive that it has come to the country."[20] Spreading and sprawling, the Generic City liberates the city from the captivity of the center, from the straitjacket of identity. It self-destructs and renews according to present needs and abilities. It is free from history. The Generic City is the post-city being prepared on the site of ex-city."[21]

There is no doubt that certain urban forms—shopping malls, entertainment zones, multiplex theaters, atriums, and airports and hotels that double as cities unto themselves—have become a common sight in cities across the world. But Koolhaas gets so caught up in the present's proclamation of its novelty and singularity that he fails to interrogate it. Consider, for example, the case of Shanghai, the paradigmatic example of China's transformation by capitalist modernization. With its gleaming skyscrapers on the Bund, the maze of highway overpasses and bridges, efficient underground transportation, and the proliferation of generic shopping malls, restaurants, and cafés, the city evokes the power of newness. Change appears weightless, free from the burden of history. To be sure, there is a historical preservation movement and a revival of interest in the Shanghai of the 1920s—focused on its Art Deco architecture, cosmopolitan literature and cultural artifacts, and the gangster world.[22] But this memory is selective; it skips over the city's imperial and communist history in order to draw a line of continuity between the cosmopolitan culture of "old Shanghai" and the global, contemporary city to suggest that the present is the reappearance of the past.[23] This ransacks the past to suit the present chimera of novelty and dynamism. Ackbar Abbas writes that Shanghai exists today as a remake, "a shot-by-shot reworking of a classic, with a different cast, addressed to a different audience, not 'Back to the Future' but 'Forward to the Past.' "[24] This remake glides over historical discontinuities and fuses the past and the present to create a single, spectacular image of Shanghai as a modern, global city. But cities have never been mere expressions of a singular logic or a dominant historical force—neither in the past nor in the present. To think of Paris as the embodiment of classic modernity, Los Angeles as the paradigmatic postmodern metropolis, and Shanghai as the typical expression of globalization is to simplify their complexity, smooth out their social and political contradictions. The excessive focus on "global cities" like New York, London, Tokyo, and Shanghai, and the ranking of cities according to their position on the scale of economic globalization also tends to flatten their urban processes and experiences and suggests that capital obliterates distinctions and functions without social and cultural differences.

Urban change is undeniable, but the historicist narrative of the rise and fall of the city is deeply flawed. Foucault wrote: "The great obsession of the nineteenth century was, as we know, history: with its themes of development and suspension, of crisis and cycle, themes of ever accumulating past."[25] Speaking this language of development, the discourse of the death of the city suppresses the spatiality of history.[26] The history of the modern city as a space of porosity, multiplicity, difference, division, and disruption is concealed when urban change is represented as the unfolding of one historical stage to another, from the bounded unity and identity of the city of industrial capitalism to the "placeless" and "generic city" of globalization— from modernity to postmodernity. We should remember that "placelessness," now attributed to postmodernity, was once identified with industrial modernity. Thus, Marx spoke of capitalism's forceful expansion across all borders and frontiers in its relentless drive to transform everything concrete into abstract measures of value: "all that is solid melts into air." The language of temporal succession forgets this history and gets caught up in the present's self-proclamation of its novelty and singularity.

The discourse of the demise of the city is also deeply elitist. Consider, for example, the sentiments expressed by Mr. Kapur, a character in Rohinton Mistry's novel, *Family Matters*, set in contemporary Mumbai. "Nothing is left now except to talk of graves, of worms and epitaphs," he says to his employee. "Let us sit upon these chairs and tell sad stories of the death of cities," he continues, grieving for the demise of his beloved Bombay. As he pronounces Bombay's death, he evokes its past life as a shining city on the sea, "a tropical Camelot, a golden place where races and religions lived in peace and amity."[27] The city appears under siege, imperiled by spatial mutations and occupation by the uncivil masses, a wasteland of broken modernist dreams of the elites. Bombay, one often hears elites say sorrowfully, is now Slumbay. Beatriz Sarlo identifies something similar in certain literary representations of Buenos Aires in the 1990s. There, too, "slumification" produces images of the multitude spreading from the periphery to the interior of the city. The city, overtaken by migrants from the interior and other parts of Latin America, is emptied of its elite and appears to return to nature. The "ruins of buildings turn into demolition sites, the demolition sites into wasteland, the wasteland into countryside."[28] The elites can no longer recognize Buenos Aires, for it no longer conforms to the contours of the imagined city of the past. As in Bombay, so in Buenos Aires, the elite memories of the city's past unity and harmony leave no place for hierarchy and multiplicity; they mistake the earlier class and ideological dominance of the urban space for the actual description of the past.

Lefebvre wrote that urban space has a structure more like that of flaky pastry than the homogenous and isotropic space of classical mathematics.[29] Layered and heterogeneous, the city can be understood as a subset of multiple urban practices and imaginations.[30] This is true as much of the so-called bounded places of the cities of an earlier time as it is of the new urban constellations of shopping malls and the displaced poor. The exploration of their "flaky pastry" structure, therefore, offers an opportunity to re-vision modernity, to bring to the surface its myths, delusions, opportunities, desires, contradictions, and conflicts. Sharing this understanding, this volume uses the dimension of space to explore the history of modern cities as diverse spatial constellations of intersecting, contradictory, and conflictual practices and experiences. It rejects the view that treats cities as organisms ordered and experienced according to an underlying logic, and engages with modernity's spatial and material forms. Thus, even as the contributors analyze modern cities against the background of capitalism, empire, and globalization, they focus on the specific historical forms of urban imaginaries, everyday life, and politics in which large social forces were expressed, experienced, and reconstituted.

GLOBAL SPATIAL IMAGINARIES

Jonathan Raban wrote: "The city as we know it, the soft city of illusion, myth, aspiration, nightmare, is as real, maybe more real, than the hard city."[31] He did not mean, I think, that the city was only a state of mind, but that it is constituted by the interplay between its spaces and its imaginations. The brick and mortar do not exist apart from representations, nor are our ideas without material consequences or take shape outside the hard city of maps, statistics, and architecture. The city is both the actual physical environment and the space we experience in novels, films, poetry, architectural design, political government, and ideology.[32] We encounter this imaginary city in Walter Benjamin's sketches of the myths, illusions, and figurative tropes that he identified in street life, shopping arcades, the display of commodities, and images.[33] But whereas Benjamin wrote only of European cities within the context of capitalism, the authors in the first section of this book chart urban imaginaries in global contexts, underscoring their location in the broader realms of both the imperial dynamic and the world capitalist economy.

David Frisby, for instance, mines the details of urban planning in fin-de-siècle Vienna to make a broader argument about contested sites and cultural formations in metropolitan modernity. This is a territory previously covered with great elegance by Carl Schorske.[34] But Frisby shows that a seemingly simple debate over street design in the Austrian city—specifically, whether they should be straight or crooked—intersected with larger issues connected to the power of capital, the circulation of commodities and individuals, traffic configurations, urban infrastructures, pathologies of urban life, and the aesthetics of the street. In short, as Frisby demonstrates, the discussion over street design was inherently part of a larger debate over Vienna's urban imaginary as a "world city," as a city of the Austro-Hapsburg Empire. This debate, which took shape as an extended comparison of Vienna and Berlin, brought to the forefront issues of history and memory, of modernity and antimodernity. Ultimately, Frisby's reading of this debate discovers different imaginaries of the modern city as the embodiment of society itself.

In his study of the global reach of modern Los Angeles, Philip Ethington chronicles a similar process unfolding in a city precisely as it came to terms with its new status as a "world city." His essay recounts the many ways in which Los Angeles first constituted itself as a global metropolis in the 1920s and 1930s through the incorporation of local histories in a global imaginary. Here, the spatial landscape of Los Angeles, itself a multiethnic and multiracial space, is connected with an unlimited array of global peripheries through economic histories of oil exploration, aircraft production, and labor. It is also represented via racial ideologies of white supremacy through cultural histories of popular fiction and Hollywood films. In a narrative that ranges from southern California across the porous frontier between Mexico and the United States and then into east Africa, Ethington tracks the ways in which the ruling powers in Los Angeles sought out familiar and friendly environments where racial and economic hierarchies mirrored their own. As he makes clear, capitalism, colonialism, and conquest combined to insert the city of Los Angeles into a global frame. But this insertion, he suggests, was ultimately framed by the white ruling class's assumptions of racial superiority and support of nonunion labor, and was driven by its larger sense of destiny.

Sheila Crane, meanwhile, explores the manifestations of architectural modernism in Marseilles and Algiers, charting their mutuality in the complex history of colonialism and decolonization. As her essay makes clear, their histories are inseparable, for the spaces of the two cities spilled into each other through the memories, experiences, and imaginations of the citizens who lived not simply inside these cities but in the blurred boundaries of an interconnected world that stretched between the French *métropole* and its north African periphery. Tracking the countless instances in which this shared culture found expression in architecture, photographs, bank notes, and museum spaces, Crane demonstrates the ways in which "fantasies of control" first took shape in the colonial context and then lingered on in the postcolonial world. In the end, her study makes a strong case for understanding the coexistence of Marseilles and Algiers in a dense interconnected web of historical and global imaginaries.

In the section's last essay, Martin Murray examines the "invented city" of Johannesburg in the aftermath of apartheid. His portrayal of the city is one that accounts for its utopian and dystopian spaces in equal measure. In some ways, Murray notes, the city represented an "urban glamour zone" of affluent residential and recreational enclaves that made ostentatious displays of global integration and a celebrated "enterprise culture" of neoliberal design. He contrasts this slice of Johannesburg with a very different world that is lived in its shadows, an "urban danger zone," defined by interstitial spaces of garrison-state confinement marked by a crumbling infrastructure, few if any amenities, and no hope of escape for its residents. In contrasting these different realities of Johannesburg and bringing them into contact, Murray demonstrates how the postapartheid metropolis shuttles between its troubled history of racial exclusion and its contemporary engagement with the global regime of capital and the spectacle of consumption. Seen from this kaleidoscopic perspective, Johannesburg appears as an intricate intersection of histories, memories, and imaginations, all taking shape at once within local and global struggles.

These essays clearly show that the city-region-nation-world framework does violence to the history of modern cities. The spatial imaginaries of Vienna, Los Angeles, Marseilles and Algiers, and Johannesburg were shaped by the histories of their global engagements. Out of such engagements, which varied from city to city, there arose "thick" local imaginaries in which capital, class, race, nation, colony and postcolony, and apartheid and postapartheid urban spaces were experienced, represented, and differentially lived.

Spatial Politics

Lefebvre writes of space as occupation. It is not geography but practice, by which he means that it is not an inert and given physical environment but a space produced by human actions. In this volume's second section, the contributors flesh out the concept of urban space as a projection of politics, as political practices. The spaces of the modern city both shaped political concerns and were in turn shaped by them. Urban spaces could generate political clashes, as conflicts rooted in, or fought over, the built environment lent themselves to larger clashes that spilled into the broader world of politics. But urban spaces were just as often reconfigured by such political clashes, as rival groups divided by distinctions of race, class, and politics sought to make such political divisions concrete in the physical structures and order of the city. Ultimately, this approach situates politics and political discourse in the spatial landscape of the city, while also identifying and highlighting the political lineaments of urban space.

Dina Khoury, for example, places contemporary Baghdad's dystopic violence and communal geography in historical perspective by excavating its spatial politics during the period between 1776 and 1810. She makes the case for considering the space of the city as a dynamic constellation—not just as geography but as an intersection of politics, society, and geography together. Examining the violent episodes in the wake of challenges to Ottoman hegemony, the encroachment of the Wahhabi movement, and Baghdad's incorporation into the post-Napoleonic world of the British Empire, she describes the new conceptualization of spaces within the city and the city's relationship with the hinterland. As her exploration of the spatial component of rebellion and violence makes clear, ethnic identities were reconstituted and reorganized through the spatial relations of the city. Noting the openly political agendas of the leaders in these incidents, their use of specifically sectarian language, and their mobilization of ever wider swaths of urban and tribal populations, Khoury argues that narratives of these violent incidents reveal that spatial distinctions were more than simply lived environments, but rather social constructs marking the boundaries of ethnic, sectarian, and political divisions within the city and between the city and its surroundings. Then as now, violence sparked by the crisis of political order transformed Baghdad's urban geography and the spatial practices of its diverse population.

Focusing on the Mexican city of Morelia between 1880 and 1926, Christina Jiménez likewise studies the ways in which public space has been constructed through popular politics. She begins with Angel Rama's influential argument about the role of writing—specifically, legal codes and municipal laws and regulations—in maintaining social hierarchy, and ingeniously turns it on its head by showing how the poor used the world of letters to extend the space of politics beyond the ballot box and newspaper.[35] She pays close attention to how street vendors lobbied municipal authorities through individual letters and collective petitions and how those authorities, in turn, responded to their pleas. The regulations that were intended to secure the place of political elites and order the city according to their needs, she argues, had the unintended consequence of empowering ordinary citizens and obli-

10

gating the city council to recognize their needs and respond in kind. Through her reclamation of the political activism of these working-class vendors, Jiménez argues that popular politics forced the Porfirio regime to accept their claims to public space and free trade. Ultimately, her work underscores the generative role of popular politics in the organization and function of urban spaces, showing how it redefined "letters" and "public space."

Belinda Davis, meanwhile, explores West Berlin in the Cold War era. She reconstructs the West Berlin of the " '68ers," bringing to life their imaginary of the city as an island of political freedom in the midst of the communist bloc. For the international student movement of the New Left, West Berlin represented a universal source of inspiration; for activist German youths, it stood as a Mecca for their political travels. The essay provides insight into the Situationists' imagination of creating a "happening" and, in a larger sense, turning West Berlin into a "world city" with connections across the globe. Davis argues that the relationship between the city and the activists who made it their home was both political and physical. Even as the city provided material for them, she contends, these activists reconstituted the city as a "scene" and a "movement" attuned to their own needs. In doing so, they helped reshape not simply West Berlin but West Germany as a whole, affecting the popular discourse on everything from how to raise a child to how to stage a protest.

In her study of postwar Los Angeles, Sarah Schrank explores the many meanings behind the Watts Towers. Literally constructed of urban debris by an Italian immigrant named Simon Rodia, the towers emerged as a potent symbol for Angelenos across the spectrum of race and class. As Schrank illustrates, the Watts Towers were invested with multiple and often contradictory meanings. Newspapers portrayed them as a public safety hazard, while civic boosters touted them as a sign of urban redevelopment and an attraction for tourists; art journals praised them as an important work of international significance, while neighboring African Americans claimed them as a metaphor specific to their own community. Ultimately, Schrank argues, the complicated meanings of the Watts Towers have proven to be a political challenge and a cultural irony, as the structures symbolize both the city's failure to ensure social equality for all its citizens and the artistic possibilities of indigenous Angelenos. Built with premodern labor in a modern city, the multiple, changing, and conflictual class and racial meanings of the towers bear testimony to Los Angeles's history as a space layered with different practices.

As these essays take us from late-eighteenth-century Baghdad to 1960s Los Angeles, they make clear that we have to take seriously the spatiality of politics. Cities were not mere sites for the political dramas; urban spaces, constituted by their political and social locations, generated and influenced the politics of empire, rebellion, and violence (Baghdad); the meanings of public space (Morelia) and freedom (West Berlin); and struggles over representations of art and race (Los Angeles). The essays suggest that we cannot think of these modern political forces and concepts without their particular locations and histories in specific cities. Nor can we understand these cities outside their constitution by their political histories.

SPACES OF EVERYDAY LIFE

The modern city is lived, above all, in everyday life. We do not mean *everyday* in the social-history sense of "ordinary life" but rather as a distinct space of routines produced and governed by modernity. It is not that premodern societies did not have daily routines, but that these were ruled by natural and ritual rhythms. Capitalism produced an altogether different space of daily life, ordered by the clock and industrial production. Max Weber referred to it as the "iron cage" of machinelike rationality; Walter Benjamin saw it as the space of the phantasmagoria of commodity aesthetics; and Lefebvre viewed it as the space for the reproduction of society.[36] It was in the realm of daily routines that radical social and cultural transformations were absorbed: the new became conventional; the unfamiliar was rendered familiar. On the other hand, it is also in the space of the everyday that the familiar is defamiliarized, where the routine can be made strange. In this sense, the everyday presents a paradox—it is the space of both the routine and strange, the familiar and unfamiliar, a domain colonized by discourse but also something hidden and evasive.[37] It serves not only as an arena for the operation of large historical forces—capitalism, the state, the bureaucracy, and so on—but also as a space of innovation, improvisation, change, and resistance. As urban residents confront the experiences of the everyday, especially through the construction and consumption of public culture, such as cinema, media reports, and artistic expressions and popular music, they remake the city and their world in countless ways. The essays in this final section approach everyday life in both these senses.

In his study of postwar London, for instance, Frank Mort explores the question of change in modern society at the level of everyday life. Rather than invoking narratives that unfold over a long time period, Mort investigates London in the 1950s through a close examination of a notorious murder case in Rillington Place, a working-class and racially mixed neighborhood in central London. In chronicling the discovery of the murder; the trial of the killer, John Christie; and the media coverage, Mort seeks to identify the catalysts of change. The murders, he argues, brought together in a visceral sense three related sets of problems that were understood to have a quintessentially metropolitan location: the symbolic relationship between the social elites of London and the disreputable characters at the city's fringe, contested understandings of pathological manifestations of an aggressive masculinity and a sexually deviant femininity, and a growing debate about the cultural impact of Caribbean migration on the indigenous character of a "problem" neighborhood in the central city. Tracking the public fantasies and personal transgressions of ordinary Londoners, Mort demonstrates that the crimes committed in the "liminal space" of Rillington Place sparked significant transformations in sexual morality and race relations in the aftermath of empire.

Mamadou Diouf, meanwhile, turns our attention to youth culture in Dakar during the 1980s. Providing a close analysis of the cultural forms favored by Senegalese youth, Diouf examines the ways in which they coped with the end of postcolonial dreams of nationalism and approached the opportunities and fantasies of globalization. The degradation of the urban environment, he argues, closely mirrored the degradation of political practices. In turn, the reconstitution of the city of Dakar and its reintegration as an integral part of Africa's global relations found a cultural counterpart in the cleansing rhetoric of the Set/Setal movement. As his essay makes clear, it was through artistic expression—in both traditional art forms such as wall paintings and, more important, musical expressions like hip-hop—that the youth culture in this Senegalese city helped rebuild the urban political culture and thereby renew the city and its residents in equal measure. Diouf's reconstruction of the Dakar youth culture's dynamic engagement with the shattering of postcolonial dreams and the commodification enforced by globalization brings into view a refreshingly different picture from that drawn by "Afropessimists."

In his exploration of Tokyo, Jordan Sand dissects the "memory projects" that proliferated in the city during its economic boom in the 1980s. Through their renaming of discarded materials, their elevation of found objects scattered across the urban landscape, and their larger reconstruction of Tokyo as the "bricolage city," groups such as the Street Science Observation Society successfully used nostalgia to offer a critique of the dominant culture. Operating determinedly outside the reach of larger historical preservation projects and choosing instead the space of the everyday, these projects provided a sharp challenge to the triumphalism of the city's "bubble culture" in the midst of a fevered economic boom. Sand chronicles the work of the individuals and groups who styled themselves as observers of urban space and urban history. Like Benjamin's rag picker and collector, their deliberate focus on the ephemeral and the "useless" objects inside the city served to project an everyday utopian vision as a counterpoint to the dominant culture of commodification.

Ranjani Mazumdar brings this section and the volume to a close with her study of 1990s Mumbai as portrayed in its cinema. At the heart of the essay is her examination of the relationship between Mumbai's representation as a quintessentially modern space and the images of poverty, misery, crime, and violence that also define the city. Globalization, she argues, has introduced a new landscape of desires and images to these contradictory representations. Treating popular films as an archive of the city, she identifies the emergence of an urban delirium of commodities and crime, of spectacle and death. Mazumdar identifies this archive in two starkly different genres of Mumbai films. First, she considers a new generation of family dramas that seek to reconcile traditional Indian values with global mobility by setting their stories in panoramic interior spaces embellished with the visual signs of global commodity aesthetics. Conceived and created by a new class of professional set designers, the panoramic interior expresses a crisis of belonging, a fear of the street, and a desire for the good life all at once. Against this, Mazumdar juxtaposes a growing canon of gangster films that invert this spatial structuring by using an elaborate exploration of the dark corners and crowded streets of the urban world to heighten the sense of danger and desperation. As her work demonstrates, the crisis of the repetitive everyday world in the "imagined city" of cinema brings about unpredictable events that both challenge the banality of daily life while projecting a new community. The quotidian experience of global mobility, consumption, and street life, reflected in the traffic between the "real" and the imagined cinematic city, emerges as an urban delirium of modernity and tradition, wealth and poverty, opportunity and its absence, freedom and violence.

Like those in the previous two sections, these chapters explore the space of the everyday in particular cities while keeping their global connections in mind. Methodologically, these essays also successfully bridge the gap that exists between the social-scientific analyses of structures and discourses and forms of representation that deal with the poetics of the everyday. They read the work of larger social forces in the relentless realm of the quotidian while also capturing its unpredictable, dynamic, and critical facets. We encounter the momentous transformations of metropolises brought about by the postcolonial aftermath, globalization, consumerism, and deindustrialization, but not the demise of the city. Instead, the authors provide us with a series of varied and vivid portraits of changes in everyday spaces of urban life, sketched to highlight the different and discrepant lived experiences of cultural modernity.

THE PROMISE OF THE MODERN CITY

Taken together, the essays in this volume present urban modernity as irreducibly global and diverse. Treating capitalism, empire, and globalization as key frames for examining urban processes, they challenge the diffusionist model according to which modernity first emerged in one center (Europe) and then spread to the peripheries. They show that there is no single city or experience that can be regarded as paradigmatic. Neither nineteenth-century Paris nor early-twentieth-century Berlin can be regarded as models of the modern capitalist city. Capitalist relations have been global and uneven since inception, and colonialism, imperialism, and globalization have operated with dissimilar effects across and within different cities. Not only do Baghdad, Berlin, Mumbai, Dakar, London, Los Angeles, Johannesburg, Marseilles, Morelia, and Tokyo look very different from each other; each one appears internally differentiated. Imaginaries and the spaces of politics and everyday life diverge. This is not to make an argument for "multiple modernities" but to suggest that urban modernity, shaped by and shaping global historical forces, must be considered differentiated and discordant.[38]

Common to these diverse experiences of urban modernity has been their functioning as spaces for generating new forms of society. In his essay on "The Right to the City," Lefebvre wrote of the city as a space of urban encounters to produce new experiences, to establish complex and transparent relations with the world.[39] These experiences and relations could be obtained neither by returning to the traditional city nor by hurtling headlong into a colossal and shapeless agglomeration, but by claiming a "transformed and renewed *right to urban life*."[40] For him, this urban was like a virtual object, a horizon to reach, not immediately identifiable in the actual city, which he thought was no longer a coherent entity.

Such a horizon struggles to surface in contemporary urbanism. The insertion of existing metropolises in vast agglomerations of production, consumption, migration, transport, finance, media, and digital networks often generates a dystopic urban imaginary. Set against it is a utopian past of coherence and unity, the transparent public space and the rational citizenry, and the simple pleasures of face-to-face urban life. Even as urban transformations speed ahead to create "placeless" imaginaries, the rationale of economic renewal and development is used to commemorate and recreate invented pasts in festivals and fairs, turning us into tourists in our own cities. Both are ruses of the present. The images of urban dystopia and utopia act together to suppress the appearance of porosity, contradictions, and the promise of urban life. This volume acts otherwise.

NOTES

Thanks are due to David Frisby, Kevin Kruse, Ranjani Mazumdar, Jordan Sand, and Ravi Sundaram for reading and making valuable comments on the draft. I should also gratefully acknowledge the excellent criticisms and suggestions of three anonymous reviewers.

1. Marshall Berman, *All That Is Solid Melts into Air* (New York: Penguin Books, 1988).

2. Georg Simmel, *Individuality and Social Forms*, ed. Donald N. Levine (Chicago: University of Chicago Press, 1971), 324–39; Siegfried Kracauer, *The Mass Ornament*, trans. and ed. Thomas Y. Levin (Cambridge, Mass.: Harvard University Press, 1995); and Walter Benjamin, *The Arcades Project*, trans. Howard Eiland and Kevin McLaughlin (Cambridge, Mass.: Harvard University Press, 1999). See also David Frisby, *Fragments of Modernity* (Cambridge, Mass.: MIT Press, 1986); and Anthony Vidler, *Warped Space: Art, Architecture, Anxiety in Modern Culture* (Cambridge, Mass.: MIT Press, 2000), 25–50, 65–80, and 81–98.

3. Henri Lefebvre, *The Production of Space*, trans. Donald Nicholson Smith (Oxford: Blackwell, 1991).

4. Gyan Prakash, "The Urban Turn," in Ravi Vasudevan et al., eds., *Sarai Reader 02: The Cities of Everyday Life* (Delhi: Centre for the Study of Developing Societies, 2002), 2–7.

5. Henri Lefebvre, *The Urban Revolution*, trans. Robert Bononno (Minneapolis: University of Minnesota Press, 2003). Originally published as *La révolution urbain* (Paris Éditions Gallimard, 1970). See also, David Harvey, *The Urbanization of Capital* (Oxford: Blackwell, 1985).

6. United Nations Population Division, *World Urbanization Prospects: The 2001 Revision* (New York: United Nations Publications, 2002), 1.

7. See Kenneth T. Jackson, *Crabgrass Frontier: The Suburbanization of the United States* (New York: Oxford University Press, 1985); Joel Garreau, *Edge City: Life on the New Frontier* (New York: Anchor, 1992).

8. D. Sudjic, *The 100 Mile City* (San Diego: Harcourt Brace, 1992), 296, cited in Ash Amin and Nigel Thrift, *Cities: Reimagining the Urban* (Cambridge: Polity Press, 2002), 2.

9. Mike Davis, *Planet of Slums* (New York: Verso, 2006).

10. For a recent overview of urbanization in China, see John Friedmann, *China's Urban Transition* (Minneapolis: University of Minnesota Press, 2005). For specific case studies, see *The New Chinese City*, ed. John R. Logan (Oxford: Blackwell, 2002). Li Zhang's *Strangers in the City: Refigurations of Space, Power, and Social Networks within China's Floating Population* (Stanford, Calif.: Stanford University Press, 2001) provides a probing account of the challenges posed by the movement of rural migrants to Beijing. Michael Dutton's *StreetLife China* (Cambridge: Cambridge University Press, 1999) is a fascinating guide to the social, cultural, and political life in the new urbanscape.

11. David Harvey, *The Condition of Postmodernity: An Enquiry into the Origins of Cultural Change* (Oxford: Blackwell, 1989).

12. Ravi Sundaram writes about the political implications of a "pirate modernity" built around the "copy" and illegal media networks in contemporary societies. See his "Uncanny Networks: Pirate and Urban and New Globalisation," *Economic and Political Weekly* 39, no. 1 (January 3, 2004): 64–72.

13. Arjun Appadurai and James Holston, "Introduction: Cities and Citizenship," in *Cities and Citizenship*, ed. James Holston (Durham, N.C.: Duke University Press, 1999), 1–20.

14. Partha Chatterjee, *The Politics of the Governed: Reflections on Popular Politics in Most of the World* (New York: Columbia University Press, 2004).

15. Paul Virilio, *The Lost Dimension*, trans. Daniel Moshenberg (Paris: Semiotexte(e), 1991).

16. Rem Koolhaas, "Postscript: Introduction for New Research 'Contemporary City,'" *Architecture and Urbanism*, 217 (October 1988), reprinted in *Theorizing a New Agenda for Architecture*, ed. Kate Nesbitt (New York: Princeton Architectural Press, 1996), 325.

17. Rem Koolhaas, "City of Exacerbated Difference ©," in *Great Leap Forward*, ed. Chuihua Judy Chung, Jeffrey Inaba, Rem Koolhaas, and Sze Tsung Leong (Cologne: Taschen; Cambridge, Mass.: Harvard Design School, 2001), 27.

18. Ibid.; Rem Koolhaas/Harvard Project on the City, Stefano Boeri, Stanford Kwinter, Nadia Tazi, and Hans Ulrich Obrist, *Mutations* (Barcelona: ACTAR, 2001); and Chuihua Judy Chung, Jeffrey Inaba, Rem Koolhaas, and Sze Tsung Leong, eds. *The Harvard Design School Guide to Shopping* (Cologne: Taschen; Cambridge, Mass.: Harvard Design School, 2001).

19. Rem Koolhaas, "The Generic City," in *S,M,L,XL*, 2nd ed. (New York: Monacelli Press, 1998), 1,248–64.

20. Ibid., 1,250.

21. Ibid., 1,252.

22. Elizabeth L. Perry, "Shanghai's Politicized Skyline," in *Shanghai: Architecture and Urbanism for Modern China*, ed. Seng Kuan and Peter G. Rowe (New York: Prestel, 2004), 106–7.

23. Ackbar Abbas, "Play It Again Shanghai: Urban Preservation in the Global Era," in *Shanghai Reflections*, ed. Mario Gandelsonas (Princeton, N.J.: Princeton Architectural Press, 2002), 37–55.

24. Ibid., 38.

25. Michel Foucault, "Of Other Spaces," *Diacritics*, 16 (1986), 22.

26. Prakash, "The Urban Turn," 5.

27. Rohinton Mistry, *Family Matters* (New York: Knopf, 2002), 263–64.

28. Beatriz Sarlo, "The Modern City: Buenos Aires, the Peripheral Metropolis," in *Through the Kaleidoscope: The Experience of Modernity in Latin America*, ed. Vivian Schelling (London: Verso, 2000), 119.

29. Lefebvre, *The Production of Space*, 86.

30. Helen Liggett, *Urban Encounters* (Minneapolis: University of Minnesota Press, 2003), xi.

31. Jonathan Raban, *Soft City* (London: Harvill Press, 1988), 4.

32. Cf. James Donald, who writes that the city is a coherence ascribed to diversity, an abstraction that emerges in the productive transactions between the physical environment and its experience and representation. "The traffic between urban fabric, representation and imagination fuzzies up the epistemological and ontological distinctions, and in doing so, produces the city between, the imagined city where we actually live." *Imagining the Modern City* (Minneapolis: University of Minnesota Press, 1999), 10.

33. Walter Benjamin, *The Arcades Project*. See also Susan Buck-Morss, *The Dialectics of Seeing: Walter Benjamin and the Arcades Project* (Cambridge, Mass.: MIT Press, 1989); and Graeme Gilloch, *Myth and Metropolis: Walter Benjamin and the City* (Cambridge: Polity Press, 1996).

34. Carl E. Schorske, "The Ringstrasse, Its Critics, and the Birth of Urban Modernism," in *Fin-de-Siècle Vienna* (New York: Vintage, 1981), 24–115.

35. Angel Rama, *The Lettered City*, trans. John Charles Chasteen (Durham, N.C.: Duke University Press, 1996).

36. Max Weber, *The Protestant Ethic and the Spirit of Capitalism*, trans. Talcott Parsons (London: HarperCollins, 1991); Walter Benjamin, "Paris, Capital of Nineteenth Century, Exposé of 1939," in *The Arcades Project*; and Henri Lefebvre, *Everyday Life in the Modern World*, trans. Sacha Rabinovich (New York: Harper and Row, 1971).

37. Ben Highmore, *Everyday Life and Cultural Theory* (London: Routledge, 2002), 16.

38. Cf. Jennifer Robinson's important book, *Ordinary Cities: Between Modernity and Development* (New York: Routledge, 2006), which outlines a postcolonial approach to cities, arguing against the opposition set up between the European cities of cultural modernity and non-European cities of development.

39. Henri Lefebvre, *Writings on Cities*, trans. and ed. Eleonore Kofman and Elizabeth Lebas (Oxford: Blackwell, 1996), 149.

40. Ibid., 158.

SPATIAL IMAGINARIES

*

CHAPTER 1

Streets, Imaginaries, and Modernity:
Vienna Is Not Berlin

DAVID FRISBY

The streets of other cities are paved with asphalt; those of Vienna
with Culture.

— *Karl Kraus*

We live for the living and not for the dead. If people wish to see dead
things then they should visit a museum. We wish to live in a modern
city that fulfills all our aesthetic and hygienic requirements.

— *Otto Wagner*

THIS ESSAY IS LOCATED within a broader comparative-historical analysis of
urban spaces, contested sites, and cultural formations in European metropolitan modernity, initially of Berlin and Vienna from around 1880 to 1914.
Focus is on the sociopolitical and cultural contexts of the *production* of urban
spaces generated by city planners and architects. Looking back over the nineteenth century, Cornelius Gurlitt identified two modern urban forms: Haussmann's Parisian boulevards and Vienna's Ringstrasse.[1] Yet other major imperial capitals such as Berlin or London do not fit neatly into either of these
forms. Berlin's dramatic expansion after 1870 was possible because the city
could expand outward without destroying its inner districts, and on the same
scale as was the case in Paris. A north-south axis, envisaged by Haussmann
for Paris, was discussed in Berlin in the Weimar Republic and in the Nazi
period, but not realized. In Vienna, attempts to introduce a grand avenue
were successfully resisted.[2]

A comparison of Berlin, Vienna, and London might produce different,
illuminating results from those examined in D. J. Olsen's influential choice
of London, Paris and Vienna,[3] and the exploration of the modernity of other
metropoles in southern Europe, for example, might challenge our conceptions of modernity that are dominated by Paris.[4] At the same time, this site
opens up an issue generated by Benjamin, and recently amplified by Harvey,

on Paris: the claim that Paris was the capital of the nineteenth century.[5] For Benjamin, the possibility of London as such a capital did not arise. For the period 1880–1914, an argument to counter the notion of a single European capital—leaving aside Benjamin's justifications for his own choice—would be that modes of globalization had already emerged, associated not merely with imperialistic expansion but also with technical and communication developments connecting urban centers and their own outward expansion. This opened up the possibility of identifying a multiplicity of metropolitan centers and potential world capitals that were represented differently. The continuous striving for world city status (in part, exemplified in world exhibition competitions) well into the twentieth century suggests either that it had not been attained or that its definition changed over time. Sometimes, as in Berlin, its representation as a world city remained ahead of its realization. In Vienna, by contrast, there was resistance to attaining such a status.

Initial work on the representations of Berlin (as new, civilized, American) and Vienna (as old, cultured, European) around 1900, and their impact on debates concerning contested sites in these cities is important. Although beyond the scope of this analysis, a comparison of the nature of imperial representations in major European cities, and a comparison of capitals with overseas and land empires would be fruitful. For the Austro-Hungarian Empire at least (the largest land empire in Europe outside Russia), its multicultural nature had important implications for its built environment. It was an empire with a plurality of metropolitan centers, most notably, but not exclusively, Budapest and Prague.[6]

As an exemplary instance that permits the comparison of Vienna and Berlin, the initial focus here is largely on streetscapes—the contested nature of the street, what is on the street, which streets and for whom, and planning streets. As a way into a comparison of the streetscapes of Berlin and Vienna, this essay takes up a controversy known as the straight or crooked streets debate. Moreover, imaginaries of Vienna and Berlin that emanate from sociological, architectural, and literary circles also have affinities with this debate.[7] The interface between the debate and these imaginaries relates to contested modernities, specifically in Vienna up until 1914.[8] The more contested Viennese modernity comes to the fore in what follows.

The debate on straight or crooked streets in the 1890s raised issues associated with the power of capital, the circulation of commodities and individuals, traffic configurations, the aesthetics of the street, historical memory, modernity and antimodernity, street infrastructure, and pathologies of urban life. The debate's initial protagonists were the German city planners Karl Henrici and Joseph Stübben, and its textual venue was the *Deutsche*

Bauzeitung, edited and published in Berlin. From a Viennese perspective, it could be read as a debate between the Viennese architects Camillo Sitte and Otto Wagner, even though neither participated directly in the controversy in the *Deutsche Bauzeitung.*[9] From a Berlin perspective, this debate could be read as a challenge to the consequences of the rapid development of a new Berlin after German unification in 1871 and a perceived extensive use of straight streets and broad grids in the city's expansion. At the same time, rather than being merely an isolated theoretical debate, it resonates in the practices of city planning and, for post-1890 Vienna, in a wider confrontation between a contested "old" and "new" Vienna, and the imaginaries of Vienna and Berlin.[10]

The debate was sparked by responses to two major works: Sitte's *City Planning According to Aesthetic Principles* (1889), and Stübben's *City Planning* (1890) which was reviewed by Henrici, a supporter of Sitte.[11] The ensuing debate between Henrici and Stübben extends into the 1890s,[12] with continuing echoes both in Henrici's review of Wagner's *Moderne Architektur* (1896),[13] and Sitte's newspaper articles.[14] Debate on traffic intersections continued much longer, whereas the title of the debate dates back to an earlier article published by Stübben in 1877.[15] In the rest of this chapter, I outline some central arguments in the works of Sitte and Stübben on city planning. I then explore some general features of the debate between Henrici and Stübben before moving on to the debate's relevance for understanding the imaginaries of Berlin and Vienna and streetscapes in the two cities.[16]

Initially acknowledging modern urban planning's technical achievements "with respect to traffic, the advantageous use of building sites, and especially, hygienic improvements," Sitte regrets that, "artistically we have achieved almost nothing, modern majestic and monumental buildings being usually seen against the most awkward of public squares and the most badly divided lots." Instead, modern city planning should "go to school with Nature and the old masters."[17] In fact, after Vienna, Florence and Rome are his most cited exemplars, ones that recall distant, aesthetic memories: "Enchanting recollections of travel form part of our most pleasant reveries. Magnificent town views, monuments and public squares, beautiful vistas all parade before our musing eye, and we savor again the delights of those sublime and graceful things in whose presence we were once so happy."[18]

This pastoral opening passage to his major work suggests the need for us to recall the past as a guide to constructing our present, where "the process of enlarging and laying out cities has become an almost purely *technical* concern."[19] Although we are at present accustomed to "the already proverbial tedium of modern city plans," "something of value and beauty" can be still constructed, if we can find "an escape from the modern apartment house block system, in order to save wherever practical, the beautiful old parts of towns from falling prey to continuing demolition, and in the end to bring forth something in the spirit of the old masterpieces."[20]

It is the function of open spaces and squares (instances from the Middle Ages, the Renaissance, and the baroque predominate) to facilitate active public life, rather than serving to provide "more air and light" or "a certain interruption in the sea of houses" in the modern city. The modern "rage" for "striving for symmetry" creates blank spaces in the modern city that yet are not city squares since, because "just as there are furnished and empty rooms, so one might also speak of furnished and unfurnished squares, since the main requirement for a square, as for a room, is the enclosed character of its space."[21]

A clearly enclosed quality of "space" is required for a square to be aesthetically effective. But there is another modern consequence of the enclosed square:

> Recently a unique nervous disorder has been diagnosed—"agoraphobia." Numerous people are said to suffer from it, always experiencing a certain anxiety or discomfort whenever they have to walk across a vast empty space. . . . Agoraphobia is a very new and modern ailment. One naturally feels very cozy in small, old plazas, and only in our memory do they loom gigantic, because in our imagination the magnitude of the artistic effect takes the place of actual size. On our modern gigantic plazas, with their yawning emptiness and oppressive ennui, the inhabitants of snug old towns suffer attacks of this fashionable agoraphobia.[22]

Those afflicted with this new disorder are those who migrate to or visit the new metropolitan centers from small, old towns.[23]

This pathology of modern urban spatial interactions is predicated on an implicit distinction between the natural development of older urban configurations and the abstract, artificial development of modern ones. Irregular old squares are aesthetically attractive, for instance, since they were not "conceived on the draught board, but instead developed gradually *in natura*, allowing for all that the eye notices *in natura* and treating with indifference that which would be apparent only on paper." In contrast, the set shape of modern squares, "laid out with a ruler . . . is only ever-so-many square yards of empty surface."[24] This arises out of the architect's abstract relationship to that which is commissioned, as "often we have never in our lives seen the square for which a competition project may be intended. Should one be satisfied then to place this *mechanically produced project*, conceived to fit any situation, into the middle of an empty place *without organic relation* to its surroundings or to the dimensions of any particular building? '*Manufactured product*' is here as everywhere the trademark of modernity."[25] Insofar as the modern planner merely offers staight lines and cubic blocks, this "manufactured product" bears no relationship to the good artistic features of the past, whose memory has been erased.

Reversing this situation in which city planning is "only . . . a technical problem" requires recalling good exemplars of past planning that create a positive artistic effect in the cityscape, and counter the cubic building block, the straight line and rectilinearity. Modern streets, continually breached by wide cross-streets, "so that on both sides nothing is left but a row of separated blocks of buildings," fail to create a unified impression. Continuity is lacking in a modern street "made up primarily of corner buildings. A row of isolated blocks of buildings is going to look bad, under any circumstances, even if placed in a curved line."[26]

Unlike earlier, felicitous, irregular creations, modern planners prefer the straight street, "the universal horizontal termination" of buildings with their "endless rows of windows of identical size and shape, . . . and the absence of large, quiet wall surfaces."[27] The harsh monotony of the modern building line emerges out of the technical approach to urban street layout dominated by traffic concerns. The disadvantage of crossing streets in the gridiron system is that traffic slows dramatically at city intersections, whereas "in the narrow alleys of the old part of town, crowded with traffic as they are, . . . [the coach driver] can proceed quite nicely at a trot . . . [because] a street seldom crosses there, and even simple street openings are relatively infrequent." For pedestrians, "every hundred steps they have to leave the sidewalk in order to cross another street" and "miss the natural protection of uninterrupted house fronts" (as in medieval streets).[28] The radial system necessitates construction of "refuges" for pedestrians, "a small safety island" that is "perhaps the most magnificent and original invention of modern city planning!"[29] It accords with "our mathematically precise modern life" in which "man himself has become almost a machine." Modern living conditions have transformed the range of possibilities for achieving an aesthetic effect by the diminution of the public sphere in which market and consumption activities have been withdrawn into "inartistic commercial structures" and artistic works "are straying increasingly from streets and squares into the 'art cages' of the museums."[30] In the *intérieur*, "we have become so sensitive . . . and so unaccustomed to the hub-bub of streets and squares that we cannot work when someone is watching us, we don't like to dine by an open window because somebody could look in, and the balconies of our houses usually remain empty."[31] This implicit retreat from the public sphere into the bourgeois *intérieur* is without reference to the stratification of the capitalist city. Similarly, Sitte's examination of traffic problems makes no reference to other forms of transport than the horse carriage and the streetcar. The city, or underground, railway receives no mention.

Modern city planning should rest on the "imperative to study the works of the past,"[32] and take account of population, traffic circulation, and social structure to facilitate city zoning. From such projections, the "number, size and approximate form of ... public buildings" should also be assessed. Lack of attention to artistic effect leads to a lack of public attachment or identification with the city, "as one can in fact see among the dwellers of the artless, tedious, new sections of cities."[33] Indeed, we modern city dwellers are forced to

> pass our lives in formless mass housing with the depressing sight of exter-nally similar apartment house blocks and unbroken frontage lines. It is probably the gentle force of habit that hardens us to them. We ought to consider, however, the impression we receive upon returning home from Venice or Florence—*how painfully our banal modernity affects us*. This may be ... why the fortunate inhabitants of those marvellously artistic cities have no need to leave them, while we every year for a few weeks must get away into nature in order to be able to *endure our city for another year.*[34]

Vienna's "banal modernity" here contrasts with a nostalgic view of Venice and Florence.

Stübben's *Der Städtebau* (1890), is more of a comparative compendium of city planning that covers in detail city plans, streets, dwellings, parks, transport, traffic, lighting, water and drainage, telegraph networks, monu-ments, and all the street "furniture" of the late nineteenth century. Al-though theoretically informed, its guiding threads do not present them-selves as a sustained theoretical argument. If Sitte's program focuses on the monumental buildings and squares in the center of the city—as if the rest of the city did not exist, except as monotonous suburbs—Stübben's work encompasses the whole of the modern city, with one significant exception: the industrial areas. Yet whereas Sitte ignores the development of an urban industrial society, Stübben is more aware of the importance of new technol-ogy in the city. Nonetheless, Stübben's conception of city building is one of

> all these building constructions ... whose purpose it is, on the one hand, to make possible the provision of appropriate dwellings and workplaces for

city dwellers, their interaction with one another and movement out of the city, on the other, to make possible for the communality the provision of built structures for administration, religious service, education, art and science, traffic and other public purposes. . . . City planning creates not merely the ground and the framework for the development of individual building activity: rather, at the same time, it is a comprehensive social activity for the physical and mental welfare of the citizenry; it is fundamental, practical, public hygiene; it is the cradle, the clothing, the adornment of the city.[35]

City planning's "creations are as much for the poor as they are for the rich." Planning participates in "equalizing justice, a co-operation in the removal of social grievances and thereby an influential co-operation in social amelioration and welfares."[36]

Within this ethical and technical modern urban project are socioeconomic reflections. In distinguishing individual family houses from multiple-occupancy apartment blocks that offer "all too often a barrack-like uniformity," Stübben, unlike Sitte, emphasises their socioeconomic foundation:

The rented apartment block, above all else, fulfills the purpose of financial investments. Resting upon the housing needs of others, its task is to extract the highest possible rent as is made obvious by the name "interest generating house" [*Zinshaus*]. . . . The rented apartment block changes its inhabitants and its owners just as the commodity does its owners; it has no intimate or, one could say, inner relationship to its inhabitants. It must suit everyone, deny all uniqueness. The inhabitants do not love their house; they only take care of the part used by themselves. The entrance hall, the stairway are really an appendage of the public street and, as a rule, open to anyone.[37]

Widespread use of this dense urban living is "a sad shadow-side of our civilization."

Stübben's alleged overemphasis on traffic is summarized in his statement that "city streets are in the first instance traffic routes; only in the second instance do they serve the extension of buildings."[38] This "density of traffic on a city street is not fortuitous or arbitrary but rather a direct consequence of its position in the city plan." Traffic is a dynamic factor in the city, acting as its focal point, "which is not something spatially fixed and unmoving."[39]

Stübben is also concerned with the interaction between public buildings and monuments and the circulation of traffic, beyond the "fully jammed narrow main streets and dead adjacent streets" found in many cities. The location of public buildings and monuments should be governed by two factors:"considerations of functional appropriateness and considerations of beauty." "Functional appropriateness [*Zweckmässigkeit*] requires easy access, ready locateability, much light and air. Beauty requires a distinctive location in comparison to the neighboring structures and an artistically effective position in the whole section of the city. It is almost always the case that considerations of functional appropriateness and beauty mutually support one another; they seldom stand in contradiction to one another."[40] Stübben thus emphasizes both utility *and* beauty in extending city planning beyond its technical features to the form of the city itself as one of humanity's outstanding accomplishments.

Stübben's volume elaborates on the significance of traffic (*Verkehr*) and its increase in both density and speed. Its facilitation requires a massive investment in a material culture for such transportation. Not merely streets and squares and their configuration but the whole range of artifacts that accompany traffic flows are explored in detail: street signs, bridges, viaducts, vegetation planted along streets, advertising boards and columns, street lighting systems, street car stands, and so forth. On the relationship between traffic and the street, Stübben maintains that

> from the standpoint of traffic, a street should be extended as long as possible in a straight line. From the standpoint of health a careful restriction of the length already recommends itself due to dust accumulation and to the sharp wind that in long straight streets, especially when they correspond to the dominant wind direction, can be quite unpleasant. Beauty dictates this restriction most of all. If a street is to correspond to a sense of beauty, and if the traffic on the street is not to tire the eye but rather guarantee a satisfying prospect, then its length must, to a certain extent, be a function of its breadth.[41]

Henrici's 1891 review of Stübben's *Der Städtebau*, juxtaposes Stübben's technical standpoint with Sitte's artistic standpoint, exemplified in Henrici's assertion that "our present day architecture strives toward the picturesque [*dem Malerischen*]." [42] Specifically, Henrici laments the modern urban planning system's preference for the "un-German": "Is it really necessary that this striving, derived from the primal German essence and directed toward the picturesque square, must make way for the un-German, Italian or French type, because the latter adapts better to the equally un-German *modern* system of 'city planning?' "[43] The attempt to preserve original beautiful squares and streets should not merely copy them in new constructs, for it is impossible to copy such old originals. Rather, this striving for copying the old is precisely what is recommended by modern city planning "with its classifications and with its squares and street figuration by means of circles and lines."[44] Yet the major defect of the modern system is the identification of streets with traffic flows. Linear grid crossing systems create significant loss of time at major intersections. Such crossings are "conceptual [*reflektiert*], *unnatural and arbitrary.*"[45] Henrici favors curved streets and indirect linear street crossings.

For Henrici, the modern straight street system is associated with "individual public buildings in a parade" and parallel housing rows. Instead, the location of public buildings should be interspersed with dwellings, because from them one should be able to appreciate and achieve the beautiful perspective. However, "the average public is in fact alienated from the artistic vision and at present finds in the richly bedecked shop display windows, above whose huge reflecting glass the monumental facades swirl in the air and in the attire which on foot, in the coach or on horseback rush by and are reflected in the glass windows complete satisfaction for the enjoyment of a cityscape. But should one concede that this is a justified and justifiable taste?" Taste should be stimulated not by foreign models such as Parisian *points de vue*, but "by taking up again genuine, old, primal German [*Urdeutsch*]" examples.[46]

In response, Stübben rejects this identification of straight streets with modern city planning systems and their opposition to the old, with a corresponding identification of irregular streets and the avoidance of street crossings as the model for a "genuine old primal German type."[47] Stübben deconstructs the "modern city planning system" that Henrici seems to abhor by pointing out, first, that his own *Städtebau* volume drew on many historical and contemporary instances of good practice from many countries and, second, that "city planning in the last thirty years has still not been incorporated into a completed 'system.' "[48] The juxtaposition of this "un-German" system with the crooked street as "primal German" is illusory in view of countless instances of irregular crossing systems in French and Italian cities. Unlike Henrici's opposition between artistic and modern systems, Stübben's concern is with the reconciliation of the demands of traffic and acquisitive interests with aesthetic interests.

The fact that many medieval churches, town halls, and the like were built on irregular plans cannot be adduced as support for following the principle of irregularity in modern constructions in order to produce an artistic effect. Indeed, both modern life and modern technology "no longer allow a true imitation of old city layouts" and, on public health grounds, such irregular arrangements should not be favored. Thus, although artistic considerations should be taken into account, "aesthetic 'reflection,' and artistic temper . . . have no right of precedence over consideration of technical traffic factors or economic and health considerations." Rather, "a city building plan is not just an ideal work of art but rather is something which decides upon important economic questions, upon mine and yours, upon the future welfare of many inhabitants."[49] It has to comply with many building regulations and other factors.

In "Individualism in City Planning" (1891), Henrici returns to the modern city planning system's one-sided privileging of traffic interests, which in turn creates traffic problems by favoring direct street crossings.[50] This arises out of "the modern mode of building cities, [which] as I believe, does not really connect with historical traditions. It commences, under the new establishment of normal street widths, with the primitive rectangular or chessboard scheme."[51] In contrast, Henrici detects a new tendency based on "a healthy individualism," in which it is not the planner's personal qualities being displayed in a city plan, but rather that "individualization must be appropriate to the distinctive features of the place that is to be built upon."[52] There can be no single, universally valid system for this approach; planners must in each case take account of traffic, building, and beauty. Of these, it is the building dimension that "represents the *bodily element* of the whole city sector, the flesh which, with the healthy content and in a beautiful form, is to produce the streets."[53]

Henrici addresses the effect of ring roads in this context. Although without specific reference to the Vienna Ringstrasse, his reflections are revealing. For him,

> ring roads are also mostly to be seen as auxilliary lines [*Nebenlinien*], and will probably only exceptionally and for only part of their length bear continuous commercial traffic. In most instances they are especially appropriate as promenade installations, because they bring with them, as one goes round them, rapidly changing images and impressions. Such promenade ring roads are largely walked on or traveled on by persons who have a great deal of time.[54]

Henrici's concern, however, is for greater differentiation of streets, dispersal rather than concentration of public buildings, and greater individualism in city planning. Stübben broadly concurs, because "it is indeed better to take into account some individual weaknesses and errors than to give over the formation of the city to schematism. Since the much repeated critique of the boring and barren nature of modern city areas is often only too true, so it is urgently to be desired that artistically trained colleagues concern themselves more than previously with the questions of city planning.[55] Again, Stübben defends his own *Städtebau* volume as reflecting diverse demands on city planning without advancing a single modern system.

The debate took a somewhat different turn in Henrici's "Boring and Pleasant Streets." ("Langweilige und kurzweilige Strassen"), in which he terms a street *"boring* if the wanderer along it gets the impression that the route is longer than it actually is; I term it *interesting* if the reverse is the case."[56] In the case of the perspective of the straight street, the more one sees of the continuous ground surface and walls of the street the more boring will a street be. The more a street is denied the endless perspective, by giving it curves for example, the more changes of perspective are available and the more interesting it will be. Between the boring and the interesting street is the "normal" street with breaks in its building line. Even the long, straight street may be broken up by artificial means such as planting bushes and trees in the middle, adding decorative street lights, or introducing irregularities into the street.

Stübben's reply again points out that he had already indicated the beneficial effect of concave lines in streets and squares to prevent boredom and encourage changing perspectives.[57] But he focuses on a deeper problem: "Major traffic arteries are unavoidable in our times. It is our modern task to construct them in an artistically beautiful manner, a task that is perhaps more difficult but nonetheless equally important than the designing of an artistic detail according to models from previous centuries."[58] The latter procedure hardly addresses the real problems faced by metropolitan traffic and the attempt to accommodate it in an aesthetically appealing manner.

Challenges to conceptions of urban modernity are also found in Sitte's newspaper articles,[59] and in Henrici's review of Otto Wagner's *Moderne Architektur,* which in his opinion

> suffers from a certain one-sidedness insofar as it focuses almost exclusively on the technical achievements of the modern period, on the anticipated ever increasing perfection of *modern means of transport* and on *metropolitan life.* But . . . this part of the spirit of the times with its *tendency toward uniformity,* penetrates through all the pores of the life of the people in such a manner that hardly any place for other things remains, that lies outside that of *world transport* and the *life of acquisition,* and which I wish to indicate with the term the *soul of the people* [*Volksgemüth*].[60]

For Henrici, Wagner's problems of modern life have already been resolved in the grid systems of America. Rather than give expression to modern metropolitan life, Henrici maintains that artists should develop a distinctive national art and style. Again, this ostensibly narrow debate was a confrontation with contested conceptions of the modern metropolis.

What are some of the general issues raised in this debate? The notion that the modern metropolis reflects the spirit of the times most commonly identifies this spirit (*Geist*) with a rational structuring of the city, whereas the aesthetic focus on the city is often identified with preserving its historical soul (*Seele*). Sitte draws this contrast in terms of the modern city as a "human storehouse" versus a "work of art."[61] The "mechanical" outline of the modern city's street network and building blocks is contrasted with a more harmonious cityscape that preserves existing irregular structures. In turn, the mechanical outline of modern urban expansion facilitates an infinitely expandable, open city in contrast to an enclosed historical core. The "rational" expansion of the city into a universal world city (*Weltstadt*) is contrasted with the historically grounded city as work of art. For some of his contemporaries, such conceptions are embodied in the contrast between Berlin and Vienna.[62]

Further, the virtues of the straight or crooked street are not confined to "linearity" versus "fantasy." Rather, the discourses on streets are embedded not merely in different conceptions of the metropolis but also in the nature of its dynamic (circulation), the nature of the practical orientations to its construction, and the perceived consequences of modern urban patterns. But other dimensions of this controversy are not highlighted. As Benjamin argued, the broad, straight boulevard might also have a political significance as potential barrier to insurrection.[63]

Another political contrast is drawn by Simmel (1896), between a "tendency towards symmetry," and "all despotic social formations. . . . The symmetrical arrangement facilitates the domination of many from a single point."[64] This contrasts with the "rhapsodic fortuitousness" of liberal state formations and other groupings whose "inner structure and boundaries of the parts are irregular and fluctuating." Elsewhere, in his essay on Rome (1898), Simmel formulates an aesthetic dimension of this controversy. The virtue of Rome's urban form lies in the "fortuitousness, contradictoriness and absence of principle" in its building history, creating a "work of art of the highest order." "This is emphasized by its streetscape just as it is determined by the hilly nature of its terrain. Almost everywhere its buildings stand in the contradictory relationship of above and below. Thereby, they relate to one another with a totally different significance than if they lay on a flat surface, merely alongside one another."[65] In the 1890s debate, "fortuitousness, contradictoriness and absence of principle" contrast with rational calculation, lack of contradiction and regulation by principles.

At issue too is the relationship of streets and squares to *circulation*. Accelerated movement of individuals, commodities, and vehicles in expanding metropolitan centers raised problems of the prioritization of vehicular traffic, the optimum street formation and width, and the maximization of traffic flows at street intersections, as well as the possibility of multilevel intersections or the construction of city railways, subway systems, and their relationship to street traffic systems. But the issue of circulation itself went far beyond straight or irregular streets and intersections. The sphere of circulation of commodities, for Marx, was associated with a free market for all that could be commodified.[66] This implied open spaces of circulation in which commodities could freely move on the surface of a capitalist economy. The sphere of commodity circulation can generate a series of attributes of its own process of mobilizing commodities and commodity signs that include interchangeability, anonymity, indifference, and uniformity. Circulation taking place on the surface of a capitalist economy could also be readily associated with superficiality. The contrary symbolic universe resisting capitalist modernity would emphasize uniqueness, intimacy, coziness, diversity, and embeddedness. Capitalist circulation generates an abstract mass of commodities, individuals, and abstract spaces. Its individuals require an appropriate urban means within which to circulate.[67] For Sitte, this was conceived by "geometric man" (an epithet he ascribed to Wagner).[68]

The negative valorization of circulation is also located in the concept of *regulation*. Both sides of the debate are concerned with regulation of traffic flows. Problems of street crossing and regulating traffic circulation became an increasingly formal problem susceptible to mathematical calculation. And traffic also affects urban land values, commercial property values, and ground rents. Beneath the streets, circulation is essential for the infrastructure of sewage, gas, water supply, pneumatic postal systems, and so forth. On the surface, the street intersection implies an interruption of circulation and a conflict of interests with respect to modes of traffic. Intersections require separation and regulation. Viewed abstractly, the indifference of the sphere of circulation in which anything can circulate is threatening to precapitalist hierarchies. The social regulation of classes of individuals requires spatial regulation. Access to centers of power became increasingly regulated, driven in part by fear of insurrections. In the 1890s debate, such political parameters remained hidden.

All this suggests a wider significance of discourses on circulation, regulation, and traffic. The German concept of traffic (*Verkehr*) has broader connotations than the English notion does. It extends from the idea of interaction in general to sexual relations. The social structure of both Berlin and Vienna in this period was a complex interaction of threatened systems of rank, associated with semifeudal and certainly precapitalist social relations, and an emergent, increasingly dynamic class society that was more in evidence in Berlin. The sphere of those with whom one associates (*verkehrt*) could not be so circumscribed as earlier. At the same time, the issue of creating boundaries and barriers to interaction could appear all the more urgent for those at the intersections of the two systems of stratification, including those who aspired to enter into the higher ranks of society. The ostensibly open system of traffic (*Verkehr*) in a capitalist market economy—combined with close regulation of the public sphere and capitalist economic relations of production—rendered the notion of interaction problematical. It is in these decades too that the barriers to accessing public spaces are increasingly transgressed. In particular, female access to the public spheres of consumption in the expanding number of modern department stores was increasing. Female access to higher education emerged in Vienna in the 1890s and a decade later in Berlin. In both cities, but especially in Berlin, powerful women's movements sought access to the public sphere of political power. For working-class women and especially the huge numbers of domestic servants, the streets were sites of work or at least of moving to and from work. The presence of expanding social movements—labor movements, the women's movement and, in Vienna, national movements—could also, on occasion, transform the street into a site of political demonstration. At a subterranean level, the transformation of sexual relations through associations with previously excluded strata rendered the openness of interactions all the more threatening.

In a broader context, several authors, such as Vidler in his *Warped Spaces*, have identified diverse discourses on urban pathologies in the late nineteenth century. Simmel for instance, names neurasthenia, hyperaesthesia, amnesia, and claustrophobia with reference to modern metropolitan life and a money economy.[69] Sitte highlights agoraphobia with reference to large, open squares surrounded by buildings from which the individual can be observed. Such "formally rational" spaces were regarded as the breeding ground of "irrational" pathological responses. Sitte also suggests that people do not wish to be observed within their homes from outside, indicative of the precarious bourgeois interior retreat and, in extreme cases, paranoia. The uniformity of the straight street and anonymous apartment block might be a source of amnesia, or at least spatial disorientation. Entrapment in the ever-momentary presentness of modernity might generate a kind of forgetting. Their opposites are claustrophobia (the negative side of Sitte's cozy squares), historically preserved memory, and nostalgia for a pastoral image of a past that is *elsewhere*, far away from "our banal modernity." The crooked, irregular streets of the city's historical core contrasted with the regular layout of modern suburbs, especially in working-class neighborhoods. The dialectics of inside and outside, old and new streets, might be resolved in their spatial separation.

Yet both Sitte and Stübben drew another analogy between inside and outside in their albeit different treatments of the outside spaces of squares as insides. Stübben, in particular, had earlier (1877) drawn a parallel between forms of squares with rooms in a house: "Just as the different kinds of construction of squares with respect to their determination and location allow themselves to be compared in an appropriate manner with the room of a house, the traffic square with the vestibule, the market square with the office, the architectonic square with the ballroom or the drawing room, the English square, finally, with the bedroom or the secluded family chamber, so this comparison equates almost completely with respect to the dimensions of size." [70]

In both instances, this outside as inside is that of a readily assembled bourgeois interior. Yet this is not a space conceived for those who live in the street, for whom the street exterior is actively transformed into an interior. This "other" group of users

is an eternally alert, eternally moving being that witnesses, experiences, perceives and devises as much between the house walls outside as do individuals within the protection of their own four walls. To the collective, the shining enamel signs of a store or company are just as good as, or better than, the decorative oil paintings on the walls of the bourgeois salon. Walls with the sign *Défense d'Afficher* are the collective's writing desk, newspaper stands its libraries, mail boxes, its bronze sculptures, benches, its bedroom furnishings, and the café terraces are the alcoves from which it looks down at its home. Where the asphalt worker lets his coat hang on the rail, that is the vestibule. And the gateway, leading out into the open from multiple courtyards is the long corridor which frightens the bourgeoisie but is to them the entrance into the chambers of the city.[71]

This "other" conception of the street or square, outlined by Benjamin, is not merely *perceived* differently but also *experienced* and *used* differently.

How is this debate relevant for the comparison of Vienna and Berlin? The debate highlights features that figure in broader architectural discourses on modernity in the 1880s, the 1890s, and beyond. A confrontation with Vienna and Berlin as sites of modernity must face the multidimensional nature of the features ascribed to these sites. In the case of the imaginaries of Vienna and Berlin, it is not merely the case that there is a perceived opposition between Berlin, as city of straight streets, other features of traffic circulation, and modernity, and Vienna as a "work of art" and harmonious cityscape. Rather, the imaginaries of Vienna as work of art are confined largely to the city's First District—its Renaissance, baroque core—and not the majority of the city. This is evident in Sitte's descriptions of the Ringstrasse and the inner core of the city, compared with the new, modern, outer developments, facilitating an opposition of "old" and "new" that embodies features of the spirit of the modern city and the soul of a cozy, old Vienna.

In the coded systems of such imaginaries, a New Vienna outside its historical core may represent Berlin, but Old Vienna can only represent itself (confirming the popular saying that "Wien bleibt Wien"—"Vienna remains Vienna"). What this implies, therefore, is that the Berlin-Vienna imaginaries, say, in the period 1890–1914, could also appear in New Vienna–Old Vienna imaginaries central to opposition to the creation of a "new" Vienna. The imaginary of Vienna, however, remains largely that of Old Vienna. The imaginaries of Vienna and Berlin as they appear in the writings of Werner Sombart (economist and sociologist), Franz Servaes (art critic), and Karl Scheffler (architecture critic) and others in this period—in this case, the first decade of the twentieth century—have been explored elsewhere.[72] They reveal imaginaries that associate Berlin with America, or even picture Berlin as "a suburb of New York" (Sombart).[73] These imaginaries of Berlin and Vienna are those generated by German and not Viennese sources. With few exceptions, from a Berlin perspective, the contrast drawn between Berlin and Vienna serves both as a positive idealization of Vienna and a critique of Berlin.

Not a few of the features in these imaginaries could be found in Old Vienna–New Vienna imaginaries in the same period. The contrast between inside and outside and soul and spirit; between historical artistic city and universal world city; between harmonious cityscape and anarchic, arbitrary spaces; between "pillars" of memory and the erasure of memory; as well as between natural inhabitants and "geometric man," are amongst the other oppositions that characterize often virulent debates between the defenders of Old Vienna and the proponents of New Vienna. This should not be surprising, because both oppositions, those between Berlin and Vienna and New Vienna and Old Vienna, draw on a more general opposition between modernity and tradition. Somewhat schematically, the Berlin-Vienna imaginaries are summarized in the list below, in which each of the individual features in the imaginaries of Berlin and Vienna cease to possess an independent existence and become dependent on their opposite as a source of longing. The more specific an individual feature becomes, the less likely is it to operate in this manner. Instead, its very specificity renders it subject to empirical investigation.[74]

Berlin	Vienna
Modern	Historical
America	Europe
Civilization	Culture
Lack of culture	Excessive culture
Male	Female
Artificial/mechanical	Natural human beings
"Indistinguishable, unsurveyable mass"	Differentiated individuals
Asphalt culture	Urban communitarian idyll
Parvenue culture	Old culture
Prussian-American stylelessness	Makart culture
Modern, new surface	Rooted old city
Spirit (*Geist*)	Soul (*Seele*)
Americanism	"German" culture as bulwark against Americanism

It should be remembered that the imaginaries of the modern are also a product of modern discourse and that the status of these imaginaries is not merely discursive. Although the Berlin-Vienna imaginaries are here drawn from German texts, Viennese literary discourses could provide some similar antinomies. Prussia and Vienna were always gendered, sometimes in a complex manner, in Viennese texts by Peter Altenberg, Karl Kraus, and Otto Weininger.[75] The imaginary of Vienna presented above is that of a natural community of city dwellers, able to develop their individuality in the context of a traditional, embedded culture that has not been invaded by the street culture of the modern metropolis, nor the Americanism of a superficial (surface) culture that emphasizes size and quantity. Some of the specific ascriptions of cultural attributes to Berlin, and Vienna—Prussian-American stylelessness in Berlin, a Hans Makart historicist culture in Vienna (both from Scheffler), and Vienna as a defense of German culture against Berlin's Americanism (Servaes)—seem either antiquated for the early twentieth century or politically disturbing. Most of the other features support more conventional, negative imaginaries of Berlin and positive imaginaries of Vienna.

At the same time, actual competition between cities, and their representations, was growing more intense both within the respective empires and between the imperial capitals. Munich was the other cultural capital city (of

Bavaria, and anti-Prussian) competing with Berlin. The rapid development of Budapest after 1867 (with its grand Andrassy Avenue *and* its Ringstrasse), and to a lesser extent Prague, was already seen as a threat to the position of Vienna in the 1890s. Competition between Vienna and Berlin manifested itself in the marketing of the metropoles and the tourist industry. More important was the competition in international exhibitions and sometimes city planning, which was often imbued with symbolic importance.

The world exhibition was usually the most significant representation of a city's status, albeit one that rested on a temporary architecture. The Vienna World Exhibition of 1873 was one of the few such exhibitions that lost money. Later imperial exhibitions of 1898 and 1908 in Vienna celebrated the monarchy, fifty and sixty years, respectively, of Emperor Franz Joseph's reign) and the Austro-Hungarian Empire rather than Vienna as world city. In this respect, such exhibitions took on the form, in part, of a regulated celebration of a multicultural, multiethnic and multilingual land empire, one that was decidedly different from the German Empire. This broader sociocultural constellation clearly had an impact on the two capital cities of Vienna and Berlin, and not merely in terms of migration sources. In the case of Berlin, the Berlin Trade Exhibition of 1896, which many viewed symbolically as indicative of Berlin's elevation to a world city, owed its more limited title to the refusal of other German cities to participate. Instead, the mayors of other cities organized the first German Municipal Exhibition in 1903 in Dresden and not Berlin.[76] Later, for its part, the international competition for the planning of a Greater Berlin in 1908–10 was anything but international, and its practical outcome was minimal.

Another implicit, contested issue was the very concept of the city itself. The ambiguity of the German concept of *Grossstadt* in contrast with the town (*Stadt*) renders possible a distinction between a *Grosse-Stadt* (big town) and a *Grossstadt* (city or metropolis). Berlin and Vienna might be described as metropoles or world cities (*Weltstädte*), to distinguish them from other cities in their respective empires (Prague and Budapest by 1900 might lay claim to this status in Austria-Hungary).[77] By the 1890s in Germany, the quantitative conceptual solution was that a city must have a population exceeding one hundred thousand inhabitants and a metropolis a population in excess of one million. By 1910, Germany possessed one metropolis—Berlin—and forty-nine cities, a statistical solution that hid other issues. In Berlin, some suburbs (Charlottenburg by 1900; Rixdorf, Schöneberg, and Wilmersdorf by 1910) were cities in their own right before incorporation into Greater Berlin in 1920 with a population of four million.[78]

The rapidity of Berlin's expansion after 1871 led many to draw a comparison, not with other major European cities, whose growth rates had slowed by the end of the nineteenth century, but with American cities such as Chicago. Both with respect to size and rate of increase of population, Vienna remained well behind Berlin.

In the case of Vienna, the creation of a Greater Vienna (Gross-Wien) in 1890 could not count on incorporating such substantial urban populations from its outer suburbs, but relied on natural population growth and migration. The city expanded in size, but the built-up area, even by 1902, was only slightly larger than that taken up by gardens, public places, and forests. Nonetheless, its population expanded from more than eight hundred thousand in 1880 to 1.4 million in 1890. The growth of population between 1860 and 1900 showed a 259 percent increase, well below Berlin's 410 percent increase. Given the nature of its empire, Vienna was a much more ethnically, culturally, and linguistically heterogeneous capital city compared with Berlin. In general, the dramatic expansion of these two metropoles and the emergence of other new cities in the last decades of the nineteenth century provides part of the context for the straight or crooked streets debate. The actual contrast—as opposed to its contrasting imaginaries—between Vienna and Berlin was also a subject for investigation, largely in Vienna.[79] In contrast, most of the influential imaginaries of Vienna emerged from Berlin. This discourse on imaginaries commenced a decade before the more theoretically and historically grounded debate on the spirit of capitalism in the work of Sombart and especially Max Weber. In turn, the "rational" spirit of capitalism had one of its sites in the rational spirit of the modern capitalist metropolis, a site likely to be the more economically dynamic and advanced Berlin than Vienna.

Metropolitan expansion in this period generated a connection between city building (Städtebau), city enlargement or extension (Stadterweiterung), and city planning or regulation (Stadtregulierung). Although the German term for city planning is Städtebau, the comprehensive plans for the city involved regulation of the city. In turn, the concept of regulation implies not merely setting boundaries for urban expansion, and the widening and realigning of streets. Rather, the regulation of the metropolis, in providing the sites of production, sites of reproduction, sites of circulation, sites of consumption, sites of state power, and so on, is a project that is no longer a technical process but is informed and governed by sociopolitical and economic agendas. A regulation of the city that creates and maintains a core and periphery, along with a segregation of social, ethnic, and gender groupings, may be guarding against the mobility of subordinate social groups in society. It is within this context that we can read the call for an aesthetic as well as an ethical regulation of the city: an aesthetic governed by sociopolitical agendas.

When we turn to major planning competitions for Berlin and Vienna, the actual outcomes are either minimal or incomplete. In the case of Berlin, the symbolic elevation of the city into a world city in 1896 with the Berlin Trade Exhibition was not matched by any major transformation of city planning.[80] In 1908, an international competition was held for the creation of a master plan for a Greater Berlin. The results, in 1910, although significant in their individual submissions and containing many monumental designs, were limited in their actual impact. As Wolfgang Sonne has argued, "the competition brought only few palpable results. In addition, a comprehensive plan . . . could not yet be officially authorized because there was no administrative and legal basis for its implementation prior to the creation of a unified municipality of Greater Berlin in 1920."[81]

Nonetheless, in Sonne's discussion of the 1908 competition, there are a number of themes relevant to the continued confrontation with the nature of streets, many of which resonate with the streets debate a decade earlier. The competition invited submissions for a master plan for Berlin "that will meet the requirements of transport as well as those of beauty, public health and economic viability."[82] Such transportation submissions included a north-south connecting line and plans for nine ring roads and four rail ring lines (Léon Jaussely and Charles Nicod). Hermann Jansen's interesting submission claimed that "it is not street lines which are needed but streetscapes."[83] His street plans contained "slight bends" to "create interesting architectural street spaces," thereby according with Sitte's notion of urban space. This was not the case with Jansen's view of traffic, in which "both children and automobiles must be given room to run wild; to confine them would be a misinterpretation of their needs, which we would certainly have to pay for later."[84] At the same time, Jansen produced original plans for Tempelhof dwellings in a substantial open green context. In its 1907 deliberations, the Berlin Architects Association had called for "setting aside appropriate spaces for public buildings."[85] Some submissions responded to this call and the desire for a monumental world city. Bruno Möhring and Rudolf Eberstadt, for instance, proposed an imperial forum with the ministry of war opposite the Reichstag, symbolizing "the army and the people, the true bearers of German greatness and power, unified in the monuments of architecture."[86] Bruno Schmitz outlined a monumental city with high-rise towers, drawing to some extent on Daniel Hudson Burnham and Edward Herbert Bennett's 1909 plan for Chicago. None of these plans for Berlin were carried out.

Almost two decades earlier, as a result of the creation of a Greater Vienna in 1890, a competition was held for a general plan (*Stadtregulierung*) in 1892–93 which was eventually won by Stübben and Wagner. However, as Eve Blau has argued, "the two winning schemes . . . emphasized communication, transportation, and technical infrastructure. Neither scheme was adopted. Rather, a new *Regulierungsbureau* (development office) was created in the city building office . . . in 1894, which was mandated to draw on the winning schemes in preparing its own workable plan for a metropolis that was expected to double in size by 1950."[87]

But it was other submissions to the Vienna competition that revealed important issues: the absent other—the working classes.[88] The submission by the Mayreder brothers was the only one to take up worker districts and housing. Such housing provision, however, was not forthcoming, because the city authority was not prepared to subsidize the building of worker housing. The Mayreders argued that "in the plans of this outline such worker districts are recommended at diverse points, yet the choice of individual districts of course depends on the initiative of the particular building contractors. . . . In order to ensure the viability of such undertakings, not very valuable land should be used for this purpose, but nonetheless due recognition should be given for a good connection by city railway or tramway, above all to the places of work."[89] The inside/outside dialectic is more explicitly revealed in their statement that

> the construction of large rental barracks should be limited because, through them the peace of the dwellings is buried by the crassest corridor traffic. It is different with respect to the construction of worker hotels . . . through which bed rentals can be reduced. It should also be noted that these worker districts should never take on such a large scale, in order that the contrast between the working stratum and the rest of the population is not so sharply drawn; a certain extension of such a district, however, offers the advantage to the working stratum of easier communal provisioning.[90]

The anxiety about the working class in the urban network is apparent in another submission by Eugen Fassbender for a "People's Ring" (*Volksring*) for the recreation of the working classes. The provision of green spaces (later a theme of Sitte)[91] would be ensured by "creating sufficiently large spaces for park and garden areas within the city boundaries, whose spaces at the same time are large and healthy reservoirs of air between the smokey, unhealthy masses of buildings." Outside the city, "leaving the desert of the sea of buildings in summer is an urgent necessity for maintaining health. . . . The upper 10,000, the middle class, can easily obtain recuperation and enjoyment. . . . They leave Vienna in the summer in search of a distant or nearby summer-fresh environment; but the poor working population cannot do so. . . . Creation of a green belt around the city for the working classes" recreation would be "not only acting humanely but also wisely [*klug*]. One would give them sufficient spaces for recreation . . . and they and their children will not only maintain themselves healthy and strong but this will also engender satisfaction in them."[92]

It is evident, therefore, that none of the urban models, existing or proposed, was merely an aesthetic project. The dialectic of the open and closed (enclosed) city and the creation of new inside/outside parameters was most evident in Vienna, with the Ringstrasse enclosing the First District with its historical irregular streets and squares and acting as a barrier to other districts. Similarly, in part for military and political reasons, the lines of the city railway went around but not into the inner core of the city. The streetcar network also hardly penetrated the core either. The regulation of the city was also accompanied by the strategic siting of the military arsenals (the two ends of the horseshoe-shaped Ringstrasse terminated in military garrisons).

The inside/outside dialectic also manifested itself in the huge discrepancy between land values and ground rents in Vienna's First District compared with the other nineteen districts.[93] This inside/outside dialectic was also played out in the aesthetic sphere. The increasingly hostile confrontation between proponents of a "new" Vienna (such as Wagner) and the defenders of "old" Vienna manifested itself in opposition to modernist architecture within the First District (Loos's Haus am Michaelerplatz, Wagner's Post Office Savings Building) and along its borders (the Secession Building, the Karlsplatz). The most obvious instance of opposition drawing directly on the inside/outside dialectic is Joseph Bayer's 1902 article against the modern movement and specifically the Secession Building (1898) and Wagner's plans for a new city museum adjacent to Fischer von Erlach's baroque church on the Karlsplatz. Bayer frames the inside/outside dialectic as follows:

> It is high time to call a stop to this adventurist architectural endeavor. Modernism is indeed much less dangerous in the private construction of villas—up to now the main achievements of the latest architectural bizarre development; *outside, one does not need to seek out its buildings. But in the city itself they cannot be avoided!* Ever since so much space has been made available here for building, we have for this reason to care the utmost for the fate of the images of the streets. Above all, what danger threatens the Karlsplatz.[94]

Bayer also cites Karl Mayreder—an important competitor of Wagner's—and his dismay at the modernist tendency that "transplants the ground of architectural experiment into the middle of the city, where its works permanently to cooperate in affecting its character in prominent squares." Such experimental works as Olbrich's Secession Building, dominated as they are by "a misunderstood individualism," are themselves uprooted from the "people," from "cultural development," and "from all tradition."[95] The explicit appeal to an *inside* of the city whose traditional beauty must be preserved against the encroachment of modernity and *outside*, where occasional "architectural experiment" is relatively harmless, reveals both the boundaries of language games and the fear of transgression of those boundaries.

Of course there was opposition to the modern in Berlin too, but because the city lacked a similar, extensive old core separated so markedly from the new as in Vienna's Ringstrasse, the topography and morphology of Berlin, in some respects at least, had more in common with Haussmann's boulevards and could not be represented so readily in the spatial mode of division of core and periphery, as in Vienna.

Vienna's inside/outside dialectic was reinforced not merely by the Ringstrasse, the intention of which was to break down the separation of the inner core from the inner suburbs but whose actual effect was to strengthen this separation, but also by the fact that the main radial streets now did not enter the inner city but terminated at the Ringstrasse. The motif of the ring was extremely powerful in Vienna's morphology. The inner suburbs were enclosed by a belt road (*Gurtel*), whose significance was enhanced by the completion of the city railway, largely elevated, designed by Wagner, with one of its routes encircling the inner suburbs along the belt road. A further rail ring was formed with an outer-city rail line, linking the western suburbs. The whole system was built between 1894 and 1901. Another belt in the Viennese woods, proposed in 1905 as a "forest and meadow belt," was finally set out as a roadway between 1934 and 1938.[96] The ring motif also surfaced in the unrealized plans for the city: in Wagner's submission for the city regulation competition in 1894, with distribution circles (after Semper) around the city; in Fassbender's People's Ring, conceived as a green belt for the same competition; and in Wagner's outline for the expanding city in 1911, with its extending circles and radial streets. The plans for unrealized radial streets of Vienna included Wagner's proposal in the 1870s for a grand avenue from the Karlsplatz to Schönbrunn, Alfred Riehl's proposal in 1895 for a grand avenue from the Stephansdom in the heart of the inner city core to the Praterstern, and Arnold Lotz's proposal for a more modest boulevard.

In addition, Wagner's 1897 conception of the Danube Canal Quayside as a boulevard was never realized.[97]

The morphology of Berlin on the River Spree—actively utilized, as was the Landwehr Kanal, but waterways that were often neglected in descriptions of the city—had been characterized by an old Berlin (elements of which appeared as reconstructions in the 1896 Berlin Trade Exhibition) and by an expanding Museumsinsel and major broad thoroughfares, most notably Unter den Linden (running east-west), intersected by the Friedrichstrasse (running north-south). Though lacking a Ringstrasse, the northern and eastern thoroughfares fanned out around and away from what had been the old city: the Brunnen Strasse, Schonhauser Strasse, Prenzlauer Allee, Greifswalder Strasse, Frankfurter Strasse, and their extensions. In the post-1871 period until the First World War, more prosperous households moved westward and southward. This movement was facilitated by the city railway, opened in 1882 and running through the center of the city from the Schlesischer Bahnhof in the east to Halensee in the west. The ring motif in Berlin was embodied in the railway around outer districts of the city—the *Ringbahn*—already completed in 1877. This line ran through the working-class districts of Wedding and Moabit, areas that did not appear in imaginaries of the city.[98] As Walther Rathenau argued in 1899, Berlin's right to the title of metropolis did not lie in its post-1871 dwellings in the west. Rather, "what gives us this title is the factory city that no one knows in the west, and which is perhaps the largest in the world. The workers' city stretches its black tentacles to the north, south and east; it envelops the slender western district with iron sinews."[99]

What Berlin did visibly possess in abundance, according to contemporaries, was straight streets. An outsider's perspective in 1892 raises some of the very same issues that were being debated on straight or crooked streets. Mark Twain, who lived in Berlin for half a year, highlighted four aspects of the city. The first is the sense of its newness and the absence of history: "The bulk of the Berlin of to-day has about it no suggestion of a former period. The site it stands on has traditions and a history, but the city itself has no traditions and no history. It is a new city; the newest I have ever seen. Chicago would seem venerable beside it."[100] A similar view is found in Walther Rathenau's (1899) reference to Berlin as "the parvenue of cities and the city of parvenues." The second feature outlined by Twain is

> the spaciousness, the roominess of the city. There is no other city, in any country, whose streets are so generally wide. Berlin is not merely *a* city of wide streets, it is *the* city of wide streets. As a wide-street city it has

never had its equal, in any age of the world. "Unter den Linden" is three streets in one; the Potsdamerstrasse is bordered on both sides by sidewalks which are themselves wider than some of the historic thoroughfares of the old European capitals; there seem to be no lanes or alleys; there are no short cuts.[101]

The width of major streets, their appropriate pathways for traffic and pedestrians, and the location of green spaces and street furniture were sources of competition between cities, and examples and discussion abound in Stübben's volume. Twain's third feature is

the straightness of the streets. The short ones haven't so much as a waver in them; the long ones stretch out to prodigious distances and then tilt a little to the right or left, then stretch out on another immense reach as straight as a ray of light. A result of this arrangement is, that at night Berlin is an inspiring sight to see. Gas and the electric light are employed with a wasteful liberality, and so, wherever one goes, he has always double ranks of brilliant lights stretching far down into the night on every hand, with here and there a wide and splendid constellation of them spread out over an intervening "Platz"; and between the interminable double procession of street lamps one has the swarming and darting cab lamps.[102]

The fourth feature highlighted by Twain is the surface terrain of the city, which contributes to one of the powerful imaginaries of Berlin, namely, the city's affinities with American cities—in this instance, Chicago:

There is one other noticeable feature—the absolutely level surface of the site of Berlin. Berlin—to recapitulate—is newer to the eye than is any other city, and also blonder of complexion and tidier; no other city has such an air of roominess, freedom from crowding; no other city has so many straight streets; and with Chicago it contests the chromo for flatness of surface and for phenomenal swiftness of growth. Berlin is the European Chicago. The two cities have about the same population—say a million and a half.[103]

For Twain, the straight, broad streets in the center of the city possessed a grandeur he did not necessarily find in other cities. The city was already known as "Chicago on the Spree" (*Chicago am Spree*).

But, for others, the consequences of a city dominated by straight streets were different in the city's new suburbs. Karl Scheffler, writing in 1910, would have concurred with Twain, insofar as "in all the new city plans the wide straight street . . . predominates, [so] that one finds in all colonial cities, the street network is as standardized as possible . . . and the squares are drawn into this geometric pattern in a theoretically arbitrary manner."[104] This is especially apparent in the new Berlin of extensive suburban areas:

> Whereas in the old city its network is arbitrarily drawn, confusion reaches its peak in the new city sections. The wanderer would not find his or her way in the radial streets leading into the suburbs if the considerable traffic did not direct them. One can live for ten years in Berlin and still wander helplessly in the northern or eastern city sections. In some neighbourhoods one is as if in a stone-built maze, without beginning or end; and the joylessness is even more enhanced by the identical width of streets, by broad spaces. In Germany, New Berlin is certainly the most monumental example of modern dilettantism in the art of planning the city.[105]

The "northern or eastern city sections" to which Scheffler refers here were often the most industrialized and home to concentrations of the working class. For Scheffler, Berlin is the epitome of the modern metropolis but lacking a positive impression: "Of course there is everything in Berlin that belongs to the basic requirements of the modern big city: broad streets, artistic squares, boulevards lined with trees, gardenlike sections, a large city park and a plethora of imposing buildings. But taken together this all makes a sad, unattractive impression."[106] This is owing to what lines these broad modern streets—the rental and commercial blocks. This is true of every suburb where "land speculation also . . . follows the same goal as in the city, . . . the same barracklike structures."[107]

The predominance of the rental apartment blocks and dwelling and commercial blocks that line urban streets and even constitute whole districts is a significant dimension of the streets debate. In Berlin, the structure of the modern street layout beyond the center can be traced back to the 1862 Hobrecht Plan for the growth of the city beyond its old core as *Residenzstadt*. James Hobrecht envisaged the extension through extensive parceling of land into substantial blocks. Although he favored the development of socially diverse occupation of these blocks and open green interior courtyards, he did not reckon with extensive land speculation, speculation that led to the maximization of housing (rental) density, socially homogeneous housing blocks, and the creation of the despised rental barracks for which Hobrecht was unjustifiably held responsible.[108]

The nature of rental blocks differed markedly in relation to their location and their potential markets—in other words, the class composition of the tenants. They also differed markedly in their interior ground plans. Indeed, in Vienna they could range from rental palaces (*Nobelmietshaus*) for an aristocratic and haute bourgeois public, to rental blocks (*Miethaus*) for bourgeois and middle-class tenancy, to rental blocks for the lower-middle and working classes (*Zinshaus*), to single- or two-room apartments with all facilities shared in a communal corridor (in Vienna, the *Bassenahaus*). The flexibility of such blocks could also accommodate mixed housing possibilities, depending on city location. Accommodation for the working classes was often in minimal spaces with dramatic overcrowding in the worst rental barracks (*Mietskaserne*). In Vienna, a mixed-function block combining retail space, offices, and dwellings (the *Wohn- und Geschäftshaus*) was not merely the location, together with the apartment block, that Wagner required his students to concentrate on in their first year of study, but it was also the increasingly most common building type in districts close to and within the city center.[109]

The apartment block may have been a problematical building type in relation to the aesthetics of the urban street, but it was what Wagner associated with its proliferation in Vienna that was cause for concern. The "rented apartment blocks, which indeed owed their existence only to the tendency for 'capital accumulation'" emerged out of new modern social circumstances.[110] These new social circumstances are often hidden in the apartment block's facades, with "the overdone apartment block facade" and "the stuck-on facade" all serving to create "the swindle-like dimensions abounding in lies reminiscent of a Potemkin village." The apartment block itself, rather than its facade, responds to a feature of modernity, namely that "people's modes of living are daily becoming more alike," a process strongly suppressing the individual dwelling and creating "our present day uniformity of apartment house blocks." Hence, compared with London, Paris, or Berlin, "in no other city than our own does the modern apartment rental block (*Miethaus*) play such a large role."[111] Wagner highlights some features of this Viennese building type: its economic foundation, its leveling tendency, and its illusory facades. In Vienna,

> objects of rent (*Miethobjekte*) correctly termed "interest houses" (*Zinshäuser*) not infrequently extend 6 and 7 stories above street level. . . . Our contemporary apartment houses, conditioned by the economic situation, pursue no other purpose than to achieve the greatest possible yield on invested building capital through the piling up of small, easily rented dwellings in a single building.
>
> Once the rental value of the individual stories becomes relatively equal as the result of introducing an elevator, a natural consequence of this must be that the external artistic design as a means of distinguishing stories can

no longer be conceived of, and that architectural designs that seek their motifs in palace architecture can be characterized as completely misguided precisely because they contradict the internal structure of the building.[112]

He recommends that apartment block facades consist of flat surfaces broken by many equally proportioned windows. This leveling process and formal equalization of living spaces is part of the standardization that Wagner associates with modernity.

Wagner's views on the rented apartment block were shared by others in Berlin, such as the architect Albert Gessner, whose volume on this building type (1909) was subtitled *A Contribution to the Urban Culture of the Present*. Gessner argues that "the big city by its very nature requires a concentration of dwellings. This concentration causes an increase in its land values, and this in turn an exploration through the building of several floors. Building in several floors leads to the unification of several dwellings in a single house and hence leads to the rented block."[113] At the same time, he defends this building type against proliferation of individual dwellings (for a minority) and against association of this building type with human misery.

For the moment, let us return to the aesthetics of the street. Gessner's volume provides several Berlin versions of what may be termed the unified block front, in which the whole block of apartments has a unified style, thereby creating a harmonious composition. This contrasts with the plethora of styles that Rathenau identified in Berlin as creating "a fevered dream . . . [in] the major thoroughfares of the west. Here an Assyrian temple structure, adjacent a patrician house from Nuremberg, further along a piece of Versailles, then reminiscences of Broadway, Italy, Egypt."[114] This contrasts too with Sitte's view, because his central concern is with questions of urban planning—the layout of squares and streets. As Hans Schliepmann argues:

> Even here, Sitte takes his stand on the beauty of the self-contained, unitary image and evidently fails to see any aesthetic merit in the modern, straight, "showpiece" street, with its emphasis on the terminating feature; this is a response that holds good, in my view, only for a *painting* of a streetscape, rather than for the real thing. The elements that make up the streetscape— the buildings and their relationship to each other—are omitted from Sitte's investigation. Modern architectural debates invariably turn on the architectural form to be used for the individual building, rather than on the way in which individual buildings combine to form a whole, or on the nature of the visual impression conveyed by that whole.[115]

But it is Wagner who draws more radical consequences for the modern streetscape. For him, simplicity and practicality should be considered when appraising the street and streetscape. He detects an important new physiological change in this context, namely the transformation of the observer's visual capacity: "The modern eye has lost the small intimate scale, and become accustomed to fewer often changing images, to longer straight lines, to more extended surfaces, to larger masses." Applied to the ubiquitous apartment blocks, this requires decorating the surface with contrasting images and simple details, deliberate highlighting of structure, and avoiding wild designs. Not considered in this context are modern transport systems, some of which, such as the elevated railway (and much of Wagner's own *Stadtbahn*), "offer the traveler some pleasure through free and rapidly changing outlook."[116]

For Wagner, the "modern eye" needs to become accustomed to the modern: the larger scale, straight lines, flat extended surfaces, larger masses. Yet rapidly changing images—the mobile gaze—are a feature of metropolitan observation. However, the emphasis on the modern implied that "a modern metropolis cannot and should not have the appearance of ancient Rome or of old Nuremberg." The picturesque effect is to be avoided in the streetscape. Wagner favors the straight line of the street where possible, because "a person always goes in a straight line" and because, for the person in a hurry, the shortest distance takes the least time in an age where the phrase "time is money" has become commonplace. Where necessary, the curved street does contribute to the variety of the cityscape and may be appropriate for traffic too. But the concern for breaking down the monotony of the straight line and making the cityscape richer in variations (*abwechslungsreicher*) contradicts Wagner's delineation of the "modern eye" or at least seeks to introduce compensations for it.[117]

Such aesthetic and practical issues emerged out of the development of new technologies of vision, including urban transit systems and the possibility of new panoramic views of the city. Important too was the impact of photography, not merely for the tourist gaze (and the massive proliferation of images of the city in photographs and postcards) but for the mobile and virtual gaze on and in the city, as well as its impact on representation of architectural forms themselves.[118] The mobile gaze in the city, in which observers themselves are in motion, was often not the starting point from which the examination of representation of architectural forms themselves was addressed. Despite the limited nature of his reflections in this context, Wagner did at least recognize the significance of mobility of viewpoint. This contrasts with the more static investigations of Hermann Maertens on the ideal optical measurement of the distance between the stationary individual observer and a monument or built structure. Not uninfluental, Maertens's model was that of a motionless flâneur, leisurely observing a monument or monumental structure in an open square.[119]

Yet not merely is vision an issue in the transformation of building blocks, streetscapes, and apartment blocks, but also the preconditions for such vision: light and air. In some of the "rental barracks" in Berlin, the density of building and the desire to maximize rental income generated apartment blocks that extended inward in several stages from the street front. The best documented and researched instance is Meyer's Hof in Wedding (1875), but there were many other instances both in Berlin and elsewhere.[120] Air and light deprivation also arose from the construction of small factories inside the quadratic street blocks. The issue is posed by Theodor Goecke (1893) as follows:

> Wide streets, large buildings—a clear path for the traffic, that is today's solution! It has brought undeniable benefits, but with the benefits have also come the huge, undivided, towering blocks of housing. Air and light are no more than catch words if they only fill the streets and plazas but are denied to people in their homes: the excessive width of the blocks of housing has gradually led to ever more rear apartments, backyard apartments and so-called garden flats; in the districts that were constructed according to the regulations that applied until 1887 it has led to generally enclosed yards, air and light shafts in the midst of built-up blocks, veritable air and light chimneys, you might say. The regulations that subsequently came into force, stipulating more generous living conditions, ensure an ample supply of air and lights. But even these appear unequal and inadequate where the population is denser; the poor people are exclusively relegated to the rear apartments.[121]

And yet in this same period as Goecke is writing, the streets debate—framed, in part, as a technical versus an aesthetic approach to city planning—was taking place, and increasing ethical concerns were being voiced. Specifically, there is a substantial discussion of the experience of dwelling conditions and inadequate housing in Berlin, Vienna, and other major cities. Questions had already been raised in the 1870s as to the social basis of the Ringstrasse zone dwelling development; in the 1880s, economist Gustav Schmoller issued a warning on the housing question and the possibility of revolution. In the 1890s, there were an increasing number of empirical studies of housing conditions in major urban centers.[122] And there were few opportunities to look backward for a solution (did cottage districts or later garden cities really address the issue?). Here it should merely be noted that substantial contributions to large-scale public housing provision largely emerged *after* 1918 in Berlin and Vienna.

Such studies of actual housing conditions and socioeconomic circumstances in Berlin and Vienna contrast with the *imaginaries* of these two metropoles, imaginaries that relate only in a mediated manner to the socioeconomic and political conditions in the two metropoles.[123] Similar imaginaries also figure in the conflicts surrounding the building of a modern metropolis in Vienna from the 1890s through the First World War, in which those seeking to create a new Vienna were often accused of attempting to transform Vienna into Berlin. As indicated earlier, one feature of Berlin's "Americanism" was the straight street, and according to Scheffler and others its proliferation in many districts of Berlin. In contrast, all attempts to create straight grand avenues in the center of Vienna were rejected.[124] Yet, another danger in Vienna perhaps lay elsewhere. Since the completion of the Ringstrasse and the Ringstrasse zone, several modernist architects in the late 1890s—notably Wagner and Loos—were referring to Vienna as a Potemkin city, in which the streetscapes were dominated by contradictory facades, by "buildings with fronts reminiscent of Potemkin villages."[125] By the time of the completion of the Ringstrasse in the first decade of the twentieth century, one modernist structure had been completed on this defining streetscape—Wagner's Post Office Savings Bank—but it was set well back from the Ringstrasse itself and faced Ludwig Baumann's overladen neobaroque Ministry of War.

Within the same period, avenues such as the Kurfürstendamm were built in Berlin, as its more prosperous population moved west.[126] The desire for Berlin to become a world city could contrast with the aim of being a beautiful city.[127] Occasionally, claims were made that both were possible in Berlin. Rathenau made this claim in 1899 at the end of his critical exploration of Berlin's lack of beauty, and a plea for a planned destruction of the existing city, to be replaced by one with "air, free prospect, perspective"—in effect a Haussmann-like project. His text concludes: "I do believe that the blind hurdy-gurdy man is still there, in whose tin box, as a child, I was permitted to deposit many a three-pfennig piece, whenever my grandmother took me to the Brandenburg Gate to watch the old Kaiser drive out. Then, he used to play's *gibt nur a Kaiserstadt, 's gibt nur a Wien'* [There's only one imperial city, only one Vienna]; now, if he has moved with the times, he probably has a new and more joyous refrain on his melodion: 'Some day, Berlin will be the most beautiful city in the world.'"[128]

NOTES

I wish to thank here members of the Davis Seminars on the city in 2005, and the Davis Center's director, Gyan Prakash, for a most stimulating intellectual environment as a visiting fellow. Thanks, too, to three anonymous reviewers of an earlier draft. Like many others, I was inspired to research the Vienna of the late nineteenth and early twentieth centuries through reading Carl Schorske's pathbreaking *Fin-de-siècle Vienna* when it originally appeared. Eventually, many years later, I had the opportunity to contribute to that research.

An earlier version of part of this article was published as "Straight or Crooked Streets? The Contested Rational Spirit of the Modern Metropolis," in Iain Boyd Whyte ed., *Modernism and the Spirit of the City* (London: Routledge, 2003). All translations are mine unless otherwise indicated.

1. C. Gurlitt, "Der deutsche Städtebau," in R. Wuttke, ed., *Die deutsche Städte* (Leipzig: Brandstetter, 1904), p. 23.

2. See D. Frisby, *Cityscapes of Modernity: Critical Explorations* (Cambridge: Polity, 2001), ch. 5. For illustrations and descriptions of specific projects, see also the informative catalog, *Das ungebaute Wien 1800–2000* (Vienna: Historisches Museum der Stadt Wien, 2000).

3. D. J. Olsen, *The City as a Work of Art* (New Haven, Conn.: Yale University Press, 1986). On London in a later, post-Nash period, 1850–70, see L. Nead, *Victorian Babylon: People, Streets, and Images in Nineteenth-Century London* (New Haven, Conn.: Yale University Press, 2000).

4. For a critical argument against a single capital, see D. L. Parsons, "Paris is not Rome or Madrid: Locating the City of Modernity," *Critical Quarterly* 44, no. 2 (2002): 19–29.

5. See D. Harvey, *Paris: Capital of Modernity* (London: Routledge, 2000).

6. See F. Driver and D. Gilbert, eds., *Imperial Cities* (Manchester: Manchester University Press, 1999). On Austria-Hungary, see A. Moravanszky, *Competing Visions* (Cambridge, Mass.: MIT Press, 1998); also, Elisabeth Lichtenberger, *Wien-Prag Metropolenforschung* (Vienna: Böhlau, 1993).

7. See Frisby, *Cityscapes*, ch. 4.

8. See ibid., ch. 5.

9. For a fuller discussion of the 1890s streets debate, see D. Frisby, "Straight or Crooked Streets? The Contested Rational Spirit of the Modern Metropolis," in I. B. Whyte, ed., *Modernism and the Spirit of the City* (London: Routledge, 2003), 57–84. For another account, see J. Rodriguez-Lores, "Gerade oder krumme Strassen?" in G. Fehl and J. Rodriguez-Lores, eds., *Stadterweiterungen 1800–1875* (Hamburg: Christians, 1983), 114–24. On German city planning, see B. Ladd, *Urban Planning and Civil Order in Germany* (Cambridge, Mass.: Harvard University Press, 1990). On Sitte, see M. Mönninger, *Vom Ornament zum Nationalkunstwerk: Zur Kunst- und Architekturtheorie Camillo Sittes* (Braunschweig/Wiesbaden: Vieweg, 1998).

On Wagner, see D. Frisby, *Metropolitan Architecture and Modernity: Otto Wagner's Vienna* (Minneapolis: University of Minnesota Press, forthcoming 2008).

10. See Frisby, *Cityscapes of Modernity*, ch. 5.

11. C. Sitte, *Der Städtebau nach seiner künstlerischen Grundsätzen* (Vienna: C. Graezer, 1889); English translation by G. R. Collins and C. C. Collins, as *Camillo Sitte: The Birth of Modern City Planning* (New York Rizzoli: 1986). Joseph Stübben, *Der Städtebau* (Darmstadt: A. Bergstrasse, 1890; reprint, Braunschweig/Wiesbaden: Vieweg, 1980).

12. The last intervention is by Stübben in 1894.

13. See Otto Wagner, *Moderne Architektur* (Vienna, Scholl, 1896). In English, see *Modern Architecture*, trans. H. Malgrave (Santa Monica, Calif. Getty, 1988). For the review, see C. Henrici, "Moderne Architektur," *Deutsche Bauzeitung* 31 (1897): 14–20.

14. Most of these pieces remain unpublished in volume form. For a recent discussion of Sitte, see K. Wilhelm, "Städtebautheorie als Kulturtheorie—Camillo Sittes 'Der Städtebau nach seinen künstlerischen Grundsätzen,'" in L. Musner, G. Wunberg, and C. Lutter, eds., *Cultural Turn: Zur Geschichte der Kulturwissenschaften* (Vienna: Turia and Kant, 2001), 89–109. In detail, see Mönninger, *Vom Ornament zum Nationalkunstwerk*; and G. Reiterer, *AugenSinn: Zu Raum und Wahrnehmung in Camillo Sittes "Städtebau"* (Salzburg: Anton Pustet, 2003).

15. See E. Schachenmeier, "Über Strassenkreuzungen," *Der Städtebau* 10 (1910): 67–71, and tables 35, 36. See, originally, J. Stübben, "Gerade oder krumme Strassen?" *Deutsche Bauzeitung* 11 (1877): 132–34. See also, in the same volume, his "Ueber die Anlage öffentliche Plätze," *Deutsche Bauzeitung* 11 (1877): 393–95; 403–6; quote on 404.

16. The classic discussion of Sitte and Wagner's positions remains C. Schorske, *Fin-de-siècle Vienna* (New York: Knopf, 1980), ch. 2. For a broader view of planning issues that touch on issues raised here, see B. K. Ladd, "Urban Aesthetics and the Discovery of the Urban Fabric in Turn-of-the-Century Germany," *Planning Perspectives* 2 (1987): 270–86.

17. Sitte, *The Birth of Modern City Planning*, 138.

18. Ibid., 141.

19. Ibid., 142. My emphasis.

20. Ibid., 170.

21. Ibid., 183.

22. Ibid., 183.

23. E. da Costa Meyer, "La Donna è Mobile," in L. Durning and R. Wrigley, eds., *Gender and Architecture* (Chichester, John Wiley, 2000), 155–70. Anthony Vidler, *Warped Space: Art, Architecture and Anxiety in Modern Culture* (Cambridge, Mass.: MIT Press, 2000).

24. Sitte, *The Birth of Modern City Planning*, 197.

25. Ibid., 213–14, my emphasis.

26. Ibid., 225.

27. Ibid., 228. For a recent discussion of the plain (white) wall, see M. Wrigley, *White Walls, Designer Dresses: The Fashioning of Modern Architecture* (Cambridge, Mass.: MIT Press, 1995).

28. Ibid., 233.

29. Ibid., 234.

30. Ibid., 243.

31. Ibid., 246.

32. Ibid., 263.

33. Ibid., 270.

34. Ibid., 271. My emphasis.

35. J. Stübben, *Der Städtebau*, 514.

36. Ibid., 515.

37. Ibid., 16.

38. Ibid., 32.

39. Ibid., 33.

40. Ibid., 40.

41. Ibid.

42. K. Henrici, "Gedanken über das moderne Städte-Bausystem," *Deutsche Bauzeitung* 25 (1891): 81–83; 86–91.

43. Ibid., 83. My emphasis.

44. Ibid.

45. Ibid., 88. My emphasis.

46. Ibid., 90.

47. J. Stübben, "Über Fragen der Städtebaukunst," *Deutsche Bauzeitung* 25 (1891): 122–28, 150–55; quote on 122.

48. Ibid., 123.

49. Ibid., 154.

50. K. Henrici, "Der Individualismus im Städtebau," *Deutsche Bauzeitung* 25 (1891): 295–98; 301–2; 320–22.

51. Ibid., 296.

52. Ibid., 297.

53. Ibid.

54. Ibid., 301.

55. J. Stübben, "Der Individualismus im Städtebau,"*Deutsche Bauzeitung* 25 (1891): 362.

56. K. Henrici, "Langweilige und kurzweilige Strassen," *Deutsche Bauzeitung* 27 (1893): 271–74, esp. 271.

57. J. Stübben, "Zur schönheitlichen Gestaltung städtische Strassen," *Deutsche Bauzeitung* 27 (1893): 294–96.

58. Ibid., 296.

59. Several newspaper articles, though not those attacking Wagner, are included in Mönninger, *Von Ornament zum Nationalkunstwerk*.

60. K. Henrici, "Moderne Architektur," 14, my emphasis.

61. C. Sitte, "Die neue Stadterweiterung," *Neues Wiener Tagblatt*, September 27, 1891, where Sitte asks: "Do we want the new city to emerge as a *work of art* or merely as a *human storehouse?*"

62. See Frisby, *Cityscapes.*

63. See W. Benjamin, *The Arcades Project* (Cambridge, Mass: Belknap Press, 1999).

64. G. Simmel, "Soziologische Aesthetik," in H. J. Dahme and D. Frisby, eds., *Aufsätze und Abhandlungen 1894 bis 1900* (Frankfurt: Suhrkamp, 1992), 197–214, esp. 204.

65. G. Simmel, "Rom: Eine ästhetische Analyse," in D. Frisby, ed., *Georg Simmel in Wien: Texte und Kontexte aus dem Wien der Jahrhundertwende* (Vienna: WUV Universitätsverlag, 2000), 115–22, esp. 117.

66. For a brief discussion of Marx on the circulation process, see D. Frisby, *Fragments of Modernity* (Cambridge: Polity, 1985), 15–27, 106–8.

67. For a brief outline of Wagner's conception of modernity, see D. Frisby, "The Metropolis as Text: Otto Wagner and Vienna's Second Renaissance," in N. Leach, ed., *The Hieroglyphics of Space* (London: Routledge, 2002), 15–30.

68. See my analysis in *Metropolitan Architecture and Modernity.*

69. See Vidler, *Warped Spaces.* On Simmel in this context, see Frisby, *Cityscapes,* ch. 3, and D. Frisby, *Simmel and Since* (London: Routledge, 1992), chs. 4, 6, 8.

70. See Stübben, "Gerade oder krumme Strassen?" 132–34. See also, in the same volume his "Ueber die Anlage öffentliche Plätze," 404.

71. W. Benjamin, cited in Christine M. Boyer, *The City of Collective Memory* (Cambridge, Mass.: MIT Press, 1994), 142.

72. See Frisby, *Cityscapes,* ch. 4.

73. Ibid., 170–71.

74. Compare the table in Frisby, "Straight or Crooked Streets," 76. On urban imaginaries in general, see J. Donald, *Imagining the Modern City* (Minneapolis: University of Minnesota Press, 1999).

75. J. Le Rider, *Modernity and Crises of Identity: Culture and Society in Fin-de-siècle Vienna* (Cambridge: Polity, 1993).

76. On the broader context for these exhibitions, see Frisby, *Cityscapes,* ch. 3.

77. G. Melinz and S. Zimmermann, eds., *Wien Prag Budapest* (Vienna: Promedia, 1996).

78. See G. Brunn and J. Reulecke, eds., *Metropolis Berlin* (Bonn: Bouvier, 1992).

79. See, for example, R. Petermann, *Wien* (Vienna: Lechner, 1909).

80. See Frisby, *Cityscapes,* ch. 3, for a discussion of the context of this exhibition.

81. See W. Sonne, "Ideas for a Metropolis: The Competition for Greater Berlin 1910," in T. Scheer et al., eds., *City of Architecture, Architecture of the City: Berlin 1900–2000* (Berlin: Nicolai, 2000), 68. See also W. Sonne, *Representing the State: Capital City Planning in the Early Twentieth Century* (Munich: Prestel, 2004), ch. 3.

82. Sonne, "Ideas for a Metropolis," 69.

83. Ibid., 70.

84. Ibid.

85. Ibid., 69.

86. Ibid., 73.

87. See E. Blau, *The Architecture of Red Vienna, 1919–1934* (Cambridge, Mass.: MIT Press, 1999), 72.

88. See W. Maderthaner and L. Musner, *Die Anarchie der Vorstadt: Das andere Wien um 1900* (Frankfurt: Campus Verlag, 1999).

89. Cited in G. Kolb, *Otto Wagner und die Wiener Stadtbahn* (Munich: Scaneg, 1989), 138.

90. Ibid.

91. See C. Sitte, "Greenery within the City," in *The Birth of Modern City Planning*, 303–321.

92. Cited in Kolb, *Otto Wagner und die Wiener Stadtbahn*, 140.

93. Detailed in Frisby, *Cityscapes*, ch. 5.

94. J. Bayer, "Die Moderne und die historischen Baustile," *Neue Freie Presse*, April 3, 1902. My emphasis.

95. Cited in ibid.

96. On these various ring motifs, see D. Frisby, "The Impact of the Vienna Ringstrasse," in C. Hermansen, ed., *Words and Deeds* (London: Routledge, 2007).

97. These plans are discussed in *Das ungebaute Wien 1800–2000* (see note 2).

98. On Berlin's architectural development in this period, see Julius Posener, *Berlin auf dem Wege zu einer neuen Architektur* (Munich: Prestel, 1979).

99. See [Walther Rathenau], "Die schönste Stadt der Welt," *Die Zukunft* 24 (1899): 36–48, esp. 38.

100. Mark Twain, "The German Chicago," in C. Neider, ed., *The Complete Essays of Mark Twain* (Garden City, N.Y.: Doubleday, 1963), 88.

101. Ibid.

102. Ibid.

103. Ibid., 88–89.

104. K. Scheffler, *Berlin-ein Stadtschiksal* (1910) (Berlin: Fannei and Walz, 1989), 150.

105. Ibid., 151.

106. Ibid., 152.

107. Ibid., 155.

108. See K. Strohmeyer, *James Hobrecht (1825–1902) und die Modernisierung der Stadt* (Potsdam: Verlag für Berlin-Brandenburg), 2000.

109. On the *Wohn- und Geschäftshaus*, see U. Prokop, *Wien: Aufbruch zur Metropole* (Vienna: Böhlau), 1994.

110. See O. Wagner, "Moderne Architektur (1896)," in O. Graf, ed., *Otto Wagner I* (Vienna: Böhlau, 1994), 278.

111. Ibid., 281.

112. Ibid.

113. A. Gessner, *Das Mietshaus* (Munich: Bruckmann, 1909), 2.

114. Rathenau, "Die schönste Stadt der Welt," 40.

115. H. Schliepmann, "Vom Strassenbilde," *Berliner Architekturwelt* 6 (1904).

116. O. Wagner, "Moderne Architektur (1896)," 282.

117. Ibid.

118. On the mobile gaze and the virtual gaze, see A. Friedberg, *Window Shopping* (Berkeley: University of California Press, 1993). On photography, in relation to Paris, see S. Rice, *Parisian Views* (Cambridge: MIT Press, 1997).

119. On the optical measure in relation to monuments, see H. Maertens, *Skizze zu einer praktischen Aesthetik der Baukunst* (Berlin: Wasmuth, 1885).

120. See J. F. Geist and K. Kurvers, *Das Berliner Mietshaus 1862–1945* (Munich: Prestel, 1984).

121. T. Goecke, "Verkehrstrasse und Wohnstrasse," *Preussische Jahbucher* 73 (1893): 85–104.

122. See, for instance, E. von Philippovich, "Wiener Wohnungsverhältnisse," *Archiv für soziale Gesetzgebung und Statistik* 7 (1894): 215–76.

123. See Frisby, *Cityscapes*, ch. 4. For a useful literary comparison of the two cities, see P. Sprengel and G. Streim, eds., *Berliner und Wiener Moderne* (Vienna: Böhlau, 1998).

124. On the plans by Wagner and Riehl, see Frisby, *Cityscapes*, ch. 5; and Frisby, "The Impact of the Vienna Ringstrasse."

125. Wagner, "Moderne Architektur (1986)," 281. For Loos's text, see his *Spoken into the Void* (Cambridge, Mass.: MIT Press, 1989), 95–97.

126. On the "Kurfürstendamm, see K.-H. Metzger, *Der Kurfürstendamm* (Berlin: Konopka, 1986).

127. See A. Endell, *Die Schönheit der grossen Stadt* (Stuttgart: Strecker and Strecker, 1998).

128. Anon. "Die schönste Stadt der Welt," *Die Zukunft* 26 (1899): 36–48; reprinted as W. Rathenau, "Die schönste Stadt der Welt" (1899), (Berlin: Philo, 1989). Translation by David Britt. For these and other texts on Berlin see D. Frisby and I. B. Whyte (eds.), *Metropolis Berlin: 1890—1940* (Berkely: University of California Press, 2008, forthcoming).

✳ CHAPTER 2 ✳

The Global Spaces of Los Angeles, 1920s–1930s

PHILIP J. ETHINGTON

A GLOBAL METROPOLIS has an unlimited periphery. It takes its populations and raw materials from anywhere on the globe, and likewise sends its
emissaries, exports its capital, and sells its commodities to anywhere on the
globe. Those commodities are often images: both visual artifacts and works
of the imagination more generally, including imaginations projected on a
global scale, as in Hollywood movies.[1] A newcomer in the 1920s to the rank
of "global city," Los Angeles, California, provides an excellent place to explore these propositions.[2]

Angelenos reached out during the first decades of the twentieth century
to establish their global presence through three key industries: oil, motion
pictures, and aircraft production.[3] But they built those industries within a
distinctive, and *regional* "borderland" political culture. That regional political culture was both a primary export of the globalizing metropolis, and
also an import generated by the very processes of establishing global foot-
prints. Like an electrical charge running back from its global hinterlands
through the new networks of global exchange, those imperial processes
supplied the energy for the exercise of power and social authority in Los
Angeles and, eventually—as two Angelenos, Richard Nixon and Ronald
Reagan, became world leaders—in the United States more generally. In a
strong sense, a globalizing metropolis is also an imperial one, whether or
not that city is a capital, such as London, Paris, or Rome. The histories of
ancient Athens and medieval Venice, no less than those of twentieth-century San Francisco and Los Angeles, show that cities can become imperial
without or within nation-states.[4]

This chapter seeks to show how a particular metropolis *became* global:
how its spaces became interlinked with those of its global periphery, so that
the social power and imaginaries of diverse global sites became mutually
shaping influences. I recount three very specific and interlocking stories
about the Los Angeles oligarchy's role in Mexico and East Africa: (1) the
story of Edward L. Doheny in the "Faja de Oro" (golden lane) oil region of

Mexico from Tampico to Veracruz; (2) the story of Edgar Rice Burroughs's implantation of the Tarzan character in Los Angeles; and (3) the massive *Trader Horn* (1931) filmmaking safari led by MGM director W. S. Van Dyke in British East Africa from 1929 to 1930. An important contention of this chapter is that the history of a global metropolis legitimately includes the local histories of the global places that become part of that metropolis's global hinterland. This chapter, therefore, ranges back and forth between Los Angeles, Gulf Coast, Mexico City, and East Africa, stopping off occasionally in Chihuahua, El Paso/Ciudad Juárez; Mexico City; Washington, D.C., London; and New York City. Los Angeles oligarchs, directing its key productive sectors, became deeply implicated in the coercive and authoritarian regimes of these regions and found congenial environments where race and labor relations articulated with their own.

But the mass populations of these extraterritorial regions were no more orderly than those who settled in Los Angeles. Crucial to my account is the dual sense of the term *borderlands*: as both a region in North America and as a type of territory that is porous and marked by cultural *mestizaje*.[5] I claim that the Los Angeles region was typified by a borderland political culture because it was the product of centuries of social relations in a highly indeterminate zone at the margins of the Spanish Empire and on the porous frontier between Mexico and the United States. To control this unruly space, the Anglo/white ruling class attempted to impose a very clear vision of white supremacy and nonunion labor. But its global territories also became part of the borderlands of Los Angeles, posing the same opportunities and threats as its more contiguous borderland region.

LA RAZA CÓSMICA CONTRA LOS ANGELES

Although few Anglos noticed, the Mexican Revolution *took place* in Los Angeles, at the corner of Seventh and Flower Streets, from November 11 to 25, 1922 (fig. 2.1). For two weeks, that location presented an exhibition called "Artes Populares en México," planned and funded at the highest levels of the triumphant Mexican government of Álvaro Obregón to celebrate the hundredth anniversary of Mexican independence from Spain (1821) and its own first year in power.[6] It was the second venue for the exhibit, the first being Mexico City itself the previous year.

The elaborate revolutionary ideology of the exhibit was the work of the greatest thinkers of the first social revolution of the twentieth century. In his new post as minister of education (secretaría de educación pública) José

Figure 2.1. Site of the Mexican Revolution, 607 West 7th Street near Flower Street, Los Angeles. Panorama, 360 degrees from north at Flower Street, clockwise. Dr. Atl curated the "Artes Populares en México" exhibit here on November 11–25, 1922. (Gallery site is marked with a white oval, upper right.) © Philip J. Ethington, 2004.

Vasconcelos brought with him into power such legendary artistic-intellectual figures as Dr. Atl (nom de guerre of Gerardo Murillo), Adolfo Best Maugard, Alfonso Caso, Manuel Gamio, Roberto Montenegro, José Clemente Orozco, David Siqueiros, and Diego Rivera. They had all spent the revolutionary decade formulating a rich political and aesthetic philosophy that exalted pre-Columbian civilization and indigenous folk art, and fused it with modernist (especially and cubist and futurist) ideals imbibed in Europe and North America. The most dramatic and lasting achievement of this cultural movement was the great fresco mural movement, launched in this same year—a movement credited to Dr. Atl.[7] Vasconcelos's idea, that a "cos-

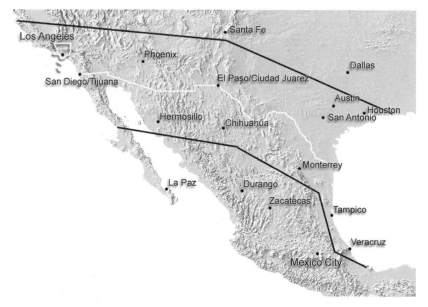

Figure 2.2. Map of the U.S.-Mexican borderlands. © Philip J. Ethington 2005.

mic race" of mestizos was poised to topple the Euro-American hegemony of the whites, could not have entered more hostile territory than it did in Los Angeles.[8]

President Álvaro Obregón was the Sonoran who had led his revolutionary armies to victory southward along the railroad arteries that had been built by California capitalists under the *Porfiriato*: regime name for the dictatorship of President José de la Cruz Porfiorio Díaz Mori—usually known as "Don Porfirio" (1876–80 and 1884–1911). The principal base for the Mexican Revolution was the tier of northern states along the U.S. border: Baja California, Sonora, Chihuahua, and Tamaulipas.[9] These states had been the most exposed to the capitalist transformation of the United States, but they were also the farthest from the power of the Mexican capital; insulated within the borderlands, a region that neither the United States nor Mexico had ever been able fully to control. The two most important Janus-faced portals of the borderlands were El Paso/Ciudad Juárez and southern California—Los Angeles in particular (fig. 2.2).[10]

The Los Angeles of 1922 into which Atl, Vasconcelos, and Obregón inserted the Mexican Revolution was very self-consciously counterrevolutionary. Its reactionary public sphere had been established by the *Los Angeles Times* owner and editor, Harrison Gray Otis. "General Otis" was a Civil War combat veteran and determined foe of all forms of labor organization. He was the principal "booster" of Los Angeles and also a leading investor. As Kevin Starr puts it, "the *Times* was more than a newspaper. It was a major real estate company" with extensive land holdings in the region, in the Pacific Northwest, and in Mexico. "The *Times* dominated Los Angeles in these years as few metropolitan newspapers have managed to do, promoting an image of Los Angeles as an upright, God-fearing, Anglo-American Protestant city, uncorrupted by foreign or immigrant influences, including unions."[11]

The Mexican Revolution was *against* Los Angeles to a significant degree, but the Mexican Revolution was also *from* Los Angeles. The brothers Enrique and Ricardo Flores Magón led the Partido Liberal Mexicano (PLM) in exile from Los Angeles, fought with the spies of Don Porfirio there, and resisted extradition in the U.S. courts. Harrison Gray Otis and Harry Chandler, his son-in-law and successor as owner-editor of the *Los Angeles Times*, had extensive property investments in Mexico. They collaborated openly with the Mexican dictatorship to round-up Los Angeles revolutionaries.[12] Just days before the Artes Populares exhibit opening, the Red Squad of the Los Angeles Police Department had raided an I.W.W. meeting at the tavern called "Bucket of Blood," arresting thirty-five labor organizers on "criminal syndicalism" charges.[13] The LAPD and the Shipowners' Association together made an "official declaration of war against radicals who infest the city's harbor." The harbor was a particular battleground not only against radicals but against racial impurity. The Ku Klux Klan counted the City of Long Beach police chiefs among their members and regularly made the news with terrorist threats.[14]

"DOHENY EL CRUEL": THE BORDERLAND STORY
OF TEAPOT DOME

In November 1921, Edward Doheny Jr. ("Ned") carried $100,000 in cash on behalf of his father to the U.S. Secretary of the Interior Albert Bacon Fall—a bribe they called "a loan"—to acquire highly profitable leases on the U.S. Naval Oil Reserves in Elk Hills, California. The bribe was revealed by the *Wall Street Journal* in April 1922 and came to be part of the Teapot Dome Scandal, a landmark in the history of the U.S. Senate and an enduring icon of the depravity of Washington politics in the "roaring twenties."[15]

Albert Bacon Fall's controversial act of leasing U.S. Naval Oil Reserves, No. 1 (Elk Hills, California) and No. 3 (Teapot Dome, Wyoming), to a pair of oil magnates, Edward L. Doheny and Harry Sinclair, respectively, was eventually exposed as proceeding from two identical bribes of $100,000, plus other financial favors.

In a transnational perspective, Teapot Dome is just the tip of an iceberg—incidental to a much deeper story about the Mexican counterrevolution and about the rise of a borderlands political culture that came to stretch from California to Cuba, if we can imagine a trajectory that runs from the story I tell here to the alliance between Richard Nixon and the anti-Castro Cubans who were caught in the Watergate Building in 1972. My retelling of this former footnote to history seeks to rewrite it as a major footprint in the global landscape of the Los Angeles, and North American, past.[16] The relationship between Secretary Fall and oil magnate Doheny began years earlier and centered on their mutual interests as investors in Mexico. It is even probable that without this shared history in the U.S.-Mexican borderlands, the Teapot Dome scandal never would have taken place.[17]

Doheny was a key member of a distinct network of southwestern politicians (known as the "Interventionists") who sought mightily to provoke a war with Mexico in order to stop the revolution, especially during the years 1914–20. Fall was the leader of these forces in the U.S. government, and Doheny was their leader among the corporate and private investor organizations. Doheny and Fall were both major targets of the Mexican Revolution; both were its fierce enemies and worked incessantly to overthrow its leftist leaders and to promote U.S. intervention, all to protect their own millions.

By the time of the Teapot Dome "scandal," Edward L. Doheny (1856–1935) had become one of the wealthiest men in the world. The son of an Irish immigrant laborer father and an Irish-Canadian schoolteacher mother, he was born and raised in Fond du Lac, Wisconsin. By all evidence a grim and determined man, Doheny learned the geology and law of mining, and then struggled to make a fortune prospecting in the silver and lead mines of New Mexico near the Mexican border beginning in the 1870s. But after nearly twenty years of sporadic success and failures, he finally gave up and followed reports of potential oil fields in the heart of Los Angeles, moving his family there in 1892.[18]

Doheny's accomplishment was not to "discover" oil in Los Angeles, nor to strike it rich by drilling the first gusher. There were at least a hundred wells in operation already by the time he entered the local market as a producer in 1892. Doheny did apply his grim determination to the "city field," gradually learning how to coax the rich reservoir of oil to the surface. Practically without capital, he and his partner actually dug their first well at the corner of Second Street and Glendale *by hand*—ore miner's style—

to a depth of 155 feet, and then rammed in a sharpened 60-foot telegraph pole to finish the job. This rustic well only produced about four barrels a day, and even this at first oversupplied the local market, where businesses had yet to learn the advantages of fuel oil over coal for operating boilers. Doheny's city field, just west of downtown (bordered by Figueroa, First, Union, and Temple) was notorious for overproduction relative to the regional demand. Gradually, however, Doheny converted local manufacturers such as brewers and even the City Hall to the use of fuel oil, as he slowly built regional dominance in oil production and refinement.

Doheny realized his first fortune not from the bounty of southern California geology, but from a shrewd alliance with the quintessential industry transforming the U.S.-Mexico borderlands: railroads.[19] When the Santa Fe railroad bought Doheny's Petroleum Development Company in 1902 for $1.25 million, he was a genuine millionaire at last, but barely so, and still a midget compared with the East Coast barons like Rockefeller. Nevertheless, he was ready to live like one, and in that same year he and his second wife, a former telephone operator named Carrie Estelle Betzold (known as Estelle) designed and built an enormous mansion in the most fashionable neighborhood of Los Angeles, the new "West Adams" district on the southern outskirts of the city.

Seeking new spaces to insert his capital, Doheny followed Otis, Chandler, William Randolph Hearst, and other California capitalists to Mexico. Hearst's father, George, had purchased the giant one million-acre Rancho Babicora in Chihuahua in the 1880s. In 1899, Harry Chandler bought an option on 862,000 acres of land in the Colorado River drainage and formed the California-Mexico Land and Cattle Company (its U.S. name) and the Colorado River Land Company, S.A (its Mexican name), which became the largest cotton plantation in the world, employing eight thousand Mexican peasants and yielding in one year alone $18 million in cotton.[20] "Ultimately," writes John Mason Hart, "Americans came to own the majority of land along Mexico's entire periphery."[21]

During the *Porfiriato* regime foreign investors poured a staggering $1.2 billion into Mexico, building its railroad infrastructure and developing its mines and agricultural estates. "Díaz's policies of keeping down popular protest, muzzling the opposition press, preventing the formation of labor unions, and not allowing strikes," writes Friedrich Katz, "greatly contributed to this enrichment."[22] Díaz also allowed foreign ownership of Mexican soil and generously exempted foreign investors from many taxes. But these policies simultaneously modernized and revolutionized Mexico. The railroads vastly increased land values and motivated a large-scale expropriation of the peasantry. Industrial and seasonal employment for market goods emancipated workers from their neofeudal *haciendas* while at the same time antagonizing them with fresh exposure to business cycles. The *Porfiriato* also sharply centralized political power in the hands of local *caudillos* (military-political chieftains) and the wealthy beneficiaries of foreign investment.[23]

Doheny's most spectacular property was the Cerro Azul oil field near Tuxpan. The fourth Doheny well, renowned to this day as "El Cuatro," spewed furiously out of control in 1916 and has remained for nearly a century one the ten most productive wells in world history, a veritable landmark of Mexican national pride. "Photographs of wells out of control, 100,000 barrels per day gushing into the air," relates Lorenzo Meyer, "circulated throughout the world, broadcasting the news of the enormous Mexican riches."[24] Mexico was, by the end of the Great War, the second-leading producer of oil in the world, after the United States. It outranked the Soviet Union, Indonesia, Iran, and Egypt, respectively.[25]

Mexicans came to know him as "Doheny el Cruel," but in Los Angeles Edward Doheny was a pious, benevolent prince, who built for himself a towering presence in Los Angeles society.[26] Eight Chester Place was no ordinary mansion. Doheny, like his contemporary, George Getty, was consciously trying to found a dynasty. As he violently extracted his immense wealth from the Mexican jungle, he built a perfectly safe replica of that jungle in his backyard. There the Dohenys kept ten thousand orchids among towering Mexican palms inside a ninety-foot-high steel and glass conservatory they called the "Palm House," an interior space so large that a full-sized canoe plied the waters of its oil-heated swimming pool (fig. 2.3).

THE CHIHUAHUA CONNECTION

The railways built during the *Porfiriato*, writes Friedrich Katz, "illustrated in the most palpable way possible that what had once been a frontier was being transformed into 'the border' and what had once been largely beyond the reach of any country was now within the reach of two countries."[27] It was within this borderland structure of political culture and economy that Doheny's indispensable ally, Albert Bacon Fall (1861–1944), rose to power.

Chihuahua was the seat of power for one of Don Porfirio's most ruthless and reactionary *caudillos*: Luis Terrazas. Terrazas and his son-in-law Enrique Creel aggressively pursued the Porfirian policies of expropriating the Indian and the free *criollo* peasants, welcoming foreign investors all the

Figure 2.3. *Top*: The "Palm House," 8 Chester Place. This oil-heated swimming pool ran less than a quarter of the length of the interior space. *Bottom*: Port of Tampico. From this port all of Doheny's Mexican oil was loaded on ships. Keystone stereoview, circa 1910. Both images courtesy of the University of Southern California, on behalf of the USC Specialized Libraries and Archival Collections.

while. The Terrazas-Creel clan amassed a vast landed empire of *haciendas*. Fighting the trend of modernization in Mexican and American labor markets (which generally expanded the realm of free-wage labor), Terrazas actually tightened the noose of debt peonage in Chihuahua. During his rule over the state as governor he filled all judgeships and local offices with loyal henchmen, making justice impossible for the masses of expropriated and exploited.[28]

Terrazas sponsored the interests of the U.S. investor William C. "Colonel Bill" Greene, who bought up huge tracts of land—made valuable by the railroads and by irrigation projects—and who ran a copper mine in Cananea in the neighboring state of Sonora. Greene, the "Cowboy Capitalist," controlled an immense $100 million empire in northern Mexico by 1906.[29] The strike by miners in that year at Cananea became a notorious precursor to the outbreak of the revolutions when it was brutally suppressed by Don Porfirio's troops, supported by two hundred Arizonans. At least 120 were killed to preserve the American capitalist's profit margins, but Greene laid the blame on an alliance of radical agitators from the revolutionary Partido Liberal Mexicano (headed by the Flores Magón brothers in Los Angeles) and the Western Federation of Miners (based in Denver).[30] At the time of the massacre of workers at the Cananea Consolidated Copper Company, Colonel Greene's partner, son-in-law, and general counsel was Albert Bacon Fall.[31]

Albert Fall's rise in New Mexican politics during the 1890s and the first decade of the twentieth century coincided, and was intertwined with, the rise of the Terrazas-Creel clan's consolidation of power in Chihuahua. Fall was one of Terrazas's major supporters and beneficiaries. He became a major landowner in Chihuahua upon marriage to William C. Greene's daughter, and was the legal representative in affairs of U.S. law for both the Greene and the Terrazas families.[32] In 1912, shortly after the downfall and exile of Don Porfirio, Albert Fall became a founding U.S. senator in the newly admitted state of New Mexico. From this platform, Fall was immediately recognized as the Republican Party's leading expert on Mexico. As Pancho Villa's revolutionary forces progressively took control of Chihuahua, they dismantled and redistributed the Terrazas empire and expropriated the holdings of Fall himself, who lost his entire Mexican fortune.[33]

Fall, a very tough operator, would not easily accept the loss of his Mexican wealth. Since 1913, he had openly lead the "Interventionist" forces attempting to roll back the revolution. He and the Interventionists, mostly major U.S. investors in Mexico, sought to establish a Mexican "protectorate" modeled on U.S. control of Cuba under the Platt Amendment ("a Cuban arrangement" Henry Cabot Lodge called it).[34] He also openly advocated the U.S. annexation of the northern Mexican states. When the Republicans regained majority control of the U.S. Senate following the 1918 elections, Fall was named to the Foreign Relations Committee (along with Warren Harding), and was authorized to chair the Subcommittee to Investigate Mexican Affairs, which held its hearings from September 1919 to May 1920.

Referred to derisively by Carleton Beals as "the Doheny Inquisition," the Fall Committee's chief mission was to assemble a case for U.S. intervention in Mexico, seeking testimony from North Americans injured and expropriated by the revolution. "From the first witness on, it became clear that Fall had no interest in fairness and would do his best to discredit the witnesses with whom he disagreed."[35] The "Fall Committee," as others called it, took place in the midst of the Red Scare of 1919–21. It began meeting in the year of the Seattle general strike, the Boston police strike, and the Chicago race riot. The leftist targets of the committee, and Fall's repeated charge that the Carranza government was "Bolshevistic," make it clear that the revolution had made a real impact on American political culture. The Left in the west was a visibly pro-Mexican Left. The leading targets of the Fall Committee were John Kenneth Turner, the Los Angeles-based socialist journalist who, in *Barbarous Mexico* (1908), had exposed the role of American capitalists in the exploitation of Mexican people, and Samuel Guy Inman, the Columbia University graduate and missionary, who wrote *Intervention in Mexico* (1919) and organized American Protestant churches against intervention through his Committee for Cooperation in Latin America.[36]

Doheny, the star witness, testified forcefully that Mexican oil was essential to American national power, that the other global sources of oil "are politically, nationally, and geographically less favorably situated than are the American oil holdings in Mexico."[37] His testimony foregrounds two other giant contextual perspectives on Teapot Dome: the Great War (including the U.S.-German-Mexican story of the Zimmerman telegram), and the military-industrial complex. Belligerents in the Great War were on a constant search for greater supplies of oil. The U.S. Bureau of Mines reported in 1920 that the U.S. Navy needed 200,000 additional barrels per day, and that "practically all of this increased quantity must be found in Mexico."[38] Understandably, Doheny enjoyed the protection of two U.S. warships anchored in the Tampico harbor, watching over his refineries and tankers.[39]

Faced with the very real possibility of expropriation after the enactment of the revolutionary constitution of 1917 and its notorious article 27 (declaring all subsurface minerals to be the property of the Mexican nation), Doheny and Fall labored fist in glove to support the counterrevolution. Fall maintained a network of spies and agents throughout the borderland region from New Orleans through Ciudad Juárez/El Paso to Los Angeles. When Porfirio's brother, Félix Díaz, made his bid to topple the Carranza government in 1918, his representative sent a letter to Fall asking his help in acquiring "air-plane guns, aeroplanes and tanks, also ammunition. $1,500,000 worth of ammunition."[40]

Doheny's oil operations not only survived but also thrived throughout the revolution. Through his Huasteca Oil Company and its parent, the Mexican Oil Company of Delaware, Doheny realized as much as $21 million in a single year.[41] Doheny's great wealth flowed only secondarily through pipelines; it flowed in the first instance from the barrels of guns. Doheny's wealth was protected also by General Manuel Peláez Gorróchtegui, *caudillo* of *Huasteca Veracruzana*, who controlled the Gulf Coast region encompassing Doheny's oil domain during the most dangerous period of the revolution, 1915–21.

Manuel Peláez was the landed and well-educated heir of a racially aloof Spanish-origin family. In "a region made up of mixed-race inhabitants, the majority of whom were mestizos with some admixture of Negro features, his appearance and [Spanish] family heritage counted for much."[42] Peláez held significant oil leases himself. But instead of aspiring to become an oil baron like Doheny, he chose instead to rule the Gulf Coast oil region as a warlord. Peláez guerrillas extorted approximately $30,000 per month from the oil producers as "loans" and "taxes," and used this money to maintain a disciplined private army. But Peláez was no mere employee of Doheny. "His ties to the petroleum industry evolved over time, from hostility and extortion to an alliance of mutual convenience." He cultivated a regional regime that refused to submit either to the logic of the revolution in Mexico City nor to the logic of the capitalists in North America and Great Britain.[43]

Thanks to the Peláez protection racket, the left wing of the revolution never gained control of the region where Doheny's Huasteca Oil Company and Lord Weetman Pearson's El Aguila Oil Company employed about forty thousand Mexicans. (Pearson's interests were later consolidated into British Petroleum). Labor organization was impossible in this repressive region. In effect, the Mexican government did not even control it. From 1916 to 1921, the Carranza forces were led by the popular "amigo de los obreros," General Cándido Aguilar. But Doheny's money saw to it that no friends of the workingmen would gain power in his Los Angeles annex. In one notorious incident Peláez guerrillas massacred eighty of Aguilar's soldiers—using knives and ropes in order to conserve scarce ammunition. Bernardo Somoneen, the founder of an early union, was assassinated in 1921.[44] Doheny maintained in the California desert a $100,000 stockpile of weapons, consisting of "nearly a million rounds of ammunition, almost enough high-power rifles to arm a regiment and enough modern machine guns to equip three batteries." He had two motives for maintaining this menacing arsenal. One was to supply the union-busting vigilantes who prevented labor organizing among his southern California oil facilities, and the other was to maintain a reserve for his *caudillo* ally Peláez.[45]

After the revolution was finally consolidated under the government of Álvaro Obregón in 1921, Doheny continued to support counterrevolutionary plots, through a network of spies and expatriates in Los Angeles.[46] He also invested heavily in Washington, D.C., to buy the influence he needed both domestically and internationally. Doheny began the process of getting out of the Mexican oil business in 1925, with a sale of $125 million to Standard Oil of Indiana. Then, in 1928, he sold the rest to Richfield Oil Company of California. Netting more than $100 million in cash from these sales, Edward Doheny reinserted this capital into Los Angeles.

His dreams of founding a lasting dynasty were abundantly materialized in the construction of a stupendous mansion for his son Ned and his family. Completed in 1928 at the staggering cost of $3.1 million ($30.2 million in 2000 dollars), "Greystone" was "a fortress-like fifty-room building in English Tudor style set on twelve and a half acres of land in Beverly Hills." Greystone offered Ned; his wife, Lucy (daughter of a Santa Fe Railroad Company executive); and their five children many comforts, including "a movie projection studio, a two-story billiard facility; a bowling alley, . . . a bar that retracted into the ceiling at the touch of a button, . . . tennis courts, swimming pools, and even a waterfall tumbling over boulders at an eighty-foot drop."[47]

But Doheny's dreams of founding a dynasty were dashed on February 18, 1929, when Ned was murdered in the guest room of the new mansion, under circumstances that remain mysterious (à la Conan Doyle) but were certainly tied to his own imminent trial as a defendant in the charge of bribing Interior Secretary Albert Fall. Fall himself had just been convicted for receiving the bribe. Before heading to Santa Fe to serve his one-year sentence, Fall stopped by Los Angeles to serve as one of the pallbearers as Ned was laid to rest in a gold-inlaid marble temple originally crafted in Rome for a second-century martyr. The Doheny fortune eventually came to rest in charities and a pair of memorial libraries: one at the University of Southern California, completed in 1930, and a second at the St. John's Major Seminary in Rancho Calleguas Hills. The grand entrance to the seminary library is a replica of the entrance to the Mexico City Cathedral, complete with an image of the Virgin of Guadalupe, the protector of the Mexican people since 1531.

Although the story of the Teapot Dome "scandal" may have ended with the imprisonment of Albert Fall and the collapse of the Dohney oil dynasty, the story of the larger metropolitan-global relations that it represents took very deep root in the borderlands, literally preparing the ground for Richard Nixon and Ronald Reagan. A more powerful Los Angeles would emerge after the Second World War, as a particularly virulent counterrevolutionary leadership arose to take Dohney's place.

TARZAN THE ANGELO

On March 1, 1919, the Chicago novelist and militarist Edgar Rice Burroughs (1875–1950) made a permanent move to Los Angeles, using the fortune he made from his Mars and Tarzan novels to purchase the giant San Fernando Valley estate of the late *Los Angeles Times* publisher Harrison Gray Otis, who had built "Las Flores" on the model of his own Mexican *haciendas*, acquired under Porfirio Díaz. Burroughs renamed the estate "Tarzana" in tribute to the source of his own fortune. The symbolic succession of Burroughs to the seat of the arch-reactionary Otis signified a profound shift in the sources of political power in Los Angeles, the United States, and eventually the world. Burroughs would insert his Darwinian, antidemocratic vision into the Hollywood culture industry, shifting the political work of Otis into the sphere of spectacular entertainment.[48]

Edgar Rice Burroughs was born and raised in Chicago while that city organized the conquest of the American West.[49] Son of an affluent Union soldier, Burroughs was educated in the classical curriculum at Andover Phillips Academy in the 1880s and then at the Michigan Military Academy in Orchard Lake, Michigan, during the 1890s. There Cadet Burroughs became the pupil of the veteran Sioux, Apache, and Nez Percé fighter, Captain Charles King. Known as "America's Kipling," King was a role model for Burroughs. The author of sixty romantic books about the European conquest of the "savage" tribes who ruled the Great Plains, King showed Burroughs how actual race wars could become profitable raw material for popular fiction. Burroughs was eventually posted with the late George Custer's 7th Cavalry in Arizona, a miserable assignment that fulfilled his hopes of military glory only in a fruitless chase of an alleged bandit known as "the Apache Kid." "I chased Apaches but never caught up with them," Burroughs remembered.[50] But Burroughs loved the military regardless and made its virtues a major theme of his life's work as a novelist and national-ist ideologue.

In fiction he did catch up with those Apaches, whose legendary ferocity he transposed into the Tharks, green men of Mars, the "anthropoid" apes of Africa, and scores of other invented races. His first product, serialized in 1912 in the New York pulp magazine *The All-Story*, was a tale called "Under the Moons of Mars" that earned him four hundred dollars.[51] Burroughs retitled the story *A Princess of Mars* for book publication in the same year, and that novel became the cornerstone of a series that eventually totaled twenty-five books. The plot of the Martian cycle revolves around a Civil War veteran named John Carter who is mysteriously transported to Mars in the midst of a desperate battle with Apaches in remote Arizona. Carter's human qualities (and strength enhanced by the weaker gravity of Mars) establish him as a master of various Martian races, eventually emerging as the supreme leader, the "Warlord of Mars" in the third novel.

The Mars series is a tour de force of the racial imagination. A once-mighty seafaring "white-skinned, blond or auburn haired race" called the Orovars had ruled the red planet for a half a million years, creating imperial, techno-logically advanced cities. "As the seas dried up, most of the Orovars entered into a cooperation with the black and yellow races, and their interbreeding over ages produced the modern red race."[52] This cooperation was necessary to fight the horrifically savage "green men," or Tharks. Tharks stand thir-teen to fifteen feet high (ten to twelve feet for the females), have "two legs and two arms, with an intermediary pair of limbs which could be used at will either as arms or legs."[53] With eyes set in the sides of their heads so that they can see backward and forward, a pair of sharp tusks, and blood-red eyes, the green men are a nightmare picture of uncivilized ferocity. Their children, hatched from eggs, are raised utterly without love. Their culture is brutal: laughter among them only signifies the appreciation of "torture, suffering, death."[54] Organized as "hordes," this race is obviously modeled on the Apaches, a comparison John Carter makes almost immediately.

Burrough's Martian allegory for the race wars of his own Age of Empire is obvious enough, but the stories also allegorize his intense hostility toward socialism, whose popularity in the United States had peaked in 1912 with the Socialist presidential candidacy of Eugene V. Debs. The Tharks had once been a civilized race, but they had lost all humane sentiments, "the victims of eons of the horrible community idea," in which all is held as common property—including the women and children. They had degraded themselves into "a people without written language, without art, without homes, without love."[55] His two main series each star a superman protagonist who rescues fair maidens from dark savages—each episode being an opportunity to demonstrate the superior manhood of whites in terms of civility, courage, refinement, and physique. "We all loved him," the opening narrator writes of the hero, Virginian John Carter, "and our slaves fairly worshipped the ground he trod."[56]

But Burroughs was only sharpening his knives with John Carter. His enduring popular masterpiece will undoubtedly remain *Tarzan of the Apes,* also published in *The All-Story,* in 1912, on the heels of the first Mars story. Burroughs would write another twenty-five Tarzan novels and license his invention to comic-strip serials and to twelve Johnny Weismuller movies produced by MGM. Burroughs created in Tarzan a truly original hero, one that combines the deepest elements of European folk narrative with the deepest anxieties of racial Darwinism.[57]

Burroughs eventually admitted that Kipling's Mowgli in *Jungle Book* was a model for Tarzan (and Kipling believed that Tarzan was the best of hundreds of rip-offs). But Burroughs was not merely rewriting Mowgli; he was tapping the same well as Kipling: the mythic story of feral man, the recurrent leitmotif of Western urban civilization since Romulus and Remus were suckled by wolves.[58] Burroughs chose apes as Tarzan's parents according to the theory of racist Darwinism, in which the English are supposedly the most highly evolved humans, and the British aristocracy the most highly evolved of these. Burroughs created a refined British lord and lady, the Greystokes, and in the novel orphans their heir in the deepest, most primeval jungle, so that their baby would be nurtured by the lowest species of protohumans—a fictional ape tribe that has language. These speaking apes are promoted on the evolutionary scale better to fit the racist scale between beasts and the African humans, who play only a wicked role in the novel. Tarzan, whose name means "white skin" in the language of this ape tribe, emerges from the jungle as a perfect Nietzschean *Übermensch.* He is master of huge beasts and of all men, physically and mentally superior in every way. Setting aside the playboy image of Johnny Weismuller, the original Tarzan is a complex mix of savagery and civilization: he is stronger than a tiger and loves to kill, but he speaks French and English and has impeccable, inbred aristocratic manners.

The 1914 outbreak of war in Europe also encouraged Burroughs to pursue nationalist propaganda. By 1918, he was not only a wealthy author of the Tarzan and Mars fantasies; he was the aggressive public foe of Huns, Communists, Bolshevists, Anarchists, and pacifists. His Darwinian worldview was inextricable now from his political expression. Burroughs denounced Germans and pacifists as "anthropoid creatures," a phrase he had invented for the advanced apes of the first Tarzan novel. "It is very possible that we shall see loosed upon the community a raft of street-corner orators of the I.W.W. and Bolshevik types. . . . We have thrashed the trouble makers of Europe and it is within the range of possibilities that we may have to deal with similar cattle here."[59]

Writing from Tarzana in 1922, on the occasion of the novel's tenth anniversary reissue, Burroughs succinctly stated his core ideology: "[T]he life of Tarzan of the Apes is symbolic of the evolution of man and the rise of civilization, during which mankind gained much in its never-ending search for luxury; but not without the sacrifice of many desirable characteristics, as well as the greater part of its liberty."[60] It can hardly be an accident that this 1922 passage almost perfectly expresses a central tenet of European fascism. The Burroughs-Tarzan opus continuously extols a master-race savagery. The lust for the hunt and joy of killing overwhelms Tarzan in many scenes. After he defeats lions, tigers, and giant apes with his bare hands and a very phallic knife (his father's sole heirloom and symbol of Tarzan's true human family), Tarzan always shouts his blood-curdling triumph-cry. An African man killed Tarzan's beloved ape foster-mother, so Tarzan hunts African humans simply for revenge. Burroughs offers no other justification nor any apology for Tarzan's many gratuitous murders. Given Burroughs's tireless exaltation of refined humanitarian sentiments, Tarzan's massacre of Africans can only signify that they do not merit human sympathies. Neither did the Jews of Europe, in the contemporary ideology of Germany's National Socialists.

Burroughs had created an instant pop-culture icon for the self-proclaimed "white" race. It is no exaggeration to say that Tarzan was a protofascist hero for the mass consumers of North American racialized capitalism. The masses who raised their children on Tarzan and John Carter were evidently unperturbed by dehumanizing, genocidal romances. But then, also unperturbed were countless generations of Europeans, for Burroughs's singular achievement was to update antique warrior heroes: Ireland's Cúchulainn; England's King Arthur; Spain's Amadis de Gaula; and his son, the Esplandían who conquered California itself and helped drive Alfonso Quijano to Quixotic madness. Those heroes also improbably slew horrific giant monsters, vanquished fierce foes by the thousands in battles of impossible odds, and behaved politely toward fair maidens. In the twentieth century, mythic heroes were to fight not *only* Muslim Moors but all the world's nonwhites. The appeal of this formula is proven by the speed with which the story of Tarzan spread through the European diaspora.

In 1918, the year of the Armistice and the onslaught of the Red Scare, the budding movie industry produced its first adaptation of *Tarzan*, and the business opportunities of Hollywood, along with the congenial climate, beckoned. Burroughs pulled up all his Chicago roots and purchased the 570-acre "Las Flores" estate of Harrison Gray Otis. "The world was combed for the greenery on this knoll," reported the *Los Angeles Times*, "hundreds of the plants coming from Asia and Africa."[61] Burroughs renamed the estate "Tarzana" and rapidly conceived plans for an entire residential community by that name (fig. 2.4).

Once he had settled himself and his family on the Tarzana estate, Burroughs of course resumed Tarzan production. *Tarzan the Terrible* (1921, manuscript finished in December 1920) is entirely about black and white races in a new fantasyland he invented called "Pal-ul-don."[62] Burroughs, now a landed squire with his own Mexican *peones*, living in the very mansion of the hated foe of the organized working class, had settled in the ideal environment for the production of the cultural hegemony of white supremacy. Tarzana became the plantation from which the Nietzschean protofascist superhero was harvested. Burroughs also joined Thomas Ince as an initial investor in Hollywoodland.

Such are the dreams that stuff is made from. Burroughs wrote the dreams of the globalizing North American "white" race into Tarzan and contributed mightily to the inscription of those racial dreams into the landscape of Los Angeles itself.

Hollywood's White Hunters in Africa

Johnstone Kenyatta and W. S. Van Dyke nearly rubbed shoulders at the port of Mombasa in February 1929.[63] Kenyatta was secretary general of the Kikuyu Central Association, setting sail for London, armed with a petition demanding the redress of wrongs perpetrated against the Kikuyu farmers of Kenya Colony, whose lands had been stolen and occupied by white settlers in the rich highlands surrounding Mount Kenya.[64] That same month, while the very nervous Colonial Office discussed ways of blocking Kenyatta's access to Downing Street, the first unit crew of thirty-five actors, technicians, cameramen, and makeup artists from the studio of Metro-Goldwyn-Mayer set sail from New York for Mombasa under the leadership of director W. S. "Woody" Van Dyke to begin a massive safari to film *Trader Horn* (MGM,

Figure 2.4. Tarzan and Tarzana, 1914 and 1928. *Tarzan of the Apes* first edition cover art by Fred J. Arting, superimposed on a 1928 U.S. Geological Survey topographic map, scale 1:24,000. Burrough's "Tarzana" development lay just south of Ventura Boulevard, traced by Tarzan's left leg. Harrison Grey Otis's "Las Flores" estate is marked here as the Caballero Country Club. USGS Reseda Quadrangle map reproduction courtesy of the Map and Imagery Laboratory, Davidson Library, University of California, Santa Barbara. © 2007, The Regents of the University of California. All rights reserved. Photomontage © Philip J. Ethington, 2005.

1931) (fig. 2.5).[65] Woody Van Dyke was the protégé and disciple of D. W. Griffith, whose spectacularly racist *Birth of a Nation* (1915) virtually founded the American motion picture industry.[66]

Trader Horn was the best-selling 1927 memoir of a grizzled African ivory trader, a Scot named Alfred Aloysius Horn. Horn had been the advance agent of London-based trading companies, partially assimilating himself into tribal cultures (especially Igbo) in the west and central African interior.

Figure 2.5. Unloading Sound Truck No. 20 at the port of Mombasa, Kenya Colony, 1929. *Trader Horn* production still, MGM Collection. Margaret Herrick Library, The Academy of Motion Picture Arts and Sciences, Beverley Hills. TRADER HORN © Turner Entertainment Co. Licensed by Warner Bros. Entertainment Inc. All rights reserved.

Horn was one of the Europeans touched by Burroughs's Tarzan story. His memoir conflates Tarzan with other white captive stories and with his own experiences among the African tribesmen.[67] He claimed to have "rescued" a white female captive, an orphaned European girl adopted and acculturated by the Isoga [Igbo] tribe and allegedly worshiped as a "White Goddess."[68] Rescuing white women from dark savages was a favorite theme for the Hollywood culture industry. The book was a best seller, so Louis Mayer and his production chief, Irving Thalberg, secured the movie rights.

Kenyatta remained in London for sixteen years, became a friend and protégé of American anticolonial leftists, including Paul Robeson and C.L.R. James, and wrote the anthropological classic *Facing Mount Kenya* (1937) under the tutelage of Bronislaw Malinowski before returning to Kenya to assume leadership of the independence movement after the Second World War in 1945.[69] The MGM crew remained in Africa for almost a year and traveled fourteen thousand miles across five European colonies: Kenya Colony, the Anglo-Egyptian Sudan, the Protectorate of Tanganyika, the Protectorate of Uganda, and the notoriously repressive regime of the Belgian Congo. They crossed the Equator seven times and built roads where none existed. Their three hundred African workers dragged a ten-ton electric generator and thousands of light bulbs to illuminate the "Dark Continent" for the European faces watching silver screens in Canada, the United States, France, Belgium, and Australia, countries in which the movie was eventually released to enormous acclaim.[70] Ernest Hemingway credited this movie for his fascination with Africa.

By taking up the subject of African colonization in the crucial years of global economic crisis, 1929–31, Hollywood made itself a powerful reactionary force supporting racist injustice. It is no accident that the African people were just at this moment becoming very dangerous to the empire. Hollywood's African savages were the nightmare rendition of the independence movement itself, which would climax for Kenya in the Mau Mau Rebellion of 1952–55 and complete independence in 1963, when Jomo (formerly Johnstone) Kenyatta became the founding president of Kenya.

As late as 1895, "Kenya" was "an overlapping patchwork of hunting, cultivating and herding peoples." These peoples included the Kikuyu and Kamba farmers and Masai herders. The British, employing "violence on a locally unprecedented scale, and with unprecedented singleness of mind," profoundly transformed the political, economic, social, and cultural landscape of East Africa.[71] One of the first tasks was to expropriate the richest farmlands, the high territory of the Kikuyu on the shoulders of Mount Kenya. In 1908, Secretary of State Lord Elgin pledged exclusive rights to these lands to the white settlers, segregated lands that would henceforth become known as the "White Highlands." (figs. 2.6).[72]

The white settlers who filtered into Kenya, largely from South Africa, were the most aggressively racist element in the new colony. They sought domination not only over the Africans, whom they considered less than human, but also over the numerous Indians, who had settled for decades in the towns of East Africa, as railroad laborers and later as an intermediary, petty bourgeois trading and professional class. The settlers won approval in 1915 of the Crown Lands Ordinance, which declared all lands occupied by Africans to be the property of His Majesty the King, authorized 999-year leases, and gave the governor the power to veto sales of lands between members of different races. Also in that year the white settlers won approval of the Native Registration Ordinance, which established the hated *kipande* system, whereby all African males over the age of sixteen were required to

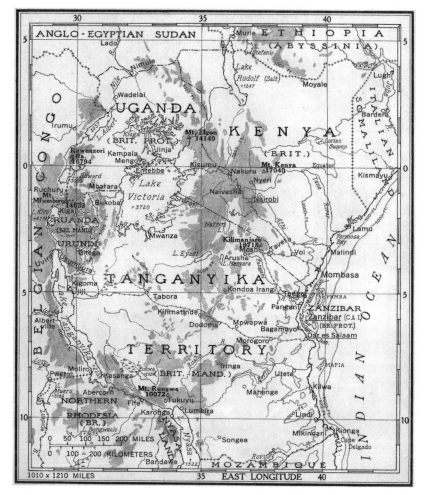

Figure 2.6. East Africa, 1920. Courtesy of Keystone-Mast Collection, UCR/California Museum of Photography, University of California, Riverside.

carry identity documents and a work record in a tin container suspended from a necklace. A negative comment ("shiftless" or "lazy") written into this record by the whim of any settler could make a man unemployable.[73] This system drove down wages and immobilized the workforce, providing the white settlers, and later Metro-Goldwyn-Mayer, with a labor force that came to be known as "the cheapest in the world."[74]

As the MGM crew established their headquarters in Kenya's capital of Nairobi and began to search for "native" labor, they entered a labor market of urbanized tribesmen whose "white" employers openly advocated forced labor. The antiunion cynicism of the Hollywood labor bosses fitted neatly with the white settlers whose compulsory labor program was openly discussed by Governor Grigg himself as "synonymous with slavery."[75] An early MGM memorandum from Charles Carlton to Thalberg and Mayer recommended using meat to keep the hundreds of African porters and extras happy. He lamented that "previous to the World War a white man could go into the interior and commandeer all the native help he would require and in most cases the natives were never paid for their services." But alas, he sighed: "Within the past seven years [i.e., the 1920s] the government has pampered these natives to the extreme." Under pressure from several humanitarian and parliamentary reports, the Colonial Office had set a minimum wage for Kenya Africans at ten cents per day.[76] The script of *Trader Horn* accepted without irony or comment both slavery and compulsory labor.

The script that Van Dyke shot in East Africa is nothing short of a genocidal fantasy. Black bodies drop like flies throughout *Trader Horn*. Thrown from cliffs, skewered by spears, burned while crucified head-down at the stake, fed to lions, and devoured by alligators, the Africans, stripped of names and all manner of dignity, are slaughtered on a genocidal scale. Of Trader Horn's expedition, no African character survives by the end of the film. All have been slaughtered by the "savage" hoards of African tribesmen encountered in the "interior." African actors portrayed crimes against themselves of which the whites were guilty.

Trader Horn's violence is not limited to humans. A sickening number of beautiful large animals were killed on-camera, for-camera. Van Dyke took special pride in the MGM safari's hunting armada. Wild animal footage was a major component of this movie project, so the crew spent as much time shooting big game with guns as they did with cameras. More significantly, they shot them with bullets and film at the same time. Guided by the four "White Hunters"—retired British soldiers who led aristocratic safaris from their base in Nairobi—and their African "gun boys," the crew killed thirty-seven big game animals in a single day (fig. 2.7).[77]

Central to the script is the relationship between Trader Horn (played by Harry Carey) and his "gun boy" Renchero (played by Mutia Omoolu). Renchero is Horn's unfailingly loyal lieutenant, and also his slave driver: he whips the expedition's carriers as a matter of routine throughout the film. Nothing is known about Omoolu, except that he was from the Kamba tribe. Presumably he lived and worked in Nairobi, drawn into the urban orbit by the time Hollywood found him. To their credit, the producers gave Omoolu

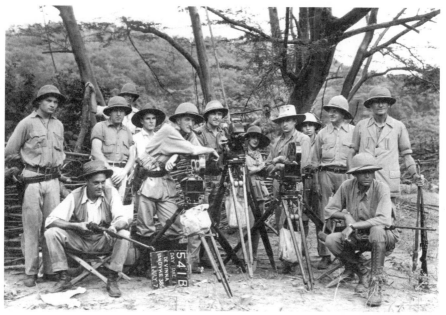

Figure 2.7. Shooting Africa, 1930. Director Woody Van Dyke is seated at far right; Director of Photography Clyde De Vinna, smoking a pipe, is leaning on his 35-mm Akley, left of center; "White Hunter" Major Edward Dickenson is seated at far left. *Trader Horn* production stills, MGM Collection. Margaret Herrick Library, The Academy of Motion Picture Arts and Sciences, Beverley Hills. TRADER HORN © Turner Entertainment Co. Licensed by Warner Bros. Entertainment Inc. All rights reserved.

title credit. Uncredited was another key figure, Riano Tindami, a Maasai who had served in the King's African Rifles. Tindami played "Riano," the lead carrier for the missionary Edith Trent (played by Olive Carey), who is seeking her long-lost daughter, the White Goddess "Nina T." (played by Edwina Booth). But Riano served the *Trader Horn* expedition in two roles. He was also the gun bearer for director Woody Van Dyke himself. Significantly, he was "Riano" in both roles.

Just as filming began, the political activities of the Kikuyu Central Association, (KCA) were generating a small panic among the settlers and colonial authorities. Labor shortages on farms were attributed by settlers to the "propaganda by Kenyatta." Murders of white settlers were now viewed as political acts, and the under-secretary of state was questioned about the apparent growth of "crimes committed against the person of white people in Kenya Colony."[78] The governor's secretary, Colonel E.A.J. Dutton, penned urgent dispatches to the Colonial Office in London, passing along secret police reports about KCA agitators, one of whom allegedly told a crowd that if their demands were not met, they should "organize rioting against the Government," and that "bands of twenty should surround out-lying farms and murder the occupants."[79] A dominant theory emerged that crime in 1928–29 was, as Police Commissioner R.G.B. Spicer stated, caused by "the accumulation of education, sophistication and detribalization of the African," which had only reached a "superficial stage in the raw African mind."[80] The theory was given its clearest expression by Governor Sir Edward Grigg himself, in a long report to the secretary of state, Lord Passfield, on the Kikuyu Central Association: "The Association consists largely of the semi-educated, the members of the younger generation who know just enough to be discontented with the conditions of barbarism in which they were born but not enough to appreciate the difficulties of emerging in a moment of time from that state of barbarism to the assumption of all the concomitants of a highly developed Western civilization."[81] Grigg was a pro-settler governor who enjoyed good relations with the leading settler, Lord Delamere, a long-haired, violent man described by Grigg himself as a man "with the racial ideas of the southern states at the time of the American civil war, who thought of old Virginia as the model."[82] Lord Delamere was the leading representative of Kenya's great aristocratic landholders, who had first expropriated the rich country of Kikuyuland. Elspeth Huxley's two-volume biography of Lord Delamere, an acclaimed bestseller responsible for establishing a romantic vision of African settlers, was titled *White Man's Country*.

But the spaces of Kenya Colony, while held generally in a state of subjection to London, were not fully controlled by any one social group or institution. An adequate account of agency in the story of colonial exploitation of East Africa requires recognition of a complex set of competing forces: white settlers, collaborationist tribal elders, a Colonial Office at odds with the goals of the settlers, humanitarian liberals in Parliament, Christian missionaries at odds with both the Colonial Office and the settlers, and most important, indigenous rights and independence activists such as Jomo Kenyatta and the Kikuyu Central Association. Kenyatta himself performed many of the "displacements" of the crucial period under consideration here.[83] A nationalist deeply influenced by the world socialist movement, he was schooled intellectually by Malinowski at the London School of Economics and politically by C.L.R. James. Kenyatta was even reported by Scotland Yard as having joined Marcus Garvey's Universal Negro Improvement Association (UNIA).[84] But among his principal political issues was defense of the "traditional" practice of clitoridectomy, or "female circumcision," a popular cause among the Kikuyu but sheer anathema to the Protestant missionaries and to feminists alike.[85] While the *Trader Horn* crew filmed their story about central Africans worshiping a white European woman, Kikuyu women demonstrated in song and dance against Kikuyu who refused to undergo the circumcision rite and operation. A Colonial Office informer reported: "Yesterday they had this dance at Kabuku and were abusing Yusufu, the teacher at Kabuku School, as this man married an un-circumcised girl. They were singing that any Kikuyu that will marry an un-circumcised woman . . . can even do illicit connection with his own mother."[86]

At it turned out, the Labour Government directly confronted the Virginia-style settlers and issued the "Memorandum on Native Policy in East Africa," which established the principle of "African paramountcy," meaning, ostensibly, that the interests of the African Kenyans would take precedence in the final policy analysis. In practice, it meant that the Colonial Office could use the interests of the Africans to justify blocking *settler* paramountcy. The policy was hated by the settlers, whose dream of an independent settler state was officially ended in the year of *Trader Horn's* theatrical release, 1931.[87]

The defeat of the extreme white supremacists in Kenya was, however, only a defeat on the precinematic landscape of the empire. Kenyatta would return to Mombasa in 1945 and mobilize the struggle for independence, operating in the interstices of power opened up by this defeat. But the work of extreme white supremacy had already been transferred to a larger landscape. For, just at the moment when leftist, liberal, and humanitarian forces were beginning to undermine the moral authority of the colonial system, Hollywood spread throughout the globe a cruel landscape of injustice, wherein all of Africa was reduced to the very vision of the "White Highlands" settlers themselves.

Indeed, the script of *Trader Horn* bears such an uncanny resemblance to the worldview of the white settlers of Kenya, that we cannot avoid recognizing their unity within concrete global networks of power, representation, and injustice. Central to the colonizing project, as with the American system of white supremacy, was the representation of "natives" as unreasoning murderers, so menacing that elaborate structures of coercion and punishment were justified. "One never knows what they will do next, " one white settler wrote to her sister during an armed confrontation in Kenya in 1912, "[and] once they think of killing they don't know where to stop; neither can any of them tell what they are doing it for—At this moment we are surrounded by 20,000 fully armed warriors."[88] Early in *Trader Horn*, the distant drums of the "ju-ju" menace the white trading party, as the vast and bloodthirsty population of jungle natives begin to pursue them, for no apparent reason. The naive Peru asks: "Horn, what is this ju-ju?" Horn replies: "Magic. God knows how it starts or where it comes from—but while those drums call, every black devil in the bush will be a homicidal maniac. And if your skin happens to be white, the witch-men are the better pleased."[89] *Trader Horn* adds a crucial element to the chronic fears of the white settlers: that Africans would love to kill Europeans just *because* they are white.

Millions of self-styled "whites" would now have their whiteness reinforced, learning that that "black" Africans were heartless savages bent on the senseless slaughter of Europeans in a generalized race war. On the Hollywood landscape, no significant cultural diversity would be permitted for "Africa." Hollywood's Africa was Hegel's: a people without history. All of Africa was reduced to a generic west and central African jungle. In cinematic Africa there are no farmers or herders, just savages with spears in jungles, without visible means of support (and therefore no legitimate claims to the soil).

At the climax of *Trader Horn*, Alfred Horn, his young visitor "Little Peru" (Duncan Renaldo), and Renchero (Olmoolu) are waiting their turn to be crucified head-down and burnt alive by their captors, the menacing Isogas. This fate had already befallen their African porters the night before. They vow to go out fighting, however, and Alfred Horn makes a curious speech in their shared cell. "At least the white race won't be disgraced by . . . " Here Horn breaks off as his eyes fall on his loyal African squire Renchero: " . . . well, any of the three of us. Why, you black hunk!" This gesture grants to Renchero a guest membership in the white race. But their only hope is the sympathy of the so-called White Goddess, "Nina T," the missionary's grown daughter, who is now a priestess of some sort, respected and feared by the Isoga. Peru and Nina are the script-destined love interest, but at this point Nina is struggling with her racial loyalties, refusing at first to show any mercy. "Don't you understand," Peru pleads with her, "white people must help each other!" (fig. 2.8).

The violence-crazed cannibals who worship the "White Goddess" are an obvious lynch mob, bent on public torture and execution for the sheer terror of it. The crucifixion scene mobilized the very iconography of Christendom to drive home the theory of pure African evil and white salvation. It also drew alarm from the Hays Office of the Motion Picture Producers Association and heavy criticism from the state censorship boards. The New York Board of Censors was not bothered by the sacrilege so much as the racial

Figure 2.8. The White Goddess: "Nina T" (Edwina Booth) whips "Gun Boy" Riano (Riano Tindami) prior to crucifixion scene. MGM studio set, Culver City. The two "Isoga" in the background are Los Angeles actors, either African Americans or Euro-Americans in blackface. Although the tribe is supposedly in the Belgian Congo, their costumes are modeled on those of the Kavirondo in Kenya Colony. Peru (Duncan Renaldo), Trader Horn (Harry Carey), and Renchero (Mutia Omoolu) stand at right. *Trader Horn* production still (1929–30). MGM Collection. Margaret Herrick Library, The Academy of Motion Picture Arts and Sciences, Beverley Hills. TRADER HORN © Turner Entertainment Co. Licensed by Warner Bros. Entertainment Inc. All rights reserved.

heresy. They required the distributors in that state to "eliminate" from reel 8 "close views where natives are choking whites, (by sound and expression) showing extreme cruelty," as they bind their captives to the crosses and place them upside down above unignited bonfires.[90]

White mobs in Alabama, Mississippi, Georgia, Louisiana, Mississippi, Texas, and many other states publicly tortured and murdered African Americans at an average rate of thirty-nine lynchings per year while this film was produced and distributed. The United States Congress blocked several antilynching bills in the 1920s and 1930s. The NAACP's antilynching campaign increased public consciousness about the horrors of lynching but failed to move even the liberal Franklin D. Roosevelt to take the problem as seriously as that of a stagnant economy. Hollywood's contribution to mass indifference among whites was to reverse the horrors of white supremacy and publicize the racist fantasies of the white lynch mobs.[91]

GLOBAL SEGREGATION

When Van Dyke entered the port of Mombasa in 1929, he scanned the shore excitedly looking for jungles and wild animals but instead "became . . . sick with disappointment. . . . My God! There dotting the hillside, standing amid beautiful gardens and wireless aerials, were some Hollywood bungalows. . . . I hid my eyes."[92] Van Dyke had laid eyes on the residential section segregated for Europeans only. The "bungalow" design (a Hindu word) originates in India, in fact, having spread to Mombasa long before California architects and home builders adopted and transformed it.[93] The global urban histories of Mombasa and Los Angeles intersected in the site and situation of these bungalows, more powerfully than merely in their familiarity to an American movie director. Kenya Colony was, just at that moment, roiled by a controversy caused by the protest of Kenya Indians against the policy of racial segregation. Following the 1908 policy of Lord Elgin, reserving the expropriated Kikuyuland as "White Highlands" for Europeans only, and a 1913 "sanitation" report recommending a "system of racial segregation," the most desirable spaces in the two principal cities, Mombasa and Nairobi, were also designated to exclude all but Europeans.

Demanding equal rights based on a 1923 Colonial Office "white paper" on "Indians in Kenya," which declared an official end of segregation of Indians in recognition of their rights as British citizens, Abdullah Wlajee Hirjee petitioned to purchase residential property in the European section of Mombasa. The Privy Council eventually ruled that conforming with the white paper was "impossible of exact fulfillment because of our previous commitment to persons who had acquired sites in particular plots with the prospect of segregation."[94]

The location shooting of the East Africa safari was completed by August 1930, but acceptable levels of sound quality had been impossible to achieve for the close-up dialogue work because soundproofed cameras were not yet available. The solution was to produce all the close-up dialogue in Los Angeles. This required the presence of Mutia Omoolu, who was part of most such scenes. Permission was obtained from Governor Grigg's office for both Omoolu and for Van Dyke's gun bearer Riano Tindami to travel from segregated Kenya Colony to segregated Los Angeles. As in Kenya, the most valuable spaces were reserved strictly for white residence, and the most valuable jobs were also reserved for whites. Spatial segregation, in fact, is the foundation for systems of white supremacy. No hotel in Culver City would accept these Africans, so they were lodged in a shack on the MGM lot for almost a full year.

Omoolu and Tindami were portrayed by the Los Angeles press as jungle savages amazed by civilization.[95] They were, instead, urbanites well acquainted with the Anglo-American system of apartheid. Segregation in Los Angeles, like that in Mombasa, however, was the target of legal contestation, as the fledgling civil rights movement denounced "restrictive covenants" in property deeds (eventually ruled unconstitutional in *Shelly v. Kraemer*, 1948). The movie that Thalberg and Van Dyke were preparing for the silver screen was utterly oblivious to the demands for racial justice. Drawing on a network of segregated talent agents, Thalberg hired uncredited African-Americans from the segregated Vernon-Central district to portray savage Africans alongside Omoolu and Tindami.

CINEMA'S GLOBAL SPACES

Trader Horn was so profitable that Irving Thalberg naturally wanted a sequel. Van Dyke and Clyde De Vinna, the film's director of photography, had shot more than a million feet of film, so there was still a store of capital in the MGM vaults ready for a Euro-American public now hungry for more enslaved Africans and man-eating lions.[96] Given the ubiquity of the Tarzan icon in popular culture by 1931—beginning that year also in syndicated daily comic strips—and the perpetual market for Burroughs's annual installments of Tarzan novels, a Tarzan movie was the obvious choice (despite the fact that six unsuccessful Tarzan movies had already been produced since 1920!). Mayer and Burroughs signed a deal within weeks of the opening of *Trader Horn*. The agreement licensed only the *characters* from the Tarzan novels—not the story—which gave MGM carte blanche to invent any story it wished.

Thalberg and Van Dyke's goal was merely to milk easy cash from the *Trader Horn* footage. Also they wanted to re-tell the *Trader Horn* story with a new twist, rather than revisit the authentic Tarzan myth. Jane Porter would be the daughter, not of a scientist (as in the Burroughs novels), but of a jaded ivory trader (as in *Trader Horn*). Instead of the traders discovering a White Goddess in the jungle, however, they would discover a White God (a mix of Adonis, Apollo, and Adam). He would be master of all the wildlife, from hippos and crocs and elephants to the African humans themselves. But MGM's Tarzan is also a fundamentally different character than the improbably educated, innately gentlemanly, yet bestial Nietzschean hero of Burroughs's novels.

MGM's Tarzan was to be, simply, a natural playboy, a model of male glamour, nearly naked and more sensuous than ferocious. Screenwriter Cyril Hume discovered the perfect specimen one day at the Hollywood Athletic Club on Sunset Boulevard: Johnny Weismuller (1904–84), a gold-medal swimmer in both the 1924 and 1928 Olympics. The plot of the MGM Tarzan movies, which paired him with Maureen O'Sullivan (1911–98) is little more than a romance beset by the dangers of both civilization and the jungle.[97]

But if the MGM Tarzan cycle softened Tarzan, it reproduced both Burroughs's and *Trader Horn's* grotesque portrayal of Africans. Even more than *Trader Horn*, *Tarzan the Ape Man* subjects the African people to the mockery of simian analogy. Every MGM movie contains the same "ju-ju" sequence, in which the jungle savages are pointlessly whipped into a murderous frenzy. Every MGM Tarzan movie also kills Africans by the dozen, often accompanied by some kind of joke.

The first and founding number of the long Tarzan series, *Tarzan the Ape Man* (1932), was directed by Woody Van Dyke, and Clyde De Vinna was director of photography. It was shot entirely in Culver City and a few standard Los Angeles–area locations, such as the lake at "Sherwood Forest." East Africa is present as rear-screen projection throughout the movie. Some Africans are played by African Americans from the segregated Central Avenue, hired through segregated labor agents. The wicked and murderous Pygmies are, however, played by Euro-American dwarfs. Woody Van Dyke detested the African Pygmies he had met in the Belgian Congo, and translated that hatred into the portrayal in Tarzan.[98] Like the malevolent blacks in *Birth of a Nation*, they are played by whites in blackface. The white characters in *Tarzan the Ape Man* are saved from a gruesome death at the hands of these "Pygmies" and their captive giant ape, by a stampede of elephants, called in by Tarzan. The Hollywood elephant supply, however, consisted of Asian elephants, so they had all been sent to the makeup department to be fitted with long African ears.[99]

In the opening scenes of *Tarzan the Ape Man*, C. Aubrey Smith (as the ivory trader James Park) and Maureen O'Sullivan (as his daughter Jane Park), on the MGM lot, become spectators of the African tribes, who appear before them as a movie. Van Dyke directed these actors to interact with the rear-screen projections, producing an eerie effect in which the North American actors speak and gesture toward East Africans, who stare back without any interaction.

The rear-screen studio amalgam is no mere fiction. It is readily mappable as a production technique (Culver City images interwoven with Kenya Colony images). It represents, almost literally, the social distance created by Hollywood between its intended white audiences and the world's people of color. The absence of communication between the two sets of "actors" reproduced the lack of intercultural communication at the point of production during the *Trader Horn* safari in 1929–30, and then reproduces the lack of intercultural communication in uncounted thousands of movie theaters, as a third set of actors—the audience—consumed the images of these "whites" and these "blacks."

CONCLUSION

The gala opening of *Trader Horn* on January 22, 1931, attracted attention unusual even for Hollywood's spectacle machine. The movie-making East Africa safari and its Culver City follow-up had been tracked in the press since February 1929. Anticipation about the "real" African scenes of wild animals and "the bushmen and various other African tribes who eat the flesh of men" was very great.[100] On stage before the lights went down, Director Woody Van Dyke mockingly fielded questions from eager reporters, who mockingly challenged the claim that the film was really shot in Africa: Reporter: "And the cannibals, Mr. Van Dyke?" Van Dyke: "I shot them in Harlem. (laughter)."[101]

In a sense he did. Harlem, during the Harlem Renaissance of the 1920s, was one of the zones, along with that of Vasconcelos's Mexico City, of *mestizaje* and interculturality that defied the Anglo-American regime of segregated colonial white supremacy. The efflorescence of that cultural milieu, produced by such figures as W.E.B. Du Bois, James Weldon Johnson, Alain Locke, Langston Hughes, Zora Neale Hurston, Claude McKay, Eugene O'Neill, and many others, was yet another example of Arjun Appadurai's "modernity at large."[102] African Americans and their Euro-American compatriots merged visions of traditional African culture with cutting-edge modernism. Jazz "is a thing of the jungles," Joel A. Rogers wrote, "modern man-made jungles."[103]

While African-Americans in Harlem and the "Harlem of the West Coast," Central Avenue in Los Angeles, searched colonized Africa for a renewed urban cultural identity, Africans such as Jomo Kenyatta drew new inspiration from the Harlem Renaissance, in the intercultural zone of London. There he met Paul Robeson, who with his wife Essie was studying African culture (Essie was studying at the London School of Economics). They wrote feverish letters to Zora Neal Hurston about the "real us." Robeson would play in several Africa films, but his characters were more complex than that played by Mutia Omoolu. His Umbopa in the 1937 British-Gaumont production of *King Solomon's Mines* is that of a nobleman who does not take orders from white men. Still, he soon rejected all such roles, seeing them as unavoidably reinforcing of colonialism and inequality.[104]

The transnational story I have told here, narrated through the spaces of its emplotment, is that of Los Angeles spreading its regional regime institutions and culture throughout the globe. But the reverse was true as well. As Los Angeles sank its teeth into the continents of the globe, its own segregated spatial regime was hardened, and it reproduced in the global cinematic spaces of representation a landscape of injustice—the contents of the borderlands political culture that it had constructed in the process of building an empire of human, material, and imaginary flows.

NOTES

The author wishes to thank Gyan Prakash, Kevin Kruse, Jeremy Adelman, Vanessa Schwartz, Steve Ross, John Laslett, two anonymous reviewers, and all the participants in the Shelby Cullom Davis Center seminar at Princeton University, at which this article was originally presented, for their comments on earlier drafts.

1. I explore questions about urban visual global culture with Vanessa R. Schwartz and colleagues in a special issue, titled "Urban Icons," of the journal *Urban History* 33, no. 2 (June 2006). See also the multimedia adaptation of this special issue at http://www.journals.cambridge.org/urbanicons.

2. The scholarship on "global cities" has exploded since Saskia Sassen's *The Global City: New York, London, Tokyo* (Princeton, N.J.: Princeton University Press, 1991). Sassen's definition is very narrow, however. She limits this class of cities to those engaged in a certain structure of global finance and service production, late in the twentieth century. Janet L. Abu-Lughod in *New York, Chicago, Los Angeles: America's Global Cities* (Minneapolis: University of Minnesota Press, 1999) showed, however, that these same economic structures were evident in New York City before the end of the nineteenth century. Both authors are mostly concerned with structures of international trade and finance. My approach is more expansive, including the role of highly regional political cultures and ideologies of race.

3. I do not deal with the aircraft sector in this chapter, but it is treated extensively, along with many other subjects not discussed here, in my book-in-progress, from

which this chapter is drawn: "Ghost Metropolis, Los Angeles: A Cartography of Time, 1542–2001."

4. The superb collection edited by Felix Driver and David Gilbert, *Imperial Cities: Landscape, Display and Identity* (Manchester, U.K.: Manchester University Press, 2003), shows how imperializing capital cities such as London, Paris, and Vienna rebuilt themselves to symbolize their imperial self-image. Two books that show powerful parallel processes in governance, infrastructure, and ideology are Steven P. Erie, *Globalizing L.A.: Trade, Infrastructure, and Regional Development* (Stanford, Calif.: Stanford University Press, 2004); and Gray Brechin, *Imperial San Francisco: Urban Power, Earthly Ruin* (Berkeley: University of California Press, 1999).

5. A classic statement of the first type is Herbert Eugene Bolton, *The Spanish Borderlands: A Chronicle of Old Florida and the Southwest* (New Haven, Conn.: Yale University Press, 1921). A classic in the second sense of *borderlands* is Gloria Anzaldúa, *Borderlands/La Frontera: The New Mestiza*, 2nd ed. (San Francisco: Aunt Lute Books, 1999).

6. Dr. Atl, *Las artes populares en México*, exhibition catalogue (1921; Mexico City: Instituto Nacional Indigenista, 1980).This important exhibit has been all but lost to history. The best details about its arrangements can be found in Porfirio Martínez Peñaloza. *Tres notas sobre el arte popular en México* (Mexico City: Miguel Ángel Porrúa, 1980), pp 91–96. Martínez Peñaloza clarifies the role of the North American author Katherine Anne Porter in the Los Angeles exhibit.

7. Jose Clemente Orozco provides a rich account of the origins of the mural movement in his *Autobiografía*. (Mexico City: Ediciones Occidente, 1945), 79–85.

8. José Vasconcelos, *The Cosmic Race: A Bilingual Edition* trans. and annotated Didier T. Jaén (1925; Baltimore: Johns Hopkins University Press, 1997), 16.

9. Linda B. Hall writes of Sonora as "the state in which the position of the Revolution was established most firmly," in *Álvaro Obregón: Power and Revolution in Mexico, 1911–1920* (College Station: Texas A&M University Press, 1981), 51; Ricardo Pozas Horcasitas, *El triunvirato sonorense* (Mexico City: Martin Casillas, 1993).

10. Of course, San Diego is the city on the border, but it was not nearly as important as Los Angeles in the geography of southern California. Dirk Raat, *Revoltosos: Mexico's Rebels in the United States, 1903–1923* (College Station: Texas A&M University Press, 1981); Hector Aguilar Camín, *La frontera nómada: Sonora y la Revolución Mexicana*, 5th ed. (Mexico City: Siglo XXI, 1986).

11. Kevin Starr, "The Great Gatsby of American Cities: Los Angeles, 1900–1930," in Sarah Vure, ed., *Circles of Influence: Impressionism to Modernism in Southern California Art, 1910–1930* (Newport Beach, Calif: Orange County Museum of Art, 2000), 17.

12. That Job Harriman and the socialists could successfully prevent the Magón brothers from being extradited is impressive testimony to the checks on the power of the capitalist oligarchy of Los Angeles. Although they controlled the police, they did not always control the courts. Edward J. Escobar, *Race, Police and the Making of*

Political Identity: Mexican Americans and the Los Angeles Police Department, 1900–1945 (Berkeley: University of California Press, 1999), 53–76.

13. "Thirty-six Reds Seized in Police Harbor Raids," *Los Angeles Times*, November 9, 1922, part 2, p. 1.

14. On November 9, 1922, former police chiefs James I. Butterfield and C. C. Cole were arrested and charged with Klan activity, but the chief who ordered these arrests was immediately suspended by the city manager. "Klan Arrests to be Sifted," *Los Angeles Times*, November 10, 1922, part 2, p. 1. In a separate incident, the Klan threatened to lynch a woman on trial for murder if she was not convicted. "Klan Menaces Mrs. Phillips," *Los Angeles Times*, November 5, 1922, 3.

15. *Wall Street Journal*, April 14, 1922; David H. Stratton, "Two Western Senators and Teapot Dome: Thomas J. Walsh and Albert B. Fall," *Pacific Northwest Quarterly* 65 (April 1974): 57–65; Hasia Diner, "Teapot Dome, 1924," in Arthur M. Schlesinger Jr. and Roger Burns, eds., *Congress Investigates: A Documented History, 1792–1974* (New York: Chelsea House Publishers, 1975).

16. The episode has been cast primarily as representing two major domestic political questions: those of natural resources and political corruption. Burl Noggle, "The Origins of the Teapot Dome Investigations," *Mississippi Valley Historical Review* 44, no. 2 (September 1957): 237–66; J. Leonard Bates, "The Teapot Dome Scandal and the Election of 1924," *American Historical Review* 60, no. 2 (January 1955): 303–22; David H. Stratton, "Two Western Senators and Teapot Dome"; Gary D. Libcap, "The Political Allocation of Mineral Rights: A Re-Evaluation of Teapot," *Journal of Economic History* 44, no. 2 (June 1984): 381–91, and "Correction: The Political Allocation of Mineral Rights: A Re-Evaluation of Teapot," *Journal of Economic History* 44, no. 4 (December 1984): 1,101.

17. I am advancing a different and inverse version of the link between Mexican oil politics and those of the United States from the one offered by Linda B. Hall in her *Oil, Banks, and Politics: The United States and Postrevolutionary Mexico, 1917–1924* (Austin: University of Texas Press, 1995). She admirably exposes, in the strongest way, the link between U.S. investment in Mexico and the Teapot Dome scandal, via Albert Fall. Hall's main object of inquiry is the political dynamics of the Mexican capital and the presidencies of Carranza and Obregón. Mine is the borderland and Washington, D.C., emplotments of these links.

18. The best account of Doheny's early years is Martin R. Ansell, *Oil Baron of the Southwest: Edward L. Doheny and the Development of the Petroleum Industry in California and Mexico* (Columbus: Ohio State University Press, 1998), 7–22. This and the following three paragraphs draw heavily on Ansell.

19. By the end of the 1890s, Doheny won a contract with the Atchison, Topeka, and Santa Fe Railroad to supply thirty thousand barrels per month to fuel their Mohave-to-San Francisco line, for ninety-six cents a barrel, which cost him less than fifteen cents a barrel to produce. Ansell, *Oil Baron*, 23–51.

20. Dennis McDougal, *Privileged Son: Otis Chandler and the Rise and Fall of the L.A. Times Dynasty* (Cambridge, Mass: Perseus Publishing, 2001), 73–75.

21. John Mason Hart, *Empire and Revolution: The Americans in Mexico since the Civil War.* Hearst's interests are discussed on 170–71.

22. Friedrich Katz, *The Life and Times of Pancho Villa* (Stanford, Calif.: Stanford University Press, 1998), 15–16.

23. John Mason Hart, *The Coming and Process of the Mexican Revolution* (Berkeley: University of California Press, 1987); John Coatsworth, "Railroads, Land-holding, and Agrarian Protest in Porfirian Mexico," *Hispanic American Historical Review* 54 (1974): 48–72.

24. "Las fotografias de pozos afuera de control, que lanzaban al aire 100,000 bar-riles diarios, circularon por todo el mundo difundiendo la noticia de la enorme riqueza mexicana." Lorenzo Meyer, *México y Estados Unidos en el conflicto petrolero, 1917–1942* (Mexico City: Colegio de México, 1968), 14.

25. Francisco Colmenares, *Petróleo y lucha de clases in México, 1864–1982* (Mex-ico City: Ediciones el Caballito, 1982), 42.

26. Gabriel Antonio Menéndez, *Doheny el Cruel: Episodios de la sangrenta lucha por el petróleo mexicano* (Mexico City: Bolsa Mexicana del Libro, 1958).

27. Friedrich Katz, *The Secret War in Mexico: Europe, the United States, and the Mexican Revolution* (Chicago: University of Chicago Press, 1981), 7.

28. The political-economic impact of the Terrazas-Creel regime in Chihuahua is carefully explained in Katz, *The Life and Times of Pancho Villa*, 27–52. For Fall's involvement with both the Greene and Terrazas, see Clifford Wayne Trow, "Senator Albert B. Fall and Mexican Affairs: 1912–1921" (Ph.D. diss., University of Colorado, 1966), 92–95.

29. David H. Stratton, *Tempest over Teapot Dome: The Story of Albert B. Fall* (Norman: University of Oklahoma Press, 1998), 75.

30. A network of labor spies supplied Greene with intelligence about the move-ments of unionists, especially those of the Western Federation of Miners. See Albert Bacon Fall Papers, Huntington Library: Frank W. Mulock to Col. Greene, June 18, 1906; Greene to *Cananea Herald/El Heraldo de Cananea*; June 14, 1906; and Daird Cole, general manager (Cananea), to W. C. Greene, president (New York), December 12, 1906, who explained: "Our Special Agent has just received a letter from some Western Federation insiders located at Denver, regarding negotiations now pending for a conspiracy to start another campaign of agitation for the purpose of embar-rassing us here."

31. El Paso reporters wrote of Fall as the "general manager" of Greene's Chihua-hua properties. Stratton, *Tempest*, 77.

32. In a remarkable autobiographical letter of July 30, 1913 to Woodrow Wilson, Fall portrays himself as someone who identified with the interests of "the common Mexican"—more so, he claims, than the many Mexican political leaders he knew. But he also explains his conviction that "the great masses of the Mexican people were not prepared to establish any government at all, or even to govern themselves locally without a central government." Albert Bacon Fall Papers, Huntington Library.

33. Hall, *Oil, Banks, and Politics*, 38; John Reed, *Insurgent Mexico* (New York: D. Appleton, 1914).

34. Clifford W. Trow, "Woodrow Wilson and the Mexican Interventionist Movement of 1919," *Journal of American History* 58, no. 1 (June 1971): 46–72, quotation at 47.

35. Dan La Botz, *Edward L. Dohney: Petroleum, Power, and Politics in the United States and Mexico* (New York: Praeger, 1991), 80; Hall, *Oil, Banks, and Politics*, 41.

36. Inman became a major figure in the Pan American Conferences and became an architect of Franklin D. Roosevelt's "Good Neighbor" policy. He later became a major critic of U.S. support for Latin American dicatorships during the Cold War. William L. Castleman, *On This Foundation: A Historical Literary Biography of the Early Life of Samuel Guy Inman* (St. Louis: Bethany, 1966).

37. Dohney quoted in Hall, *Oil, Banks, and Politics*, 43.

38. Mark Requa to U.S. Army, Navy, and Shipping Board, January 9, 1920 (forwarded to secretary of state on February 27, 1920), quoted in La Botz, *Edward L. Dohney*, 97.

39. La Botz, *Edward L. Dohney*, 80–107. Katz, *Secret War in Mexico*, 159–61.

40. Quoted in La Botz, *Edward L. Dohney*, 66.

41. No wonder he dismissed his $100,000 "loan" to Secretary Fall as "a mere bagatelle." The figure of $21 million for the Doheny interests is cited in George Creel, *The People Next Door: An Interpretive History of Mexico and the Mexicans* (New York: John Day Co., 1926), 361. Creel, the Wilson administration's last diplomat to Mexico, was sharply critical of the Harding administration policies.

42. Jonathan Brown, *Oil and Revolution in Mexico* (Berkeley: University of California Press, 1993), 256.

43. Peter Shuey Linder, "Every Region for Itself: The Manuel Peláez Movement, 1914–1923" (M.A. thesis, University of New Mexico, 1983), 48–66, 89–104, 139–44; quotation at v. Jonathan Brown's assessment agrees with Linder's: while the *pelacistas* constituted a private counterrevolutionary army, they were in no way controlled by the oilmen. Peláez, Brown explains, was "the perfect *caudillo*" because he never ran out of resources for the people of his region and prevented demands for land reform that characterized the areas controlled by the left wing of the revolution. Brown, *Oil and Revolution in Mexico*, 255–72.

44. On Somoneen, see Colmenares, *Petróleo y lucha de clases in México*, 42–45.

45. As Martin Ansell explains, Dohney suddenly revealed this arms cache and offered it to the California National Guard in order to avoid the new U.S. neutrality laws. *Oil Baron of the Southwest*, 152.

46. Two of Doheny's lieutenants met at a dinner party on July 1, 1921, in a Los Angeles home to plot an alliance between General Manuel Peláez and General Esteban Cantú, the reactionary *caudillo* of Baja California. The venue was the home of Cantú's brother-in-law, in honor of General Manuel Peláez, the aim of which was to raise money for the proposed pincer-assault on the Mexican capital from opposite corners of the country. La Botz, *Edward L. Dohney*, 103–4. Cantú met in Washington

with Interior Secretary Albert Fall in the months preceding this Los Angeles meeting. Esteban Cantú to Albert Fall, February 21, 1921. Albert Bacon Fall Papers, Huntington Library.

47. La Botz, *Edward L. Doheny,* 168.

48. Irwin Porges, *Edgar Rice Burroughs: The Man Who Created Tarzan* (Provo, Utah: Brigham Young University Press, 1975), 305.

49. This biographical sketch is based primarily on Porges, (ibid.); Erling B. Holtzmark, *Edgar Rice Burroughs* (Boston: Twayne Publishers, 1986); and Richard A. Lupoff, *Edgar Rice Burroughs: Master of Adventure* (New York: Carnival Press, 1965).

50. Quoted in Lupoff, *Edgar Rice Burroughs,* 8.

51. John I. Tucker, "Tarzan Was Born in Chicago," *Chicago History* 1, no. 1 (1970): 18–31.

52. Clark A. Brady, *The Burroughs Cyclopaedia* (Jefferson, N.C.: McFarland and Co., 1996), 249.

53. Edgar Rice Burroughs, *A Princess of Mars* (New York: Modern Library, 2003), 16.

54. Ibid., 58.

55. Ibid., 42, 60.

56. Ibid., xxi.

57. Erling B. Holtzmark, *Tarzan and Tradition: Classical Myth in Popular Literature* (Westport, Conn.: Greenwood Press, 1981).

58. Maximillian E. Novak, "Robinson Crusoe's Fear and the Search for Natural Man," *Modern Philology* 58, no. 4 (May 1961): 238–45; Julia Douthwaite, "Rewriting the Savage: The Extraordinary Fictions of the 'Wild Girl of Champagne,' " *Eighteenth-Century Studies* 28, no. 2 (Winter 1994): 163–92.

59. Quoted in Porges, *Edgar Rice Burroughs,* 299.

60. Quoted in ibid., 359–61.

61. Quoted in ibid., 305.

62. His preparatory notes make the premise clear enough: "*At-den*—(Tall-Tree) White, hairless warrior, Tarzan's first acquaintance. *Om-at* (Long-Tail) black, hairy warrior, Tarzan's second acquaintance." Quoted in Porges, *Edgar Rice Burroughs,* 345.

63. The same month that Ned Doheny was murdered at Greystone Mansion in Beverly Hills.

64. Telegram dated February 6, 1929; Kikuyu Central Association, "Petition to Secretary of State for the Colonies," February 14, 1929, Public Record Office, London (hereafter PRO), CO 533 384/9.

65. W. S. Van Dyke, *Horning into Africa* (Los Angeles: California Graphic Press, 1931), 55–56; Robert C. Cannom, *Van Dyke and the Mythical City of Hollywood* (Culver City, Calif.: Murray and Gee, 1948), 193.

66. Van Dyke began working for Griffith as his key grip on the set of *Intolerance* (1916). After directing scores of B westerns, he became a first-line director after his

success with *White Shadows of the South Seas* (1929), MGM's first big experiment with shooting an entire film overseas. Van Dyke became one of MGM's most valuable and prolific directors. At his death of a heart attack in 1942, he had directed eighty-nine films, including the popular *Thin Man* series starring William Powell and Myrna Loy. The scholarship on *Birth of a Nation* is immense, but there is near unanimity that it set the basic standards for artistic excellence in production values and demonstrated the commercial viability of feature-length films. Although the film's racism is beyond question, the importance of this racism to Griffith's achievement has long been a matter of controversy. See Fred Silva, ed., *Focus on "Birth of a Nation"* (Englewood Cliffs, N.J.: Prentice-Hall, 1971).

67. Jon Tuska observes that Alfred Aloysius Horn admitted influence of the Tarzan story on his own, and speculates that he also borrowed the white captive story from William Selig's 1922 movie, *The Jungle Goddess* (Export-Import Film Company). *"Trader Horn*: A Cinematograph," *Views and Reviews* 3, no. 1 (Summer 1971): 51–58.

68. By the 1920s, Horn was working as an itinerant peddler in Johannesburg, where he was discovered by the South Afircan novelist Ethrelda Lewis. Lewis persuaded Horn to write out his reminiscences, and she patched them together into the book that was released with her as "editor." Ethrelda Lewis, ed. *Trader Horn: Being the Life and Works of Alfred Aloysius Horn with Illustrations from the Metro-Goldwyn-Mayer Production* [1927]. (New York: Gorsset and Dunlap, 1932).

69. George Delf, *Jomo Kenyatta: Towards Truth about "The Light of Kenya"* (Westport, Conn.: Greenwood Pres, 1961), 66.

70. The thousand light bulbs is an actual statistic, but it echoes Ralph Ellison's *Invisible Man*. The European could use a thousand light bulbs and still could not see the African as a person.

71. John Lonsdale, "The Conquest State, 1895–1904," in Willam Ochieng', ed., *A Modern History of Kenya, 1895–1980* (London: Evans Brothers, 1989), 6.

72. Robert Maxon, "The Years of Revolutionary Advance, 1920–1929," in Ochieng', *A Modern History of Kenya*, 86.

73. Ibid., 72–73.

74. Tiyambe Zeleza, "The Establishment of Colonial Rule, 1905–1920," in Ochieng', *A Modern History of Kenya*, quotation at 53.

75. George Bennett, "Settlers and Politics in Kenya," in Vincent Harlow and E. M. Chilver, eds., *History of East Africa* (Oxford: Clarendon Press, 1965), 265–332; quotation at 303.

76. Charles Carlton to M.J.J. Cohn, "Technical Notes," June 22, 1928, MGM Collection, University of Southern California, Cinema-Television Library.

77. Van Dyke, *Horning into Africa*, 159.

78. Kenya Register of Correspondence, 1929, CO 628 24, pp. 163, 224. PRO, London.

79. Dispatch, E.A.J. Dutton, November 26, 1929, CO 533 384/9, PRO, London.

80. R.G.B. Spicer to Chief Native Commissioner, July 21, 1929, CO 533 384/9, PRO, London.

81. Governor Edward Grigg to Secretary of State, October 12, 1929. CO 533 392/ 1, PRO, London.

82. Grigg quoted in Bennett, "Settlers and Politics in Kenya," 301.

83. The term is from Gyan Prakash, "Introduction: After Colonialsm," in Prakash, ed., *After Colonialism* (Princeton, N.J.: Princeton University Press, 1995), pp. 3–20.

84. E. Park, Scotland Yard, to Col. E.A.J. Taylor, June 19, 1929, CO 533 384/9, PRO, London.

85. The practice is defended in Kikuyu Central Association, Petition, February 14, 1929, CO 533 384/9, PRO, London. The practice was roundly condemned by the National Council of Women of Great Britain, "Circumcision of African Girls," CO 533 392/10.

86. "Kagwnarwa," N.D. [1929], CO 533 392/1, PRO, London.

87. The new tough line was delivered by the new governor, Sir Joseph Byrne, "a strong man for a tough job" who was best remembered as a policeman during the "Troubles" in Britain's oldest colony, Ireland. He did not appreciate independence movements of any kind. Bennett, "Settlers and Politics in Kenya," 311–13, 315–16.

88. Lucy Langridge, c. 1912, in Lucy Langridge Papers, Royal Commonwealth Society Library, quoted in Dane Kennedy, *Islands of White: Settlers Society and Culture in Kenya and Southern Rhodesia, 1890–1939* (Durham, N.C.: Duke University Press, 1987), 132.

89. *Trader Horn* screenplay, temporary final script (October 1, 1930), scene 10, MGM Collection, Academy of Motion Picture Arts and Sciences.

90. Jason S. Joy to Irving Thalberg, February 25, 1931, MPAA Production Code Administration Files, Margaret Herrick Library, Academy of Motion Picture Arts and Sciences, Beverly Hills, California.

91. Statistics on lynchings are drawn from the NAACP's contemporary research. "Lynchings 1918–1934 Inclusive," NAACP Papers (microfilm), Library of Congress. President F. D. Roosevelt's indifference to the antilynching bills is shown in Eleanor Roosevelt to Walter White, May 2, 1934, Eleanor Roosevelt Papers (microfilm) Library of Congress. The principal antilynching bills under consideration were the Dyer Anti-Lynching Bill of 1921 and the Costigan-Wagner Bill of 1937. By 1940, the NAACP gave up on the Costigan-Wagner Bill. Philip Dray, *At the Hands of Persons Unknown: The Lynching of Black America* (New York: Random House, 2002); Robert Zangrando, *The NAACP Crusade against Lynching, 1909–1950.* (Philadelphia: Temple University Press, 1980); John Lewis, et al., *Without Sanctuary: Lynching Photography in America* (Santa Fe, N.M.: Twin Palms Publishing, 1999).

92. "I had come twelve thousand miles to savage Africa to see the posterior of civilization assume all the likes and proportions of civilization's brow and scalp lock." Van Dyke, *Horning into Africa*, 55.

93. From *bangla*, meaning literally "in the Bengal style," according to the Merriam-Webster Dictionary Online, http://www.m-w.com/dictionary/bungalow, accessed October 2006.

94. "Indians in Kenya" (London, 1923); "Segregation in Townships: Correspondence, 1930–31," CO 533 394/1, PRO, London.

95. " 'Trader Horn' Film Natives Leave Soon," *Los Angeles Examiner*, January 19, 1931; Louella O. Parsons, "Jungle Film at Chinese Thrills First-Nighters," *Los Angeles Examiner*, January 23, 1931.

96. Jerome Beatty, "He Brings 'Em Back in Cans," *American Magazine*, August 1934, 76–77, 106–8.

97. Story conference notes show that the screenwriters, who included director Van Dyke, were concerned primarily with perfecting the love interest between Tarzan and Jane. Rudy Behlmer, *W. S. Van Dyke's Journal: "White Shadows in the South Seas 1927–1928" and Other Van Dyke on Van Dyke* (Lanham, Md.: Scarecrow Press, 1996), 75–84. The twelve MGM Tarzan movies are *Tarzan the Ape Man* (1932); *Tarzan and His Mate* (1934); *Tarzan Escapes* (1936); *Tarzan Finds a Son!* (1939); *Tarzan's Secret Treasure* (1941); *Tarzan's New York Adventure* (1942); *Tarzan Triumphs* (1943); *Tarzan's Desert Mystery* (1943); *Tarzan and the Amazons* (1945); *Tarzan and the Leopard Woman* (1946); *Tarzan and the Huntress* (1947); and *Tarzan and the Mermaids* (1948).

98. "A pygmy has one distinction above every other native in Africa," Van Dyke wrote in his memoir: "Above every other [*sic*] animal of five continents, above every sulfur spring or city sewer, above our croc pool or African water holes—of all the smells I have ever smelled, the pygmies have the smelliest smell. Their stench rises to the high heavens. It is not dirt or filth, because no filth or dirt could possibly smell as evil as they do." Van Dyke, *Horning into Africa*, 129.

99. Rudy Behlmer, "*Tarzan* at MGM," in George E. Turner, ed., *The Cinema of Adventure, Romance, and Terror: From the Archives of American Cinematographer* (Hollywood: ASC Press, 1989), 115–37.

100. "*Trader Horn* Players Back from Africa," *Los Angeles Examiner*, December 11, 1929. Quotation is from Louella O. Parsons, "Jungle Film at Chinese Thrills First-Nighters," *Los Angeles Examiner*, January 23, 1931.

101. Cannom, *Van Dyke and the Mythical City of Hollywood*.

102. On the modernism of New York's writers and their milieu, see Christine Stansell, *American Moderns: Bohemian New York and the Creation of a New Century* (New York: Henry Holt, 2001); and Ann Douglas, *Terrible Honesty: Mongrel Manhattan in the 1920s* (New York: Farrar, Straus and Giroux, 1995).

103. Joel A. Rogers, "Jazz at Home," in David Levering Lewis, ed., *The Portable Harlem Renaissance Reader* (New York: Viking Penguin, 1994), 52.

104. Martin Bauml Duberman, *Paul Robeson* (New York: Alfred A. Knopf, 1988), 169–71.

CHAPTER 3

Architecture at the Ends of Empire: Urban Reflections between Algiers and Marseille

SHEILA CRANE

Following the French conquest of Algeria in 1830, transportation networks created as part of the colonial enterprise positioned the port cities of Marseille and Algiers as key points of contact between the north African colonies and the French *métropole*. Although geographically separate from "mainland" France, the city of Algiers, as the capital of "French Algeria," was nevertheless imagined to be unusually close, owing in part to its relative proximity on the opposite shore of the Mediterranean Sea. Perhaps most important, Algeria held an unusual status within the French colonial empire, following its official redesignation in 1848 as an integral part of France, an understanding that was reinforced by the significant numbers of Europeans who resettled there on at least notionally permanent terms.[1] As the requisite port of transit to north Africa, Marseille was similarly imagined to occupy a liminal position. Descriptions of the city repeatedly characterized it as a microcosm of the French Empire, as if the colonial exhibitions held there in 1906 and 1922 had been absorbed into its very social and architectural fabric.[2] In the early decades of the twentieth century, a seemingly endless array of literary and pseudo-journalistic descriptions repeatedly emphasized the "dangerous" cosmopolitanism of the city known since the midnineteenth century as "the door to the Orient."[3]

The blurring of boundaries between Marseille and Algiers, based on their geographical proximity and on movements of people back and forth across the Mediterranean Sea, did not simply come to an end at the moment of Algeria's independence in 1962. Not only did many of the thousands of so-called *repatriés*, or French colonists who left Algeria around this time, resettle in the Marseille region, but the influx of north African immigrants to Marseille in the decades that followed also created ongoing, dynamic connections between these cities. In the face of migrations, buildings from the colonial era in Algiers remained as significant symbolic presences within the urban landscape. At the same time, the pressing need to accommodate waves of *repatriés* and Algerian immigrants had important effects on the architecture of Marseille. Travel posters from the early twentieth century that presented Algiers and Marseille as veritable mirror images of one another have today been replaced by new representations of these cities' shared Mediterranean identity, whether articulated through the culture of soccer or the sounds of *raï* musicians.[4] As much as significant differences between Algiers and Marseille have marked their postindependence histories, perceived resemblances between them remain constitutive aspects of both cities' urban imaginaries and architectural legacies.

Despite these connections, histories of architecture have long examined Algiers and Marseille, as well as France and Algeria, in isolation from one another. By contrast, significant attention has been paid to the instrumental role that urban planning and architecture played in the establishment, maintenance, and expansion of the French colonial empire, particularly in north Africa.[5] As much as it is widely acknowledged that beginning in 1830 invading French troops attempted to physically inscribe their authority into Algiers by radically altering its physical structure, the subsequent history of architectural interventions has similarly been characterized as a seemingly endless parade of French architects projecting foreign architectural forms onto the city.[6] The work of Kristin Ross has begun to redress this unidirectional framework by tracing the long-lasting effects that the colonial venture had on France itself, particularly as processes of intensive modernization were redirected inward during the 1950s and 1960s.[7] From a rather different perspective, Patricia Morton has shown that attempts to represent clear distinctions between France and its colonies in architectural form frequently collapsed in the face of much more complex interactions and hybrid constructions.[8] While these studies have shifted the focus from the impact of the *métropole* on the colonies to the reabsorption of colonial cultures into metropolitan cities, such intersecting dynamics continue to be examined separately. Even in the face of now well-established investments in borderlands, negotiated meanings, and hybrid constructions, studies of colonialism and its effects on cities continue to be framed from either the perspective of the colonies or of the *métropole*, even outside the context of the French Empire, so that the range of intersections and dynamic transfers across these borders have yet to be fully explored.

In this chapter, I take seriously Anthony King's trenchant observation that "the extensive relations of colonialism must themselves be seen not only as a particular mode of production, but also a space of production, affecting cultural practices and products in the metropole as much as in the colonies."[9] Such dialogic processes were particularly vivid between Algiers and Marseille, in no small part because as port cities, they functioned as key sites of transfer and connection. As King has also noted, port cities in colonial contexts resemble each other more than they do other interior cities. Here I explore the degree to which port cities at the very meeting point between colonial and metropolitan cultures might themselves share important characteristics. Within such liminal terrain, architecture was particularly active in shaping urban experience, given the sheer physicality and the important symbolic role of buildings. Expanding on these observations, I trace the circulation of architects and transfers of architectural ideas between Algiers and Marseille as well as the transformations of discrete architectural projects during the long period of decolonization. By analyzing the changing structural forms and symbolic meanings of these interventions, I argue that intersecting colonial pasts and postcolonial futures have significantly shaped the urban landscapes of Marseille and Algiers.

This chapter focuses on the work of two architects, Fernand Pouillon and Roland Simounet, as it responded to and was significantly altered by the changing urban and political conditions of decolonization. By tracing the relationship between Pouillon's housing complexes in Algiers, designed during the early stages of the French-Algerian War, and his earlier projects in Marseille, it is possible to untangle the complex trajectories of his architectural translations. Here the etymological roots of the term *translation*, understood as the "removal or conveyance from one person, place, or condition to another" suggests the relevance of this concept to Pouillon's own process of formulating architectural models between sites as well as to the mutability of his completed projects.[10] In fact, Pouillon's buildings were significantly recreated both before and after independence—through the actions of their inhabitants, through appropriations by the postindependence government, and in the hands of the architect himself. Finally, I consider Roland Simounet's re-finding of Algiers in Marseille in a series of projects from the 1980s and early 1990s as architectural longings for a lost Algerian past, akin to what the French novelist Henri de Montherlant, playing on the terms *nostalgia* and *Algeria* has called *nostalgérie*.[11]

From Marseille to Algiers: "The Battle for Housing"

Shortly after his election in April 1953, the new mayor of Algiers, Jacques Chevallier, initiated an extensive and highly publicized building campaign repeatedly described as his own "battle for housing," with Fernand Pouillon as his favored architect "imported" from Marseille. Three years earlier,

Chevallier had led a brief and ultimately failed attempt to forge a liberal alliance with moderate leaders of the nationalist movement. Although Chevallier advocated the tempered liberalization of the colonial regime to accommodate some degree of local autonomy, he imagined that such expanded institutions for self-governance would nevertheless operate within the administrative framework of a Franco-Algerian federation.[12] As mayor of Algiers, Chevallier chose a more indirect means of simultaneously acknowledging and redirecting increasingly virulent calls for Algeria's independence, by focusing his attention on the physical structures of the city.

Diar es-Saada ("city of happiness"), the first housing complex Pouillon designed for Chevallier, was constructed in the Clos Salembier quarter on a plateau at the summit of the hills that formed the southeastern perimeter of the city (fig. 3.1). With apartment units housed in low-rise structures and in a single sixteen-story tower block, Diar es-Saada accommodated more than three thousand residents and included such amenities as a parking garage, an elementary school, and a post office.[13] The complex was organized in a series of terraces linked together by elaborate staircases, while individual buildings were dispersed around open courtyards, each with its own distinctive embellishments, including a reflecting pool with sculpted dolphins cavorting in the water, a courtyard filled with rows of palm trees, and a series of vaulted stone canopies forming an open-air marketplace. The apartments themselves ranged from one- to four-bedroom units, equipped with remarkably up-to-date appliances. From the exterior, the monumental scale, starkly classicizing forms, and massive limestone walls of Pouillon's buildings contrasted sharply with their surroundings, particularly given the provisional nature of much of the neighboring architectural landscape.

The Clos Salembier quarter's dramatic topography had long discouraged concentrated development, given its severely sloping terrain of deep ravines and the area's relative distance from the city center below. In the decades following the French invasion of Algeria in 1830, the area adjacent to the port at the foot of the Casbah had been radically recreated as the representational core of colonial authority. However, by the early twentieth century, the notional heart of the city had been effectively displaced further eastward along the waterfront, in the direction of the Clos Salembier quarter. At the same time, the city was expanding exponentially, in large part through mass migrations of people moving from the countryside into the city in search of better economic opportunities.[14] As in other peripheral areas of the city, extensive shantytowns sprung up in the Clos Salembier quarter, particularly in the ravines that had long been designated by urban planners as empty spaces unsuitable for building. Until Pouillon's project was inaugurated, the

Figure 3.1. Fernand Pouillon, Diar es-Saada, Algiers, 1953–54. From Alberto Fer-
lenga, "Fernand Pouillon: Le pietre di Algeri," *Casabella* 66, nos. 706–7 (December–
January 2002–3): fig. 5. Photo courtesy of the Canadian Centre for Architecture,
Montreal.

colonial administration had only gestured to the growing housing shortage
with a series of haphazard projects and temporary barracks. In 1955, one
observer disparaged this phenomenon, characterizing this neighborhood as
a veritable museum of failed housing types.[15] In this setting, Diar es-Saada
appeared as a new, monumental city within the city.

Construction of Diar es-Saada was completed in November 1954, the
same month the National Liberation Front (FLN) initiated as series of coordinated actions against the colonial regime that effectively inaugurated the
war for independence, even if it was never formally acknowledged as such
by the French government. A new census published the previous month
registered the fact that, for the first time since the early stages of colonization, several districts at the edges of the city had a clear majority of Algerian inhabitants over Europeans.[16] Among these, the Clos Salembier quarter had one of the highest proportions of Algerians—more than 80 percent
of its total residents.[17] Both in terms of its exploding population and its
inadequate housing stock, the Clos Salembier quarter exemplified the pressures placed on the city's urban landscape that marked the years leading

up to independence. In response to these conditions, Mayor Chevallier attempted to use architecture to redress what he perceived as convergent crises. To this end, the industrialization of mass housing production would both provide jobs and halt the explosion of shantytowns on the city's periphery, strategies imagined together to be effective tools of pacifying the rapidly expanding Algerian population. Although Pouillon's first housing complex in Algiers, Diar es-Saada, was reserved for European residents, his second project, Diar el-Mahsul ("city of plenty"), was heralded from the moment of its initial design in 1954 as the city's first intentionally mixed housing development, with 982 of the 1,630 apartments designated for Algerian residents. As much as Chevallier emphasized the new attention his administration was bringing to the plight of Algerians, both of Pouillon's housing projects simultaneously contributed to rebalancing the population at the city's periphery by guaranteeing the reverse migration of Europeans to the Clos Salembier quarter.

At Diar el-Mahsul, distinct hierarchies nevertheless remained in place, as the European section was clearly separated from the complex for Algerians by the new through the Clos Salembier quarter that ran between them (fig. 3.2). Structurally, the European section incorporated grand architectural flourishes both in terms of scale and elaboration. As in Diar es-Saada, low-rise apartment buildings of varied heights lined terraced spaces. A ten-story tower stood in the center with an elaborate fountain at its base featuring Neptune in his chariot being lifted out of the water by four horses, while an arcaded passageway, called "the door to the sea," led from the central courtyard to an expansive esplanade overlooking the Mediterranean. By contrast, the Algerian section was set back behind the crest of the hill, and its smaller buildings were crowded together around much more modest open spaces. Whereas the generous loggia and balconies in the European section were similar to those in Diar es-Saada, the apartments across the road were extremely small by comparison, with only minimal kitchenettes and restrained fenestration. The original designs called for the construction of a Catholic church in the section designated for Europeans and a mosque in the area for Algerians, although the Saint Jean-Baptiste Church was the only religious structure actually erected. Two covered, open-air marketplaces were created for this new community of more than seven thousand people, each clearly distinguished by its material: brick for the Algerian section and stone across the road.[18]

Although it is tempting to regard Pouillon's designs as entirely coterminous with new demands for segregated habitations, the generation of these forms suggests a more complex story. Both of Pouillon's projects in Algiers

Figure 3.2. Fernand Pouillon, Diar el-Mahsul, Algiers, 1954–55. From Alberto Ferlenga, "Fernand Pouillon: Le pietre di Algeri," *Casabella* 66, nos. 706–7 (December–January 2002–3): fig. 6. Photo courtesy of the Canadian Centre for Architecture, Montreal.

shared compositional elements with La Tourette, the apartment complex that he had designed in 1949 as part of the postwar reconstruction of Marseille (fig. 3.3). Like La Tourette, Diar es-Saada was organized around a central courtyard and activated by the projecting volume of a single tower block rising above one end of the complex. While Diar el-Mahsul did not replicate the composition of La Tourette as closely, buildings in both sections of the complex were organized around a series of terraced courtyards. The similarity of Pouillon's projects in Algiers to his earlier complex in Marseille was rendered even more palpable by the fact that Diar es-Saada and Diar el-Mahsul were built of limestone shipped across the Mediterranean from a quarry near Marseille. Despite these compositional and material connections, Pouillon subsequently took pains to clearly separate his projects in Algiers from his previous projects in Marseille. In his autobiography, he claimed that the Ottoman fortifications he had seen during his first driving tour of Algiers with Mayor Chevallier had inspired the placement and volumes of Diar el-Mahsul at the crest of the hill overlooking the port.[19] Pouillon's insistence that his buildings in Algiers were inspired by local architectural references was clearly intended as a means of asserting their

105

Figure 3.3. Fernand Pouillon, La Tourette, Marseille, 1949–51. Photo by the author.

authenticity as well as the architect's supposedly intuitive understanding of such foreign terrain.

Historians have generally taken Pouillon at his word, echoing his insistence that his projects in Algiers were inspired by architectural models he encountered there.[20] Certainly the architect self-consciously asserted connections to local place through the design of his buildings, but these structures were not simply products of a dramatic encounter with the landscapes of Algiers. Instead, Pouillon's retrospective narration of his first glimpse of fortifications in Algiers pointed to a formula that the architect had already begun to articulate in Marseille. There, the hulking silhouette of La Tourette overlooking the sea was specifically intended to echo the form of the seventeenth-century Saint-Jean Fort guarding the entrance to the old port. The stone mass of Diar el-Mahsul inscribed into the hillside above the port of Algiers not only created a similar relationship between building and landscape, but also mimicked at various points the narrow windows in the seaward walls of La Tourette, designed to protect against the forceful winds of the mistral.

Select architectural details featured in Pouillon's projects in Algiers were products of equally convoluted genealogies. In both of his complexes in Algiers, Pouillon incorporated elements that he claimed responded to local architectural traditions that he described as a combination of Ottoman and Andalusian influences.[21] In this regard, the wooden corbelled balconies at

106

Figure 3.4. Detail of buildings in the European section of Diar el-Mahsul in Algiers. Originally published in Bernard Félix Dubor, *Fernand Pouillon* (Milan: Electa/Moniteur, 1986), fig. 47. Photo by Bernard Félix Dubor; courtesy of the Canadian Centre for Architecture, Montreal.

Diar el-Mahsul would seem to reference elements characteristic of buildings in the Casbah (fig. 3.4). However, Pouillon had already incorporated similar elements into his designs for La Tourette in Marseille (fig. 3.5). Similarly, Pouillon designed intricately patterned facades for the focal buildings of his projects in Algiers, whether in the form of highly elaborated balustrades that formed a striking sculptural presence on the tower at Diar es-Saada or in the staggered patterns of projecting stones and recessed openings in the tower at Diar el-Mahsul. Whereas the *claustra* (or screen wall) that he created as a focal point of his buildings in Marseille was rendered more abstractly in standardized concrete blocks, this earlier structure likewise gestured toward the *moucharabeih*, a screenlike element and spatial division associated with Islamic architecture.

Given these echoes of his previous work in Marseille, Diar es-Saada and Diar el-Mahsul must be understood not simply as direct responses to north African architecture but as translations of key elements through Marseille to Algiers. My aim here is neither to substitute one account of architectural origins with another nor to suggest that the story ends with the proper identification of the authoritative stylistic or geographical source. The point is not to displace the Casbah as the essential referent of Pouillon's architecture in order to claim such a role for Marseille. Rather, the fact that Pouillon's architecture in Algiers was not simply generated from his initial visual encounter with this city, but also constructed in relation to his architectural imaginary in and of Marseille necessitates a more careful examination of the projections of place and claims for authenticity that Pouillon directed toward both cities.

Pouillon's repeated assertions that the architectural landscape of Algiers formed the inspiration for his housing complexes were echoed in his descriptions of the extensive renovations he made to his own residence there, the Villa des Arcades. Named for the private aqueduct that brought water to its fountains and extensive gardens, this structure was built in the seventeenth or eighteenth century as a summer residence for successive Ottoman *raïs* of Algeria, including the renowned *corsaire* Raïs Hamidou, whose name had long been associated with this structure.[22] During his tenure there in the 1950s, Pouillon oversaw numerous modifications. As the architect himself explained: "I radically suppressed everything in the structure that my predecessors had added to it, and at the same time I gave back to it what had been diminished."[23] Far from merely removing what he deemed to be "inauthentic" elements, Pouillon made extensive changes, including a new wing featuring a swimming pool, the installation of modern amenities, and the replacement of large areas of destroyed or damaged glazed, ceramic tiles with

Figure 3.5. Detail of buildings at La Tourette in Marseille. Photo by the author.

new ones. Following his detailed study of the structure in the early 1990s, Alessandro Sartor praised what he described as Pouillon's "subtle architectural mimesis."[24] However, I would argue that Pouillon's interventions did not aim to replicate the existing architecture exactly but instead strategically negotiated the seemingly opposing aims of emulation and differentiation.

Despite Pouillon's attempt to blend new elements into the historic structure by imitating its forms, his additions were visibly modern in their materials and execution. The loggia leading to the new swimming pool, for example, gestured toward the original structure's horseshoe arches, even as the new streamlined, rounded arcade and unornamented columns introduced a subtle difference. According to Pouillon, the pool "integrated itself in form and in spirit into the composition, adding a supplementary charm to the ensemble."[25] While appearing to submit his architecture to the dictates of history, Pouillon aimed to add qualities that he deemed were lacking. In other words, his modifications were intended to seduce the viewer not simply as seamless renovations, but as elements that would simultaneously assert their distinctiveness.

At the Villa des Arcades, Pouillon attempted to demonstrate his architectural prowess through a kind of masquerade as native architect. At the same time, however, he intentionally left legible marks of himself on the structure, such as the new arcade framing the swimming pool, in his bid to outdo Islamic architecture at its own game. In this respect, Pouillon's renovation of the Villa des Arcades was less subtle mimicry than an expression of what Kaja Silverman has called double mimesis. In her analysis of Lawrence of Arabia, Silverman argued that his adoption of native dress and advocacy of Arab self-rule were strategies through which he sought "to imitate the Arabs to the point where they might be prompted to imitate him back."[26] Although Pouillon occasionally performed similar travesties at the Villa des Arcades, the house itself served as a stage set in which the architect envisioned himself stepping directly into the shoes of the legendary *corsaire* Raïs Hamidou. Similarly, in his aim not simply to master, but to perfect the original structure of the Villa des Arcades, Pouillon framed his renovations as an improved and superior model of indigenous architecture.

Like the Villa des Arcades, Diar es-Saada and Diar el-Mahsul were imagined as structures that might perform transformative work. Pouillon's mass housing projects aimed to acculturate their inhabitants, who would ideally absorb the well-ordered, hierarchical arrangement of the buildings and thereby be remade into modern, urban dwellers.[27] The section of Diar el-Mahsul designated for Algerians, like similar projects constructed in Algiers in the 1950s, was officially called "evolutionary" housing, a term that

110

clearly communicated the special aims of recreating this sector of the population.[28] Of course, one of the ironies of this transformative project was that
by the time Pouillon was designing his projects in Algiers, most Algerian
residents already occupied European-style housing.[29] In addition to Mayor
Chevallier's desire to placate the indigenous population broadly speaking,
Diar el-Mahsul aimed to guarantee the creation and implantation of a new
Algerian elite in the Clos Salembier quarter. Given the relatively high rents
that were charged for these apartments, the project seems to have been fairly
effective in these terms, although it was less successful in persuading this
"quasi-aristocracy" (as one bureaucrat described it) to acquiesce to the
claims of "French Algeria."[30]

At first glance, it would appear that the forms of Pouillon's architecture
were uniquely suited to the task of constructing ideal inhabitants differentiated by ethnicity, given his own investment in using architecture to assert
claims of authenticity and difference. In his housing complexes in Algiers,
the most spectacular architectural embellishments were staged in the areas
intended to house Europeans. These gestures toward north African architecture thus worked to confer importance and authority on these buildings
and their inhabitants by way of their visual distinctiveness, following tactics
similar to those employed in the Villa des Arcades. Nevertheless, the architectural forms of Diar es-Saada and Diar el-Mahsul resist absolute distinctions between "Algerian" and "European." In this regard, Pouillon's
buildings diverged significantly from contemporaneous models of "evolutionary" housing, which presumed direct equivalencies between architectural style and ethnic or religious categories, so that different populations
were not only assigned separate housing types, but these distinctions were
also clearly represented in the building's external facades.[31] In Pouillon's
projects, the most vivid signs of indigenous architecture were used as clad-
ding for modern housing destined for Europeans.

Madani Safar-Zitoun has analyzed the unusual structure of Pouillon's
"evolutionary" housing in Algiers in the following terms: "In effect, the
stakes [of these buildings] consisted in making Muslims accept European-
type dwelling units and in making Europeans live in buildings taking their
external symbolism from 'Arab' architecture. With a single stone, one in
some way delivered two blows: without mixing populations in the same
building or in the same housing block, it was possible to bring one closer to
the other in an indirect manner by immerging each community in the culture and architectural symbolism of 'the other.' "[32] These tactics might be
seen to resonate with Chevallier's vision of "cohabitation" as a means of
appeasing both European and Algerian populations while nonetheless main-

taining the colonial structure of dependence. At the same time, however, Safar-Zitoun's observation provides a useful framework through which to reconsider not simply the relationship between Pouillon's buildings on either side of the road that ran through the Clos Salembier quarter in Algiers, but also the dialogue between the architect's projects that notionally faced one another across the Mediterranean Sea. Seen in this light, we might imagine that the inhabitants of La Tourette in Marseille were also to be acculturated into modern urban dwellers whose location and cultural identification was oriented toward north Africa. Pouillon's housing complexes between Marseille and Algiers were thus structured by redoubled mimetic strategies, as the interior and exterior forms of his buildings constructed intersecting and potentially contradictory projects of imitation. Of course, these were never fully equivalent evolutionary schemes. Ultimately, the North African references in the European dwellings at Diar el-Mahsul were simply decorative flourishes applied to building facades, not intended to alter patterns of everyday life within their interiors.[33] The residences for Algerians, by contrast, were explicitly conceived as enclosed spaces that would forcibly adapt and control their inhabitants.

In his work between Marseille and Algiers, Pouillon emphasized similarities between these sites and created buildings that visibly projected an imagined cultural affinity across the Mediterranean. These projects might then be understood less as the transposition of an "original" architectural form clearly rooted in one site into a new locale, than as products of assimilative translation.[34] That is, projected similarities between these two sites allowed the architect to reiterate isolated details and compositional strategies deemed appropriate to both cities. Although Pouillon used seemingly localized references as means of legitimating his buildings in Algiers, their "origin" was rooted as much in the forms of his earlier buildings in Marseille as in what the architect described as his dramatic discovery of the Casbah after his arrival in Algiers. From the outset, Pouillon perceived Marseille as already somewhere else, an understanding made evident in his observation that the built fabric and geography of Marseille's old port resembled that of the Casbah in Algiers.[35] In turn, he experienced Algiers through the lens of anticipated expectation. When he arrived in the city, he found what he had imagined would be waiting for him—familiar models for monumental fortification and orientalizing embellishment. Nevertheless, the afterlives of Pouillon's buildings in Algiers belied the architect's visions of harmonious equivalence.

From the terrace of the Villa des Arcades, Pouillon was able to watch the construction of Diar el-Mahsul and monitor its progress. As in his own residence, gestures of mastery and distinction informed the highly publicized, spectacular construction feats he orchestrated in his housing complexes, such as planting fifty palm trees in a single day at Diar es-Saada or building a fourteen-story tower in thirty-six days at Diar el-Mahsul.[36] The battles Pouillon imagined himself waging on the construction site reiterated the hypermasculinist language that Chevallier and his administration repeatedly used to aggressively promote these projects as the evident victories in his "battle for housing."[37] Images of Diar es-Saada and Diar el-Mahsul were widely circulated in Algeria and in France, in photographs published in newspaper articles, glossy publicity brochures created by the mayor's office, and film clips incorporated into newsreels screened in the *métropole*.[38] Postcards depicting similar views of Diar es-Saada and of the European section of Diar el-Mahsul were sold during this period alongside those representing more conventional monuments of Algiers, suggesting that these two sites in the previously remote Clos Salembier quarter had rapidly been transformed into tourist destinations.[39] Official representations of Pouillon's projects, however, contrasted sharply with more informal appropriations on the ground.

Diar es-Saada and Diar el-Mahsul were repeatedly represented during this period in aerial views that dramatized their difference from the surrounding environment, in part by emphasizing their monumental scale and starkly rationalizing, geometric forms.[40] Photographs composed on the ground included a series of nighttime views in which dramatic lighting transformed buildings and sculptures into mysteriously animate presences. When people were included, they were frequently dwarfed by the architecture (particularly in views in which the angle of the camera deliberately exaggerated the height of the towers) or depicted in harmonious scenes of communal celebration. Despite their differences, these images almost invariably framed Pouillon's buildings as iconic premonitions of the future architectural landscape of Algiers. Chevallier's administration aggressively circulated such images with accompanying texts describing them as visual evidence that Algeria could only be successfully transformed into a modern city under the beneficent guidance of the French colonial administration. These images were explicitly intended to persuade their viewers, in Algeria and in France, that the project of "French Algeria" was worth pursuing at all costs. At the same time, these photographs represented Algiers as a pristine, modern city. Such a vision contrasted sharply with contemporaneous images circulating around this time in newspapers and newsreels that depicted the city as a site of violent conflict, including photographs of French troops patrolling the courtyards of Diar el-Mahsul.[41]

113

Pouillon's own recollections of the project may be seen as symptomatic of the colonialist ideology of control that framed his work in Algiers. In his memoirs, the architect recounted an evening promenade he took with Chevallier and the prefect of Algiers through Diar es-Saada as its construction was nearing completion, noting that they "strolled through this city created for ten thousand inhabitants, like kings of an imaginary and abstract city."[42] Such fantasy images of Diar es-Saada and Diar el-Mahsul as ideal urban landscapes might have been easy to evoke before actual inhabitants occupied these spaces or might have even been possible to stage thereafter in carefully choreographed photographs. They were, however, more difficult to sustain once these structures were inhabited and incorporated into the city. Publicity photographs insistently separated these buildings from their surroundings, whether framed from an aerial perspective or from within the solid enclosures of courtyards. However, when viewed from the streets running through the Clos Salembier quarter, one obtained a quite different view of the relationship of Pouillon's buildings to the wider cityscape. Indeed, these developments were intimately connected to the temporary housing barracks that stood precariously at the very edges of Pouillon's and Chevallier's ideal cities, hovering just outside the frame of authorized imagery.[43]

Fantasies of control given physical form in the monumental stone walls of Pouillon's apartment buildings and in Chevallier's vision of housing as an instrument of pacification were further transformed in the wake of the city's outright militarization. Notably, an office of the Urban Administrative Section (S.A.U.) was installed near Diar el-Mahsul in the late 1950s. Organized in 1956, this new administrative agency and surveillance force attempted to forge Franco-Algerian solidarity by providing education and other services to underserved Algerian populations while simultaneously policing their everyday activities.[44] In part owing to the effectiveness of the S.A.U. in controlling the outlying areas of Algiers, including the Clos Salembier quarter, violent confrontations were largely confined to the city center until December 1960. Early that month, ultrarightist European militants led a series of demonstrations, protesting General de Gaulle's announcement that a referendum would be held regarding the possibility of self-governance in Algeria, that led to a series of violent incidents in the majority-European quarter of Belcourt, just below the Clos Salembier. In response, thousands of Algerians joined in counterdemonstrations that were met by extreme violence that continued over several days throughout the city.[45] Mouloud Feraoun, who taught in a school in the Clos Salembier quarter until October of that year, described the events of December 11, 1960, in the journal he kept throughout the war: "So today the Arabs are in the streets. These are the people 'from my neck of the woods'; I mean from the Clos [Salembier]. They have taken over [Diar-el-] Mahçoul and [Diar-es-] Saâda, along with those from Belcourt and the Ruisseau."[46] Its intended function as a structure of containment temporarily inverted, Diar el-Mahsul became a rampart from which attacks were launched onto the surrounding city, as supporters of the liberation movement breached the walls of the complex and poured into the streets below.

Many demonstrators from the Clos Salembier quarter and elsewhere were killed by extremists and by the military that day and in the months that followed. While these events marked a turning point in the conflict, they also effectively heralded the transformation of Diar es-Saada and Diar el-Mahsul into battlegrounds, as both complexes became sites of bomb explosions, acts of vandalism, and assassinations.[47] On several occasions, European extremists used the upper floors of the towers in both of Pouillon's complexes as shooting galleries, in one instance killing a two-year-old girl who was standing with her mother on the balcony of their apartment across the road in the Algerian section of Diar el-Mahsul.[48] These events pushed the militarized structure and segregationist logic of Pouillon's architecture to a horrifying extreme. However, conflict was simultaneously inscribed into these structures in more subtle ways, through the territorial claims of graffiti scrawled onto the buildings themselves and by repeated attacks from within these walls launched through the medium of sound, as whistles for "French Algeria" were answered by cries of "Muslim Algeria." Even the insistent interiority of Pouillon's courtyards was challenged by the coordinated choruses of women in the Algerian section of Diar el-Mahsul who, not only from the streets but also from their individual apartment interiors and balconies, joined their voices together in ululations and used household objects to orchestrate *"concerts de casseroles."*[49]

In Marseille, the equation of housing with fortification might have been understood as a relatively straightforward historicizing gesture rather than a largely militarizing one. In the context of war in Algiers, the creation of an inhabited fortress had altogether different implications. In this way, Pouillon's attempt to seamlessly transfer the notion of housing as fortification from Marseille to Algiers raised the specter of cultural untranslatability that threatened to undermine the imagined connections between these sites on which the French colonial project was built. In Diar es-Saada and Diar el-Mahsul, the architect's claims to authenticity and mastery were challenged by the violent incorporation of Pouillon's and Chevallier's imaginary cities into the everyday, contested urban spaces of Algiers. In this way, the conjoined military and civilian occupations of these buildings during the French-Algerian War dramatically emphasized their very real distance from Marseille.

REMAPPING ALGIERS AT THE END OF EMPIRE

Clearly, attempts to rewrite Fernand Pouillon's buildings did not simply begin when Algeria officially became independent in early July 1962. Along with relatively ephemeral reinscriptions of graffiti and voice, the events of the French-Algerian War initiated longer-term transformations of these spaces. In the months leading up to independence, many residents of Diar es-Saada and Diar el-Mahsul departed Algiers, leaving numerous apartments vacant in their absence.[50] According to reports of the S.A.U. in the Clos Salembier quarter, by early 1961 there were so many people living in apartments they had not been authorized to occupy, either as illegal squatters or through unofficial transfers of property, that the authorities had given up any systematic efforts to control these movements. Widespread reclamations by Algerian residents of buildings formerly occupied by Europeans thus went hand in hand with the mass exodus of French settlers. In "The Horses of Diar el-Mahsul," a short story serialized in the weekly journal *Algérie-Actualité* from 1968 to 1969, the Algerian writer Saïd Belanteur described the nightly repossessions that took place in the European section of Pouillon's second housing complex:

> The [nearby] shantytowns . . . and the luxurious apartments of Diar el-Mahsul were emptied simultaneously, at the same rhythm, at night, in a feverish haste! At the same time that a wealthy [French] family was engulfed into a powerful car and drove, with its lights off . . . , a poor [Algerian] family, bundles and old tools in a handcart, quietly approached, stopped, stood watch, calculated their chances, noticed which light had just been turned out, waited a few minutes more—enough time to watch a car drive away—and climbed the stairs to shamelessly take possession of a bit of paradise.[51]

The most radical transformation of Algiers's built environment during the period of decolonization was its actual repopulation by Algerians. By 1962, Europeans had vacated more than fifteen thousand dwellings that were then acquired by Algerians. Although the new Algerian government declared in 1962 that the state had the right to preempt any transfers of dwellings and that no single person could acquire more than two properties, no firm mechanisms were put in place to control these exchanges. After new legislation was passed in 1966 and 1967, the state became the official title-holder of all vacated properties (*biens vacants*), and an additional 12,200 dwellings formerly owned by Europeans officially changed hands.[52]

In addition to their expropriations through both unofficial and lawful means, Pouillon's buildings in Algiers were transformed through everyday processes of inhabitation even as the broader landscape of hastily constructed temporary barracks that surrounded them remained dominant elements of the Clos Salembier's architectural landscape. According to Madani Safar-Zitoun's research, many new residents of abandoned buildings seem to have transformed the spaces and functions of their dwellings in similar ways. Often, apartments were split into two sections, with one room set aside as a formal reception area, frequently furnished following European traditions and often incorporating objects left behind by former residents.[53] The everyday life of inhabitants was confined to the remaining rooms, often organized quite differently with objects brought from previous dwellings. Such divisions re-created the physical spaces and patterns of habitation originally designed in complexes like Diar es-Saada and Diar el-Mahsul. Whereas Pouillon had assigned specific functions to individual rooms based on French conventions of modern dwelling, new inhabitants of these apartments transformed compartmentalized rooms into multifunctional, polyvalent spaces.

Such hybrid practices inscribed into expropriated apartments formerly inhabited by Europeans also engendered new phenomenological experiences of the same spaces. Safar-Zitoun has provocatively characterized this phenomenon as the simultaneous coexistence of the more familiar Algerian practice of "life at ground level" with "life perched up high," oriented in relation to the height of the windows.[54] In this way, "by consuming extroverted European housing, Algerians symbolically appropriated the attributes and signs of modern technology and of material progress that had constituted the foundations of the colonizer's power."[55] Far from simply adopting the dwelling practices of the former inhabitants, these expropriated dwellings were simultaneously remapped through divergent practices of habitation.

Similar dynamics seem to have informed a rather different expropriation of Pouillon's apartments shortly after independence. In January 1964, the postindependence government led by Ahmed Ben Bella chose to feature an image of Pouillon's first construction in Algiers, Diar es-Saada, on the new 100-dinar banknote that was issued that month (fig. 3.6).[56] Given the propagandistic function that Pouillon's project performed for Chevallier's admin-

Figure 3.6. One hundred-dinar banknote, back, issued in Algeria in 1964. Collection of the author.

istration, this choice is particularly remarkable. When this image was created, Diar es-Saada had been radically transformed by its physical reoccupation. As such, the image of the apartment complex that appeared on the currency of the newly independent nation must be seen as a reference to the dramatic expropriation of these buildings and all of the structures the French left behind.

However, the new 100-dinar banknote did not simply clad the Algerian state in the outward symbols of its now displaced colonial predecessor, since the bill's opposite face, inscribed in the new nation's official language of Arabic, presented a distinctly different vision of Algiers (fig. 3.7). Rather than an aerial view from the hills, the city is framed by the activity of the port with the distinctive forms of two minarets dominating the narrow slice of the urban landscape visible in the background. The massive boats docked at the port tower above the figures of workers whose labor is nonetheless dramatized in the foreground. In contrast to the stark, modern forms of Pouillon's housing blocks, the wooden scaffolding and hand-pulled cart create a vision of postindependence Algeria self-consciously oriented toward the past. In this way, the new banknote did not simply represent the state in the image of its colonial predecessor, but it simultaneously embraced visions of the city predicated on both forward-looking modernization and select recuperations of an imagined precolonial past.

The concerted publicity campaign through which Chevallier promoted Pouillon's new housing projects as icons of his administration and its success in the so-called battle for housing effectively positioned Diar es-Saada as a potent contemporary symbol of French colonial power. By choosing a

Figure 3.7. One hundred-dinar banknote, front, issued in Algeria in 1964. Collection of the author.

familiar image of present-day Algiers, Ben Bella's government advanced its own program of modernization, one that echoed the rhetoric of Chevallier but rearticulated its significance under the banner of Algerian socialism. During the years following independence, the apartments that Pouillon had designed for European inhabitants were not simply repopulated by Algerians, but also legally redefined. In this regard, Diar es-Saada was representative of the massive redistribution of property by and for the state, which eventually became the owner and landlord of much of the housing stock in the capital city.[57]

In 1966, Pouillon returned to Algiers and designed a series of hotel and resort complexes for the Ministry of Tourism under the new government of Houari Boumediene.[58] Shortly after his return to Algeria, Pouillon was asked to transform the Saint Jean-Baptiste Church, which he had built in 1954 as part of the Diar el-Mahsul complex, into a mosque. Here, the reinscription of Islam into the topography of Algiers was a critical means of redefining the city's urban landscape. Pouillon's redesign called for the construction of new exterior walls following the rectangular perimeter of the existing structure's base. However, rather than submerging the church's visible cross plan beneath entirely new facades—which would have in turn allowed for a more practically and symbolically appropriate interior plan for the mosque—the exterior remained largely the same (fig. 3.8). The only change to the structure visible on the exterior was the conversion of the bell tower into a minaret. Although these were relatively minimal changes in terms of the building's structure, the consequences of transforming the

Figure 3.8. Fernand Pouillon, Saint-Jean-Baptiste Church, as transformed into a mosque, Algiers, 1966. Originally published in Bernard Félix Dubor, *Fernand Pouillon* (Milan: Electa/Moniteur, 1986), fig. 57. Photo by Bernard Félix Dubor; courtesy of the Canadian Centre for Architecture, Montreal.

church into a mosque were nonetheless profound in terms of both its function and meaning.

The transformations of Diar es-Saada and Diar el-Mahsul in the wake of independence might be understood as *retranslations*, in the sense that Tejaswini Niranjana has used this term. As Niranjana argues, the transformative practice of retranslation works less to completely erase the marks of the colonizer's presence than to reframe those traces as part of an ongoing process of decolonization.[59] Following Walter Benjamin, Niranjana asserts that the more literal the retranslation, the more radical its potential effects.[60] Indeed, the transformation of the church into a mosque, like the rearticulation of Diar es-Saada on the postindependence banknote, aimed to translate iconic symbols of the colonial regime into palpable figures of its displacement in the most literal terms possible. In this way, the retranslations of Pouillon's buildings were also means of rewriting history, both through the actual appropriation of structures and the reinscription of their functions and symbolic meanings.

Although architecture was an important tool that governmental authorities used both before and after independence to reshape the city's image, such physical and symbolic transformations were never fully contained by official discourses. Saïd Belanteur's serialized short story of 1968–69 that describes the nightly expropriations of apartments in Diar el-Mahsul provides a different lens through which to consider these changes as more than merely a struggle between colonial and postcolonial authorities. Belanteur's story follows a young Algerian boy named Mounir, whose father leaves his village on the outskirts of Algiers to join the FLN and the independence movement. Before his father departs, he promises Mounir that he will bring him a horse of his own once the fighting is over. During the war, along with all the other inhabitants of their village, Mounir, his mother, and grandmother are forcibly resettled into barracks hastily erected in the Clos Salembier quarter near Pouillon's housing complexes. In order to support the family, Mounir's grandmother works as a housekeeper for a French woman who lives in the European section of the nearby Diar el-Mahsul. After much urging, Mounir persuades his grandmother to let him accompany her to work, where he discovers an impressive fountain off the main courtyard. In Mounir's eyes, its four horses, dramatically pulling the water god Neptune and his chariot out of the water, recall his father's promise.

For Mounir, the horses of Diar el-Mahsul represent both the dream of independence that will return his father and his promised horse to him and the transformative potential of the city. Ultimately, Mounir and his friends celebrate the moment of independence by clambering onto the backs of Pouillon's stone horses. Belanteur describes this act of taking possession of Diar el-Mahsul—its fountain, its courtyards, its apartments—not as the justifiable theft of the possessions of Europeans, but as the reappropriation of objects and spaces that rightfully belonged to the Algerians whose labor originally created them. Diar el-Mahsul was thus being returned to those to whom it rightfully belonged.

Whereas one could easily understand Diar el-Mahsul—particularly the section built for Europeans and the classicizing forms of its water god and horses—as immutable symbols of "French Algeria," Belanteur's story provocatively suggests that complex workings of imaginative and actual appropriations did not simply begin at the moment of independence. Although these sculptures were clearly positioned by the architect Pouillon as symbols of the French presence that distinguished this section of his complex from the comparatively unornamented habitations on the other side of the freeway, for Mounir, they represented an entirely different vision of freedom and escape. Even as the fountain embodied colonial power, the possibility of laying claim to it in different terms allowed Mounir to invest the horses with his own associations. Their meaning was not transformed merely by the transfer of ownership, but by the realization—at least momentarily—of Mounir's originary understanding and fantasy image of these horses as Arabian stallions.

In his analysis of the architecture and ideology of the postindependence capitol complex in Chandigarh, India, designed by Le Corbusier, Vikrama-ditya Prakash observes that "origins . . . are not ends, and therefore are not the only ways of deriving identity and ownership."[61] If the relationship of architecture to decolonization is conceived solely as a process through which postcolonial authorities appropriated cultural signs whose meaning was fully determined by the desires of their authors, we ignore the possibility that inhabitants of these structures might understand themselves and the spaces they occupied in different terms. The advent of independence transformed Mounir's experience of Diar el-Mahsul. However, neither the hierarchies originally created by Pouillon's buildings nor the changes that followed independence completely determined the way he understood these spaces. Mounir's imaginative engagement with the horses at Diar el-Mahsul suggests the powerful ways in which architecture may be invested with divergent, even if ultimately more ephemeral, meanings through processes of everyday habitation. In similar terms, the Algerian architect and urban planner Rachid Sidi Boumediene has asserted that decolonization may be possible less through the creation of new buildings than through the reoccupation of places that once were inaccessible.[62] By extension, Mounir's subjective reimagining of the horses and Diar el-Mahsul suggests that reoccupations may take various forms, even those that are conjectural and contingent.

The end of "The Horses of Diar el-Mahsul," recounts the removal of the fountain from the courtyard of Pouillon's housing complex, following a decision by the city's postcolonial administration to erect it elsewhere in the city.

While the four horses were moved to a more prominent, prestigious location along the November 1st Avenue, near the center of the city and the recently renamed Place des Martyrs, "Neptune, whose horses they had taken, [remained] alone, planted at the bottom of his basin, with one arm raised in a ridiculous manner."[63] In the eyes of the now adult Mounir, this lamentable event signaled the failure of the Algerian revolution to reinvest the city's disenfranchised residents with the power and autonomy that the horses of Diar el-Mahsul had seemed, in the eyes of the young boy, to guarantee.[64]

In fact, the physical relocation of the fountain was later followed by an even more dramatic displacement of Diar el-Mahsul and Diar es-Saada. In 1984, on the twentieth anniversary of the liberation struggle, a new monument to the martyrs of the revolution, the Makkam-Echahid, was constructed in the hills above the city center not far from Pouillon's housing complexes (fig. 3.9). Erected on a vast, open esplanade looking out over the surrounding city and the water below, this massive monument was shaped in the abstract forms of three intersecting palm fronds. The towering form of this enormous structure not only aggressively asserted its presence within the familiar topography of the city, but it also formed the cornerstone to the adjacent development of Riad el Feth, which included a museum documenting the liberation struggle, a shopping center, and a new hotel. Although this complex continued the efforts initiated shortly after independence to redefine the city of Algiers as a memorial topography organized in relation to the events and official heroes of the war, it simultaneously marked the liberalization of the Algerian economy by Boumediene's successor, Chaldi Bedjedid. That this structure was specifically imagined to displace Pouillon's buildings is evident not only in the way the new monument dwarfes the nearby towers of Diar es-Saada and Diar el-Mahsul to become the most prominent architectural landmark in Algiers, but also in the use of its image on a new banknote issued that same year. However, even as the Makkam-Echahid attempted to fully dislodge the symbolic importance of these monuments of the colonial era, it nevertheless reiterated the relationship of Pouillon's buildings to the surrounding city. Their authoritative monumentality was effectively reinscribed into the representational heart of postindependence Algiers.

FROM ALGIERS TO MARSEILLE: SIMOUNET'S NOSTALGÉRIE

As much as the urban landscape of Algiers was physically and symbolically redefined in the wake of independence, the city of Marseille and its sur-

Figure 3.9. Makkam-Echahid (Monument to the Martyrs), Algiers, 1984. From Lavalin, Inc., ed., *Mastering Water, Earth, Air and Fire in Only 50 Years* (Montreal: Lavalin, 1987), 47. Photo courtesy of the Canadian Centre for Architecture, Montreal.

roundings were radically transformed during this same period. When Algeria officially became independent, the vast majority of French residents, thereafter known as the *repatriés*, left for France, where many settled in Marseille and the surrounding region. Although it had long been reputed as a city of immigrants, Marseille also became home to growing numbers of north African immigrants in the decades that followed. While new pressures had been placed on architecture in Algiers during this period to represent the changing identity of the city and its inhabitants, Roland Simounet's architecture articulated a rather different quest to redefine Marseille's relationship to the end of empire. His work, which began in Algiers and moved to Marseille—in the opposite direction from that of Pouillon—traces an intersecting trajectory of architectural responses to the colonial past. Born near Algiers into a family descended from a pharmacist who was among the first generation of French colonists, Simounet designed a wide range of projects in Algeria in the 1950s and early 1960s, including individual villas, prototypes for mass housing, a cultural center dedicated to his friend Albert Camus, and a new town erected near the vestiges of the ancient Roman settlement in Timgad.[65] No single project served as a model that Simounet later replicated in the way that Pouillon's La Tourette in Marseille had formed the foundation for his subsequent work in Algiers. Instead, the structural components Simounet consolidated in his work in Algeria became the organizational principles of his later projects in France.

The defining elements of Simounet's architecture are especially evident in Djenan el-Hassan ("the beautiful gardens"), a housing development designed for the challenging site of a ravine in the western hills of Algiers, in a quarter whose topography and population resembled that of the Clos Salembier (fig. 3.10). Built in two sections, the first in 1957 and the second shortly after independence in 1962, Simounet's modular dwellings, designed as temporary, transitional housing for Algerians, follow the dramatic contours of the topography. Each unit, with its own balcony and vaulted roof, was stacked in a staggered formation to provide an outdoor terrace for the apartment below.[66] The housing model Simounet developed at Djenan el-Hassan self-consciously responded to the work of Le Corbusier, who had created an extensive new urban plan for Algiers in the 1930s.[67] At Djenan el-Hassan, the interior courtyards that Le Corbusier had privileged as the structural and social heart of the north African house were transformed into external balconies, while terraced roofs were designed as outdoor living spaces, in reference to the architecture of the Casbah. Whereas Pouillon created discrete, external decorative flourishes for his buildings in Marseille and Algiers that were notionally inspired by north African architecture, Simounet distilled a series of essential, structural devices that were variously reiterated in his buildings in Algeria and in France: interior courtyards, roof terraces, and monolithic walls.

Simounet left Algiers in 1963 and relocated his architectural practice to Paris. His subsequent projects in France repeatedly returned to the elements he had established in Algiers, but the connections between his architecture and his Algerian origins were pushed to the foreground in a project he

Figure 3.10. Roland Simounet, Djenan el-Hassan, Algiers, 1957–62. Originally published in "Djenan-El-Hassan (Alger)—Cité de recasement," *Techniques et Architecture* 20, no. 6 (September 1960): 113. Photo by Photo Studios P.A.I.R., Algiers; courtesy of the Canadian Centre for Architecture, Montreal.

helped to develop for a site in L'Estaque, a former fishing village turned industrial suburb on the coast north of Marseille. In 1983, Raymond Courvière, the minister charged with overseeing the affairs of the *repatriés*, invited Simounet to design a museum that would contain not only exhibition galleries but also a library and research center. The project took its name from the group organized to guide its development, the Association for the Conservation and Development of the Cultural Patrimony of the French Natives of North Africa. Although the museum was supposed to address all the repatriated French residents of north Africa, in the hands of Simounet and the association members, French-Algerians quickly became its privileged referents.[68]

The proposed museum project was part of a broader shift in the terms through which *pied-noir* identity was articulated and understood during the 1980s. French residents of Algeria, the majority of whom joined the mass exodus to France during the months leading up to independence in 1962, "returned" to a country that many of them had never even visited. There they faced extreme housing shortages, few available jobs, and no little resentment from their metropolitan compatriots, particularly in the Marseille region where many of them settled.[69] After 1962, the term *pieds-noirs* (literally, "black feet") was increasingly adopted in reference to the former Euro-

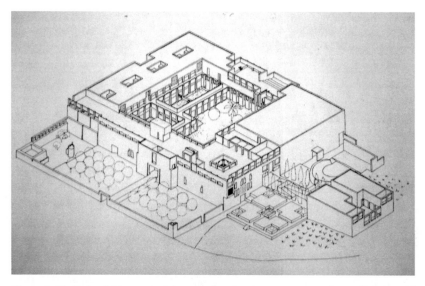

Figure 3.11. Roland Simounet, Museum for the Conservation and Development of the Cultural Patrimony of the French Natives of North Africa, L'Estaque, axonometric drawing, 1983–86. Photo from the Roland Simounet Collections (1997017 P124), Centre des Archives du Monde du Travail, Roubaix.

pean settlers of Algeria. Although the origins of the term are still debated, it seems to have referred either to the black boots worn by the soldiers of the first French occupation forces or to the dirty feet of the poor European settlers who followed them. The group formed to guide the development of the proposed museum, an early attempt to challenge silence and ambivalence regarding both the French-Algerian War and the *repatriés*, marked a departure from earlier organizations of *pieds-noirs* that had largely been interested in fostering social networks among former French residents of Algeria. By contrast, the proposed museum represented a new commitment to cultivating and promoting *pied-noir* identity through cultural productions aimed at a more general audience.[70] To this end, the museum intended to represent the *pieds-noirs* as a model minority culture that, in the two decades since 1962, had been successfully assimilated into the universalizing aims of the French Republic.[71]

Simounet's initial designs for the museum drew on the building blocks he had consolidated in Algiers. The entire walled complex was organized around a central outdoor courtyard with an accessible rooftop terrace that provided a panoramic view of the Mediterranean Sea (fig. 3.11). In contrast to his earlier projects in Algiers, however, this structure gestured toward north Africa not simply in its forms but also through sensorial experiences, with the landscape and climate of the Marseille region providing a final touch of imagined authenticity. Entering through the main portal, a ramp led the visitor past miniature orange groves—intended to recall those planted by French colonists in Algeria—and through the fortresslike walls of the museum interior.[72] From the entrance foyer, the museum circuit began in a room called the wall of images. In this enclosed space, the visitor was to be immersed in photographs covering the entire room, along with the sounds and smells of changing Algerian and north African landscapes where, according to design documents, "the visitor would have the impression of being incorporated into the landscape and of being a living actor in these images."[73] Rather than encouraging direct engagement and activity, these spectacular displays were intended to overwhelm and absorb the viewer.

The museum thus aimed to transport visitors to a distant place and immerse them in a timeless vision of the past, an experience that was repeated throughout the building: in the visual material displayed in enclosed galleries, in the fragrant vegetation of its outdoor courtyard and gardens, and even in the *hammam* constructed in the museum annex. By self-consciously staging an experience of dislocation and reorientation, Simounet's building transformed the Mediterranean landscape of Marseille into an elaborate simulacrum of, and memorial to, a lost *French* north Africa. In turn, visitors were invited to surrender themselves to the receptive, sensorial experience of *nostalgérie*. As in the writings of Henri de Montherlant, where the term first originated, the museum enacted a melancholic longing for a lost, innocent past similar to the one that permeated Montherlant's fictional accounts of *pied-noir* life before independence and the trauma of repatriation.[74] By invoking the mythic Mediterranean ciphers of land, sun, and sea, the museum's building and landscape worked together to create the impression of being *"là-bas,"* of returning to a far away, yet familiar place, safely drained of historical specificity and political conflict.

Although the museum project was put on hold in 1986, that same year, Simounet won an architectural competition to design the National School of Dance in Marseille. Like the museum, this building was to be organized around a central courtyard, with imposing solid walls punctuated only by a few small openings. The staggered volumes of the building in turn created a complex and variegated roofscape. Whereas the site of the museum in L'Estaque had provided dramatic views of the sea that Simounet used to his advantage in the building's design, the location proposed for the National School of Dance posed a rather different challenge. The school was to be erected in the Saint-Just quarter, on the periphery of the city center in an area that had increasingly become home to Marseille's growing immigrant population, many of whom were from Algeria. Like other areas on the northern periphery of the city, the urban landscape was increasingly dominated by sprawling public housing complexes recently erected in the hopes of accommodating Marseille's exploding population.

From the outset, Simounet focused particular attention on the articulation of exterior walls, emphasizing their important role in creating a sense of enclosure and protection. The external form of the building was also connected to the practical problem of creating what Simounet referred to as an acoustically neutralizing building. In this way, the architect worked to actively protect and disengage the dance studios from the noise and activity of the surrounding city, including the metro station and transit hub standing directly across the street. His own understanding of north African architecture as fundamentally oriented around the interior courtyard, and thereby profoundly interiorizing, provided a productive model for the very introverted space of learning he hoped to create for the National School of Dance.

A drawing from 1987, created as Simounet was developing his designs for the school, details the lessons the architect claimed to have first absorbed in Algiers and that clearly informed his projects in Marseille, including the lyrical qualities of the port as well as the whitewashed walls and terraces of the Casbah. In the drawing and accompanying text, Simounet's memories of his childhood and the landscapes of Algiers merge with a poetic lament for modern architecture as articulated in the city's palm trees, which the architect calls "the *pilotis* of my youth."[75] Here Simounet recalled not only the landscapes of his childhood, but more specifically his affiliation with Le Corbusier and the older architect's earlier abstraction of the Casbah into the foundational elements of modern architecture. The *nostalgérie* of Simounet's projects in Marseille thus articulated intersecting longings for originary, lost pasts, both those of the *pieds-noirs* and those of modern architecture's own colonial history. In this way, Simounet's encounter with Marseille elicited an unusually direct mapping of his projects there in relation to Algiers as an imagined, multilayered architectural origin.

In the case of the National School of Dance, such a mythic re-finding of Algiers in Marseille was facilitated by the decision to move the proposed site of its construction from the densely constructed, cosmopolitan neighborhood of Saint-Just to a park in a largely bourgeois residential neighborhood on the southern side of the city. Detached from its surroundings, the building's imposing white walls, central courtyard, labyrinthine interior spaces, and interlocking roof terraces create the impression of a miniature, abstracted Casbah floating dreamlike in the park's verdant enclosure (fig.

Figure 3.12. Roland Simounet, National School of Dance, Marseille, 1986–91. Photo by the author.

3.12). In its new pastoral location, it was certainly easier for Simounet to project a mythic vision of Algiers in Marseille, one that could represent a nostalgic longing for a lost home and the recuperation of an imagined history of modern architecture. In this setting, the School of Dance was physically detached not simply from noisy intrusions, but perhaps even more crucially from the dense fabric of the city in which traces of Algiers and memories of north Africa were not solely the province of the *pieds-noirs,* but of French-Algerians of various origins, including the Algerian immigrants whose histories were absent from the museum's memorial aims. In this way, the *nostalgérie* of Simounet's projects for Marseille suggests that these buildings might be understood in part as mythic mistranslations disconnected from both the contemporary complexities of Marseille and the historical realities of Algiers.

Simounet's understanding of Marseille as a site for recuperating a particular vision of France's colonial past was more than simply a personal project. By the time the National School of Dance was being completed, city officials had reconceived Simounet's abandoned museum project for L'Estaque as a means of promoting Marseille by way of its historical connections to the colonies. In 1992, as the construction of the National School of Dance was coming to an end, the city of Marseille held an architectural competition to design a "Museum for the Memory of the Overseas French." The new project was to be housed in the Fort Saint-Jean adjacent to Pouillon's La Tourette housing complex, a site chosen in part for symbolic reasons, given its imagined history as a silent witness to departures of colonists leaving from the nearby port of Marseille to resettle overseas. The competition program was based on Simounet's earlier proposals, with significant shifts in focus, encouraged by the current mayor of Marseille, Robert Vigoureux, from the conservation of patrimony to the cultivation of memory and from *pied-noir* experience to the history of French settlers in colonial territories around the world.[76] At the same time that these modifications were undertaken with the recognition that living memories of the colonial experience were quickly fading, Vigoureux also wanted the project to appeal not simply to the *pied-noir* community or even solely to the *repatriés* of various countries, but to a significantly broader public.

In his competition entry, Simounet revisited his earlier project for the site in L'Estaque, transposing its elements into the dramatically different contours of the Fort Saint-Jean (fig. 3.13). Entering the museum from a door at the base of its massive fortifications, the visitor would first encounter a wall of images, followed by a multimedia room featuring changing projected images that covered the walls and ceilings. These elements were adapted from Simounet's previous designs with the aim of "immersing the spectator in an environment from the past."[77] After this initial encounter, the visitor would be led in a spiral from the entrance spaces through galleries and multimedia displays at different levels to finally emerge onto a terrace with its dramatic view of the port and the sea. The museum's restaurant was the only interior space that projected above the fortifications, notionally orienting the visitors' gaze toward north Africa. Substituting couscous for Proust's madeleine, with a panoramic view of the Mediterranean as an appropriate backdrop, the restaurant intended to function as the crowning experience of displacement and nostalgic immersion featured in the early project for L'Estaque.

In Simounet's hands, Marseille's memory of its "overseas" past was submerged and only faintly visible within the engulfing form of one of the city's most prominent monuments. Despite the fact that his earlier museum project for L'Estaque had been used by Mayor Vigoureux to persuade authorities in Paris that Marseille should be chosen as the site for the new cultural center, Simounet's revised proposals were rejected in favor of the project by Denis Froidevaux, an architect based in Paris who specialized in historic preservation. However, given the severe effects of deindustrialization and resultant skyrocketing rates of unemployment in Marseille, Froidevaux's project was discarded shortly thereafter, as it was judged to be too costly. Ironically, the roots of this economic crisis were themselves inti-

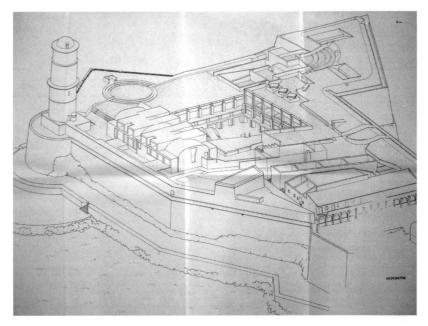

Figure 3.13. Roland Simounet, Museum for the Memory of the Overseas French, Marseille, perspective drawing, 1991–92. Photo from the Roland Simounet Collections (1997017 P53), Centre des Archives du Monde du Travail, Roubaix.

mately tied to the history that the museum was intended to memorialize. What was notably repressed both in Simounet's project and in debates surrounding the museum was any reference to rising tensions in Marseille regarding immigration, particularly from north Africa, with the result that these intersecting histories were framed as absolutely distinct from one another. In this way, the architectural form of Simounet's proposed project might be seen to dramatize the submerged archaeology of the city's own colonial history and the ambivalent relationship to its postcolonial present that has profoundly marked Marseille's contemporary identity.

Architecture at the ends of empire, in Algiers and in Marseille, is haunted in potent, if often divergent ways, by colonial legacies that continue to shape the postcolonial present of both cities. To recognize the mutability of forms and meanings between these sites, we need only think of the many incarnations of fortifications in Algiers and Marseille, as architectural structures and ideological propositions. These various projects, from Diar el-Mahsul and the Makkam-Echahid to the National School of Dance and the Museum to the Memory of the Overseas French, were all rooted in the desire to create self-contained spaces detached from the broader urban landscape. Although such structures of protected enclosure were necessary to transform imagined, mythic constructions of identity into architectural form, such visions were repeatedly challenged by the near impossibility of sealing off these structures from their surroundings.

Even though Montherlant's notion of *nostalgérie* was defined in relation to a specifically *pied-noir* project, I want to suggest that this term could speak to the broader recuperative strategies that have fueled the arguably ongoing process of decolonization in both Algiers and Marseille. As much as Simounet's longings for lost Algerian origins were radically different in substance from the desire by Algeria's postindependence administrations to resurrect a purified precolonial past and to rewrite more recent history, Mounir's imaginative longings for freedom invested in the horses at Diar el-Mahsul diverged from Pouillon's projections of authenticity and mastery. Nevertheless, these intersecting architectural imaginaries underscore the degree to which the urban histories of Algiers and Marseille have been and continue to be forged in relation to one another. The processes of translating, appropriating, erasing, or recovering traces of colonialism during the French-Algerian War and following independence created intersecting networks of associations and identifications built on the often uncanny architectural legacies of France in Algeria and Algeria in France.

Even within the broader history of the French empire, the circumstances of Algiers were exceptional, particularly in terms of its imagined and administrative incorporation into the French nation, the experience and aftermath of settler colonialism, and the extreme violence and repressions that accompanied the war for independence and that continue to fuel its contemporary reverberations. Despite their distinctiveness, the urban dynamics that have linked Algiers and Marseille might usefully be considered in relation to what Michael Dear and Héctor Manuel Lucero have described as the postborder condition between San Diego and Tijuana. Dear and Lucero draw attention to the dramatic cross-border consolidation evident in the sprawling new megacity of "Bajalta, California," an area that effectively functions as "a single, integrated city-region that just happens to straddle an international boundary."[78] The asymmetrical and relatively less intensive phenomena of urbanization and migration between Algiers and Marseille, particularly in the wake of the mass repatriation of French and other European residents of Algiers around the time of independence, have resulted in a greater separation between these two cities. Nevertheless, continued connections across the Mediterranean—whether manifest physically in architectural form or in phantasmatic projections—might be understood to represent a related "postborder condition," where "elements of different worlds coexist and mutate," effects that are particularly palpable in the built landscapes of both cities.[79] As much as borders create material divisions, they also structure points of contact, conflict, and passage. The histories of Algiers and Marseille speak to such conditions and suggest the importance of writing urban histories that treat cities not as simply as self-contained entities, but as sites significantly shaped by broader regional, transnational, and translocal dynamics.[80]

By examining Marseille and Algiers in dialogue with one another, I aim to contribute to a broader rethinking of the tendency to separate the histories of cities in metropolitan centers from those in colonial or formerly colonial territories that continues to guide analysis of colonialism and the city. This study constitutes one piece within a larger puzzle of reconsidering the shared histories and legacies of colonialism as they have significantly reshaped cities at the tumultuous boundaries between colonial and metropolitan terrains. Recent scholarship has begun to gesture to connections that might be charted between Dublin and Glasgow or London and Bombay, and such interconnections are certainly worthy of further examination.[81] Urban reflections between Algiers and Marseille might then find provocative counterpoints in related processes of architectural transfers and symbolic rewritings between Jakarta and Rotterdam, Brussels and Kinshasa, Tripoli and Naples, Tangier and Cádiz, or Tokyo and Shanghai.

NOTES

This essay and the larger project from which it is drawn have been transformed in innumerable ways by conversations with and suggestions by many members of the extraordinary community of scholars at the Shelby Cullom Davis Center and in the History Department at Princeton University who pushed me to think about cities and about writing comparative histories in new ways. I am especially grateful to Gyan Prakash and Kevin Kruse for organizing this volume and the seminars in which it first germinated, to James McDougall for his generous and extremely insightful reflections on an earlier draft of this paper, and to the two anonymous readers for their suggestions. Thanks are also due to the Davis Center, the Western Society for French History (Millstone Research Fellowship), as well as the Arts Research Institute and the Committee on Research at the University of California, Santa Cruz for providing funds essential for my research.

1. The constitution adopted by the French administration on November 12, 1848, declared Algeria to be an integral part of France. In 1881, Algeria was integrated directly into France through the establishment of a new administrative system dividing the territory into communes. See Benjamin Stora, *Histoire de l'Algérie coloniale*,

2nd ed. (Paris: La Découverte, 2004), 114. A statute adopted in 1947 officially defined Algeria as a "group of French *départements*," that is, as an administrative region understood as a subdivision of the nation. Guy Pervillé, "Une capitale convoitée," in Jean-Jacques Jordi and Guy Pervillé, eds., *Alger, 1942–1960: Une ville en guerre* (Paris: Éditions Autrement, 1999), 126. On the exceptional status of Algeria in the French metropolitan imaginary, see Éric Saravèse, *L'invention des pieds-noirs* (Paris: Éditions Séguier, 2002), 161.

2. Yaël Simpson Fletcher discusses this phenomenon in " 'Capital of the Colonies': Real and Imagined Boundaries between Metropole and Empire in 1920s Marseille," in Felix Driver and David Gilbert, eds., *Imperial Cities: Landscape, Display and Identity* (Manchester: Manchester University Press, 1999), 136–54.

3. One such publication from 1941 claimed that if you wandered through the markets near the city center, you would think you were in "the middle of Arabia and Kabylia [the northern mountains of Algeria]. . . . In sum, the entire oriental basin of the Mediterranean [was represented], with all its languages, all its dialects, all of its idioms. In the center of Marseille, one finds oneself transported thousands of miles away." Louis Blin, *Marseille inconnu* (Avignon: Edouard Aubanel, 1941), 12, 14. Unless otherwise indicated, all translations are by the author.

4. A recent exhibition organized through the cooperation of institutions in both cities has made much of these historical and contemporary connections: *Parlez-moi d'Alger: Marseille—Alger au miroir des mémoires*, exh. cat. (Marseille: Mission pour le Musée National des Civilisations de l'Europe et de la Méditerranée, 2003).

5. Pioneering studies of French colonial urban planning and architecture include Gwendolyn Wright, *The Politics of Design in French Colonial Urbanism* (Chicago: University of Chicago Press, 1991); Paul Rabinow, *French Modern: The Norms and Forms of the Social Environment* (Cambridge, Mass.: MIT Press, 1989); and François Béguin, *Arabisances: Décor architectural et trace urbain en Afrique du Nord, 1830–1950* (Paris; Dunod, 1983).

6. Such a framework pervades the existing literature on architecture and colonialism in Algeria. See, for example, Jean-Louis Cohen, Nabila Oulebsir, and Youcef Kanoun, eds., *Alger, paysage et architectures, 1800–2000* (Paris: Éditions de l'Imprimateur, 2003); Zeynep Çelik, *Urban Forms and Colonial Confrontations: Algiers under French Rule* (Berkeley: University of California Press, 1997); Marc Bédarida, "L'influence française," *Techniques et Architectures* 430 (1997): 91–95; and Xavier Malverti, "Alger: Méditerranée, soleil et modernité," in *Architectures français d'outre-mer* (Paris: Institut Français d'Architecture, 1992); and Michèle Lamprakos, "Le Corbusier and Algiers: The Plan Obus as Colonial Urbanism," in Nezar AlSayyad, ed., *Forms of Dominance: On the Architecture and Urban Planning of the Colonial Enterprise* (Brookfield, Vt.: Avebury, 1992), 183–210.

7. Kristin Ross, *Fast Cars, Clean Bodies: Decolonization and the Reordering of French Culture* (Cambridge, Mass.: The MIT Press, 1995).

8. Patricia Morton, *Hybrid Modernities: Architecture and Representation at the 1931 Colonial Exhibition, Paris* (Cambridge, Mass.: MIT Press, 2000).

9. Anthony King, "Rethinking Colonialism: An Epilogue," in Nezar AlSayyad, eds., *Forms of Dominance: On the Architecture and Urbanism of the Colonial Enterprise* (Brookfield, Vt: Avebury, 1992), 353.

10. John Simpson and Edmund Weiner, eds., *The Oxford English Dictionary*, 2nd ed. (Oxford: Oxford University Press, 1989).

11. Henri de Montherlant, *La Rose de Sable*, in *Romans*, vol. 2, ed. Michel Raimond (Paris: Gallimard, 1982), 179; cited in Philip Dine, *Images of the Algerian War: French Fiction and Film, 1954–1992* (Oxford: Clarendon Press, 1994), 149–50.

12. Chevallier came from a bourgeois family in Lyon with long-standing ties to the colonies, as his grandfather had built his fortune importing wood, wine, and other products from Algeria. Jean-Louis Planche, "Jacques Chevallier, député-maire d'Alger," in Jean-Jacques Jordi and Guy Pervillé, eds., *Alger, 1940–1962: Une ville en guerres* (Paris: Éditions Autrement, 1999), 160–65; and Benjamin Stora, *Algérie 1954* (Paris: Le Monde and Éditions de l'Aube, 2004), 25–31. For Chevallier's own account of his political career, see Jacques Chevallier, *Nous, Algériens* (Paris: Calman-Lévy, 1958).

13. According to administrative records from 1961, Diar es-Saada was home to 3,406 residents. See Centre des Archives d'Outre-Mer [hereafter CAOM], series 2SAS, file 60; Centre Algérien d'Expansion Économique et Sociale (C.A.E.E.S.), "Budgets familiaux dans le quartier du Clos Salembier," unpublished report, May 1960–June 1961.

14. The population of Algiers expanded dramatically from 214,520 residents in 1931 to 357,753 in 1954. If anything, the figures from the 1954 census may have been underestimated, given the ubiquity of illegal and quasi-legal settlements. See Jean Pelletier, *Alger, 1955: Essai d'une géographie sociale*, Cahiers de Géographie de Besançon, no. 6 (Paris: Les Belles Lettres, 1959), 6–7. Migrations of large numbers of people to Algiers only increased in the years that followed. From the beginning of the war in 1954 to independence in 1962, the population of Algiers rose to 869,946 inhabitants. Larbi Ichboudene, *Alger: Histoire et capitale de destin national* (Algiers: Casbah Éditions, 1997), 333. For discussion of the endemic, structural dynamics of the housing crisis in Algiers during this period, see Madani Safar-Zitoun, *Stratégies patrimoniales et urbanization, Alger, 1962–1992* (Paris: Éditions L'Harmattan, 1996), 40–43.

15. In his 1955 study of the urban geography of Algiers, Jean Pelletier described the Clos Salembier quarter as "a veritable museum of housing conceded to Muslims by the Administration: *Ghorfas* in more or less disastrous condition, barracks of the 'Cholet' type, well constructed and rather spacious, but also cabins made of wood planks that are already deteriorating less than a year after their construction." Pelletier, *Alger, 1955*, 80. Also see Robert Descloitres, Jean-Claude Reverdy, and Claudine Descloitres. *L'Algérie des bidonvilles: Le tiers monde dans la cité* (Paris: Mouton, 1961), 13–14.

16. See Pervillé, "Une capitale convoitée," 126.

17. According to Pelletier's study, the Clos Salembier quarter had 20,748 Algerian and 2,890 European residents. *Alger, 1955*, 76. See also M. Sgroï-Dufresne, *Alger, 1830–1984: Stratégies et enjeux urbains* (Paris: Éditions Recherches sur les Civilisations, 1986), 36.

18. "Les réalisations de l'Office public d'H.L.M. de la ville d'Alger: Diar-es-Saâda—Diar-el-Mahçow—Climat de France—Eucalyptus," *Chantiers: Revue Illustrée de la Construction en Afrique du Nord* 23 (1956). In 1961, 7,704 people lived in Diar el-Mahçoul, 5,210 of whom lived in the area designated for Algerians and 2,494 in the area for Europeans. See CAOM, 2SAS/60: C.A.E.E.S. report.

19. Fernand Pouillon, *Mémoires d'un architecte* (Paris: Éditions du Seuil, 1968), 172.

20. See Çelik, *Urban Forms*, 1997, 145–46; Alberto Ferlenga, "L'histoire comme matériau," in Jean-Lucien Bonillo, ed., *Fernand Pouillon, architecte méditerranéen* (Marseille: Éditions Imbernon, 2001), 119; Bernard Felix Dubor, *Fernand Pouillon* (Paris: Electa Moniteur, 1996), 56; and Alberto Ferlenga, "Fernand Pouillon (1912–1986): New Foundation of the City, New Foundation of a Discipline," *New City: Modern Cities* 3 (Fall 1996): 74.

21. Pouillon, *Mémoires*, 205. In this respect Pouillon diverged from previous evaluative mappings of Algeria's architectural landscapes by French architects insofar as he did not privilege Algiers's Andalusian or "Moorish" (*mauresque*) architectural heritage over its Ottoman legacy as many of his predecessors had tended to do. See Nabila Oulebsir, *Les usages du patrimoine: Monuments, musées et Politique Coloniale en Algérie (1830–1930)* (Paris: Éditions de la Maison des Sciences de l'homme, 2004), 296.

22. For a brief history of the Villa des Arcades, see Alessandro Sartor, "Villa des Arcades: Original Structure and Its Transformations," *Environmental Design: Journal of the Islamic Environmental Design Research Center* 15–16, nos. 1–2 (1994–95): 136; and Lucien Golvin, *Palais et demeures d'Alger à la période ottomane* (Aix-en-Provence: Édisud, 1988), 121–23.

23. Pouillon, *Mémoires*, 212.

24. Sartor, "Villa des Arcades," 142. The few commentators who have analyzed Pouillon's interventions likewise concur that they were sensitively handled and successfully blend into the overall complex as the architect had intended. See Golvin, *Palais et demeures d'Alger*, 123; and Jean-Jacques Deluz, *Alger, chronique urbaine* (Paris: Éditions Bouchène, 2001), 51.

25. Pouillon, 212.

26. Kaja Silverman, "White Skins, Brown Masks: The Double Mimesis, or with Lawrence in Arabia," *Male Subjectivity at the Margins* (New York: Routledge, 1992), 312.

27. The strict logic of segregation that structured Diar es-Saada and Diar el-Mahsul was never fully realized in practice. See, for example, Jean-Jacques Deluz's de-

scription of the people who were his neighbors in one of the buildings included in the European section of Diar el-Mahsul in the late 1950s: Deluz, *Alger*, 46–47.

28. Architects and urban planners in Algiers thus adopted the terminology that had been developed in Morocco by ATBAT-Afrique in its development of housing types designed for different ethnic categories with the aim of gradually training Moroccans to live "properly" in European-style accommodations. See Monique Eleb, "An Alternative to Functionalist Universalism: Écochard, Candilis, and ATBAT-Afrique," in Sarah Williams Goldhagen and Réjean Legault, eds., *Anxious Modernisms* (Cambridge, Mass.: MIT Press, 2000), 55–73.

29. See Pelleltier, *Alger, 1955*, map of Clos Salembier quarter; and Safar-Zitoun, *Stratégies patrimoniales*, 35.

30. CAOM, 2SAS/60: C.A.E.E.S. report. See also Safar-Zitoun, *Stratégies patrimoniales*, 61.

31. The studies by ATBAT-Afrique in Morocco in the early 1950s are paradigmatic in this regard. See, for example, the studies from 1953 for housing types designated for "Muslim," "Israelite," "European," and "mixed" populations in the Archives d'Architecture du Vingtième Siècle, Institut Français d'Architecture, Paris, Georges Candilis collection, 236 IFA 608/10.

32. Safar-Zitoun, *Stratégies patrimoniales*, 168.

33. Here Pouillon's strategy might be usefully to compared with what the British architect Edwin L. Lutyens, who designed the Viceroy's House complex in New Delhi, India, in 1918–31, described as "emblematic ornament." For a related critical discussion of this concept and its relationship to colonial ideology in architecture, see Catherine Ingraham, "Architecture as Evidence," in Stephen Cairns, ed., *Drifting: Architecture and Migrancy* (London: Routledge, 2004), 65–67.

34. See Maria Tymoczko, "Post-colonial Writing and Literary Translation," in Susan Bassnett and Harish Trivedi, eds., *Post-colonial Translation: Theory and Practice* (London: Routledge, 1999), 21.

35. Pouillon, *Mémoires*, 83.

36. Ibid., 195–96. Alberto Ferlenga has observed that these spectacular construction feats provided a kind of ready-made epic history for Pouillon's new buildings. Ferlenga, "L'histoire comme matériau," 119–20.

37. Jacques Chevallier, "La bataille du logement sera livrée jusqu'à la victoire complète," *Alger: Revue Municipale*, no. 4 (April 1955): 10–12; and "Alger: Premier chantier de France livré et gagné—La Bataille du Logement," *Alger: Revue Municipale*, no. 5 (May 1955).

38. See Pouillon, *Mémoires*, 214; Centre des Archives Contemporaines, Fontainebleau, file 13: l'Office Public d'H.L.M., "Alger, Diar-es-Saâda," photographic album, ugust 14, 1953; and Françoise Espel, *Alger: Deuxième ville de France* (Paris: Éditions Pensée Moderne, 1959). In the mid-1950s, a seemingly constant parade of dignitaries toured these completed projects, and their visits were invariably documented in photographs intended for publication. Zeynep Çelik notes that such ceremonial tours

were not without incident: "As reported by *L'Echo d'Alger* in March 1957, a visit by Mayor Chevallier and a group of schoolteachers to the construction site of Diar el-Mahsul had ended with the 'salutations of about one hundred little Muslims who shouted "Algeria is ours" and who threw stones at the visitors.' " Çelik, *Urban Forms*, 1997, 150.

39. See Ferlenga, "L'histoire comme matériau," 121. A report describing the Clos Salembier quarter in 1958–59 explicitly claimed that Diar el-Mahsul was a key site in the contemporary tourist landscape of Algiers. CAOM, 2 SAS/59: summary report of the S.A.U. of Clos-Salembier, 1958–59. According to Jacques Gandini, a guidebook to the city published in 1957 insisted that tourists should not miss "the unforgettable spectacle" of the city lit up at night that one could view from the esplanade of Diar-el-Mahsul. Jacques Gandini, *Alger de ma jeunesse, 1950–1962* (Calvisson: Éditions J. Gandini, 1995), 163.

40. In addition to their frequent use in the municipal administration's official publications, aerial photographs of Diar es-Saada were included as key examples in two articles on aerial photography and its uses for urban planning in Algiers. "La photo aérienne et ses resources insoupçonnés," *Alger: Revue Municipale* no. 3 (March 1955): 38–42; and M. E. Pasquali, "La photo aérienne au service de l'urbanisme," *Travaux Nord-Africains*, September 22, 1955.

41. See photograph by Nicolas Tikhomiroff, a photojournalist working for Magnum, taken in the days following the mass demonstrations and subsequent violence that marked the first weeks of December 1960 and reproduced in Henri Alleg et al., eds., *La guerre d'Algérie: Des complots du 13 mai à l'indépendance* 3 (Paris: Temps Actuels, 1981), 3:271.

42. Pouillon, *Mémoires*, 196.

43. In 1953, the houses of the shantytowns in the Clos Salembier quarter known as "La Victoire Sifaoui" and "El Mansah" were destroyed and their eight hundred residents were rehoused in prefabricated barracks nearby. Although the land that was liberated by this operation was used to construct Diar el-Mahsul, none of these displaced inhabitants were accommodated into the new buildings. Instead, their temporary quarters became semipermanent dwellings. Safar-Zitoun, *Stratégies patrimoniales*, 43. In the decade before independence, only ten percent of petitions for public housing filed by Algerians were satisfied, as compared to seventy-five percent of requests by Europeans. Safar-Zitoun, *Stratégies patrimoniales*, 57.

44. For an account of the S.A.U. and its active role in the colonial administration's policy of pacification, see Grégor Mathias, *Les sections specialisées en Algérie: Entre ideal et réalité, 1955–1962* (Paris: L'Harmattan, 1998).

45. Benjamin Stora, *Histoire de la guerre d'Algérie (1954–1962)* (Paris: Éditions la Découverte, 2004), 58; Alleg, *La querre d'Algéne*, 265–74.

46. Mouloud Feraoun, *Journal, 1955–1962: Reflections on the French-Algerian War*, trans. Mary Ellen Wolf and Claude Fouillade (Lincoln: University of Nebraska

Press, 2000), 279. From 1955 until his assassination by extremists of the O.A.S. (Organisation de l'Armée Secret) on March 15, 1962, Feraoun kept a journal recording his observations and responses to the events of the French-Algerian War that was first published posthumously in 1962.

47. The monthly reports of the S.A.U. office in the Clos Salembier quarter from December 1960 through early 1962 catalog many of these events. See CAOM, 2SAS/59–60. Feraoun's journal provides a dramatically different narration of similar incidents; Feraoun, *Journal, 1955–1962*, 277–84.

48. CAOM, 2SAS/60, "Message regarding the events that took place in the Clos Salembier from December 8th–16th," December 17, 1960. See also Feraoun, *Journal, 1955–1962*, 281–82.

49. See CAOM, 2SAS/60, "Message regarding the events . . . " and monthly report, November 20, 1961.

50. By 1965, more than 80 percent of the French population of Algeria, about 950,000 people, had departed. Jacques Fremeaux, "Le reflux des français d'Afrique du Nord (1956–1962)," in Jean-Jacques Jordi and Émile Témime, eds., *Marseille et le choc des décolonisations* (Aix-en-Provence: Édisud, 1996), 14–15.

51. Saïd Belanteur, *Les chevaux de Diar el-Mahsul* (Algiers: S.N.E.D., 1975), 39.

52. See Safar-Zitoun, *Stratégies patrimoniales*, 74–81.

53. Ibid., 90. Such reappropriations were not new in the postindependence era. A 1960–61 report on the Clos Salembier quarter described a similar situation: A *salon*, furnished in European manner "is in effect the first purchase that a Muslim family undertakes when they acquire a modern dwelling, but, in fact, this room remains a showroom [*une pièce de parade*] where no one lives. The room everyone occupies remains, by contrast, furnished in the 'Arab' style: high benches covered in satin cushions are pushed against the wall, with platters and various silver objects occupying the center, fabrics are placed around the room, and the entire space is rounded out by a magnificent television set." See C.A.E.E.S. report.

54. Safar-Zitoun, *Stratégies patrimoniales*, Ibid., 90.

55. Ibid., 89.

56. Nabila Oulebsir and Xavier Malverti both mention the prominent image of Diar es-Saada on the first postindependence 100-dinar banknote, but do not discuss the image on the reverse side of the banknote. Oulebsir, *Les usages du patrimoine*, 312; and Xavier Malverti, "La saga algérienne," in Jean-Lucien Bonillo, ed., *Fernand Pouillon: Architecte méditerranéen* (Marseille: Éditions Imbernon, 2001), 66.

57. The Algerian state eventually owned 90 percent of the housing stock in Algiers that had been the property of Europeans. Safar-Zitoun, *Stratégies patrimoniales*, 64–68.

58. Fernand Pouillon's return to Algiers, like his initial stay there, was facilitated by former mayor Jacques Chevallier, who remained in Algeria after independence, chose to adopt Algerian citizenship, served as the vice-president of the Chamber of Commerce in Algiers from 1963 to 1966, and founded "la Société pour l'aménage-

ment et l'équipement du tourisme en Algérie" that was intimately involved in the construction of new tourist facilities undertaken by Boumediene's government. See Stora, *Algérie 1954*, 30–31; and Planche, "Jacques Chevallier," 164. See also Juliette Minces, *L'Algérie de Boumediene* (Paris: Presses de la Cité, 1978), 82–83.

59. See Tejaswini Niranjana. *Siting Translation: History, Post-structuralism and the Colonial Context* (Los Angeles: University of California Press, 1992); and Douglas Robinson, *Translation and Empire* (Manchester: St. Jerome Publishing, 1997), 88–89.

60. Walter Benjamin, "The Task of the Translator," trans. Howard Zorn, in *Theories of Translation*, ed. Rainer Schulte and John Biguenet (Chicago: University of Chicago Press, 1992), 71–82.

61. Vikramaditya Prakash, *Chandigarh's Le Corbusier: The Struggle for Modernity in Postcolonial India* (Seattle: University of Washington Press, 2002), 25.

62. Rachid Sidi Boumediene, quoted in Deluz, *Alger*, 182.

63. Deluz, *Alger*, 62.

64. The Swiss-born architect Jean-Jacques Deluz, who worked in Algiers from the late 1950s until the early 1990s, also read this decision in a light similar to Mounir's interpretation. According to Deluz, moving the horses to an appropriately prominent location was a misguided attempt to put everything in its proper place. In effect, already marginalized residents on the city's periphery were robbed of their familiar sculpture. Ibid.

65. For an overview of Simounet's career, see Roland Simounet, *Dialogues sur l'invention*, ed. Richard Klein (Paris: Moniteur, 2005); Richard Klein, ed., *Roland Simounet à l'oeuvre: Architecture, 1951–1996* (Villeneuve d'Asq: Édition Musée d'Art Moderne Lille Métropole and Institut Français d'Architecture, 2000); *Roland Simounet, d'une architecture juste* (Paris: Le Moniteur, 1997); and *Roland Simounet: Pour une invention de l'espace* (Paris: Electa France, 1986).

66. Zeynep Çelik has discussed the relationship between Djenan el-Hassan and Simounet's extensive studies of architecture and social practices in la Mahieddine, then the largest shantytown in Algiers, that he presented at the 1953 meeting of CIAM (the International Congress of Modern Architecture) in Aix-en-Provence. Zeynep Çelik, "Learning from the *Bidonville*: CIAM Looks at Algiers," *Harvard Design Magazine* 18 (Spring–Winter 2003): 70–74; and Çelik, *Urban Forms*, 157–61.

67. Although Le Corbusier's plan for Algiers was officially rejected by the municipal administration in 1941, his experiences in Algeria and development of this project was central to his subsequent architecture, as numerous scholars have argued. See Alex Gerber, "Le Corbusier et le mirage de l'Orient: L'influence supposée de l'Algérie sur son oeuvre architecturale," *Revue du Monde Musulman et de la Méditerranée* 73–74 (March–April 1994): 363–77; Jean-Pierre Giordani, "Le Corbusier et les projets pour la ville d'Alger, 1931–1942" (Master's thesis, University of Paris, 1987); Mary McLeod, "L'appel de la Méditerranée," in Jacques Lucan, ed., *Le Corbu-*

sier, une encyclopédie (Paris: Éditions du Centre Pompidou/CCI, 1987), 26–32; and Mary McLeod, "Le Corbusier and Algiers," *Oppositions* 19–20 (1980): 55–85.

68. The tendency to present *pied-noir* experience as equivalent to that of all French *repatriés* was not unique to this project, but a common phenomenon during this period. See Jean-Jacques Jordi, *1962: L'arrivée des pieds-noirs* (Paris: Éditions Autrement, 1995), 200 and Saravèse, *L'invention des pieds-noirs,* 227–41.

69. See Saravèse, *L'invention des pieds-noirs,* 235; Jordi and Témime, eds., *Marseille et le choc des décolonisations;* Jordi, *1962;* and Benjamin Stora, *La gangrène et l'oubli: La mémoire de la guerre d'Algérie* (Paris: La Découverte, 1991), 258.

70. See Jordi, *1962,* 199–209; and Stora, *La gangrène et l'oubli,* 247.

71. See Centre des Archives du Monde du Travail, Roland Simounet collection (hereafter CAMT/RS), file P124/2: Association pour la Conservation et le Développement du Patrimoine Culturel des Français Originaires d'Afrique du Nord, *La mémoire des français originaires d'Afrique du Nord,* vol. 1: "Texte du rapport," unpublished manuscript, September 20, 1984. In this way, the museum was developed on the heels of similar rearticulations of *pied-noir* identity in the early 1980s. See, for example, Emmanuel Robles, ed., *Les pieds-noirs* (Paris: Éditions Philippe Lebaud, 1982).

72. Éric Saravèse has shown that the imagined tradition of French settlers in Algeria as agricultural pioneers was formative to constructions of *pied-noir* identity in France. This militant strain that he describes did, however, diverge significantly from the universalizing claims of Simounet's museum. See Saravèse, *L'invention des pieds-noirs,* 147–74; and Dine, *Images of the Algerian War,* 149–53.

73. CMAT/RS, file P124/5.

74. Montherlant, *La rose de sable,* 179; cited in Dine, *Images of the Algerian War,* 149–50. Montherlant uses this term at the end of a long passage recounting a former colonist's highly romanticized memories of peaceful interactions between north Africans and European settlers (including himself).

75. Quoted in Klein, *Roland Simounet à l'oeuvre,* fig. 12.

76. See CAMT/RS, P53/5, competition program, 1991; "Fort Saint-Jean: Recherché en paternité," *Le Méridionale,* December 22, 1990; and "La maison de repatriés de tous pays," *Le Provençal,* March 10, 1993.

77. CAMT/RS, P53/4, letter from Jean-François Delorme, the scenographic artist Simounet hired as a consultant for his new project, November 2, 1992.

78. Michael Dear and Héctor Manuel Lucero, "Postborder Cities, Postborder World: The Rise of Bajalta California," *Environment and Planning D: Society and Space* 23 (2005): 318. See also Michael Dear and Gustavo Leclerc, eds., *Postborder City: Cultural Spaces of Bajalta California* (New York: Routledge, 2003). I am grateful to the anonymous reader who suggested this connection.

79. Dear and Lucero, "Postborder Cities," 319.

80. For an important discussion of the "translocal" as a category of analysis, see James Clifford, *Routes: Travel and Translation in the Late Twentieth Century* (Cambridge, Mass.: Harvard University Press, 1997).

81. See Mark Crinson, *Modern Architecture and the End of Empire* (Burlington, Vt.: Aldershot and Ashgate, 2003), 10; and Anthony King, *Global Cities: Post-imperialism and the Internationalization of London* (London: Routledge, 1990).

CHAPTER 4

The City in Fragments: Kaleidoscopic Johannesburg after Apartheid

MARTIN J. MURRAY

> Johannesburg seemed to me just about at the ends of the earth, in
> the middle of the lions and the Negroes, that is to say—inaccessible.
> —Le Corbusier, July 1939

BECAUSE IT HAS LONG BEEN the country's premier urban landscape, Johannesburg after apartheid is the one place where the evolving story of the "new South Africa" is most fully played out, and where it is most carefully monitored and vigorously appraised.[1] It is here where the hopes and desires, the fears and anxieties, of millions of people find concrete expression in the unfolding drama of everyday life. The generative imagery of Johannesburg—or its "invented tradition"—has always laid considerable stress on its energizing qualities, its kinetic dynamism, and its seemingly limitless opportunities for self-enrichment. Despite the relative blandness of its topographical surroundings, Johannesburg has always traded in glamour and illusion, ephemeral traits that never cease to lure countless numbers of expectant newcomers into its captivating orbit.[2]

For more than a century, this glittering "City of Gold" has been the most telling touchstone for South Africa's extremes and excesses, the true-to-life mise-en-scène for conspicuous displays of ostentatious wealth in the midst of deplorable impoverishment and depravation, a resplendent playground for affluent white consumers, most of whom have never set foot in any of the literally dozens of dreary, sprawling black townships and informal settlements that remain hidden on the urban periphery. One can easily attribute much of the city's license, or its profligacy, to its originating frontier mentality, an atavistic response to the edgy lawlessness of the early digger days.[3] To the extent that it reflects the insouciant, unrepentant crassness of late capitalist consumerism, Johannesburg after apartheid is a bustling, frantic city of somewhat superficial excitement with little congeniality and human warmth, an unforgiving place of unfulfilled expectations, squandered opportunities, and broken promises. Viewed from the wide-angle lens of South Africa's turbulent and bitter history, "Joburg," "Jozi," "Egoli," or whatever nickname seems to fit at the moment, is a contradictory place where the genuine desires for racial harmony and equality have come face to face with the enduring legacies of racial antagonism and distrust. It embodies at once the utopian dreams of the racially reconciled "rainbow nation" that has struggled to overcome its odious past and the dystopian nightmares of deracinated urban space under siege, a dyspeptic "fortress-city" at war with itself. It is this incongruous mixture of the old and the new, the strange and the majestic, the visible and the invisible, and the carefree and indifferent, that gives this untamed, kaleidoscopic "Golden City" its distinctiveness as the quintessential metropolis in the "new South Africa."[4]

Although the demise of white minority rule has unburdened South Africa of its odious distinction as a widely despised "international pariah," the exposure of its markets to the competitive vagaries of the world economy has subjected its premier urban landscapes to the centrifugal pressures of globalization. Like other aspiring "world-class" cities where the yawning gap between the anxious rich and the desperately poor is an integral feature of urban life, Johannesburg after apartheid has come to exhibit the morphological characteristics of what urban theorists have referred to as the "garrison city," the "dual city," or the "carceral city," where the urban landscape is partitioned into what Saskia Sassen has called an "urban glamour zone"—a new hyperspace of global business and finance with streamlined airports that double as fancy shopping malls catering to affluent travelers, advanced telecommunications networks, state-of-the-art corporate headquarters facilities, luxurious hotel accommodations, and an absorbing culture of "world-class" entertainment diversions—and an "urban danger zone"—the interstitial spaces of confinement, with their broken-down infrastructure, few social amenities, and restricted opportunities for escape, where vast legions of service workers and the casually employed compete with the unemployed, the unemployable, and the marginalized and "socially excluded," for survival.[5] In short, Johannesburg simultaneously conveys seemingly contradictory images: on the one side, distinct "affluent enclaves" that proudly display the ostentatious symbols of global integration and the celebrated "enterprise culture" of neoliberal design; and, on the other, peripheral, stigmatized zones characterized by embryonic forms of what Loïc Wacquant has called "advanced marginality."[6]

Unraveling "Spatial Politics" in
Johannesburg After Apartheid

> Like the nobles of feudal Europe, white South Africans are retreating
> behind fortifications. In the leafy avenues in Johannesburg's rich
> [northern] suburbs, defensive walls around the houses are climbing
> upwards, usually topped off with what South Africans call siege ar-
> chitecture: crenellations, electric fencing or just plain razor wire.
> —*Economist*, July 1995

Broadly speaking, spatial partitioning of urban landscapes has long been a
defining feature of South Africa's cities.[7] The white middle classes have always sought to carve out their own places of work, residence, and leisure,
and, in the process, have tried to create barriers—both physical and semiotic—between themselves and the segmented layers of the black working
class and haphazardly employed. The visible patterns of differentiation,
fragmentation, and separation that have come to characterize the Johannesburg urban landscape after apartheid did not come into existence all at once
but instead are the result of long, drawn-out, and incremental processes of
spatial restructuring that only accelerated with the transition to parliamentary democracy. These new patterns of differentiation, fragmentation, and
separation have not only reinforced the structural inequalities already
deeply ingrained in the cityscape, but they also reflect the inchoate symp-
toms of an emergent spatial logic governing the organization, uses, and
meanings of urban space in Johannesburg after apartheid.[8]

On balance, the mainly white, wealthy urban residents of Johannesburg
have largely sidestepped the question of their civic responsibilities toward
the new democratic order, retreating into sequestered places that put a premium on personal safety and comfort. To a certain extent, the reluctance of
the property-owning elite to bear the financial burden of bottom-up "up-
liftment" has contributed to urban polarization, fragmentation, and exclusion. National political strategies of financial empowerment of the nouveaux-
riches rather than the hoped-for redistribution (the so-called postapartheid
dividend) have played an important part in stimulating this new form of
urbanism. It is not only real estate developers, property speculators, and
wealthy, white urban residents who have selected this form of privatized

urbanism, but a committed neoliberalizing state administration that has established certain priorities and agendas, especially at the national level.[9]

The social consequences of these new spatial dynamics are multiple and often contradictory. On the one hand, white middle-class residents, who rarely ventured out of the confines of their racially segregated cocoons during the apartheid years, have come to experience firsthand an inescapable proximity to the harsh realities of the "other" South Africa: homelessness and vagrancy, high levels of unemployment, informal street economies, and an upsurge of reported street crime—along with the fear, resentment, and anxiety it engenders. For those urban residents who appreciably benefited from the system of formalized racial discrimination either because of their active participation or their passive acquiescence, the end of apartheid and the transition to parliamentary democracy has come at a price: as they negotiate their daily lives, they are no longer able to avoid the kinds of annoyances, anxieties, and disruptions that threaten the entrenched leisurely lifestyles to which they had become so thoroughly accustomed—and to which they believe they are entitled. On the other hand, new modes of spatial management, regulation, and organization that have come into existence after apartheid have transformed the urban landscape into a contested terrain, a battleground for bitter struggles that used to be considered political or economic. Whereas the lines of cleavage during the apartheid era typically crystallized around the polar extremes of white affluence and black impoverishment, the new divisions are sliced much more thinly, where a new postapartheid rhetoric of rights and entitlements has been translated into a spirited defense of property, privilege, and social status. Despite the uplifting egalitarian discourses of nonracialism, nation building, and the "rainbow nation," what has emerged in Johannesburg after apartheid is a new kind of Gramscian, positional warfare revolving around the uses and meanings of urban public and private space, where fluid battlelines have been drawn not just between the rich and the poor and the "haves" and "have-nots," but also between the aspiring middle classes and less affluent layers of the working class, and against newcomers to the city—transient work-seekers, the poor and homeless, women and children, internal migrants, and foreign immigrants.[10]

No longer capable of falling back on the old orthodoxies of racial segregation and apartheid, the white propertied elites have turned to new means to protect their class interests. In the aftermath of the transition to parliamentary democracy, political stabilization has meant reestablishing the contested legitimacy of the overlapping hierarchies of power, wealth, and status that derived primarily from property ownership. "Spatial politics" in Johannesburg after apartheid has slowly but surely coalesced around the interdictory practices of boundary making. Space, like class, becomes racialized when the capacity for access to it is a matter of privilege and when it masquerades as the natural attribute of an entrenched white elite or the inherent property of vested interests. The introduction of new techniques of spatial management has reshaped the urban landscape in novel and unanticipated ways, supplanting meaningful urban public space with cocooned, privatized surrogates and putting into motion entirely new dynamics of separation, exclusion, and marginalization. The intensification of new and insidious kinds of symbolic racism, discrimination, and prejudice has reinforced the segregation of the white rich from the black poor—social groups who are kept apart in exclusive and luxurious spatial enclaves, on the one hand, or in ramshackle townships on the urban fringe, blighted inner-city ghettoes, or featureless squatter settlements, on the other.[11]

Put broadly, the overall design of urban space is not simply a matter of context and aesthetics, but it is also a complex sociospatial process that encodes power relations, value orientations, and symbolic meanings into the routine practices of everyday life.[12] The built environment—its shape, contours, and accessibility—sets limits and possibilities for the conduct of everyday life. Because of their capacities to alternatively attract and repel, actually-existing places influence behavior, shape opinions, and regulate social action. The organization and management of urban space restricts and "decides" what activities, behaviors, and practices can take place, "authorizing" some while delegitimating and condemning others.[13] Such monumental "sites of assembly" as corporate office complexes, enclosed shopping malls, gated residential communities, and other "privatized" enclaves designed exclusively for the use of the monied classes do not constitute inert backgrounds to the production of meaning, or passive contexts within which the practices of everyday life take place. Instead, the carving out of these distinctive "luxury spaces" in Johannesburg after apartheid is an integral part of an active ordering, organizing, and legitimating process that transforms the uses of the cityscape, restructures social relations, and shapes the subjective identities of urban residents.[14]

Spatial Patterning after Apartheid:
Place Making as Boundary Marking

Johannesburg is where the money is. And the action. It's the most powerful commercial center on the African continent. It is an

African city that works: the phones dial, the lights switch on, you can drink the water, there are multi-lane freeways, skyscrapers, conference centers, golf courses. If you should get lost, ordinary people on the street speak English. Cell phones are everywhere. You can send e-mail from your hotel room, you can bank any foreign currency, you can watch CNN, and should you fall ill, the hospitals have world-class equipment and doctors who can be trusted with a scalpel.

—"City of Johannesburg," official Web site

In writing on the city, Walter Benjamin treated the built forms of the modern metropolis as compressed microcosms of the social world, emblematic expressions of hidden social relations and their antinomies. Rather than taking the built environment at face value, he insisted on looking behind the semblance of the ordinary to draw attention to those marginal, repressed, and ignored features of the cityscape that typically escape notice. Benjamin looked on these taken-for-granted built forms of the cityscape as vast repositories of eclipsed relics, outmoded remnants, and obsolete fashions, something akin to archaeological sites containing clues to understanding the ephemeral transitoriness of modernity. Just as cities are invariably subjected to transformation and erasure, urban spaces are always haunted by the specter of their historical past. Not only extending in space but stretching across time, cities accumulate metonymic objects and discarded artifacts as a kind of "archive of involuntary memory." Put in another way, the built environment connects places and activities. Thus, the meaning of city-sites resides not in their architectural forms alone, but in their use and the collective memory of that use.[15]

In his allegory of modernity, Benjamin regarded city-sites as transitory objects, invariably evolving over time into ruins, transformed into the discarded and forgotten dream-images of a long-lost, bygone era. Although looking backward at the decaying, crumbling residues of a lost dreamworld provided Benjamin with a useful vantage point from which to understand the failure of modernism to realize its imagined utopia, the exploration of new, postmodern, architectural confections like citadel office complexes, enclosed shopping malls, themed entertainment destinations, and gated residential communities enables us to steal a fleeting glimpse as to where Johannesburg-in-the-making might be heading. As the embodiments of the desire for unreal places not fully realized, these new, highly stylized architectural edifices contain in embryonic (and attenuated) form the phantasmagoric dream-images of the Johannesburg Future City.[16]

149

Throughout its turbulent history, Johannesburg has been torn between the extremes of utopian dreamworld and dystopian nightmare. At its founding in the late 1880s, the city acquired its original schizophrenic urban identity that has long oscillated between the sacred and the profane, or between a bountiful Garden of Eden and a frightening Paradise Lost, the contemporary prototype of ancient Babylon and Nineveh.[17] These extremes have a way of exaggerating differences, contributing to fears and anxieties, and fostering distrust and resentment. The self-promoting city-boosterism that can at one moment glorify and mythogize Johannesburg as the epitome of urban swank and cosmopolitan sophistication can just as easily metamorphosize into its opposite. Dystopian images of the city as a miasmic cesspool of abject misery, rampant disease, and interminable strife have often lent legitimacy for various kinds of municipal intervention into the existing social fabric of the city. The noir-image of urban dystopia has frequently served as the administrative justification for the "creative destruction" and the rebuilding of the urban landscape. Grand urban renewal plans—from racial segregation to forced removals, from demolition of old buildings to the elimination of whole city blocks and erasure of streets, and from inner-city revitalization to glitzy experiments with the New Urbanism—have derived their raison d'être from the imagined disorder, mis-use, and deteriorization of urban space.[18]

In the popular imagination of local residents, Johannesburg after apartheid is at once an exhilarating site of exotic adventure and excitement, and a foreboding place of imminent danger and criminal violence. These twin narratives of sensuous pleasure and bodily harm parallel each other, existing in the unstable space that is neither entirely factual nor thoroughly fanciful. The utopian dreams of a genuine "rainbow nation" contrast sharply with the dystopian nightmares of impending social breakdown and racial discord. Seen through the alternating gaze of these opposing visions, the urban landscape seems like a schizophrenic place, without coherence or clarity, stability or predictability. But there is more to the story than competing image categories. Johannesburg is, of course, not simply a mental construct, or a fleeting figment of a fertile imagination. It is an actual place with its own location and peculiar climate, its own history and architecture, its own spatial dispositions, its own distinctive topographical features and surface appearances, its own distinctive cacophony of languages, its own traffic sounds and musical rhythms, its own idiosyncratic smells and characteristic tastes, its own colors, and its own problems and enjoyments.[19]

For all its jaunty verticality, frantic pace, and cosmopolitan vitality, Johannesburg has always been a rather gritty and unglamorous city, without the natural beauty of the seashore and the majesty of Table Mountain that endow Cape Town with its attractiveness. Exuberant city boosters boast about the tallest skyscraper (Carlton Centre), the loftiest structure (Brixton Tower), and the highest apartment complex (Ponte City) on the African continent. But "bigness," "tallness," and "best" do not add up to the kind of genuine urbanity that even the most optimistic urban planners admit does not yet exist and can only be hoped for in the future. Like all cities, there is no "essential" Johannesburg. In short, the city is not a coherent entity easily reducible to a single quality or monochromatic category. From its rather inauspicious start, Johannesburg has always been a kaleidoscopic city, where complex processes and multiple images coexist in uneasy tension and contradiction at the same time and place.

Focusing attention on "place-making" activities at work at two different sites enables us to explore how city building processes in Johannesburg after apartheid have been highly uneven and contradictory. Rather than trying to grasp the city in its totality, narrowing our gaze to these two particular localities enables us to respond more sensitively to the sociocultural politics of agency (or the "microphysics of power") as these take shape on the ground, involving as they do the dense web of relations between negotiation and compromise, coercion and force, complicity and affiliation, mimicry and contagion, and resistance and refusal. Put in theoretical terms, urban space is not an a priori constant or a fixed and inert container for social action, but rather it is the ever-changing medium through which social processes and practices take place. As a result, urban space itself has a history. Tracing transformation and evolution of particular sites over historical time— whether blossoming into "spectacle" or, conversely, falling into ruin— allows us to unpack the metropolis as a loosely assembled ensemble of diverse places in constant motion: a heterogeneous landscape where localities come and go, are grafted onto others, are layered on top of what came before, or disappear into oblivion.[20]

Because it is a city of fragments, the story of Johannesburg can only be told in vignettes, or micro-stories. The two sites explored in detail here can be treated as "spatial stories": each contains a narratological coherence, a dramatic emplotment, and a cast of characters. These two sites are not only material locations but also symbolic "place-markers," or what Henri Lefebvre called "representational spaces," that convey shared meanings about city life.[21]

The first site—the Montecasino entertainment complex, upscale shopping mecca, and gaming resort—is a quintessential exemplar of cocooned, sanitized space, a material embodiment of the "post-public" city where the construction of barriers, walls, and partitions enforce the adoption of new rules of inclusion and exclusion governing who is authorized to make use of such places and who is denied entry. Sites like Montecasino celebrate the compartmentalization of space, highlighting exclusivity as a mark of urban distinction. The fashioning of such urban "spectacles" not only represents the power of real estate and money markets, but also reflects the strategic choices of powerful city-builders intent on entering Johannesburg into the headlong race with the aim of claiming world-class status as a "global city." These places are showcases for the display of cosmopolitan urbanity and repositories of postmodern aesthetics and architectural design.

As an urban "spectacular" designed to add distinction to the urban landscape, Montecasino is an exemplary expression of conventional boosterist fantasies of a radiant and stable urban future. It reflects the impulse toward what Robert Fishman called "bourgeois utopias": partitioned and sealed-off places that signify a retreat into the Arcadian dreamworld of harmonious exchange, leisured living, and conspicuous consumption. In order to convey the uplifting message of the frictionless "rainbow nation," such sites figuratively erase the past. In conjuring up images of a comfortable future organized around commodity consumption, they necessarily deny the persistent presence of the past in the present.[22]

In contrast, the second site—the shabby Huguenot Hotel located in the inner-city "hyperghetto" of Hillbrow—represents the inability of city planners, municipal authorities, and policing agencies to tame the "disorderly city." Because it is a disreputable house of prostitution, this place reflects the failed promise of the "rainbow nation" to rescue young women from a dismal life on the ravening streets. As an allegory for what has gone wrong with the city after the demise of white minority rule, such places as the Huguenot Hotel raise the specter of the dystopian nightmare of impending urban decay and collapse. These localities serve as grim reminders that the rights of citizenship have not triumphed over oppressive relationships and that the uplifting message of the postapartheid city as the site of harmony and opportunities for betterment has not yet materialized for all.

Just as Walter Benjamin was not interested in the Parisian Arcades for their own sake but rather for what they signified about urban modernity, these two "spatial stories" connote something about the meaning of everyday life in Johannesburg after apartheid. Because these two sites convey such powerful, value-laden images about where Johannesburg might be heading, they can easily be read as allegories for what is right and what is wrong about urban living in the postapartheid city. This hermeneutic approach does not pretend to speak for the city in its entirety, but only for selected fragments that seem to symbolize its extremes.[23]

Yet these contrasting urban images of comfortable utopia at Montecasino and abysmal dystopia at the Huguenot Hotel do not represent hermetically sealed oppositions. They are integrally interconnected, and the production of one presupposes the production of the other. The simultaneous fashioning of the urban landscape into cocooned "fantasy" playgrounds for the well-to-do and fetid wastelands for the impoverished involves the striation of urban space, or the division of the cityscape into attended zones of affluence and neglected sites of decay. Whether by conscious design or ingrained habit, the active work of enclosure and segmentation—by walling, fencing, partitioning, and guarding—has separated the agoraphobic rich from the resentful poor, thereby undermining the uplifting, utopian vision of the city as a properly organized and managed space. Rather than harmonizing city spaces, city-building processes in Johannesburg after apartheid have led to the polarization of the city into "radically antagonistic spaces," each with its own actual modes of existence and normative rules of conduct.[24]

The spatiality of city-building processes is also intimately connected with the uneven rhythms and diverse temporalities of everyday life. Investigating these two sites can also provide useful insights into the different temporal experiences of urban life, or what Ben Highmore has called the "unevenly developing city." Whereas the tropes of rapid movement, accelerating pace, and speedy circulation are associated with the City of Spectacle, the metaphorical, figurative language of stasis, stagnation, and entropy are typically linked with the Miasmal City. In Johannesburg after apartheid, spectacular, hypermodern sites like the Montecasino "gaming resort" are dominated by, even overwhelmed by, swift movement and the uninterrupted flow of commodities, money, and people. In contrast, the dynamics of ghettoization that have taken hold in the Johannesburg inner city—of which places like the Huguenot Hotel are an integral part—are characterized by the decelerated pace and languid tempo of everyday life, or, as Highmore puts it, "by slowing-down rather than speeding up, more by stagnation than by circulation."[25]

In a real sense, then, it is only through such comparisons of different "place-making" processes in the city that the alternating speeds, multiple directions, and patterned regularities of urban life can be fully grasped and deciphered. The uneven and contradictory impulses of real estate capitalism have rendered slowness a severe penalty in the frenetic global race for accelerated hypermodernity. The hypermodern city of scenographic "swagger buildings," "rainbow" cosmopolitanism, and the spectacle of conspicuous consumption offers a counterpoint to those dismal places that, in the language of developmental modernism that still dominates the discourse of urban planning, "lag behind," "fail to progress," or "fall by the wayside," thereby requiring intervention to get them back on course.[26]

GLORIFIED FANTASIES, MASTERPIECES OF DECEPTION:
ON IMPORTING LAS VEGAS TO THE "NEW SOUTH AFRICA"

Julius Caesar would have enjoyed indulging in the pleasures of the magical fantasy offered at the mini-Roman Empire created at Caesars Gauteng. More than 2050 years after the demise of the Great Roman Empire, it has come back to life, with lots of artistic license—this time at the Gateway to Africa.
—*Marian Giesen*

In Johannesburg after apartheid, it is becoming increasingly difficult to distinguish between the real fake and the fake fake.[27] Surely, all fakes are not equal; there are good fakes and bad fakes. The standard is no longer "real" versus "phony," but the relative merits of the imitation. What makes the good ones better is their improvements on reality, that is, their ability to entice consumers to actually prefer the copy to the original.[28] The real fake has reached its apogee in places like the Las Vegas strip where ersatz imitation has been perfected to a high art form. As Robert Venturi, Denise Scott Brown, and Steven Izenhour pointed out in their once controversial and now classic study, *Learning from Las Vegas*, an entire vocabulary and language of architectural forms has been invented to satisfy new social, commercial, and cultural requirements for design motifs grounded in pastiche, mimicry, and parody.[29] Giant billboards, decorated sheds, the use of moving light and bold coloration, and continuous, competitive frontages of evocative fantasy and novelty, all meant to attract the automobile traveling at highway speed, seduce with visual wonders, beckoning passersby to the hotels and gaming tables. In the desire for "normality," such frantic city building makes it difficult to remember that apartheid ever existed. With so much "happy talk" of the radiant future, it is sometimes impossible to engage in a conversation about the past.[30]

Buildings are political statements as well as architectural accomplishments. With its stress on rank consumerism as social life and entertainment, and as wish- and dream-fulfillment, the casino resort is the quintessential real fake, fantasy-place in urban South Africa after apartheid.[31] There is no lack of capital to support the construction of these make-believe, made-from-scratch environments. In a wholesale bid to tap into the global tourism market, South Africa's corporate "culture-entertainment industries" have feverishly set about building casino resorts all over the country. With Carnival City Casino and Entertainment Complex (at Brakpan, east of Johannesburg), Gold Reef City Casino (south of Johannesburg), Champions Casino (Witbank), Montecasino (Fourways), and Caesars Gauteng (next to Johannesburg International Airport), it has been said that virtually every middle-income household in the Greater Johannesburg metropolitan region is never more than twenty minutes by automobile away from the nearest gambling casino. The competition for business is intense. The proliferation of these places, to borrow a phrase from Reyner Banham from another context, marks "the total surrender of all social and moral standards to the false glamour of naked commercial competition."[32]

The cultural landscape is a medium of representation that serves to erase history and legibility, and to naturalize power relations. In the typical case, South Africa's newest casino resorts construct a collage of themed destinations, which borrow from other places and other times, and are juxtaposed in the built environment with little attention to logical, historical, or geographical ordering principles. Their attention-getting place names evoke images of innocent landscapes, harmless places from a bygone era. Analogous to the Foucauldian idea of heterotopia, casino resorts combine attributes of theater, cinema, garden, museum, holiday camp, honeymoon motel, brothel, penal colony, sporting event, and cruise ship. Like enclosed shopping malls, casino resorts are artificial environments that pretend to be natural, and they help their patrons forget about the fragile underpinnings of the highly inequitable social order. Johannesburg's permanent state of flux means the transience some experts associate with high levels of urban crime is a given condition of city life. All these factors contribute to an underlying insecurity that permeates the ethos of Johannesburg after apartheid. Yet there is also a creative energy, similarly born out of these unsettled conditions. So if the casinos around the Johannesburg metropolitan area are more glitzy and gaudy than those elsewhere, it is only because they express everything that the city is. From the quaint insularity of Montecasino to the over-the-top garishness of Caesars Gauteng, casino resorts are part of the spirit of reckless abandon that characterizes Johannesburg and the fantasies that urban residents devise to counteract their fears about city life. They live in the present and project themselves into the future. With their classical stylistics and "timeless" themes, these new casino complexes exemplify the avoidance of historical memory. They construct an imaginary utopia outside of history.[33] Their reworked, "post-public," social spaces are common sites not for disinterested interactions, but rather of commercial exchanges.[34]

Architecture deals with promotion of fantasy as well as the organization of space. Casino resorts are subjected to a make-believe historiographical staging, whereby they are totally absorbed into a kind of fictive architectural discourse, a mythologized fable that follows a stepwise progression of logical movements, or what Sarah Chaplin, in her interpretation of the Las Vegas Strip, calls the "name-tame-same-game" sequence. At the initial stage, there is the discovery of an exotic "other" place, one that has faded into history: a quaint Tuscan village (Montecasino), ancient Rome (Caesars Gauteng), legendary early Cape Town (Grand West Casino and Entertainment World), historic Johannesburg at the time of the gold rush (Gold Reef City Hotel and Casino), Victorian heritage in a waterfront/seaside setting (Boardwalk Casino and Entertainment World, Port Elizabeth). Naming has the effect of bringing back into existence those distinctive qualities of place that have intrinsic aesthetic value: the insular communities of northern Italy, the grandeur of the Roman Empire, the strike-it-rich *mentalité* of the Johannesburg gold rush, or the festive ambience of the seaside boardwalk. Second, the identification and marking of the attributes of this long-lost place effectively call attention to its "otherness." This stress on "difference" only highlights the distinctiveness of place when juxtaposed against the ordinariness of everyday life. Third, residual traces of "otherness" are reduced or made to disappear by rendering these differences similar to what is already known: leisured entertainment, excitement, consumer spending. This process takes place both in the fashioning of discourse and in the tailored construction of the built environment: new terms are invented, new concepts are identified, theoretical neologisms are coined, and eventually these semantic constellations of words are incorporated within sanitized public relations discourse. The corporate owners of casino resorts promote these places as "family-friendly" amusement centers with something for everyone, or sites "dedicated to organized vacationing," as Umberto Eco put it in another context. What were once known as "gambling casinos" have resurfaced as less offensive "gaming" resorts, cleansed of all pejorative connotations and rendered euphemistically harmless. This renaming marks the triumph of skillful public relations. Lastly, in order to compensate for the inevitable assimilation and disappearance of the "otherness," there is an attempt to reproduce or manufacture differences with reified images or appropriated and recontextualized examples, as a form of textual, visual, or spatial gaming that camouflages the profit-seeking motives that lay behind the construction of these places in the first place.[35]

Casino resorts present an allegorical rejection of the spatial geography of urban uncertainty, replacing the outside world with their own internal hyperreality, where, to borrow from Umberto Eco, "everything looks real, and therefore it is real; in any case the fact that it seems real is real, and the thing is real even if, like Alice in Wonderland, it never existed."[36] This flattening of an entertainment and shopping experience against fake historical settings betrays a nonchalant indifference toward authenticity, despite the *accuracy* of the reconstructions. This hallucination serves to blend quite different historical periods and to erase the distinction between historical reality and pure fantasy. Entertainment sites like Montecasino, Gold Reef City Hotel and Casino, Grand West Casino, and the Boardwalk Casino and Entertainment World are backward-looking places banking on nostalgia, or "staged chaos," as Christine Boyer puts it in another context.[37] As at Disneyland, casino resorts not only present a set of illusions, but also a set of illusions that are glorified as fantasies, as masterpieces of falsification.[38]

Marketing Illusion at Montecasino

What was once the gambling casino and is now being transformed into the "gaming resort" has become on its own terms, the real thing. The outrageously fake fake has developed its own indigenous style and lifestyle to become a real place.

—*Ada Louise Huxtable*

Built on a thirty-eight-hectare site at the intersection of William Nicol and Witkoppen Roads in the rapidly expanding development node of Fourways, Montecasino is one of the most ambitious private commercial adventures ever undertaken in Africa, incorporating leisure, entertainment, and retail components in a vast multipurpose complex.[39] This huge, heavily capitalized project, with its artful, stylish, and even daring design, is more than just another casino development: composed of equal parts of nostalgia, superficiality, and calculated guile, it is an important card for metropolitan Johannesburg in the highly competitive game of urban supremacy played against Cape Town, its "tourist-destination" rival, which has the distinct advantage of a naturally beautiful setting at the southern tip of the African continent. Through its sheer size and detailed architectural design, Montecasino has already contributed a new dimension to the upscale tourism, entertainment, and leisure industries of the Greater Johannesburg metropolitan region. The corporate owner of the Montecasino Resort complex is Tsogo Sun, a newly formed partnership bringing together Tsogo Investments, a black empowerment investment group, and Southern Sun Gaming Interests. This corporate entity holds five gaming licenses: the flagship development at Montecasino, the Emnotweni Casino in Nelspruit, the Champions Casino in Witbank, the casino on the Durban Village Green site, and the recently awarded East London license. As major players in the South African gaming industry, this partnership has managed to bring the "complete Las Vegas experience" to the once pastoral outskirts of Johannesburg's rapidly expanding northern suburbs. Together with the Sandton Convention Centre, which formed part of the Tsogo Sun bid, the Montecasino development represents a 1.8 billion-rand investment in construction and equipment costs, as well as professional services, local and provincial contributions, and infrastructure costs.[40]

The MGM Grand Corporation, the Las Vegas casino operating group, was integrally involved in the overall planning of the facilities and the spatial layout of the whole complex and the casino area. Creative Kingdom, an architectural firm from the United States, developed the external design concept, and local architects Bentel Abramson were responsible for the actual implementation of the project. Situated on a gently sloping site, the Montecasino project is designed to imitate a thirteenth-century hilltop village in Tuscany, surrounded by a protective wall sheltering it from menacing outside forces. The vernacular buildings around the entire perimeter of the complex and inside the walled compound have artificial facades that were constructed in exacting detail to resemble the cracked stones, water-stained walls, and multicolored patina of a centuries-old village in northern Italy.[41] Not only did the architects, designers, and builders seek to faithfully represent the details, texture, and the look of actual buildings and their surroundings, but also to reproduce objects from the past and project them onto the present. To achieve this "perfectly imperfect" look, the developers selected building materials from a large palette (rugged-face brick, terrazzo, colorful mosaic, travertine, random rubble stonework, timber, wrought iron) and applied construction techniques that accelerated "the hundreds of years of weathering inflicted on the walls of any Tuscan village" in "just a few months."[42]

Montecasino has been fashioned from a set of design guidelines that extrapolate from the realism of a centuries-old Tuscan village and reproduce a simulated replica of it for contemporary visitors who can relish the imitation in a sheltered and sanitized environment. Manipulated for commercial purposes, architecture no longer determines the unique visual identity of a place but is drawn into a vicious circle of self-referentiality. By plagiarizing from other times and other places in a desperate search for authenticity, the built environment is reduced to nostalgic stereotypes.[43] Built on just eighty-five thousand-square meters of the expansive site, the Montecasino complex is literally a miniature village inside city walls. Like the Borgota shopping mall in affluent Scottsdale, Arizona, this imitation Tuscan village provides a leisure-entertainment venue in a secure and uniquely themed environ-ment. The spatial layout of Montecasino resembles the operatic scale of a gigantic theatrical stage-set consisting of an assemblage of indoor paved streets and cobbled walkways, a central piazza or main market square, and inward-facing buildings with real windows and wrought-iron balconies pointing toward the center, and with immense, solid, weathered walls rising to meet semitransparent arched ceilings and a central glass dome. Although giving the impression of a centuries-old village open to the elements, Mon-tecasino is in effect an enclosed seven-story building, covered by a massive roof spanning three levels, which reaches a height of fourteen meters at the peak. This ceiling structure is the largest in the southern hemisphere, hold-ing beneath it 18,500 square meters of retail space, artfully designed to cater to different consumer tastes. As an architectural device, this weatherproofed skyscape protects against unpredictable vagaries of climate. Built with a unique curvature that enhances light, the ceiling structure ensures moderate temperatures throughout the year, day and night.[44]

The stress on fantasy theming is intensified within the complex, and the fastidious attention to detail is evident "in every street corner and open window." Once inside the enclosure, the visitor is mesmerized with a daz-zling spectacle of scenographic attractions and entertaining diversions. The effect of this iconic invention of a centuries-old Tuscan village is one of almost unreal perfection, or what the trade journal *Architect and Builder* called an "authentic re-creation."[45] Who needs to actually visit Tuscany, when the reconstructed imitation, the authentic reproduction, is just as good as the original? As if by magic, an enclosed village metaphorically "comes to life," with several piazzas, pavement eateries, and seven different Tuscan neighborhoods, ranging from an affluent uptown to the less opulent sur-roundings of a quaint imitation fishing village. Those interior designers who have meticulously "planned its spontaneous unplannedness" are keenly aware that Montecasino is selling escapism to affluent consumers with dis-posable incomes.[46] The widespread use of artificial props, including fake but realistic-looking items such as drainpipes strangled with bougainvillea, bicy-cles leaning against lampposts topped with nesting pigeons, TV antennas, lines of washing flapping in the breeze, ornamental crests, wall murals, fountains, and assorted street furniture, adds a kind of sensory playfulness to this surreal concoction. The illusion is carried out with such dedication that even the bricks were imported from Tuscany and the shop signs and menus are printed in Italian.[47]

The appeal to different audiences dictated the location of more than eighty individual stores. In an effort to break from rigid uniformity that characterizes most themed entertainment venues, the interior designers adopted a hybrid approach that coalesces around three different commercial settings: a high-end neighborhood of fashionable boutiques and upscale restaurants; a middle range of intermediate shops; and an imitation downtown area, with a "more local, community feel," and a "colourful, domestic look." This distinction between retail environments was a way to effect a change of appearance for the visitor, while facilitating flexibility in the use of exterior design, textured finishes, and paint colors.[48]

The main entrance from the seven-level parking garage leads to the grand staircase, which is situated five meters above the gaming floor and offers visitors an ideal viewing platform over the imitation village square that is in actuality the theatrical setting for the casino. The continuous, flowing environment at Montecasino makes little or no reference to the outside. Instead, it establishes a surreal sense of an enchanted, special world, one that encourages a kind of unity of sensory experience within an effortless enclosure that functions like the blending of time, place, and action in classical theater. For theater, after all, is largely a matter of light and darkness. Montecasino at night suggests this principle most strongly. The idea is to darken all distractions and to focus audience attention with light.[49]

Mimicking a Tuscan village square, this central hub consists of an 8,500-square meter floor outfitted with 1,700 slot machines and 70 gaming tables. With the insistence on authenticity, cobbled paving stones and facades are real, and the stone vases are individually carved and molded to resemble the "real thing." The pillars and the arches leading into the Salon Privé and the VIP high stakes gambling areas are constructed of steel, individually cast, and covered in stone to give them a look of their own. The Salon Privé covers an area of 1,400 square meters, with 91 slot machines and 15 tables to entice the gambler. Elegant features include marble-tiled bathrooms, fireplaces, and four wrought-iron chandeliers that cast light onto the deep-colored cherry wood, which in turn accentuates the finishing touches of gilded picture frames, crystal decanters, and antique shaving brushes. Complimented by an entertainment lounge, an upscale restaurant, and four bars in the immediate vicinity, the "gaming" area becomes a completely self-contained zone. A 150-meter stream gives spatial definition to the casino floor by dividing it from the spacious promenade. Traversed by arched bridges at all the entry points to the slot machines and gambling tables, this flowing water cascades over rocks, "brushing the drooping branches of the weeping willows and creating a current for the numerous ducks and their ducklings to swim in." Although constructed entirely from artificial materials, these "replicas of nature" seem so genuinely real, "one cannot help but wait for the squawk of the fishing herons or the fall of an oak leaf."[50]

Thirty-five imitation trees, ranging from pin oaks and birches to moon maples and gingkos, are scattered around the floor. With materials imported from the United States, these sculptured fakes were constructed in a process that transformed them from a jumbled mass of steel bars to towering structures that resemble tapering autumn-colored trees. The bars were welded together from thickest to thinnest, creating the general configuration of bare branches and trunks and were then covered in a fiberglass bark, covered in epoxy putty to create texture and character. Finally, each imitation tree was plastered with one hundred thousand plastic leaves, "giving birth to an unbelievably realistic piece of nature."[51]

These realistic-looking trees are scenographic imitations of nature that enhance the structured feeling of an authentic village square. Strategically placed not only in the casino area but throughout the streets and the food court, they provide an ideally camouflaged structure within which to conceal security cameras and to locate the acoustic equipment necessary for the creation of a complete "surround sound" system. Tsogo Sun has an exclusive management and development agreement with MGM Mirage, a Las Vegas-based casino-resort operator with considerable experience in casino security. There are approximately 720 surveillance cameras scanning the gaming area, with eight members of staff on duty per shift to monitor any suspicious movements on the floor. Other security systems are hidden in the cover of the immense ceiling above the floor of the complex. The use of impressive coverings includes an acoustic ceiling above the casino area, and an eight thousand-square meter handpainted diorama ceiling, airbrushed to create the effect of a blue, cloud-dappled sky.[52]

Although the casino is central to the entire development, the aim of the architects was to design and build a leisure-entertainment venue in which the gaming area did not overpower everything else. Casino resorts operate on the principle of mall salesmanship called "adjacent attraction," where, as Richard Sennett put it, "the most dissimilar objects lend each other mutual support when they are placed next to each other."[53] What makes places like Montecasino work is not only the architectural facades that imitate street life in other times and other places, but the selective importation of "entertainment" from all across the globe, including internationalist cuisine, as well as films, electronic devices, or video games borrowed willy-nilly from the United States and Europe. Chosen specifically for the complex, the various restaurants offer dining styles ranging from pan-asian cuisine, steakhouse-style eating, Mediterranean and Eastern fusion, Latino and wine bar–style dining, Cuban food, and quaint coffee shops. Located under a six-ton glass dome ceiling constructed on the ground and hoisted into place in one piece, the food court area emphasizes family-style eating in a ambient setting designed to resemble a centuries-old Tuscan courtyard. The fountain bubbling in the center and hydrangea-lined walkways surrounding the area create a social gathering place for weary shoppers. Within this area, branded outlets such as Spur, McDonald's, KFC, Steers, and the Ocean Basket operate, where "fabrics and flags in the colours of Italy" conjure up the festive atmosphere of old Tuscany.[54]

Glamorous and pretentious, the brand-new casino resorts that have sprung up around the greater Johannesburg metropolitan region are the quintessential architectural marvels of the postapartheid age. Unlike the functionalist megastructures that gave substance to modernism, these garish casino resorts are profit-making enterprises built on excess, where subtlety and understatement are dwarfed by the relentless pursuit of dilettantish chic, and where nothing is quite what it seems. The architects and interior designers who have constructed these places bring together material objects and visual displays to conjure up imaginary worlds that bear only the slightest resemblance to what existed in the past. As tiny fragments of larger cities, these cleverly themed environments seek to capitalize on what casino entrepreneurs refer to as the "wonder factor," or the kind of attractions analogous to the "old circus sideshow—something exotic to lure [visitors] into the main tent."[55]

THE MIASMAL CITY: THE INVISIBLE UNDERSIDE
OF THE GLITTERING "CITY OF GOLD"

In the aftermath of World War II, city-builders set in motion a feverish process of restructuring the downtown business district that sought to both embody the economic dynamism of the Greater Johannesburg metropolitan region and reflect the "world-class" aspirations of its most vociferous city-boosters. Pillaged and plundered from North America and Europe, these ambitious urban renewal projects bore the distinctive hallmarks of modernist city-building: functional specialization, efficient and rational use of (vertical) space, and rapid movement. The driving force behind these urban revitalization programs was a vision of streamlined and heroic modernity where the historic downtown business district, the main shopping thoroughfare extending along the north-south axis of Eloff Street, and the emergent residential zone in Hillbrow—with its multistoried apartment blocks, upscale restaurants, and fancy shops—at the northeast corner of the central city were integrated into a coherent whole. In the 1950s and 1960s, Hillbrow, and the adjoining areas of Berea, Joubert Park, and Yeoville, became a "vast testing-ground" for real estate speculation in building stock. In their haste for quick returns on speculative investment, corporate builders constructed large, high-rise apartment buildings that multiplied dozens of times over, producing tightly packed, overcrowded residential neighborhoods largely lacking in open, social spaces of meaningful public congregation. Yet from the start, Hillbrow attracted newcomers to the city, especially (white) aspiring middle-class professionals in search of genuine urban ambience lacking in the culturally homogeneous northern suburbs. By the late 1960s, Hillbrow had metamorphosized into one of the most densely populated residential areas in the southern hemisphere. Its concentrated mass of rentable apartment blocs made it an attractive point of arrival for yet another generation of European (particularly Jewish) immigrants seeking a fresh start in Johannesburg. Yet this fleeting moment of genuine cosmopolitan urbanity—when Hillbrow was known as the "Manhattan of Africa"—was short-lived. The gradual slide that began when large numbers of middle-class residents, including first-generation Greeks, Italians, Germans, and Jewish people, left the country in panic following the 1976 Soweto uprising, eventually turned into a rapid downward decline in the 1990s.[56]

Today, the inner city of Johannesburg is a place in ruins.[57] With an official estimate of one hundred thousand residents squeezed into an area of 10.28 square kilometers, Hillbrow has perhaps the highest population density of any area in the southern hemisphere. The actual crowding is undoubtedly much worse, because a substantial portion of the residents are undocumented migrants, squatters, and runaway children—groups likely to evade official census–taking. Unlike other neighborhoods in Johannesburg, Hillbrow has acquired a distinctly pan-African atmosphere, as Africans from all over the continent arrive in large numbers, with pulsing music popular in places like Lagos and Kinshasa emanating from the bars, seedy nightclubs, and apartment buildings. Drug-pushers loiter at street corners, competing for space with hawkers who have commandeered the sidewalks for displaying their meager wares. Many of the high-rise buildings, owned by absentee landlords trying to wring the last drop of profit from lifeless shells, teeter on the edge of virtual collapse, without water, electricity, or refuse collection. The interiors of most of the buildings range in quality from "quaintly tatty to positively post apocalyptic."[58]

In contrast to the proactive stance toward the hoped-for revival of the central city, urban planners have practiced a strategy of containment in high-density residential neighborhoods of the inner city. Although the built environment of Hillbrow, Berea, and Joubert Park has experienced a steady downward spiral into decay, disrepair, and ruin, this process has been both contradictory and uneven. Some building sites have deteriorated at a rapid pace, while others have retained at least a modicum of their former glory. In a number of instances, municipal authorities have seized buildings whose owners have failed to pay their property taxes. These municipal interventions have resulted in the refurbishment of a number of apartment buildings. Yet despite the fanfare that has accompanied these efforts at building reclamation and rehabilitation, they have failed to keep pace with the ongoing degradation of the built environment.

At first glance, the Huguenot looks like any other multistory hotel sandwiched between row after row of high-rise apartment buildings that make up much of the streetscape of Hillbrow, Berea, and Joubert Park.[59] Located on a side street, away from the congested sidewalks of Kotze and Pretoria Streets, the main east-west arterial roadways that bisect the heart of Hillbrow, it has the tired, run-down look of gradual deteriorization. Like other buildings in the surrounding area, the Huguenot Hotel suffers from transitory neglect. After all, it is part of the city in ruins. Its shabby exterior functions like a mask, concealing what takes place inside.

The Huguenot Hotel is a brothel, and a particularly seedy one at that. The building accommodates somewhere between one hundred and two hundred women and girls who make their living in the sex-work industry. Inner-city brothels are the grim stage-sets for the theatrical performance of transactional sex, gendered places where female bodies only exist to be used and discarded. These are perverse places inhabited by impermanent people with ephemeral and inconstant relationships, continuously on the move, and wanting to be somewhere else. These are places of shattered dreams and broken lives, where the instinctual survivalism of truly desperate people has replaced all hope.

In conventional terms, "inside (or interior) space" is the site of the intimate and the personal, the private and the inalienable, whereas "outside (or exterior) space" is the realm of money, exchange, and public social interaction. What endows the brothel with its sociospatial significance is that it reverses this conventional distinction between interior and exterior by pulling the "public" inside. The architectural design of the interior spaces of the Huguenot Hotel operates not only as a platform that accommodates the choreographed performance of transactional sex, but also as a generative mechanism that produces the gendered subjectivities that commingle there.[60]

A look inside the Huguenot Hotel provides a fleeting, furtive glance into the seamy underside of the "City of Gold." One gains access to the interior of the building by climbing several stairs to reach wide double-doors protected by a locked metal gate. Burly male guards block the entryway, turning away those considered "troublesome" or suspicious-looking, and permitting the rest to enter. Ever on the lookout for knives, guns, or other weapons, armed men frisk everyone, including women, seeking to enter. The sequence of interior rooms is designed for the most efficient use of available space. The ground floor consists of three main spatial enclosures differentiated principally by their functional usages. In its visual language, the interior of the Huguenot Hotel is a dreary, cold, and haunting place. The main reception room is located to the left of the entrance hallway, and this windowless enclosure serves as the designated gathering-place for customers and "hostesses." This large, cavernous room consists of a long bar at one end and a pool table at the other, and is capable of accommodating perhaps as many as one hundred people. Cast in shadow and darkness, it evokes feelings of claustrophobia and disorientation.

The interior spaces of the Huguenot Hotel display a modicum of class distinction, if not differentiation. The brothel owners constructed another meeting-room at the back of the building—named the VIP Room—where admittance is reserved for "preferred customers," that is, those who dress smartly and spend plenty of cash. This slightly upgraded space is outfitted with tables and chairs and a fully equipped bar. Finally, there is also a well-stocked commissary of sorts, where sex workers can purchase incidental items like soap and additional toiletries, and can rent clean towels and sheets.

By late afternoon, as the Huguenot begins to fill up with curious customers and expectant "hostesses," the place is transformed into a crowded, noisy, and smoke-filled marketplace for physical encounters of the carnal kind. Individuality is subsumed in the cash-nexus. The prostitutes who work in places like the Huguenot are mainly black women. The few white women who work there are old well beyond their years, haggard and sometimes toothless, and almost always drug-addicted.

Prostitutes and hotel management operate under a system of monetary exchanges that resemble a perverse kind of urban sharecropping. At the top, a shadowy "management company" oversees the operations, providing protection, anonymity, and a (relatively speaking) "safe" environment off the dangerous streets. The prostitutes who live and work at the Huguenot rent individual rooms located in the upper floors. These rooms function as both living quarters and sites of transactional sexual activity.

The brothel operates as a distinct site for the working out of the microphysics of gendered power. The bodies of women and young girls are accessible through the payment of money. Once a bargain has been struck and payment is received, "hostesses" accompany clients to their dingy rooms in the ten-story building. Individuals gain access to the upper floors through a locked iron gate that blocks access to the elevators. Clients accompany sex workers to their upstairs rooms via an elevator located on the other side of a locked gate protected by more armed guards.

Prostitutional activities organized in hotels like the Huguenot take the form of a modern-day "putting out" system, where payment is linked to "piecework" artisanal production. Sex workers require at least six clients a day to cover their rent, food, and incidental expenses. Competition is intense, and this bitter rivalry often leads to what health researchers term "unsafe sexual practices." When clients demand it, sex workers will often forgo the use of condoms in order to attract customers away from their competitors. Drugs, particularly crack-cocaine, are integrally connected with prostitution, and many drug-addicted prostitutes often supplement their unpredictable incomes by selling drugs to clients. These shabby, long-stay hotels provide the kind of anonymity and flexibility required for all sorts of criminal commerce. Drug addicts do not always have cash, but they can always find something to barter. So Hillbrow has become a flourishing conduit for stolen property. Drug couriers need false travel documents, and this leads to a broadening web for forgery and fraud.[61]

If rapid circulation and impetuous movement govern city life in the hypermodern city, then lethargy and stagnation, entropy and stasis characterize the interior world of the brothel.[62] Sex workers—trapped in the seeming timelessness of the "world's oldest profession"—become stationary objects, fixed in place, lying in wait, where boredom and anticipation commingle in a temporal pattern defined by a repetitive cycle, a seemingly endless loop, of physical attention in exchange for money. The grim choreography that takes place in this confined (and confining) space puts women and young girls at grave risk. Sex workers are imprisoned in these hellholes of despair where HIV-AIDS and other sexually transmitted diseases are the inevitable and invisible outcome of the social circumstances within which they find themselves. According to medical researchers, the estimated twenty thousand sex workers in the inner city have exhibited the key characteristics of a core transmitter group for HIV-AIDS.[63] According to research conducted by the Southern Metropolitan Local Council in 2000, it was estimated one in four adults living in the inner city were HIV-positive, double the statistic for the same area four years earlier. A staggering 40 percent of people attending the main AIDS center in Esselen Street, Hillbrow, tested HIV-positive. In 1999, seventy thousand people were buried or cremated in the Greater Johannesburg metropolitan area, compared with fifteen thousand in 1994—a dramatic increased attributed largely to the spreading AIDS epidemic.[64]

In some brothel-hotels, seasoned sex workers often assume a dominant role in maintaining order and discipline. They introduce newcomers to the business and oversee the conduct of sex workers who live on the premises. These women—commonly known as "head mamas"—are either self-appointed or elected by the sex workers living in the hotel. When sex workers learn through the grapevine that one of their "colleagues" is not using condoms with clients, they typically respond with verbal abuse and sometimes violence. Yet even in the midst of this wretchedness, sex workers often develop bonds of solidarity and cohesiveness to protect themselves and their colleagues from abusive clients, the ravages of sexually transmitted diseases, and chronic material instability.

The public discourse dealing with prostitution oscillates between two wildly different tropes: the terms *sex worker* and *sex slave* connote two very different images. On the one hand, *sex worker* suggests a seller of labor-power on the market, one who is entitled to the formal rights granted to wage earners under law. The trope of *sex worker* seeks to normalize prostitutional activity, to make visible what is essentially an invisible practice. It calls for decriminalization if not outright legalization of prostitution. On the other hand, *sex slave* connotes a noir image of human bondage, women trapped in a degrading life-world from which there is no exit. This trope calls for aggressive policing, prosecuting brothel-owners, and releasing women from modern-day enslavement. In truth, both these relationships point to what is actually happening on the ground.

Just like the levels of Dante's Hell, prostitutional activities assume different positionalities in the spatial geography of virtue and vice. At the risk of oversimplification, it is possible to classify sex work into three main types: first, there are autonomous "entrepreneurs," women who typically work either alone or in small groups under the "protection" of bodyguards and drivers. These women typically operate from private homes or gated apartment buildings in the plush, middle-class northern and eastern suburbs.

Second, there are the sex workers who operate from brothels, usually in groups ranging from a dozen or more to several hundred. These women typically work in shifts. As horrible as this situation is, there are conditions far worse for street-walkers who operate from curbside or street corners throughout the inner city. Their ranks include some foreign immigrants, but they are mainly poor and desperate women and girls escaping the poverty, drudgery, and insecurity of the surrounding townships and rural areas. For women, risk of danger escalates on the streets. There is little protection against predators of all kinds.

What complicates this rather neat picture is the importation of foreign immigrants. At one end, there are brothel owners who have located upscale brothels in middle-class areas and have filled them with woman from places like Bulgaria, Ukraine, Russia, and Thailand, "marketing" them as "exotic." At the other extreme, inner-city brothel owners have lured countless numbers of impoverished, and often underaged, girls from surrounding countries like Mozambique, Zimbabwe, Lesotho, and Swaziland to work in the sex industry. Truly disreputable places like the Chelsea Hotel (corner of Catherine and Soper Roads, Berea), the Europa Hotel (corner of Smit and Claim Streets), the Dorchester Hotel (Quartz Street), the Jungle Inn (Quartz Street), the Golden Key, and Little Roseneath have acquired much-deserved reputations as confined places where girls as young as ten or twelve were held against their will—sometimes shackled to their beds and kept naked and drugged—in situations akin to bonded servitude. These are sites of socioeconomic misery, social isolation, and moral degradation.[65]

South Africa has become the regional center of an endemic trafficking ring of women and children for the sex industry. According to the International Organisation for Migration, local syndicates, along with Russian organized crime gangs and globally connected Chinese triad organizations, are involved, luring women from Russia, Bulgaria, and Thailand to work in "high-class" brothels in the northern suburbs. In addition, Angolan, Congolese, and Nigerian syndicates were responsible for much of the trafficking in women from African countries.[66] It has been estimated that criminal syndicates smuggle as many as one thousand women and girls (age fourteen to twenty-four) from Mozambique across the border, where they are forced to work in restaurants or in brothels catering for the mass market in the sex trade. According to the report, "white, Afrikaans-speaking men" have abducted street-children in Lesotho, bringing them illegally across the border into South Africa, where they are held against their will and forced into prostitutional activity.[67] Human traffickers typically try to recruit women and young girls in bars, clubs, and at taxi stands in large cities in neighboring countries, luring them to Johannesburg with promises of good jobs and lots of money. According to a report issued in 2000 by Zurayah Abass, director of Molo Songololo, an estimated thirty-eight thousand child prostitutes, with girls as young as four years of age, were forced into the sex industry. Researchers link the rise in child prostitution with increased poverty and unemployment, which has led some parents to force their own children into prostitution as a source of income. The report also contended that a southern African myth—that AIDS can be prevented or "cured" by having sex with a virgin—also contributed to the increase in child prostitution.[68]

THE DISJOINTED METROPOLIS

> Place-making based on exclusion, sameness or nostalgia is socially poisonous and psychologically useless; a self weighted with its insufficiencies cannot lift the burden by retreat into fantasy.
> —*Richard Sennett*

In *Invisible Cities*, Italo Calvino recounts the apocryphal tale of a Venetian traveler, Marco Polo, who regales the aged Tartar emperor Kublai Khan with stories about the cities he has visited in his wayward travels around the empire.[69] Eventually it becomes clear that each of the fantastic cities that Marco Polo dutifully describes is really one and the same place: the city of Venice. The Johannesburg dissected here resembles Calvino's invisible Venice, for this place contains many different cities in one as well. It is at once a city of collective memory and of amnesia, a city of unfulfilled promises, a city of hopes and desires, a city hidden from view, a city of wondrous and frightful signs, a city of spoken and unspoken words, a city of the living and of the dead.[70]

Johannesburg is the undisputed economic and cultural capital of the "new South Africa"—a distended, bloated metropolis (with "world-class" aspirations) rivaled only by Cape Town as a site of cosmopolitan urbanity. This sprawling urban agglomeration—crowded, dirty, noisy, disorganized, and pulsating with life—is home to more people of different ethnic and religious backgrounds than anywhere else on the African continent. The Greater Johannesburg metropolitan region is a sprawling amalgam of a dozen or so medium-size towns, edge cities, and nodal clusters that sprouted in the barren veldt and then spread, fueled by population growth, real estate speculation, and suburban development. What looks more or less like a seamless urbanscape from the air is in fact a handful of rival cities bumping up against each other. Johannesburg offers a pullulating collage of competing images: canyonlike streets dwarfed by huge skyscrapers, homeless squatters inhabiting Art Deco masterpieces, glue-sniffing runaway children begging outside entrances to upscale shopping malls, and underpaid private security guards watching over huge, walled-in mansions. Its blend of frontier entrepreneurialism and perpetual greed acts as a stimulus of frightening power. From a distance and at night, the soaring office towers seem to lose touch with reality and take on magical powers as phantasmagoric images. With the end of apartheid and the transition to parliamentary democracy, the affluent white middle classes, poised for the promise of segregation by flight, responded to their fears of urban disorder by building ever outward. So in this way, some of the racial tensions of the city—and they are legion—were eased far more by sprawl than by accommodation. The restructuring of urban space in Johannesburg after the end of apartheid still depends on powerful and interlocking exclusions. The rapid extension of exclusionary spatial forms—citadel office complexes, gated residential communities, and other enclosed places—represents a deliberate reaction to the opening of the public places to multiclass participation. The propertied middle-class retreat to fortresslike redoubts is motivated in part by a great fear of the dangerous classes, by the insecurity of chance encounters, and by the nostalgic longing for the restoration of an imagined respectable middle-class order.

The steady accretion of downtown citadel office complexes, sleek skyscrapers for the corporate elite, glitzy "shoppertainment" extravaganzas for the idle rich, and gated residential estates constructed around top-of-the-line golf courses have significantly restructured the urban landscape of the Greater Johannesburg region, urbanizing the periphery, and extending the tentacles of the city in all directions. City boosters boast of the world-class features of Johannesburg after apartheid, promoting it as a vibrant business center, a thriving hub for arts and culture, and a hospitable tourist destination. Yet the early warning signs of a possible nightmare future are clearly visible. It is the spatial juxtaposition of urban glamour zones and urban danger zones that makes the relationship between the built environment and social well-being most evident. To a significant degree, Johannesburg after apartheid has become a cocooned city of urban fortresses. These enclosed places are scattered across the urban landscape, creating an intricate, labyrinthine maze of sealed-off urban cells. Wealthy urban residents live, work, and play in these formidable bastions of brick and mortar, wood and iron, and steel and glass. Many of these fortified enclosures are connected by enforced bridges that span busy public thoroughfares below. However, when the residents of these sequestered enclaves are forced to leave their safety zones, they do so within the protective amour of their cars, dreading every moment they are "out there" in the illegible public spaces of the city, exposed to the mercy of unknown predators who lie in wait for victims. In the popular imagination, these public spaces are the perceived "war zones" of the city—dens of iniquity and violence that threaten the very existence of those seeking a safe haven in their private fortresses. They are also the living (and breathing) spaces of the urban poor, who have no choice but to face the everyday dangers of the "disorderly city" with little or no protection. The urban poor have filled in the voids, the underutilized and empty spaces of the cityscape, abandoned by the anxious middle-class residents who have retreated behind walls, barriers, and fortifications. Urban residents have discarded the utopian ideal of sharing and using the public spaces of the city in equal measure. Only those who do not have a choice are left to fashion their everyday lives in these derelict and dangerous areas. Like shadowy microgovernments, private agencies operating with the blessing of municipal authorities have assumed command over designated zones of the cityscape, renaming them "city improvement districts," while the urban poor, the homeless, and the unfortunate are all left to fend for themselves outside the grid of enclosed fortresses for the privileged.[71]

Putting Cities in Their Place

> In reality they all lived in a kind of hieroglyphic world, where the real thing was never said or done or even thought, but only represented by a set of arbitrary signs.
> —Edith Wharton, *The Age of Innocence*

Cities are not monolithic or fixed entities, whose "essence" can be captured simply by reference to a priori categories, abstract typologies, or schematic ideal-types.[72] Similarly, the transformation and metamorphosis of cities over time is not the result of a singular logic, a unilinear teleology, or a universal process of urbanization. City-building processes are contradictory and uneven. Hence, the understanding of cities cannot be reduced merely to an assessment of relative geographical size, demographic trends, population statistics, topographical characteristics, morphological forms, cartographic representations, or surface appearances. It follows, then, that there is something misleading about classifying or arranging cities in a single, hierarchical rank-order according to which some are endowed with characteristics that make them more "global" or "world-class" than others.

Instead, cities are complex and impermanent aggregations, or, as Nick Prior has put it, "contiguous assemblage[s] of built forms, everyday practices, and spatial discourses" that intersect, overlap, and intermingle with one another in historically specific ways. Viewed from this angle, it makes more sense to view the urban landscape as an evolving spatial form that brings together elements of the material and the corporeal, along with the symbolic and the imagined, in particular places, sites, and locations. Rather than looking on cities as inert containers or theatrical stage-sets within which social relations are constituted and social action and exchange take place, it is much more fruitful to look on urban space itself as part and parcel of the constitutive process of constructing social relations and shaping (post)modern identities and subjectivities. This understanding conforms to the view of the city (shared by Michel de Certeau and others) as palimpsest—a multilayered space where traces, ruins, and remnants of past city-building efforts coexist in the present with the early signs of an imagined Future City, embryonic glimpses of what is to come.[73]

In *The Practice of Everyday Life*, Michel de Certeau distinguished between what he called the "concept-city" and "urban practices." These contrasting paradigms are rooted in two different epistemological stances, or "ways of knowing" the city. The concept-city conjures up a panoramic image of the cityscape as abstract geometric space, capable of being mapped as a connected grid, pictured as a unified field measured as a fixed entity, or represented as a rational totality. In contrast, urban practices refer to an active engagement with city-life: negotiating the variegated uses of the streetscape, experiencing the everyday, and moving from one place to another. Captivated and mesmerized by this scopic drive to visually comprehend the city as a unified totality, urban planners, city officials, cartographers, and city boosters alike project onto the haphazard urban agglomeration a fictive coherence, connectedness, and robust wholeness that is largely not there. Moving from a panoramic vision of the city—with its panoptic pretensions of capturing "essences" subsumed under a single "totalizing" logic—to a more quotidian perspective on urban life enables us to grasp and hence more fully understand the processes of "place making" and "boundary marking," or everyday practices of partitioning and enclosure, and inclusion and exclusion. In short, inspecting what takes place in the interstices of the urban social fabric provides us with the opportunity to uncover spatial networks and modes of exchange often hidden from view in the city, and hence to make sense of spatial relations as lived and contested in the conduct of daily life.[74]

NOTES

In addition to expressing my appreciation to Robert Tignor, Bill Jordan, Anne Pitcher, Sarah Shrank, and Gyan Prakash for comments on earlier versions of this paper, I would also like to thank the three anonymous reviewers for this volume who offered important suggestions for revisions.

1. This epigraph is from a letter from Le Corbusier to Rex Marthienssen, July 1939. Cited in Gilbert Herbert, *Marthienssen and the International Style: The Modern Movement in South African Architecture, Architectural Education, Professional Practice, Journalism, and Achievement in Johannesburg, Pretoria, 1920–1940* (Cape Town: A. A. Balkema, 1975), 243.

2. The descriptions and arguments made in this paper are based on my own extensive field research, including interviews with key city officials and property developers, along with on-site visits to various locations, carried out over a five-year period.

3. See Andrew Donaldson, "Whoring," in Heidi Holland and Adam Roberts, eds., *From Jo'burg to Jozi: Stories about Africa's Infamous City* (London: Penguin, 2002), 77–80, esp. 78.

4. For some ideas in the above paragraph, see David Robbins, *Wasteland* (Johannesburg: Lowry, 1987), 195–96; and Jennifer Robinson, "(Im)mobilizing Space— Dreaming of Change," in Hilton Judin and Ivan Vladislavic, eds., *Blank _____: Architecture, Apartheid, and After* (Rotterdam: NAi, 1999), 163–71.

5. See Saskia Sassen, *Globalization and Its Discontents* (New York: New Press, 1998), xxxiii. For a comparison with other "divided cities," see Martin J. Murray, "The Spatial Dynamics of Postmodern Urbanism: Social Polarisation and Fragmentation in Sao Paulo and Johannesburg," *Journal of Contemporary African Studies* 22, no. 2 (2004): 139–64; Jon Connell, "Beyond Manila: Walls, Malls, and Private Spaces," *Environment and Planning A* 31, no. 3 (1999): 417–40; Mike Davis, *City of Quartz: Excavating the Future of Los Angeles* (New York: Vintage, 1992); and Teresa Caldeira, *City of Walls: Crime, Segregation, and Citizenship in Sao Paulo* (Berkeley: University of California Press, 2000).

6. Loïc J. D. Wacquant, "The Rise of Advanced Marginality: Notes on Its Nature and Implications," *Acta Sociologica* 39, no. 2 (1996): 121–40; and Loïc Wacquant, "Urban Marginality in the Coming Millennium," *Urban Studies* 36, no. 10 (1999): 1,639–47. For a critical treatment of global integration, see M. Christine Boyer, "Cities for Sale: Merchandising History at South Street Seaport," in Michael Sorkin, ed., *Variations on a Theme Park: The New American City and the End of Public Space* (New York: Hill and Wang, 1996), 181–204.

7. The epigraph is from "South Africa: Murder and Siege Architecture," *Economist*, July 15, 1995. For an excellent review of the relevant literature on spatial parti-

tioning, see Jonathan Crush, "Scripting the Compound: Power and Space in the South African Mining Industry," *Environment and Planning D* 12 (1994): 301–24.

8. See Jo Beall, Owen Crankshaw, and Susan Parnell, *Uniting a Divided City: Governance and Social Exclusion in Johannesburg* (London: Earthscan, 2002), 29–62; and Lindsay Bremner, "Closure, Simulation, and "Making Do" in the Contemporary Johannesburg Landscape," in Okwui Enwezor et. al., eds., *Under Siege: Four African Cities*, Documenta 11_Platform 4 (Kassel, Germany: Hatje Cantz, 2002), 153–72.

9. Some of these ideas are derived from personal communication with Jennifer Robinson.

10. For urban South Africa, see Jennifer Robinson, "Spaces of Democracy: Remapping the Apartheid City," *Environment and Planning D* 16, no. 5 (1998): 533–48. For a wider discussion, see Neil Smith, *The New Urban Frontier: Gentrification and the Revanchist City* (London: Routledge, 1996).

11. See Jennifer Robinson, "The Geopolitics of South African Cities: States, Citizens, Territory," *Political Geography* 16, no. 5 (1997): 365–86.

12. See Henri Lefebvre, *The Production of Space*, trans. Donald Nicholson-Smith (Cambridge, Mass.: Blackwell, 1991), 1–67. See also Sharon Zukin, "The Postmodern Debate over Urban Form," *Theory, Culture, and Society* 5 (1988): 431–46, esp. 435.

13. See Susan Parnell, "The Built Environment: Neglected Frontier of South African Studies," *Urban Studies* 55, no. 2 (1986): 91–92.

14. These ideas are adapted from James Epstein, "Spatial Practices/Democratic Vistas," *Social History* 24, no. 3 (1999): 294–96, 301. See also M. Christine Boyer, *The City of Collective Memory: Its Historical Imagery and Architectural Entertainments* (Cambridge, Mass.: MIT Press, 1996): 5–29; and Ali Madanipour, "Urban Design and Dilemmas of Space," *Environment and Planning D* 14, no. 3 (1996): 331–55.

15. See Paul Jaskot, "Berlin, Capital of the Twentieth Century," *Design Book Review* 44/45 (2001): 62–67, esp. 64.

16. For the source of some of these ideas, see Helen Hillis (with Paul Tyrer), "The Fetishized Past: Post-industrial Manchester and Interstitial Spaces," *Visual Culture in Britain* 3, no. 2 (2002): 103–17, esp. 103, 115; Rajeev Patke, "Benjamin's *Arcades Project* and the Postcolonial City," *Diacritics* 30, no. 4 (2000): 3–14, esp. 4–5, 7; and Susan Buck-Morss, "The City as Dreamworld and Catastrophe," *October* 73 (1995): 3–26.

17. For the creative use of these early image-categories for Johannesburg, see Charles Van Onselen, *Studies in the Social and Economic History of the Witwatersrand, 1886–1914, vol. 1: New Babylon*, and vol. 2, *New Nineveh* (London: Longman, 1981).

18. Guy Baeten, "Hypochrondriac Geographies of the City and the New Urban Dystopia," *City* 6, no. 1 (2002): 103–16, esp. 111–12.

19. Jonathan Crush, "Darkness Falls: Imagining the South African City," *Social Dynamics* 19, no. 2 (1993): 128–48. See also James Donald, *Imagining the Modern City* (Minneapolis: University of Minnesota Press, 1999): 8, 10–11.

20. See Victor Burgin, "Geometry and Abjection," in James Donald, ed., *Psychoanalysis and Cultural Theory: Thresholds* (London: Macmillan, 1991): 12.

21. Lefebvre, *The Production of Space*, 100–101.

22. Robert Fishman, *Bourgeois Utopias: The Rise and Fall of Suburbia* (New York: Basic Books, 1987).

23. It is important to point out that treating these spaces in allegorical terms enables me to avoid a narrowly *metonymic* argument whereby a singular form in the built environment is taken, by a process of inflation and conflation, to be emblematic not only of a general condition but expressive of an essence. These ideas (and the quotation) are borrowed root-and-branch from Meagan Morris, "Great Moments in Social Climbing: King Kong and the Human Fly," in Beatriz Colomina, ed., *Sexuality and Space* (Princeton, N.J.: Princeton University School of Architecture, 1992): 1–53, esp. 18–19.

24. Lindsay Bremner, "Crime and the Emerging Landscape of Post-apartheid Johannesburg," in Judin and Vladislavic, *Blank _____*, 48–63. See Mike Davis, "Urban Renaissance and the Spirit of Postmodernism," *New Left Review* 151 (1985): 106–14; and Setha Low, "The Anthropology of Cities: Imagining and Theorizing the City," *Annual Review of Anthropology* 25 (1996): 383–409.

25. See Ben Highmore, "*Street Life in London*: Towards a Rhythmanalysis of London in the Late Nineteenth Century," *New Formations* 47 (2002): 171–93, esp. 172–73, 175. These contrasting tropes of speed and circulation versus stagnation and entropy form part of the rhetorical arsenal of city officials who work with a moralizing policy and planning discourse with which to stereotype parts of the urban landscape.

26. See ibid., 190–91.

27. The epigraph is from Marian Giesen, "Caesars Gauteng Resort Complex," *Planning* 172 (November/December 2000): 40.

28. See Umberto Eco, *Travels in Hyperreality: Essays*, trans. William Weaver (New York: Harcourt Brace Jovanovich, 1986): 30–31, 40–44; and Ada Louise Huxtable, *The Unreal America: Architecture and Illusion* (New York: New Press, 1997): 75.

29. See Robert Venturi, Denise Scott Brown, and Steven Izenhour, *Learning from Las Vegas: The Forgotten Symbolism of Architectural Form* (Cambridge, Mass.: MIT Press, 1972).

30. Huxtable, *The Unreal America*, 75–76.

31. This idea owes its origin to Eco, *Travels in Hyperreality*, 40–44; and Huxtable, *The Unreal America*, 97.

32. Reyner Banham, "Mediated Environments or: You Can't Build That Here," in C.W.E. Bigsby, ed., *Superculture: American Popular Culture in Europe* (London: Paul Elek, 1975): 80.

175

33. For a comparative perspective, see William Kowinski, *The Malling of America: An Inside Look at the Great Consumer Paradise* (New York: Morrow, 1985): 207; and Jonathan Raban, *Soft City* (London: Hamish Hamilton, 1974): 122–23. For the analogical similarity between gambling and consumption and the dissimilarity between gambling and work, see David Clarke, *The Consumer Society and the Postmodern City* (London: Routledge, 2003): 11–13, and 21–22.

34. See Laura Podalsky, *Specular City: Transforming Culture, Consumption, and Space in Buenos Aires, 1955–1973* (Philadelphia: Temple University Press, 2004): 182–83.

35. Huxtable, *The Unreal America,*76; and Sarah Chaplin, "Heterotopia Deserta: Las Vegas and Other Spaces," in Iain Borden and Jane Rendell, eds., *InterSections: Architectural Histories and Critical Theories* (London: Routledge, 2000): 203–20, esp. 207–8.

36. For a wide discussion of these kinds of ideas, see Eco, "*Travels in Hyperreality*," 1–58.

37. See M. Christine Boyer, "Twice-Told Stories: The Double Erasure of Times Square," in Iain Borden, Jane Rendell, and Joe Kerr (with Alice Pivaro), eds., *The Unknown City: Contesting Architecture and Social Space* (Cambridge, Mass.: MIT Press, 2001), 30–53, esp. 33–35.

38. See Rob Shields, "Social Spatialization and the Built Environment: The West Edmonton Mall," *Environment and Planning D* 7, no. 2 (1989): 158; and Eco, *Travels in Hyperreality,* 39–44.

39. The following discussion of Montecasino is based on my numerous on-site visits to the premises between 1999 and 2006. The epigraph is from Huxtable, *The Unreal America,* 75.

40. "Montecasino," *Architect and Builder* (January/February 2001): 30–31; and "A Tuscan Village in South Africa," *Economist,* April 7–13, 2001.

41. At least one critic noted the irony and "insensitivity" in the choice of the name: "Monte Casino was a 15-th century Benedictine monastery, a great centre of European learning, before it was tragically destroyed by Allied bombing in one of the bloodiest battles of World War II. Many thousands of German, Polish, and American soldiers died in its assault and defense. Parodying its name for the purposes of running a gambling joint is rather like naming a dental practice after Dachau or a pyrotechnics business after Dresden." (David Le Page, "Gauteng's Newest Citadel of Sin," *Economist,* January 5, 2001: 41. To add one irony on top of another, the original Monte Casino was not located in Tuscany at all, but is south of Rome. Thanks to Pamela Long for pointing this out to me.

42. See "Montecasino," *Architect and Builder* (January/February 2001): 33–34; Cara Pauling, "Montecasino, Fourways," *Planning* 173 (January/February 2001): 14; and Achille Mbembe, "Aesthetics of Superfluity," *Public Culture* 16, no. 3 (2004): 373–405, esp. 396–400.

43. Boyer, "Twice-Told Stories," 49.

44. Pauling, "Montecasino, Fourways," 14.

45. "Montecasino," *Architect and Builder* (January/February 2001): 36.

46. This phrase is taken from Boyer, "Twice-Told Stories," 31.

47. Pauling, "Montecasino, Fourways," 16–17.

48. Ibid.; and "Montecasino," *Architect and Builder* (January/February, 2001): 36.

49. See Kowinski, *The Malling of America*, 62–63.

50. Pauling, "Montecasino, Fourways," 15.

51. See "Montecasino," *Architect and Builder* (January/February, 2001): 37; and Pauling, "Montecasino, Fourways," 15.

52. "Montecasino," *Architect and Builder* (January/February 2001): 37.

53. The notion of "adjacent attraction" is taken from Margaret Crawford, "The World in a Shopping Mall," in Sorkin, *Variations on a Theme Park*, 15. For the quotation, see Richard Sennett, *The Fall of Public Man* (New York: Vintage, 1976): 144–45.

54. Pauling, "Montecasino, Fourways," 17–18.

55. See R. W. Apple, "Spinning Mirages like Cotton Candy," *New York Times*, October 27, 2000, E43, E46.

56. Real rents in inner-city neighborhoods have declined by over a third from 1976 to 2000. "Hillbrow Rents Are Down in Real Terms but That Will Change," *Business Day*, March 28, 2001.

57. This metaphor is borrowed from AbdouMaliq Simone, "People as Infrastructure: Intersecting Fragments in Johannesburg," *Public Culture* 16, nos. 3 (2004): 407–29, esp. 407.

58. Ted Leggett, "Rainbow Tenement: Crime and Policing in Inner-City Johannesburg," *Institute for Security Studies*, monograph 78 (April 2003): 1–4.

59. I would like to thank Josephine Malala and Mashadi Dumelakgosi for introducing me to the Huguenot Hotel. My observations are based on two on-site visits in May 2001.

60. Some of these ideas are derived from Beatriz Colomina, "The Split Wall: Domestic Voyeurism," in Colomina, *Sexuality and Space*, 73–128, esp. 85, 94.

61. Leggett, "Rainbow Tenement."

62. See David Trotter, *Circulation: Defoe, Dickens, and the Economies of the Novel* (Basingstoke: Macmillan, 1988); and Susan Buck-Morss, "The Flâneur, the Sandwichman and the Whole: The Politics of Loitering," *New German Critique* 39 (1986): 99–140.

63. H. Rees, M. E. Beksinska, K. Dickson-Tetteh, R. C. Ballard, and Ye Htun, "Commercial Sex Workers in Johannesburg: Risk Behavior and HIV Status," *South African Journal of Science* 96, no. 6 (June 2000): 283–85.

64. "Aids 1000% Up in Jo'burg Inner-City," *Daily Dispatch* , July 4, 2000; and Alan Whiteside and Clem Sunter, *AIDS: The Challenge for South Africa* (Cape Town: Human and Rousseau, 2000).

65. "Police Raid Hillbrow Brothels," *SABC News*, February 3, 2001. Many of these hotels are now closed for business. With the exception of the refurbished Eu-

ropa, many remain as derelict, hollowed-out hulks. This observation is based on my on-site visits to most of these places in May–June 2006.

66. "S. Africa's Child Sex Trafficking Nightmare," *BBC News,* November 23, 2000.

67. "SA Sex Trafficking Widespread," *BBC News,* March 25, 2003.

68. Abass is quoted in Jacques Pauw, director, "Sold Sisters," *Special Assignment: SABC News,* April 1, 2003.

69. The epigraph is from Richard Sennett, "The Search for a Place in the World," in Nan Ellin, ed., *Architecture of Fear* (New York: Princeton Architectural Press, 1997), 69.

70. See Filip de Boeck, "Kinshasa: Tales of the "Invisible City" and the Second World," in Enwezor, *Under Siege: Four African Cities,* 243–86, esp. 243.

71. See Abdou Maliq Simone, "Straddling the Divides: Remaking Associational Life in the Informal City," *International Journal of Urban and Regional Research* 25, no. 1 (2001): 102–17. These ideas are taken from Karina Landman, "The Urban Future: Enclosed Neighborhoods?" paper presented at the Urban Futures Conference, Johannesburg, July 10–14, 2000.

72. The epigraph is from Edith Wharton, *The Age of Innocence* (New York: D. Appleton and Co., 1920): 42.

73. These ideas are shaped from Nick Prior, "Urban Portraits: Space/Body/City in Late Georgian Edinburgh," *New Formations* 47 (2002): 194–216, esp. 194–95; Ida Susser and Jane Schneider, "Wounded Cities: Destruction and Reconstruction in a Globalized World," in Jane Schneider and Ida Susser, eds., *Wounded Cities: Destruction and Reconstruction in a Globalized World* (Oxford: Berg, 2003): 1–24, esp. 3–4; and Michel de Certeau, *The Practice of Everyday Life* (Berkeley: University of California Press, 1984), 200–202.

74. These ideas are fashioned from a reading of de Certeau, *The Practice of Everyday Life,* 91–110; and Prior, "Urban Portraits," 194–95, 214.

SPATIAL POLITICS

*

Violence and Spatial Politics between the Local and Imperial: Baghdad, 1778–1810

DINA RIZK KHOURY

Modern Baghdad is dying a long and violent death according to most press reports. Gone is the rich, secular, cultural life that characterized the cafés of its two oldest modern thoroughfares, Rashid and Mutanabi Streets. Gone as well are the mixed neighborhoods of middle-class professionals drawn from across the sectarian divide. In their stead, the city is acquiring a new communal geography as Sunni and Shi'i militias and their leaders inscribe sectarian politics into space. While the state had controlled much of the spatial politics in the city before 2003, it is now confined to a barricaded zone and protected by U.S. power. Baghdad seems to epitomize the postmodern dystopic city in the new imperial age. Communal violence, receding state controls, free market cleptocracy, and imperial hubris combine to produce new geographies of power.

But Baghdad is not simply a symbol of postmodern dystopia. Its current crisis is bound to the specific and local spatial practices of its diverse population's encounter with modernity. This encounter had its beginnings some two hundred years ago at the cusp of what historian C. A. Bayly has called the age of "archaic globalization."[1] Then, as now, the urban geography of Baghdad and the spatial habits of its various residents were transformed by violence that wracked the city during a period of crisis in the old political order. Baghdad was incorporated into the Anglo-Indian sphere of British imperial thinking in the midst of the Napoleonic wars, the first global wars of the modern period. As a frontier city in the Ottoman Empire, it was soon reconfigured in the Ottoman imperial imagination. No longer a locus of old imperial rivalries between Islamic empires, it became the scene of Ottoman negotiations with British modern imperial ambitions. Compounding the turmoil created by this new global order was the challenge presented to the legitimacy of Ottoman Sunni ruling traditions by the Wahhabi movement, a Sunni revivalist movement, which acquired followers in Baghdad. These imperial and regional factors, I argue, impinged on local politics and transformed spatial practices and politics within the city and between the city and its hinterland. Openly political agendas often characterized the episodic violence in the city. Leaders of rebellions and factional struggles now employed a vocabulary of sect and "utopia" and were able to mobilize wider sectors of the urban and tribal populations. Narratives of these violent episodes penned by local literati exhibited a new conceptualization of spaces as constructs denoting ethnic/sectarian and political markers between ideological communities.

Sectarian violence is embedded in Middle Eastern societies' experience of modernity. As Ussama Makdisi has argued, it was neither solely the product of European manipulations nor the result of primordial identification. Rather, it marked the politicization of subaltern populations seeking voice in what had hitherto been elite-dominated traditional politics.[2] Rarely, however, has there been an attempt to understand this violence as spatial practice, not simply as movement contained within the geographic confines of the city. Furthermore, there have been few consistent attempts by historians to study the transformation of the urban population's conceptualization of space during the transition from the early modern to the modern period. In what follows, I explore the ways in which space was represented by different protagonists and observers during three episodes of sustained violence, in Baghdad spanning the years 1778 to 1810. The story however, begins in the early modern period.

The social and economic causes of violence and what Charles Tilly has called the "repertoires of contention" have been the subject of studies by historians of the early modern Middle East in the past three decades.[3] However, the spatial component of rebellion and violence has received less attention. Historians have often pointed to the importance of spatially defined solidarities in mobilizing sectors of the urban population in interelite factional struggles as well as in food and tax riots.[4] Following historians of early modern Europe, they have searched for clues for the motivation of rebellious urban populations by locating the targets of their anger in the spatial grid of the city. Their work has been valuable to our understanding of urban politics. However, they have tended to write about space as a neutral and stable category, one that contains social action but retains an unchanging social meaning over time. For example, despite the centrality of quarter solidarities in mobilizing populations during periods of violence, and the disruption that this violence created in the habitual use of space, historians often assumed that the appropriation of space by urban rebels retained the same meaning over time and reproduced stable community relations.

Part of the problem of writing about the meaning of space during the early modern period is the nature of the literary sources we use to understand the meaning and agendas of the rebels and rioters. They were often written by urban elites drawn from the local religious community whose descriptions of rebellion were often couched in hostility to the rebels and the disruption of the moral and political order that they had brought. Chronicles of such violence in Baghdad lacked teleology; events were recorded to inform, entertain, and edify. When violence was reported, the language employed was restorative and deeply ambivalent about the actions of both the elites and commoners who were involved. It is as if the story of social upheaval was set up from its inception in preparation for the restoration of the old order.[5] The ritualistic recounting of violence, and the coexistence of what David Nirenberg has described in the context of communal violence in the Middle Ages as "rhythmic time" and "successive events," allowed for the illusion of stability and restoration of order.[6] In many cases, these stories of rebellions were recorded to be read or told to an audience interested in the moral and action of the narratives.

However, when rebellious and riotous populations inverted the habitual use of such public sacred and secular spaces as mosque, sufi lodge, and quarter, their acts not only imbued these spaces with political meaning but changed the spatial and social hierarchy in the city.[7] Spatial politics, by which I mean, to quote David Harvey, the ways in which "well established spatial practices and discourses are 'used up' and 'worked over' in social action,"[8] played an important role at two levels. First, they reflected the transformation of economic and social weight of different communities in the city. The use of space during periods of violence became a venue for the assertion of this new social power through the disruption of the tenuous stability of the political order. Second, violence—whether generated and narrated as discord/sedition (*fitna*) brought on by the factional struggles of elites, or as rebellion to preserve or challenge the Ottoman political order—was a venue for the enactment in public spaces of rituals of power and popular contestation of that power. Insofar as violence, particularly sustained violence, disrupted the habitual use of space, it also helped recalibrate the communal identities in spatial terms. It simplified and helped map with stark lines identities that were complex and contingent.[9]

SPACES OF POWER, SPACES OF CONTENTION, 1600s–1770s

The Ottoman imperial imagination conceived of Baghdad in military and sacred terms. Its conquest from the Shi'i Safavid dynasty in the sixteenth century established it as the largest fortress of the Ottoman Empire along the Persian/Ottoman frontier. Threats to the territorial sovereignty of the Ottoman state from Persia or from rebellious local governors were almost always seen as threats to its legitimacy as a Sunni power and bulwark against Persian Shi'ism. When a rebellious military officer surrendered the city to the Persians in 1622, the Ottoman state organized several campaigns to retrieve it, culminating in a 1638 campaign led by the sultan himself.[10] Baghdad was also a sacred space. Described in many official Ottoman documents as the "Abode of Saints," it was home to a number of mausoleums of sufi saints and Islamic scholars, all recorded with meticulous detail by Nasuh Matrakci, who accompanied Suleiman the Magnificent on his campaign to conquer Baghdad in 1534. Of the many mausoleums in the city, the Ottomans were particularly interested in the tomb of Abu Hanifa, the founder of the Islamic legal school to which the Ottomans subscribed; the tomb of the founder of the Qadiriyya sufi order; and the tomb of Musa al-Kazim, the sixth imam of Shi'i Islam.[11] In an attempt to integrate Baghdad into the sacred space of empire, Suleiman the Magnificent renovated and enlarged the Abu Hanifa mosque, building a school and establishing a large endowment for its support.[12] Situated outside the city walls, three kilometers from the citadel and the Maydan quarter, its *ulama* (religious scholars) were sometimes the targets of the wrath of rebels who associated them with the state in the seventeenth century.[13] Much of imperial and local politics mapped Baghdad's place in the empire as a special city, one that is of utmost strategic importance in controlling the frontiers between Sunni and Shi'i Islam, but also a place of significance in Islamic sacred history, be that Shi'i or Sunni.

Ottoman hegemony in the city was established spatially. At the apex of the Ottoman provincial order was the governor and the military regiments. They formed what was known in Ottoman government literature the *askeri* estate. The citadel, the center of military power was where the military regiments, the janissaries, were stationed. Around it, a hippodrome, the Maydan, gradually developed into a residential and commercial quarter catering to the military regiments. In the seventeenth century, the Ottoman traveler Evliya Çelebi deemed the citadel and the hippodrome one of the largest in the empire. Measuring 20,800 steps (nearly 2.5 leagues), it was surrounded by several towers. Until the early eighteenth century it housed the governor and his private military retinue.[14] It continued to be the center of Baghdad's military community well into the nineteenth century, a small city within a city, housing at one time or another thousands of military men.[15] These constituted separate communities organized into regiments, each with its own leader and special dress and subject to its own laws in criminal matters. Exempt from a slew of taxes, their salaries and provisions were paid through a complex system of rural and urban tax farms, through transfers of funds from other provincial capitals, and direct payment from the provincial treasury.[16] For much of the seventeenth century, these regiments controlled the politics of the city. By the beginning of the eighteenth century, the factional struggles between these communities took the form of struggle over rural and urban resources between imperial janissary regiments rotated occasionally from the southeastern parts of the empire and the locally recruited regiments who had been infiltrated by Baghdadis and other rural elements in the area and appear to have had a large percentage of Shi'is among them.[17] The locally recruited regiments were often allied with the guilds, particularly the powerful coffee-grinders guild, the water-carriers guild, and the butcher's guild.[18] These were trades closely associated with the provisioning of the janissaries (coffee houses and meat provisions being central to the well-being and acquiescence of the military regiments), and many of the local janissaries engaged in these trades.[19] Members of guilds enrolled in the janissary regiments to obtain tax and legal exemptions. During the seventeenth century, a number of these regiments belonged to the semiheterodox Bektashi sufi order associated with the janissaries of the empire. After the conquest of Baghdad, the Bektashi sufi lodge was erected on the opposite side of the southern part of the citadel, across the Tigris River and near the pontoon bridge that served as a gateway from the western side of the city. At the head of the western end of the bridge, a small citadel called the Bird's Citadel, housed a small military regiment responsible for the collection of tolls on goods entering the eastern part of the city.[20] Standing outside the heart of the city, and separate from its more orthodox sufi convents, the Bektashi lodge and its visitors were often associated with the disorder and heterodoxy brought on by the unruly followers of the order. For the military regiments who hailed from different parts of the empire, however, the lodge helped create a community of believers from disparate military regiments.

The *mahkama*, the Islamic courthouse, and center of Ottoman judicial as well as administrative power over its subjects, was located south of the pontoon bridge and the Maydan. It was in the court that issues pertaining to commercial, inheritance, and marriage disputes were adjudicated. The judge, often appointed by the central government, was also the enforcer of the moral order within the community, ensuring that goods were produced and sold according prescribed quality and price, and punishing drunkenness and prostitution. In addition, the judge acted as the intermediary between the government and the populace, ensuring that state law was implemented and

185

drafting petitions to the central government on the part of subjects complaining of heavy taxation or abuses by administrators. This was at least how the judicial system worked in other parts of the empire.[21] As most of court records of Baghdad have been lost, we have to assume that the same process was at work in the city. Indeed, petitions sent by the subjects of the city to the central government and orders sent by the central government to the various officials in the city point to the centrality of the court as a space of interaction between the state, intermediaries, and the various sectors of the population. It was a space where locals could go to lodge complaints against the abuses of certain officials or file petitions concerning commercial, administrative, and political matters. Thus, the weight of Ottoman power was concentrated alongside the northeastern bank of the Tigris River. When rioters and local power groups sought to redress wrongs or usurp power, they walked and fought in this spatial grid. The strip of territory between the Maydan and the Islamic court (approximately 1.5 kilometers), witnessed the majority of the battles between different groups in Baghdad from the seventeenth to the early nineteenth century. Even when conflict revolved around quarter and factional solidarities, these conflicts were only resolved after a confrontation, no matter how brief, in this arena.

The Tigris formed both a barrier and a link to the various parts of the city. It divided the city between its eastern and more populous part, known as Rusafa, and the sparsely inhabited and rural western part, the Karkh. Until the eighteenth century, the western part of the city was not regarded by the inhabitants of Rusafa as part of its landscape.[22] Connected to the eastern side of the city by a pontoon bridge, and guarded by a citadel, the Karkh was the gateway to the tribal hinterland and the weakest defense of the city against tribal and Persian invaders. Until the early eighteenth century it appears to have had a Shi'i character and perhaps population. It had the largest concentration of Shi'i mausoleums and shrines devoted to the descendents of Ali.[23] It was at various times a space defined by danger as well as a refuge for rebels and governors trying to escape threats to their own power. Ottoman governors tried to encourage its settlement during the seventeenth century by building a mosque, a hostel, and some shops, but these soon became a center for highway robbers.[24] The shrine of al-Kazim, a few kilometers north of the Karkh was a small hamlet catering to the thousands of Shi'i pilgrims who visited the city annually.[25] But perhaps the most potent dividing line between order and disorder for Baghdad was that between the city, confined by walls and the Tigris, and the hinterland (barr) that lay outside the safety of the river and the walls. Local histories as well as official documents portray the hinterland as the vaguely defined space where rebels who disgorged from the city fled to find supporters among tribesmen and came back to threaten city folk. It is where the rules of justice and politics did not apply and the support that the rebels obtained from the populations outside these walls could be attributed to the latter's moral deficiencies. Until the second half of the eighteenth century, this view of the countryside continued to dominate the mental universe of urbanites across the social and political divide.

Baghdad had long been the center of trade and pilgrimage linking Asia, the Mediterranean, and India through the Persian Gulf. Ottoman and European visitors commented on the ethnic and linguistic diversity of its population. The eastern part of the city had a large Shi'i population, some of whom had come as pilgrims from Persia and other parts of the Muslim world and had settled in the city. There was also a substantial Jewish population and a smaller Christian community.[26] Baghdadis spoke Arabic, Persian, Turkish, and sometimes Urdu. However, outside of the concentration of Jews and Christians in their own quarters, we have no indication that the sectarian divisions between Shi'is and Sunnis were reflected in residential patterns of settlement. The southern part of the city, the quarter dominated by the mausoleum of Abd al-Qadir al-Gaylani, founder of the influential Qadiriyya order was the center of pilgrimage and scholarly life. The leaders of the Qadiriyya order, responsible for the maintenance of its rich endowment, claimed descent from the house of the Prophet Muhammad. The Shaykh quarter that grew around the mausoleum and its mosque was often the center of seditious politics in the seventeenth century. It had the largest concentration of sufi *tekkes* (lodges) in the city, and these might have been the primary spaces where rebellions were organized.

The quarter of Ras al-Qurayya, situated close to the market district on the southeastern bank of the Tigris, south of the Christian quarter, was the home of craftspeople working in the cloth and copper trades. The *tekke* for the Rifa'i sufi order, associated with charismatic practices of worship favored by craft corporations, as well as three mausoleums of minor saints of local significance serviced the spiritual needs of a community of merchants and craftspeople associated with the bazaars.[27] The quarter marked the southernmost end of the commercial district of Baghdad and was dominated by its main bazaars, its customs house, and the court. In its confrontations with those in power, its inhabitants were always allied with those of the Shaykh quarter from whose leaders they drew legitimacy for their rebellion.

Quarter solidarities dominated popular politics in Middle Eastern cities well into the late nineteenth century. During the early modern period, these solidarities were bolstered by the web of administrative and legal practices that invested the quarters and their leaders with abilities to represent and mediate between the quarter's inhabitants and the outside world and located each nonelite resident in the spatial grid of the city. The leader of the quarter, its *shaykh* or *kahya*, was responsible for the assessment and collection of taxes from different members of the community. Except for elite households and those belonging to the highest echelons of the Ottoman provincial bureaucracy, every urban litigant or claimant in the Islamic court identified himself or herself by his or her quarter (*mahallat*). Thus, one's legal personality, particularly for Muslims, was located spatially in one's quarter.[28] Yet this spatially constructed legal and administrative definition of Baghdadis simplified the complex web of communal interactions and spatial divisions within the quarter itself. Almost all the quarters of Baghdad, particularly on its eastern side, were divided into small, more compact communities centered on a neighborhood known as the *'aqd* (literally, a necklace, designating the enclosed space) made up of several families related to one another by kinship, geographic origin, or religious belief (particularly in areas surrounding sufi lodges). Thus, within the larger quarter there must have existed a spatial hierarchy of power and privilege defined by a multiplicity of factors such the residents of the most notable families and those with communal or religious authority along with the presence of a floating population of military men who had access to arms and allocated for themselves the function of protecting the quarter. Yet the narrative sources on violence of the period, like the court records, do not usually mention these hierarchies within the quarter. They speak of divisions in the city in the shorthand of quarter, glossing over the particular location of differences and points of tension within the quarter and lending textual stability to a changing use and meaning of space. However, by the beginning of the second half of the eighteenth century, several factors contributed to the emergence of new quarter solidarities that reflected the recalibration of hierarchies of power within the quarter and between the quarter and other sections of the city.

THE TRIBE IN THE CITY: THE "OTHER SIDE" ASCENDANT

The first period begins rather spectacularly with a plague that devastated the city in 1771–72. Abd al-Rahman al-Suwaydi, one of the leaders of the 1778 rebellion and its chronicler, begins his narrative of the rebellion with the devastation wrought on Baghdad by the plague, locating the beginning of what he calls the "Events of Baghdad and Basra" with the plague and the Persian occupation of Basra. The plague had led to the disruption of trade and the loss of qualified officials to rule the city as well as military men to subdue its countryside. Hence, when the Persian invasion came three years later, the governor of the province of Baghdad, Omar Pasha, was unable to fend off the enemy.

The 1778 rebellion came in the wake of a severe crisis in Ottoman imperial authority in Iraq accompanied by a realignment of power between different urban constituencies in the city and its tribal hinterland. Emerging from a debilitating war with Russia in 1774, the Ottoman government was unable to turn its resources to protect its eastern frontier from the twin dangers of recalcitrant tribal populations or Persian occupation. In 1774, Karim Khan, a Persian ruler based in Shiraz, occupied Basra, disrupting the flow of Indian Ocean trade into Ottoman territories and threatening the Ottoman hold over Baghdad.[29] That the prospect of a Persian occupation of *irak-i arab*, as Iraq was known to the Ottomans, was an imminent possibility was reinforced in the minds of Baghdadis and of the imperial government by a history of such attempts dating back to the seventeenth century, and ending in 1743 when the forces of Nadir Shah were repulsed at the gates of Baghdad. The rebellion took place within the context of the breakdown of state authority and the severe economic and social dislocation resulting from the Persian occupation of Basra. Although the imperial context provides the explanation of the rebellion and, as will become clear, explains the manner in which the rebels chose to articulate their claims to legitimacy, it does not explain the ways in which communal identities were constructed and deployed in the heat of the rebellion. For that we have to turn to the transformations in patterns of urbanization in the city, the emergence of new elites, and the shifts in the tribal world of southern and central Iraq in the first seventy years of the eighteenth century.

Eighteenth-century Baghdad was the provincial capital of an area that extended south to Basra, southeast to the marshes of Arabistan and northeast to the mountains of Kurdistan. Its western boundaries extended as far north as Mardin in present-day Turkey. Like many other major cities in the Middle East, it was ruled by a local political/military elite who developed their own community and monopolized the office of governor for more than a century. Drawing their legitimacy from the Ottoman state, they ruled by manipulating the different local groups, particularly the mercantile and tribal groups that had settled in the city. The politics they introduced into Baghdad, as into other cities in the Arab parts of the Ottoman Empire, has been dubbed the politics of households.[30]

In 1704, Hasan Pasha, a bureaucrat from the imperial palace, was sent to Baghdad to restore order and limit the power of the janissaries who had effective control of the machinery of local government. His son, Ahmad Pasha, proceeded to build a dynasty of provincial governors based on the recruitment of Georgian boys, purchased as slaves and attached to his households. One of his Mamluks, Sulayman Abu Layla, institutionalized the practice and created a military order as an alternative to the janissaries. Distinguished by special dress and residing mostly in the governor's compound until they married and set up separate households, the new praetorian guard became the primary administrators of the province and the beneficiaries of its largest tax farms.[31] They were, by the end of the eighteenth century, a distinct community, and Baghdadis alluded to them as the *kurj*, the Georgians, to distinguish them from soldier and Ottoman officials.[32]

As a consequence, the military regiments, the janissaries, who had the upper hand until the early eighteenth century, became increasingly disempowered.[33] Concomitant with the loss of political hegemony was the erosion of their regimental officers' monopoly of the rural and urban resources that they had controlled through tax farms.[34] While the Mamluk households and their dependents allocated the most lucrative of the urban and rural tax farms to themselves, they also channeled some of the rural resources to the mercantile and religious elite of the city. Furthermore, they contracted partnerships with merchants in Baghdad and Basra, thus cementing their ties with a wider local elite constituency. By the 1760s, it became evident to the leadership of the janissary regiments that the consolidation of Mamluk power had come at their expense and the expense of the sectors of the artisanal urban population they represented. Their conflicts with the Mamluks were particularly evident in the transition between the rule of one Mamluk governor and his successor. The janissaries had control of the main spaces of power in the city, the inner citadel where the treasury and provisions of the regiments were located, and the Maydan quarter, where they organized petitions to the central government on behalf of their own candidate. Outbreaks of violence were engineered with the support of their constituencies among the guilds closely associated with janissary monopolies, particularly the butcher's guild, and other sectors of the population who were primarily based in the northern section of the city. To maintain their acquiescence, the Mamluk elites co-opted some of the officer corps, who became part of the governing elite of the city. Despite a clear division between the officer corps and the rank and file of these regiments, the former were often able to draw on the support of the latter in times of conflict.[35]

The rise of new political elite in the city and the marginalization of the old military establishment coincided with a number of developments in the tribal landscape of southern and central Iraq and northern Arabia that had a profound impact on the political culture of the city. A tribal resurgence caused by the loss of imperial control over frontiers in the wake of three Persian invasions was accompanied by the rise of a flourishing regional economy based on the establishment of tribal market towns.[36] Hala Fattah dates the beginning of this transformation in the political economy of the tribal world of southern Iraq and central Arabia to the mideighteenth century and finds that a literary culture that stressed local and regional networks of merchants and scholars was its hallmark. While the imperatives of expanding markets played a role in the ascendance of tribal aristocracies and the articulation of a tribal regional identity, tribesmen also became part of what Kolff has called, in the Indian context, a "military labor market" in which men, organized in bands, were recruited by the Mamluk governors of Baghdad as well as by the central state, as infantry and cavalry to subdue the countryside and fight off enemies of the state.[37] The militarization of the tribal society led to the reconstitution of tribal identities. We know little about this transformation, but the 'Uqail tribe, which played an important role in the 1778 rebellion, offers the clearest example of the impact of such militarization. The men of the 'Uqail were drawn from the different tribes of Najd, in central Arabia. When they migrated as gangs of fighting men into Iraq, they lost the protection of their own tribe and were unable to return to their tribal domain. They became good soldiers, settled on the outskirts of the western part of Baghdad, created a fictive kinship, and were led by a *shaykh* appointed by the Ottoman government.[38] The Mamluk governors of Baghdad pioneered the use of this military labor market to offset the power of the janissaries.

Changes in patterns of urbanization during the first seventy years of the eighteenth century reflected the changes in the political economy of the city and its hinterland. By the second decade of the eighteenth century, the settlement of the western part of Baghdad by families claiming tribal descent either from southern Iraq or from small towns in the middle and upper Euphrates region began to change the social composition of the city. Whereas the eastern part of Baghdad had an ethnically and religiously diverse population, the western part of the city became almost exclusively inhabited by Sunni families claiming descent to one of the tribal groups of Iraq.[39] Some families migrated into the city because their agricultural lands had fallen into disuse as a result of the unsettlement of frontiers between Persia and Iraq. Others seem to have come from smaller provincial towns to establish a link with merchants centered in Baghdad and the tribal world that served as a conduit for a trade that connected Arabia to Aleppo in the north. Some, like the fictive 'Uqail tribal group, came to settle as military contingents.[40]

For the Mamluk rulers of Baghdad, the settlement of the western quarter by Arab tribal and landowning/commercial/religious elites was a mixed blessing. To deal with the tribal confederacies, the Mamluk governors created an office called the "Door of the Arabs," a title bestowed on the aristocratic al-Shawi family of the 'Ubaid tribal federation. The family settled in the quarter, and its patriarchs became the mediators between the government of Baghdad and the tribes of Ottoman Iraq. The governors soon utilized the predominance of other Sunni religious families drawn from the mid-Euphrates towns. The al-Suwaydi family was among the first to be patronized by the Mamluks, particularly when ideological threats from Shi'i Persia surfaced. Yet the relationship between the leaders of the quarter and the center of power in the northern part of the city remained troubled. At various times in the eighteenth and nineteenth centuries, the al-Shawi family attempted, often unsuccessfully, to translate its power as mediators and as leaders in the Karkh quarter into a power-sharing arrangement with the Mamluk/Ottoman elite. The other leaders of the quarter were often careful to distinguish themselves from the Mamluk/Ottoman elite.[41] They tried to remain neutral in the factional struggles going on in the eastern part of the city. They were, in the words of one of their leaders, the people of good pedigree (asl), whereas those among the Ottoman/Mamluk elite were possessors of government and good conduct, (siyasah wa adab).[42]

The emergence of new elites and the entry of the Arab/tribal/Sunni groups as political actors in Baghdad were accompanied by a transformation in the spatial politics. In addition to the settlement of the western quarter and its incorporation into the mental and political space of the city, the coffeehouse and the majlis, or literary salon, became the centers of contention. In the course of the seventeenth and eighteenth centuries, the number of coffeehouses more than doubled in the city, and the new coffeehouses were located in southern and central sections of the city, areas not infiltrated by the military communities of the northern quarter, where much of the violence of the seventeenth century was concentrated.

The coffeehouse represented a space outside the confines of the citadel, tekke, or mosque that socialized inhabitants of the quarter in ways less circumscribed by the behavioral strictures of sacred spaces. It also represented a place for various factional leaders to recruit followers, buy support, and create a mob. In Baghdad, for example, an imperial order issued to a janissary officer in 1762 called on him to control certain elements (kimsiler) who, full of seditious intent, were using coffeehouses to recruit riff-raff into his regiment for a small fee. This was something the government had repeatedly warned against in the past, and it was the main reason for the breakup of social hierarchies in the empire.[43]

Of the ten coffeehouses in Baghdad at the end of the seventeenth century, five were located in the Maydan quarter, in and around the citadel, one was near the courthouse, two near the customs house and two across the bridge on the western bank of the Tigris.[44] Clearly, these were located to service the commercial and military communities in the city, and outside of those located in the Maydan, all were on the banks of the Tigris, close to the markets. By the second decade of the nineteenth century, there were twenty-eight coffeehouses. Of these, four were located in the Maydan quarter, and four others were in the Mahdiyya quarter, dominated by the butcher's guild. More significant was the location of the remaining twenty coffeehouses. Five were on the southeastern bank of the Tigris, close to the Shaykh and Ras al-Qurayya quarters; the rest were in the middle quarters the city, sections that would become increasingly visible in the politics of Baghdad in the last decades of the eighteenth century.[45]

Whereas the coffeehouse was a secular public arena for the recruitment of followers, the *majlis* became the secular space, outside and alongside the mosque and the *tekke*, for the meetings of the civil elite of Baghdad. Held at homes of families, at times different families of the same lineage, the salons met regularly, certain families in neighborhoods hosting them on set days of the week. Like the *dhikr* (remembrance) meetings at sufi *tekkes* and mosques, they were attended by a relatively stable group of people. We have more detailed information on these salons for the first half of the nineteenth century when they seem to have become fairly widespread in many neighborhoods of Baghdad.[46] We do know, however, that as early as the first half of the eighteenth century, three families in the western side of Baghdad set up literary salons. The patriarchs of two of these families played a leadership role in the 1778 rebellion. The al-Shawis, the "Door of the Arabs," had set up at least two salons, as did the al-Suwaydis, who represented the most prominent religious scholars in the quarter.[47] Although we have no direct evidence of the kind of intellectual debates that took place in these salons, it is safe to say from the sort of literature produced by their patrons that the subjects ranged from literature and genealogy to theology and politics.[48] More important, these salons offered the civil elite an alternative to the cultural patronage of the salons of the government/military elite and played an important role in creating solidarity among the quarter's population.

Despite their integration into the economy and politics of the city, the residents of the Karkh quarter remained distinct; they were outsiders. The mental geography that mapped the new settlers' identity extended from Arabia and the Persian Gulf to the Syrian desert. Unlike the more ethnically and religiously diverse residents of the eastern part of the city, whose mental geography encompassed Persia, the Caucasus, and India, the arriviste residents of the Karkh were bound by ties of fictive or real kinship to the tribal world of market town, mid-Euphrates agricultural settlements and military bands. They occupied a liminal space between urban and rural, tribal and sedentary. Even their houses carried the stamp of their origin: poorly built and similar to the houses in rural small market towns, they were surrounded by date palms and were weakly fortified.[49] Their entry into the urban politics of Baghdad in 1778 was at first hesitant, but in the end it established their leaders for some time as arbiters of Ottoman political power in the city and allowed them to assert a distinct identity. What follows is an account of the rebellion by one of its leaders, Abd al-Rahman al-Suwaydi.[50]

The violence of 1778 lasted several months. In its initial stages it pitted the city's northern section around the Maydan, which now encompassed other quarters attached to the janissaries—such as the Mahdiyya, dominated by meat merchants and the butcher's guild, and the Qaraqol quarter, named after the night guards of the city—against the southern and southeastern quarters of Shaykh and Ras al-Qurayya. The demands of the rebels were clearly articulated. They wanted the government in Istanbul to remove the governor, Abdallah Pasha, who was mentally deficient, and his cohort, the treasurer Ajam Muhammad. The former had been unable to do anything about the Persian occupation of Basra and its disruption of trade. To make matters worse, Ajam Muhammad had confiscated the fortune of the preceding governor, distributed tax farms among his followers, and extorted merchants for money. Furthermore, Selim Efendi, the emissary sent by the government to investigate the inability of the governor of Baghdad to fight off the Persians, had purchased his position from the government, through funds provided by the Abdallah Pasha. His role was compromised by his debt to the governor and his cohort.[51]

The Shaykh and Ras al-Qurayya quarters were led by the foremost religious figure of the Qadiriyya sufi order and the Shafi'i jurisconsult. The leaders of the rebellion did not seek to overturn the either the Mamluk/ Ottoman order or challenge the legitimacy of the state. Their demands were quite specific. They wanted to put an end to corruption and to ensure that Abdallah Pasha, Selim Efendi, and Ajam Muhammad, did not submit the city to the Persians if they failed in their bid to retain power in the city. At best, the rebels wanted those three to contract a peace treaty with the Persians that would ensure they stay out of Baghdad in exchange for accepting their rule in Basra. They found that Isma'il Kahya, a leader of a faction of the Mamluk/Ottoman elite, was ready to become their leader. They asked that Selim Efendi, the Porte's emissary in Baghdad, submit their request to appoint him governor in place of Abdallah Pasha.

Selim Efendi refused to submit to the request of the rebels. Drawing on the support of the janissary officers stationed in the citadel, the governor, Ajam Muhammad, and the quarters dominated by the night guards and the butcher's guild, he proceeded to bomb the rebel's quarters. Barricades were set in the Maydan quarter, and the rebels tried to breach them. Unable to break the impasse that ensued, Isma'il Kahya appealed to Abd al-Rahman al-Suwaydi, the leading notable and religious scholar of the Karkh quarter for help. Al-Suwaydi agreed after some hesitation. Eventually, the leadership of the rebellion was shared by al-Shawi of the Karkh quarter and the leader of the Qadiri sufi order. The latter was also the *naqib al-ashraf*, a man who derived his legitimacy from the sanctity of his lineage and his leadership of the corporate group who claimed descent from the Prophet's family. What started out as a routine confrontation between the northern quarters and the southern quarters, widened to include almost all of the population of the city, its central quarters allying with the southern and western quarters. The rebels used the vocabulary of legitimate dissent, that is to say, they sought to restore just order to the city and to resolve the stand-off with Persia that had disrupted trade and compounded the misery brought by the plague. However, the spatial practices of the rebels and the representations by our informant about these practices were determined and constrained by a set of textual tropes of self and other that drew on the habitual representations of space and inverted their meaning. Thus, the quarter, in this case the Karkh, separated by the boundary of the river became the container of virtue and the upholder of legitimacy, while the Maydan, the center of Ottoman military power, became the den of iniquity and the locus of sedition. The other quarters of Baghdad, the allies of the Karkh, became appendages in a struggle that pitted the Karkh against the forces of disorder. Al-Suwaydi's description of the rebellion marked in spatial terms the practices of the rebels as they asserted their control over the agenda of the various actors.

The leaders of the rebellion coordinated the defense of barricades. They ensured that food was available to those who guarded these barricades and other parts crucial to the defense of the spaces under their control. The Shaykh and Karkh quarters were to split the amount of cooked pilaf they were to provide to the rebels. Al-Shawi himself paid the neighborhood toughs and paramilitary tribal groups settled in the northern edges of Karkh ('Uqail and Najjada) to guard certain sectors of the city, including the bridge, which was set on fire by the government's forces in order to control the flow of goods and men between the eastern and western banks of the Tigris. Moles were planted in the Maydan quarter and in Abdallah Pasha and Selim Efendi's houses. They listened closely to rumors about the evil intentions of the unjust and made sure that these rumors were circulated among their followers. Outgunned by the janissaries and the forces of the Maydan, who controlled the munitions depot as well as the cannons that sent balls flying into their neighborhood, the rebels enlisted the help of an Indian sufi, who had come to live in the mausoleum of Abd al-Qadir al-Gaylani. He had expertise in cannon and ammunitions and proceeded to help the rebels build makeshift cannons and recycle cannonballs.

The rebels and those upholding the Ottoman order expanded their use of space to include areas not used in previous confrontations. Sacred spaces were commandeered in the conflict. Locally recruited soldiers fighting on the side of the government used the minaret of Hasan Pasha mosque on the eastern bank of the river to shoot at rebels on the western side. The rebels set up barricades at the Mevlevi *tekke* near the bridge to defend their quarters. It became the green line between the rebels and the forces of the "enemy." When this barricade was breached a few weeks into the rebellion, the women of the Ras al-Qurayya and Shaykh quarters went out to the river wailing and calling on the help of the people of western Baghdad.

The pontoon bridge connecting the eastern and western quarters of the city was transformed into a battlefield for the first time. Ushering in as it did the cooperation between the eastern and western parts of the city, it became imperative for Selim Efendi's and Ajam Muhammad's forces to cut this connection. But it was also a means for the rebels to help their more embattled comrades on the other side. Particularly after the barricades at the Mevlevi *tekke* were breached, al-Shawi hired irregulars from his quarter to cross the bridge and help the other side.

The new use of old spaces became the venue for the assertion of the social power of the western quarter and its inhabitants and of the development of alliance between different spatially defined communities in Baghdad, alliances that would continue to develop over the next half century. Furthermore, the spatial politics of the rebellion helped communities construct their identities by giving spatial fixity to the "other." Al-Suwaydi's narrative of the event is biased, but it is an indication of the way identities that hitherto had been part of the group mentality became politicized and recast as communal markers. The "other" in al-Suwaydi's narrative is Selim Efendi, dubbed the Rumi, a euphemism for Turk. Al-Suwaydi used it to denote the lowly and corrupt nature of Selim, not his presence as an official. Had he intended his insult to designate the Ottomans, he would have used the term Osmani. Al-Suwaydi used the same designation to discredit the religious adviser, the *mawla bashi*, of the janissaries. The latter could barely speak Arabic, so how could he then issue *fatwas* calling the rebels unbelievers, something he had done to discredit them? But our informant's wrath was most strongly directed at Ajam Muhammad, who was not only corrupt and debauched, but also a Persian and a Shi'i and therefore a traitor to the Ottoman Sunni state. It was hard to understand, according to al-Suwaydi, how the Sunni inhabitants of the northern quarters who supported Ajam Muhammad could do so given both his sect and his ethnicity. Most prominent in al-Suwaydi's story, however, was the identity of his quarter as a bastion of Arab courage and honor, traits he associated with the tribal origins, true or fictitious, of its inhabitants. Despite the alliance of the Karkh with the southern sections of the city, they were designated as "our comrades" (*rufaqa'una*), whereas those of the western quarter were "our people" (*qawmuna*). Although the "other" in al-Suwaydi's narrative was the Turk, the Persian, the Shi'i, it was the Arabness of his quarter, its heroic and ultimately crucial stand in support of a just Ottoman order that mattered most. In this narrative, which he presented to the governor chosen by al-Shawi, he made sure that his quarter's role as a player in Baghdadi as well as imperial politics was recorded.

The rebellion marked the entry of the Karkh and its inhabitants into Baghdadi politics. It also signaled for the first time a wide popular participation across sectors of Baghdad. Unlike the bread riot or the short factional conflicts that continued to reappear in the city for some time, the rebellion was a well-orchestrated attempt at restoring what was perceived as a real threat to the city in face of Ottoman weakness and official corruption. Led by a new community in the city, it heralded a period of troubled cooperation and integration between the Ottoman/Mamluk elite and the civil and tribal leaders of various communities in the city and its tribal hinterland. Furthermore, it marked the beginning of the ideological construction of a tribal Arab identity, intimately bound, for the leadership of the Karkh quarter, with a Baghdadi identity. That this identity was in large part constructed in spatial terms that linked the quarter to the city and to its tribal hinterland had much to do with the attempts of its leading inhabitants to negotiate a place for themselves in the old spatial distribution of power in Baghdad.

IMPERIAL CONFLICTS, UTOPIA, AND THE POLITICS OF SECT
AND TRIBE, 1802–1810

Whereas the 1778–79 rebellion was marked by sustained violence and a clear articulation of demands, the two episodes of violence in 1802 and 1810 took place in a radically altered regional and international context that introduced new elements into the political equation and the spatial distribution of power both within the city itself and between it and its hinterland. Perhaps the three most significant were the spread of Wahhabi doctrine, the establishment of a Wahhabi state, and the presence of Europeans in the city. The Wahhabi state presented the Ottomans with a severe challenge to their legitimacy within Sunni space and overshadowed their perennial ideological struggle with Persian Shi'ism. Thus, southern Iraq and Baghdad were reconfigured as a new ideological and military frontier, one that needed to be controlled not only to combat Shi'ism, but also to combat challenges to the state from within its territorial boundaries. As early as 1800, the precariousness of Ottoman legitimacy in the heartland of Sunni Islam, in the holy cities of Mecca and Medina, had made the Ottomans and their British allies aware of the ways in which the new political realities were remapping the ideological and territorial order of the area. When the local ruler of Mecca and Medina was asked if he would side with the Ottomans and the British against the French in Egypt, he found that the economic ties he had with Egypt made it difficult for him to support the Sunni sultan against the infidel French.[52] The Napoleonic occupation of Egypt in 1798 and the period of global uncertainty that followed it transformed Baghdad into a strategic space for the East India Company, the French, and the Ottomans and augured a period of modern imperial discourse and control on both the European and Ottoman sides. When the representative of the East India Company in Aleppo wrote to Harford Jones, its first resident in Baghdad, that "the seeds of discord have long been beyond the limits of Europe, and it is hardly to be expected that the short span of our lives should suffice to restore even the imperfect degree of tranquility, of which we have been once spectators," he was expressing the sense of rupture in time and space that pervaded the writings of the Europeans and Ottomans.[53]

The Wahhabis spearheaded a puritanical religious/political movement inspired and led by Muhammad ibn abd al-Wahhab in mideighteenth-century Najd (Arabia). Its founder, influenced by a community of scholars centered in the holy cities of Arabia who stressed the primacy of a scripturalist interpretation of the Quran, and a strict adherence to the example *(sunna)* of the Prophet and his early followers, called for the individual interpretation of the primary texts of Islam. He rejected the accretions of a great number of legal works produced by the scholarly legal establishment that were developed in the early centuries of Islam and was adamantly opposed to all kinds of mystical practices that gave human beings the power to intercede between the individual and God.[54] By the end of the eighteenth century, Ibn abd al-Wahhab had succeeded in forging an alliance with a tribal princely kinship group, the house of Saud, and together they created a state, a political *imamate*, that threatened the legitimacy of the Ottoman state.

Wahhabis had an ambiguous impact on southern and central Iraq. What was most problematic for the community of scholars who had some sympathy for their call for reform was their insistence on declaring all those who did not follow their doctrines unbelievers, and therefore subject to attack by their forces. Those who followed sufi practices, the Shi'i, as well as religious scholars engaged in what they believed to be the sophistry of theological argumentation were not true Muslims. The politicization of religious practice, its removal from the domain of the personal to the political, together with the disdain the Wahhabis exhibited for the exegetic learning of religious scholars earned them many enemies. However, the state they set up in Najd, based on light Islamic taxes and strict adherence to law, and their management of the pilgrimage to Mecca and Medina when these had fallen to them, contrasted with the weakness and corruption of the empire and the rulers of Baghdad who were engaged in continuous disruptive factional struggles. Furthermore, the comportment of their adherents—their simple dress and the apparent artlessness and defiance of habitual rituals of secular power—provided tangible alternatives, within Islamic prescribed traditions, to the system of power created by the Mamluk/Ottoman elite.

Harford Jones, in a telling vignette, reports on a peace treaty contracted between the governor of Baghdad and the Saudi ruler of the Wahhabi state in 1798. Preparations for the conclusion of the peace treaty, which took place at the governor's palace on the banks of the Tigris, south of the Maydan quarter, were extensive. Richly adorned and flanked by hundreds of his colorful guards, the governor sat on his diwan to welcome the envoy of Ibn Saud. The envoy, barefoot and in simple white dress, entered the governor's room. The officers of the court tried, in what was the diplomatic tradition of the time, to hold the envoy's arms to assist him up the stairs. He refused their assistance, proceeded up the stairs himself, and sat himself down in front of the governor and proceeded to address him unceremoniously: "Hoy Suleiman! Peace be upon on all who think right. Abdul Aziz has sent me to deliver to you this letter, and to receive from you a ratification of an agreement made between his son, Saoud, and your servant Ally; let it be done soon, and in good form; and the curse of God be on him who acts treacherously. If ye seek instruction, Abdul Aziz will afford it."[55] The envoy's transgression of the spatial and sartorial decorum that governed the relations of power between subjects and rulers, between the tribal world of Baghdad's hinterland and the city's elite, and his insistence that the governor might seek instruction from a tribal ruler in the heart of territories hitherto associated in the minds of Baghdadis with disorder, provided a concrete utopian vision to those who had sought an alternative political order within the paradigm of Sunni orthodoxy.[56]

Wahhabism entered the political lexicon of ordinary Baghdadis in the last two decades of the eighteenth century but became a factor in local politics especially after the sack of Karbala in 1801.[57] It exacerbated Shi'i/Sunni tensions; it redefined the spatial sectional politics of a city divided between the Arab/tribal western part and the more diverse eastern part; it alerted the governors to the threat that tribal elites armed with a new ideology presented to the political order; it allowed the Ottoman government to impose a measure of administrative reform by brandishing accusations of Wahhabism against its enemies; and finally, it introduced the concept of *takfir* (declaring nonfollowers apostates) to the political lexicon of different factions in Iraq.

The Wahhabi sack of Karbala, one of the holy cities of the Shi'is, horrified the Sunni scholarly establishment, but the Wahhabi sectarian attitude toward Shi'is did find support among certain sectors of the scholarly community who were influenced by their ideas. These ideas were discussed with more intensity when one of the leading residents of the Karkh quarter converted to Wahhabism. A benefactor of the cultural elite of the city, his literary salon (*majlis*) provided the venue for intense discussions on the difference between Wahhabism and the call to an adherence to a more scriptural interpretation of Islamic practice. By the first decade of the nineteenth century, the debates on these issues had become the major topic of the different literary salons in the city.[58] Compounding the tension between sects in the city was the conscious attempt by the Wahhabis to recruit supporters among Baghdad's population. In 1801, when another treaty between the governor of Baghdad and the Wahhabis was being negotiated, the spokesman of the Wahhabis demanded that every "true Muslim," that is to say Wahhabi, residing in the governor's jurisdiction be charged only religiously sanctioned taxes and "not a penny more." According to Harford Jones, this call had great impact on the population of Baghdad, where "without so strong a temporal inducement, many have already embraced the Doctrines of the

Wa-ha-by."[59] Furthermore, the conversion of tribes in southern Iraq to Shi'-ism through the proselytizing overseen by Shi'i religious scholars in the holy cities of Najaf and Karbala compounded tensions created by the Wahhabis' exclusivist stance.[60] The polarization of the religious map of southern and middle Ottoman Iraq, characterized by the construction of religious identity as ideology, sundered the delicate balance that had existed between its various communities.

Wahhabi expansion in Iraq and Arabia threatened the trade routes that connected the Indian Ocean-Persian Gulf trade to the Mediterranean. Although the local merchants suffered most from such disruptions, the British East India Company's ships along the Persian Gulf were subject to attack by Wahhabi pirates.[61] The company sent its representative in Persia to ask the governor of Baghdad to subdue the Wahhabis. At the same time, the Napoleonic occupation of Egypt in 1798 and the threat of French expansion into India made Baghdad, for the first time, a strategically important city for the Europeans. The British in particular were visible in the ways that East India Company envoys projected their presence. Envoys were received as heads of state, their power augmented by their distribution of money to the populace lining the streets from the East India Company Residency to the government center. Flanked by Indian soldiers and dressed in distinctive clothes, the East India Company employees brought the theater of Anglo-India to Baghdad for the first time.[62] Located near the popular quarter of Ras al-Quraya on the banks of the Tigris, the British Residency in Baghdad gradually became a visible actor in the politics of the city.

The extent to which British presence in Baghdad in the late 1790s and early 1800s disrupted the balance between non-Muslim and the Muslim population is hard to gauge. In 1801, the drums and fifes that were used by the *sepoys* and guards of the Residency for morning and evening roll call had elicited the anger of the population and compelled the assistant governor to the city to discontinue the practice, as Baghdad was "a sacred city and that its inhabitants were particularly strict on the article of religion to suffer an infidel to beat a drum in his house, and this could not fail to incense the populace"[63] This incensed population could have made a connection between the infidel and its local Christian and Jewish population. During the 1802 civil war, an attack on the Jewish and Christian quarters and businesses was launched by sectors of the population for the first time. Particularly galling to the Muslim inhabitants was a rumor circulating in plague-infested Baghdad that the governor was allowing some Jewish and Christian families to flee the city while Muslims were locked in.[64]

201

It is within the context of heightened sectarian politics and the disruption wrought by the Napoleonic invasion that the violence of 1802 should be placed. Two Baghdadi witnesses, a Christian merchant and a lowly Sunni preacher in one of the mosques in eastern Baghdad, portray the conflict in ethnic or sectarian terms. However, the spatial dimensions of their narrative of the violence offer different perspectives of the meaning of the new geography of belief and identity.

The conflict was a struggle between two factions of the military/political elite over who would succeed Sulayman the Great, the deceased Mamluk governor of the city. The plague, the provincial government's mishandling of it, and the continued unrest in the countryside was compounded by the death of the governor who had brought a measure of stability to the city during his twenty-two years of rule. The governor had relied on the support of the tribal military contingents resident in the Karkh quarter and cultivated the support of the quarter's leader, Muhammad beg al-Shawi. He had effectively created an alternative center of military power situated in the Karkh quarter to counter the declining power of the janissaries in the Maydan quarter. The civil war, according to historians of the period was the last attempt by the politically weakened janissary regiments to take control of the city. It soon divided the city along spatial lines that echoed in some respects the earlier divisions. This time, however, the center of the violence was in the eastern and central parts of the city where a large Shi'i population lived and where some of the local janissary regiments with ties to the artisanal population had some support. The Karkh, the western part of the city, was involved and spoke in the name of the restoration of an Ottoman order attacked by a janissary leader, Ahmad Agha, of "dubious" ancestry and moral character. Like his predecessor, Ajam Muhammad in the 1778 rebellion, he threatened to surrender Baghdad to the Persians, who were clamoring for an end to Wahhabi attacks on Shi'i shrines.

For the Sunni preacher who wrote his sermon as a lesson in the ways of the unjust, what marked the ascendance of this particular rebel leader was the increased power of the Shi'i community in the city. Unlike the narrative of the earlier rebellion, where the enemy was conceived of as Persian and Shi'i, an imposter from outside the city, this cleric found the enemy within its fold.[65] Furthermore, the vocabulary that the preacher used to describe the various factions in the city used ethnicity as a marker of distinction. Thus, the paramilitary contingents employed by the leaders of the western quarter of Baghdad were Arabs, whereas the Mamluk faction was referred to as a *kurj*, a designation that highlights their Georgian origins. His sermon was a clear wish for a recalibration of ethnic and sectarian hierarchies established by the previous Mamluk rulers of Baghdad over the past twenty years, hierarchies that had been sundered by the civil war and by the ascendance of Shi'i as well as tribal/Arab elites and their military followers in the western quarter.

The perspective of Yusuf Aboud, the Christian merchant, was somewhat different. The struggle, he wrote, began when the Arab tribal leader of the western quarter of Baghdad and the head of the janissary regiments disagreed on the division of the power in city. What ensued was a conflict over the ascendance of the tribal/Arab elements in the western part of the city, in alliance with the Mamluk elite, and the janissary elements. No accusations of Shi'ism were leveled against the janissaries. Rather, they were accused of drunkenness and disorderly behavior. Those who ultimately suffered in this episode of violence were the Christian and Jewish merchants, whose shops were attacked first by the janissaries and then by the Arab tribal contingents fighting under the leaders of the western quarter. More significant, when order was restored and a governor chosen and installed by a consensus of the notables of Baghdad, Aboud made it clear that this was made possible only through the cooperation of the tribal Arab contingents controlled by the leaders of the western quarter.[66] In contrast to the preacher who was more interested in narrating the violence as a story of restoration of an Ottoman/Mamluk order in the city, Aboud's account was based on another mental geography of southern and central Iraq. A merchant whose connections spanned the world of tribal market towns and cities as far north as Aleppo, his description of the violence was not invested in the victory of one protagonist or the other. Rather, as an oblique commentary on the state of the chaos in the city, he offered a sympathetic description of the Wahhabi state in Arabia.[67] Its ruler, ibn Sa'ud, imposed low taxes, he established a political order with minimum distinctions between ruler and ruled, and in the areas where Wahhabi rule was effective, tribes were not allowed to raid merchant caravans. In the midst of complete breakdown of Ottoman power, when merchants like Aboud could not sell their stocks of coffee because of Napoleon's occupation of Egypt, the Wahhabi/tribal state seemed like a viable alternative to the Ottomans and their Mamluk vassals. For Aboud, protection and peace were no longer located in the city, but had migrated into the tribal world—a utopian society where security reigned, social distinctions were minimal, and low taxes were the norm.

By 1810, the Wahhabis had occupied of the holy cities of Mecca and Medina. Pilgrimage caravans coming from Ottoman territories under official Ottoman banners were prohibited. The Wahhabi utopian order, envisioned as an alternative to the Ottoman order, was now ensconced in the sacred space of Islam and offered a severe political challenge. Characterized in the official narratives and orders emanating from Istanbul as a belief system espoused by ignorant tribesmen, the government now saw the need to control this new ideological frontier by direct intervention. Despite the persistence in the official documentation of the Wahhabi space as one dominated by inherently disobedient and ignorant tribesmen, the Ottoman government now issued orders to its religious scholars to engage the doctrines of the Wahhabis and to reeducate Muslims who had fallen prey to Wahhabi propaganda.[68]

Furthermore, the Ottoman government was increasingly aware of the strategic importance of southern Iraq and Baghdad to the British and began looking at Baghdad as a new kind of frontier, one that pitted its interest as a modernizing Islamic power against the imperial interests of Britain. Baghdad, in other words, was no longer simply a sacred city, nor a bulwark against Persian Shi'ism. It was now a new kind of space, threatened by a "tribal resurgence" that derived its legitimacy from the "correct" practice of Sunni Islam, and its politics increasingly dominated by East India Company representatives who viewed it as an extension of British India. Thus, the 1810 rebellion took place within this changed regional and imperial context and had a number of new elements. The rebellion marked the first attempt by the Ottoman government to articulate a vision of Iraq (understood as encompassing central and southern areas of present Iraq) as a new kind of frontier. Halet Efendi, the Ottoman emissary to Baghdad, penned a series of reports to the central government in which Iraq and its major city, Baghdad, were now represented as a linchpin in the maintenance of an imperial space threatened by Wahhabi-infested tribal rebellions and British interests.[69] The central government's attempt at dislodging Sulayman the Little, the governor of the province, augured its first effort to map a more centralized modern empire. Sulayman the Little refused to comply with the government's orders to surrender his position. He declared a rebellion. However, rather than justify his rebellion as an attempt to redress a wrong inflicted on him by the state, he challenged the political legitimacy of the state. He issued a religious opinion (fatwa) declaring that the sultan had lost his right to rule because he was not in control of Mecca and Medina.[70] Sulayman the Little became, in the local narratives of his rebellion and his violent death at age twenty-four, a tragic figure who had tried to reform but failed, owing to the machinations of the representative of the Ottoman state and the treachery of his supporters. He had, according to some of these narratives, been successful in winning the support of the scholarly community, particularly the Sunni reformist one, and of the local civilian elite.

When the rebellious governor was killed in 1810, his tenure in Baghdad was described by Ibn Sanad al-Basri in this manner:

> When Sulayman the killed (*al-qatil*) took over Baghdad he followed a good path and ruled it according to the *salaf* (the early Muslim community) in belief. And he shunned injustice. He was interested in the arts of *hadith* and he disallowed those that were not accepted and made sure that they conformed to *shari'a*. He prohibited tax collectors from taking *ushr* (a land tax sanctioned by Ottoman law) taxes, and gave them a monthly salary from *bayt al-mal* (treasury). He was particularly liked by the *ulama* and the one who was in his favor was Ali ibn Muhammad al-Suwaydi, known for *hadith* studies. He read *hadith* in a number of meetings. When he became aadviser (*sadr*) to Sulayman he became even more modest.[71]

Finally, despite the reformist measures undertaken by the deposed governor, his program appears to have been espoused by limited sectors of the civilian population. He lived in the narratives of the Sunni local literati as an example of the fate of ambitious governors who defy the state's orders. However, the circumstance surrounding his rebellion and the vocabulary he chose to gain legitimacy for his challenge of the state's prerogatives, demonstrate the radical shift in the configuration of local and imperial politics between 1778 and 1810.

Conclusion

I have argued that the forging of new political identities in eighteenth- and early-nineteenth-century Baghdad involved the reconstruction of embedded mentalities such as tribe, sect, and religion into ideological communities. These ideological communities were forged through spatial practices and representations of the spaces of the city and the tribal world of which it was part. These identities developed in the context of imperial breakdown and shifts in the economic, political, and ideological realities of southern and central Iraq. Particularly during periods of violence, Baghdadi political culture became increasingly polarized around ethnic and religious identities. Whereas the seventeenth-century narratives of rebellions rarely mention ethnic or religious communities as repositories of virtue or corruption, the narratives of the eighteenth and early nineteenth centuries do. The articulation of the "Shi'i" as an "other" became more prominent when Wahhabi doctrines began to have some followers among the tribal and Sunni elites quartered in Karkh. At the same time, the ethnic distinctions of Arabness became a more important factor in the politics of Baghdad. Despite the fluidity of these communal identities in everyday spatial practices, they acquired stability during periods of violence. To paraphrase E. P. Thompson's characterization of class, an identity is "not a thing . . . it is a happening."[72]

The transformation of the spatial politics of the city reflected the interests of an emerging land-owning tribal elite allied with the older mercantile and religious groups in the older sections of the city. The alliance between these two groups reached its heyday in the early nineteenth century and was cemented in literary salons and marriages between these two groups. The spectacular performance of this land-owning/tribal/Sunni elite during the rebellion marked their entry into the commercial and religious establishment of Baghdad, as it did into the Ottoman official politics of the city, which were centered in its northern sections. The expansion in spaces of contention meant that a wider sector of the population had a stake in challenging or supporting Ottoman rule or its local representatives. Whether they challenged it or spoke in its name, the vocabulary they used in expressing their dissent and the spaces they used to mobilize and challenge it, were integrated into a larger Ottoman domain in a way they had not been in the seventeenth century.

Finally, Baghdad and Iraq became conceptualized as a different kind of space by the Ottoman imperial government and the British. It was now a frontier of a different kind, one that bound the interests of two modernizing empires. For the Ottomans, Baghdad's sacred history and its position as a frontier against the Persians was less significant than its position as a contested space, a frontier, between visions of reform within the abode of Sunni Islam.

Notes

Research for this chapter was supported by grants from the American Research Institute in Turkey, the National Endowment for the Humanities, and the American Council of Learned Societies.

1. C. A. Bayly, *The Birth of the Modern World, 1780–1914* (Oxford: Blackwell, 2004), 27–49.

2. Ussama Makdisi, *The Culture of Sectarianism, Community, History, and Violence in Nineteenth-Century Ottoman Lebanon* (Berkeley: University of California Press, 2000).

3. See Doug McAdam, Sidney Tarrow, and Charles Tilly, *Dynamics of Contention*, particularly "What Are They Shouting About?" (Cambridge: Cambridge University Press, 2001), 3–37; and Sidney Tarrow, "The People's Two Rhythms:

Charles Tilly and the Study of Contentious Politics. A Review Article," *Comparative Studies in Society and History* 38 (1996): 586–600. For the Middle East, see Madeline Zilfi, "The Kadizadelis: Discordant Revivalism in Seventeenth-Century Istanbul," *Near Eastern Studies* 95, no. 4 (1986): 251–69. Soraiya Faroqhi, *Coping with the State, Political Conflict and Crime in the Ottoman Empire, 1550–1720* (Istanbul: ISIS Press, 1995); and Karen Barkey, *Bandits and Bureaucrats, the Ottoman Route to State Centralization* (Ithaca, N.Y.: Cornell University Press, 1994) focus on the state as an agent of oppression and co-option of rebels and criminals—in stark contrast to their counterparts who study rebellions in from within the "urban studies" perspective and focus on factional and communal mobilization within an urban space in which the state has little impact and urban actors and identities are paramount. See André Raymond, "Une révolution au Caire sous les Mamouks: La crise de 1123/ 1711," and "Quartier et mouvements populaires au Caire au XVIIIème siècle," in P. M. Holt, ed., *Political and Social Change in Modern Egypt*, (London: Oxford University Press, 1968), 104–16. For Palestine, see Adel Manna', "Eighteenth- and Nineteenth-Century Rebellions in Palestine," *Journal of Palestine Studies* 24 (1994): 51–66; and Mina Rosen, "The Naqib al-Ashraf Rebellion in Jerusalem and Its Repercussions on the City's Dhimmis," in *Asian and African Studies*, 18 (1984): 249–70. For Aleppo, see Abraham Marcus, *The Middle East on the Eve of Modernity, Aleppo in the Eighteenth Century* (New York: Columbia University Press, 1989).

4. See, for example, James Grehan, "Street Violence and Social Imagination in Late Mamluk and Ottoman Damascus (ca. 1500–1800)," *International Journal of Middle East Studies* 35 (2003): 215–36.

5. See Makdisi, *The Culture of Sectarianism*, 28–50 for an insightful description of such history writing. In chronicles of violence in Baghdad, binary moral and religious categories—of good and evil, ignorant and learned, just and unjust, legitimate and illegitimate, heretic and believer—appeared to describe rebels and the rabble in times of great disruption only to disappear in describing these populations when order was restored. I shall come back to this point a little later in this chapter.

6. David Nirenberg, *Communities of Violence: Persecution of Minorities in the Middle Ages* (Princeton, N.J.: Princeton University Press, 1996), 228.

7. William Sewell, "Space in Contentious Politics," in Ronald R. Aminzade et al., eds., *Silence and Voice in the Study of Contentious Politics* (Cambridge: Cambridge University Press, 2001), 52–88.

8. David Harvey, *The Condition of Post-Modernity: An Inquiry into the Origins of Cultural Change* (Cambridge: Basil Blackwell, 1990), 227.

9. See Sandra Freitag, *Collective Action and Community* (Berkeley: University of California Press, 1989), for the relationship of the construction of ideological communities and collective action in public spaces in India.

10. Abbas al-Azzawi, *Tarikh al-Iraq bayn Ihtilalayn* (Baghdad: al-Matba'at al-Ahliyyah, 1939), 4:165–236.

11. Nasuh-Silahi Matrakci, *Beyan-i Menazil-i Sefer-I Irakeyn-i Sultan Suleyman Khan* (Ankara: Turk Tarih Kurumu Basimivi, 1976).

12. Evliya Çelebi, *Seyahatname* (Istanbul: Iqdam Matbasi, 1898), 4:393–432. The author recounts how the lost body of Abu Hanifa was found and given a proper burial place when Suleiman the Magnificent came.

13. Ahmad bin Abdallah al-Baghdadi Ghurabzade, " 'Uyun al-akhbar al-'ayan bi man fi salif al-'asr wa al-zaman," British Library, ADD 23309/I. The Mevlevi *tekke*, situated between the bridge and the customs house on the river, became by the end of the sixteenth century a magnet to a literate, Ottomanized Baghdadi elite that contributed to the rich calligraphic, miniature, and poetic Ottoman tradition. See Rachel Milstein, *Miniature Painting in Ottoman Baghdad* (Costa Mesa, Calif.: Mazda Press, 1990).

14. Evliya Çelebi, *Seyahatname*, 4: 396–432. Pedro Teixeira, *The Travels of Pedro Teixeira with His "Kings of Hormuz," and Extracts from His "Kings of Persia,"* trans. and ann. William Sinclair (London: Hakluyt Society, 1902), 63.

15. According to Teixeira, who visited Baghdad in 1603, the city's military regiments constituted 14,000 men, mostly "Turks" from other nations. About 4,000 to 5,000 lived in the city, of which 1,500 were imperial janissaries (*kapi kul*). At the end of the seventeenth century, one document states that there were 5,122 imperial janissaries stationed in Baghdad, of which 3,629 were stationed in the ammunition depot and the citadel that surrounds it (*uç kale*). Başbakanlik Osmanli Arşivi (BOA), Istanbul, Bab-ı defteri, Baş Muhasebe, #40885). By 1699, mobilization of troops to fight tribal insurgents called for the upkeep of some 10,629 troops (*sirdengectis*). BOA, Bab-ı Defteri, Baş Muhasebe, #40885.

16. The figures for imperial janissary regiments (*kapi kul*) stationed in Baghdad in the seventeenth century varies according to documents. Estimates range from three thousand to more than five thousand, depending on mobilization and funding. Members of these regiments rotated between fortresses on the eastern frontiers of the empire. BOA, Bab-ı defteri, Yeniceri Kalemi, #33817 (for the year 1641), #33862 (for the year 1657). For funding of these imperial janissaries in 1693, see BOA, Maliyeden Müdevver, #4396. *Tax farms* are revenues accruing to the government through the sale or assignment to individuals of tax collection rights. By the mid-eighteenth century, Ives estimated that there were forty thousand janissaries, many of them tradesmen and presumably drawn from the local population. They were almost impossible to mobilize in war. They "enjoy many privileges over other subjects, occasionally wear a special cloak and at the bazaars and markets they purchase duty free most commodities. They are never punished for, a crime in public." Edward Ives, *A Voyage from England to India in the year MDCCLIV, and A Journey from Persia to England by Unusual Route* (London: Edward and Charles Dilly, 1773); 2:284.

17. Evliya Çelebi, *Seyahatname*, 4, 393–432.

18. BOA, Mühimme 78–253-3, 78–697-2, 79–364-2. All these orders were issued in the first years of the seventeenth century during an uprising headed by a local strongman.

19. Thomas Lier, *Haushalte und Haushaltspolitik in Bagdad 1704–1831* (Wurzburg: Ergon Verlag), 21–32.

20. Evliya Çelebi, *Seyahatname*, 4:400–420.

21. Leslie Peirce, *Morality Tales, Law and Gender in the Ottoman Court of Aintab* (Berkeley: University of California Press, 2004); and Bogac Ergene, *Local Court, Provincial Society and Justice in the Ottoman Empire* (Leiden: Brill, 2003) are among the latest monographs examining the Ottoman court system.

22. Teixeira, T*he Travels of Pedro Teixeira*, mentioned three thousand inhabited houses as opposed to twenty thousand in the eastern part of the city.

23. Murtaza Nazmizadeh Efendi, "Menakib-i merakid-i ziyaretina enbiya ve evliya bagdat'," Suleymaniye Kütüphanesi, Bagdatli Vehbi #1259; and Imad Abd al-Salam Ra'uf, *Ma'alim Baghdad fi al-qurun al-muta'akhirah fi daw' al-waqfiyat wa al-I'lamat wa al-hujaja al-shar'iyah al-mahfuzah fi arshif wizarat al-awqaf bi-Baghdad* (Baghdad: Bayt al-Hikmah, 2000). The author lists mosques, *tekkes*, coffeehouses, and their endowments based on endowment and court records kept in the Waqf archives in Baghdad.

24. Ra'uf, *Ma'alim Baghdad*, 108–9.

25. Evliya Çelebi, *Seyahatname*, 4:428–29.

26. Teixeira, *The Travels of Pedro Teixeira*, p. 65 for a report from the early seventeenth century; and James Fraser, *On the Present Condition of the Pachalik of Baghdad, and the Means It Possesses of Renovation and Improvement*, British Library, L/P&S/9/98, for an 1834 view of Baghdad and its diverse population.

27. Ra'uf, *Ma'alim Baghdad*.

28. Dina Rizk Khoury, "Slippers at the Door or Behind Closed Doors: Domestic and Public Spaces for Mosuli Women," in Madeline Zilfi, ed., *Women in the Ottoman Empire, Middle Eastern Women in the Early Modern Era* (Leiden: Brill, 1997), 105–27.

29. For the disruptive impact of this Persian occupation on the trade in Basra, see Thabit Abdullah, *Merchants, Mamluks and Murder: The Political Economy of Trade in Eighteenth-Century Basra* (Albany: State University of New York Press, 2001).

30. See Jane Hathaway, *The Politics of Households in Ottoman Egypt: The Rise of the Qazdaglis* (Cambridge: Cambridge University Press, 1997). For Mosul, see Dina Rizk Khoury, *State and Provincial Society in the Ottoman Empire, Mosul 1540–1834* (Cambridge: Cambridge University Press, 1997); and Tom Nieuwenhuis, *Politics and Society in Early Modern Iraq: Mamluk Pashas, Tribal Shayks and Local Rule between 1802 and 1831* (The Hague: Martinus Nijhoff, 1981). More recently, for Baghdad, Thomas Lier has applied the model of politics of the household to the Mamluks who ruled Baghdad for a nearly a century. Lier, *Haushalte und Haushaltspolitik in Bahdad*.

31. Adila Khatun, the wife of the first Mamluk ruler of Baghdad is said to have ordered all his supporters among both the military and civilian population to wear a special headdress. Imad Abd al-Salam Ra'uf, *Adila Khatun: Safha fi tarikh al-Iraq* (Baghdad: Maktabat Jawad, 1997).

32. Abd al-Rahman al-Suwaydi, *Hadiqat al-zawra' fi sirat al-wuzara'*, ed. Safa' al-Khulusi (Baghdad: Matba'at al-za'im, 1962), vols. 1 and 2. Rasul al-Kirkuli, *Da-*

what al-wuzara' fi tarikh waqai' Baghdad al-zawra', trans. Musa Kadhim Nawras (Beirut: Dar al-Kitab al-Arabi, n.d.).

33. The janissaries suffered a reduction in their numbers. In the year 1776–77, the list of janissaries supplied with meat and goods by the tax farm of Baghdad numbered 4,482 (BOA, Baş Muhasebe Kalemi, #41429), whereas in 1790 the number was down to 2,586 (BOA, Baş Muhasebe Kalemi, #5961). These numbers are at best rough estimates. They might reflect only the number of janissaries provided for in one provisioning cycle, usually three months. They should be used with caution.

34. Lier, *Haushalte und Haushaltspolitik in Baghdad*, 64–113.

35. The officers, known as *aghas*, intermarried with the children of Mamluk elite and with those of the civil elite. By the beginning of the eighteenth century, they had become part of the literary and commercial life of the civil elite of eastern Baghdad. See Abd al-Rahman Hilmi al-Suhrawardi, *Buyutat Baghdad fi alqarn al-thalith 'ashar*, ed. Imad Abd al-Salam Ra'uf (Baghdad: Maktab Jawad, 1990).

36. C. A. Bayly, "India and West Asia, c. 1700–1830," *Asian Affairs* 19 (1988): 3–19, finds that Nadir Shah's invasion of north India and Iraq in the first half of the eighteenth century severely strained the Ottoman and Mughal imperial states, and allowed tribal bands, often recruited as military contingents to become feudatories, creating their own mini-states on the edges of empires. Hala Fattah carries Bayly's argument a bit further by positing that Arab tribal populations established flourishing commercial towns and mini-states that were based on trade in horses, coffee, and grain. Their chroniclers expressed a sense of regional identity that was distinctly Arab and non-Ottoman. See Hala Fattah, *The Politics of Regional Trade in Iraq, Arabia and the Gulf, 1745–1900* (Albany: State University of New York Press, 1997).

37. Dirk Kolff, *Naukar, Rajput and Sepoy: The Military Labor Market of Hindustan, 1450–1850* (Cambridge: Cambridge University Press, 1990). A late-eighteenth-century estimate places the number of standing forces of the governor at about thirteen thousand (including janissaries, irregular forces, and Mamlukso, whereas tribal cavalry and infantry that could be mobilized by the ruler could climb up to forty thousand men. See Abd al-Aziz al-Nawwar, *Dawud Basha wali Baghdad* (Cairo: Dar al-Kitab al-Arabi, 1967) 307–8. The Ottomans called on the governors of Baghdad and other provinces of what is now Iraq to mobilize tribal infantry to fight the Persians. See, for example, a series of orders sent to Omar Pasha, then governor of Baghdad, as well as leaders of Amadiye, Cizre, and Mardin, between January and October 1776, in which the government called for the mobilization of Kurdish and Arab tribes, some two thousand to six thousand men to fight off the Persians in Basra and subdue other tribes. See BOA, Şikayet defterleri, 189–94–269, 189–106–296, and 189–136–359. Jean Baptiste Louis Rousseau, *Description du Pachalik de Bagdad* (Paris: Treuttel et Wurtz, 1809), 28–29, puts the number of all military forces in the employ of the governor in 1807 at thirty thousand.

38. Abd al-Karim al-Ghani Ibrahim *Najdiyun wara' al-hudud, al-'Uqaylat* (London: al-Saqi Press, 1991), 68–79.

39. Evliya Çelebi, who visited Baghdad in 1656, commented on the ethnic diversity of the city's population as well as the predominance of shi'a among its commercial and artisanal classes. European travelers—starting with Tavernier in the midseventeenth century to Niebuhr in the eighteenth—continued to comment on the ethnic and religious diversity of the eastern part of Baghdad, where Turkish, Arabic, Persian, and Urdu were spoken.

40. The development of the Karkh quarter as an area of settlement for families of Arab/tribal ancestry is attributed to Abd Allah al-Suwaydi, who as a religious scholar of modest means settled in the northern part of the west bank near the mausoleum of Khidr Elias sometime in the 1720s. See Imad Abd al-Salam Ra'uf, *Abd Allah al-Suwaydi, siratahu wa rihlatuhu* (Baghdad: Dar al-Tiba'a wa al-Nashr, 1988), 20. Other families such as the al-Shawis, the Ghannams of the Shammar tribe, the Duris, and the Jubur settled in the quarter.

41. The best description in English of the conflict between the al-Shawis and the can be found in Tom Nieuwenhuis, *Politics and Society in Early Modern Iraq*, 46–107. A biographical dictionary of the most important civilian families in Baghdad in the early eighteenth century provides a fairly clear picture of the ethnic divisions between the western and eastern quarter. Whereas the civil elite residing in the eastern quarter were drawn from Kurdish, Ottoman/Turkish, central Asian, and Arab families, those on the western side were dominated by families of Arab tribal descent. See al-Suhrawardi, *Buyutat Baghdad*, 114–15.

42. In his description of a particularly "debauched" claimant to political power, Abd al-Rahman al-Suwaydi describes him as being without pedigree (*asl*), without the capacity to know what is acceptable and what is not (*adab*), and without *siyasa* (the ability to rule through experience and moderation). Abd al-Rahman al-Suwaydi, *Tarikh hawadith Baghdad wa al-Basra*, ed. Imad Abd al-Salam Ra'uf (Baghdad: Wizarat al-Thaqafah wa al-Funun, 1978), 65.

43. BOA, Mühimme defteleri, 162–456–3.

44. Drawn from Imad Abd al-Salam Ra'uf, *Ma'alim Baghdad*; and Ya'qub Sarkis, *Mabahith Iraqiya* (Baghdad: Shrikat al-Tijara wa Tiba'a al-Mahdudah, 1948), 2:180–95.

45. Imad Abd al-Salam Ra'uf, *Ma'alim Baghdad*.

46. Al-Suhrawardi, *Buyutat Baghadad*, records the salons of the civil-elite in the eastern section of the city, mentioning primarily the salons of the most prominent families in the western quarter. See also Ibrahim al-Durubi, *Al-Baghdadiyun, akhbaruhum wa majalisuhum* (Baghdad: Matba'at al-Rabitah, 1958). For the role of the salon in Cairo, see Peter Gran, *The Islamic Roots of Capitalism: Egypt 1760–1840* (Syracuse, N.Y.: Syracuse University Press, 1998); and more recently, Nelly Hanna, *In Praise of Books: A Cultural History of Cairo's Middle Class, Sixteenth to Eighteenth Centuries* (Syracuse, N.Y.: Syracuse University Press, 2003).

47. See al-Suhrawardi, *Buyutat Baghdad*, 114, for the al-Shawis, and Ra'uf, *Abd Allah al-Suwaydi*, 27–28.

48. The al-Suwaydis were the propagators in Baghdad of a particular brand of reformed Islam associated with a more scripturalist reading of foundational texts. Various members of the family produced treatises on reform of sufi orders, on tribal genealogies, on poetry, and on a particular brand of Islamic literature called *maqamat*. The al-Shawis were scholars and poets as well as tribal leaders.

49. Rousseau, *Description du Pachalik de Baghdad*, 5.

50. Al-Suwaydi, *Tarikh hawadith Baghdad wa al-Basra*. For a good description of the rebellion in English, see Nieuwenhuis, *Politics and Society in Early Modern Iraq*, 63–71.

51. BOA, Cevdet Dahiliye, #2306.

52. British Library, OIOC/IOR/H/Misc.474, pp. 108–12.

53. British Library, OIOC/IOR/H/Misc.478, letter from Barker to Harford Jones, 200.

54. The literature on the Wahhabis is voluminous. For a brief and succinct discussion on the connections of ibn abd al-Wahhab to other reformist Hadith scholars in Mecca and Medina, see John Voll, "Muhammad Hayya al-Sindi and Muhammad ibn abd al-Wahhab: An Analysis of an Intellectual Group in Eighteenth-Century Medina," *Bulletin of the School of Oriental and African Studies* 38, no. 1 (1974): 32–39. For an analysis of the social and political background of the Wahhabi movement in Najd and Iraq, see Hala Fattah, *The Politics of Regional Trade* (Albany: State University of New York Press, 1997).

55. Harford Jones Brydges, *An Account of the Transactions of His Majesty's Mission to the Court of Persia in the Years 1807–1811 to Which is Appended A Brief History of the Wahauby's* (London: James Bohn, 1834), 2:26.

56. This is evident in the description of the Wahhabi state by a Christian merchant, Yusuf Aboud. See "Laqt al-mafqud fi athar aal Aboud," in Yaqub Sarkis, *Mabahith Iraqiya* (Baghdad: Sharikat al-Tiba'ah al-Mahdudah, 1948), 1:53.

57. Wahhabi forces had been attacking market towns in southern Iraq as early as the 1750s. In 1788, an emissary of the Wahhabis requested a debate with a religious scholar in Baghdad who was to be appointed by its governor to discuss matters of Wahhabi dogma. See "Commentary on a Book in Refutation of the Wahhabis, Being an Answer to Certain Questions Which the Wazir Suleiman Sent to the Author," Cambridge University Library, Or. 738. The manuscript is untitled and unattributed and dated 1203/1788. I have not had a chance to read the printed response of Sulayman ibn Abd al-Wahhab, *Tawhid al-Khallaq fi Jawab Ahl al-Iraq* (Cairo: al-Matba'a al-Sharqiyya, 1804–5). The manuscript, although devoted in large part to the Wahhabi responses, appears to have been written by an Iraqi scholar rather than by the son of Ibn Abd al-Wahhab. For the Shi'i perspective on this raid, see Meir Litvak, *Shi'i Scholars of Nineteenth Century Iraq: The 'Ulama of Najaf and Karbala* (Cambridge: Cambridge University Press, 1998), 1,201–26. The first Ottoman document that expresses awareness of the Wahhabis as presenting a doctrinal, albeit at that time, limited challenge is dated 1776. Orders for Sulayman Pasha, the governor of Baghdad, to deal with the Wahhabis were issued at several points before their sack

of Karbala. However, he was unable to deal with them. For a discussion of the impact of the ways in which the Ottoman government dealt with the Wahhabi challenge in Iraq and the response of its local literati, see Dina Rizk Khoury, "Who Is a True Muslim? Exclusion and Inclusion among Polemicists of Reform in Nineteenth-Century Baghdad," in Virginia Aksan and Daniel Goffman, eds., *The Early Modern Ottomans: Remapping the Empire* (Cambridge: Cambridge University Press, 2007).

58. 'Uthman Ibn Sanad al-Basri, "Matali' al-su'ud fi akhbar al-wali Dawud," Suleymaniye Kütüphanesi, Bagdatli Vehbi #1116 29–33.

59. British Library, OIOC/IOR/L/P7S/9/6, 174b.

60. Yitzhak Nakash, *The Shi'is of Iraq* (Princeton, N.J.: Princeton University Press, 1994), 13–48.

61. Fattah, *The Politics of Regional Trade*, 91–122.

62. See "Laqt al-mafqud fi athar aal Aboud," 1: 45–64.

63. British Library, OIOC/IOR/H/Misc.474, 209.

64. British Library, OIOC/IOR/L/P7&s/6, 217.

65. Anonymous, "Nuskha fi ma hadatha fi akhbar al-buwash," Landberg Library, Yale University, #616.

66. "Laqt al-mafqud fi athaar aal Aboud," 1:53–59.

67. This reaction to the Wahhabis by Jews and Christians of Baghdad is further reinforced by a Jewish merchant who reported to Claudius James Rich that his caravan was raided by Wahhabis, but that they let him go when they found out that he was Jewish. Their quarrel, they said, was with those "non-muslims" within their faith. Claudius James Rich, Journal, British Library, OIOC/MSS/EUR/A13, p. 11.

68. Khoury, "Who Is a True Muslim?"

69. BOA, Hatt-i Humayun, #20296 and Lier, *Haushalte und Haushaltspolitik in Baghdad*.

70. Claudius James Rich, "Account of the Revolution of Baghdad in 1810," British Library, IOIC, MSS. EUR. D. 30, 1–16. Rich, the East India Company Resident in Baghdad, played the role of intermediary between Sulayman the Little and Halet Efendi. He was consulted by Halet Efendi over his preferred choice of a successor to the deposed governor.

71. Al-Basri, "Matali' al-su'ud," 40.

72. E. P. Thompson, *The Making of the English Working Class* (New York: Vintage Books, 1966), 10.

CHAPTER 6

From the Lettered City to the Sellers' City: Vendor Politics and Public Space in Urban Mexico, 1880–1926

CHRISTINA M. JIMÉNEZ

ENTERING THE LETTERED CITY: PETITIONS, PEDDLERS, AND PUBLIC SCRIBES

In *The Lettered City*, Angel Rama suggests that in Latin American societies writing was "so revered as to take on an aura of sacredness."[1] The proliferation of legal codes, municipal ordinances, and regulatory laws through the nineteenth century increasingly codified acceptable behaviors, practices, and standards in modernizing cities. Codes and regulations exemplify how the "prestige of writing and other symbolic languages" represented primary mechanisms for the exercise of power in Latin America.[2] Tracing the prestige of writing back to the colonial period, Rama argues that because writing was solely the domain of the *letrados* (educated middle- and upper-class bureaucrats and lawyers), power was concentrated in their hands, reifying the elitist and hierarchical aspects of political power in Latin America, and creating a perpetual "distance" between the literate, educated *letrados* and "the rest of society." Rama concludes: "it was this distance—that separated the written from the spoken word, the rigidity of letters from the fluidity of speech—that reserved the manipulation of legal protocols to the tiny group of letrados."[3] Although writing certainly formed a central mechanism for the dissemination of power and order, as Rama describes, learned and literate men were *not* the only people who had access to it.

Contrary to ideas about the state- or elite-centered nature of writing, the political sphere, and the construction of citizenship, in this essay I describe how poor, working, and even illiterate men and women in the Mexican provincial city of Morelia, Michoacán, generated a dialogue with local authorities about their rights to public space and political claims through letters and collective petitions. Thousands of letters sent between city residents and urban authorities illustrate how a wide range of urban dwellers actively exchanged ideas with state officials about their different visions of the city and urban life. By circumscribing "politics" to the realm of the ballot box, the newspaper, the trade guild, the political party, the riot, or the salon, scholars often overlook how everyday petitioning between subjects/citizens and the state, often mandated by state-generated regulations, constituted an accessible and legitimate form of political engagement for popular groups.

Granted, petitioning authorities had been a part of the repertoire of political action for indigenous communities and other subaltern groups in Latin America since the early colonial period.[4] However, in the mid- to late-nineteenth century, the proliferation of municipal and state codes generated countless new everyday moments/events when residents had to correspond with the state to establish micro-contracts under the liberal regime about their rights, obligations, behavior, and appearances. These legal protocols *required* residents to write to the city council or state government in order to secure official permission—often including the purchase of a "license"—before embarking on numerous activities in the city. Licenses were required to sell in public places, change the facade of a house, make improvements to household pipes, cut down trees, post flyers, and put on a theatrical drama or bullfight. Although regulations, at times, constrained and compromised private interests, they compelled residents to write to authorities and, conversely, obligated local authorities to respond, which they often did. Moreover, petitioners regularly cited article 7 of the 1857 constitution which guaranteed the "right to petition authorities and to get a response," a central tenet of liberal representative government. Extended dialogues between the city council and city residents often ensued as each side negotiated and debated the terms of a particular permit or license. Although many petitions have a similar format, these letters were not just mundane, formulaic exchanges. Rather, residents often used a basic letter of request as a platform to ask for additional concessions from the city council or to inform authorities about other problems in their neighborhood, ranging from police abuses to sewer spills. Similarly, the city council tailored its responses to each petitioner, often noting that an on-site inspection had been made of the area in question before the writing of its response. In these exchanges, residents argued about their rights, often holding authorities accountable to protect their right to conduct commerce freely in public space.

If mandated urban regulations served as the pretext for popular petitions to local authorities, public scribes provided a means for nonelite residents to access the "lettered city." With the help of a public scribe or literate friend or neighbor, even illiterate residents could correspond with authorities about legal protocols, often negotiating the terms of any given license. Owing to the very low literacy rate of the Mexican population in this period (estimated at minimally 85 percent illiterate), many of the letters sent to the city council were written through a literate third party.[5] These petitions raise an important interpretative issue. Public scribes usually worked at an open table in the main markets or along central avenues of the city. For a few cents, illiterate city residents could hire a scribe to write or read their correspondence.[6] Much of the documentation that we historians use to write about nonelite actors forces us to rely on sources generated through secondary actors, like scribes or notaries. Public scribes were very different from registered notaries, however. Scribes served poorer and working-class residents; they did not preserve documentation of their work; they were often regulated only minimally, if at all; they left no official acknowledgment of their work on the letters they transcribed; and there are few historical records of public scribes in nineteenth- and early-twentieth-century Mexico. Thus, we know little about their level of education, social backgrounds, or daily functions. Although the public depended on literate neighbors, patrons, or scribes to engage authorities in written correspondence, through their petitioning a wide range of city dwellers entered a dialogue and discussed politics in their letters, thus entering the Lettered City.

Examining how everyday petitioning about city space and its regulation generated opportunities for popular groups' insertion into urban politics is particularly relevant given the limits of political citizenship during this period. During these decades, nonelite urban Mexicans are often depicted as political actors only when they were protesting government or industry, thus reinforcing the characterization of an unruly mass of reactive, passive, or manipulated lower classes. By requiring residents to write to authorities for official approval of various urban activities, municipal regulations served to reinforce the political relationship and, as I argue elsewhere, an urban moral economy between city dwellers and city authorities.[7] Although writing may be the "handmaiden of bureaucracy" and thus of the power of the state wielded through it, one historian astutely observes that "writing must, at the same time, be viewed as a means for ordinary people to practice their citizenship."[8] In the context of turn-of-the-century Mexico, corresponding with authorities through petitions opened a critical space for popular political engagement to a majority of the Mexicans who were not granted the right to vote under the 1857 constitution because they were not included in the definition of "Mexican citizen."

All Mexican nationals were guaranteed the rights outlined in the 1857 constitution, but the right to vote was not a constitutional right for all Mexicans. In contrast, Mexican "citizens" were individuals who qualified as

"Mexicans," and who were also at least eighteen years old if married, or at least twenty-one years old if single, and who "possessed an honest way of making a living."[9] Mexican citizens had similar obligations as Mexican nationals, but they were given the right to vote, the right to engage in formal politics, and the duty of serving local governments, all rights denied to noncitizen Mexicans. This distinction extended nationality and constitutional protections to all Mexicans, but reserved the right to vote only for those males who qualified as "citizens." Significantly, the 1917 constitution perpetuated this legal requirement of citizenship in article 34. I suspect that the importance of demonstrating an honorable reputation and "honorable occupation" for vendors and other working-class men was directly linked to the subjective requirement that "citizens" possess an "honest occupation." Moreover, the right to petition authorities and the right to free trade enabled urban vendors to legitimate their occupations as "honest" by gaining the approval of the municipal council for their businesses and by contributing to municipal coffers with their monthly vending fees.[10] Given these political limitations, the dialogue between popular residents and local authorities that resulted from popular petitioning and regulation requirements represented a primary method for women and other noncitizen Mexicans to engage in the political process.[11]

Through this analysis of the communications between street vendors and the political elite of Morelia, I argue that certain aspects of urban politics during the *Porfiriato* contributed to the dynamics of Mexican politics and state-society relations in the postrevolutionary era. This interpretation suggests how several overlapping, yet seemingly contradictory, conclusions about the *Porfiriato* (1876–1910), the Mexican Revolution (1910–1920), and the consolidation of the postrevolutionary state (1920s and 1930s) could be reconciled. In short, this research indicates that urban residents were able to secure many vital concessions or protections from local authorities during the *Porfiriato*. In the 1880s, for instance, public sellers effectively embedded themselves and their businesses in central public spaces of the city, arguing for their own contributions to the aesthetics of urban modernity, local commerce, and consumer culture. Although arguments based on aesthetics, public health, and public morality increasingly were used against poorer vendors after 1890, vendors continued to negotiate with government officials, employing vertical and horizontal networks to defend their claims to city spaces. Informal social networks formed on the streets of the city laid a vital foundation for the subsequent organization of vendors into unions, as well as for the effective vendor politics that emerged after 1917.

Notably, the post-1917 revolutionary government in Morelia granted vendors concessions and protections from the state, including the right to sell in the informal economy and, conversely, access to affordable consumer goods, as well as recourse to the state government through group organizations, such as unions. These concessions are often presented as the positive "outcomes" of the Mexican Revolution and are thus historically associated with the alternatively populist and corporatist nature of the postrevolutionary Mexican state (1920–present). In Morelia, however, the roots of the informal economy, urban consumer culture, popular access to the state through group associations, and collective petitioning rest in the late-nineteenth-century reign of Porfirio Díaz (1876–1910), prior to the Mexican Revolution. Based on their active politicking in the late nineteenth and early twentieth centuries, street vendors forced the postrevolutionary state and local merchant elite of Morelia to take seriously their claims to public space and their right to free trade.

THE PUBLIC CITY: TRANSFORMING PEOPLE AND SPACES

As the capital of the state of Michoacán, Morelia underwent processes of urban growth, modernization, commercialization, and beautification similar to those transforming many capital cities. The city also experienced many of the fundamental shifts marking the history of Mexican cities during these years. The urban population of the municipality of Morelia grew from 23,835 in 1882 to nearly 60,000 in 1930. Similarly, the population of the District of Morelia, a larger territorial unit, increased from 111,000 in 1882 to about 200,000 inhabitants by 1930, an expansion just below average for a Mexican provincial capital and its hinterland during this period.[12] Descriptive evidence strongly suggests that a significant portion of this population increase in the city of Morelia resulted from rural to urban migration, as rural people seeking refuge in the city from the violence, political chaos, and economic instability of the countryside built shacks and huts along the urban periphery.[13] Particularly after 1890, the state and local elite responded to the influx of rural migrants by adopting policies of social control common in urban centers during this period.

Throughout this period, Morelia served as the administrative, service, and commercial hub for Michoacán's regional economy. The city's position as state capital reinforced its identity as a modern, urban center in contrast to the surrounding countryside. Although fundamental realignments in regional power occurred during the Mexican Revolution, the city itself was largely spared from revolutionary violence, as were many Mexican cities.[14] In the early 1920s under the leadership of Governor Francisco Múgica, Michoacán, especially the countryside, became a laboratory for some socialist-inspired policies of the postrevolutionary Mexican state. A strong regional tradition of trade unionism, *agrarismo* (peasants organizing for land reform), and state populism culminated through the 1920s and 1930s under the governorship of Lázaro Cárdenas (1928–32) who subsequently became president of Mexico (1934–40). Although Morelia's history is exceptional in some ways, it is certainly typical in others.

As in other Mexican cities, material improvements changed the way city dwellers thought about and used public space in Morelia. The regional and local elite along with urban-dwelling landowners, commercial elite, and the emerging professionals and middle classes constituted the *gente decente* of the city.[15] Members of this European-oriented cultured class were strongly invested in controlling appearances and public spaces. Modernized and beautified public spaces represented a public stage for these status-conscious residents to display their moral, modern, cosmopolitan lifestyles through their consumption of certain kinds of "transforming" goods and experiences. Transforming commodities, like certain European imports, public recreational activities such as bicycling, and spectator-oriented novelties like movies represented modernity in Morelia owing to "their association with Europe, the very center of modernity, and because of their evident contrast with local practice."[16] In growing cities like Morelia control over centrally located public spaces thus became central to the aspirations and identities of the upper and middle classes.

In this vein, Morelia's *zócalo*, the Plaza of Martyrs, and several other downtown plazas, patios, and parks were renovated in order to create more paved, open, tree-shaded public space in the city.[17] Public spaces increasingly became places where "decent" ladies and gentlemen could spend time strolling along newly paved streets, sidewalks, or garden-lined paths without muddying their shoes. Park benches were installed to provide people with a place to rest during their promenades. Outdoor activities also changed as new public lighting stretched beyond dusk the hours of active street life. Although Morelia had some street lighting as early as 1810, when the first public oil lamps were established at the corners of the cathedral of Morelia, the number of street lamps increased substantially over the mid- to late nineteenth century, from 25 lamps in 1825 to 332 lamps by 1870. The new innovation of the 1880s was the installation of eighty electric light bulbs in 1888.[18] The beautification and lighting of central public spaces symbolized progress and modernity for local elites, as evidenced by the amount of money invested in creating and maintaining these spaces.

Increasing numbers of municipal employees were hired to preserve this vision of the city by regulating people and public behavior in them. At the turn of the century, four different police forces patrolled the city: the night guards of public lighting, the municipal sanitary police, the regular municipal police, and the state gendarmes.[19] Each branch of the police forces had specific duties, but all operated in the spirit of preserving the elite developmentalist vision of their modernizing city.[20] Sanitary policemen served as street cleaners and garbage collectors, doubling as agents of public works, collecting debris from construction sites and repairing city roads, especially when the municipal road crew was overloaded with work.[21] In contrast, the regular police and state gendarmes policed the behavior of city residents in public and ensured that residents abided by the numerous state and municipal regulations decreed over these decades.[22] Similarly, teams of municipal gardeners cared meticulously for the gardens of the city during the day, while guards stood watch over the parks' saplings and flowers by night.[23] Official efforts to preserve and protect trees illustrate the importance of these green spaces to the ruling elite of the city.[24] Municipal policemen were required to plant trees in the plazas and urban promenades at the appropriate season of the year. Moreover, trees were not to be cut down without the expressed approval of the municipal council, and city residents were legally responsible for the watering and care of the trees in front of their residences, according to Morelia's 1881 Edict of Police, article 48.[25] By the early 1890s, the state government of Michoacán had officially inaugurated July 1 as the "Day of the Tree." State-sponsored festivals involving parades and collective tree planting ceremonies were organized on that date for the next several decades.[26]

As public spaces were progressively beautified, sanitized, and regulated, they came to represent vital spaces for the display, advertising, and merchandising of products and events in the city. Glass showcases, window displays, advertising leaflets, store front placards, billboards, electric signs, and background musical enticements were gradually added to the repertoire of entrepreneurs in the late nineteenth and early twentieth centuries. Leaflet advertising was one of the earlier forms of marketing to take off. By the late 1880s, additional space for announcements and advertisements was needed to accommodate the needs of advertisers. One promoter, Francisco Carrillo, wrote to the city council complaining that "the available bulletin boards are insufficient . . . because with great frequency, one's announcement does not remain visible for the length of time necessary in order for the desired result to occur."[27] Competition for advertising in public spaces and especially on public bulletin boards forced advertisers to post their advertisements on any available wall space in the city center. Photographer Arcadio Calderon, for instance, went to lengths to obtain what he believed to be the "exclusive right" to post flyers on the trees of the central park. Upon seeing "other advertisements on trees in the park," he complained to the city council that other people were posting flyers in the parks, thus violating his "exclusive right" to this space. The city council responded that his permission was being withdrawn because "these ads may only be posted on the announcement boards."[28] Aestheticized public spaces themselves thus became commodities over which competing groups vied.

Despite efforts to impose a certain vision on city spaces, people, behaviors, appearances, and movements were not easily contained, especially as urban public spaces became coveted spaces for production, commerce, and consumption. The shared nature of urban space in the growing, modernizing city tended to bring people of diverse social classes together, thus subverting simple systems of social control. In fact, elite notions of the modern, ordered city depended on a large body of poor, indigenous, and mestizo manual laborers who worked to maintain physical appearances and to service the leisure lifestyles of the upper and middle classes. For the men and women who earned their livelihood working in public spaces as gardeners, night guards, street sweepers, vendors, petty entrepreneurs, shoe shiners, newspaper hawkers, leaflet distributors, porters, water carriers, domestic servants, prostitutes, latrine cleaners, and public works agents, as well as in numerous other low-level service jobs, city life embodied other experiences, agendas, and aspirations. Specifically, the transformation of urban public space offered new potential sources of employment, access to public services, exposure to new experiences, and new possibilities for popular politicking. Thus, in addition to survival strategies, new urban identities, alternative forms of political engagement, and popular urban activism were produced in relation to urban space.

The transformation of central public spaces literally created more physical space for new production and employment opportunities. It also generated possibilities for new forms of political engagement for working residents. From the 1880s onward, public vending in the informal sector of the city sustained many working-class residents and recent migrants from the countryside.[29] Vendors quickly became the most visible and controversial workers in shared city spaces. Although space in city markets remained available, increasing numbers of sellers sought to locate their businesses in the bustling, newly transformed urban spaces of the city. In Morelia, parks, plazas, and especially the *portales* (the central arch-covered walkways) were the most desireable locations for vendors who catered to strolling consumers. For many decades, these archways were considered to be the prime vending location because of their centrality to the hustle and bustle of the city. The spots under the covered archways also provided protection for vendors from the sun, heat, and dust in the summer, and shelter from the wind, rain, mud, and cold in the winter, an important consideration for vendors deciding where to set up their stands. Other public sellers worked itinerantly or located their businesses along the central streets, in a corner of the park, or near the entrances of Morelia's many churches.

In the late nineteenth century, many sellers were granted permission to sell in public areas and to build permanent stands in those places, literally claiming a piece of public space for their private businesses. To legally work in the public spaces of the city, prospective vendors had to write a letter to the city council requesting permission to establish their stall, counter, table, or floor mat. These letters usually explained precisely where sellers sought to set up shop, what they were going to sell, the dimensions of the area they would occupy, and/or a design of the stall. Most letters also provided several arguments for why the council should grant them permission. An example of a typical request was that of José de la Guzmán, a small merchant in handkerchiefs and *rebozos* (large shawls that were ubiquitous apparel for middle- and lower-class women). In 1884, Guzmán sent a letter to the city council explaining that in order to expand "the honest occupation for my livelihood to which I have dedicated myself," it was necessary for him to set up an *alacena* (literally, a cupboard or closet) in the Portal Allende. He argued that if he was going to "take advantage as much as possible of this operation," it was "indispensable for [him] to establish this storage area" where he could "keep for the night in rigorous deposit the valuable commercial effects under lock and key." Guzmán reassured the authorities that the dimensions of his stand "will not obstruct in any manner the transit of the inhabitants." Moreover, he promised to "religiously pay the respective pension." Eleven days after receiving the letter, the city council decided that "because the petition was good and convenient for the petitioner as well as for public beauty, and given that the stand will be well-constructed, the requested license should be granted."[30] As Guzmán explained, permanent stands offered several advantages over the mere blanket, *petate*, cart, or small table, as sellers could store goods overnight, relieving them from the task of transporting their wares home each night.[31]

Guzmán's letter to the city council highlights several typical arguments used by vendors to persuade authorities to allow them to sell in public spaces. Other vendors argued for their contribution to public beauty, their contribution to local trade and municipal tax revenue, and their dependence on vending—an "honest occupation"—to provide for their "numerous families." Adopting the constantly repeated rhetoric of the city council, vendors also promised to maintain decorum in their public interactions, promote public morality, and faithfully serve their customers. Other public sellers asserted, their legal right to "free trade" under article 124 and the right "to dedicate oneself to whatever livelihood one chose" under article 4 of the 1857 Mexican constitution.[32] Vendors also echoed elite concerns that stalls be "permanent," "well constructed," "properly designed," and of the "correct dimensions," all phrases continuously used in the city council's exchanges with potential stall builders. The city council thus encouraged the building of permanent vending stalls, because permanent stalls were regarded as an improvement over vendors hawking their piled goods from dirty *petates* and blankets in the city's archways. Notably, vendors would later defend permanent stalls as their private property, citing constitutional article 27, which established the "sanctity of private property." Sellers used multiple strategies to assert and defend their claims to public space. They employed the rhetorical discourses of modernity, beautification, morality, public health. They argued about their rights, needs, and contributions to city life, and associated their small businesses with consumer culture, local trade, and revenue.

In the late nineteenth century, despite official efforts to control public space, the city council of Morelia allowed numerous vendors to set up their stalls in central locations. In the eyes of the local political elite, public selling embodied both the liberal principle of free trade in action as well as the expansion of capitalist consumer culture.[33] Financial considerations also seemed to motivate the bankrupt municipal government to permit public selling, as all exhibitors, vendors, service providers, and entrepreneurs were required to pay a monthly fee to municipal coffers. Even musical groups and minstrels who strolled through the park and streets of the city playing their instruments had to acquire the proper license and pay a small fee.[34] However, municipal rents were negotiable. In 1884, Pedro Arroyo, for example, not only secured a permit to sell cigarettes and cigars in the Archway of Aldama, but he also requested that his monthly rent be reduced from four to two *reales* a week, arguing that "what I sell is entirely too little . . . and my sales do not correspond to the assigned rent." In addition, he pointed out that some other vendors paid only two *reales* in rent each week and he thus believed that it was only fair that he be assigned the same amount. The city council agreed to reduce his rent.[35] Thus, despite concerns about controlling public spaces, the city council gave vendors considerable leeway to establish their businesses in central spaces during the 1880s and early 1890s, a situation that shifted after the turn of the century, and then again after the fighting phase of the revolution in 1917. Through the letter and petition, vendors were able to argue, individually and collectively, for their right to the public spaces of the city.

THE VISUAL CITY: CENTRAL SPACES AND THE POLITICS OF AESTHETICS

Conflicts over the uses (or perceived abuses) of beautified public spaces had long been a concern of the ruling classes and *gente decente* of the city. Sensibilities clashed in the 1890s and 1900s as waves of rural migrants sought refuge in the city from the political and economic instability of the countryside. The situation reached a boiling point in the 1910s, however, with the onset of revolutionary violence in rural Michoacán. Many new arrivals to the city turned to street selling as a source of income, overwhelming Morelia's walkways, parks, and plazas in the process. The growing urban poor were perceived as dangerous threats to the city's morality, sanitation, public health, aesthetics, and fluid pedestrian traffic. One city councilman lamented: "It is not possible for the council to placate the pretensions that it receives daily from the petty merchants. To do so would mean that, within a few days of granting their desires, vendors would be situated around all of the main gardens of the city."[36] Notions of modern civility were rooted in the moral-environmental theory, the theory that the presence of filth and, thus conversely, the lack of beauty, in an environment contributed to the spread of disease, an increase in immorality, and a rise in criminal behavior. Thus, promotion of "public beauty" was justified by its ability to bolster public morality and safeguard public health. Although eliminating scourges to public health was a top priority of the municipal government, the politics of aesthetics allowed elites and the state to justify the relocation and removal of the urban poor from public areas in the name of public beauty and the greater public good.

Zoning policies were pivotal to the council's attempt to create certain boundaries within the city that increasingly limited the access of the urban poor to central areas.[37] Since the 1890s, commercial zoning had emerged as an informal practice, but it was quickly formalized near 1900 as a way to order and control public spaces in the downtown area. As a result, the city council started to relocate vendors in congested areas, like the archways, to other parts of the city. Based on zoning laws, new vendors requesting selling licenses were not allowed to sell in central locations. The city council did allow petitioners to suggest an alternative location before they were officially designated a spot.[38]

Relocation quickly emerged as a new point of contention between vendors and the city council from 1890 through the 1910s. The city council largely abandoned the principle of historical precedent. Vendors traditionally had been able to claim their right to a particular location based on the fact that they had sold in that very spot for many years. Increasingly after 1900, and especially in the 1910s, even long-established sellers were relocated, usually receiving fifteen days notification before their stalls had to be removed.[39] Most were relocated either to the Market of San Agustín, a fairly central semicovered market, or to newly built plazas on the peripheries of the city where they could sell drinks, prepared foods, produce, and even alcoholic beverages to a working-class clientele. Yet, often sellers complained about the drop in sales they experienced after moving their stalls to these working-class *colonias*, and many asked to return to their original locations.[40] Nonetheless, the city council justified this policy by citing its responsibility to maintain an uninhibited flow of pedestrian traffic. One councilman explained: "It is necessity to encourage among these vendors the tendency to establish their small businesses in outlying plazas, such as the Plaza Carrillo, in order to localize them and stop them from invading the public walkways as they do now."[41] Preserving free circulation in the city (an idea inherently wed to the liberal concept of free trade) was just one rationale for vendor relocation.

Although zoning and relocation were ostensibly aimed at controlling traffic and commercial activity in Morelia's historic district, these policies also placated vocal downtown shop owners and enabled the council to enforce a certain aesthetic in the city center. Through these decades, downtown store merchants repeatedly condemned vendor stalls and display cases as "nuisances," because they blocked natural light from their stores and caused the walkways to become completely unpassable at times.[42] In 1910, a prominent member of the local elite, José Osegura, spearheaded a petition from ten store owners to remove the vendors situated in front of their storefronts in the archways. Appealing to the council's concern with public beauty, public health, and the protection of private property, they described how their businesses as well as the aesthetics of the city suffered: "No one can ignore the very poor appearance of these improvised stalls made of blankets, straw mats, and dirty boxes, nor the damage that they do to the buildings when nails are used to secure these badly made stalls." Their letter continued to describe the imminent threat these stalls posed to public health and public morality as well: "There are also more serious inconveniences presented . . . by these improvised stores in the public walkway. The owners have turned their stalls into kitchens and dormitories that serve as their bedrooms. This situation could clearly give rise to acts of immorality in prominent public areas."[43]

Complaints of downtown store owners about the "prejudices" they suffered on account of vendors reached a peak in the revolutionary years.[44] Tellingly, however, vendors were obviously posing competition for downtown stores. In 1913, a response by the commission of markets explained that "with great frequency consumers linger for rather long periods of time in front of these stalls, thereby implying that the vendors were not only" contributing to overcongestion, but also creating market competition by luring away customers with their lower prices.[45] Although established merchants used similar rhetoric about "public" priorities, it is clear that vendors also posed significant commercial competition for customers to centrally located shopkeepers.

Around 1900, the strength of the informal vending economy and the competition felt by store owners from vendors literally pulled their merchandise and employees onto the streets. The sidewalk display case thus emerged as a new selling technique. Display and window cases—usually consisting of glass-topped shelves placed just outside of storefronts—clearly suggest how public space had become a vital commodity. In 1900, for instance, the Port of Liverpool, an early department store, got permission to construct a display case "to better exhibit the effects of our business." Other shopkeepers and petty merchants followed its lead.[46] Entrepreneurs assured the municipal authorities that their glass displays would add to the "public beauty" of the city and would not obstruct the *vía pública*.[47] By the late 1920s, department stores were sending their employees out onto the streets with merchandise for the express purpose of meeting vendor competition head on.[48]

Historians have connected the adoption of glass windows and displays at the turn of the century to new attitudes about consumption and public space. As William Leach asserts: "The new exterior glass environment began to change the way people related to goods." In contrast to open markets where the buyer could "touch, smell, and examine the goods," and "where there was access and movement from all sides as contact between customers and goods flowed undisturbed," during the 1890s and beyond glass windows and displays created a new shopping experience. Showcase merchandising aimed to protect the goods and the merchant's capital investment in them "from pilfering hands, but also from the weather and street grime," while simulta-

226

neously fostering "the impression of intimacy" between the consumer and the commodity. Leach further explains: "Glass closed off smell and touch diminishing the consumer's relationship with the goods. At the same time, it amplified the visual, transforming the already watching city person into a potentially compulsive viewer. It must have altered the character of the relationship between goods and people by permitting everything to be seen yet rendering it beyond touch. . . . Perhaps more than any other medium, glass democratized desire even as it dedemocratized access to goods."[49]

In early-twentieth-century Mexico, the creation of desire and exclusivity in relation to publicly displayed, glass-encased commodities further reinforced the politics of aesthetics and visuality in the city. Initially, display cases and window cases exhibited manufactured goods, both local and imported, such as ready-made clothes, shoes, hats, crystal, leather goods, or artistic crafts like photographs and pottery. Quickly, however, street vendors and small business owners selling a wide range of goods appropriated the concept of a free-standing display case to present a more modern, sophisticated image to the public. As sellers began requesting permits for kiosks, stands, and display cases, new standards of stall construction and aesthetic design were used to exclude poorer sellers in the urban core.[50]

As the city's population grew, people recognized fewer residents by name or reputation. As a result, city council members increasingly seemed to rely on nonpersonal clues in a writer's letter to determine his or her social standing, which, in turn, influenced their decision about their requests. One of the basic clues that indicated a vendor's social class was the kind of stand he or she could afford to construct. Sellers were required to submit detailed descriptions of their proposed stalls, including the stall's exact dimensions, the type of construction materials that would be used, and the proposed location. In addition, petitioners had to include an architectural design of their stall. These submitted designs alone revealed the diverse financial standings of petitioners; some designs, complete with ornamented details, were drafted by professional architects, whereas others were simple, crude sketches of stalls drawn on small pieces of paper. In fact, García Gómez, a particularly stringent council member, confirmed that the city council followed an unwritten policy to give more modern display cases and window displays preferential treatment. In an internal report by the commission of markets, he justified the removal of vendors, saying: "I think that it should be insisted that the public walkway remain unhindered, and if necessary, its obstruction should be tolerated only when pleasant-looking display cases which are well-made and of smaller dimensions are constructed." He believed that display cases of modern designs could be tolerated if they lined the walls and were fit around the pillars. Acknowledging how humbler petty merchants suffered when relocated, he reasoned that, "the particular must sacrifice for the general good, as in the case of the invaded archways." Echoing the council's common refrain, he stipulated, however, that in no way should cases "block traffic, look ugly, or block the light in the most central location of our city."[51]

Between 1907 and 1913, fifteen different entrepreneurs approached the city council asking to build kiosks or cottages in one corner or another of the Plaza of Martyrs or along the Morelos Esplanade. Seven of the requests were granted without limitations. All of these seven petitioners proposed to build quaint cottages and kiosks, many of which were depicted for the council in fine architectural drawings.[52] Considering the general atmosphere of regulation and control in the city during these years, the city council did not appear to have many qualms about relinquishing control of these prominent public spaces to a certain type of vendor, namely, one that was going to invest significant amounts of money to build the type of structures the council believed would further beautify the plaza. Nevertheless, even these sellers were obligated to present a design of the kiosk and received all of the regular warnings from the council: "do not ruin the pavement," "do not block public transit," "do not exceed the dimensions agreed upon," and "be sure the kiosk conforms to the style and design of the preexisting ones." Most of these sellers sold printed and manufactured items such as cigarettes, newspapers, and candies.

In contrast, most of the eight requests denied or granted only temporarily were submitted by public sellers who did not have much money to invest in stands.[53] Two petitioners were flatly denied. The other six requests were granted for only a very limited period of time, averaging about four months. Few of these sellers included designs with their letters to the city council showing off the stylish manner in which their stands would embellish the plaza. Several described their kiosks as simply "being made of wood," and thus distinguishing them from a few of the requests describing stalls made primarily of cloth or canvas. During these years prior to the revolution, the city council's preferential treatment of sellers with financial resources was subsequently condemned as evidence of Porfirian "caprices," a legacy against which postrevolutionary governments sought to define themselves.

Similar standards of aesthetics applied to display cases. When merchants proposed to construct window displays out of glass and metal, the city council was quite agreeable. The use of these modern materials appealed to the council members' desire for a more modern, sophisticated appearance of the city center. In contrast, the council was not as accommodating toward poorer vendors who proposed to construct display cases out of less expensive materials, like wood and canvas, because it believed these kinds of display cases too closely resembled vending stalls. The modern form of the display case seemed to warrant higher quality materials in the eyes of the council. It clearly distinguished between requests to build lower-quality display cases and requests to build "elegant" glass and metal window displays, thus favoring sellers with more resources to invest in their displays. When vendor Vicente Alvarez, for example, asked permission to built a display case out of wood and canvas the council suggested that rather than building a display case, he should "just use a table," like the other vendors in the archways. Apparently, the city council preferred not to have display cases at all rather than to have displays made out of wood and canvas.[54]

This distinction between the quality, materials, and design of stalls, stands, and display cases continued to be of utmost importance to the city council through the next twenty years. Through the 1910s and 1920s, it openly reminded established merchants building display cases to be sure that their "display cases always present a better appearance than the ordinary vending stalls."[55] The city council encouraged these merchants to use their resources to enhance the city's appearance of worldliness and modernity with their shiny glass and metal cases, always insisting that display cases "should not in any way present an obstacle to public transit," and should "be of regular dimensions and have a nice appearance."[56] In 1925, for instance, when local photographer Rubert Martínez wanted to set up a showcase to exhibit his "works of artistic merit," he promised that the display would be "a public adornment owing to the material construction of the display case as well as the artistic works exhibited in it."[57] After the turn of the century, merchants' ability to provide "public adornment" via their kiosks and display cases clearly allowed them greater leeway and privilege in relation to public space.

THE CONTESTED CITY: VENDORS NETWORK TO DEFEND PUBLIC CLAIMS

Just as the stance and strategy of the city council changed during these decades, so too did the strategies of public sellers. Faced with new aesthetic standards that threatened their central vending locations, petty merchants continued to use petitions to engage with prevailing discourses of public health, aesthetics, consumer culture, and morality. However, increasingly in their written communications with various city councils, vendors presented themselves collectively as a group with common interests. Just as other urban residents had organized collectively to demand resources and services from local government based on their shared neighborhood identities, vendors used similar strategies to defend their claims to public space.[58]

As rural to urban migration altered the demographic and spatial dynamics of the city, new forms of sociability beyond formal group associations, including mutual aid societies, voluntary associations, patriotic juntas, religious groups, peasant communities, or political parties emerged as vital urban networks. As Hilda Sabato suggests, in the space of the city, people engaged in new "modes of sociability," thus expanding social networks.[59] New forms of sociability also encompass the broad range of informal interactions that occurred as more people were brought into close relation with each other. Numerical and descriptive evidence illustrates that neighborhoods, markets, parks, plazas, *cantinas*, and other public spaces brimmed with new and old residents. During their daily interactions, they exchanged ideas and gossip, shared common complaints and stories of their experiences, and circulated information about life, work, and politics in Morelia. These informal forms of sociability were not based on any formal membership nor political status as a Mexican "citizen." Rather, urban networking included people based on their presence and their residence in the city. Residency, not citizenship nor social status, enabled people to participate in these urban social networks.

Negotiations between a group of shoemakers and the city council typify the rhetorical and networking strategies of vendors through the 1890s and 1900s. Before the application of new zoning laws, the shoemakers had occupied space in the downtown archways surrounding the *zócalo*. They had been relocated to the Market of San Augustín around 1890. By the following year, however, the shoe sellers wrote to the council requesting to move back to their previous location in the archways. In their letter, the cobblers explained how their sales had been "much better" before they were relocated "because [in the archway] we were in immediate contact with the public." By contrast, in the "hidden corner" in the Market of San Augustín, they were "cut off from [their] circle of known consumers." Apart from the detriment to their own businesses, the persistent sellers argued that "municipal funds would surely benefit from their return to the *portales* [archways]" because more of their same profession would be encouraged to sell if they could sell in such a desirable location. They explained that "the number of shoe sellers has substantially dropped since their relocation to the Market of San Augustín," owing to the distance from the center and the "narrowness" of that market.[60] Essentially, the cobblers were arguing for a change to zoning laws that excluded shoes from list of goods that could be sold in the central archways.

In an effort to strengthen their case further, the petitioners pointed to their relationships with reputable merchants, drawing on these social networks like personal references; the shoemakers had obtained the signatures of "respectable persons with commercial establishments in the portal" in order to illustrate the "support and cooperation" they had from the surrounding business community. By drawing on the respectability and support of these store merchants, the shoe sellers were automatically offering witnesses to their proper behavior and morality by establishing these store owners as their informal guarantors, like those required for the municipal registration of service workers, such as porters and domestic servants. The cobblers also demonstrated to the city council that these store merchants supported their commercial efforts, thus allaying the council's concern about potential conflicts between these groups over market competition. In addition, the cobblers urged to be moved back to the *portales* for the sake of their health and for public health in general, because, they noted, "the humidity of the market is causing grave illnesses among us." In light of these compelling arguments, the council granted the shoemakers' request and returned them to the Portal Matamoros. As part of the compromise, however, the council stipulated that the cobblers had "the obligation of building some stalls or other decent apparatuses where customers could try on the shoes without being in the view of the public."[61] Apparently the public display of unclad feet, especially women's bare feet, could not be allowed in such a central location, as it posed a threat to public morality and disturbed the city council's vision of Morelia as a moral, progressive city. Nonetheless, the message was clear: if the cobblers wanted to return to the *portales,* they had to make capital investments to improve the aesthetic quality of their stalls.

This dialogue between these shoemakers and the city council evidences not only the arguments employed by vendors in these negotiations but also the importance of both horizontal and vertical social networks. These sellers networked horizontally with other vendors to form collective petitions to the city council, but they also networked vertically with upper- and middle-class shopkeepers in order to boost their respectability in the eyes of the council. Other vendors used similar strategies. In 1911, for instance, a group of ice cream sellers enlisted the help of the Liberal Youth Club of Michoacán to defend their right to sell somewhere in the city. On behalf of this group of displaced ice cream vendors, the Liberal Youth Club explained: "A delegation of individual owners of ice cream stalls approached the club, protesting against the order issued by the city council obligating them to unoccupy their stalls in the Esplanade without assigning them another place to go." The letter signed by thirteen young liberals argued, however, that given the actual circumstances of commerce, it was essential for these vendors to be in popularly frequented places; therefore, "in order to be just, their stalls must be advantageously located."[62] In response, the commission of markets offered to move them to the Market of San Agustín. Through their social networking, these vendors successfully enlisted the aid of the Liberal Youth Club and secured a place for themselves in a public market.

This type of back-and-forth negotiation was quite typical of the correspondence between vendors and municipal officials. Although many sellers wrote individually to the city council, many opted to present and argue their case as a group, using the power of numbers on their side. Nonetheless, this strategy was not always effective. A group of twenty small merchants of clothing, namely *rebozos* and *sarapes* (cloaks for women and men), for example, collectively negotiated with the city council in 1911. Immediately after being told by the council that they were going to be relocated, these clothing dealers offered to reduce the size of their stalls so they would not block public traffic. They then argued that it would not be necessary to transfer them to "very distant places." They explained that such a transfer would cause their businesses, "which provide the bread for our families" to fail. Moreover, they explained that if they were relocated, as suggested, to the streets outside of the Market of San Agustín, they would have to worry about the "unhygienic conditions, the unpleasant appearance, and bad smells" of the market owing to the presence of many food vendors.[63] In this last argument, these vendors were echoing the city council's repeatedly voiced concern about putting food vendors together with nonfood vendors. Despite these arguments, their petition was denied.

Numerous examples attest to the power, yet accessibility, of the "lettered city" by evidencing how public sellers did engage political authorities in dialogue and debate. In a particularly notable exchange from 1914, sixteen vendors (composed of five men and eleven women) reacted quite strongly to the news that they were being relocated to the plaza outside of the market. They argued for their right to remain in the Archway of Allende by presenting themselves as honorable, hard-working, but poor *vecinos* (neighbors) of Morelia. They explained: "Our small businesses honorably attribute ourselves and our families the subsistence by which we live without causing harm to anyone and without giving any motive for complaints of scandals or of any kind." They urged the council to allow them to stay for the sake of their health: "We will be exposed to the sun and the force of the rain, especially in the rainy season when the rain showers are strong." Finally, reminding the newly seated municipal government of the historical precedent of public selling in Morelia, they wrote: "We should warn you that since time immemorial it has been the custom that in this archway there have always been vending stalls, so much so that historically the archway used to be commonly called the 'Archway of the Vendors.' This decree would break this tradition that all of the public is accustomed to, as they go there to do their shopping for small items."[64]

Despite their use of arguments about how their move would adversely affect their health, threaten their livelihood, break with local traditions, and disappoint urban consumers, the vendors were forced to relocate. Three months later, in May 1914, this same group wrote a second letter appealing to the city council's sense of social responsibility and social consciousness. They reiterated their arguments about the detrimental effects of their move to the outdoor Market of San Augustín, emphasizing the financial ruin they faced in this second letter. The vendors explained that "we are extremely poor people" and in the new location "we sell almost absolutely nothing." Consequently, "we do not make any profit from our sales. Therefore, we can not cover our other financial obligations that we paid for from our small profits, nor can we afford to pay the rent for our houses where we live." In addition, the rent collector in the market "demands excessive rent from us, and these demands are like forced loans that absorb almost all of the truly insignificant amount that we make from our sales." These sellers concluded by appealing to the council's mercy, saying it would be "an act of charity" if they allowed them to return to the archways. Although the vendors were not permitted to return to the archways, they were successful at gaining something; their plight and arguments about the weather spurred the state government to authorize the construction of an overhang to cover the south side of the market.[65]

The organizing and petitioning strategies of sellers represent an important, often overlooked, form of political engagement during the *Porfiriato* and revolutionary periods. As I have argued above, vendors successfully asserted themselves as political agents by persistently engaging the state in dialogue about their claims to public space. These popular sellers also used social networks to advocate for their claims. These nineteenth-century practices were translated into formal political activism after the revolution with the founding of vendor associations and unions in the 1920s. Thus, I argue that in the case of urban vendors, the creation of unions and group associations—a trend often associated exclusively with the Mexican Revolution and the postrevolutionary Mexican state—was rooted in popular politics over public spaces and other associative practices generated in nineteenth-century Porfirian political culture.

The Sellers' City: Redefining the Politics of Public Space

By 1917, vendor politicking and activism in Morelia had generated such leverage in the political and physical terrain of the city that the postrevolutionary Mexican state was forced to reckon with vendor claims to public space. Although the revolution had clearly changed the rhetorical discourse and political orientation of local government, decades of sustained politicking among vendors enabled them to position themselves and their claims as the legitimate rights of the "people" or the "public" to city space. With the consolidation of constitutionalist power at the national and regional levels in Mexico after 1917, the state of Michoacán in Morelia began to issue policies to court the loyalties of the popular classes, in particular, public sellers. In February 1917, for instance, the state government reduced the fees paid by all of the city's public vendors by 30 percent, covering the lost expenses with public debt.[66] Vending permits for many of the previously "off limits" central areas of the city, such as the archways, were redistributed as well. Between July and December 1917, the city council issued ten permits for several women and a few men to set up stalls to sell sweets and tobacco in the archways, a stark contrast to the continuous efforts to clear out the archways a few years earlier.[67] By July 1919, numerous vendors and ice cream sellers filled the Plaza of Martyrs and the Esplanade Morelos again. In contrast to the policies of tight control and policing during the 1900s and early 1910s, in 1919 the city council granted many requests from people wanting to sell everything from fruit to ice cream to prepared foods, such as *tortas* (sandwiches), in different areas of the city.[68] The city council appeared to be courting the political loyalties of lower-class residents. In the wake of the revolution, local officials nurtured vertical political alliances across class divisions.

The leeway granted to vendors to reestablish themselves in these central locations resulted in new and renewed conflicts among vendors and downtown store merchants and homeowners. One particular dispute between a downtown homeowner and a street vendor illustrates how the municipal government constructed these vertical political alliances by defending vendors' right to sell in public spaces. In addition, the city council was able to fiercely defend its own boundaries of authority. The homeowner, Francisco Estrada, wrote to the council in 1919, hoping to get Magdaleno Pérez, a small vendor of toys, removed from the front of his house which was located along the archways. In a letter to the city council, Estrada lamented how for two years Pérez had situated his stall in front of his house "without his permission." He explained how Pérez had "extended his stall so it now blocks free transit under the archways, often causing disputes and disruptions." Estrada hoped to have the entire archway cleared of sellers. He seemed to realize that he might get a negative response from the city council, however, because he stated: "Even if Pérez has an official license from the Municipal Corporation," it should take into account that "the license] was granted without the knowledge of how [Pérez] is an obstacle to my own rights as a property owner." In his own defense, Pérez wrote to the council charging Estrada as being an "enemy of the revolution."[69] Both Estrada and Pérez argued for their rightful claims to this central city space. Estrada argued for Pérez's removal based on the fact that he was blocking public transit and disrupting social order. Conversely, Pérez called on the city council to uphold the ideals of the Mexican Revolution and to stop the exploitation of the poor by the rich.

The city council jumped on this last assertion, further accusing this upper-class homeowner of unlawfully usurping the powers of the city council by collecting rent on public space. In the internal report from the Commission of Markets regarding this dispute, the councilmen got straight to the point. They wrote: "In the first paragraph of his letter, this gentleman [Estrada] confesses that he gives out permits and collects some type of rent from the small industrialists and entrepreneurs who hang poster boards, announcements, and display cases in the Portal Galeana," in front of his house. Estrada was, therefore, guilty of collecting rent that should have been destined for municipal coffers. The commission explained: "The Portal Galeana forms part of the public walkway. Moreover, there is no doubt that it is exclusively the property of the city and that the *ayuntamiento* [municipal government] has absolute domain over it." They concluded: "Therefore it can be deduced that this gentleman [Estrada] who makes these collections and issues permits is usurping functions for which he has no legal power or authority." The report articulated the council's belief that "there is no doubt that if there were enough market spaces to accommodate all the sellers that are presently found in the streets and *portales*, they would all be gathered together and condensed in market places properly prepared for commerce." Yet, the city council asserted, "that is impossible for now," because there was not sufficient market space to accommodate all of the vendors. The council thus defended Pérez's right to sell in public and denied Estrada's request to have him removed. In addition, Estrada was warned: "You must stop issuing false permits and collecting rent of any kind for the public space in front of your house; if you continue to do so, you will pay a fine for illegally usurping functions of the *ayuntamiento*."[70] As this example illustrates, the city council protected vendors in the *portales* from eviction and exploitation at the hands of homeowners, such as Estrada. Although new political positioning and public discourse about claims to these central spaces highlighted the impact of the revolution in Morelia, these discourses and positions clearly drew on the historical precedent vendors themselves had established.

In the 1920s, as municipal and state governments further expanded systems of regulation and standardization, negotiation between street vendors and the city council was the norm. Uniform standards were enforced: all vending stalls had to conform to a certain design provided by the city council, giving the *portales* an ordered appearance. Under the new municipal procedures, vendors were given an official blueprint for their stall design, literally reversing the practice of the preceding forty years when vendors presented their own designs to the council for approval.[71] Similar to efforts in the late 1890s and early 1900s, vendors were organized and grouped together in commercial zones according to the type of merchandise they sold. With the emergence of these standardized procedures in the 1920s, vendors harkened back to the openness of the city council during the years from 1917 to 1919.

By claiming their rights based on the recent precedent of the revolutionary government of 1917 and praising the protection certain revolutionary governments gave to urban sellers, vendors articulated a standard of what they considered "good government," namely, a government committed to the ideals of the revolution and to protecting the interests and livelihood of *el pueblo*, the people. Vendors also addressed the council in a way that assumed its "honorable" or "charitable and just" spirit, thus aiming to shame the council into adopting a charitable stance toward their petition: "Taking into consideration that this Honorable Corporation is motivated by the highest desires to protect small business, as well as in their spirit of rectitude and justice," petitioners assumed the council would give them aid.[72] Vendors also commonly drew on revolutionary rhetoric to suggest that the seated city council either was, or was not, supportive of the ideals of the revolution and, by association, the interests of popular groups. Despite new government structures of regulation through the 1920s, negotiation and compromise remained a central part of official interactions between the city council and vendors.

In addition to new rhetorical arguments, vendors were able to reestablish much of their negotiating power after 1917 and into the 1920s by drawing on vertical and horizontal social networks. Informal organizing networks laid a foundation for the first official unions of sellers, who increasingly described themselves as small-business owners in Morelia. By 1930, at least two different unions represented sellers, stall owners, and vendors: the Union of Independent, Small-Scale Employees and Owners and the Union of Small Business Owners.[73] Through the 1920s, the city council continued to grant concessions to vendors, such as allowing them to reclaim coveted public space in the *portales*. The state and municipal governments, however, developed an elaborate structure of regulating bodies to ensure that vendors adhered to local regulations. This regulatory power of the state came to be the predominant factor defining the relationship between workers in the informal sector and the state through the twentieth century. Although clients of an increasingly complex corporatist state, public sellers in Morelia secured official support for their claims to urban public spaces. Public space in growing cities continued to be a valuable commodity extended to (or withheld from) the lower and middle classes in postrevolutionary urban Mexico.

By the 1920s, vendors had clearly moved negotiations over citizenship and political representation, as well as the commercial struggle for customers, onto the streets and public spaces of Mexican cities. Vendor persistence at selling in public also transformed city spaces with the mushrooming of the informal economy in cities across Mexico. The prominence of public selling and the strength of the informal vending economy is indicated by the level of competition they posed to established stores. In 1926 competition from street vendors spurred the National Council on Commerce, a body representing merchants' commercial interests, to write a letter to the municipal president of Morelia articulating the profound effect street vendors had on their businesses. The letter explained: "The competition of street vendors toward the commercial establishment is quite substantial, and the negative effects that we receive from it are publicly well known. The advantages of itinerant vendors obstruct established businesses. In addition, they are invading the important neighborhoods." The National Council of Commerce then recommended that "a commission be appointed to study the manner in which established commerce could be best protected." This commission researched how various municipalities were regulating the vending economy. As a result of the commission's queries, the municipal vending regulations from the city of San Luis Potosí were obtained and studied.[74]

The articles of the San Luis Potosí regulations outlined various steps that established businesses could take to better compete with street vendors as well as the ways the city council could better police vendors and thus stop illegal vending. Vendors' selling strategies were so successful, cost-effective, and efficient that stores had to reinvent how they were going to attract customers and sell their goods. The streets and public spaces of the city became the showcases for their products. The five central articles of these regulations are as follows:

1. ... Employees from the department store modeling the store's clothing should go out onto the streets to sell the store's merchandise, being considered like street vendors ...
2. ... Store employees should go out on the streets with pieces of fabric and other merchandise to solicit interest and orders from pedestrians;
3. All itinerant vendors selling clothing should be required by the municipal government to have a license with a picture as identification for the inspectors of the municipal government and inspectors from the National Council of Commerce. Vendors would be required to display the identification whenever asked for it ...;
4. All itinerant vendors regardless of their merchandise must pay a daily fee of 5 pesos to be paid ten days in advance for a legal license to remain in effect;
5. Itinerant vendors who clandestinely sell merchandise will be punished with a fine four times more than the normal fine or arrested"[75]

The local Morelia branch of the National Council of Commerce turned these recommendations over to the municipal government of Morelia for consideration. The *ayuntamiento* debated the articles at length before deciding to commission a local study of the issues in Morelia before accepting this slate of probusiness articles. The degree to which these propositions were incorporated into municipal law remains unclear. However, this debate prompted clear political lines to be drawn, because that same year, 1926, Morelia's first official vendor union was formed.[76]

CONCLUSION

In this chapter I explore how contestations and negotiations over urban public space in the late nineteenth and early twentieth centuries created a foundational dynamic of popular organizing vis-à-vis the Mexican state. Vendors embedded themselves in central public space in the nineteenth century during the years of modernizing urban transformation. Although increasingly marginalized from central areas of the city, they refused to be pushed out of public spaces by the politics of aesthetics from 1888 through 1917. Public sellers drew on long-established traditions of collective petitioning to leverage their claims to public space after 1917 and through the 1920s. Informal social networks in the city served as a basis for this process of urban politicking. Moreover, access to the "lettered city" through the petition thus generated a pivotal means of political engagement and collective organizing around public space that continued throughout the twentieth century.[77]

NOTES

1. Angel Rama, *The Lettered City*, ed. and trans. John Charles Chasteen (Durham, N.C.: Duke University Press, 1996); 29. Also see Román de la Campa, "The Lettered City: Power and Writing in Latin America," in. Benigno Trigo, *Foucault and Latin America: Appropriations and Deployments of Discursive Analysis* (New York: Routledge, 2002), 17–43.

2. Rama, *The Lettered City*, 57.

3. Ibid., 29.

4. See Martin Lienhard, "Writing from Within: Indigenous Epistolary Practices in the Colonial Period," in Rosaleen Howard-Malverde, ed., *Creating Context in Andean Cultures* (Oxford: Oxford University Press, 1997), 171–84. Also see Sara Castro-Klarén and John Charles Chasteen, eds., *Beyond Imagined Communities: Reading and Writing in the Nation in Nineteenth-Century Latin America* (Washington, D.C.: Woodrow Wilson Center Press, 2003).

5. Ramon Eduardo Ruíz, *Mexico: The Challenge of Poverty and Illiteracy* (San Marino, Calif.: Huntington Library, 1963), 8. Ruiz estimates that illiteracy in many rural villages was closer to 100 percent in 1910.

6. For brief discussions of public scribes in Mexico, see Pablo Piccato, *City of Suspects: Crime in Mexico City, 1900–1931* (Durham, N.C.: Duke University Press, 2001), 31, 38; and Susie S. Porter, *Working Women in Mexico City: Public Discourses and Material Conditions, 1879–1931* (Tucson: University of Arizona Press, 2003), 150, 190.

7. Christina M. Jiménez, "Making an Urban Public: How the City Revolutionized Citizenship in Mexico, 1880–1930," book manuscript in progress.

8. Ian F. McNeely, *The Emancipation of Writing: German Civil Society in the Making, 1790s-1820s* (Berkeley: University of California Press, 2003), 1–2.

9. See Seventh Constitutional Congress, *Constitutión federal de los estados de México por el congreso constituyente el día 5 de febrero de 1857* (Mexico City: Imprenta del Gobierno Federal, 1896), article 2 of Section 4. Hilda Sabato discusses similar occupational restrictions in Peru. See Hilda Sabato, "On Political Citizenship in Nineteenth-Century Latin America," *American Historical Review* 106, no. 4 (2001): 1290–1315.

10. These ideas are elaborated on in Christina M. Jiménez, "Their Right to the City: Political Uses of Public Space in a Mexican Provincial Capital, 1880–1910s," *Urban History* 33, no. 3 (2006): 435–56.

11. For recent studies that explore these overlapping links between citizenship, popular politics, liberalism, and in some cases urban formation in Mexico, see Andrés Lira, *Comunidades indígenas frente a la Ciudad de México: Tenochititlan y Tlatelolco, sus pueblos y barrios, 1812–1919* (Mexico City: Colegio de Mexico, Centro de Estudios Históricos, 1995); Carlos Illades and Ariel Kuri Rodríguez, eds., *Ciudad de México: Instituciones, actores sociales y conflicto político, 1774–1931* (Zamora: Colegio de Michoacán, 1996); and Peter Guardino, *The Time of Liberty: Popular Political Culture in Oaxaca, 1750–1850* (Durham, N.C.: Duke University Press, 2005). For similar studies on other regions of Latin America, see Sarah C. Chambers, *From Subjects to Citizens: Honor, Gender, and Politics in Arequipa, Peru, 1780–1854* (University Park: Pennsylvania State University Press, 1999); Brooke Larson, *Trials of Nation Making: Liberalism, Race, and Ethnicity in the Andes, 1810–1910* (Cambridge: Cambridge University Press, 2004); and Antonio Annino and François-Xavier Guerra, eds., *Inventando la nación: Iberoamérica. Siglo XIX* (Mexico City: Fondo de Cultura Económica, 2003).

12. Gerardo Sánchez Díaz, *Pueblos, villas y cuidades de Michoacán en el Porfiriato* (Morelia, Mexico: Universidad Michoacana de San Nicolás de Hidalgo, 1991); and Enrique Florescano, ed., *Historia general de Michoacán*, vols. 3 and 4 (Morelia, Mexico: Instituto Michoacano de Cultura, 1989). Robert M. Buffington and William E. French, "The Culture of Modernity," in Michael C. Meyer and William H. Beezley, eds., *The Oxford History of Mexico* (New York: Oxford University Press, 2000), 425, note that "between 1877 and 1910, Chihuahua City's population grew from 12,000 to 30,000, Monterrey's from 14,000 to 79,000. The Federal District more than doubled, to house in excess of 700,000 people, with nearly half its 1910 population originating from elsewhere in Mexico."

13. José Alfredo Uribe Salas, *Morelia, los pasos a la modernidad* (Morelia, Mexico: Centro de Investigaciones Históricas, Universidad Michoacana de San Nicholas de Hidalgo, 1993), 8.

14. Studies of the political and economic conflicts surrounding the Mexican Revolution, particularly those treating urban groups, include Alan Knight, *The Mexican Revolution*, vols. 1 and 2 (Cambridge: Cambridge University Press, 1986); John Hart, *Revolutionary Mexico: The Coming and Process of the Mexican Revolution* (Berkeley: University of California Press, 1987); Barry Carr, *El movimiento obrero y la política en México*, 2 vols. (Mexico City: Sepsetentas: 1976); and Adolfo Gilly, *La revolución interrumpida, México 1910–1940* (Mexico City: El Caballito, 1971). Regional studies of export economies, political conflict, and political consolidation include Gil Joseph, *Revolution from Without* (Cambridge: Cambridge University Press, 1982); Aguilar Héctor Camín, *La revolución sonorense, 1910–1914* (Mexico City: Instituto Nacional de Antropológica e Historia, 1975); and Allen Wells, *Yucatan's Gilded Age: Haciendas, Henequen, and International Harvester, 1860–1915* (Albuquerque: University of New Mexico Press, 1985).

15. For studies on the regional history of Michoacán, see Margaret Chowning, *Wealth and Power in Provincial Mexico: Michoacán from the Late Colony to the*

Revolution (Stanford, Calif.: Stanford University Press, 1999); Eduardo Nomelí Mijangos Díaz, *La revolución y el poder político en Michoacán* (Morelia, Mexico: Universidad Michoacana de San Nicolás de Hidalgo, 1997); Martín Sánchez Rodríguez, *Grupos de poder y centralización política en México: El caso Michoacán, 1920–1924* (Mexico City: Instituto Nacional de Estudios Históricos de la Revolución Mexicana, 1993); and Christopher R. Boyer, *Becoming Campesinos: Politics, Identity, and Agrarian Struggle in Postrevolutionary Michoacán, 1920–1935* (Stanford, Calif.: Stanford University Press, 2003).

16. Arnold J. Bauer. *Goods, Power, History: Latin America's Material Culture* (Cambridge: Cambridge University Press, 2001), 152–53; and Benjamin Orlove, ed. *Allure of the Foreign: Imported Goods in Postcolonial Latin America* (Ann Arbor: University of Michigan Press, 1997), 13.

17. See Archivo Histórico del Municipio de Morelia (AHMM), box 252, file 233, 1881–1882, box 252, file 283, 1881–1882; box 253, file 158, June 6, 1884; box 261, file 165, July 23, 1887. As early as 1882, the city council was budgeting money for expenditures on seeds and saplings to plant in the gardens and walkways of the city. AHMM, box 252, file 165, March 27, 1882.

18. Uribe Salas, *Morelia*, 32–33, 96–99.

19. In contrast to Mexico City's, these urban police forces were small: "By the late *Porfiriato*, [Mexico] City's police forces consisted of 422 mounted police, 1,872 gendarmes on foot, and a corps of secret police." See John Robert Lear, "Workers, Vecinos, and Citizens: The Revolution in Mexico City, 1909–1917." (Ph.D. diss., University of California, Berkeley, 1993), 129–30.

20. Alan Knight uses the term *developmentist/developmentalism* in "Popular Culture and the Revolutionary State in Mexico, 1910–1940," *Hispanic American Historical Review* 74, no. 3 (1994): 396. For a theoretical discussion of racism in Mexico in the early twentieth century, see Alan Knight, "Racism, Revolution, and *Indigenismo:* Mexico, 1910–1940," in Richard Graham, ed., *The Idea of Race in Latin America, 1870–1940* (Austin: University of Texas Press, 1990). For a treatment of these ideas in Brazil, see Dain Borges, " 'Puffy, Ugly, Slothful, and Inert': Degeneration in Brazilian Social Thought, 1880–1940," *Journal of Latin American Studies* 25 (1993): 235–56; Howard Winant, "Rethinking Race in Brazil," *Journal of Latin American Studies* 24 (1992): 173–92; and Thomas Holloway, *Policing Rio de Janeiro: Repression and Resistance in a Nineteenth-Century City* (Stanford, Calif.: Stanford University Press, 1993); These ideas are explored in the U.S. context by Alan M. Kraut, *Silent Travelers: Germs, Genes, and the "Immigrant Menace"* (Baltimore: Johns Hopkins University Press, 1994).

21. This was certainly the case through the 1890s, as exemplified in AHMM, book 321, exp. 184, October 31, 1894. Depending on the availability of municipal funds, the city employed between forty and fifty night guards, roughly ten regular policemen, and twelve sanitary police at any given time from the late 1880s to the revolution.

22. AHMM, box 252, file 257, 1881–1882. All of these municipal employees were paid an average of ten to twelve pesos per month, a salary slightly higher than the typical wage of manual laborers hired to work on private and public construction projects during the 1880s. According to this municipal budget, in 1882 the forty regular night guards employed by the municipality earned twelve pesos per month. In contrast, a handful of head night guards earned nearly double, at twenty-five pesos per month, and the inspector of night lighting earned thirty pesos per month.

23. See AHMM, box 261, file 93, March 1888 for various inventory lists and other records.

24. This concern for trees within the city is coupled with a concern about deforestation more generally in the region. The prefect of Morelia kept records on the "conservation and propagation" of the wooded lands in the district. Local police chiefs were responsible for preserving local forest lands and reporting to the prefect on the condition of forests. By 1896, the governor's office expressed concern about the state of deforestation in the district. See AHMM, book 336, file 82, December 26, 1896.

25. See articles 48–51 of the 1881 Edict of Police, AHMM, box 249, file 76, 1881–1882. Other trees would be cared for by sentenced prisoners laboring under the public works inspector. Since 1873, local law specified that persons who cut down a tree in a public park without the express permission of the city government had to pay for the cost of replacing the tree in addition to a twenty-five-peso fine or spend ten days to one month in jail, during which time they were required to plant at least six trees under the instructions of the public works inspector. The council consistently enforced this law, both imposing fines for violations and regularly denying requests to cut down trees through the 1920s. Although fines were regularly imposed, the abundance of requests for such permission also attests to the attention paid to this decree by Morelia's residents. For example, upon asking if he could cut down a tree whose branches were blocking the sun from his alfalfa field, Victoriano Mendieta was informed by the city council that he could not cut it down, as doing so would "remove some of the most beautiful trees that landscaped the one side of the Paseo San Pedro." See AHMM, book 332, file 196, August 5, 1896. For various requests for permission to cut down trees and related fines, see AHMM, box 261, file 194, May 18, 1888; box 261, file 195, June 1, 1888.

26. Some of the files on the Día del Árboles include: AHMM, book 319, file 53, December 22, 1893; book 316, file 132, June 10, 1893; book 338, file 213, July 4, 1897; box 372, file 21, 1904; box 324, file 15, 1927. Every July 1 schoolchildren, preparatory students, invited guests, local politicians, and the governor of Michoacán paraded along the main street, followed by five carts and two urban trolley platform cars carrying numerous tree saplings to be planted in the central plaza gardens as well as along the main boulevard. While the governor of Michoacan headed the procession, the festivities were planned and hosted by the municipal government. By the 1890s, festivities for Arbor Day were publicly announced through circulated flyers and official programs. Such celebrations continued through the 1920s.

27. AHMM, box 261, file 47, December 6, 1887.

28. AHMM, box 21, file 155, March 6, 1911.

29. Although few studies in Mexican history have been solely dedicated to the history of vending and street peddlers, several historians of Mexico and Latin America have recognized the importance of street vending to urban popular groups, particularly among recent migrants to the city; see Pablo Piccato, "*Urbanistas, Ambulantes,* and *Mendigos*: The Dispute for Urban Space in Mexico City, 1890–1930," in Carlos A. Aguirre and Robert Buffington, eds., *Reconstructing Criminality in Latin America* (Wilmington, Del.: Scholarly Resources, 2000), 113–48; and Susie Shannon Porter, "In the Shadows of Industrialization: The Entrance of Women into the Mexican Industrial Work Force, 1880–1940" (Ph.D. diss., University of California, San Diego, 1997), esp. chap. 4. On the role of urban selling for slaves in Peru, see Christine Hünefeldt, *Paying the Price of Freedom: Family and Labor among Lima's Slaves, 1800–1854* (Berkeley: University of California Press, 1994). For a study of street peddlers in the context of U.S. urban history, see Daniel M. Bluestone, " 'The Pushcart Evil': Peddlers, Merchants, and New York City's Streets, 1890–1940," *Journal of Urban History* 18, no. 1 (1991): 68–92. Problems and debates surrounding street vending continue to the present in many Mexican and Latin American cities. For more contemporary studies, see John C. Cross, *Informal Politics: Street Vendors and the State in Mexico City* (Stanford, Calif.: Stanford University Press, 1998); and Gareth A. Jones and Ann Varley, "The Contest for the City Centre: Street Traders versus Buildings," *Bulletin of Latin American Research* 13, no. 1 (1994): 27–44. The deepest research on the issues surrounding late-twentieth-century urban selling has been dedicated to Peru; see Ivan Alonso, Fernando Iwasaki, and Enrique Ghersi, *El comercio ambulatorio en Lima* (Lima: Instituto Libertad y Democracia, 1989); Ximena Bunster and Elsa M. Chaney, *Sellers and Servants: Working Women in Lima, Peru* (New York: Praeger, 1985); Florence E. Babb, *Between Field and Cooking Pot: The Political Economy of Marketwomen in Peru* (Austin: University of Texas Press, 1989); Gavin Smith, *Livelihood and Resistance: Peasants and the Politics of Land in Peru* (Berkeley: University of California Press, 1989); and Romeo Grompone, *Talleristas y vendedores ambulantes el Lima* (Lima: DESCO, Centro de Estudios y Promoción del Desarrollo, 1985). For a comparative history of peddling in Europe, see Laurence Fontaine, *History of Pedlars in Europe,* trans. Vicki Whittaker (Durham, N.C.: Duke University Press, 1996).

30. AHMM, box 254, file 64, January 18, 1884. For a similar request, see AHMM, box 261, file 145, June 8, 1888.

31. Permanent stalls usually consisted of a tabletop with a built-in cabinet underneath constructed of wood with zinc or cloth siding. *Petates* are traditional woven straw mats. AHMM, box 254, file. 64, January 18, 1884. For a similar request, see AHMM, box 261, file 145, June 8, 1888.

32. See Seventh Constitutional Congress, *Constitutión federal.*

33. Mauricio Tenorio-Trillo, *Mexico at the World's Fairs: Crafting a Modern Nation* (Berkeley: University of California Press, 1996).

34. See AHMM, box 247, without file number, 1879; box 55, bundle 1, file 10, January 22, 1920.

35. AHMM, box 253, file 140, May 29, 1884.

36. The councilman made this request to a petition from nine sellers of ceramics to return to their old central location, see AHMM, box 29, file 134, September 25, 1914.

37. For an interesting comparative study on municipal policies aimed at controlling the urban poor and homeless, see Gilles Vandal, "The Nineteenth-Century Municipal Responses to the Problem of Poverty: New Orleans' Free Lodgers, 1850–1880, as a Case Study," *Journal of Urban History* 19 no. 1 (November 1992): 30–59.

38. AHMM, box 17, bundle 2, file 8, December 29, 1909; box 23, bundle 2, file 138, June 23, 1913; box 308, file 16, 1924.

39. AHMM, box 27, bundle 1, file 86, November 19, 1913.

40. AHMM, box 25, bundle 1, file 72, November 20, 1912; AHMM box 29, file 123, October 1, 1914; box 29, file 22, November 16, 1914. box 29, file 134, September 1914; and box 30, bundle 2, file 49, November 27, 1914.

41. AHMM, box 25, bundle 1, file 104, November 5, 1912. The Plaza Carrillo was a working- and middle-class neighborhood close to the Chiquito River on the south side of the city, precisely the kind of neighborhood where the city council hoped to relocate many vendors in order to get them out of the center and overcrowded markets. For an analysis of the development of these peripheral plazas and the role played by popular groups, see Christina M. Jiménez, "From Plazas to Colonias: Popular Claims to Urban Development in Mexico, 1880–1955," paper presented at the Center for Latin American Studies, Princeton University, February 17, 2004.

42. AHMM, box 17, bundle 2, file 112, April 29, 1910; box 25, bundle 1, file. 5, September 21, 1912; and box 23, bundle 1, file 46, May 14, 1913.

43. AHMM, box 17, bundle 2, file 89, June 18, 1910.

44. For many more of these complaints, see AHMM, box 26, various files, 1913.

45. AHMM, box 25, bundle 1, file 5, September 21, 1913.

46. Among the first requests were those from "La Violeta," owned by José Trevino, AHMM, box 13, file 43, July 4, 1904; "La Criolla," owned by Luis G. Calderón, box 17, bundle 2, file 84, July 7, 1910; and "El Puerto de Liverpool," owned by the Indiffred Brothers Company, box 17, bundle 2, file 83, July 6, 1910.

47. For files regarding display cases, and window cases see AHMM, box 13, file 43, July 1, 1901; box 17, bundle 2, file 84, July 7, 1910; box 17, bundle 2, file 83, July 6, 1910; box 23, bundle 1, file 31, March 11, 1913; box 17, bundle 2, file 112, April 29, 1910; box 23, bundle 2, file 138, June 23, 1913; box 315, file 19, 1925; and box 315, file 18, 1925.

48. This practice, discussed in the last section, was part of a proposal made in 1926 by the National Commission on Commerce to local business owners as one way to effectively compete with street vendors, who were perceived as taking away much of their business.

49. William Leach, *Land of Desire: Merchants, Power, and the Rise of a New American Culture* (New York: Vintage Books, 1993), 61, 62–63.

50. AHMM, box 17, bundle 2, file 83, July 6, 1910.

51. AHMM, box 22, bundle 2, file 104, October 17, 1911.

52. For files regarding permits that were unconditionally granted to construct kiosks, see AHMM, box 17, bundle 1, file 101, April 17, 1908; box 21, file 162, March 10, 1911; box 21, file 126, August 29, 1911; box 21, file 208, August 12, 1912; box 23, bundle 2, file 21, August 25, 1913; box 25, bundle 1, file 54, November 29, 1912; and box 26, bundle 2, file 50, January 31, 1913.

53. For files regarding permits denied or limited, see AHMM, box 17, bundle 2, file 50, February 28, 1910; box 17, bundle 1, file 115, March 30, 1908; box 27, bundle 1, file 59, December 10, 1913; box 26, bundle 1, file 3, September 18, 1913; box 23, bundle 2, file 54, January 18, 1913; box 23, bundle 2, file 140, April 7, 1913; box 17, bundle 1, September 27, 1907; and box 17, bundle 1, file 16, November 25, 1907. For a long-term temporary seller, see box 27, bundle 1, file 59, December 10, 1913. One man, Vicente Tovar, noted that he had been erecting his stall to sell candies during Christmas for the past ten years.

54. AHMM, box 17, bundle 2, file 112, April 29, 1910. Also see AHMM, box 23, bundle 1, file 31, March 11, 1913.

55. AHMM, box 23, bundle 2, file 138, June 23, 1913.

56. AHMM, box 17, bundle 2, file 84, July 7, 1910.

57. AHMM, box 315, file 19, 1925. Another example in 1925 was the request by José Carrillo and his son, who were opening a leather goods store. Notably, the letter was drafted by his legal representative, José Hurtado Júarez, who wrote to the city council about this permit on his behalf. See box 315, file 18, 1925.

58. Christina M. Jiménez, "Popular Organizing for Public Services: Residents Modernize Morelia, Mexico, 1880–1920," *Journal of Urban History* 30, no. 4 (May 2004): 495–518.

59. Hilda Sabato, *The Many and the Few: Political Participation in Republican Buenos Aires* (Stanford, Calif.: Stanford University Press, 2001). See the epilogue for a discussion of these ideas and also Sabato, "On Political Citizenship."

60. AHMM, book 317, file 189, September 22, 1891. Also see other letters in same file.

61. Ibid.

62. AHMM, box 22, bundle 2, file 111, October 21, 1911.

63. AHMM, box 22, bundle 2, file 104, October 17, 1911.

64. AHMM, box 26, bundle 2, file 12, February 24, 1914.

65. AHMM, box 28, bundle 3, file 25, May 8, 1914.

66. AHMM, box 42, bundle 2, file 2, February 18, 1917.

67. AHMM, box 42, bundle 1, file 8, July 17, 1917. This file contains several letters and permit approvals for this year. Also see box 32, bundle 2, file 53, February 12, 1916; book 112, file 19, July 25, 1919.

68. AHMM, book 112, file 19, 1919. This thick file contains numerous requests of this sort, many of which were granted.

69. AHMM, book 112, file 19, 1919.

70. Ibid. In his letter, Estrada accused the city council of denying his request because his political affiliation opposed that of the seated council. Although this may certainly have been true, I do not have enough information about these political factions within Morelia to draw concrete conclusions from this assertion.

71. AHMM, box 308, file 10, file 77, and others, 1924.

72. AHMM, box 308, file without number, 1924. Quoted from a letter written by José Viveros, dated October 24, 1924.

73. See AHMM, box 321, bundle 2, file 1, 1926; box 95, files 42 and 48, 1929; box 418, file 24, 1930.

74. AHMM, box 321, bundle 1, file 8, October 26, 1926.

75. Ibid.

76. AHMM, box 321, bundle 2, file 1, 1926.

77. See John C. Cross, *Informal Politics, Street Vendors and the State in Mexico City* (Stanford, Calif.: Stanford University Press, 1998); and Jérôme Monnet, *Usos e imágenes del centro histórico de la Ciudad de México* (Mexico City: Centro de Estudios Mexicanos y Centroamericanos, 1995).

CHAPTER 7

The City as Theater of Protest:
West Berlin and West Germany, 1962–1983

BELINDA DAVIS

WEST BERLIN/"THE CITY"

Since its explosive growth at the turn of the twentieth century, Berlin has both shared many characteristics with other German, European, and "world cities" (*Weltstädte*) and boasted many unique associations. The latter was all the more the case for the two "half-cities" in the post–World War II Germanies, each side representing the last, best bulwark, physical and ideological, against incursions from the Cold War enemy. West Berlin in particular captured the popular imagination of millions, in West Germany and elsewhere, though its formal geopolitical status was entirely anomalous, and though its residents suffered the effects of its peculiar "island" existence, all the more once East German authorities erected the Wall in August 1961. "Front City Berlin" or "Cold War Island Berlin" represented for many young West Germans and others a potential beacon of freedom and democracy—in sharp contrast to its actual circumstances, "hard" in many senses. Though not a capital like Paris or Tokyo, West Berlin shared with those cities the symbolism of a powerful modernity—and postmodernity—and the characteristics of the "new urbanism," with its "electrifying atmosphere."[1] But, beyond this, it represented an especial mutability; indeed, it was largely the imposition of fantasy that made the gray, hardscrabble city seem alive. The physical space of the city was in the postwar era a kaleidoscope of enduring (if competing) symbolisms and open signifiers. From the early 1960s through the early 1980s particularly, protestors drew on that space in its complexity to inform particular forms of activism. Further, activists mapped characteristics and qualities of themselves onto the city's surfaces, and adopted the same in turn from the city. Politics made the space; activists "made" West Berlin; West Berlin in turn made the activists.[2] Its peculiar uprooting from established meanings made it a site particularly accommodating of activists' fantasies.

The broad spectrum of "New Left" activism had already begun in the early to mid-1960s in some forms around West Germany/West Berlin, but contemporary popular narrative situated the activism squarely in West Berlin, radiating out to the west beyond its walled borders, but remaining the hub of such activity. The accepted story is that the New Left began in West Berlin in the cramped office of the Socialist German Student Organization (SDS) at the Free University, in the placid southwest of the city, remaining primarily a campus-based phenomenon, though one closely observed by student organizations at other universities, at least until June 1967.[3] In an example of West Berlin at its worst, on June 2 a policeman fatally shot a peaceful student demonstrator, thereby mobilizing and unifying broader populations. Frankfurt on the Main, national headquarters of the SDS, arose in popular vision as the "second city" of New Left protest. But West Berlin remained the capital (of this, if of nothing else).

The attempt by a right-wing activist to assassinate student leader Rudi Dutschke in the city some ten months later sparked a dissolution of the larger "extraparliamentary" movement (Außerparlamentarische Organisation, or APO) in most narrations.[4] Still, one hastens to mention the successes of these years, on issues from broad educational reform to making the wider public aware of injustices abroad. This activity contributed to an indefinite transformation of West German (then German) political culture, including significant democratization. Moreover, 1968–69 marked the beginning of the critical "new social movements" (women's, antinuclear, and environmental movements, among others) that spread throughout the city in the 1970s, under its "surfaces," in turn forming a critical part of the mammoth peace activism of the early 1980s. In this context, alongside the pitched discussion of the new, marginal, but closely watched violent protest, West Berlin remained a critical physical and symbolic center. This activism remained tightly imbricated with a set of desires about personal "liberation" that were closely connected with political liberation worldwide, and that were in turn represented by and through language about "the city," and West Berlin above all. Understanding how West Berlin played this role, as a city and as a particular city, how activists—not just leaders—interacted with and used the city, and how this affected and remade the city in turn is the mission of this chapter.

DREAMSCAPES: *DRANG NACH BERLIN*

> So I lived at that point in Frankfurt. Then I realized things were really happening in [West] Berlin. . . . Everything was possible. . . .

So I just came here [to West Berlin]. There was so much going on. There were lots of . . . that is, above all, lots of people from Italy, just lots of people.

—"Silke"

The dream is out.

—*Punk music band Ton Steine Scherben, 1982*

The "pull to West Berlin" was a complex and contradictory impulse: born of excitement and fear, politics and personal desire, these characteristics fit closely together. West Berlin symbolized a potential utopia; particularly after June 1967 and April 1968, it represented an actual dystopia. It seems to have been in part the distance between these poles that so attracted the tens of thousands of young people who poured into the anomalous *Weltstadt* in the 1960s and '70s, even as so many older citizens deserted the walled city.[5] Despite its lost formal geopolitical status, West Berlin represented a center of world politics; as many informants observed, "big politics" were simply unrelentingly "present" (*präsent*) there. Cold War rhetoric, and official propagandistic deployment of the city, contributed to making the former Third Reich capital a mecca for thousands of non-Germans. This in turn contributed substantially to the imaginary geography in which younger West Germans situated it. Despite its especial remoteness by some measures, swallowed on all sides by the German Democratic Republic (East Germany), it was somehow closely connected to the "rest of the world"— to elsewhere in western Europe; to the United States; and to Latin America, Africa, and Asia. This wholly new city, in which the markers of the past bobbed about like jetsam, laid itself open to be remade by young West Germans and others, who sought through this process to remake themselves.

Many determined to come to West Berlin, beginning especially in the early 1960s, to change their lives and prospective life paths, for what they perceived to be this sense of freedom, including freedom to speak out. There was a generalized atmosphere of excitement, a feeling that this was where things happened, if not always easy things. Precisely the range of young people in the city created the admixture of experiences and ideas that promoted the intense level of discussion initially associated with the Free University (FU), in particular, but also well beyond its confines. Activist Hanna Kröger wrote in 1969 in the SDS journal *Neue Kritik* that nowhere was activism so exciting—or so effective—as in the city of West Berlin.[6] The city's perceived character as a site for such excitement in turn became a self-fulfilling prophecy, as throughout the 1960s and into the next two decades, young Germans flocked to the city because it was, if no longer the national capital, the "capital of politics," the "capital of leftist debate," and "capital of the 'scene' [Szene]."[7] Activists in the city and outside onlookers saw West Berlin as a crucible, a white-hot vessel literally difficult to escape. "Tulla," who came to the city in 1970 as a student, remembered the city's "unbeliev-ably heated atmosphere." Peter Mosler, FU student and activist, wrote that in turn the movement was constituted by the "talk of the cities in which the pavement was the hottest, Berlin and Frankfurt"—and he saw the former as considerably surpassing the latter.[8]

The image of "hot pavement" raises another set of metaphors instrumen-tal in mobilizing young activists. The image resonated with the readiness of activists to take to the streets, in small and larger numbers, in more and less "well-behaved" fashion, and with the willingness of such activists at a cer-tain point to avail themselves of paving stones, a primary symbol of the '68 movement in Europe, in defense of their right to be in the street. It hints at the situationist notion of the "beach" that lay beneath the paved streets, the city's liberatory—and liberatable—potential, despite as well as because of its external structures. Herbert Vesely's 1959 short movie Die Stadt (The City) anticipates 1960s West Berlin's contradictions and the need to work around them, directly connecting these characteristics to activists' own para-doxical feelings of impotence and potential to imagine and realize change, as well as their fear of and rage toward those who sought to quiet them.

Indeed, the degree to which these activists created this fantastic character must be emphasized: the West Berlin of the 1960s and '70s was a difficult place to live on many counts. The Wall built in August 1961, still more severely circumscribed movement in and out of the city (fig. 7.1). If West German and Allied funding contributed to the rebuilding of this north Ger-man "half-city," in demonstration of the virtues of capitalism in the midst of residual Stalinist communism, it remained bleak and gray, dotted with areas of still bombed-out and bullet-pocked buildings, and of ugly new mass housing projects. Despite the subsidy of "cultural life," as in the building of the new opera, and of the America House, the city seemed overall lifeless, even in the early 1960s. "Gaby," arriving in the city first in 1974, described it still then as a "very hard city," on the "front lines of the Cold War." She and many others believed this contributed to the singularly "hard" nature of activists' battles there, for example, in contrast to those in Munich, where fun (Spaß and Gaudi) prevailed. There were other particular reasons for this. Christian Semler among others, who spent his youth commuting between Munich and Berlin, noted that the city had boasted a notably liberal bent in the initial postwar decades. But, reversing the path residents in other regions took, older West Berliners grew less tolerant and less accommodating by the

Figure 7.1. West Berlin (districts in East Berlin are outlined but not labeled). Map by Sophia Appelbaum.

mid-1960s. Protestors claimed they often feared "being beaten almost dead" when they demonstrated: "the population there was against us. . . . [We] always had to reckon with being persecuted."[9] Certainly the beefed-up police "standby forces" (*Bereitschaft*), developed in both halves of the divided city to ward off external enemies, had a powerful effect on policing more broadly in the western part.[10] The police execution of a peaceful protestor on June 2, 1967, was only one example of this affect of besiegement—a sentiment that spread among resident populations.

And yet what is remarkable is that young people—students and others—crowded in anyway, seeing in this dismal reality particularly great possibilities. Though an avowed Frankfurt resident and activist, "Susanne" acknowledged being convinced by her brother's reports from the city to the east, averring that, if revolution would come anywhere in Germany, it would be in West Berlin. "Tulla" remembered: "Well, of course I wanted to come to Berlin: that's where everything was happening. . . . It had a burning interest for me. . . . I absolutely wanted to do something." "Heinrich," leaving the

251

Munich scene for West Berlin in 1972, saw it more as an obligation than as a fantasy: he recalled that, when he wanted to "do the right thing . . . [it] only made sense to come to Berlin. . . . Berlin simply constituted the summa" of potential for transformation. Leading SDS and later Maoist activist Christian Semler, a native of both Munich and West Berlin, chose for this reason to stay in the latter with his sister even as a teenager—while his mother moved back to Bavaria. "People just came to Berlin . . . yeah, we were packed in pretty tightly," and that was exciting. Some informants remark on the particularly divisive politics among activists in that city. But others speak of how the existing "hard life" was a unifying force, melding activists together over the heat of opposition to them.

Thus, the dream of the city was a complex fantasy for many activists, far removed from the simple hedonism described by some members of the press in their own imaginings of activist desires. To be sure, such lurid tales as many articles recounted contributed for some to West Berlin's draw, just as did the hard life. Activist leaders (a designation created at least in part by the press) above all in West Berlin achieved celebrity status, winning hundreds of letters expressing love, adoration, willingness to engage in sex—and testimony to the writers' own political practices and dreams.[11] The authors of such letters represented a notably broad range of age, region of residence, and other demographic characteristics. Some wrote to establish a kind of vicarious connection to the activities of these "stars"—and to the city itself. But for others, the dream was to travel physically to the city themselves. Indeed, many treated the apartment of West Berlin's famous (or infamous) living commune, Kommune I, located in a pleasant petit bourgeois area of the city, as a kind of shrine to which they hoped to make pilgrimage. Writing often to "Kommune I, Stuttgarter Platz, Berlin," or even simply to "Kommune I, Berlin," West Germans—alongside many non-German nationals— requested permission to come "hang" with commune members for a while, or even simply announced their imminent arrival for indefinite periods. "Dear Kommune-Gang!" wrote one typical enthusiast, "can I come by you in January [1968] for a 'sleep-in' for about two weeks? . . . Am formally politically bound to you. What I'm going to do in Berlin, I don't know exactly. Maybe experience, fun, etc. . . . Do I need to bring a sleeping bag?" (Indeed, in the process of projecting their fantasies, many apparently took the Kommunards for a travel agency, announcing a whole range of plans and demanding accommodations and other arrangements—and even job placement in West Berlin, as one French bookseller requested.)[12]

Some letters were clearly from star-struck teenagers—though the role of personal fantasy and what it represented in terms of playing out an alternate reality should not be discounted. Many of these authors wrote of their own increasing political engagement as well, which they seemed to seek to validate through even this attenuated form of connection with West Berlin. Most seemed to admire these activists' vision of doing things differently. In the case of the Kommunards, correspondents seemed fascinated by their position as "life artists" (*Lebenskünstler*): those who take themselves on as a creative and recreative project, defying their own pasts and the constraints around them to remake themselves, as part of a political project.[13] "The city" generally was a critical element in this: before coming to West Berlin, Kommunard Dieter Kunzelmann asserted the sense that "cities are sandboxes for grown-up children."[14] One correspondent penned a request that member Fritz Teufel, recently released from prison, write to "tell about how freedom tasted," seemingly a reference both to the contrast in Teufel's own recent experiences and to that between Teufel's and the writer's own lives.

This latter disparity—as between the hard reality in West Berlin and the fantasies activists sought to realize—is reflected as well by memoirs and interviews that refer to a kind of "double life" and "double existence" many young West Germans felt they led in this period. There was the "everyday" life led according to parents' demands and tight constraints, and a second life of dreams and desires, often realized in part, sometimes in fantasy only—for the time being—but tied either way to a specifically urban excitement. West German teenager Gabriele Huster described this double life in a 1967 diary entry in which she describes her experience sneaking out of her rural home to see the Rolling Stones in concert in "big city" Dortmund.[15] Others more physically proximate to urban areas describe regularly crawling out of bedroom windows at night or on weekends to go to concerts, dance, or just walk with friends "in the city," a first step toward creating something different for themselves. (A few would leave home at midnight and return at dawn, in time to get to school by seven, unbeknownst to parents.)

But this allure applied particularly to West Berlin. If contemporaries imposed on that city an imagined geography, a sense of its proximity somehow to the rest of the world that defied physical geography, this pull was about going where things were "happening," where the "action" was—and where one could be a part of it.[16] This conception was not completely unfounded: West German and Allied politicians regularly used West Berlin as a staging ground for propagandistic pageantry, offering performances by individuals from Lucius Clay and John F. Kennedy to a host of world leaders; at the same time, spies were exchanged on the city's Glienicker bridge. This official glamour was also part of its appeal, and, critically, became in turn a self-fulfilling prophecy. Cities generally, like universities, are more likely to attract people from outside; West Berlin was particular attractive to the thousands who brought new ideas and cultures with them and thereby added to the glamorous as well as gritty strangeness that West Berlin represented.[17] The presence, moreover, of the exotic and fantastic, offering tastes of how things could be, came not only from individual people. Movies like Louis Malle's *Viva Maria* (1965) made a particular impact across West Germany and West Berlin, connecting the European protagonists (Brigitte Bardot and Jeanne Moreau) to the Mexican Revolution, which these characters led to its success while simultaneously fulfilling themselves sexually.[18] The film played for months in West Berlin cinemas; the movie actually contributed to drawing to West Berlin key activists from West Germany, who came together in 1966 to form the "Viva Maria" group. This presence of "the world" was reflected through other seductive means as well, including, for example, through American culture and consumer goods, available above all in big cities. The Kufürstendamm, or Kudamm, the newly prominent West Berlin avenue with its shop windows alternating the newest gadgets and appliances and peep shows, symbolized for all West Germans the apotheosis of postwar consumption and globalization, in both its most positive and increasingly negative senses.[19]

But there was something more to this process of "opening up," for which West Berlin became such a powerful symbol, a "total global city," the true "center of politics," despite the city's lack of an official political role.[20] Many West Germans came specifically to West Berlin after "tramping" widely for months and even years, finding it the only German city to reflect the "world experience" they felt they had gained—and to which they in turn contributed.[21] West Berlin–born "Franz" stayed in the city after moving from home in 1974: unlike many counterparts born outside the city, he asked why he would think of leaving his "home town" for any length of time. Attending classes at the Free University, he spent his evenings at a bar in Schlachtensee, a quiet, comfortable neighborhood in southwest Berlin, drinking with Iranians, Chileans, and Palestinians: the role of "international" students and other residents, far more critical than is recognized throughout the movement in western Europe, was visible everywhere in this city. "Bärbel," who came to West Berlin alone as a young teenager in 1973, felt she had left the country entirely: for over a decade in the movement she lived and worked in the city entirely among non-Germans. She spoke specifically of West Berlin's role in creating these critical international contacts—a circumstance of Cold War-inspired scholarships and other programs hardly motivated by interest in bringing young West Germans and West Berliners to challenge conditions and circumstances around them.

This was all "unbelievably exciting" for many of those involved, as informants suggest. But life was no less hard—and quotidien—for the most of them. Behind many protestors of 1969 and later, adorned in straggly hair and blue jeans, stood the suit or dress image of their earlier years, and all the conventions that went along with it.[22] The reality of many West Berliners on their own often looked far removed from fantasy in many respects. Movement leader Rudi Dutschke had a wife (activist Gretchen Dutschke-Klotz) and children; his first child was born in 1967 at the height of his political involvement. Activists Helke Sander and Annette Schwarzenau both bore the burden of single parenthood as the price of their coming to West Berlin, and this characteristic became a central piece of their political work, in large part a function of necessity. Even the Kommunards spent days billing and collecting payments for the mimeographs of their flyers and other material, by which they earned money, as well as pursuing tedious tasks necessary to members' legal troubles. If writers to Kommune I hungered for the "fun" that was the watchword of *provo* and *sponti* (*provocative* and *spontaneous*) antiauthoritarian activism, one must acknowledge the limits of such "fun" in the Kommunard's daily lives.

Indeed, symbol of *gaudi* hedonism, Dieter Kunzelmann, the driving force behind Kommune I, described his own departure from Munich to West Berlin in 1966 as necessary to creating a meaningful political movement that joined personal and broader political "liberation," precisely because Munich was "too hedonistic" a city.[23] When in 1962 Kunzelmann theorized "the city" as the best site for activism in his *Unverbindliche Richtlinien* (Nonbinding Guidelines), citing both situationist and Frankfurt School inspirations, he noted the negative as well as positive qualities in cities, a difficulty of carrying out everyday life that actually contributed to their virtues for political action, qualities that obtained particularly in West Berlin. Many other contemporaries have made a similar case.[24] It was, once again, this combination of fantasy plus the impossibility of fully realizing it that made West Berlin, the walled city, the perfect site for these politics.

Mixing descriptions of personal fulfillment and the West Berlin housing occupations of the late 1970s and early '80s, the lyrics of punk group Ton Stein Scherben (Tone Stone [Glass] Splinters) expressed this same sense, as in the lines "we have to get out of here/this is hell" and "we have to take a step into paradise." Poet and longtime activist Peter-Paul Zahl, coming from Frankfurt to West Berlin via prison in the same period, described the city as "a pile of shit. Of course. But on this pile of shit bloom the most beautiful roses."[25]

It is also important to see this in the context of the German past. A number of activists saw the Berlin Wall as a "late result" of the war, important to acknowledge and contend with in that context. The grittiness and toughness of West Berlin life was part of its functionality for activists and even part of its charm. But, more than this, it seemed that only a city that had sunk so low had the potential for such heights. The dystopia operated as part of the allure. Segments of the West Berlin audience kept Jean-Luc Godard's menacing 1965 *Alphaville* in the theaters as long as the starkly contrasting *Viva Maria*. (The name was later adopted by a West Berlin punk band). One activist claimed that in June 1967 murdered demonstrater Benno Ohnesorg had "died of this city" (not *in dieser Stadt*, but *an dieser Stadt*), contrasting perceived aspects of the city's reality—including remnants of its past—with its potential.[26]

THE CITY AND THE PUBLIC: NOT THE "BERLIN MODEL"

It is well known that initially the situationists wanted at the very least to build cities, the environment suitable to the unlimited deployment of new passions. But of course this was not easy and so we found ourselves forced to do much more.
—*Guy-Ernest Debord*

Here in Berlin I first realized that we could . . . provoke monster demonstrations, through which we make our ideas known to the greater public. We storm a department store or something, take all the goods, and distribute them on the street . . . Or we engineer a crazy scene (*Vögel-Szene*) in the middle of a big shopping area.
—*Dieter Kunzelmann*

Perhaps the foremost fantasy represented for younger West Germans by West Berlin and "the city" more broadly was that of belonging, of being able to communicate, of being listened to.[27] From the early 1960s, students at the Free University argued over the "Berlin Model" and its virtues and limits. The Berlin Model was part of West German and Allied leaders' efforts to make West Berlin a showcase of Western democracy, to define the "new Berlin" in a very particular way. Students at this newly constituted university were to participate ostensibly in decision making at the university: officials and administrators conceived of reasoned, sober discussion as a part of the students' curriculum as well. But many students claimed this was after all old wine in new bottles. Segments of the mainstream press were rather remarkably attentive to student politics, above all in West Berlin, and reported regularly and usually respectfully on decisions students reached through their governing bodies. But most professors and university administrators treated such decisions patronizingly and dismissively when they concerned any substantive issues, such as a demand for action against a professor who spewed anti-Semitic invective in his classroom, or for reconsideration of administrators' "disinvitation" of an outspoken and critical guest speaker. Many students claimed to find the residual authoritarian structures visible in the Berlin Model emblematic in turn of the greater society—and claimed too the right to say what a new Berlin Model should mean—indeed according to presumed Allied principles of democracy. Some among these actively searched for new and more provocative forms of activism toward this end.

On many levels these activists succeeded, both in making their voices heard and in eliciting some form of positive response. The widespread image of activists' "pinned-up" mouths (borrowed from the French *atelier populaire* placard from May 1968) paradoxically loudly bespoke on posters and in demonstrations through the 1970s a broad sentiment of an inability to be heard. Into the 1980s, *Sprayers* (graffiti artists, the name a homophonic pun on the Spree River, connecting West and East Berlin) painted such phrases as "here speech has been whitewashed" and "here words have been painted over" on walls in the Kreuzberg and Schöneberg districts—once more precisely making the message of silencing seen.[28] These activists sought to use West Berlin as both actor in and stage for this activism, moving quickly beyond the university campus to exploit the kinds of spaces and surfaces that cities provide.

The "myth" of Berlin, among other myths, helped bring these "outsiders" into the city to practice their *détournement*, their "rerouting" and "misappropriation" of objects, acts, and places to call particular attention to their message.[29] The fact that so much of its symbolism was up for grabs, while at the same time familiar, reinforced the "publicizability" of such acts; the attention cities attracted generally, compounded in the case of West Berlin's high profile, all but guaranteed a wide audience. This was a central piece of the success of the activists in these decades in transforming the "public sphere," as it had become defined most recently for West Germans in Jürgen Habermas's 1962 *Structural Transformation of the Public Sphere*. For these activists, the limited availability of space for "reasoned debate," and the nature of this debate itself, was insufficient to democratic expression—and, in a more personal sense, to "being heard." A broadened space of expression, alongside an expanded view of the nature of appropriate political expression, was essential to the transformation of West German/German political culture that remains in place to this day. The forms themselves, quite aside from the content, reinforced this breadth and enlarged the scope of action that so well exploited the city's spaces.

From the 1960s and into the early '80s, hundreds of thousands of mostly younger people flowed into West Berlin, for longer and shorter periods of time, to become part of the "scene," their own presence and activism contributing toward maintaining the image and thereby the flow, through a wide range of student-centered and far broader organizations. It was, among other things, in recognition of the variety of activists within and outside the student body that, in 1966, Rudi Dutschke announced a broader "extraparliamentary organization," formally transcending the narrower description of a student movement, though to be sure the university remained one major staging area for "the movement's" planning and actions. Key early actions took place in and in front of the FU rector's office and the university's Henry Ford Building (the name important as well as the building's capacity to hold large groups, such as the international "Vietnam conference," and the area outside it, in which the first sit-ins in Germany took place. The Otto Suhr Institute, named for the popular former West Berlin mayor, and the Mensa, or student cafeteria, were also important sites. But by mid-decade, both planning and "actions" had spread out from the campus in the quiet, prosperous Dahlem district to areas including the Kudamm and the new nearby opera building; to petit bourgeois Wilmersdorf; and, in the next years, to working-class Moabit (and its infamous courtrooms); mixed-class Charlottenburg and Schöneberg; and to poorer Kreuzberg, home to the city's Turkish and other "guest" workers, marked by the Wall and by the despised Springer Press.

One thing was clear: West Berlin could always get attention, and an "action" in this city was almost never a wasted effort. Different parts of the city gave different inflections to actions taken. One activist noted the new "tone" adopted by the SDS once it moved away from campus into an office right on the Kudamm in 1966, parts of the group now more defiant, confrontational, and "radical." This simultaneously glamorous and seedy avenue provided ample general public and official attention for key actions even before the SDS move, from the 1964 demonstration against visiting Congolese leader Moise Tshombe (the first time movement protestors defied police orders); to the 1965 protest against screening of the violent *Africa Addio*, showing in cinemas on the avenue; to the 1966 Christmas *Happening* in which East German leader Walter Ulbricht and American president Lyndon Johnson were burned in effigy. The avenue remained a premier site for actions through the 1970s, during which period some "autonomist" activists, housing occupiers, feminists, and others "strolled" the avenue, or blocked traffic, and broke shop windows to protest perceived West German consumerism.

Likewise, members of Kommune I adopted a site in Charlottenburg very near the Wilmersdorf district as their home, in this case as both a practical and an ironic gesture. Though members performed few actions there, and those who lived nearby admitted they were good enough neighbors, the very presence of the commune in Stuttgarter Platz ("the Stutti") in 1967–68 gave new meaning to the area, a source of concern for many local residents, who proudly conceived of the neighborhood as "respectable," and feared a besmirching of this character. Likewise, this district formed the base for a key West Berlin *sponti* newspaper, *Agit 883*, the name of which derived from the Wilmersdorf telephone exchange, and thus once more made an ironic connection to place in the city, though the original source of the choice was simply an affordable and convenient building. Overall, movement throughout the city was largely pragmatic: if one were relatively poor, as the overwhelming majority of activists were, one rented an apartment or office space where the price was right. Again taking a practical approach, if one wanted to protest the visit of the shah of Iran, one would sensibly demonstrate not on campus but before the city hall and the Opera, where he, city officials, and the press would be, and where the public eye would be focused. At the same time, activists attempted to play with and on localized symbols and surfaces.

The public eye was indeed focused when, in June 1967, a policeman shot first-time demonstrator Benno Ohnesorg at point-blank range in the back of the head while Ohnesorg knelt on the ground, chased from the Opera for the crime of protesting West Berlin's hosting of the Iranian shah. But, as this event made clear, on the stage of this city, no single set of directors and actors controlled how the plot played out. The event effected a coalescence of disparate activists, also bringing hundreds of thousands outside the city into sympathy with the demonstrators. At the same time, it also sharply polarized West Berliners, many of whom believed Ohnesorg "got what he deserved," and that "students should study, and shut up."[30] The effect within the movement was, moreover, as much anxiety- as energy-producing, and the event deepened old fissures, particularly over political strategies and forms. Still, in its unpredicted plot development, the event brought even greater attention to West Berlin—far more so, naturally, than to the other cities in which demonstrators protested the Shah.

Such fissures opened still more in April 1968 after the attempt on Rudi Dutschke's life on the Kudamm by a young man from Munich, who claimed that the goading Springer Press paper *Bild*—and the "success" of the Martin Luther King assassination—inspired him. The frenzied violence in West Berlin in the weeks following this second attack—by demonstrators, primarily against Springer property, by police, primarily against demonstrators—splintered the movement over the questions of tactics, goals, and possibilities for reform. That, alongside the official ban on demonstrations that attempted to move the focus away from West Berlin, effected a retreat by the movement.[31] It also left a mark on the city in the minds of all West Berliners, transforming the meaning of the space around Koch Street and the newspaper district indefinitely. Indeed, emblematic of the lasting (if long-conflicted) memory attached to the area, that piece of Koch Street has now been renamed Rudi Dutschke Street. At the same time there soon developed an even broader proliferation of both performers and stages in the city, as well as across West Germany, in the form of the "new social movements," anti-hierarchical "basis groups," and citizens' initiatives. (Simultatneously, the growing Eastern Bloc–oriented German Communist Party [DKP] turned its focus out of major cities, not least because it did not pursue the publicity-oriented, provocative tactics that operated best in the metropolitan setting.)

The range of practices activists developed in the 1960s through early 1980s was remarkably broad. In terms of sheer quantity, most of the manifestations were written, taking forms from the vast proliferation of newspapers to the ubiquitous flyers and banners, to the graffiti, stamps, buttons, and stickers that increasingly marked the "vertical" as well as the "horizontal": on buildings, on bodies, lofted high into the air. The flyer above all was the hallmark of the movement: cheaply reproducible via mimeograph and easily distributed through the city, these eye-catching if often impossibly wordy documents made an enormous impact. The spoken word was also central, through *Happenings* and the wide range of political "theater."[32] But *Happenings* were about more than just words: such theater was about action as well, as in the notions of "direct action" and "demonstrative action."[33] Bodies sitting or standing where they would not "normally" be, were provocation—as in the innumerable sit-ins, go-ins, and teach-ins, as well as love-ins, smoke-ins, die-ins, and a "Switcheroo-Go-Out," in which a convicted activist switched places with an acquitted one in the courtroom, necessitating that both be let go and subjecting the legal system to ridicule. Filmmakers and artists adopted such techniques with relish. Yet it is important to emphasize that these were not the politics exclusively of the kind of elite that could produce such works. Certainly provo-politics did not belong to anyone exclusively; such forms were *Bild*'s stock and trade as well, and indeed activists borrowed such strategies from the newspaper. Here the importance of the city, and particularly of a city with the symbolic importance of West Berlin, comes into play.

"Provo" actions reflect politics that take advantage most commonly of the urban surface, because of its limitless public spaces, the difficulty (not through lack of effort) of controlling those spaces, and the number of viewers, both direct and indirect. It is worth noting how little it took to be perceived as practicing "provocative" politics in the city: through the end of the 1960s, having long hair or playing guitar in public was enough to elicit charges of disturbance of public order and of antiauthoritarianism.[34] Again, in a city such as West Berlin, not only did such actions win publicity that protesters could scarcely have dreamed of elsewhere, but these actions also meant so much more—and, to be sure, so many more, overdetermined messages—than they would have elsewhere, as activists were well aware. New Left leader Daniel Cohn-Bendit characterized such actions as all about "getting attention," thereby broadening "the public sphere"; he claimed they were effective as such, even when creating "negative" attention.[35] Rudi Dutschke declared retrospectively, despite the attack on him his activism elicited, that the "consciousness-constituting role of provocative acts can be seen as breaking through the hermetic set up by the manipulation system," and was thus an essential part of the "long march," working within existing channels but stretching the existing confines as a means to ultimately superseding them.[36]

The editors of *Agit 883* saw their work contemporaneously as a "practical contribution to a counter-public sphere."[37] But such actions also clearly reached the hegemonic public sphere, when they took place in West Berlin—as some recipients of such "communications" understood. Writing in the major national newspaper *Die Zeit*, journalist Gisela Stelly reported on Dieter Kunzelmann's 1967 "Disturbance Action" during the memorial service for former Reichstag president Paul Löbe, in which Kunzelmann jumped out of a coffin carried aloft to distribute flyers demanding fellow Kommunard Fritz Teufel be released from prison (fig. 7.2). Describing his combination of "provocation and funny clownery," she observed in appreciative tones, "if the art *Happenings* have taken place primarily in a relatively small circle of initiates and celebrated in closed rooms, now 'the public sphere' is being brought into it. The 'action' is transferred to the street." West Berlin, she concluded, was "the center of th[is] culture-revolutionary outbreak"; few other sites could have served the function as well.[38]

Figure 7.2. Members of Kommune I run across heavily trafficked Berlin streets toward a spot near a memorial service for West German eminence Paul Löbe, in a *Happening* to demand freedom for imprisoned "Kommunard" Fritz Teufel (August 12, 1967). Photo courtesy of Michael Ruetz/Agentur Focus.

Perhaps surprisingly, such acts were also regularly "positively" received in some quarters for their intended message, despite officials' commentary and Springer Press's screaming headlines that endlessly proclaimed the satanic acts of a "small, radical minority." One example is the overwhelmingly sympathetic public response to the building-squatting campaigns in West Berlin from the late 1970s (a strategy borrowed from Frankfurt, Hanover, and elsewhere). Ultimately the campaigns won many concrete desired legal and policy remedies, precisely concerning urban policy, including the availability of affordable and attractive housing and the functioning of the city for its inhabitants.[39] One West Berlin occupier noted that for her situation as for many other like instances, "there was always a great lot of support, precisely for the occupiers themselves, as well as for the general [campaign]."[40] In this regard activists managed to convince broad populations that their concerns were valid on many scores, and to persuade a large piece of West German society of the legitimacy of their registering their voices in the public domain.

Many activists have observed the direct benefit for themselves as well, in the form of emotional satisfaction and of the playfulness that they felt in relation to their surroundings. *Szene* life, broadly, a feeling of both fitting in and being somehow connected with the larger world, fed the imagination along with giving activists agency and voice. This was what made it "extremely beautiful" to throw eggs at Amerika-Haus, "euphoric" to be part of a demonstration, what spurred *Feelings* (used in the English) more generally that wakened what many felt to be somnolent lives.[41] One activist described participating in such activities as creating a life "densely filled with experiences, never spent from the deadly emptiness, like before." He related this specifically to "the city," as when "he [threw] himself into his rusty VW, [turned] on the motor, and tore through the city with his gasping machine, Dylan's music in [his] ear."[42] Artifacts of the era brim with both emotional language and discussion of that emotion—especially fun, excitement, and a sense of being part of something—and including a deep need to communicate, to be heard, understood, and acknowledged, opportunities that cities richly afforded. This emotion also included raw fear, real fear of physical danger, from fellow civilians as well as from police, who likewise sought to control the image and symbolism of West Berlin, all the more as police weapons moved from billy clubs to pistols, tear gas, and water cannons. But, while this fear pushed thousands of erstwhile activists into retreat, such actual and prospective danger confirmed for others the need for such acts, perceived as the only strategies—aside from terrorism—for civilians to make a powerful public statement in response.

BERLIN IN PRIVATE: NOT THE "BERLIN LINE"

> How does one create a maintainable cloud in one's living room?
> —*Hartmut Sander*

Can Berlin be saved?
—Extrablatt, *January/February 1983*

Indeed such strategies were so effective, despite government countermeasures, that officials rapidly retracted the "Berlin Line," as they had put it: the policy that had criminalized housing squatters in response to pressure from landlords. But protest in the streets, "spraying" the buildings themselves, and other such uses of the external West Berlin landscape were not the only means of protest, and indeed these often became difficult and even dangerous to pursue in the crackdown era of the 1970s. Movement activists sought both to remake their society and remake themselves: the private was, after all, political—and vice versa. They sought not only new and newly vitalized forms of public expression of their concerns. As a function of this concern for "innerness" (*Innerlichkeit*), intensified by a partial retreat from provocative public expression in the "leaden" years of 1968–78, protesters looked "inside"—behind the scenes—away from public spaces as much as in them, to achieve broad movement visions. Many contemporary activists describe a dull, tightly constrained, often oppressive and even physically violent upbringing, promising lives with limited options, a prospect that moved many into the New Left. Activists sought communication with their "elders," parental and more broadly, but they also sought escape from some of the notions their parents represented: ideals of the petite nuclear family (even when, in the initial postwar era, this scarcely corresponded to any reality), and a related set of morals and mores. But what activists sought in practice as alternatives scarcely corresponded to the sensationalist views of commentators. Although sexual experimentation and use of illegal drugs clearly figured into the "scene," most activists seem to have sought sources of emotional and practical support in small groups and extended family-style structures that reflected far older practices as much as anything revolutionary—though such relationships contributed in principle to building new, more democratic, and less hierarchical patterns of everyday life. Activists on the whole constituted a remarkably hard-working bunch, willing to spend their days in often tedious tasks in pursuit of a larger (if often inchoate) vision. Sympathizers knew West Berlin housing occupiers as *Instandbesetzer*, combining *besetzten*, "to occupy," and *instandsetzen*, "to care for, preserve, and restore" the neighborhoods the latter worked in, in contrast, as they saw it, to slum landlords. Activists, definable by a great range of activities, mapped both these dreams and the everyday means to reaching them onto gritty West Berlin as well as other cities, now increasingly inspired by and taking advantage of the city's internal spaces, its possibilities for networks, and that lay behind the surfaces, mirroring what they saw as the city's own potential, and contrasting the latter with the existing, often despairing reality.

The "insides" in which the general alternative movement and its components grew flourished not only and not even largely in the great assemblies held in the cavernous Henry Ford Auditorium (*Audimax*), but rather as often in smaller, more intimate settings on a more human scale. The Republican Club, with its comfortable couches and chairs, was one early such site. Later, FU SDS executive board member Sigrid Fronius recalled her entrance

Figure 7.3. Squatters' Café Krautscho, Willibald-Alexis Street, Berlin. Photo by Wolfgang Krolow, reproduced with permission of the artist.

into the movement through such meetings, spurred initially by a crush on one of the club members. Particular bars became nightly hangouts, starting with intense theoretical discussions, but, as the evening and the drink wore on, becoming more personal and, for many, more comfortable and interesting—enough so that young men and women with babies in tow, with work obligations in the morning as well as classes, often stayed till late in the night. These included "scene pubs" (*Szene-Kneipen*) and cafés, such as the one in Steinplatz near the Technical University (TU) that Rudi Dutschke most often frequented early on; the Aschinger, just off the Kudamm (where the Viva Maria group was formed, and, Kunzelmann recounts, "where we pursued contact with normal Berliners [*Normalo-Berliners*]");[43] and the Schwarze Katze in Yorckstrasse, on the gritty Schöneberg/Kreuzberg border, among scores of other such meeting places. This practice mirrored the quite traditional German custom of establishing a table of regulars (*Stammtisch*) at one's local bar, as well as the explicit political affiliation over time of certain bars. The bars underscored for activists, moreover, as they had long done for other city residents, the "local" nature of one's life in the big city.

Drawing on this experience, housing occupiers in West Berlin often opened "occupied bars" nearby or on the ground floor of the buildings they

Figure 7.4. Close-up of the door of a squatters' café, Winterfeldt Street, Berlin. Top sign proclaims a welcome; below, a bear (the symbol of Berlin) dressed in police riot gear, with the words "we must unfortunately stay outside." Photo by Wolfgang Krolow, reproduced with permission of the artist.

squatted. These included the well-known Wedding district "Café Barrikade," which functioned to create a comfortable place for the larger community who wished to endorse the occupiers but did not share their living space—and to expand community and sociability in the neighborhoods. For "Tulla," living in Wedding was critical to her discovering a kind of "hidden Berlin" where prewar-style working-class culture still thrived and through which she felt she deepened her understanding of politics—and of herself. The bars served as both emotional and political support sites for the housing occupiers. Many "occupied bars" were notoriously difficult for "outsiders" to find (for some, one had to bring one's own door handle). A few, though otherwise welcoming, were marked with the comical sticker of a bear, the city's symbol, in riot gear, with a line through it, captioned "we have to stay outside," a twist on the sticker banning dogs from bakeries and grocery stores, and referring also to some activists' sense that, like Jews, African-Americans, and other "unwanteds" in other eras and places, they themselves were banished to the outside—and now remade their own new "inside" (figs. 7.3 and 7.4).

Kitchen tables were one of the most popular meeting places for activists, offering a highly desired intimacy, requiring no one else's "permission" to use them, and demanding little outlay of cash (though refreshments were always part of making such meetings comfortable and appealing). The entire West German women's movement started around kitchen tables in West Berlin in 1968, such as that of film student Helke Sander, while those in attendance took turns watching children.[44] But this was hardly a defining feature of women's meetings only, and, although, naturally, living quarters outside of cities have kitchens too, it was such spaces in cities that provided these particular inner oases. One informant remembers discussion meetings in the mid-1960s, at the home of one M. "He was an older student. . . . What he lived from is unclear. Because he was disgustingly poor. He was so poor that—he served people of course, one had to do that—he had only dry bread and Quark [spreadable fresh cheese]. And some very weak tea, so that it could suffice for lots of people. But there sat forty people and drank this weak tea and ate this bread . . . cut very small." That many students were older, that activists were not necessarily students, that dormitories did not exist at the two West Berlin universities, the FU and the TU, or at other West Berlin institutions of higher education, contributed to the possibility and likeliness of these practices. In another instance, students at the FU invited to their table five of their sociology professors, known as sympathetic to—and formative of—their views. "Although we were so poor, we had only spaghetti with catsup, but they came. And stayed the whole evening or half the night, and we discussed and discussed. And at some point my daughter came out, all disoriented [and said], 'Mommy, I can't sleep!' " Kommune I was known for its dinners with a wide range of eminences; they would be sure to steal their supplies from the luxurious food concession at the famous KaDeWe department store on these occasions. Rudi Dutschke counted many family suppers with the likes of Ernst Bloch and Herbert Marcuse, when the latter were in West Berlin. In the 1970s, such private tables were the site of discussions with and among those living "underground." But most such gatherings were among the far less celebrated (or infamous), and these formed a central basis for the long-term movement: by drawing people in, by creating something people wanted to be part of, and could be part of. In many ways, this was the movement, spread out in kitchens around the city, the inside of the movement's public face.

By the 1970s, as the fractured movement was pushed inward, entire subcultures and alternative cultures developed, largely inside the city: in the alternative newspaper offices, bookstores, festivals, concerts, parties, self-help classes, and, above all, the "centers," initially women's- and youth-based, that acted as physical sites for great ranges of activities and that physically bound these interests together. These formed a dense and broad network of connections below the surface that only a larger city could support. They drew, moreover, on West Berlin's many and particular offerings, in the form of buildings such as the deserted former Nazi film studio, the UFA-Fabrik in Tempelhof, and the former Bethanien hospital in Kreuzberg. Even by the mid-1960s, there were networks created out of telephone numbers: that was the "real Berlin experience." When the phone numbers of some of the best-known *Revoluzzer* were printed in the front section of copies of flyers from the movement, available for purchase around the country, many responded as though they had received a map of the homes of Hollywood stars. But such lists were of course far more about bringing and holding people together "below the surface." Although newspapers likewise might seem less bound to physical space because of their ease of distribution, the literal thousands of smaller and larger publications coming out of the movement in West Berlin and throughout West Germany tended to be both global in scope and intensely local, providing, in part because of their numbers, opportunities not just for reporting or for humorous send-ups, as in such West-Berlin organs as *Oberbaumblatt* (named for a bridge in Kreuzberg), *Agit 883*, and *Extrablatt* (with its send-up of *Bild*), but also for intense and "private" discussions and debates among movement members. These included active exchange on topics from how "alternative" a local "alternative bookstore" really was, considering how it treated patrons, to how appropriate were particular discussions of sexuality within the movement.

"Centers" were all the more a function of their urban space, acting as magnets both for neighborhoods and for particular communities and populations.[45] Here too, levels of activity "beneath the surface" were quite extraordinary: the women's center in Berlin might host some thirty events in a week. This might include everything from regular get-togethers to mount the feminist magazine *Courage* or the lesbian paper *Unsere kleine Zeitung* (Our Little Newspaper); to meetings planning the next action against section 218 of the Civil Code, which banned abortions, or for a battered women's shelter (a concept new to this time, connected to the city's capacity to let one hide behind the scenes); to self-defense classes and consciousness-raising groups; to "women's music evenings," in the cozy women's bar; to lavish, often women-only festivals. Not only did such centers, newspapers, and other organizations bring different and overlapping populations together (key for example in helping overcome divisions such as the gay/straight and separatist/nonseparatist splits), but they also influenced the way in which "networks of networks" created coalition politics over the space of the city, transcending the focus on any single site.

Likewise, group housing (*Wohngemeinschaften*, or WGs), including, but not limited to, squatted houses, acted as a major site of the movement from the beginning, hidden from public view. Indeed, to the extent that the broader public had a view, it was extremely misleading. Almost never the site of wild sexual experimentation they were imagined to be, WGs originated even before the "Kommunes," out of purely practical needs. Housing was expensive, despite price controls intended to prevent the population from flowing out of the walled city, and, for single people without large incomes, or for couples (especially unwed) who wanted to cohabit, group housing was often the only affordable or legal choice, including for many outside the movement. However, WGs did very much act as living communities that centrally included the discussion and practice of politics in the city. In general, inhabitants of WGs emphasized nonhierarchical living (in principle, at least) and open communication. The level of communication was remarkable: in many houses, every issue had to be democratically decided, and much of the political work of these houses was in trying to live through such democratic practices. Not surprisingly, informants report, there were regular and considerable arguments as well. But, for many, then, the benefits included an equally "practical" emotional element: a way to live with others, to defy loneliness and permit communication in a comfortable private space, without either living with one's parents or having to get married.

WGs functioned then predominantly as extended families. This sociability mirrored that of the city, writ small. One of each day's greatest joys in many WGs was a common evening meal.[46] ("Katrin," who moved to West Berlin after studying at the University of Marburg, complained in retrospect that, in the 1970s, several of the women in her house went on diets and ruined this concept. "Anna" claimed members of her WG lived on fast food (*Curry-Wurst*)—but they did try to eat it together.) To be sure, everyday life was often infused with "outside" politics—all the more so as time went on. Particularly in German Communist Party WGs, group house members tended to do everything together, from meetings and study groups in the house to recruitment and other activism outside the house. The political and politicized aspect also bore some negative consequences: under the sectarian nature of post-1968 politics, one could scarcely imagine "sharing a bathroom and a kitchen with someone who didn't think the same way you did." But far more commonly these sites of comfort reflected the very heterogeneity of the city. They remained vital loci inside the city, behind its facades, permitting in principle the development of the self and new societal structures along with the city itself, from the outside in.

The city provided the stage and backstage for activists to try to create and present themselves and their community, to envision a different life. One cynical graffito on the walls of a Kreuzberg building read: "Hurray, I've been normalized." Movement activists held themselves in distinction from the *Normalos*, as they called them. But these activists contributed to setting new norms for West German society and politics, concerning everything from child rearing to accepted sites of political practice, and, one can argue, contributing to producing a basis to approach the democracy West Berlin and West German officials had proclaimed existed decades earlier. These activists contributed too to remaking (West) Berlin into a "world city" (*Weltstadt*). Far removed from contiguity with West Germany physically, West Berlin can be seen as having been a major center of national interest, and international life, politically, socially, and culturally. New Left activists drew inspiration from the city and in turn kept the city alive; West Germany and—in the new "Berlin Republic," Germany as a whole—has felt the effects of this activity.

NOTES

1. Cf. informants "Susanne" and "Klaus." Sources for this paper include my interviews with more than fifty contemporary activists. Except for the best known, informants are identified by pseudonym, at their request.

2. This chapter follows approximately the same time span as my larger book project, *The Inner Life of Politics: The New Left in West Germany, 1962–1983* (forthcoming). Numerous specific events mark the two dates of the range, but none of these has particularly signficant import. My larger point is to suggest a transformation of German political culture that took place over this longer period, and certainly fording such "break points" as 1968 and 1978.

3. The organization serendipitously had the same initials as the American student organization (Students for a Democratic Society); the role of the two was in some respects comparable.

4. The APO, first announced formally in 1966 in response to the Grand Coalition (and referring to an idea a few years older still, out of the West German peace movement) was a more accurate title from the beginning than the narrower characterization of "student movement." The variability in age and life position that marked the range of activitists, as well as the longer stretch of time, makes using existing terms difficult: *student movement*, or still more narrowly, *SDS activity* is clearly insufficient; even designating this as a single movement over the long period may be highly suspect, though together, these movements had a collective and cumulative effect.

5. Certainly avoiding military service was not the least of the advantages that living in West Berlin offered for young West German men. West German men were obligated to perform eighteen months of service in the Bundeswehr. West Berlin was technically not part of West Germany.

6. Hanna Kröger, "Die organisatorische Situation in Berlin," *Neue Kritik* 54 (1969): 49–61.

7. Interview by author with "Heinrich" and "Silke"; see also Klaus-Jürgen Scherer, "Berlin (West): Hauptstadt der Szenen. Ein Portrait kultureller und anderer Revolten Anfang der achtziger Jahre," in Manfred Gailus, ed., *Pöbelexzesse und Volkstumulte in Berlin: Zur Sozialgeschichte der Straße 1830–1980* (Berlin: Verlag Europäische Perspektiven, 1984), 197–222. See also Joseph Scheer and Jan Espert, *"Deutschland, Deutschland, alles ist vorbei": Alternatives Leben oder Anarchie? Die neue Jugendrevolte am Beispiel der Berliner "Scene"* (Munich: Bernard and Graefe, 1982).

8. Peter Mosler, *Was wir wollten, was wir wurden: Studentenrevolte—zehn Jahre danach* (Reinbek: Rowohlt, 1977), 9. See on Frankfurt, Wolfgang Kraushaar, *Fischer in Frankfurt: Karriere eines Außenseiters* (Hamburg: Hamburg Edition, 2001), 24–25.

9. Cf. interviews with "Richard" and "Rüdiger."

10. Cf. Norbert Steinborn and Hilmar Krüger, *Die Berliner Polizei 1945 bis 1992: Von der Militärreserve im Kalten Krieg auf dem Weg zur bürgernahen Polizei?* (Berlin: A. Spitz, 1993); also Klaus Weinhauer, *Schutzpolizei in der Bundesrepublik: Zwischen Buergerkrieg und innerer Sicherheit. Die turbulenten sechziger Jahre* (Paderborn: Schoeningh, 2003); and Thomas Lindenberger, *Volkspolizei: Herrschaftspraxis und öffentliche Ordnung im SED-Staat 1952–1968* (Cologne: Boehlau, 2003).

11. Cf. Stefan Reisner, ed., *Briefe an Rudi D.* (Frankfurt on the Main: Editions Voltaire, 1967); and Kommune I (hereafter K1), files 03.01, 03.10 Letters, Hamburger Institut für Sozialforschung (hereafter HIS).

12. See ibid., file 03.01 . Dieter Kunzelmann organized these files himself for HIS in the late 1990s (before his faked death, a more recent *Happening*), out of the yards of files Kommunards had carefully kept contemporaneously. Members' reference through this self-description to participants in the Paris Commune was intentional.

13. Jörg Fauser, letter to parents, March 1, 1970, reproduced in Ulrich Ott and Friedrich Pfäfflin, eds., *Protest! Literatur um 1968* (Marbach: Deutsche Schillergesellschaft, 2000), 217; cf. Ralf-Rainer Rygulla, "Fuck You (!)," translation of American underground poems, ibid., 229; and interview with "Harald."

14. Attributed collectively to Gruppe Spur, of which Kunzelmann was a leading member: "Kanon der Revolution," *Spur-Buch* 7 (1962), n.p.; the citation continues: "every person owns a global Volkswagen."

15. Gabriele Huster, "Ich habe Mick gesehen!" in Eckhard Siepmann et al., eds., *CheShahShit: Die sechziger Jahre zwischen Cocktail und Molotow* (Berlin: Elefanten Press, 1984), 87–89. Cf. K1, files 03.01, 03.10 Letters HIS.

16. Cf. Saskia Sassen, *The Global City: New York, London, Tokyo* (Princeton, N.J.: Princeton University Press, 1991); also Philip Ethington, "The Global Spaces of Los Angeles, 1920s–1930s," in this volume. There is, of course, an enormous literature on imagined geographies: see David Harvey, *Consciousness and the Urban Experience* (Oxford: Blackwell, 1985); Harvey, *Spaces of Hope* (Berkeley: University of California Press, 2000); Ian Cook et al., eds., *Cultural Turns/Geographical Turns: Perspectives on Cultural Geography* (New York: Prentice Hall, 2000); and S. C. Aitken and L. E. Zonn, eds., *Place, Power, Situation, and Spectacle: A Geography of Film* (Lanham, Md.: Rowman and Littlefield, 1994).

17. This was a surprisingly large population, a function of many circumstances, including the symbolism of West Berlin, and in part a function of Allied powers to draw people to and keep people in Berlin, particularly after the Wall was erected in August 1961, as well as postwar diplomatic, economic, and other relations between West Germany and America, West Germany and other European nations, and West German diplomatic relations more broadly. There was also a significant population of former refugees from the Nazi regime and their children, as well as refugees from Soviet territory and former East Germans. Finally, many younger West Germans and West Berliners had themselves spent time outside the country—"tramping," spending a year in an American high school (as did SDS national head K. D. Wolff as well as SDS leader Michael Vester), acting as an *au pair* elsewhere in Europe, and so forth.

18. Such movies played almost exclusively in big cities and acted as another source of draw to these cities.

19. Cf., generally, S. Jonathan Wiesen, "Miracles for Sale: Consumer Displays and Advertising in Postwar West Germany," in David Crew, ed., *Consuming Germany in the Cold War: Consumption and National Identity in East and West Germany, 1949–1989* (New York: Berg, 2003), 151–78.

20. Interviews with "Tulla," "Harald," and "Gaby."

21. See Dieter Kunzelmann, *Leisten Sie kein en Widerstand! Bilder aus meinem Leben* (Berlin: Transit, 1998); and cf. Inga Buhmann, *Ich habe mir eine Geschichte geschrieben* (Munich: Trikont-Verlag, 1977).

22. Cf. Sigrid Fronius, "Als Frau stand ich nicht unter dem Zwang, jemand sein zu müssen," in Ute Kätzel, ed. *Die '68erinnen* (Berlin: Rowohit, 2002), 35; and Susanne Schunter-Kleemann, "Wir waren Akteurinnen und nicht etwa die Anhängsel," ibid., 101.

23. Kunzelmann, *Leisten Sie kein en Widerstand*. Cf. Frank Böckelmann and Herbert Nagel, eds., *Subversive Aktion* (Frankfurt on the Main: Neue Kritik, 1976), 23–25; 78–9; 128–29; 150–51; 176–77; see also Diethard Kerbs, ed., *Die hedonistische Linke: Beiträge zur Subkultur-Debatte* (Neuwied: Luchterhand, 1970).

24. Cf. interviews "Gaby," "Harald," "Tulla," and "Rüdiger."

25. Cf. songs with the same titles: "Wir müssen hier raus," "Schritt für Schritt ins Paradies," as well as "Der Traum ist aus" and "Rauch-Haus-Song," among others. Also, Peter-Paul Zahl, "Vorwort," in Wolfgang Krolow, *Häuserkämpfe: Instandbesetzer Bilderbuch* (Berlin: LitPol, 1981), n.p.

26. Mosler, *Was wir wollten*, 27.

27. In the epigraph, Kunzelmann is writing from West Berlin in 1964 to New Left theorist Frank Böckelmann in Munich (Böckelmann and Nagel, *Subversive Aktion*, 126). In this particular letter he refers to Munich, where he still lived.

28. Cf. Krolow, *Häuserkämpfer*, n.p.; also Helmut Schmitz, *Spray-Athen: Graffiti in Berlin* (Berlin: Rixdorfer Verlagsanstalt, 1982), 108.

29. Cf. Simon Sadler, *The Situationist City* (Cambridge, Mass. MIT Press, 1999).

30. Readers letters to *Der Spiegel*, June 12, 1967.

31. Cf. Anna K. Kuhn, "Berlin as Locus of Terror: *Gegenwartsbewältigung*," in Barbara Becker-Cantorino, ed., *Berlin in Focus* (Westport, Conn. Praeger, 1996), 159–86. Dutschke died of delayed effects of his wounds in 1979.

32. Daniel Cohn-Bendit, *Der große Basar* (Munich: Trikont, 1975), 10, 17.

33. Cf. Thomas Balistier, *Straßenprotest: Formen oppositioneller Politik in der Bundesrepublik Deutschland zwischen 1979 und 1989* (Münster: Westfälischer Dampfboot, 1996); and Ruud Koopmans, *Democracy from Below: New Social Movements and the Political System in West Germany* (Amsterdam: Institute for Social History, 1993).

34. Compare Ralf Reinders, "Unbeugsamen an der Spree," in Rolf Reinders and Ronald Fritzsch, *Die Bewegung 2. Juni: Gespräche über Haschrebellen, Lorenzentführung, Knast* (Amsterdam: ID Archiv, 1995); Michael "Bommi" Baumann, *Terror or Love? Bommi Baumann's Own Life Story as a West German Urban Guerrilla* (New York: Grove Press, 1979); and Daniel Cohn-Bendit and Reinhard Mohr, *1968: Die letzte Revolution, die noch nichts vom Ozonloch wusste* (Berlin: Wagenbach, 1988). See also memoirs in Kätzel, *Die '68 erinnen*.

35. Cohn-Bendit and Mohr, *1968*, 36.

36. Rudi Dutschke, *Geschichte ist machbar: Texte über das herrschende Falsche und die Radikalität des Friedens*, ed. Jürgen Miermeister (Berlin: Klaus Wagenbach, 1981). Cf. Belinda Davis, "Provokation als Emanzipation: 1968 und die Emotionen," *vorgänge* (December 2003): 41–49.

37. *Agit 883*, March 13, 1969.

38. "Happening, Love-in, Sit-in, u.s.w.," *Die Zeit*, November 3, 1967. See also "Teufel auf freiem Fuß," *Frankfurter Allgemeine Zeitung*, August 11, 1967. Cf. poet Peter Handke, who noted the effects of such acts, such "engaged theater" taking place outside formal theaters, to spur new ways of thinking in the Brechtian tradition, "until reality itself becomes a particular site of action [*Spielraum*]," while making the terror of existing reality evident by " 'terrorizing' it, theatricalizing it, and quite properly making it ridiculous."

39. "New Social Movement" scholars have documented patterns of winning public support, often resulting in official capitulation to protestors' demands. See Dieter Rucht, ed., *Protest in der Bundesrepublik: Strukturen und Entwicklungen* (Frankfurt on the Main: Campus, 2001); Roland Roth and Dieter Rucht, eds., *Jugendkulturen, Politik und Protest: Vom Widerstand zum Kommerz?* (Opladen: Leske and Budrich, 2000); and Roger Karapin, "New Left Social Movements and Public Policy in West Germany, 1969–1989" (Ph.D. diss., M.I.T., 1993). In the case of West Berlin housing

occupations, for example, authorities came to work together with occupiers effectively in rebuilding the local community and housing stock. In a somewhat different dynamic, Robert Stephens has observed the strange bedfellows created when "alternative types" and officials worked together to create detox centers for drug users in Hamburg, and how ambivalent both parties felt about the cooperation. Robert Stephens, *Germans on Drugs: The Complications of Modernization in Hamburg* (Ann Arbor: University of Michigan Press, 1007).

40. Interview with "Silke."

41. Schunter-Kleemann, "Wir waren Akteurinnen," 108; Mosler, *Was wir wollten*, 20ff; Baumann, *Terror or Love?* Cohn-Bendit and Mohr, *1968*, 26. A 1985 French television documentary by Daniel Cohn-Bendit telegraphs the strength of this emotion in the various national movements: *Nous l'avons tant aimee—la révolution Revolution*, whereas *Autonomie* (April 1977) cited Jerry Rubin's observation that it was more "fun" to practice than to watch revolution.

42. Cited in Mosler, *Was wir wollten*, 20.

43. Kunzelmann, *Leisten Sie kein Widerstand*, 51.

44. This was likewise the case with the Frankfurter "Weiberrat," the core of the women's movement in that city, with the "women's" peace movement in the early 1980s—as well as with the Independent Women's League in late-1980s East Germany. Some women who played active and important roles in this last group claimed they felt uncomfortable after the revolution, when politics no longer took place "around Bärbel Bohley's table." See I. Miethe, "From 'Mothers of the Revolution' to 'Fathers of Unification,' " *Social Politics* 6, no. 1 (1999): 87–101. Such a sentiment was not, however, unique to women, of course.

45. Not everyone inspired by such ideas ran to a few concentrated urban centers. The "center" movement of the 1970s, comprising particularly "youth" and "women's" centers, blossomed in small towns too and acted as a kind of substitute for the concentration of an urban "scene," as one informant characterized it. But tens of thousands still migrated for the shorter or longer term. "Detlef" described his politicization as a ten-year-old in 1968 during highly unusual protests in his "provincial" home town of Bremen: "This kind of thing just didn't happen here. And then [the demonstration] went forward, at the beginning maybe five hundred people, who then said. . . , 'what they do in Berlin, we can do here too!' " Just a few years later, he had moved on his own to West Berlin. There were a minority of activists who resented West Berlin's dominance in the political imagination and the sense that activists there knew something they did not. Many activists in Frankfurt, West Germany's "second city" of protest in this era, refuted that there was anything special about Berlin.

46. Cf. Klaus Hartung, "Die Psychologie der Küchenarbeit: Selbstbefreiung, Wohngemeinschaft und Kommune," in Siepmann, *CheShahShit*, 102–6; cf. also with activists' preference for meeting at kitchen tables, as above.

CHAPTER 8

Nuestro Pueblo: The Spatial and Cultural Politics of Los Angeles' Watts Towers

SARAH SCHRANK

IN EXPLORING THE SPACES of the modern city, Los Angeles provides as rich a venue as any for asking important questions about the relationships between culture and identity, history and society, politics and community, and the power dynamics inherent in those couplings. Philip Ethington reminds us that this is a city of high modernist conceit, with its freeways and archetypal modernist buildings, yet is a city replete with "the spontaneous profusion of the unique and the particular—those unplanned social relations that people form in the everyday."[1] It is a city that has produced its own field of inquiry, the so-called L.A. School, which managed to hang itself on a rhetorical split between hyperbolic exceptionalism and paradigmatic normalcy.[2] Volumes of new historical work, however, have moved us out of this knot by avoiding regional sunshine/noir mythologies, with no disrespect to Mike Davis who articulated them but never intended us to create historiographical bedrock out of them.[3]

Los Angeles is also a city whose political economy is embedded in what David Harvey has called a dialectical relationship between the human body and the effects of globalization.[4] It is a city where a global economy has helped mark ever-sharpening divisions between rich and poor, white and nonwhite, citizen and noncitizen while continuously selling images of the black gangster body, the Latino laborer body, the porn star body, and the white Hollywood Barbie body to the world. Bodies themselves, and the concomitant images of them, do important cultural and economic work in southern California; building a local economy while naturalizing exploitative social relations in racialized and sexualized forms. At the same time that Los Angeles has deployed the body as the key to its cultural and economic development, the city, historically, has also invested in an art-based civic culture in its bid for prominence as a global cosmopolitan entity. Nowhere does the body, the city, and the artistic merge more completely into a complex symbol of the civic than at the Watts Towers (fig. 8.1).

Figure 8.1. Sabato Rodia, *Nuestro Pueblo* (Watts Towers), 1921–54, detail. Photo by the author.

Watts Towers: The Making of a Modern City Space

While Los Angeles sought for decades to project the self-image of a modern city with an internationally significant art center, far on the margins of civic officialdom an unassimilated and self-educated Italian laborer worked alone in his backyard building the city its best-known artwork. Using nothing more than premodern tools and the weight and strength of his less

276

than five-foot-tall body, Sabato Rodia bent steel, broke glass gathered in a wheelbarrow pushed through the streets of Watts, and hauled tons of cement up and down the towers he built to one hundred feet and from which he could see far into downtown, the Hollywood Hills, and perhaps even the ocean. So often did Rodia work with the detritus of the growing city that journalists and students who interviewed him in the 1960s reported that tiny glass shards were embedded in the skin of his hands and arms. Rodia literally embodied the modern city while the towers, with their artful beauty born of immense human labor, bore lengthy witness to the historic urban shifts from multiracial integration to segregation and violence that have plagued Los Angeles' southern neighborhoods. Together, Rodia and his towers exemplified the creative vision and brutalizing physicality of the modern urban experience.

From 1921 to 1954, on an awkwardly shaped triangular space on East 107th Street, Rodia lived and worked until the day he deeded his property to a neighbor and abruptly moved to Martinez, in northern California. During his thirty-three years in this historically multiracial neighborhood notorious for its ghetto and its race riot, Rodia hand-built his fantasy city of seven towers, a gazebo, two fountains, two cactus gardens, and a boat. Embedded in tile on one of the towers is *Nuestro Pueblo*, Spanish for *Our Town*, but the structures remain best known as the Watts Towers. They have received international acclaim as a masterpiece of engineering, folk art, junk sculpture, and mosaic tiling, while recent scholarly interest in outsider art has led to their appearance in hundreds of catalogues and guidebooks.

In part because Rodia preferred not to specify what they meant (or explained and was misunderstood) and in part because their sheer size and eccentricity lend them to the imagination, the Watts Towers have become a modern urban space laden with shifting cultural and political meanings. Whether portrayed in newspapers as a public safety hazard or in art journals as an important international artwork, appearing as a metaphor for the African-American community in movies and music videos, adorning the cover of municipal financial reports as a symbol of urban redevelopment, or showing up in guidebooks as a tourist destination, the towers exist as an ever-increasing collection of images.[5] Because the Watts Towers are irrevocably linked to the racial politics of Los Angeles, the meanings of these images slip and change depending on the prominence of Watts, or matters of race in general, in the American popular imagination. This point is underscored by the fact that whereas some Angelenos know of the towers, most people who visit them are not from Los Angeles, or even California, at all. *Nuestro Pueblo*'s geographical location in South Central has proven a deterrent for local visitors. The towers' fame as an artwork juxtaposed with their physical presence in Watts have led them to become a convenient stand-in for Los Angeles and an emblematic symbol of postwar American blackness; they have served as cultural place markers in hundreds of literary pieces, movies, music videos, and television shows, from Don DeLillo's *Underworld* to HBO's *Six Feet Under*. As such, political efforts to claim, preserve, and celebrate the towers have been tightly connected to postwar struggles for space and power in the city. Reading the startlingly varied interpretations of Rodia's work, one is introduced to the contested meanings of Los Angeles' promise and limitations for diverse people in the city.

This representational layering of an urban-based spatial idiom is certainly visual, but it also emerges from the language surrounding Rodia's creation. He called it *Nuestro Pueblo*, but few know the work by this name, a provocative take on Los Angeles' original name, "El Pueblo de Nuestra Señora la Reina de los Ángeles de Porciúncula." By inscribing his towers in Spanish, Rodia honored his Mexican neighbors and the pre-American history of Los Angeles, and claimed the towers and the city for others than himself alone. The Italian origins of Rodia's inspiration and his conscientious effort to incorporate the language of his Mexican neighbors have largely been obscured by "Watts Towers," a name that stuck during the 1959 Building and Safety hearings involving their imminent demolition.

As a landmark placed historically and geographically at the nexus of Los Angeles' suburban promise and socioeconomic failure, the history of the Watts Towers also offers a unique commentary on American postwar urban policy. Once seen by thousands of daily train commuters, the towers faded from the landscape as new freeway routes and rapid economic decline in the 1950s contributed to what Norman Klein has called Los Angeles' "urban erasure."[6] As private automobiles replaced trains and trolleys, the towers and the neighborhood disappeared from the city's popular consciousness. In the historical struggle to render them visible to a local as well as an international public, the towers have become important for understanding how Los Angeles' struggles over civic identity are connected to the city's politics of race and representation. In Los Angeles, a city that has sought recognition as a reputed artistic center on a par with New York and other world cities, the Watts Towers have proven a political challenge and a cultural irony. At once symbolic of the city's failure to ensure social equality, the towers have also served as a testament to Los Angeles' indigenous creative merits. The City of Los Angeles has always had a conflicted relationship with the towers, working almost as hard to destroy them as to harness their cultural value. The towers have evolved into a political space in which the meanings of the modern city are negotiated, contested, and inscribed.

Watts and Los Angeles' Postwar Urban Policy

In the early 1900s, Watts, originally a Mexican land grant named Tajuata, grew into a multiethnic, working-class transportation hub (known as the "crossroads of Los Angeles"), as Mexicans, African Americans, and Asian Americans joined Anglos working on the railroad tracks. Processes of segregation combined with the black migration of the World War II era made Watts, and the surrounding area known as South Central Los Angeles, a largely African American neighborhood. Known for its high rates of black home ownership and solid middle class, Watts would, by the late 1950s, suffer the effects of white and middle-class black flight, the early erosion of a heavy manufacturing base, and the dissolution of public housing. Restrictive housing covenants and Federal Housing Authority redlining policies meant black residents were limited in where they could go in Los Angeles, and Watts residents who found access to new suburban areas left as quickly as they could. A once stable community, Watts in 1959 was an early example of what American ghettos would look like later in the century, as regional, national, and global economic restructuring widened class disparities among African Americans and between African Americans and other ethnic groups. Growing unemployment, decreased rates of home ownership, and a loss of a once superb public transportation system in favor of private automobiles and freeways that cut across the residential area meant Rodia's old neighborhood was in rapid decline. Josh Sides, in his excellent history of black Los Angeles, points out that these social changes also "encouraged many of South Central's remaining white residents to abandon their efforts at 'neighborhood preservation' and simply move out [while] well-employed black families . . . sought to flee the rising crime and poverty, and the declining schools, of South Central."[7]

Watts was not the only community in postwar Los Angeles to struggle with urban restructuring, nor were redlining and freeways the only factors contributing to increased racial segregation. George Sánchez demonstrates in his work on Boyle Heights that the 1950s represented a difficult time for multiethnic communities like Watts as right-wing politics pressured Jews, among other white ethnics, to leave peacefully integrated neighborhoods for white suburbs. Even when dedicated to civil rights, the combination of racialized housing policies, increasing economic pressures, and fears of voicing political opposition in the censorious early 1950s pushed even progressive Angelenos out of their communities, leaving behind the more impoverished and less assimilated.[8]

As Sánchez, Eric Avila, Josh Sides, and others have argued, the postwar period in Los Angeles is best characterized as one of urban relocation, rarely at the behest of city residents. In one of its most egregious examples, the Los Angeles City Council gave its final approval to the Bunker Hill Renewal Project in March 1959. The 136-acre downtown project razed nineteenth-century mansions that were home to pensioners and the poor and replaced them with financial and civic buildings that became Los Angeles' downtown civic center. The "substandard rooming houses and cheap hotels" were removed by city authorities because of their "inevitable earmarks of crime, disease, fire, and excessive public housing costs."[9] This was followed by the razing of Chavez Ravine, a Mexican barrio dating back to the nineteenth century, and the eviction of its last residents, the Arechiga family, to make way for the building of Dodger Stadium.[10] As Angelenos ate lunch and watched on television, the family members were led (or carried) to waiting police cars.

Los Angeles also enacted the slum clearance policies trumpeted by New York's Chairman of the Committee on Slum Clearance, Robert Moses, whereby "blighted" areas, often hosting thousands of private residences, were razed to the ground. These long-established working-class neighborhoods were replaced by commercial districts, or sometimes nothing at all, rather than by new and affordable housing units. Watts was such a target of postwar slum clearance. In the fall of 1959, at precisely the same time that Los Angeles' Building and Safety Committee reissued the order to demolish the towers, the *Los Angeles Examiner* reported that the area east of Central Avenue, on 103rd Street, was the subject of municipal "housing rehabilitation." About two blocks from where *Nuestro Pueblo* stood, almost three thousand properties, mostly African American residences, were to be cleared away as part of Building and Safety's bid "to clean up slum and blight conditions."[11]

A critical part of urban renewal was the freeway system that allowed suburbanites rapid access to and from commercial and leisure districts. As part of postwar urban renewal programs instituted in Los Angeles, freeway construction was symptomatic of nationwide federal support of white suburbs at the expense of minority neighborhoods. The freeways built under the auspices of the 1956 Interstate Highway Act (many of which were begun earlier as WPA projects) often cut through poor areas, destroying limited low-income housing, obliterating public space, and forcing property values to plummet.[12] Roads like Los Angeles' Harbor Freeway (Route 110) and the Santa Monica/San Bernardino Freeway (Route 10) were especially damaging to minority communities in Los Angeles by creating a geography of ethnic invisibility as commuters drove over and past neighborhoods like Compton, Watts, and East L.A. without ever seeing the segregated consequences of southern California's suburban growth. The loss of the "Red Cars" (Henry Huntington's electric trolley line) that followed the embrace of freeways meant that Watts, the former transportation hub, had grown obsolete. Rodia's towers, which for thirty years had been seen by thousands of daily passengers on their way to work, were no longer a prominent feature of the Los Angeles landscape. Like so many minority residents, the towers too disappeared in the shadow of the freeway system. Bud Goldstone has astutely pointed out that "this sudden lack of an audience and the increasing urbanization of his neighborhood probably influenced [Rodia's] decision to leave."[13] Like Bunker Hill's residents and Chavez Ravine's Arechiga family, the Watts Towers were simply in the way.

Sabato Rodia and the Building of the Towers

The towers, and the surrounding smaller structures, are built from steel rebar that Rodia bent into his desired shapes by placing it under the nearby railroad tracks and bending it with his body.[14] The shaped rebar was overlapped with heavy wire and wrapped with another layer of chicken wire to secure the joint. Rodia then created his own unique mixture of durable cement (currently unmatched by preservationists) with which he encased the wire wrapped joint and pressed broken glass, dishes, tiles, shells, found objects, and tools into the mortar. Most of the objects were left to stick permanently while others, like tools and household objects such as faucet knobs, fire screens, and baking tins were used to create imprints and removed, leaving Rodia's signature heart and floral designs in the 140-foot wall and along the cement floor (figs. 8.2 and 8.3).

The physical feat of Rodia's accomplishment is usually the first quality to impress the novice viewer. Not only did he bend steel with his body, Rodia built his towers without scaffolding, blowtorch, or power tools. Instead he used a window washer's belt and devised a system of pulleys that he used to haul himself, and thousands of pounds of cement, up and down the metal towers as he wrapped the joints and stabilized each level before moving on to the next. Rodia built ladders into the towers' form to facilitate his movement, possibly a foresight of the maintenance the structures would constantly require (fig. 8.4).

When Rodia was not working on *Nuestro Pueblo* he labored for a tile company, collecting the leftovers of expensive tile used in homes in more

Figure 8.2. Sabato Rodia, *Nuestro Pueblo* (Watts Towers), 1921–54, detail of steps. Photo by the author.

affluent parts of the city, or gathered broken glass, shells, and miscellaneous objects from the neighborhood and the beach. To have envisioned the project at all is remarkable, but to have tenaciously stuck to it for more than thirty years is what makes the Watts Towers so impressive. Having completed his project, Rodia gave the property away and left Los Angeles, never to see his handiwork again. Located by art history students from the University of California in 1961, Rodia granted interviews and made a warmly received appearance at a discussion of his work at Berkeley.[15] He died on July 16,

Figure 8.3. Sabato Rodia, *Nuestro Pueblo* (Watts Towers), 1921–54, detail of tool impressions and tile work. Photo by the author.

1965, at age eighty-six, less than a month before Watts would erupt in violent civil protest.[16]

Why Rodia built *Nuestro Pueblo* has been a source of great speculation ever since he began work on it in 1921. A native of Ribottoli, a village twenty miles east of Naples, who came to the United States in the 1890s to work in the Pennsylvania coal mines, Rodia kept most details of his personal history vague.[17] Reasons for why he might dedicate his adult life to such a solitary endeavor also remained obscure. Local newspapers interpreted the towers as an immigrant's homage to his adopted homeland, a gift to America.[18] A 1939 *Los Angeles Times* piece reported that the project helped Rodia through his alcoholism, his new sobriety meaning he no longer used his own bottles but those of other drinkers.[19] In 1952, the papers reported that neighbors who once found the towers eccentric now took pride in their local landmark.[20] Those who lived with the towers as part of their daily urban experience also speculated that Rodia had built a radio tower, possibly one transmitting the wartime propaganda messages of Ikuko Toguri (Tokyo Rose), who grew up in Watts. Student filmmaker, William Hale, documented Rodia working in 1953, arguing that "inner necessity" caused the craftsman to obsessively "build toward the sun."[21] Richard Cándida Smith has noted how art critics have deemed Rodia an outsider artist, spontaneously spinning his steel and cement like a spider, arms encrusted with broken glass like the very sculpture he was building.[22] In 1971, Reyner Banham declared the Watts Towers

Figure 8.4. Sabato Rodia, *Nuestro Pueblo* (Watts Towers), 1921–54, inside view of spire. Photo by the author.

"almost too well known to need description" and Rodia himself as "very much at one with the surfers, hot-rodders, sky-divers, and scuba-divers who personify the tradition of private, mechanistic *satori*-seeking in California."[23] Rodia himself was recorded saying, "I want to do something big."[24]

There is another compelling explanation. In 1985, two folklore scholars, I. Sheldon Posen and Daniel Franklin Ward, published the findings of a lengthy investigation into the Feast of St. Paulinas, an Italian American festival that took place each June in Brooklyn, New York. The highlight of the festivities was the carrying of a three-ton, six-story tower called a *giglio* through the streets on the shoulders of more than one hundred men. Other festival participants carried a giant galleon. Atop both the tower and the boat stood a statue of St. Paulinas. What Posen learned while conducting his research was that the festival originated in Nola, near Naples in southern Italy. Paulinas had been a fifth-century bishop of Nola captured by invading Vandal marauders and taken to north Africa. There he was made a slave but through divine gifts was able to interpret the future for the Vandal king. As a reward, the king set Paulinas and his fellow captives free. They returned to Italy by ship and were greeted by villagers bearing mounds of lilies (or *gigli*). The contemporary annual festival celebrated the miraculous return of Paulinas to his village. Ward realized that Los Angeles' Watts Towers, the topic of his own doctoral research, bore a startling resemblance to these *gigli* ceremonial towers.[25] Adding together Rodia's own origins in a town not far from Nola and his inclusion of a boat in his complex of structures lends credibility to their argument that he was recreating the *gigli* of his youth in his backyard. The Committee for Simon Rodia's Towers in Watts argues that this plausible explanation was long overlooked because a reporter misunderstood Rodia as pointing to his boat and saying the "ship of Marco Polo," obscuring any obvious connection to Nola or St. Paulinas. Given the strength of the *gigli* festival evidence, the committee believes Rodia actually told the reporter that the sculpture was "il barca di Paolo" or "the boat of Paulie, Paulinas."[26] A 1937 *Los Angeles Times* article did state that the structures were "modeled after quaint towers which Rodilla remembered from his native Italy," but does not elaborate on what those "quaint towers" might be.[27] Someone early in the towers' construction had part of the story but years of reinterpretation and misunderstandings have rendered the towers' meanings elusive, infinite, and deeply personal to those who engage with them.

No one is certain why he left Los Angeles, although surviving interviews imply that Rodia left because of his age and his deteriorating relationship with the neighborhood, as teenagers tossed garbage over the fence or threw rocks, breaking his carefully placed tiles and bottles.[28] After he moved north, Rodia's next-door neighbors tried to turn *Nuestro Pueblo* into a taco stand ("Tower Tacos"), but the city refused to grant them the building permit. The towers stood in vandalized disrepair until the Committee for Simon Rodia's Towers in Watts fought to protect the towers from the city's demolition order, beginning work to permanently conserve and exhibit them to the public.[29]

The Politics of Art in Los Angeles

Art preservationists first invested the towers with symbolic and political meaning in 1958 when the Committee for Simon Rodia's Towers in Watts—composed mostly of middle-class art students, teachers, artists, architects, and engineers—led the grassroots effort to save Rodia's towers from demolition by the city's Building and Safety Department. Formed by film student William Cartwright and actor Nicholas King, the committee's goal was to ensure effective and permanent guardianship of Rodia's work. Shortly thereafter, Cartwright and King sought out the towers' owner, Rodia's former neighbor, Joseph Montoya, and bought the property for about three thousand dollars.[30]

It quickly became clear that caring for the towers would be more complicated than any of the students involved had thought. When the committee (whose name was shortened to the Committee for Simon Rodia's Towers in Watts) applied for a permit to construct a caretaker's cottage on the site, its request was refused.[31] Unsure about what they were and finding no building permit, in 1957 the Building and Safety Department had issued a demolition order for their removal. Because of the vandalism occurring after Rodia's departure from Los Angeles, Building and Safety also declared the property unsafe and a public hazard. Neighbors reported to investigating students that local teens made sport of throwing rocks and chipping away at the bottles and tiles pressed into the towers' mortar, probably searching for treasure rumored to be hidden within. At the subsequent July 1959 public hearing regarding the towers' future, Deputy City Attorney W. E. Wilder argued that their "workmanship was of poor quality [and that] the towers have begun to deteriorate rapidly in recent years," adding "the structures are broken in places and in danger of collapsing."[32] Assured of the towers' strength, the committee challenged the city to test them. The committee's engineer, Bud Goldstone, whose expertise in aeronautical structures convinced him Rodia's skilled craftsmanship would withstand a ten thousand-pound-pull stress test, persuaded the committee's volunteer attorney, Jack Levine, to put forth the stress test challenge. The city accepted, agreeing if the towers survived, Building and Safety would withdraw the demolition order. On October 10, 1959, the widely publicized test was held and, with hundreds watching, the towers survived a truck's ten thousand-pound-pull intact.[33] The next day H. L. Manley, chief of the Building and Safety Department, announced the city would drop its efforts to have the towers torn down. For the moment, the towers were saved.[34]

In preparation for the 1959 demolition hearings, the Committee for Simon Rodia's Towers in Watts launched an international campaign of letters and petitions to define the towers not as an eccentric local curiosity, but as a significant artwork. The committee hoped that if the towers could be understood as art rather than an unusual novelty, then perhaps the City of Los Angeles would grant them civic landmark status, ensuring their protection. This was a risky strategy, given the city's general campaign to restrict, remove, and even destroy artworks and art spaces throughout the city. As the committee phrased it later in 1966, "in spite of dramatic changes during the last decades, there is still a strong backlog of sentiment against the arts as useless if not outright corrupting."[35] In Los Angeles this was an especially dubious legacy, as the 1950s had been marked by nasty public art controversies.

For a brief period from 1948 to 1951, Los Angeles had hosted a remarkable art program of festivals, community centers, galleries, and children's classes, all sponsored by the publicly funded Municipal Art Department. Kenneth Ross, the department's dynamic director, placed emphasis on community art projects and local cultural centers.[36] In the spring of 1951, the *Los Angeles Times* announced Ross's introduction of a new program that promised "to give art exhibits, lectures, films, forums, painting demonstrations, and instructions in arts and crafts in community buildings . . . in every community area."[37]

Buoyed by public sponsorship, the Municipal Art Department encouraged a decentralized civic culture that annually brought art and music festivals to public parks in diverse neighborhoods, from Beverly Hills to Compton. Ross so believed in the social benefits of public art in public space that, as early as 1950, he secretly funded festivals in Compton and Watts, appointing Beulah Woodard, the first African American to exhibit at the County Museum, director of the art shows.[38]

Working in the long shadow of the 1947 Hollywood blacklist, a conservative attack on the Municipal Art Department undermined the new art program. Together with the anti–public housing real estate lobby, the Building and Safety Committee accused Ross of permitting a "heavy Communist infiltration" of the All-City Outdoor Art Show, the cornerstone of Ross's program.[39] After weeks of public hearings, the council refused to authorize funds for the city's art department unless Kenneth Ross banned abstract modernist art from all future public art exhibits.[40] This, combined with an internal audit, meant that by the mid-1950s, Ross could no longer count on public funding in order to offer free exhibits, inexpensive art classes, and art festivals.[41]

With public art spaces closed and modernist art suspect, many artists were pushed out of the city completely or into the cultural margins. Some went to Venice Beach, which since the early 1950s, had been a retreat for artists and bohemians. By 1959, however, publicity generated by Beat literature, movies, and popular magazines made Venice an attraction for both tourists and young, stylish beatniks, pitting artists against homeowners in disputes over coffeehouses like the Venice West Café and the Gas House, both of which were private businesses hosting poetry readings and exhibiting artwork. Stories of the economic threat to bar and nightclub owners and tales of thousands of teenagers flocking to late-night racially integrated dens of iniquity made the newspapers frequently enough to pressure both city and county authorities to look into the "coffeehouse problem."[42] In the fall of 1959, the Los Angeles City Council passed an ordinance requiring all coffeehouses to have entertainment licenses, giving the Los Angeles Police Department the power to grant permits at its own discretion.[43] As a result, local police had the power to control sites of cultural activity, usually by making arrests, orchestrating drug searches, planting spies, and through general surveillance.

It was artwork, however, that fell under the greatest suspicion. Coffeehouses displaying paintings and sculptures attracted the most attention from the Los Angeles Police Department and the County Sheriff's office. An anonymous coffeehouse owner reported in the *Los Angeles Times*, "the average cop thinks there is something subversive about any place with paintings on its wall. He thinks an artist is a suspicious character partly because of the way he may dress and partly because the officer holds art itself suspect."[44] The Watts Towers thus came under municipal scrutiny at precisely the same time that Building and Safety and the Los Angeles Police Department were shutting down alternative art spaces in other parts of the city.

Once Building and Safety declared the towers safe to stand, the city cautiously (and briefly) tried to parlay the towers into a tourist attraction. Following a 1960 fundraiser by Kenneth Ross and the Municipal Art Department, titled "The Significance of the Watts Towers in the Community Landscape," a number of articles appeared in the *Los Angeles Times*, arguing for the towers to be a site included in guidebooks along with the Rose Bowl, Forest Lawn, Grauman's Chinese Theater, and the recently opened attraction, Disneyland. As one piece put it, "Watts Towers is the one local landmark guaranteed to raise a few eyebrows, whether in approval, awe, or amazement."[45] Professional claims that the Watts Towers were indeed art, combined with Ross's support, were successful in achieving some municipal recognition. In March 1963, the City of Los Angeles recognized the site as a cultural heritage monument.[46]

RACIAL POLITICS AND THE WATTS TOWERS ART CENTER

The troubled relationship between Watts and broader Los Angeles led the towers' protectors to try to separate them symbolically from the neighborhood in which they stood. Images promoting the towers' artfulness were usually shot from the ground up, obliterating their surrounding urban environment. Photographs exhibited by the Museum of Modern Art (1961) and the Los Angeles County Museum of Art (1962) show the towers in a rural setting with barely a hint of the city that has always surrounded them.[47] Photographed from peculiar angles, the towers were shorn from Watts and recontextualized in the discourse of postwar modernism. Conversely, neighborhood activists and community leaders historically have tightly linked the neighborhood to the towers. Once saved from the municipal wrecking ball, they have served as an uneasy liaison between white liberals invested in their artistic merits and predominantly black community activists hoping to parlay the towers into federal and state funding for local cultural and commercial facilities. The Watts Towers Art Center (WTAC), a separate building originally purchased by the committee in 1959 and serving community youth as a space for free arts and music education since 1961, has competed with preservation efforts for state funding. The quality of this codependent relationship between the towers' preservationists and the community center has ebbed and flowed through the decades, depending greatly on the broader political and socioeconomic context.

Neither the push to make the towers a tourist attraction nor the granting of official monument status was done with much municipal enthusiasm, and the city made no move to support the WTAC. The second part of the committee's preservation campaign, in fact, was the maintenance of this community center. Committee member Eve Echelman recruited African American artists Noah Purifoy and Judson Powell, and teacher Sue Welsh, to set up and run the center. Purifoy, who had a background in social work, ran the WTAC with a powerful sense of community activism and a commitment to art education. Although much of the towers' publicity had focused on preservation and aesthetics, he insisted that the WTAC function as a material connection between the towers and the community of Watts, with art the medium through which a child could learn "he is part of the community of man, and that he is no more and no less than any other."[48] With two full-time teachers on staff, Debbie Brewer and Lucille Krasne, the center offered drawing and painting classes every day for children aged four to eighteen. The community role of the WTAC would attract significantly more state and municipal attention after the Watts riot, but in the years prior there was little support beyond Teen Post, a program funded in 1964 through Lyndon Johnson's War on Poverty.[49] Some federal funding also came through a research project titled "The Aesthetic Eye" to study black youth and the connections between the learning process and art education.[50]

As early as 1963, the committee began work to propose an ambitious expansion of the WTAC. The new cultural facility would be better staffed, offer a broader range of classes, and host a social services office. Hoping that the unification of art attraction and community-at-large would help build much-needed cultural, social, and commercial facilities in Watts, the committee thought that the State of California would be instrumental in supporting to such a project. This strategy was articulated in a committee pamphlet: "After removing the demolition danger, [the Committee] has turned its attention to larger purposes —long-range preservation of the towers as a cultural monument; development as a community facility."[51] In the spring of 1965, the architecture firm of Kahn, Farrel, and Associates, on behalf of the committee, submitted to the California Department of Parks and Recreation a proposal to build the "Simon Rodia Community Arts Center," which included a teen center, social services office, food facility, exhibition spaces, outdoor amphitheater, dance studios, a theater seating two hundred, and a parking lot for four hundred cars. If adopted, the plan would have overhauled one square block of Watts.

The expansion was overly ambitious, and some committee members had voiced doubts about whether it was even appropriate for "a small, self-constituted committee to have control of something like the towers," let alone create and run an entire arts and culture center.[52] The new name, Simon Rodia Community Arts Center dropped any immediate association with Watts, and its size and scope spoke to some committee members' loss of perspective in their preservationist zeal. Noah Purifoy, the original director of the WTAC, stated in interviews that the planned expansion was a mistake, that such a program would weaken the relationship between the community and the art center. Purifoy felt an enlargement designed to draw people from outside Watts to what was hoped would eventually become a credential-granting art school was too sophisticated an art program for the focused goals of the WTAC.[53] He feared that such a project would alienate Watts' residents and defeat the original goal of the WTAC, which was to provide a safe place for black youth to learn about the creative process. In addition, he disliked the proposed new name, because he had always been reluctant to identify the art center as a community center, recognizing that neighbors would see it one more government agency making an intrusion akin to urban renewal and redevelopment.

Judson Powell shared Purifoy's concern that they not pose as an agency. He remembers Watts residents often came to the WTAC asking for money, bail bonds, medical assistance, and other aid far beyond the abilities of a community art facility. The WTAC and the committee found itself in the situation of offering a cultural site useful to an impoverished urban neighborhood but neither equipped nor prepared to provide the basic facilities and infrastructure residents needed. Powell felt that the role of the WTAC was to tie art to public education by creating outreach programs with the Los Angeles Unified School Board. The Watts community felt it ought to play a greater role, creating further tension between the art center and the neighborhood.[54]

The tension over the expansion was for naught,, as the state rejected the plan outright and refused the towers both state park and landmark status. The California Department of Parks and Recreation concluded "the Simon Rodia towers are definitely a sort of bizarre art form. . . . However, their preservation is not a matter of statewide concern."[55] In its report, the state encouraged private ownership and maintenance of the towers and helpfully recommended "that the proper local agency enlarge and develop the area into a Community Art Center," thereby kicking financial responsibility back to the committee, which was surviving from grant to grant without any secure fiscal base.[56]

THE TOWERS AND THE 1965 WATTS UPRISING

The summer that California rejected the Watts Towers as a state park and crushed hopes of a permanent source of funding was the same summer that Los Angeles hosted the so-called Watts Riot, one of the largest civil uprisings in U.S. history. The event began on Wednesday, August 11, 1965, during a scuffle between police and onlookers after twenty-one-year-old Marquette Frye's arrest for drunk driving at 116th Street and Avalon, several blocks south of Watts. Violence escalated after Marquette was bloodily struck in the head by a cop's nightstick and rocks were thrown at the departing police car. As remaining police called for backup, growing numbers of young men took to the streets, lighting fires and throwing stones, moving on to overturn cars and break windows of white-owned shops and businesses. By Thursday, the Los Angeles Police Department and the County Sheriff were out num- bered, and on Friday, August 13, Governor Pat Brown called in the National Guard. It was on Friday that the uprising moved north into Watts, burning two full blocks of 103rd Street near Central Avenue. Throughout the day, Noah Purifoy maintained considerable calm over the WTAC as crowds of kids gathered for their regularly scheduled art classes. According to Jeanne Morgan, the phone rang off the hook as admirers from all over the world called to find out if the towers were surviving the violence outside. Purifoy stationed children at the phones so callers would hear their small voices telling them all was well but also reminding them that there were people there too who might be cause for concern.[57]

At 3 a.m. Saturday morning, 3,356 National Guardsmen were in the streets of South Central. At 8 p.m., Governor Brown instituted a curfew, and by midnight on Saturday there were thousands of National Guardsmen on active duty in Los Angeles. The curfew was finally lifted on Tuesday, August 17. A frustrated response to high unemployment, a dire educational system, a lack of social services, a history of police violence, and a dearth of public transportation in a neighborhood where less than 14 percent of residents owned cars, the riot left 34 people dead, 1,032 injured, and approximately 4,000 arrested, 500 of whom were under eighteen years of age. The McCone Commission estimated damage to stores and automobiles to be over $40 million, and the numbers of dead, wounded, and arrested in Los Angeles far outnumbered the totals for all of the uprisings combined in New York, Rochester, Jersey City, Paterson, Elizabeth, Chicago, and Philadelphia during the bloody summer of 1964.[58] As shocking as the televised images were to Americans from all over the country, black Los Angelenos knew trouble had been brewing for a long time. As Chester Himes put it: "The only thing that surprised me about the race riots in Watts in 1965 was that they waited so long to happen. We are a very patient people."[59]

The Watts riot forever changed national perceptions of American urban race relations, dulled Los Angeles' sunshine booster image, and reoriented how Rodia's towers would be publicly represented as the city was catapulted into the American popular consciousness as an emblem of urban blight and black revolution. With the national spotlight on Los Angeles, Watts, and anything associated with it, the area had become too charged a place for lighthearted editorials about an eccentric Italian tile-setter and too dangerous to attract art-loving tourists. Rodia's grateful immigrant gift to America seemed more appropriate as an emblem of urban failure. In a radical contrast to the art discourse surrounding the towers prior to 1965, post-riot mentions of the towers did so in direct conversation with recent events, emphasizing their unavoidable geography. The year 1966 proved a pivotal one for the City of Los Angeles' renewed interest in Watts, art production in the community, and publicity for the city and the towers.

THE COMMUNITY REDEVELOPMENT AGENCY
AND SPATIAL POLITICS, POST-1965

Noah Purifoy's fears that outside interests in Watts could do more damage than good were realized when less than six months after the riot, in January 1966, headlines splashed across the *Los Angeles Times* promising that "Visions Point to Park-like Future for Watts."[60] While residents voiced anxiety that the burning of South Central facilitated urban renewal (or "Negro removal"), city planners began work to transform the neighborhood into "the concrete and trees of pedestrian malls, sparkling new commercial structures and even garden apartments." The city's Community Redevelopment Agency (CRA) proposed long-term plans for new housing but suggested that commercial development was the most important strategy in rebuilding the area.[61] The most dramatic component of the CRA plan for Watts was its appropriation of the Committee for Simon Rodia's Towers in Watts's 1965 plan for an expanded community center. In this new, post-riot rendition, the burned out 103rd Street business district was transformed "into a tree-lined pedestrian mall with a park corridor connecting it to the Watts Towers as a cultural monument."[62] The CRA plan kept the originally proposed name "The Simon Rodia Community Arts Center," removing direct associations with Watts, black Los Angeles, or the original goal of the center to create a safe cultural space for black and Latino kids.[63] In fact, CRA drawings of the center show a safe cultural space for *white*, middle-class Angelenos. Appalled, the committee insisted that the WTAC be black-run, arguing "federal or local support cannot be expected unless greater Negro participation is achieved."[64]

CRA money did not come through for the new WTAC, and it is unclear what happened to $3 million earmarked for Watts's redevelopment. Instead, the committee regrouped and launched a campaign to raise $75,000 for a new building. Jack Levine, the attorney for the committee since the 1959 Building and Safety hearings, stated at a press conference that it only wanted to sponsor an expanded art center and leave its operation to the community.[65] Despite millions of federal dollars being pumped into the neighborhood through the U.S. Department of Housing and Urban Development (HUD), the War on Poverty, and other offices such as the Economic Youth Opportunity Agency, Teen Post, and Job Corps, the committee was unable to raise the necessary funds and, almost a year later, staged a "dig-in" whereby two hundred people, mostly Watts residents, worked in shifts to dig the twelve-inch trench needed to lay the building foundation. Unable to afford the necessary heavy equipment, neighbors and committee members put in the concrete foundation by hand. Plans for the new center were donated by sympathetic architects in the Los Angeles area. Though the committee hoped to open the center in August 1967, the new building would not be dedicated until March 1, 1970.[66] By surviving for at least forty-eight years (1959–2007), the WTAC may be the oldest nonprofit community art space in the country and certainly the model for the radical Los Angeles arts centers of the 1960s and 1970s such as the Studio Watts Workshop, Watts Happening House, the Performing Arts Society of Los Angeles, the Compton Communicative Arts Academy, as well as Chicano centers found mostly on the other side of town: Mechecona Arts Center, the Mexican American Center for the Creative Arts, and Plaza de la Raza.

COMMUNITY POLITICS AND COMMUNITY ARTS, POST-1965

If flawed commercial redevelopment plans represented Los Angeles' approach to addressing the "Watts problem," a focus on the arts represented the neighborhood's. In the spring of 1966, representatives from the WTAC and local high schools planned the "Watts Festival of Arts" to be held at Markham Junior High with the intention of exposing "Watts artists to the general community and expos[ing] the general community to Watts."[67] The festival included theatrical productions, a parade, and various workshops on painting, dance, music, and sculpture. The big draw, however, was the exhibit, "66 Signs of Neon," organized by Noah Purifoy and Judson Powell. While still running the WTAC in 1964, Purifoy and Powell had thought of creating a sculpture garden around the towers made of found objects from the neighborhood. The one thing the Watts revolt produced in unlimited quantities were piles of burned and trashed materials that those with a creative eye could gather and mold into sculpture. Thus, the exhibition was born. "The riot," explained Powell to the newspapers, "was the first thing this community ever did together."[68] After collecting three tons of charred riot detritus, the artists invited four friends to join them in their project named for the drippings and casings from broken neon signs.[69] The artworks also included assemblages of shattered windshields, torn sheet metal, and ghoulish montages of children's shoes and broken dolls. The exhibit at Markham Junior High attracted an enormous amount of attention, traveled to Washington, D.C., and onward to Germany—in an ironic twist, as bloody American ruins were shipped abroad.[70] In the accompanying catalogue, *Junk*, Purifoy tied the exhibit, the riot, and his goals as the director of the WTAC together. Basically agreeing with the findings of the McCone Commission, the governor's report that blamed unemployment and a lack of educational resources for the revolt, Purifoy felt that art and culture should also have been emphasized. By having few outlets for artistic creativity, education in South Central was further failing its youth. "66 Signs of Neon" was shown again at the 1967 and 1968 Watts Arts Festivals but, by 1969, had been dismantled with the individual pieces scattered and lost.[71]

Purifoy's dark vision was echoed in a widely read account of postrevolt Watts, "A Journey into the Mind of Watts," Thomas Pynchon's 1966 *New York Times* exposé. Pynchon described a neighborhood that went from national obscurity to national obsession and yet remained virtually unchanged as an impoverished ghetto in which government intervention is resented, the police feared, and communication between black activists and white liberals poor. It is a place ("Raceriotland," a dark play on Disneyland) that America wants to forget: "Somehow it occurs to very few of them [white Americans] to leave at the Imperial Highway exit for a change, go east instead of west only a few blocks, and take a look at Watts. A quick look. The simplest kind of beginning. But Watts is country which lies, psychologically, uncounted miles further than most whites seem at present willing to travel."[72] Pynchon knows, however, that the one thing that *has* historically drawn white visitors to black Los Angeles is Simon Rodia's backyard fantasy. But he is not willing to let a curious, art-loving public off so easily. No pat on the head for *Times* readers on June 12, 1966. Instead, Pynchon foregrounds Rodia and the Watts Towers as more evidence of Los Angeles' urban decay. Pynchon respects Rodia, admiring his "dream of how things should have been: a fantasy of fountains, boats, tall openwork spires" but also sees the mortared broken glass as a specter of failure: "A kid could come along in his bare feet and step on this glass—not that they'd ever know. . . . These kids are so tough you can pull slivers of it out of them and never get a whimper. It's part of their landscape, both the real and the emotional one: busted glass, busted crockery, nails, tin cans, all kinds of scrap and waste. Traditionally Watts. Next to the Towers, along the old Pacific Electric tracks, kids are busy every day busting more bottles on the street rails. But Simon Rodia is dead, and now the junk just accumulates."[73]

Little publicity for the towers followed the Pynchon article or Purifoy exhibition of 1966, with a few exceptions. One was a children's book written in 1968 by Jon Madian depicting a kindly old gent schooling a black kid on the artistic value of garbage. Distributed to elementary schools around the United States, Madian's picture book shows an actor playing Rodia (the real Rodia already dead three years) in a romanticization of the relationship between an elderly white man and a racially charged neighborhood. A second public image of the towers in the post-riot years was their appearance on the cover of *Time* in 1969 in celebration of California's population explosion. Two years later Reyner Banham celebrated the architectural landscape of Los Angeles, featuring the towers as one of the few orienting emblematics in his maps of the city.

POLITICAL BACKLASH: DAMAGED CITY, DAMAGED TOWERS

With a general lack of publicity and the stigma of 1965 preventing the fund-raising campaigns possible in 1959, the Committee for Simon Rodia's Towers in Watts could no longer afford to keep the towers or the WTAC. After sixteen years of maintaining them on private donations, in 1975 the committee turned the towers over to the municipal government. The city promised to care for them and repair weather damage, and hired a contractor to do so. Untrained in the skilled work needed to reinforce Rodia's unique structure, the contractor and his associates badly damaged the towers, performing what is known as a "savage restoration," whereby a work of art or historical landmark is "preserved" in such a way as to purposely destroy or irreparably damage the original work. What the ten-thousand-pound-stress test could not do in 1959 was achieved sixteen years later by chipping away the mosaics, ripping apart the foundation, attempting to pour plastic onto the face of the towers, and leaving flammable waste in barrels within the towers' base. Fortunately, the towers did not explode, and the Center for Law in the Public Interest sued the city, on behalf of the committee, to stop the damaging restoration and force the city to pay reparations. In a complex lawsuit that would finally end in 1985, the committee donated the Watts Towers to the State of California with the stipulation that $207,000 of state funds would go to the city for their preservation and upkeep. As part of the settlement, Watts Towers was finally proclaimed a California Historic Park while responsibility for restoration was assigned to Los Angeles' Cultural Affairs Department.[74]

The municipal government's neglect of the towers reflected the national attitude toward the inner city in the 1970s—a lack of empathy combined with diminished financial support (fig. 8.5). The conservative backlash against the social upheaval of the 1960s was pronounced in California, as exemplified by the passage of Proposition 13. In 1978, landlord lobbyist Howard Jarvis gathered more than a million signatures to put the proposition limiting property taxes for suburban homeowners on the state ballot. The passage of Proposition 13 severely limited the funding of schools, public services, and urban infrastructure in inner-city neighborhoods and had an immediate effect on the Watts Towers.[75] In a letter to a concerned resident of Watts, the Office of the Mayor wrote: "All of us in [the city government] share your concerns regarding the safety of the Watts Towers. However we

Figure 8.5. Sabato Rodia, *Nuestro Pueblo* (Watts Towers), 1921–54, detail of chipped shell and dinnerware. Photo by the author.

cannot give any assurances for 24 hour security. . . . With the passage of Proposition 13 it may be necessary for the city to have fewer security officers than we had before to guard all of our public facilities."[76]

THE TOWERS IN THE AGE OF CIVIC RENEWAL

The 1970s and 1980s represented a shift in the political infrastructure of the city. Conservative mayor Sam Yorty lost in 1973 to the first (and, to date, only) African American mayor of Los Angeles, Tom Bradley. He would win four consecutive terms before his retirement in 1993. Properly criticized for acquiescing to corporate land grabs, susceptibility to foreign payoffs, and not supporting affordable housing, Bradley was also responsible for putting Los Angeles on the international map as a financial center, and the 1984 Summer Olympics were his career's major coup. As Roger Keil argues in his work on Los Angeles as global city, downtown Los Angeles underwent an immense transformation during the Bradley years, becoming dominated by skyscrapers and the symbols of global capitalism: "Bradley's ability to smooth out the waves of social unrest in Los Angeles during [the 1970s and 1980s] enabled new concepts of an urban future to surface, and opened the space of the city to the fantasies of developers who had their eyes on the downtown prize."[77]

Bradley's vision of a rejuvenated Los Angeles, with racial and economic distress behind it, included an emphasis on the arts as part of a new, invigorated civic identity. In anticipation of the 1984 Olympics, he commissioned forty-seven murals, painted along major stretches of the Routes 110, 101, and 10 freeways. Often showing runners or other sports participants, the murals "officially" resurrected an art form that the City of Los Angeles had destroyed in the 1930s as communistic and overly critical of racial and class inequities. David Siqueiros's *Tropical America*, whitewashed in the 1930s, is the most famous of the city's Mexican murals. By the 1960s and 1970s, of course, murals had become a major visual component of the Chicano movement and of radical social movements in Los Angeles, and other cities throughout the United States. The irony of Los Angeles' Cultural Affairs Department adopting a highly politicized and historically marginalized art form to represent the new global Los Angeles as a seat of international financial prowess was not lost on local artists. To this day, the Bradley-era murals are a favorite target of graffiti artists and taggers who see these freeway wall paintings as unwelcome marks of the "civic official."[78]

This strange separation of art and history in the name of a new civic identity continued through the 1980s when the Los Angeles papers, the *Herald Examiner* in particular, sponsored a fundraising campaign in support of the towers. Pulling together an impressive roster, including representatives from the Committee for Simon Rodia's Towers in Watts, local art critics and commentators, museum curators, newspaper editors, state assemblymen, prominent American architects, and a couple of Watts activists, the *Herald Examiner* hosted "The International Forum for the Future of Sam Rodia's Towers in Watts," which ran for three days in June 1985 at the Davidson Conference Center at the University of Southern California. Avoiding the 1965 revolt and the social history of Watts, the press instead used the towers to obscure racist power relations that defined living conditions in South Central and to promote Bradley's civic campaign of "community affirmation." The *Herald-Examiner* adopted the language of the 1950s preservation campaign, writing: "No symbol in Los Angeles carries more meaning than these sparkling spires. A testimony to immigrants' dreams. . . . Today that vision towers over Watts, high above the railroad tracks, the little houses and the human struggle—a tribute to a community's inner strength."[79] This commentary, combined with photographs that rarely showed the neighborhood, served to separate the "towers as community" symbol from the history of Watts. Moreover, the romantic mythology surrounding an immigrant building such a monument obscured Watts's new Latin American immigrants from view. With all the trappings of an official and possibly productive meeting, little came of it other than plans to host an international design competition to commercially redevelop the area surrounding the towers. Mike Davis has pointed out that at the very moment that Los Angeles came into its own as a global city, with the trappings of shiny buildings and plans for new museums, "such vital generators of community self-definition as the Watts Towers Art Center . . . had to make drastic cutbacks to survive the 'age of arts affluence.' "[80]

The Cultural Politics of the Towers

While Los Angeles' municipal government and the newspapers deployed the towers as a deracialized, deracinated, and depoliticized symbol of community, popular culture increasingly adopted the towers as a symbol of American blackness in the 1980s and 1990s. Pop cultural appropriations of the towers were not new. Musicians who lived or performed in postwar Watts, for example, often had close affiliation and nostalgia for *Nuestro Pueblo*. Jazz and rhythm-and-blues greats respectively, Charles Mingus and Johnny Otis, have commented in their autobiographies on the towers' significance as a neighborhood landmark and a testament to artistic endeavor. Visual artists have been captivated too; Jann Haworth and Peter Blake featured Simon Rodia amid the crowd of faces assembled on the Beatles' 1967 *Sgt. Pepper* album cover.

What changed in the 1980s was the infusion of hip-hop into mainstream American popular culture with graffiti, urban dance moves, and rap music together articulating "a black cultural expression that prioritizes black voices from the margins of urban America."[81] The social effects of neglecting the inner city increasingly played out in movies, with Los Angeles emerging as the filmic trope of black urban unrest in the late twentieth century in much the same way that New York served as the symbol of American ethnic conflict and urban blight in 1970s films like *Taxi Driver, Mean Streets, Serpico*, and *Saturday Night Fever*. And with the Watts Towers physically located in Watts, ground zero for gang warfare and a historical touchstone for popular conceptions of Los Angeles' "South Central," Rodia's life work became a common spatial reference for Hollywood. In *Colors* (1988), Dennis Hopper deployed the towers to metaphorically show how a black neighborhood is torn apart by gang warfare, police violence, and drugs.[82] In *Ricochet* (1991), starring Denzel Washington and John Lithgow, encodes the towers as symbols of "blackness," black community, and Black Power.[83] In the 1992 cheese-ball buddy film, *White Men Can't Jump*, the towers signal a white man's arrival in the ghetto, while the 1996 movie, *Courage under Fire* deploys the towers to new effect. Displayed as a black-and-white print hanging on a bedroom wall, the towers serve, for a middle-class black family functioning in the upper echelon of white Washington, D.C., political culture, as an ambiguous marker of black authenticity, one's roots in the 'hood, or perhaps a sign of a finely tuned aesthetic sensibility.

The towers have increasing, and significantly embodied, resonance in hip-hop. Since the Los Angeles gang wars of the 1980s (and possibly before), the thrown hand sign for Watts is three fingers of the right hand pointed down, symbolizing Rodia's three main towers. In very recent years, they have been featured in advertisements, music videos, and computer games. Rhythm-and-blues performer Tyrese appears gleaming, and well-sculpted, with his body placed in geometrical alignment with the towers on the cover of his 2001 CD release, commenting in the liner notes: "I use the Watts Towers as a symbol of freedom, history, struggle, independence, strength and a high level of confidence."[84] L.A. hip-hop artist, The Game, prominently features the towers in several of his videos. In 1999, the towers appeared in a Levi's print ad in which a young hipster sits on a stool in the lot behind the towers holding a sign that says "Restoration, Rejuvenation."[85] Levi's appropriation of the Watts Towers helps render them an icon of popular culture while a multinational corporation profits by cashing in on a real social and political history. Globalization and the denim-clothed youthful body emphasize the growing socioeconomic space between those living near the towers and those able to buy Levi's latest offerings. Removed from their urban context in high-art discourse, popular representations of the towers in the hyperviolent video game "Grand Theft Auto–San Andreas" and Boost Mobile's ubiquitous "Where you at?" advertising campaign exploit the towers for their authenticating street credentials. As hip-hop has main-streamed through our broader popular culture, representational icons like the towers have become increasingly part of an urban vernacular landscape whose meanings are loosely tied to pop notions of black cultural identity and tightly secured to commercial products. Far beyond any intention of

Simon Rodia, the Watts Towers increasingly embody the globalized process whereby an urban space's commercial value makes a profit for those well outside the reach of the social ills originally rendering that space its consumerist marketability.

Conclusion: *Nuestro Pueblo* as Political Space

Representations of the Watts Towers in artwork, advertising, municipal reports, art journals, and popular culture are inscribed with the contrasts between high art and community art, black public space and white safe space, art removed from its urban context and art made of urban debris, towers of power and towers of poverty. Underlying much of the "officially civic" language surrounding the towers is an inarticulate but obvious discomfort with the evolution of the towers into a nationally recognized civic landmark in a city with a long history of painting over, literally and figuratively, representations of nonwhite and poor people.

The political climate of the 1990s helped formulate new uses for the towers. In 1990, Arloa Paquin Goldstone successfully applied for the towers' National Landmark status. On the heels of this achievement, the City of Los Angeles Watts Redevelopment Project used the towers to decorate its cover in the fall of 1991. It is yet another ironic twist that proponents of urban renewal would use the towers as a symbol of a rejuvenated neighborhood when so much more energy has gone into preserving the towers than rectifying social and economic inequities. This irony is especially pronounced, given that urban renewal helped destroy Watts as an economically viable neighborhood and led to the early efforts to tear down the towers in the first place.[86]

The 1991 CRA project evaporated first with the brutal beating of Rodney King by officers of the Los Angeles Police Department, then with the "not guilty" verdict that sparked looting and violence across a wide band of southern Los Angeles. With riots focusing national attention again on Los Angeles' black neighborhoods, the failure of programs, grants, and contracts that followed the aftermath of 1965 were shown in stark relief. James Woods, founder of the Studio Watts Workshop, has said: "If funding had concentrated on establishing institutions rather than temporary programs, we could have accomplished much more."[87] Short-term funding of community art could not maintain such programs any more than fixing Watts Towers could fix Watts.

301

Figure 8.6. Sabato Rodia, *Nuestro Pueblo* (Watts Towers), 1921–54, detail of heart-laced earthquake reinforcement bridge. Photo by the author.

Since the summer of 1999, Watts, and the towers, have become state-recognized tourist attractions. Through the nonprofit Watts Labor Community Action Committee and the California Council for the Humanities, local activists have organized bus tours of Watts with an extended stop at Rodia's towers. The hope of tour organizers is that by educating outsiders on the cultural merits of Watts, commercial interests might start investing in the area. In July 1999, President Clinton visited the neighborhood as part of a national tour of economically depressed areas. Work on the large Watts Towers community art center, proposed and rejected by the state in 1965, began in 1998, but the project is riddled with design problems and moves slowly. The new building, begun in 2006, has obliterated the parking lot, and WTAC staff fear few will visit if they have to park on the street. The WTAC continues to offer classes, mount exhibitions, and host art and music festivals, now under the direction of Rosie Lee Hooks.[88] Watts faces new challenges as its Latino population has overtaken the African American population. The new residents of Watts are also poor, and the social services that exist in the area are ill-equipped to handle Spanish-speaking clients.[89] In 2001, the Cultural Affairs Department's eight-year, $2 million renovation ended, with help from the Getty Conservation Institute, and the towers' scaffolding was removed with great fanfare in the local media.[90] Today, the Committee for Simon Rodia's Towers in Watts is trying to get either the city or the state to issue a "stop work" order to end another bout of damaging restoration practices that have inalterably erased unique examples of Rodia's handiwork (fig. 8.6).

Midway through Rodia's construction of *Nuestro Pueblo*, in 1938, Lewis Mumford published his epic history of the origins of the modern city, *The Culture of Cities*. He wrote in his introduction, "the city, as one finds it in history, is the point of maximum concentration for the power and culture of a community. . . . With language itself, it remains man's greatest work of art."[91] *Nuestro Pueblo* has proven such a point, an art-based space that acts as a galvanizing force for a politics grounded in cultural identity and loud claims to social equity. Its towers have been both generative of community and symbols of community in political fights over funding and territory. *Nuestro Pueblo* represents the penultimate modern metropolis, as it embodies premodern labor while holding the multitudinous meanings, multilingual names, and commercial promises of the postmodern world city.

NOTES

I would like to thank Judson Powell, Bud Goldstone, Seymour Rosen, Michael Cornwell, Jeanne Morgan, and Joan-Claire Kleihauer for their help in the writing of this chapter. I must also thank all the members of the Committee for Simon Rodia's Towers in Watts, SPACES, and the staff of the Watts Towers Art Center who have worked so hard to keep *Nuestro Publo* intact.

1. Philip J. Ethington, "Ghost Neighborhoods: Space, Time, and Alienation in Los Angeles," in Charles G. Salas and Michael S. Roth, eds., *Looking for Los Angeles: Architecture, Film, Photography, and the Urban Landscape* (Los Angeles: Getty Research Institute, 2001), 29.

2. Roger Keil, *Los Angeles: Globalization, Urbanization and Social Struggles.* (New York: John Wiley and Sons, 1998), xiv.

3. Mike Davis, *City of Quartz: Excavating the Future in Los Angeles* (1990; New York: Vintage, 1992).

4. David Harvey, *Spaces of Hope* (Berkeley: University of California Press, 2000), 12–15.

5. Sarah Schrank, "Picturing the Watts Towers: The Art and Politics of an Urban Landmark," in Stephanie Barron, Ilene Fort, and Sheri Bernstein, eds., *Reading*

California: Art, Image, and Identity, 1900–2000 (Berkeley: University of California Press, 2000) 373–86.

6. Norman M. Klein, *The History of Forgetting: Los Angeles and the Erasure of Memory* (London: Verso, 1997).

7. Josh Sides, *L.A. City Limits: African American Los Angeles from the Great Depression to the Present* (Berkeley: University of California Press, 2004), 170.

8. See George J. Sánchez, " 'What's Good for Boyle Heights Is Good for the Jews': Creating Multiracialism on the Eastside during the 1950s," *American Quarterly* 56, no. 3 (September 2004): 633–61.

9. Los Angeles County Museum, Los Angeles History Division 1900–1961, California file no. 371134, Huntington Library. San Marino, Calif., 53.

10. Eric Avila, *Popular Culture in the Age of White Flight: Fear and Fantasy in Suburban Los Angeles* (Berkeley: University of California Press, 2004), 166–67.

11. "L.A. Shows World How to End Slums." *Los Angeles Examiner,* special edition reprint, October 11–12, 1959, in California Ephemera Collection 200, box 61, UCLA Department of Special Collections.

12. See Avila, *Popular Culture in the Age of White Flight*, 206–23; George Lipsitz, *The Possessive Investment in Whiteness: How White People Profit from Identity Politics* (Philadelphia: Temple University Press, 1998).

13. Bud Goldstone and Arloa Paquin Goldstone, *The Los Angeles Watts Towers* (Los Angeles: Getty Conservation Institute, 1997), 84; and "Watts Towers Face Threat from Freeway," *Los Angeles Times*, June 1963, 25.

14. Jeanne Morgan, "Rodia's Towers: Nuestro Publo, a Gift to the World," in Daniel Franklin Ward, ed., *Personal Places: Perspectives on Informal Art Environments* (Bowling Green, Ohio: Bowling Green State University Popular Press, 1984), 80.

15. Leon Whiteson, *The Watts Towers of Los Angeles* (Oakville, Ont.: Mosaic Press, 1989), 25.

16. Goldstone and Goldstone, *The Los Angeles Watts Towers*; Jeanne Morgan, "My Life with the Watts Towers," n.d., Jeanne Morgan Papers, Archives of American Art, Smithsonian Institution, West Coast Regional Center, Huntington Library, San Marino, Calif.; Calvin Trillin, "I Know I Want to Do Something," *New Yorker,* May 29, 1965, 72–120; and Leon Whiteson. *The Watts Towers of Los Angeles* (Oakville, Ont.: Mosaic Press, 1989).

17. Goldstone and Goldstone, *The Los Angeles Watts Towers*, 25–28.

18. There is exciting new work on the towers' meaning as an immigrant intervention into the American cultural landscape, particularly that of Teresa Fiore, "Preoccupied Spaces: Re-configuring the Italian Nation through Its Migrations" (Ph.D. diss., University of California–San Diego, 2002).

19. Joe Seewerker and Charles Owens, "*Nuestro Publo*: Glass Towers and Demon Rum," *Los Angeles Times*, April 28, 1939, sec. 2, p. 2.

20. "Immigrant Builds Towers to Show His Love for U.S.," *Los Angeles Times*, June 8, 1952, pt. 1A, p. 26.

21. *The Towers*, directed by William Hale (Los Angeles: University of Southern California, 1953).

22. Richard Cándida Smith,"The Elusive Quest of the Moderns," in Paul Karlstrom, ed., *On the Edge of America: California Modernist Art, 1900–1950* (Berkeley: University of California Press, 1996), 32.

23. Reyner Bahnam, *Los Angeles: The Architecture of Four Ecologies* (1971; Berkeley: University of California Press, 2000), 111.

24. *The Towers*, 1953.

25. I. Sheldon Posen and Daniel Franklin Ward, "Watts Towers and the Giglio Tradition," in *Folklife Annual 1985* (Washington, D.C: American Folklife Center at the Library of Congress, 1985), 143–157.

26. Jeanne Morgan, correspondence with author, August 6, 2005.

27. "Flashing Spires Built as Hobby," *Los Angeles Times*, October 13, 1937, pt. 2, p. 2.

28. "Immigrant Builds Towers to Show His Love for U.S." *Los Angeles Times*, June 8, 1952, sec. 1A, p. 26; Paul V. Coates, Confidential File, *Los Angeles Mirror-News*, October 4, 1955, sec. 1, p. 6; and Cándida Smith, "The Elusive Quest of the Moderns."

29. Goldstone and Goldstone, *The Los Angeles Watts Towers*.

30. Ibid., 88; Jo Farb Hernandez, "Watts Towers," *Raw Vision* 37 (Winter 2001): 34.

31. Goldstone and Goldstone, *The Los Angeles Watts Towers*, 85.

32. Are They Fine Art or Junk?" *Los Angeles Examiner*, April 3, 1959; "Hearing to Preserve Watts Towers Opens at City Hall," *Los Angeles Examiner*, July 7, 1959; "Watts Towers Pass Safety Test," *Los Angeles Examiner*, October 11, 1959. Interviews with Rodia in the Jeanne Morgan Papers.

33. Goldsone and Goldstone, *The Los Angeles Watts Towers*, 92–95.

34. See note 32.

35. Committee for Simon Rodia's Towers in Watts, "The Simon Rodia Arts Workshops," 1966, Department of Special Collections, UCLA, collection 1388, Committee for Simon Rodia's Towers in Watts, box 2, folder 1.

36. Author's interview with Sandra Rivken, Public Relations Office, Cultural Affairs Department, City of Los Angeles, February 20, 2001.

37. "City Takes New Approach to Art," *Los Angeles Times*, April 23, 1951.

38. "Outdoor Art Shows Chairmen Appointed," *California Eagle*, September 14, 1950; "South Park Festival Success," *California Eagle*, October 19, 1950; microfilm reel no. 37, Southern California Library for Social Research, Los Angeles, California.

39. Building and Safety Committee Report, November 5, 1951; Los Angeles City Archives, city council file no. 50460.

40. "Second Round of Art Row before Council," *Valley Times*, October 31, 1951; "City Tightens Art Exhibit Purse Strings," *Los Angeles Mirror*, November 7, 1951. These clippings are in the Fletcher Bowron Papers, Huntington Library, San Marino, Calif. box 92. (Bowron was mayor of Los Angeles, at this time.)

41. Letter from the city clerk to the Municipal Art Commission, filed September 1, 1955, Los Angles City Archives, city council file no. 64886; letter from the mayor's office to the Municipal Finance Committee, June 24, 1957, Los Angeles City Archives, city council file No. 79872.

42. Nightclub owners' concern about the popularity of the coffeehouses encroaching on their businesses went as far as a $100,000 damage suit lodged against Herb Cohen for purposefully turning a nightclub into a "beatnik hang-out." "Judge Hears 'Beat' Café Suit," *Los Angeles Examiner*, December 17, 1959.

43. "All-Night Coffeehouses to Pay Entertainment Tax," *Los Angeles Examiner*, January 28, 1959; Patrick McNulty, "Beatniks and Venice Square Off in Fight," *Los Angeles Times*, August 3, 1959; "Police Oppose Permit: Beatnik Hearing Becomes Fuzzy," *Los Angeles Examiner*, September 2, 1959; "Gas House Defended," *Los Angeles Examiner*, September 3, 1959; "Beatniks 'Cut Out' of Hearings: Police Examiner Biased, They Say," *Los Angeles Examiner*, September 9, 1959; "Squareville Heatnik Scorches Beatniks," *Los Angeles Examiner*, October 28, 1959; "Judge Hears 'Beat' Café Suit," *Los Angeles Examiner*, December 17, 1959.

44. Frank Laro, "Tourists Make Beatniks Flee Coffeehouses," *Los Angeles Times*, June 2, 1959, pt. 2, p. 8.

45. Marylou Luther, "L.A. Has Many Attractions Not Included in Guidebooks," *Los Angeles Times*, March 17, 1960, A1; "Watts Towers Topic of L.A. Art Panel," *Los Angeles Times*, March 13, 1960, 16; Beverly E. Johnson, "The Watts Towers," *Los Angeles Times*, April 24, 1960, L28.

46. Whiteson, *The Watts Towers of Los Angeles*, 83. The towers were officially designated a Los Angeles Cultural Heritage Monument in 1963. Their current status as a National Landmark was achieved in 1990.

47. Willaim C. Seitz, *The Art of Assemblage (New York: Museum of Modern Art, 1961)*, 77; Seymour Rosen, *Simon Rodia's Towers in Watts: A Photographic Exhibition* (Los Angeles: Los Angeles County Museum of Art, 1962).

48. Noah Purifoy, quoted in Ronald H. Silverman, "Watts, the Disadvantages, and Art Education, 19, no. 3 (March 1966): 16–20.

49. Noah Purifoy, interviewed by Karen Anne Mason in African-American artists of Los Angeles oral history transcript, 1990, UCLA Special Collections; and transcript of interview with Dale Davis, John Outterbridge, and Cecil Ferguson, July 29, 1994, John Outterbridge Papers, Archives of American Art, Smithsonian Institution.

50. Purifoy, African-American artists of Los Angeles oral history transcript, 58–63.

51. Committee for Simon Rodia's Towers in Watts, *The Watts Towers*, pamphlet, n.d.

52. Trillin, "I Know I Want to Do Something," 107.

53. Purifoy, African-American artists of Los Angeles oral history transcript, 69.

54. Author's interview with Judson Powell, April 15, 2007.

55. California. Department of Parks and Recreation. *Watts Towers Study*. June 1965, 3.

56. California Department of Parks and Recreation, *Watts Towers Study*, June 1965, 3–4.

57. Jeanne Morgan, correspondence with author, March 7, 2005.

58. Governor's Commission on the Los Angeles Riot, *McCone Commission Report: Complete and Unabridged, December 2, 1965* (Los Angeles: Kimtrex Corp., 1965); and Gerald Horne, *Fire This Time: The Watts Uprising and the 1960s* (Charlottesville: University Press of Virginia, 1995).

59. Chester Himes, *The Quality of Hurt: The Autobiography of Chester Himes* (Garden City, N.Y.: Doubleday, 1972), 73–74.

60. Jack Jones, "Visions Point to Park-like Future for Watts," *Los Angeles Times*, January 17, 1966, A1.

61. Peter Bart, "Center Planned at Watts Towers," *New York Times*, March 20, 1966, 84.

62. Jones, "Visions Point to Park-like Future."

63. Drawing of "The Simon Rodia Community Art Center," Department of Special Collections, UCLA, collection 1388, Committee for Simon Rodia's Towers in Watts, Watts California, miscellaneous, box 1, folder 2.

64. "The Simon Rodia Arts Workshops" (see note 35).

65. "Rodia Towers Art Center Drive Begins," *Los Angeles Times*, August 10, 1966, A2.

66. "Watts Holds 'Dig-In' for Community Art Center," *Los Angeles Times*, June 25, 1967; and *McCone Commission Report*.

67. Art Seidenbaum, "Cultural Approach to Watts," *Los Angeles Times*, December 8, 1965, D1.

68. Quoted in Art Berman, "Watts Easter Week Art Festival Puts Riot Debris to Cultural Uses," *Los Angeles Times*, April 8, 1966, A1.

69. Joyce E. Widoff, "Out of the Ashes . . . Art and Understanding," *Tuesday Magazine*, August 1968, 5–15. Lizette LeFalle-Collins, *Noah Purifoy: Outside and in the Open*, exhibition catalogue (Los Angeles: Afro-American Museum Foundation, 1997), 10–11.

70. Thanks to Victoria Holly Scott for pointing out the irony of exporting American ruins to Europe.

71. The Watts Art Festival at Markham Junior High may have helped lay the organizational groundwork for the more radical Watts Summer Festival in August 1966, a fete attended by more than ten thousand in a musical tribute to the thirty-four killed the year before. The Watts Summer Festival still takes place each year.

72. Thomas Pynchon, "A Journey into the Mind of Watts," *New York Times*, June 12, 1966. I gratefully thank Brett Mizelle for pointing out the value of this piece for understanding post-1965 views of Los Angeles.

73. Ibid.

74. "City Council File No. 71-3270," April 18, 1975, SPACES archives; "Suit Assails City's Handling of Watts Towers, Calls for Private Ownership," *Los Angeles*

Times, October 27, 1978, pt. 2, p. 8; "Private Boost for Watts Towers," *Los Angeles Times*, February 22, 1985.

75. Davis, *City of Quartz*, 182–86.

76. Letter to Mae Babitz from the office of the mayor, June 28, 1978, Department of Special Collections, UCLA, collection 1388, Committee for Simon Rodia's Towers in Watts, box 12, folder 16.

77. Keil, *Los Angeles*, 82.

78. It is significant that the city now claims its murals as important emblems of cultural activity and "diversity" or "multiculturalism," particularly since the 1984 Olympics when the Bradley administration commissioned forty-seven freeway murals as part if its controversial downtown "cleanup." In appropriating murals, the city has acknowledged, even legitimated, the wall as civic space. But even as the city cleaves art from its politics (this is made obvious by the appalling police murals on the 110 freeway) graffiti writers remind us when they tag officially civic murals that wall space is at a premium and claims to the exterior wall are hotly contested, despite city efforts to render murals conflict-free. I am grateful to the work of Marcos Sanchez-Tranquilino for his discussion of the political conflict between Chicano muralists, representing an "official" form by the late 1970s and graffiti artists who, in Los Angeles, remain on the margins. This is useful for understanding why civic appropriation of the mural form attracts so much attention from taggers throughout the city. Marcos Sanchez-Tranquilino, "Space, Power, and Youth Culture: Mexican American Graffiti and Chicano Murals in East Los Angeles, 1972–1978," in Brenda Jo Bright and Liza Bakewell, eds., *Looking High and Low: Art and Cultural Identity* (Tucson: University of Arizona Press, 1995), 55–88.

79. "Save the Watts Towers," *Los Angeles Herald-Examiner*, April 22, 1985, sec. 2, p. 1.

80. Davis, *City of Quartz*, 78.

81. Tricia Rose, *Black Noise: Rap Music and Black Culture in Contemporary America* (Middletown, Conn.: Wesleyan University Press, 1994), 2.

82. *Colors*, directed by Dennis Hopper (Los Angeles: MGM Studios, 1988), with performances by Sean Penn, Robert Duvall.

83. *Ricochet*, directed by Russell Mulcahy (Los Anlgeles: Warner Brothers, 1991), with performances by Denzel Washington, John Lithgow, and Ice-T.

84. Tyrese, *2000 Watts*, RCA Records, 2001.

85. Levi's advertisement, *The Big Issue*, Summer 1999, 20–21.

86. Community Redevelopment Agency of the City of Los Angeles, *Watts Redevelopment Project Biennial Report: November 4, 1991*, John Outterbridge Papers; and William Fulton, *The Reluctant Metropolis: The Politics of Urban Growth in Los Angeles* (Baltimore, Johns Hopkins University Press, 2001), 297–98.

87. Quoted in Daniel B. Wood, "Activists Build Culture from the Ground Up," *The Christian Science Monitor*, June 8, 1992, 9.

88. Elizabeth Christine Lopez, "Community Arts Organizations in Los Angeles: A Study of the Social and Public Art Resource Center, Visual Communications and the Watts Towers Art Center" (Ph.D. diss., UCLA, 1995), 49.

89. Matea Gold. "A New Watts Awaits Visit by President," *Los Angeles Times*, July 7 1999, pt. A, sect 1; Steve Schmidt, "Watts Shows Off New Look: Tourists Invited to Site of '65 Riots," *The San Diego Union-Tribune*, August 29, 1999, A3; Paul Chavez, "Promises Linger in Watts: Despite Federal Pledge to Help, Area Still a Blight," *San Diego Union-Tribune*, November 4, 1999, A3.

90. Jennifer Kelleher, "In Watts, Towers Stand for Hope," *San Diego Union-Tribune*, September 27, 2001. E1.

91. Lewis Mumford, *The Culture of Cities* (San Diego: Harcourt Brace, 1938), 3–5.

SPACES OF EVERYDAY LIFE

*

Morality, Majesty, and Murder in 1950s London: Metropolitan Culture and English Modernity

FRANK MORT

How do modern societies change—morally, sexually, and culturally? One obvious historical response is to say complexly, following no guaranteed blueprints, driven by diverse and competing interests, and with highly unpredictable consequences. Social historians and historians of sexuality working on the liberalization of moral beliefs and attitudes in England after the Second World War have highlighted a number of familiar themes that they have identified with the so-called permissive moment of the 1960s. The expansion of political struggles over "dangerous" or "deviant" sexualities; shifting boundaries between public, private, and family life; more individualized versions of femininity, and the renewed impact of expert opinion have all been variously associated with the formation of a post-Victorian, secular morality.[1] Although such issues are acknowledged to have histories with "long *durées*," they have been closely associated with a distinctively postwar narrative of modernization. Historians have documented these shifts as evidence of a renewed phase of liberal reform, assessing their outcomes as legislation driven by parliamentary or pressure-group politics and as policies that reshaped sexual habits and moral behavior.

My aim is also to address changes to postwar morality, but I view English society from a different vantage point, with the aid of different methodological tools, and in doing so highlight contrasting processes of transformation. The ambition is not to displace existing accounts, for I return to a number of themes highlighted in these histories, but rather to destabilize them by bringing into focus events, lives, and urban environments for which many of the central interpretative devices that are available do not really work.[2] My account is an exercise in microhistory; it uses the multiple resources of a socially grounded cultural analysis, informed by the exegeses of place and setting, to raise a set of larger questions about the dynamic work performed by narratives of sexual and moral transgression in reshaping English society during the postwar years.

My focus is on one *cause célèbre* murder case in London; the serial killing of six women by John Christie in Rillington Place, a working-class and racially mixed area of north Kensington, in 1953. Told in the language of the police report, by the sanitary inspector, by local prostitutes, and ultimately by the pathologist and the barrister in the courtroom, these murders were a contemporary dramatization of a very traditional poetics of the city as an encounter with poverty, deprivation, and death, and they drew heavily on a set of genres for understanding urban life that had first been rehearsed in London more than a hundred years before.

Claiming significance for a seemingly small-scale, if sensationally horrific, event involves highlighting the resources offered by such micro-histories. As Carla Hesse has posed the question recently: "How can we move from the analysis of a single narrative to make broader claims about the discursive construction of social categories?" and, I might add, the ways in which such incidents can lead to the identification of larger patterns of cultural change.[3] My response to this challenge involves adopting a dual approach that is familiar to cultural historians who aim to integrate a detailed analysis of specific events with a wider understanding of social and cultural processes. I focus on a close reading of the Rillington Place murders, analyzing their formal structures of meaning that were organized through the representational resources of narrative, iconography, and so on. Simultaneously, I identify the larger generic significance of the episode; the ways in which the social morphology of the case points to strong continuities with a range of other transgressive events during the same period.

The Rillington Place murders were one of a series of highly publicized metropolitan incidents, variously involving homicide, sex, treason, Cold War espionage, and political scandal, which precipitated and an extensive public debate about contemporary morality in the period from the late 1940s to the early 1960s. Other sensational murder stories included the trial and execution of the faux London playboy, Neville Heath, in 1946, and the "acid bath killer," George Haigh, in 1949, as well as the *crime passionnel* of Ruth Ellis, the last woman in England to hang, for shooting her lover in 1955.[4] Exposés of sexual scandal centered on the show trial of Lord Montague of Beaulieu, Michael Pitt Rivers, and Peter Wildeblood for homosexual offences in 1954, as well as the Profumo affair, in 1963, which compromised the Conservative government, as a result of the sexual entanglement of the war minister, John Profumo, with the call girl Christine Keeler.[5] The Profumo affair also had a double plot that coupled sex with the geopolitics of the Cold War, and it therefore needs to be seen in relation to the other genre of public scandal dominating the postwar years, the high-profile cases of

314

spying that characteristically twinned homosexuality and espionage. Episodes in this latter category included the defection of British Foreign Office officials Guy Burgess and Donald Maclean to the Soviet Union in 1951, together with the fallout from the Vassall spy scandal in 1962–63.[6]

Although all of these events had very specific origins, there was a remarkable continuity of subject matter and setting that linked their various concerns. They frequently highlighted high politics and elite society, but in ways that drew attention to the moral deficiencies of these arenas, rather than to their operation as enlightened spheres of influence. It was no accident that so many of the cases crescendoed in courtroom dramas, for the modern English courtroom stands as "one of the great social spaces for the enactment of access to the secrets of sex."[7] All of the incidents were characterized by the mutual dependence of high and low cultures that were depicted as promiscuously interrelated in the diverse public and entertainment spaces of central London. All of them condensed competing beliefs about transgressive and pleasure-seeking sexuality, set against marriage and the family, with highly unstable definitions of public and private life. Many of the cases probed the psychology and motivations underpinning the nature of evil, treason, sex, and passion—forms of human behavior that were frequently seen to be stimulated by London's urban environments. A number of these exposés also brought into play anxieties about the capital's cosmopolitan and migrant cultures, and about the ways in which cosmopolitan milieus were being transformed under the impact of decolonization.

In their dramatic enactment as disruptive narratives of urban life these events became elevated to the status of transgressive fantasies, occupying a prominent position in postwar English politics and culture. I am using the linked terms of *fantasy* and *transgression* here in a social rather than a psychoanalytic sense, to delineate the collective formation of a series of imagined scenes, constructed on the back of real historical events, that breached the boundaries of what was socially and morally acceptable, or politically possible. Fantasies of this kind were transgressive not simply in terms of their concern with various immoral, treacherous, or murderous deviations from normative conduct, but also in the more precise sense defined by Peter Stallybrass and Allon White, as events that, though positioned as socially marginal, frequently became symbolically central to national life.[8]

This was by no means the first time that metropolitan scandals had functioned in such a way. Throughout the nineteenth century a plethora of murder cases and intrigues had permitted diverse constituencies to engage in struggles over meaningful stories about social danger and moral truth.[9] The cases that erupted during the immediate postwar years were complexly shaped by those earlier events and drew heavily on their cultural and political resources. But they also orchestrated decidedly contemporary versions of moral truth-telling, functioning as major interpretative devices within English society. Overwhelmingly, these postwar incidents dramatized quintessentially modern anxieties that eventually led to changes in social mood, in attitudes toward criminal conduct and sexual mores, as well as to some of the key markers defining English national identity. Yet the character of the cases was in no sense unproblematically progressive or forward-looking. This was because the factors shaping them were drawn from some very traditional elements within public life: murder, treason, and sexual scandal. An important and relatively neglected part of the history of cultural change in England during the postwar years centers on the significance of these transformative events, whose long-term impact on social beliefs and moral attitudes was profound.

The Rillington Place murders brought together three related sets of concerns that were understood to have a quintessentially metropolitan location: the symbiotic relationship between London's social elites and the capital's "low life," contested understandings of pathological forms of masculinity and of sexually wayward femininity, and an accelerating debate about the cultural impact of Caribbean immigration on the indigenous character of one problem zone in the inner city. By focusing in detail on the discovery of the murders and on the trial of the killer, John Christie, together with the attendant media coverage, I show how the case represented a distinctive elaboration of these moral anxieties. It functioned as a grotesque site of social and moral disturbance, acting as a catalyst to a prolonged debate about the social and sexual pathologies that were embedded within contemporary urban life. These discussions were taken up in subsequent scandalous episodes throughout the following decade.

Two months before the coronation of Elizabeth II in the spring of 1953, four Jamaican families were living in the end house of an insignificant Victorian cul-de-sac in north Kensington.[10] Contemporary photographs show Rillington Place as a shabby street lying close to the Metropolitan Railway; its dilapidated late-nineteenth-century houses, with their bay windows and soot-blackened brick, were dominated by the chimney of an abandoned iron foundry. It was a street where the average wage was about eight pounds a week, where most of the families had to share a toilet, and where more often than not there was no bath. In the row of terraced houses there was at least one resident, a seventy-seven-year-old-widow, Margaret Ploughman, who could not even write her own name.[11] This part of north Kensington was characteristic of the type of inner-city zone that loomed large in contemporary public debate about the so-called twilight areas of London. In the 1950s urban planners, social workers, psychologists, public moralists, journalists, and filmmakers all pointed to the emergence of new configurations of social and moral problems that were no longer wholly shaped by the traditional demarcations of social class and metropolitan poverty.

These investigations disrupted both the traditional class divisions that had dominated the social geography of the Victorian city as well as the functional versions of urban modernity that were written into the midtwentieth-century projects for the rebuilding of London in the aftermath of the Second World War.[12] Twilight zones, or zones of transition, were characteristically squeezed between the established infrastructure of the metropolitan core and the settled residential communities of the Victorian inner suburbs. An arc of these problem areas was seen to run from Islington, Holborn, and King's Cross, in the north, westward across to Marylebone, Paddington, and Kensington.[13] Official and expert discussion of such districts regularly focused on the "unsettled" or "disturbed" nature of their populations, which were seen to epitomize an urban world in which the markers of class and community had been profoundly dislocated.

Rillington Place was one of London's liminal spaces. Only a bus ride away from Marble Arch and the heart of the West End, it was caught on the borders of a district of traditional, white working-class poverty, known as Notting Dale, and the more mixed and culturally exotic, though equally dilapidated, location of Notting Hill. Notting Dale's reputation as a London slum had an extensive pedigree, dating back to the early nineteenth century. Noxious local industries, repeated outbreaks of cholera and typhoid, and a gypsy settlement had all contributed to the area's long-standing negative reputation.[14] "The Dale," as it was invariably known locally, had a defensive proletarian character, and in the 1950s groups of local residents increasingly projected this defensiveness as racially homogenous and white. Part of the reason was to be found in the adjacent area. Notting Hill, immediately to the east and south, had been developed originally in the 1860s as a proposed westward extension of genteel squares and crescents along the fashionable Bayswater Road, situated on the north side of Hyde Park. By the interwar period, with the accelerated middle-class exodus to London's new western suburbs, the area's imposing villas had been converted into cheap flats and rooming houses.[15] Notting Hill became one of the major sites for Caribbean settlement in the 1950s, as well as for smaller numbers of Cypriot and Maltese immigrants.

Public anxieties about the condition of areas like north Kensington high-lighted long-standing connections between social and moral decline and the urban environment, but during the 1950s a range of experts and professionals also began to reconfigure these associations in new ways. Reporting in the 1890s, Charles Booth and his team of metropolitan researchers mapped poverty in Notting Dale via a conceptual framework that was derived from his vast sociological survey of life and labor in London's inner ring. Booth viewed the pauperized, transitory inhabitants of north Kensington as a subcategory of the collective entity of the metropolitan poor, namely, "the residuum" or submerged tenth.[16] By the midtwentieth century, local social workers and council officials argued that north Kensington's problems could no longer be viewed through the template of class-specific models of social deprivation. The presence of the Caribbean population, and the emergence of new phenomena such as "unmarried mothers" and local Teddy Boy gangs, the first of the flamboyant postwar youth subcultures, meant that north Kensington became defined as one of the capital's inner-city problem zones.

Number 10, like most of the other houses in Rillington Place, showed all of the outward signs of landlord neglect, with peeling paint and rotting stucco. It was not let out as flats, but, in the desperate conditions of postwar overcrowding, as rooms. In microcosm, living conditions in the house condensed social tensions that were becoming increasingly prevalent in these inner-city areas, as Caribbean immigrants began to compete with the local working-class population for scarce material resources. Housing was the most significant element in the volatile crucible of postwar English "race relations," which erupted only five years later as the Notting Hill Riots, involving clashes between local fascist groups, elements within the white working-class population, and Jamaicans and Trinidadians.[17] The house at 10 Rillington Place, let through a West End property agency, had long been occupied by poor but "respectable" whites. In 1950, it was bought by a West Indian landlord who began renting the accommodation to his fellow Jamaicans.[18] By the following year, seven Jamaican men and women were living on the upper floors of the house, through a process of rooming or subletting. The roots of this overcrowding, and of embryonic Jamaican landlordism, lay in a situation where most of the rented accommodation in London was filtered by a "whites only" housing policy, which was tacitly sanctioned by the local Kensington council.[19]

On March 24, 1953 the rooms on the ground floor of number 10 were empty, after the previous tenant had left hurriedly a few days earlier. Neighbors knew John Christie and his wife, Ethel, who had lived there for fifteen years, as a quiet, reserved Yorkshire couple, who cut a respectable pose in

318

the decaying area. Yet judged in terms of income and access to the most precious of postwar commodities, housing, the Christies' social status was extremely precarious. Repeated bouts of ill-health and criminal convictions for petty theft and assault had confined John Christie to a variety of low-grade clerical jobs. Despite their downward mobility, the couple maintained a superior social tone in the street. Working-class neighbors were impressed by Christie's quiet, genteel voice, by his neat appearance and mock club tie, and by an assumed air of social authority.[20] Most of the locals, especially the Jamaican tenants, believed that the couple "didn't like colored people."

One of the new tenants in the house, a Jamaican laborer, Beresford Brown, was also something of a handyman, and he asked the landlord's permission to do up the back room of the empty ground floor as a kitchen. When he went downstairs on that March afternoon he found a scene of dereliction and squalor. Overlooking the overgrown back garden full of weeds, newspapers, and rubbish, the room contained only a dirty mattress and an ancient, cast-iron kitchen range. Tapping one of the walls, Brown noticed that it sounded hollow, and he pulled away the wallpaper to find a hole in the lath and plaster about two inches across. Peering in with his torch, he could just make out the "bare back of a human being."[21] In a state of shock he ran out of the house and called the police. Brown's account, which he later told in court, enacted a significant feat of cultural ventriloquism. Privileged by the law as an embryonic "good colored citizen," the Jamaican immigrant rehearsed his evidence as an outsider, as an extraneous commentator on the indigenous urban poverty that he found in the rooms below his home. Brown was aware that he had stumbled across a scene of multiple murder, and he evoked its atmosphere through a series of powerful images—images of the all-pervasive odor of decomposition, of the scene of violent domestic disorder, and of death, personified as unidentified female detritus. He rehearsed his story across a sensory borderline between smell and vision and through a spatial poetics that dramatized his discoveries as a journey from the external world into a small claustrophobic space, or lair. Alain Corbin has described this type of tight spatial metaphor as a device used predominantly by official agencies to simultaneously delineate and distantiate the habitus of the urban poor.[22] More unusually in Brown's testimony, this language was drawn on by a subaltern subject to describe an interior that was suffocating, derelict, and suffused with death.

Scotland Yard, the center of London's criminal police investigations, decided to excavate the whole of 10 Rillington Place. It was literally taken to pieces, floor by floor and wall by wall. Chief Inspector Law, from the photographic department, was immediately called in to record the scene, which resembled a charnel house. Working with the well-established visual codes of criminal photography, Law produced images that were used as part of the forensic evidence to map the mise en scène of the crime.[23] They depicted a sequence of corpses—all of them women—encased, quite literally, in the decayed Victorian fabric of the building, or buried in the back garden. Forensic tests showed that all of the victims were, with one exception, the remains of young women in their twenties or early thirties who had died either a few months previously or long before, sometime in the 1940s. On the basis of detailed postmortems, Dr. Francis Camps, the police pathologist and an expert in forensic medicine, confirmed suspicions already circulating in the press and in the local community that the murders were "sex crimes."[24] Three of the women had been subjected to sexual intercourse, immediately before death by a lethal dose of carbon monoxide poisoning. Police records identified them as prostitutes who had worked the streets, pubs, and rooming houses of north Kensington and the nearby Edgware Road. Camps's provisional conclusion was that the women had been the victims of "systematic" murder "with a sexual basis." Meanwhile, the remains under the floor boards were identified as those of Ethel Christie, the wife of the previous tenant.[25]

Police photography and forensic science released powerful negative images of the killings that were in excess of their representation as scientific and legal evidence.[26] In the Rillington Place case, as in so many modern serial murders, the fact that all the corpses were female immediately endowed the murders with an erotic charge. Images of transgressive urban horror were evoked by the association of the women's bodies with decay and putrefaction.[27] The press was quick to point out that 10 Rillington Place had already gained a reputation as a "chamber of horrors."[28] In 1949, the bodies of Mrs. Beryl Evans and her baby daughter, Geraldine, had been found lying together in the washhouse. They had been strangled, and Timothy Evans, the husband and father, had been hanged for the murder of his daughter. The hunt was now on for the missing man who had left the ground-floor rooms so suddenly—John Reginald Halliday Christie.

The Christie case was the macabre sensation of the coronation season. Ruth Fuerst, Muriel Eady, Ethel Christie, Rita Nelson, Kathleen Maloney, Ina MacLennan, Beryl and Geraldine Evans—the press and the police repeatedly circulated the names and the mug shots of these murdered women like a sinister counterpoint to the pictures of visiting foreign dignitaries and heads of state arriving in London for the royal event. In the popular and middle-market daily papers and in the evening editions Christie's trial and subsequent execution ran as a macabre counterpoint to the coronation. The

London Evening Standard covered the Rillington Place story as a front-page leader more than a dozen times between March and June, in the teeth of fierce competition from royal news.[29] In May the *Daily Express* showed pictures of London jammed with spectators watching the coronation rehearsals, side by side with the grisly police exhumation of the bodies of Mrs. Evans and her daughter from Kensington Cemetery.[30] This double-imaging was a long-standing media device for producing sensational news copy; the juxtaposition of the sublime and the monstrous suggested that these stories of majesty and murder were in some uncanny way related, or at least that they existed in the same topos or space.

Starkly contrasting versions of "high" and "low" London were generated at John Christie's trial and in the powerful cultural imagery that circulated throughout the case. Media organization of Christie's story played a major role in centering the case on the capital's bifurcated social topography, thereby shaping the moral anxieties unleashed by the killings. The highly wrought cultural rituals of the courtroom drama were cross-fertilized with the equally elaborate codes of publicity to produce an expansive commentary on postwar London society and its social instabilities. As in earlier notorious homicides, London was constructed as lying at the epicenter of murderous crime; the case was seen as an international scoop, with leading crime reporters from as far afield as New York and Sydney arriving to cover the case in person.[31] Albert Pierrepoint, the nation's public executioner, noted perceptively how serial killings like Christie's were reported to a readership "greedy for details of death and the dealers of death," a public who had become habituated to violence by world war and the horrors of the concentration camps.[32]

Overwhelmingly, this was coverage in which print journalism shaped not only the transmission of information about the affair, but also its overall gestalt. The public spectacle of the coronation, the first major televised public event in Britain, was heralded as beginning the "television age," yet, in reality, press media still dominated news communication throughout the 1950s. This was especially true in a classic murder story like Christie's. The case demanded continuous reporting of a kind still beyond the technological scope of the newer medium of television, but ideally suited to the hour-on-hour editions circulated by the popular dailies and the London evening papers.[33] Equally important were the established codes of crime reporting, with their generic framework of cultural meanings and readership expectations derived from late-nineteenth- and early-twentieth-century popular culture. Social documentary reportage jostled for space with the multiple genres of melodrama, horror, and detective fiction.

Coverage of the Rillington Place murders drew together many of the subjects that dominated public debate about the condition of inner London during the 1950s: issues about traditional forms of power, wealth, and social hierarchy, about the dubious glamour of the West End and its metropolitan characters, and about the racial and sexual pathologies that were generated by adjacent areas in the inner city. In the Christie case these themes were also framed by discussions of history and geography—in particular, by discussion of the way many of the inhabitants and the spaces of the contemporary city were shadowed by the legacy of a Victorian past.

Christie was tried for the murder of his wife at the Old Bailey, London's principal showcourts, in the middle of June 1953.[34] Coming midway through the social calendar of the season (London's elite spring and summer social round), and taking place within weeks of the coronation of the new queen, Christie's appearance was framed by the press both as a popular spectacle *and* as part of the rituals of elite society.[35] This dual focus was immediately apparent from the diverse character of the audiences who were drawn to the trial. Outside the entrance to the court's public gallery in Newgate Street, overnight queues formed fourteen hours before the opening day. However, the *London Evening News* observed in its "Society" column that a different constituency was also eager for seats, gossiping that getting into the court was proving more difficult than gaining access to the Royal Enclosure at Ascot races. The paper noted that reserved seating, just above the well of the courtroom, had been set aside for "forty specially invited guests of the City."[36] A large part of the audience at the Old Bailey were celebrities, precisely that section of a national and international social elite who were already in London for the coronation. Eminent foreign tourists wrote in pleading for courtroom passes.[37] Closer to home, socialite and royal photographer Cecil Beaton came every day; so did Lady Lowson, wife of a former lord mayor of London. American dramatist Terrence Rattigan and Fryniwyd Tennyson Jesse, the famous crime writer, both covered the case. The *Daily Express* reported how "fashionable women," including the actress Margaret Leighton, strained forward in their seats when psychiatrists entered the witness box to testify about the state of Christie's mind.[38]

The sense of social atmosphere and occasion was hightened by the fact that Number 1 Court, scene of some of the most famous trials in English criminal history, with its particular atmosphere of intimate theater, was specially reopened for the case, restored after wartime bombing. This prominent staging reinforced the trial's significance as a spectacular event; part of the orchestrated theater of the criminal law as public spectacle and metropol-

322

itan entertainment. Postwar restoration work on the court preserved intact the intricate networks of juridical and social power and the forms of urban spectatorship that had their origins in much earlier periods of London's social and political history. According to legal custom, Mr. Justice Finnemore, the presiding judge, left the high-backed center chair on his bench vacant, reserving it for the City of London's most prominent dignitary, the lord mayor.[39] To Finnemore's left, the seats held for members of the bar and their distinguished visitors were raised at a higher level than the counsel benches and directly confronted the jury at eye level. The octagonal-shaped dock, topped with glass panels in black wooden frames and capable of holding up to twenty prisoners, dwarfed individual defendants. Above them all, removed from the court on a different floor, were the thirty seats of the public gallery. The American playwright and Anglophile Robert Sherwood marveled at the "dignity and majesty" of English justice, all superbly calm and businesslike, he reported, with an air of distinguished ceremonial about it, which was quite different from the modern histrionics of a courtroom in New York or Chicago.[40]

In an postwar world of mass democracy and extended citizenship rights, Christie's trial, like the Montague-Wildeblood case and the Profumo scandal, appeared to dramatize a more traditional and hierarchical view of English life. Leading members of metropolitan high society made significant appearances in many of these affairs, as active participants, energetic spectators, and via the authority awarded to selected forms of gentry or aristocratic symbolism. Why was this the case?[41] In order to understand how social life mapped onto these scandalous events, I want to look at historical interpretations of English society in the years after 1945, which have charted the relative decline and partial disintegration of the country's traditional elites.

The political and social power wielded by the "upper class" is generally understood to have been substantially curtailed in the immediate postwar period, under the impact of the combined democratizing effects of the Second World War, the Labour Government's own postwar program of social redistribution, and the changing dynamics of public life. Ross McKibbin extends this argument about upper-class decline not simply to its formal institutions, but also to the informal rituals of social honor that centered on the idea of metropolitan elite society. Inasmuch as part of the upper class defined itself, and was defined by others, by its symbolic capacity for public display in the capital city, then, McKibbin argues, the failure of these practices to survive into the postwar period was a serious symptom of high society's decline.[42]

There is plenty of contemporary evidence from the doyens of London society in the late 1940s and early 1950s to lend weight to McKibbin's thesis. Yet many of its rituals and some of its personalities underwent an energetic revival and a partial transformation during the early 1950s. This renaissance was encouraged by the dynamic forms of cultural conservatism linked to the coronation and to the Tory general election success of 1951, which ushered in a thirteen-year-period of Conservative political hegemony.[43] The reappearance of key milestones in London's social season (Ascot, Wimbledon tennis, the Henley regatta), linked to elite personalities, such as the man-about-town, the society hostess, and the denizens of Pall Mall's and Mayfair's clubland in the West End, were among the most significant features of this reassertion of cultural authority by the metropolitan gentry.

The counterpoint to this elite revivalism was the way that a number of elite society figures, and their society settings, were seen to be implicated in London's underworld or its demimonde, via their sexual tastes or politically motivated actions. Guy Burgess's public and private career gained notoriety not simply because he was a Soviet spy, but because of the way his life criss-crossed elite institutions, such as the Foreign Office, the BBC, and the literary salons of London, on the one hand, and the homosexual underworld of nearby Soho and Piccadilly, on the other[44] John Profumo, the ambitious Conservative minister par excellence, with a family history rooted the Italian nobility and on friendly terms with members of the English royal family, epitomized another version of this story of social and sexual transgression, via his links with West Indian pimps and local call girls in Mayfair and Notting Hill.

Many of these scandalous events pointed to explicit and disturbing connections between members of the social elites and London's multiple forms of "low life," reconfiguring a version of the overworld/underworld dichotomy that had been a regular feature of Victorian social encounters. Christie's trial dealt in a related though differently nuanced version of these cultural and spatial divisions. The murderer's career began from the opposite end of the social spectrum; a life that was lived for nearly twenty years in the extremely localized world of north Kensington. It was the distinctiveness of this social setting, as well as the eight particularly gruesome murders, that provided part of the attraction for the high-society audience who flocked to the case. When Lady Lowson was asked on the last day of the trial if she had found the revelations horrifying, she replied: "Not at all, because the *location*, the motion and the interest of it all was so absorbing that it took way all the horrors."[45]

324

Yet Christie's story did more than focus public attention on the decaying inner city, it also kaleidoscoped the divergent social spaces of "high" and "low" London in a troubling yet reciprocal relationship. Christie's murders pushed together polarized worlds, making visible the grotesque and the monstrous in a city that was marked out as special that summer by royal ritual. In this sense the case was distinctively different from other serial killings that took place in the capital during the same period. Whereas the other postwar celebrity murderers, Haigh and Heath, were personified as faux London playboys who operated from the gentility the suburbs and the Home Counties, John Christie was overwhelmingly depicted as the product of inner-city decay, but through a narrative and a set of visual images that juxtaposed his world against the environmental settings of elite London.

The concomitant of criminality is its association with place, argues Adrian Rifkin: in order to represent crime, it is necessary to have a space to configure it.[46] These suggestive remarks about crime and its attendant spatial imagery apply in a distinctive way to the Rillington Place killings, where the territorially based nature of the murderer's crimes featured as a central interpretive device in the case. It was through the representations of John Christie's own character that the courtroom audience and a wider reading public encountered a map of London that centered on the capital's contiguous but polarized social milieus. Camps, the police pathologist, noted later that Christie's trial exemplified a particular category of murder, where the motive and criminal seemed securely established but where the murderer's identity became "the central problem of the case."[47] For much of the trial Christie was represented as the archetypal "little man," entirely fixed by custom and locality to a few north Kensington streets. Christie himself embellished this persona in his own carefully crafted newspaper story: "I am a quiet humble man who hates rows or trouble. . . . I come from a solid, respectable old-fashioned type of Yorkshire family. . . . I am the sort of chap you would never look twice at in a bus."[48] With her trained eye for courtroom history, Tennyson Jesse believed that the murderer's character most closely resembled that of an earlier beleaguered "little man," Dr. Crippen. Crippen's trial for killing his wife, Cora, in 1910 had projected the murderer as a subaltern antihero; the representative of a form of lower-middle-class masculinity that was becoming increasingly squeezed in the rapidly changing social and gender dynamics of Edwardian London.[49] John Christie represented a midtwentieth-century reworking of the story of subaltern man, who was the combined product of urban decline, the precariousness of lower-middle-class existence, and the sexual and racial instabilities of postwar London.

Time and again as the evidence unfolded, Christie was depicted in situ, as the product of the degraded cultures that existed close by Rillington Place itself: the cafés, street-corner pubs, and rooming houses of north Kensington where he picked up women. It was here that the jury also encountered many of the murderer's victims, pathologized by both the prosecution and the defense lawyers as prostitutes and street characters. These were precisely the images of the inner city that planners and urban sociologists highlighted as the source of so many of London's contemporary problems; a world in which poverty and moral blight existed side by side with traditional wealth, and where isolated men and women like Christie and his young female victims were identified as the products of profound urban dislocation.

Yet as Christie's story unfolded in court, it became clear that there was a counterweight to these exposés of inner-city horror. Supposedly sighted as far afield as Tangier and Vancouver, the murderer appeared to have doppelgängers all over London and across the world.[50] Christie's speed of movement and his seeming ability to mesmerize his female victims before killing them was also redolent of Svengali-like evil. Now, Christie was transformed into a figure of metropolitan modernity, a character who juggled time and space compression with disguise and masquerade.[51] In terms of London's social geography, Christie and a number of his victims were seen to move outside the confines of Notting Hill and into the dubious glamour of the West End. It was at this point that the murderer's itinerary collided with the world of elite London, social environments that must have been recognizable to many of the celebrity audience in the courtroom. Now, the "bluebeard of Notting Hill" appeared to take on the characteristics of a cultural and sexual sophisticate who mingled in the pleasure grounds of the metropolis.[52]

Christie's excursions into the West End were not confined to the capital's deluxe sexual economy; he had also been spotted in more genteel venues, apparently stalking female members of the concert audience at the Royal Albert Hall and lady shoppers in St. James's.[53] Some of the itineraries of the murdered women also extended beyond north Kensington's street corners and low houses of sexual assignation, or "knocking shops," across into central London's nightclub scene. Rita Nelson had been spotted many times at the Benelux Club, near Piccadilly, and at the infamous 21 Club in Marylebone.[54]

Throughout the trial the prosecution barrister and Attorney-General Sir Lionel Heald worked strenuously to isolate Notting Hill for the jury, portraying its inhabitants as part of a "strange country," or an exotic district, that was distant both from the quotidian city and from the world of official or "landmark" London represented by the coronation.[55] Christie's appearances in and around the West End blurred that distinction, suggesting that the demarcations between elite London and its dangerous or troublesome spaces and characters were porous and not clearly boundaried.

One important effect of this combined media treatment was to bring together the high and low cultures of the metropolis in a series of powerfully resonating visual oppositions, which were themselves part of wider pictorial techniques for representing the city during the immediate postwar years. The north Kensington district of Christie and his victims was invariably depicted in monochrome, as a world of chiaroscuro tones, of half-light and shadow, where human endeavor was drained of warmth, color, and vibrancy. The press photographs that were selected as iconic representations of the murders were invariably shots of the bleak frontage of the terraced house and the derelict back garden. These were images of a city still caught in the grip of postwar austerity, where life was dominated by the sheer struggle for existence. Familiar from the media treatment of many other wartorn European metropoles, they became typical visual representations of London in a series British crime-thriller films and in detective fiction produced in the late 1940s and early 1950s, where the capital was imaged as a city of gray shadows, derelict bomb sites, and treacherous moral quicksand.[56]

The Rillington Place murders continually evoked a pictorial contrast between this monochrome vision of the metropolis and the Technicolor magic of a city bustling with purposeful or ceremonial movement in preparation for the coronation. Lavishly illustrated press supplements for the royal event, together with the Pathé News coronation footage released in the summer of 1953, depicted London as a site of glamorous international and imperial spectacle.[57] This urban world was triumphantly "in color," where the members of the metropolitan elites, from the royal family down, were represented as vibrant and high-spirited. For one moment, in early June 1953, these worlds of majesty and murder were brought into a social and representational relationship. In her postcoronation drive through west London, the queen passed close by Rillington Place, which had come to resemble a charnel house. Gaudily festooned with flags and patriotic ribbon, the local press noted how the queen's smile and her regal presence momentarily dispelled the horrors of the murders.[58]

The Christie case, together with many of the other exposés and public scandals of the postwar years, oscillated between depictions of a metropolitan world of traditional luxury and one of extreme social deprivation. Almost entirely absent from the coverage of these events was any acknowledgment of the new world of postwar social reconstruction as evidenced in the replanned city, with its optimistic reordering of the urban environment, mass democracy, with its extended access to social citizenship and welfare rights, or popular consumerism, and its implied democratization of cultural relationships. The meanings that were generated by the Rillington Place killings were anchored in much more traditional social hierarchies. In particular, a legacy of "Victorianism" was drawn on by many of the commentators to explain the character of contemporary events. This was an accretive and eclectic version of the nineteenth-century past that was sufficiently composite to include images and environments from the Edwardian period as well. Experts and the police, as well as the press, continually raided the resources of the Victorian city in order to render the case socially meaningful. Such uses of history were not simply residual; the past was understood to be an active presence in the development of contemporary social and sexual relationships. How was this past-present relationship articulated and what were its consequences?

Much of the material environment for the murders was quintessentially nineteenth century, with corpses buried in the decrepit Victorian house and the narrow streets and terraces providing the dominant setting for the action. Many of the social actors in the affair were also presented through the language of nineteenth-century urban typologies. There were the workers and local residents of Notting Dale's street scene: pawnbrokers, secondhand furniture dealers, seamstresses, and street women, whom Christie had met with or accosted. There were also the charity workers, city missionaries, and other moralizing agents, with their legacy of philanthropic reform, who appeared in the reconstructed itineraries of a number of the dead women. Christie's own murderous travels through the city at times resembled a bizarre progress of the late-Victorian swell, or man-about-town, with his assumed right to move freely across the metropolis. Here were a set of people and metropolitan environments that were endowed with significance partly as a result of their connectedness to a Victorian past.

In the months before the coronation there were a number of other events, natural disasters and human dramas that along with the Rillington Place murders were vivid reminders of how the nineteenth century continued to ghost present-day London. In December 1952 a dense fog had settled over the capital. Combined with industrial pollution and the freezing weather, it recalled memories of the great Victorian smogs of 1873 and 1880, especially in its spiralling death rates.[59] Early in the New Year floods hit the east coast of England, submerging large parts of the Thames estuary, threatening the capital, and reminding Londoners about those great Victorian engineers who had embanked the river. Then in March the queen's grandmother, Queen

Mary, hailed as the "last of the great Victorians," died at Marlborough House. This was the cue for an outpouring of romantic nostalgia, celebrating a London life that had spanned the salons of Disraeli and the world of the London County Council's housing estates.[60]

Each of these events dealt in a version of the city in which a nineteenth-century inheritance was used define the contemporaneity of events and people in the present, and where Victorianism figured as an active presence in the development of the new. There were multiple and competing ideas about England as a post-Victorian society in circulation after 1945. The progressive version, championed by public intellectuals and politicians intent on using the state to modernize restrictive nineteenth-century social policies, invariably stressed the distance between the world of the Victorian past and the present. Examples of a more recidivist idea of England were the complex forms of nostalgia written into the burgeoning (and inherently nostalgic) heritage and conservation movements, which from the early 1960s endowed Victorian objects and artefacts with authentic cultural significance.[61] Victorianism as it appeared in the Rillington Place murders and in the other scandals represented a different rendering of historical truth. These episodes were heavily influenced in their organization and content by nineteenth-century narratives of moral danger, but they drew on the resources of the urban past in order to generate specifically modern ideas about sexual behavior.

Nowhere was this dynamic articulation of past and present more apparent than in the sexual treatment of the principal characters in the Rillington Place episode, for the gender-specific readings of deviant, wayward, or dangerous sexuality formed one of the central explanatory principles shaping the case. Writing about London's most infamous sexual monster, Jack the Ripper, Judith Walkowitz has demonstrated how the Whitechapel murders in the inner East End during the late 1880s drew on a "transitional language" in order to represent sex crime. The characterization of the Ripper as monster, Walkowitz has argued, with its roots in the cultural codes of gothic horror and melodrama, coexisted with an emergent scientific discourse that eventually transformed the figure of the sex beast into that of the medicalized sexual deviant.[62] Sixty years later, the Rillington Place murders pointed to the ongoing instability of social perceptions used to define deviant and transgressive male sexuality. The whole apparatus of postwar sexual science was mobilized to reveal what were in reality multiple scientific explanations about the killer, as different genres of medical and psychiatric knowledge competed for attention. These were disseminated to both professional audiences and to a mass public in an overall climate in which the scrutiny of the sexual criminal was becoming part of a much broader movement by the postwar welfare state toward the interrogation of the behavioral characteristics of the socially recalcitrant.[63]

The murderer's pathology was overwhelmingly located in his mind: "Is Christie Sane? Three Doctors Argue the Vital Question," "Doctors Clash at Trial," announced the daily and evening papers part way through the case.[64] This interpretative framework was partly set by Christie's own plea of insanity, but specific discussions of the murderer's mental state triggered a much more expansive intellectual discourse about the etiology and the mental capacities of sex offenders. Older, but nonetheless influential, notions of mania, sadism, and hysteria essentially derived from late-nineteenth- and early-twentieth-century sexology and clinical psychiatry, competed for attention with the claims of modern psychology and psychoanalysis. Dr. Desmond Curran, a leading clinical psychiatrist who pioneered treatments for homosexual men, was brought in from Harley Street, the West End center of English medicine, to adjudicate on the competing claims about Christie's mental state. Curran's own report was a mixture of behaviorist psychology and clinical judgment, spiced with Freudianism, a combination that reflected the pluralistic understandings of many categories of sex offenders during the 1950s. Christie showed all the signs of an overdeveloped ego and a highly abnormal character, yet, rather than being the victim of a psychiatric disease, Curran typed him as an "inadequate psychopath with hysterical features." Drawing directly on psychoanalysis, he argued that at root Christie's abnormality lay in his repressive childhood and family background.[65]

Medical opinion, with its strong endorsement of expert authority in speaking about sex, collided with popular media coverage in the Christie case. The daily and Sunday papers traded their own distinctive rendering of the drama of popular science, coupling a celebration of modern technology with the frisson of medical terror. Journalists reported that Christie was taken "in conditions of complete secrecy" to the Maudesley Hospital, London's psychiatric treatment center, where he was subjected to "electro-encephalogram tests." Placed on a couch with "his head covered with a complicated 'hair-net' of solid silver leads," white-coated assistants prepared to operate the "brain machine."[66] These aspects of the trial's coverage positioned Christie as a quintessentially modern antihero, disaggregating the case from its roots in earlier moments of criminal history.

In a remarkable twist to the endless dissections of his character, Christie turned this process self-reflexive, appropriating a popular psychological language to read his own personality. He proved to be particularly adept at scripting his own lead role in this scenario, deliberately courting the attention of various news agencies while he was in prison and eventually selling his "confessions" from the condemned cell to the *Sunday Pictorial* in order to achieve maximum effect.[67] Smuggled out to journalists, his serialized autobiography was released only days before he was due to hang. Christie chose to frame his life as a Freudian narrative of guilt, shame, and psychosexual damage. It dealt in scripts of the unconscious, narrating "the strange dark dreams . . . which haunted me for so many years."[68] There were primal scenes, seduction theories, and unresolved Oedipal conflicts. Christie in his autoanalysis, the expert witnesses who examined him in prison, and most of the later commentators on the case were all agreed on one significant point: the impact of a psychic legacy of Victorian morality. "My parents were Victorians of the old school," Christie recounted, "I always lived in dread of my father. He was stern, strict, and proud."[69] The murderer was portrayed, and portrayed himself, as a post-Victorian casualty, the victim of a repressive sexual culture that had demanded unattainable moral standards. The result was psychosexual damage, guilt, and sexual murder.

Christie's modernity was defined by his simultaneous distance from and links to a nineteenth-century past. His career was seen to be tied to a Victorian legacy inasmuch as family, class, and background all pointed to the continuing impact of nineteenth-century beliefs and attitudes. Yet simultaneously he was cast as post-Victorian, particularly via many of the resources that were used to understand his character. In that sense he embodied a hybrid form of modern masculinity that was seen to be compromised by its allegiances to competing models of social conduct.

A different transitional language of female sexuality was used to understand the character and the motivations of the young murdered women. The most significant difference between the treatment of Christie and the treatment of his victims was the identification of their respective sites of cultural and sexual disturbance. Whereas Christie's behavior was firmly located in his aberrant psychology, in the case of his victims it was their bodies, handed over to the mortuary and the coroner, that were scrutinized for signs of sex and then read back to the unstable social environments that had produced them. Christie's victims were not gynecologically mutilated, as victims so often are in cases of modern sex crime, but the bodies of the murdered women were read for what Jane Caputi has called "fetishized," "absolute sex."[70] They testified not only to the monstrous nature of Christie's acts, but also, in a number of cases, to their own wayward sexuality. Camps, the police pathologist, examined the stomach contents of the dead women, analyzing them for what he termed signs of their "erratic life."[71] With the exception of Christie's wife, their bodies were always represented as potentially suffused with sexuality. Accompanied by all of the visible signs of decomposition as they were exhumed, the women's corpses evoked negative female body images of the prostitute as putrid, confirming the strongest associations between sex and death.

Yet the treatment of the lives of some of the murdered women pointed to a more unstable handling of female sexuality, in which traditional moralizing definitions competed with contemporary portrayals of young women's less abject and more mobile social location in the city. Christie's first victim, Ruth Fuerst, was a young Austrian women from a small town near Vienna who had come to London at seventeen as a student nurse in search of the big city. Fuerst switched to munitions work during the early part of the Second World War, living in a single furnished room only a few minutes walk from Rillington Place. Christie met her in a Ladbroke Grove snack bar, where she told him that "she used to go out with American soldiers and one of them was responsible for a baby she had previously."[72] Attractive, feisty, and sexually assertive, Ruth Fuerst was well known to a number of local moral rescue workers and welfare agencies. She was precisely the type of "wayward girl" turned "amateur prostitute" whose profile loomed large in the files of London's reclamation and purity associations. Fuerst was young, culturally mobile, and unattached; her short adult life was played out as a series of ambiguous sexual episodes that were part of a wider search for metropolitan excitement and a degree of feminine independence. Her biography did not fit the traditional categories of prostitution; it demonstrated what Sonya Rose has described as a relatively continuous and frequently shifting public discourse about appropriate norms of female sexuality throughout the first half of the twentieth century, and especially during wartime.[73]

When it came to the three known prostitutes, Ina MacLennan, Rita Nelson, and Kathleen Maloney, the police were on more familiar territory, framing these women through a comprehensive language of social pathology that linked long-standing concerns about active female sexuality with more recent anxieties about miscegenation and delinquency. Nelson and Maloney had a record of convictions for prostitution, disorderly behavior, and petty theft dating back to the 1940s. Seen as "uncontrollable," a succession of juvenile courts had placed care and protection orders on Maloney, and she had been sent to a Catholic mission.[74] The cellarman at a pub on Edgware Road had watched her with punters in the streets around Marble Arch in the West End, while police witnesses confirmed that she was known to associate with "Lascars," seafaring men, Irish navvies, and "men of all nationalities."[75] The press depicted MacLennan as a "bright lights girl" and also reported on her supposed taste in foreign men. Playing up this sense of the sexually exotic, the *Daily Mail* informed readers that her real name was "Mrs. Klim Mauny Soe Hla," as she had once married a Burmese airman.[76] Nelson's record of petty crime was similar to that of the other two girls, and the police portrayed her as a modern deviant "with a kink for men."[77]

The treatment of the social and sexual character of London and its inhabitants throughout much of the Christie case suggested a compromised or hybrid version of modernity. However, one feature of the murders was much more resoundingly contemporary; race, or to use the contemporary lexicon *color*, ran through the events like a leitmotif. The intrusion of London's Caribbean populations and cultures into an episode that was in other respects so profoundly shaped by traditional narratives of Englishness disrupted the social categories written into the affair. Overwhelmingly, the racialized element differentiated the killings from most of the other sensational English murder cases of the early twentieth century, such as the Crippen homicide, or the famously domestic *crime passionnel* of the Thompson-Bywaters case in the 1920s. This component also distinguished the Christie murders from many subsequent English serial killings, such as the Yorkshire Moors murders in the 1960s, the "Yorkshire Ripper" case in the 1980s, or the Gloucester serial killings by Fred and Rosemary West a decade later.[78] In both the earlier and the later murderous episodes, the killers and their victims were wholly circumscribed by extremely localized, racially homogenous settings. Although this was also partly true of the Christie murders, the immigrant presence suggested a cultural milieu that was less fixed by the traditional markers of class and community, and where Englishness was itself a problematic category.

This aspect of the affair was shaped by north Kensington's rapidly changing social and material character, as the area became one of the main sites for Caribbean settlement after the war. By the early 1950s, an emergent sociology of "race relations" was beginning to give a distinctive intellectual gloss to the impact of postcolonial immigration on British cities. Much of this work amplified a version of the debate about twilight zones that already characterized the treatment of inner-city districts. What was distinctive about this sociological agenda was the way it produced more overtly racialized definitions of the urban environment, in which districts, streets, houses, and even rooms were marked by the problem of color.

The emergent sociology and anthropology of postwar British race relations viewed immigrants from the Caribbean, India, and Pakistan predominantly through the lens of *cultural difference*, rather than difference as marked by physiology or genetics.[79] In Britain, official and intellectual discourses on race through to the 1960s overwhelmingly privileged the social and anthropological rather than the biological register of racial difference, where the problem of cultural assimilation was defined through the opposition between the national host community and the "out group" of the immigrant. Drawing on Chicago School sociology, British anthropologist Kenneth Little observed in his study of Cardiff's docklands area in 1947 that it was in the "rooming house quarters" that the great metropolitan centers had their "racial colonies." Removed from the tightly knit family and neighborhood organization of traditional working-class areas, these were districts where "community" was especially difficult to define, because of the "peculiar mobility of the modern city."[80] Anthony Richmond's research on color prejudice in Liverpool, based on material collected between 1941 and 1951, built on the work of his mentor Little to give a similar spatial definition to the city. Looking to Robert Park's model of urban sociology (Park had defined prejudice as "an instinctive and spontaneous disposition to maintain social distance"), Richmond warned of a potential "similarity with the American situation" in terms of the "definite tendency for the colored population to congregate in a particular part of the city," a phenomenon that provoked feelings of resentment and hostility from the indigenous population.[81] In areas like north Kensington, as in Stepney and Liverpool, immigrant difference was defined as a problem of environment and setting. This was a spatialization of race, and it was overwhelmingly in play in the Christie case.

Christie's defense team drew on these professional languages of race relations in order to bolster his plea of insanity, as a condition that had been exacerbated by growing cultural tensions in the inner city. But medical experts and lawyers, along with Christie himself, also raided more popular forms of contemporary racism that were being forged in the interstices of frontline areas like north Kensington. Christie's trial played out in embryonic form a highly charged version of the phenomenon that Bill Schwarz has termed the reracialization of England and its white urban populations.[82] The geopolitics of the postcolonial encounter in north Kensington, as elsewhere in English cities, produced a cultural syntax of white Englishness that was different from both the older languages of popular domestic imperialism and the newer sociologies of race. As Schwarz has noted, two interrelated sentiments cohered around this formation in the quotidian rituals of everyday life: the fantasized figure of the white man as victim and, commensurably, a conception of white womanhood as prey to the rapacious and uncontrolled appetites of black men.[83]

334

Christie's defense was that his insanity had been brought on by persecution from his Jamaican neighbors, and his lawyers ran through the gamut of postwar "color prejudice" to demonstrate the "terrible pressures" that he had been living under. The murderer and his dead wife were positioned as little people, striving to maintain respectability and social standards in a district facing an alien culture. When Christie's new landlord began letting out the upper floors of the house to his fellow Jamaicans, Christie's stream of letters to Kensington Council drew on powerful cloacal imagery to make a direct connection between the degraded conditions of his own environment and the presence of the Caribbean population.[84]

Color, for John Christie, was an odor, a noise, a sex, a proximity, a persecution, indeed anything that was other, and he drew on a moralized environmental language, with its origins in nineteenth-century public health fears, to come to terms with his neighbors. Damp, overcrowding, and filthy sanitation were not simply blamed on "these colored people," as Christie called them, the people and their conditions became metonymically identified.[85] In an expansive courtroom exchange, Christie's defense lawyer insinuated to Franklin Stewart, one of the new Jamaican tenants in the house, that the reason his client continually sprinkled the hallway with disinfectant was not because he was deliberating trying to hide the smell of the corpses, but because of the filthy habits of colored tenants like himself![86] Much was made in court of one of Ethel Christie's letters, written to her sister in Yorkshire, in which she complained: "It is awful with these 'people' here," comparing London's negative cosmopolitanism with the northern values of homeliness and neighborliness.[87] Grounded in the dispossessed streets of Britain's decaying urban areas, stories like that of John and Ethel Christie became a catalyst for the new forms of popular racism that characterized the 1960s.

This vision of whiteness, a belief about "living in a white man's country," was built on miscegenation fantasies of an extraordinary virulence. Christie had clearly wanted to talk about race during and after his killing spree. "I know the Notting Hill district very well," he had confided to Ena Baldwin, a secretary whom he had approached in a Lyons tea shop, "it has changed a lot lately, a lot of colored people, foreigners there." Christie embellished his account by highlighting the universal predatory sexual characteristics of black men: "The blacks are hated in parts of America. . . . Where there is a white family living, and if they have any young children, especially little girls, they have to watch the black boys. . . . Do the same to them as they do to Tom Cats."[88] In court he claimed he was "terribly upset" when his landlord let the upstairs rooms to "colored people and to white girls."[89]

335

The Rillington Place murders and their associations with cosmopolitan Notting Hill fueled wider popular fears about London as a center for interracial sex. One father from Liverpool wrote to the police anxious to trace the whereabouts of his missing daughter, a girl with fair hair and blue eyes who, he confessed, was "a sex maniac towards colored people." Her disappearance had led her father to think that she might have made "her way to London with some black" and then fallen into Christie's hands.[90] Sexual anxieties of this kind, about Notting Hill as a flashpoint for interracial sex, surfaced again and again throughout the 1950s. A catalyst to the 1958 race riots, they also informed the defensive proletarianism of local Teddy Boy gangs, who enforced informal codes of sexual honor in white working-class communities.[91]

In the spring and summer of 1953 these miscegenation fears were given an international resonance as the Christie case unfolded. The Rillington Place murders took place at the height of the Mau Mau raids in Kenya. The British press was replete with stories about terrorist attacks on the farms of European settlers, with their inhabitants tortured, mutilated, and then massacred in an implied return to African savagery.[92] In March, the first reinforcement of British troops left London for Nairobi, and in April, Jomo Kenyatta, leader of the Kenya African Union, was sentenced to seven years hard labor for his part in orchestrating the Mau Mau movement. Though most of the violence was directed at other African Kenyans, in Britain the obsession was with the threat to white women and their children. Nuns and other female missionary workers were portrayed as under attack from forest gangs who, it was claimed, drank human blood and regularly engaged in shocking sexual orgies.[93] In London the colonial secretary, Oliver Lyttleton, stuck doggedly to the official line that Mau Mau was not a politically inspired, anticolonial movement, but was essentially an "anti-European and anti-Christian" force that had committed the worst crimes "you can imagine."[94] The new governor of Uganda, Sir Andrew Cohen, characterized the movement as wholly atavistic: "a reversion to tribalism in a perverted and brutal form."[95]

Coverage of Mau Mau involved a deep projection of British fantasies about African culture and African masculinity, and its impact shaped metropolitan politics at home. Fears about black insurgents slaughtering whites, with their subtext of interracial sexual violence, began to be transferred onto anxieties about the growing presence of Caribbean settlers in London. The symbolic interaction between images of the disintegration of British colonialism, and the domestic world of inner-city areas like north

Kensington, produced fears of cultural and sexual disturbance that would reshape the boundary lines between black and white. In microcosm, Christie's trial represented an early working through of these newly racialized urban fault lines.

The philosopher Paul Ricoeur suggested that the horror genre is one of the ways that we understand ourselves as human. It is part of the myths humanity lives by; one of the stories societies tell in order to help make sense of the world and to derive reassurance about actions and things that pose a threat to control, happiness, or even survival.[96] Ricoeur's insights are a significant but partial truth, for "being human" and "being monstrous" are not universal conditions; they are shaped by particular historical circumstances. The Christie case, and its setting in the coronation year, was a very specific version of a horror story. I want to propose, by way of conclusion, that the case returns us to the questions I posed at the opening, about the character and direction of moral and cultural change in England during the postwar period.

John Christie hung for the murder of his wife in Pentonville Prison on July 15, 1953. Pierrepoint, the executioner, remembered that blinking behind National Health spectacles as he approached the scaffold, Christie was "no trouble."[97] A crowd of about two hundred people waited outside the gates, some pressing their ears up against the prison walls in the hope of hearing the trapdoor slam open in the execution shed.[98] Despite this sense of narrative ending to the murder story, the Rillington Place affair offered no closure or resolution to the ethical and moral problems that it raised and to the city that had produced them. The case was characterized by the instability of its cultural registers and by the way that it intensified but did not close debate about the excesses of deviant sexuality in the context of postwar London.

It was not an isolated occurrence. Read in conjunction with the other metropolitan cases of scandal, treason, and murder that punctuated London society during the postwar years, these episodes performed significant cultural work. They repeatedly problematized moral and sexual values that were understood at the time to have Victorian or nineteenth-century origins. The impact of these incidents was more diffuse than the progressive accounts that dominate postwar English history. They were not centered on policy or legislation, nor were they driven by the doyens of liberal opinion, nor were they framed by a conception of reformist politics, and their settings were local and particular rather than conceived on a national stage. Nonetheless, their long-term impact on moral beliefs and attitudes was profound.

Taken together, they represented what Victor Turner has defined as "social dramas," where a sense of crisis invariably involves a complex infraction of the rules of morality, law, or custom, followed by the overt or implicit recognition of schism and social division.[99] The transformations they initiated were not straightforwardly modernizing. Indeed, the Byzantine ways in which they unfolded contrasted sharply with the more overtly progressivist versions of postwar social change. Sexual narratives of political and social transgression, acted out in quasi-Victorian locations that juxtaposed metropolitan overworlds and underworlds, appeared on first reading to confirm a backward-looking agenda. Yet in almost every instance the net effect of these episodes was to destabilize traditional moral and sexual certainties via narratives, dramatis personae, and settings that drew heavily on the resources of the past.

What these scandalous events highlight is the continuing force and adaptability of nineteenth-century cultural forms in a period and a society that was repeatedly characterized as post-Victorian, especially on issues of sex and morality. Victorian moral codes, and perceptions of their embeddedness in particular aspects of the metropolitan environment, were transformed but not wholly abandoned by the social actors who participated in these scandalous affairs. Such uses of history problematize in equal measure established readings of postwar modernization, and they complicate conventional cultural periodizations that have been used to distinguish the nineteenth from the twentieth century. Recognizing the impact and the consequences of these events involves historians in constructing a more complex narrative of contemporary sexual and moral change, as part of a revision of the history of twentieth-century English modernity.

Notes

The author acknowledges that an earlier version of this article has been published as "Scandalous Events: Metropolitan Culture and Moral Change in Post–Second World War London," *Representations* 93, Univrsity of California Press (Winter 2006): 106–37.

1. See Jeffrey Weeks, *Sex, Politics and Society: The Regulation of Sexuality since 1800* (London: Longman, 1981); Noel Annan, *Our Age: Portrait of a Generation* (London: Weiderfeld and Nicolson, 1990); Ross McKibbin, *Classes and Cultures: England 1918–1951* (Oxford: Oxford University Press, 1998); and Arthur Marwick, *The Sixties: Cultural Revolution in Britain, France, Italy, and the United States c.1958–c.1974* (Oxford: Oxford University Press, 1998).

2. For discussion of the restricted nature of the existing historiography of postwar Britain see Carolyn Steedman, *Landscape for a Good Woman: A Story of Two Lives* (London: Virago, 1986); and Becky Conekin, Frank Mort, and Chris Waters, eds., *Moments of Modernity: Reconstructing Britain 1945–64* (London: Rivers Oram Press, 1999), 1–40.

3. Carla Hesse, "The New Empiricism," *Cultural and Social History* 1, no. 2 (2004): 204.

4. For coverage of Heath and Haigh, see Conrad Phillips, *Murderer's Moon: Being Studies of Heath, Haigh, Christie and Chesney* (London: Arthur Baker, 1956). For Ruth Ellis, see Laurence Marks, *Ruth Ellis: A Case of Diminished Responsibility?* (London: Penguin, 1990).

5. For the Montague-Wildeblood case, see Peter Wildeblood, *Against the Law* (London: Weiderfeld and Nicolson, 1955); and Chris Waters, "Disorders of the Mind, Disorders of the Body Social: Peter Wildeblood and the Making of the Modern Homosexual," in Conekin, et. al., eds., *Moments of Modernity*, 134–51. For Profumo see Ludovic Kennedy, *The Trial of Stephen Ward* (London: Victor Gollancz, 1964).

6. On Burgess and Maclean, see Cyril Connolly, *The Missing Diplomats* (London: Queen Anne Press, 1952); and Tom Dreiberg, *Guy Burgess: A Portrait with Background* (London: Weicherfeld and Nicolson, 1956). For the Vassall case, see Home Office, *Report of the Tribunal to Inquire into the Vassall Case and Related Matters*, Cmnd. 2009 (London: HMSO [Her Majesty's Stationery Office], 1963).

7. Kali Israel, "French Vices and English Liberties: Gender, Class and Narrative Competition in a Late Victorian Sexual Scandal," *Social History* 22, no. 1 (January 1997): 1.

8. Peter Stallybrass and Allon White, *The Politics and Poetics of Transgression* (London: Methuen, 1986). For discussion of social fantasy in the context of postwar London, see Frank Mort, "Fantasies of Metropolitan Life: Planning London in the 1940s," *Journal of British Studies* 43, no. 1 (January 2004): 120–51.

9. See Israel, "French Vices and English Liberties"; and Nancy Erber and George Robb, "Introduction," in George Robb and Nancy Erber, eds., *Disorder in the Court: Trials and Sexual Conflict at the Turn of the Century* (Basingstoke: Macmillan, 1999), 2.

10. The following account is based on Francis Camps, *Medical and Scientific Investigations in the Christie Case* (London: Medical Publications, 1953); R. T. Paget and Sydney Siverman, *Hanged—And Innocent?* (London: Victor Gollancz, 1953); Lord Altrincham and Ian Gilmour, *The Case of Timothy Evans: An Appeal to Reason* (London: The Spectator, 1956); F. Tennyson Jesse, ed., *Trials of Timothy John Evans and John Reginald Halliday Christie* (London: William Hodge and Co., 1957); Ludovic Kennedy, *Ten Rillington Place* (London: Victor Gollancz, 1961); John Eddowes, *The Two Killers of Rillington Place* (London: Little Brown and Co., 1994); Rupert Furneax, *The Two Stranglers of Rillington Place* (London: Parker, 1994); and anon., *Rillington Place* (London: Uncovered Editions, 1999).

11. Statement of Margaret Ploughman, March 28, 1953, in Metropolitan Police, Office of the Commissioner, Correspondence and Papers, Murders of Ethel Christie and Other Women at 10 Rillington Place, London, by John Reginald Halliday Christie, 1953–1965, The National Archives (TNA), Public Record Office (PRO) MEPO 2/9535, part 1B.

12. For the classic planning accounts of Greater London, see J. H. Forshaw and Patrick Abercrombie, *County of London Plan* (London: Macmillan, 1943); Standing Conference on London and South East Regional Planning, *Greater London Plan 1944 . . . A Report on Behalf of the Standing Conference on London Regional Planning . . . at the Request of the Minister of Town and Country Planning* (London: HMSO, 1945).

13. See Peter Sainsbury, *Suicide in London: An Ecological Study* (London: Chapman and Hall, 1955), 89–92. For analysis of twilight or intermediate zones in the 1950s, see Mort, "Fantasies of Metropolitan Life."

14. Barbara Denny, *Notting Hill and Holland Park Past: A Visual History* (London: Historical Publications, 1993), 86. See also *The Survey of London*, vol. 37, *North Kensington* (London: N.p., 1973); Oliver Bailey and Harold Mollier, *The Kensingtons* (London: Regimental Old Comrades' Association, 1935); and Mary Borer Cathcart, *Two Villages* (London: W. H. Allen, 1973).

15. Edward Pilkington, *Beyond the Mother Country: West Indians and the Notting Hill White Riots* (London: I. B. Tauris, 1988), 56.

16. Charles Booth, ed., *Life and Labour of the People in London*, 3rd series, *Religious Influences*, vol. 3, *The City of London and the West End* (London: Macmillan, 1902), 152–53.

17. For discussion of housing as a critical factor in English "race relations" during the 1950s and 1960s, see: James Wickenden, *Colour in Britain* (London: Oxford University Press, 1958); Ministry of Housing and Local Government, *Report of the Committee on Housing in Greater London*, Cmnd. 2605 (London: HMSO, 1965).

18. See Kennedy, *Ten Rillington Place*, 210.

19. See evidence of Franklin Stewart, Home Office, Criminal Files, Christie, John Reginald Halliday: at Central Criminal Court on 25 June 1953 Convicted of Murder; Sentenced to Death; Executed 15 July 1953, 1949–1953 [Christie's trial transcript], TNA PRO HO 291/228, p. 36. For evidence of the "whites only" housing policy in Notting Hill, see Ruth Glass, *Newcomers: The West Indians in London* (London: Centre for Urban Studies and George Allen and Unwin, 1960), 44–92; and Mike Phillips and Trevor Phillips, *Windrush: The Irresistible Rise of Multi-Racial Britain* (London: HarperCollins, 1998), 120–42.

20. For the Christies' background and precarious social position, see Kennedy, *Ten Rillington Place*, chapters 1–3; and Eddowes, *Two Killers of Rillington Place*, chaps. 1–2.

21. Ibid.

22. Alain Corbin, *The Foul and the Fragrant: Odour and the French Social Imagination*, trans. Miriam Kochan (Cambridge, Mass.: Harvard University Press, 1986),

151–53. See also Carolyn Steedman, *Dust* (Manchester: Manchester University Press, 2001), 117–18.

23. The original photographs are preserved at TNA PRO HO 291/228. For the evidence of Percy Law, the police photographer, see Tennyson Jesse, *Trials of Timothy Evans and John Christie*, 134–37.

24. Camps, *Medical and Scientific Investigations*, 40.

25. Ibid.

26. For the contradictory character of modern documentary photography see Allan Sekula, *Dismal Science Photoworks 1972–1996* (Normal: University Galleries, Illinois State University, 1999), 122.

27. For the these negative erotic associations in the history of modern sex crime, see Judith Walkowitz, *City of Dreadful Delight: Narratives of Sexual Danger in Late-Victorian London* (Chicago: University of Chicago Press, 1992), chap. 7; Deborah Cameron and Elizabeth Frazer, *Lust to Kill: A Feminist Investigation of Sexual Murder* (Cambridge: Polity in association with Basil Blackwell, 1987); and Jane Caputi, *The Age of Sex Crime* (Ohio: Bowling Green State University Popular Press," 1987).

28. "Crowds Wait All Night Outside Rillington Place Charnel House," *Kensington News and West London Times*, March 27, 1953, 1.

29. See "Christie: Bodies in Cupboard," *Evening Standard*, April 22, 1953, 1; and "Is Christie Sane? Doctors Clash," *Evening Standard*, June 24, 1953, 1. During the period April to June 1953, months that were dominated by coverage of the coronation, the Rillington Place murders appeared twelve times as headline news in this London paper alone, second only to the royal event.

30. See "London Jammed 14 Hours in Coronation Preview," and "Mrs. Evans: Dawn Exhumation," *Daily Express*, May 18, 1953, 1.

31. For the international press coverage of the trial, see Applications for Press and Visitors Passes Regina v John Christie April–June 1953, TNA PRO CRIM 8/22.

32. Albert Pierrepoint, *Executioner Pierrepoint* (London: Harrap, 1974), 169.

33. For the primacy of print journalism in news transmission throughout the 1950s and the ongoing importance of the "human interest story," see Arthur Christiansen, *Headlines All My Life* (London: Heinemann, 1961); and Hugh Cudlipp, *At Your Peril . . . A Mid-Century View of the Exciting Changes of the Press in Britain* (London: Weidenfeld and Nicolson, 1962).

34. Christie was tried only for the willful murder of his wife. Under English law at that time, even if accused persons had been committed for trial on more than one murder charge, they were only tried for one offense at a time. See Tennyson Jesse, *Trials of Timothy Evans and John Christie*, lvi.

35. On the celebrity nature of the trial, see ibid.; Furneaux, *The Two Stranglers of Rillington Place*, 9; and Eddowes, *Two Killers of Rillington Place*, 93.

36. "The Christie Judge," *London Evening News*, June 22, 1953, cutting preserved in Central Criminal Court, Miscellaneous Books and Papers, John Christie, Applications for Press and Visitors Passes, April–June 1953, TNA PRO CRIM 8/22.

37. See A. Klapras to Central Criminal Court, Old Bailey, June 6, 1953, TNA PRO CRIM 8/22.

38. "Christie's Mind," *Daily Express*, June 25, 1953, 1.

39. See Kennedy, *Ten Rillington Place*, 140–41.

40. Robert Sherwood, "If Christie Had Been Tried in New York," *Evening Standard*, June 26, 1953, 6.

41. The trials of Stephen Ward and Christine Keeler in 1963, as part of the denouement of the Profumo affair, aroused much high-society interest, as the case also actively involved London's social elites. See Kennedy, *The Trial of Stephen Ward*. In the Montague-Wildeblood case much was made in the courtroom and in the press of the links between the metropolitan gentry and homosexuality; see Wildeblood, *Against the Law*.

42. See especially McKibbin, *Classes and Cultures*, 1–43. McKibbin gives a working definition of the upper class as a network that included the monarchy, the extended royal family and senior functionaries of the court, the old aristocracy, the political class attached to the peerage, a good part of the gentry, and many of the very wealthy.

43. For complaints about the decline of elite society in the late 1940s and 1950s, see Robert Rhodes James, ed., *Chips: The Diaries of Sir Henry Channon* (London: Weidenfeld and Nicolson, 1967), 470–71. For a more dynamic view of elite London in the 1950s from the perspective of a younger generation, see Douglas Sutherland, *Portrait of a Decade: London Life 1945–1955* (London: Harrap, 1988).

44. See "Guy Burgess Stripped Bare," *People*, March 11, 1956, 3; and "He Kept Blackmail Letters in His Room," *People*, March 18, 1956, 3.

45. "Express Diary," *Daily Express*, June 26, 1953, 6 (author's italics).

46. Adrian Rifkin, *Street Noises: Parisian Pleasures 1900–1940* (Manchester: Manchester University Press, 1993), 123–24.

47. Francis Camps, with Richard Barber, *The Investigation of Murder* (London: Joseph, 1966), 51.

48. John Christie, "My Dream and My First Victim," *Sunday Pictorial*, July 5, 1953, 6.

49. See Julie English Early, "A New Man for a New Century: Dr. Crippen and the Principles of Masculinity," in Robb and Erber, eds., *Disorder in the Court*, 209–11.

50. See Maria Fuchs, astrologer, Bremen, to the chief detective to the Assize Court, Old Bailey, June 5, 1953, TNA PRO MEPO 2/ 9635, part 3B.

51. For Christie as Svengali, see Mrs. L. Hay to Superintendent Peter Berridge, March 26, 1953, TNA PRO MEPO 2/9535, part 3A. For a cultural reading of the Svengali phenomenon in terms of urban modernity, see Daniel Pick, *Svengali's Web: The Alien Enchanter in Modern Culture* (New Haven, Conn.: Yale University Press, 2000).

52. Arrest of the London "Landru," newspaper cutting extracted from *Le Soir*, April 4, 1953, trans. P. C. Langford, contained in TNA PRO MEPO 2/ 9535, part 3A.

53. Statement of Arthur Turner, March 25, 1953, PRO MEPO 2/9535 Part 1A.

54. Statement of Mariana Demetra Papajotou-Jarman, TNA PRO MEPO 2/9535, part 1B.

55. Sir Lionel Heald, closing speech for the prosecution, June 24, 1953, quoted in Tennyson Jesse, *Trials of Timothy Evans and John Christie*, 253.

56. These films included *They Made Me a Fugitive*, 1947, directed by Alberto Cavalcanti; *Noose*, 1948, directed by Edmond Greville; and *The Blue Lamp*, 1949, directed by Basil Dearden. See Charlotte Brunsdon, "Space in the British Crime Film," in Steve Chibnall and Robert Murphy, eds., *British Crime Cinema* (London: Routledge, 1999), 148–59.

57. For the spectacularization of the metropolis during the coronation, see "River Mirrors London's Feu-de-Joie," *Daily Telegraph*, June 3, 1953, 1; and "The Queen Turns on the Lights," *Daily Express*, June 3, 1953, 1.

58. "And the Queen Smiled," and "Gay Rillington Place," *Kensington News and West London Times*, June 5, 1953, 5.

59. See Ministry of Health, Reports on Public Health and Medical Subjects, *Mortality and Morbidity during the London Fog of December 1952*, no. 95 (London: HMSO, 1954).

60. "Mr. Churchill's Broadcast," *Times*, March 26, 1953, 8; and "The Genius of Queen Mary," *Daily Mail*, March 25, 1953, 5.

61. For progressivist strategies, see—among very many—*Report of the Committee on Homosexual Offences and Prostitution*, Cnnd. 247 (London: HMSO, 1957); and C.A.R. Crosland, *The Future of Socialism* (London: Jonathan Cape, 1956). For heritage and conservationist versions of the Victorian past, see Patrick Wright, *On Living in an Old Country: The National Past in Contemporary Britain* (London: Verso, 1985); and Raphael Samuel, *Theatres of Memory: Volume 1, Past and Present in Contemporary Culture* (London: Verso, 1994).

62. Walkowitz, *City of Dreadful Delight*, 197–98. See also Cameron and Frazer, *Lust to Kill*; and Jane Caputi, *The Age of Sex Crime*.

63. See Nikolas Rose, *Governing the Soul: The Shaping of the Private Self* (London: Routledge, 1996); and Peter Miller and Nikolas Rose, eds., *The Power of Psychiatry* (Cambridge: Polity, 1986).

64. "Is Christie Sane? Doctors Clash," *Evening Standard*, June 24, 1953, 1; and "Three Doctors Argue the Vital Question—Is Christie Sane?" *Daily Mail*, June 25, 1953, 1.

65. Dr. Desmond Curran, Report on John Reginald Halliday Christie, June 4, 1953, TNA PRO PCOM 9/1668.

66. "Doctors Give Christie Secret Brain Test," *Sunday Empire News*, June 7, 1953, cutting preserved in TNA PRO PCOM 9/1668.

67. See W. Montgomery, on behalf of Central London News Service, to J. Christy [*sic*.], April 1, 1953, TNA PRO PCOM 9/1668.

68. "Girls Laughed at Me," *Sunday Pictorial*, July 12, 1953, 6.

69. "Christie's Own Story: My Second Victim . . . We Kissed and Cuddled," *Sunday Pictorial*, July 12, 1953, 6.

70. Caputi, *The Age of Sex Crime*, 129.

71. Camps, *Medical and Scientific Investigations*, 39.

72. Second statement of Christie, June 5, 1953, quoted in Camps, *Medical and Scientific Investigations*, 200–201.

73. Sonya Rose, "Sex, Citizenship, and the Nation in World War II Britain," *American Historical Review* 103, no. 4 (October 1998): 1,148.

74. Statement of Lillian Maloney, TNA PRO MEPO 2/ 9535, part 1C.

75. Statement of George Noakes, March 30, 1953, TNA PRO MEPO 2/9535, part 1B.

76. "Multi-Killer: Police Fear," *Daily Mail*, March 27, 1953, 1.

77. Report of Sergeant J. Brown, March 28, 1953, TNA PRO MEPO 2/9535, part 3A.

78. For coverage of these other homicides and serial killings, see René Weis, *Criminal Justice: The Story of Edith Thompson* (London: Hamish Hamilton, 1988); Fred Harrison, *Brady and Hindley: The Genesis of the Moors Murders* (Bath: Ashgrove Press, 1986); Nicole Jouve Ward, *"The Streetcleaner": The Yorkshire Ripper Case on Trial* (London: Boyans, 1986); and Colin Wilson, *The Corpse Garden: The Crimes of Fred and Rose West* (London: True Crime Library, 1998).

79. See especially Chris Waters, " 'Dark Strangers' in Our Midst: Discourses of Race and Nation in Britain, 1947–1964," *Journal of British Studies*, 36 (April 1997): 207–38.

80. K. L. Little, *Negroes in Britain: A Study of Racial Relations in English Society* (London: Kegan Paul, 1947), 2–3.

81. Anthony Richmond, *Colour Prejudice in Britain: A Study of West Indian Workers in Liverpool, 1941–1951* (London: Routledge and Kegan Paul, 1954), 18; and Barbara Ballis Lal, "The 'Chicago School' of American Sociology, Symbolic Interactionism and Race Relations Theory," in John Rex and David Mason, eds., *Theories of Race and Ethnic Relations* (Cambridge: Cambridge University Press, 1986), chap. 13.

82. Bill Schwarz, " 'The Only White Man in There': The Re-Racialization of England 1956–1968," *Race and Class* 38, no. 1 (1996): 65–78.

83. For these versions of "white England" as they were played out in Notting Hill during the 1950s, see Majbritt Morrison, *Jungle West 11* (London: Tandem Books, 1964); Pilkington, *Beyond the Mother Country*; and Charlie Phillips and Mike Phillips, *Notting Hill in the Sixties* (London: Lawrence and Wishart, 1991).

84. See statement of Derek Kennedy, sanitary inspector, March 26, 1953, TNA PRO MEPO 2/9535, part 1A.

85. See statement of Christie, March 31, 1953, TNA PRO MEPO 2/9535, Part 1B.

86. Derek Curtis Bennett to Franklin James Stewart, trial transcript, June 22, 1953, TNA PRO HO 291/228, 36.

87. Ethel Christie to Mrs. Lily Bartle, December 15, 1952 [date altered by Christie], Exhibit no. 4, TNA PRO HO 291/228.

344

88. Statement of Ena Baldwin, March 27, 1953, TNA PRO MEPO 2/9535, part 1B.

89. Evidence of Christie, trial transcript, June 23, 1953, 109.

90. John McGowan to Metropolitan Police, March 25, 1953, TNA PRO MEPO 2/9535, part 3A.

91. For the Teddy Boy presence in Notting Hill, see Racial Disturbances, Notting Hill Activities of Extremist Organizations, Deputation of MP's to the Secretary of State, 1959–61, TNA PRO HO325/9.

92. See "Women Fight Intruders—Courageous Action Succeeds," *Times* (London), January 6, 1953, 6; and "Settler Killed by Mau Mau," *Times* (London), February 9, 1953, 8. See also Colonial Office, *Historical Survey of the Origins and Growth of Mau Mau*, Cmnd. 1030 (London: HMSO, 1960).

93. "Mau Mau Massacre of Loyal Kikuyu," *Times* (London), March 28, 1953, 8. See also "Nairobi Declared a Special Area," *Times* (London), April 25, 1953, 5.

94. Oliver Lyttleton, *Times* (London), November 7, 1952, quoted in Wunyabari Maloba, *Mau Mau and Kenya: An Analysis of a Peasant Revolt* (Bloomington: Indiana University Press, 1993), 101–2. For the impact of Mau Mau on race relations in north Kensington, see Anthony Richardson, *Nick of Notting Hill* (London: George G. Harrap and Co., 1965), 144–45.

95. Sir Andrew Cohen, *British Policy in Changing Africa* (London: Routledge and Kegan Paul, 1959), 55.

96. Paul Ricoeur, *Hermeneutics and the Human Sciences: Essays on Language, Action and Interpretation* (Cambridge: Cambridge University Press, 1981), 143.

97. Pierrepoint, *Executioner Pierrepoint*, 205.

98. "200 Crowd at Prison as Christie Dies," *Star*, July 15, 1953, 1.

99. Victor Turner, "Social Dramas and Stories about Them," *Critical Inquiry* 7, no. 1 (1980): 159.

CHAPTER 10

(Re)Imagining an African City: Performing Culture, Arts, and Citizenship in Dakar (Senegal), 1980–2000

MAMADOU DIOUF

Two points of view generally frame analyses and various descriptions of the African city. The first, a rather pessimistic perspective, stresses the severity of the crisis rocking African societies and urban spaces and infrastructures.[1] In contrast, the second viewpoint emphasizes urbanites' ingenious ways of reinventing a uniquely African destiny for the African population.[2] According to the first approach, the city is often a strangely hostile place to African populations, thus the second perspective presents a vision of an urban dynamic that allows Africans to appropriate and domesticate the city. The pessimists think in terms of political analysis and administrative intervention, measures that they hope will render the city simultaneously productive, governable, well ordered, sanitized, hospitable, and stable. The optimists, on the other hand, strive to re-create the city by tracking its aesthetic and cultural expressions, and the political, architectural, and economic practices of certain groups, in particular youth and marginalized groups who are cultivating domestic and public spaces through indigenous and cosmopolitan practices that isolate them from both the nationalist administrative social sphere and reinvented traditional virtues and values. These practices inscribe themselves in a political economy introduced by colonial domination and ruled by the logics of extroversion, which have been reinforced considerably by economic stagnation and the interventions of international financial institutions. At the present moment, we are witnessing an increase in the tension between local and global resources. Since the end of the postcolonial enterprise of social and ideological totalization, the gauges of local authenticity and the imperatives of globalization are at stake in a conflict that is essential in determining the future of African societies.

African urban societies have evolved considerably through time and space. New dynamics are being created today, most notably in light of the role that youth play and an increasingly difficult level of competition for rare economic, realty, and symbolic resources. Authority over spaces abandoned by the state is disputed more and more frequently, and the groups that seize them control these spaces in a discriminatory and brutally violent fashion. The fragments of the population that either avoid the community or strive to control it include ethnic and religious associations, associations from certain quarters of the city, and certain age groups. They open up gaps and pathways to other processes of identification. Depending on one's interpretation, these new appropriations reveal either the depth of the crisis or the extraordinary rapidity of the reconstructions that either rock or reconfigure cities faced with decreased state involvement and subsidies, as well as the chaos provoked by political regrouping and economic adjustments. Forgetful of historical contingency, formulas of identification that contradict each other also present themselves as timeless prophecies. These formulations of identity accompany a discourse of legitimization that draws from the plural registers of religion, ethnicity, and urban loyalty, choosing indigenous and foreign elements (or drawing on both) in order to create a memory and narratives capable of capturing the twisted history and current state of an Africa adrift between a fabricated authenticity and an evasive global presence. In this chapter, I hope to follow the contours of this geography of memory as it plays out in Dakar and its suburbs. Senegalese youth make the narratives, tonalities and histories traced on the walls and set to music that this study attempts to order and classify.

Dakar is located in the Cap Verde peninsula, the westernmost point of Africa, advancing deep into the Atlantic Ocean. With the island of Gorée off its coast, it played a crucial role in the early stages of the "making of the Atlantic world" and the political economy of the slave trade. The inclusion of Senegambian inhabitants, the Lebu, into the Atlantic space generated new forms and formulations of community, cultures, languages, religions, and political and social codes—borrowing simultaneously from European, Arab Muslim and African resources. Through a steady building of their economic and military power in collaboration with the European traders, the Lebu became an Atlantic community and won independence from the kingdom of Kajoor in the late eighteenth century. Since then, the autochthonous inhabitants of the Cap Verde peninsula, the Lebu, have been cultivating a rebellious spirit that became one of the defining features of their identity. Associated with this rebellious culture is a landownership system combining indigenous resources and French landownership legal codes, therefore setting the Lebu apart from other Senegalese groups. They are not an ethnic group; they are a *collectivité* (community) because of their experience with European education, institutions, and culture.[3]

347

Prior to the establishment of colonial rule in this region of Senegal during the early nineteenth century, Dakar was a collection of dispersed villages along the coast. The colonial city of Dakar was founded in 1857 at the southern tip of the peninsula. It became in 1895 the political and administrative capital of French West Africa, attracting over the years a growing number of migrants (individuals and communities) from the hinterland of Senegal, the larger west African region, the Ottoman Empire (Syria and Lebanon), and France. The completion of the harbor—the principal link between Europe, the African colonies, and South America—and the completion of the railway networks connecting the city and the cash crop production areas gave a new impetus to economic development, population increase, and the ethnic and national diversity of the city. The convergence of different communities, cultures, and religions, is reflected in the architecture, the organization and allocation of space, and the modes of inhabiting, imagining, and representing the fragmented and very tightly policed territories constituting Dakar as a colonial space: a space of hybrid identities and plural exchanges produced by a network of power relations that were unstable, unpredictable, ambiguous, and disorderly.

Within the changing context of all these interventions in the heart or the periphery of the city, by marginal or active agents for the urban changes and development, a manifest and implemented pale of settlement has been enacted, with the Plateau (European city/the downtown area), the Medina (the colonial native area, largely dominated by the Lebu until the late 1970s), and the irregular settlements of migrants from the rural areas (the *bidonvilles* [slums]) affecting the level and the quality of infrastructures as well as access to social services. The new spatial design and land allocation were the result of a policy of residential segregation that replaced an "earlier pattern of co-existence, if not integration of the African and European populations" before the outbreak of a severe epidemic of bubonic plague in 1914.[4]

The converging and diverging trajectories and subsequent physical and cultural changes that have been (re)configuring each area and the city as a whole have been continuously making Dakar a cosmopolitan city, caught between the designs and aspirations of the migrants it is attracting and the desire of an urban and orderly metropolis of its elites, shaping continuously the cultural, artistic, and criminal life of one of the largest urban stages of west Africa.

Dakar is still growing, both demographically and territorially, becoming at the end of the 1980s a large urban hub connecting Senegalese and west African globalization. To satisfy the housing demands, many public housing projects were successfully executed from the 1960s until the late 1970s to satisfy the growing middle class of civil servants and private firm clerks. During the same period, which covers Leopold Sédar Senghor's presidency (1960–80), "Dakar . . . has been a vibrant and dynamic 'art world,' a particular site for the production, interpretation, and collection of modern art . . . when Leopold Sédar Senghor established its national art school, the Ecole des Arts du Sénégal. Artists working during the post-independence period pioneered an expressive genre of painting whose distinctive themes and styles were associated with the cultural ideology of Negritude and its promotion by President Senghor."[5] The city is more and more attractive, not only because of its infrastructures and concentration of industrial, administrative, and services jobs, but also as a consequence of the economic crisis Senegal has been experiencing since the 1970s. Henceforth, migration, unemployment, and street peddling led to the presence of slums close to the Plateau, putting an unbearable pressure on the urban resources and infrastructures. Today basic public services such as garbage collection, drainage, and transportation often break down; many of the formal urban institutions and processes are turned into informal sites of bargaining, corruption, and struggles. Spaces and procedures abandoned by the state are taken over by actors based on their ethnicity, age, religion, and/or political positions.

During 1988–89, the walls of Senegalese cities—and especially Dakar and its suburbs—were transformed by paintings. As representations, these murals are productive moments in the construction of a new historical memory. These stammerings of an emergent memory issue out of a desire to break with the historical memory that guided the nationalist generation to power at the end of the Second World War.[6] This study is concerned with the imaginary and consciousness of the social movement that attacked the ruling class and its historical foundation (*historicité*) through stone throwing and frescoes. By clearing a path through the city, this sweeping movement redefined the spaces and logics of sociability in public places.[7] While it does not, of course, represent an abrupt break with nationalist memory, these demonstrations attest to the reorganization/recomposition of historical heritage. This procedure involves "invention" or "imagination"; it entails the production of a new historical mode. For now, this movement can be qualified as particularly urban in view of the nature of the values inscribed in the drawings and in the organization of space (or the representations that constitute this historical memory). Iconography devoid of text presents an interpretive situation—for viewers as much as for analysts—that might be thought of as recreation. Interpretations sanctioned by neighborhoods are often lodged in their own collective memories, which crystallize around a historical person (marabout, football player, politician) and are expressed in songs and festivals (*foural*) organized by the youth.[8] Furthermore, the writing of history through the practices of these social movements is often ambiguous owing to their historicist excess, their overburdening with Senegalese cultural references and political discourse. With the rise of the technocracy to power and the implementation of a structural adjustment program in 1981, "history" has become a substitute for negritude and African socialism.[9]

DEGRADATION OF THE URBAN ENVIRONMENT, DEGRADATION OF POLITICAL PRACTICES

This double subtitle could be reversed because, as simplistic as this "game" might seem, the order of the title is a perfect expression of the difficult beginnings of the Set/Setal movement. Literally, *Set* means "clean" and *Setal* "to make clean." Together, the two terms also refer to notions of order and "moral cleanliness" in the face of the corrupt ruling class. It designates a circumscribed and orderly territory—the neighborhood—against marginality and informal trade and nonregulated economic activities. Is this movement, above all, an opposition to environmental degradation or a violent reaction to the crisis of the democratic transition? The movement aims to improve the environment of the neighborhoods, to remove the garbage and dirt. But it also seeks to clean up—or reform—political and social practices. The first analysis of this movement refers quite explicitly to the combination of motivations:

> February 1988–April 1989. Senegalese youth burst, full speed ahead, onto the political scene. No one expected them, but no one particularly cares. Fear of the future is expressed in a formidable, destructive rage. Between two stone throws, a seventeen year-old student lets loose: "We are going to break everything in order to reconstruct it better." Idle words? Indeed. Since July 1990, juvenile violence has become a sort of raving madness that has remained an enigma. Before dumbfounded adults, groups of youth, who were once given over to chasing Mauritanians, put their new credo to work: order and cleanliness. The most dreadful city on the continent, the most infested with erring characters and traffic jams, is cleaned from top to bottom. The public gardens, which had become sordid public toilets, were fixed up, decorated, and restored to their original vocation.[10]

The historical frame that emerges here to mark out the founding events of Set/Setal could be enlarged to include the crises of the schools and universities; the lost school year (1987–88), for instance, was a clarion call for a series of strikes, demonstrations, and riots during which students, the unemployed, and the marginals attacked urban symbols and signs of power on the Plateau. In the beginning of 1990, before the cleanup operations began, violent attacks against alcohol drinking establishments in the Medina and on the borders of the Plateau and the assault against the "hooligans" (*voyous*) who occupy the Corniche represent the "moralizing" and political aspects of this same movement.

Clearly, this emergent network is inscribed in a larger framework: that of postcolonial Senegal and, more specifically, Dakar, the largest Senegalese city, the site of power and the center of attraction for young migrants fleeing agricultural crisis and drought. This context is also marked off by the advent of Senghor's successor, Abdou Diouf (1981), the extremely difficult democratic transition, the controversial 1983 presidential and legislative elections, and a dismal economic situation. While undergoing an economic and financial recovery, Senegal implemented a structural adjustment program. In many cases, the state withdrew from health, education, and public works. The public administration and public or parastatal institutions were "cut back" (*dégraisser*), and impoverishment followed. Furthermore, the state chose this moment to accelerate the application of local and territorial administrative reforms begun in 1972. The municipal status of the city of Dakar was restored. At this point, the state's financial disengagement from local structures took on a juridical form; responsibility for the management of public space was returned to local populations via the mediations of their representatives.

According to its most current definition, Set/Setal is a human investment in cleanliness (in the sense of hygiene, but also having a moral sense— against corruption, prostitution, delinquency). To be sure, it involves improving the quality of life in neighborhoods, removing garbage and dirt. But it also involves embellishing places, sometimes naming them, often marking them with monuments bearing witness to moments or figures of local history or to solicit the private memories of families and youth associations. This follows from the fact that Set/Setal is both a youth movement and a local movement (as opposed to a national movement or even that of parties and urban sections of parties). It is centered in and on the neighborhood, the *koogn* (the hood) of Wolof urbanites. It is a direct response to the rapid degradation of public infrastructure, the almost nonexistent collection of garbage in popular neighborhoods and the Plateau owing to the crisis of

SOADIP (a private garbage collection company), and poor relations between this company and the new municipality. The new municipality's lack of technical and financial means lasted until the creation of a new semiprivate cleanup company (SIAS).[11] Dakar had been left in a repulsive condition owing to the state's desertion of the public service sector and the municipal authorities' incapacity to pick up the slack.

There are historical antecedents to Set/Setal's call for "cleanliness" and "human investment"; its genealogy goes back to the nationalism and voluntarism marking the first decade of postcolonial Senegal. Action undertaken under these two rubrics was deemed a matter of "human investment." Insistence on human resources in Africa (today we speak of the "valorization of human resources," in the words of the technocrats), as opposed to its material and technical poverty, is indicative of the unanimous vision of, and consensus of opinion about, this historical sequence, or African socialism. This continuity is underscored in the study carried out by Enda Tiers Monde: "Set/Setal is primarily concerned with cleanliness. No doubt, there were attempts to take over for the public service sector, to back it up. Mamadou Dia mobilized the youth of the UPS in order to make the capital pleasant and clean, and to get rid of undesirables—especially prostitutes, who were rounded up and sometimes married, in the same stride, to former combatants. Afterward, the administration undertook several mobilizing operations, such as *set weec* or project *Augias*."[12]

This last program took place during the second decade of independence. It was characterized by disillusion, the crisis of authoritarianism, and violent reactions among the popular classes and the petite bourgeoisie. Public authorities began to promote the more technical and political (*politicienne*)—as opposed to ideological—*set weec* and *Augias* projects.[13] They illustrate the failure of the routinization of cleanup and hygiene services. Nonetheless, these programs invested the domain of public health and sanitation with moral connotations and incited the exclusion and marginalization of certain social groups that were qualified as "human congestion" (*encombrements humains*), obstructing the needs of tourism and jeopardizing the status of Dakar as a crossroads and a site of international meetings.[14] The ruling class profited, each time, from the *Augias* operations to affirm its liberality (*munificence*), its indisputable power, and its authority over populations caught in the circuits of power. These interventions affirmed the political party's power at the local level, its articulation with the logics of legitimation in regions and neighborhoods, the centrality of clientelist constructions, and their languages in Senegalese political trajectories. They allowed the ruling class and the party to prove its magnanimity and repeat the nationalist impulse.

Beyond their intended purpose to organize and clean, these projects were occasions for (re)dramatizing, in a vigorous and spectacular manner, the nationalist gesture. They were moments for inscribing, in a punctuated way, through commemoration, its incontestable regime of truth. At times, they were also instances in which some aspects of the latter were negotiated so as to enhance its seductive power. Must one, then, conclude that Set/Setal is simply a part of this history of interventions, that it is inscribed in the nationalist political project of human investment? Or is it naturally part of the affirmation of African socialism, its rhetorical and laudatory figures and its modes of mobilization and embodiment (operations *Augias*)? Does it imply historical continuity, ideological continuity, or rupture? In any of these cases, the inscription of all these practices in the city leads us to examine the contemporary political stakes of urban control, the workplace, and leisure, as well as the city's history and the traces left by social actors. Can one locate relationships between the stylistics of power and the style of Set/Setal, the logics of *Sopi*, and the open-ended nature of the democratization of Senegalese society?[15] And what are these relationships in the context of state disengagement and appeals to ethnic, religious, and regional identities that are constantly being reformulated? Can Set/Setal be read as a form of strategic syncretism liable to organize an alternative space for social relations? Does it promote the redefinition of relations between the state, the ruling class, and the youth, or is it simply a new move made by Senegalese youth in their quest for a reference point that would root them in a changing urban landscape?

Deconstructing Nationalist Memory

The Set/Setal movement emerged just after the violent crises of Sopi, which followed both the campaign and the February 1988 elections.[16] Set/Setal marks the failure of the institutionalization of certain modes of political action and defines the youth as the "accursed segment" (*la part maudite*) of Senegalese society. In order to defuse the postelection crisis, the president-elect, Abdou Diouf, decided to use "the youth" as the symbol of his five-year term. The constant wavering of official discourse between a negative and a positive tenor attests to the ruling class's ambivalence with respect to youth practices and its incapacity to take economic or social responsibility for them. And the youth, for its part, registered and magnified itself in the

Sopi movement without having any pretension or ambition to save the world. The young participants allowed themselves to be carried by the storm they themselves created in order to wash (*set* = clean, *setal* = to make clean) the city and Senegalese society. The violence seemed to be a sign of enormous distress, profound anguish, and fear in the face of an uncertain future and the increasingly unequal redistribution of power and wealth in a society under adjustment. Perhaps, beyond political motivations, the stylistics of power and its incontestable signs of force—its contemptuousness and symbols (*xeesal*, stature, gold, generosity, fast cars)—were decisive for the mobilization of the youth, for their attack against the ruling class and representations of the state. Since 1983, the profound and lasting destabilization of the institutionalization of mechanisms for the democratic transition by the young and marginalized people (symbolized by *Sopi*) inaugurates a new era in Senegal. This was an outright refusal of outcomes imposed by the democratization process as implemented through institutions established by the new ruling class. And this dissonance presupposes modes of expression, multiple strategies, and especially new narratives of the city. It entails, more precisely, the production of history that counters nationalist fictions and fables about the radical alterity of African desires, wishes, and practices. The dissonance between the style and the discourse of the ruling class, the tactics of democratization, and the living conditions of an entire population destined to increasing marginalization and impoverishment, precipitated the activation and updating of powerful and sometimes novel symbols, contributing to both the nationalist historical stock and a world open to African world music and Western referents.

The endeavor to destabilize "master fictions" had been set in motion.[17] Moreover, if political strategy necessitates identification, for those excluded from the political scene (those who emerge in Set/Setal), the production of alternative references is indispensable to their capacities to act and think as alternative political subjects. This act, which aims to shake the foundations of nationalist memory, goes hand in hand with a new approach to space— that is, investing it with local memory. And this is the composition of identity that can be read off the walls of Dakar. Here, I am interpreting this as a mode of deconstructing nationalist memory and its myth, which couples development and social justice. And since the 1950s, history has played, and continues to play, a large role in the construction of all variations of this myth. These metamorphoses were often linked to the state's constant invention of a politically charged rhetorical space—a space of territorial scale, for the construction of the nation with restored dignity. In doing so, it instituted a central regime of truth, which claims to subordinate all discourse. During the time of negritude and African socialism, no interstice was left untouched, including that of artistic wandering. The state under Senghor dictated not only its rhetorical version of the nationalist era, but also its aesthetic version (whose imported medium and technique—"beaux arts"—negates the painting and sculpture developed by artists who were cut off from state subsidies).[18] From this, adjustment has inspired the invention of a new technique and a new aesthetic by using salvaged materials.[19] The city emerges in painting as it does in song.[20]

With the rise of the technocracy, the state's disengagement from the cultural sphere has liberated certain spaces. For example, the inclusion of painting on glass in the petite bourgeois contemporary modernist aesthetics relocated such a cultural production in Senegal modern arts. Glass painting therefore lost its ethnological identity as an expression of African traditional art as well as its function of religious marker for new urban groups forcefully attempting to preserve the dominant rural elements of their brotherhood identity. The dissolution of the heritage of negritude and African socialism, the disappearance of places for expositions (Musée dynamique, village des Arts), the financial crisis, and the orientation of the École des Beaux Arts all contributed—along with the degradation of the urban environment and the failure of the law on illicit accumulation—to the quest for the reorganization of the alarmingly obsolete nationalist vision of the past. Moreover, this very retreat from the official sphere of culture underscored efforts being made to destabilize nationalist memory.

These efforts were constructed around three reference points. The first is an intellectual reference. Its Senghorian facet is supported by the ethnolinguistic writings of Cheikh Anta Diop, and it is circumscribed by rationalization through scripture. The second is the historical discourse of the traditionalist (a *griot*). Its narrative is inscribed in the construction of an independent state, and it supports and discloses a historical continuity that is not troubled by anachronisms. It gives a popular and mobilizing color to the construction of historical consciousness as posited by the logics of the nationalist generation—or to the affirmation of nationalist identity. These two poles were pillars for the mobilization of the *évolués*. They also allowed for the articulation of traditional or religious legitimacies by inventing a genealogy worthy of memory and hence essential to the founding of the nation-state. And, following that, the third pole is the brotherhood's narrative of the dawning of Muslim families and holy places in "a nation blessed by God, Senegal."

These three narratives are not mutually exclusive. To the contrary, they are constantly in conflict, dialogue, and sometimes even complicity. Like the

355

colonial narrative (the Faidherbian hagiography of the builders of empire who established the Senegalese colonial territory),[21] they construct Senegalese identity on the basis of the Wolof identity of the *ndiggel* (the groundnut basin and the regions around Touba and Tivaouane) and the Atlantic commercial ports (Dakar, Rufisque, Saint Louis).[22] The production of the postcolonial territory through the dramatization of these three narratives, which are often surreptitiously associated with the colonial referent, structured the discourse of the state—which is standing for Senegalese national discourse. The state became central, then, to the production of symbols initially selected from the regions described above. Through this, civic rituals were institutionalized. After Senghor's departure, the names of places were indigenized, as was official iconography. Colonial statues have been toppled and *Ceddo* statuary has gained ground.[23] Nelson Mandela and Soweto are now inscribed on the squares and boulevards to materialize Senegalese mobilization against apartheid. The reworking of representations and the repackaging of the referents of Senegalese nationalism through the contributions of ethnic, religious, and urban peripheries are constantly reformulating the historical bases (*historicité*) of the postcolonial situation.

SIGNS AND IMAGES: (RE) NARRATED HISTORY

Unbridled liberalism demands, in response, the production of a history linked to the brutality of the crisis, which has intensified the marginalization of youth and women, increased urban poverty and crowding, and magnified the deplorable state of living conditions and hygiene.[24] This is why, in these history lessons, historical knowledge is first political, and then practical.

The important epistemological question is the following: can one delimit and locate a unified doctrine in a movement that is being constantly reconfigured? Should we look for references in Youssou Ndour's song, "Set"?[25] Is there continuity between the Set/Setal movement and the cultural and sports expressions of the Associations culturelles et sportives (ACS)? The ASC were sites of refuge for political dissidence during the time of the single party, and they always have been sites of political and ideological competition in the neighborhoods. They have often been at the origin of informal economic activities and the mobilization of huge numbers of participants in rainy season football championships (*Navetaan*), which include teams from all neighborhoods. Is it best, from a purely heuristic point of view, to disassociate Set/Setal from organizations that have their bases in the refusal of state intervention and the weight of hierarchical, ethnic, or religious traditions, or to disassociate it from the productivist concerns of public institutions? Can the sometimes democratic, sometimes conservative—but always social and cultural—character of rural youth and women's associations be read as manifestations of Set/Setal?

If the environment is a preoccupation shared by both participants in this urban movement and rural folk, who have been greatly affected by the crisis in the groundnut economy, then the aesthetic profusion of the former (that is, Set/Setal) is much more territorial and gestural than plastic. Their frescoes trace out the lines of a new history and a new aesthetic of the city. And in this process, a new urban culture emerges.[26] The murals, like *Mbalax*, mobilize and express new idioms that account for unprecedented situations.[27] It is possible that the Set/Setal movement and the signs that accompany it are indicative of a dynamic that was always thought to have been stifled by autocratic politics and the reigning mediocrity of an aborted democracy whose Westernited leadership is incapable of managing economic and social crises.

Through a good look at this wall of signs—or what I refered to as a mode of marking identity—one is struck with ecological concerns about the standard of life in, above all, the neighborhood. This inscription is the founding mark of the Set/Setal movement; it creates a public urban space devoid of village referents and the moral and cultural discrediting of "African" status in the city. Concerns about the order and cleanliness (or "making clean") of the neighborhood go beyond questions of hygiene; they posit other problems, such as embellishment, as well. This aesthetic pursuit has given rise to quite astonishing statues and decorative objects. Colored tires—half-buried in straight lines along the road or stacked up in the form of a monument—speak to a culture of rebellion whose referents are Soweto, the Palestinian occupied territories, and the test of riots to come. Here, we find a will to reconstrue and reimagine that seems highly indebted to the dramatization of the riot in South Africa and the Middle East.[28]

The spectacular character of these statues, which have taken over the space of the neighborhood, issues out of a heterogeneous ensemble of signs that are "cultural and historical references." The materials—salvaged objects from urban everyday life (metal, plastics); carved tree trunks, twisted and erected on stilts, like monuments, bearing calabashes and canaries (the village)—are diverted from their usual, and often religious, functions. In their commentary on this aspect of Set/Setal, the authors of Set, the walls that speak, note that: "There are many authentic echoes. For the *Ceddo*, the authentic defender of "genuine" Africa, certain positions of stones and branches evoke the cults that we call 'fetishistic,' and a sculpted tree trunk refers to the art of the forest."[29] This very work of diversion, subverting functions and symbols, is a manner of re-creating the past. It works by telescoping, maintaining pluralist references (the Wolof spirit of *Ceddo*, the *Sereer pangool*, the *Lebu tuur*, the Sirens, etc.) so as to redefine a symbolic anchor and reorganize the nationalist regime of truth and its appropriation of space. The substitution of associative logics (plurality) for militant logics (recuperation/manipulation) informs these procedures of ordering, which include the active work of selecting, toning down, and censuring what is at the heart of Set/Setal.[30]

To a certain degree, recentering on the neighborhood reflects the quest for an inscription having neither colonial nor nationalist origins. Baptizing streets in the Medina or the Gueule Tapée/Fann-Hock quarters of Dakar with the names of local personalities (soccer players or marabouts), which take the place of the letters of the alphabet (A or E street), is a manner of erasing a certain memory. It also entails tactics of identity that re-create categories of a new sociability, being distinct from those produced by the nation and the ethnic group. In the end, this is an attack on the state's management of urban space and its mode of carving it up. The groups that have emerged through the course of the movement have thus produced private, local memories by selecting their own pasts, their own "founding fathers," and by inscribing their own signs in the sand and in monoliths. The list of stars (those whose names were assigned to streets) reveals a reconstruction of the past that is socially significant as an elaboration of their present.

The reorganization and restructuring of urban territory according to pluralist norms also involves confrontation with the state's spatial inscription—its geometric totalitarianism linked to a repressive apparatus and the project of organizing populations. Through this confrontation, a truly "public space" has been opened up.[31] The population seems to have found the means to fill the void left by the state. And the sites they have localized are now places for meetings, debates, and certainly for the evaluation of politics. The appropriation of space is accompanied by speech (*prise de parole*), by the palaver as re-creation—that is, not only the village palaver, under the tree, but the palaver in front of a stylized baobab, "the symbol of dialogue, of negotiation and hard work."[32]

A more or less exhaustive census and thematic catalogue of the frescoes has been presented by Enda-Tiers Monde. This work allows one to glean certain general characteristics from the ensemble. For one, the features of the drawings (or paintings) and some notations express a connivance with fast food culture and comic strips. The annotations attest to the large place of "riot culture," and characters' positions activate a memory that posits them as youth (references to the youth of the Intifada and Soweto are manifest). It should be noted, however, that to ignore the artistic dimension of these works would imply reductionism with respect to their meanings. Following the predominant hygiene-sanitation rubric (17.15 percent), the historical rubric (13.2 percent) is an important thematic of Set/Setal.[33] In the former category, it is interesting to note that the drawings have an educative function; they are often accompanied by texts that require reading. And, from this perspective, the iconography is reformulated, giving a new dimension to a message (on hygiene, vaccinations, treating and preventing diarrhea) that the project Santé pour Tous en l'An 2000 (Health for All in the Year 2000) had outlined but failed to popularize.

The youth compensated for the shortcomings or absence of the media. On the other hand, the historical register is composed of two repertories, one religious (11.7 percent)—and very Islamic—and the other political. The first centers on the character of the marabout, which no longer evokes brotherhood affiliations, but rather seems to signal the end of the era of the Senegalese saints and their groundnut economy. In that sense, the history that can be read in these drawings is a history of the Wolof brotherhoods—now reorganized, they consecrate the entry of the marabouts into the city and modernity. And this modernity affirms the conquest of autonomous ideological space by the marabouts. The writing of history thus promulgated is an ordering of memorable objects, as well as the invention of signs that give access to codes for deciphering.[34]

If the first repertory is indigenous, the second is more syncretic. The latter is informed by systems of representation marked by certain perceptions of the outside world; it parades political personalities and national or international sports figures. Its symbolics are entirely heterogeneous: from Leuk-le-Lievre (that is, cunning) of Senegambian children's stories to the House of Slaves, its spiral staircase hugging a Statue of Liberty whose features hesitate between the French Marianne and Fatou, to the Senegalese (wall of a high school in Dakar).[35]

The historical depth of these repertories varies. Apart from the reference to slavery, the oldest referent dates to the nineteenth century (the heroes of the struggle against the colonial conquest and founders of the brotherhoods, El Hadj Malick Sy and Ahmadou Bamba). And the most contemporary figure is El Hadj Abdoul Aziz Sy, the leader of the Tijani brotherhood in the 1980s. It is difficult to decode these messages because of the superimpositions and ruptures in style, temporality, geographic loci, and registers. Nonetheless, one can advance certain hypotheses, because the Set/Setal movement has a subtext, or an imagined message. Commentary is quasi-absent; the drawings (or paintings) speak for themselves. Hence, the act of deciphering is free. And, likewise, youth interventions in the social field are totally unpredictable; their texts are unintelligible to the political class.

From this reading of frescoes, one can deduce that Set/Setal inspires the continual (re)fabrication of history and the city. The latter two become "territories" for the construction of identities and the invention of a tradition and a memory adjusted and informed by the economic and social crisis. This is the violent work of "indocility." Indeed, when these narratives bring together figures like the Statue of Liberty and Leuk-le-Lievre, morality is displaced, giving way to a new semantic foundation that calls on variable knowledge and the diverse referents of democracy—a democracy by cunning (Leuk) or by consensus (Abdoul Aziz Sy or the Statue of Liberty).[36]

The murals also dramatize politicians, like the past generation of Senegalese leaders (Blaise Diagne, Galandou Diouf, Lamine Gueye, Leopold Sédar Senghor) who are often depicted. They seem to bear witness to a lack, a certain nostalgia, and, most obviously, radical disillusionment with respect to the technocracy—which concluded its first ten years in power in 1991—and the failure of *Sopi*, or its foundering in political manoeuvres. They indicate notable absences: Mamadou Dia, Majmout Diop. Perhaps they are informative as to the real power of the expressive gestures and genealogical fabrications of El Hadj Mansour Mbaye?[37]

In any case, the modes of expressing history—or the nature of history (*historicité*)—as revealed by these wall paintings make use of diverse material (Martin Luther King, Nelson Mandela), which is proof of a "mixing" (to use the term of Dakar Rappers) of histories: the city thus creates a new culture, disconnected from the values of the village and the peasantry. It becomes *métisse*, ridding itself of its original complexes—that of colonial detribalization and the conception of the city as a site of debauchery and vice. The important stakes lie between national memory and local memories. The new urban order is being elaborated in the very democratic innovations and crises that overwhelm postcolonial Africa today. The imaginary and the conscience of a social movement—the youth and the marginalized peoples of Dakar—are projected onto the walls, marking space in order to oppose the historian-state of the nationalist period, which is, for today's generation of adjustment, antiquity.

THE PRODUCTION OF AN URBAN CULTURE

Youth and other marginalized people project their imagination and conscience onto the walls of the city; they brand the land in a manner that opposes the state's historical claims and its panoptic ambition, carved out through surveillance and repression during the first two decades of independence. By contrast, the city creates a new and hybrid culture that is disconnected from rural values and rejects the inferiority complexes left by the epithets like "detribalized," "urban den of vice," and "places of perdition" that had been associated with urban culture. What is at stake, then, is the crucial relationship between the national memory and local memories. Set/Setal's interrogations, just like its peremptory and insolent assertions, take as their targets precisely those founders that invested the city with meaning and manners whose guiding concepts were taken from their experience of colonization as the defining moment of African/Senegalese identity. In the eyes of the youth involved in Set/Setal, all of the other postcolonial paths, including those of the heirs of independence, are wasted time marked by ignorance, manipulation, and an impatience that relies on a single-method discipline and control. In this sense, Set/Setal expresses the sentiments of a disillusioned generation that is projecting its heartaches onto the sad, cracked walls of the postcolonial city.

The city sketches its own image, but it takes form in song as well; the Set/Setal movement thus privileges images and sounds to the detriment of words, constructing a library in which makeshift narratives borrow from the registers of violence, sexuality, politics, and the economy.[38] This analysis confirms Célestin Monga's affirmation that all undertakings that attempt to make sense of African realities must be as concerned with seeing (*le voir*) as they are with listening (*l'entendre*).[39] The well-known singer Alpha Blondy confided to a journalist from the *Washington Post* on January 10, 1999, a day after the military coup against the regime of the Parti Démocratique de Côte d'Ivoire, "in authoritarian situations, musicians act as journalists. They talk about stories that certain journalists kill because they belong to the political elite. We're the voice of those who don't have a voice."

Set/Setal cannot be reduced to its iconographic and sculptural dimensions. It is a movement that literally makes some noise, introducing *mbalax* into the public space. With steadfast determination, it picks up the rhythmic discourses and narratives of the *griots* and epic traditions, most notably Wolof and Halpulaar, updating them and making them relevant in the current context. In this way, Set/Setal creates a new genre of music. Its rhythms invite listeners to dance and display their bodies and the fashions that cover them. During the 1990s, *mbalax* music came to be the emblem and banner of an establishment that was merging the opposition and the party in power, indirectly favoring the slow ideological transformation of the ruling classes through the adoption of a national costume (3 Abdou and *grand boubou* for men; *grand boubou, camisole* or *ndöket* for women) and a traditional form of sensuality (*nemali*, an artisanal type of incense that Senegalese women

361

prepare).[40] Such shifts are an attack on colonial references and promote an ideological alternative to the daily attempts to redirect the political, cultural, and religious imagination from Dakar toward Touba. *Mbalax* performance interprets, interpolates, contradicts, and amplifies a text that presents itself on different registers. These are not texts of denunciation alone—*mbalax* texts relate to the lives and deaths of youth; to their disappointments, their dreams, their fears, and their anxieties; to their expectations and their sacrifices, and to their cries of pain and joy, in a continuity that resists the linear nature of conventional nationalist and traditionalist texts. The ambition hidden behind this cultural production is the restoration of Senegalese values. Mixing the anonymous epic of the life of the "little people" and the epics about heroic historical figures, *mbalax* performances conform to the rules of the praise poem in order to salute the sometimes doubtful success of government officials, politicians, and merchants, yet all the while seek to contrast them, awkwardly and obliquely, to the heroes of the street—soccer players, artists, deceased or lost friends—all models of the trajectories and daily pain of African youth at the end of the past century.

Similar to the text, dance is the other side of *mbalax*'s indigenous character. Sounds and rhythms unite to titillate the body, making it vibrate and liberating it from the chains of social constraint and religious morality. On the dance floor, flexible bodies, free of all constraints, trace figures free of any commitment and of any stress, but this conditional and temporary freedom disappears as soon as the dancers step outside of the magical circle. Women's bodies above all are celebrated, but this celebration reveals facets of masculine identity as well. In finery and clothes that flaunt the feminine form, women's bodies can be both a sign of male success and the chasm of sadness and failure in which masculine vanity and arrogance are broken. In the eyes of men, the femininity liberated by *mbalax* is dangerous, because it can be bought and sold and has a price.

Mbalax reconditions women in an economy of desire that juxtaposes the indigenous prose of sexuality alongside the amorous discourses of the films and soap operas of Europe, America, Brazil, Mexico, and above all, India. Masculine or feminine, the body is also a site of the unprecedented violence of skin-lightening products (*xeesal*) and excision; it is also the target of severe beating and deadly lynching of those rumored to be "stealing" the male genital parts. In this new sexual economy, men ask themselves some essential questions. Who is the seducer's intended audience? Who is the prey? Who is the hunter? Who is the bait? If only these questions were nothing more than those of males who are like febrile, gauche actors drunken on scents and colors, but who consent to enter women's monologue in this fashion to the rhythm of *mbalax*! But this music has also accompanied movements of cultural and political contestation and has transmitted new models of social success. Finally, in the 1990s, it became the sound of the establishment that took the reins of power and proposed a philosophical alternative deeply inspired by the values of *mbalax*: an open economy sustained by individual and collective initiatives, constantly traveling, but firmly rooted in the local. *Mbalax* seems to play to perfection the role of bridge or link between the logics of economic and cultural globalization, and its adaptation by the most flexible and open indigenous culture.

The Boul Falé Generation and the American Dream

During the 1980s, the hip-hop movement and its musical expression—raps—developed in the margins of *mbalax*. Unlike *mbalax* musicians, rappers have little interest in mending the social fabric. Nor does rap propose a philosophy and way of life that could reconstruct society through local and indigenous resources in order to confront the economic and nationalist crisis whose universalizing tendencies have left room for the informal sector's makeshift efforts (*bricolage*) and for migration. On the contrary, rap slides into the gaping fissures created by economic and social collapse, the degradation and corruption of social mores, enlarging the social gaps and participating in a systematic way in the fragmentation of Senegalese society.

The hip-hop movement is also that of the *Boul Falé* generation (rude generation).[41] Its participants are men and women, youthful and not so youthful, who now live "nowhere, neither inside nor outside." In particular, they come from the "zone," to use Jean-François Lyotard's terminology, from the working-class districts and the urban peripheries of Dakar.[42] Bad boys and loose girls, outsiders and outlaws, they roam the city's margins, breaking in from time to time to dance, to struggle, and to steal.[43] They offer and put to the test the only commodity they control—their bodies. Rap replaces the historical narratives of the Set/Setal generation with the present and the ephemeral.[44]

One of journalist Malick Diagne's lively feature articles provides an exact list of this type of phenomenon and the cultural "channel surfing" that produced this spontaneity. These "channels" include the *khombeul, tanebeer,* and *Podium rap*. *Khombeul* is a cultural performance staged by an association that often brings together youth who dress in traditional costumes for the occasion. The *tanebeer* reaches a much larger audience than the *khombeul* and seeks in contrast to highlight the neighborhood's political and economic elites (men and women whose genealogies are worth singing about), in whose honor the celebration is organized. *Tanebeer* is laudatory and provides a cultural site for the circulation of money, the allocation of prestige, and the organization of the social hierarchy.[45] *Podium rap* attracts youth who are a bit more with it; they wear micro-minis, American fashions, and the inevitable sneakers and baseball caps, all displayed with American ghetto "attitude."

The title of a PBS (Positive Black Soul) song, "New Generation Boul Falé," has become the rallying cry of a generation that has emerged in the violence of words and the aggressive nature of music in order to break with the festive and joyous music of Set/Setal and the inventive dances linked to *mbalax*. An English word here, a French word there, a Wolof expression, and the feat is accomplished! These rappers mix an elusive identity in order to give their own sense to an unstable life whose ephemeral nature is revealed in the rapper's art, which is produced through a form of "channel surfing" in the global cultural supermarket. This improvisatory mode of expression of a culture of collage takes into account the cultural hybridity and cross-cultural transactions that take place in the Senegalese entertainment market. Distancing itself from the soft sensuality of the *khoumbeul*, the PBS song is enough to take one's breath away: "We are in a republic of bastards. What use is democracy if there aren't any jobs or sweets? We are all descendants of Adam and Eve, but that's not what you see. Some guys cruise in Mercedes, while others get around on foot. To have peace, we need to shoot everything up, they sing." Despite the denunciation, certain segments of the *Boul Falé* generation flaunt the signs of globalization. Youth illustrate the slogan "everything is foreign and nothing is foreign," adopting the American flag and American fashions as symbols.

Rap groups have a precise geography that influences their themes, the grammar, and the style of their products. They hold an ideology of loyalty to neighborhoods and traditional cultures mixed with the rhythms of the world. As PBS's members point out about Senegalese rap, "it's American, African, European ... African rhythms and an American beat."[46] This "world" music includes words in English, French, and Wolof. Different groups are particularly popular in certain neighborhoods, and each is devoted to its locale—Positive Black Soul to Amitié 2 and Liberté 6; Sunu Flavor to the HLM (originally intended as Habitations à Loyer Modéré—welfare housing—these housing estates are actually coveted properties); Dabrain to Liberté 5, Bok Sagn Sagn; and BNP to Thiaroye; Bouln' Bai to Rebeuss; Pee Froiss to Fass; Jant bi to Dieuppeul, and Sacré Coeur 3, and Colobane; Bamba J Fall to Rufisque, and so on.[47]

364

Precisely because of its style and its performers, rap attacks almost anything, breaking the rules and taking everything out on the authorities, beggars, *talibés*, politicians, or women.[48] Rap constructs and reconstructs these varied and shifting targets to fit rhythms and phraseology in which alliteration and poetic merit matter more than the accuracy of the characterizations or their fairness. A pluralistic art form colored by the location of a youth population in dire straits, at loose ends, and faced with an economic crisis that deepens daily, rap music, like its discourse and tonalities, pushes the limits of music and sounds that depict the harsh living conditions endured by most Senegalese. At the same time, rap constructs an imaginary geography of departure that erases the Atlantic Ocean, making North America contiguous with Senegalese territory. In addition to the U.S. flag and greenbacks, Senegalese youth borrow American idols, ways of speaking, walking, and, above all, American dreams for the future. The narratives and sounds of Senegalese rap are not bound to bear the same message. Nevertheless, they do share two common elements: denunciation and recourse to various languages. These narratives draw on Wolof in particular, as on French (the colonial language), and English (the language of globalization).

The differences in the narratives and preoccupations of various rap groups reflect their diverse social origins, the quality of education that the performers have received, and the culture of the neighborhood where they live. PBS is active in the residential neighborhoods of the petite bourgeoisie made up of civil servants and teachers (Amitié 2 and Liberté 6). The principal leads of PBS attended the University Cheikh Anta Diop in Dakar at the end of the 1980s, a time that was dominated by violent riots in schools and at the university. A two-fold preoccupation, local and global, manifests itself in their musical productions. On the local level, their project is essentially one of denouncing the flaws of Senegalese society. They identify social questions that demand urgent solutions—beggary, delinquency, and the corruption of true love by money—and produce a quite accurate sociology of the city. On a second level, PBS inscribes itself in the pan-African heritage by referring to nationalist history and thought ("Lou tax pourquoi," *Senerap*, 1997). Their lyrics refer to prestigious thinkers or artists like Aimé Césaire, Cheikh Anta Diop, and Kwame Nkrumah, and revolutionaries like Thomas Sankara ("L'Afrique," *New York Paris Dakar*, 1997) to show the Egyptian and Nubian roots of African cultures and civilizations and favor an aesthetic that renews the pan-Africanist narrative. They highlight the way oppression structures shared pan-African experience and forms of resistance, as well as the grammar of common roots and appropriations that found the common project of the liberation of Africans and people of African descent (African Americans and Caribbean peoples).

By comparison, other groups have chosen to inscribe themselves in the local, and thus in a less pan-African dynamic, but one that is aesthetically just as open to rhythmic and tonal globalization. Each group proposes themes that are based on or inspired by the preoccupations of its neighborhood. In an idiom that mixes French and Wolof with style, Pee Fross (the group identified with Fass) offers rather didactic messages, as in the song "Sida" [AIDS], which praises fidelity. Taking a more political tone through references to the seventeenth-century philosopher and political figure Kócc Barma, who affirmed that "politicians are not worthy of trust" [un politicien n'est pas digne de confiance], BNP of Thiaroye exposes the importance of ruses to political life ("Yow Miledal," *Senerap*, 1997). In response, a group from Thiés called Siki Sakana invites us to listen to the truth about, "the management of the country, the liars and incompetents who run the country, the tired old men, the exhausted old women, and the children who yell and cry" ("Deuguebi," *Senerap*, 1997).[49]

The group Jant bi, from Colobane, adds accusations of corruption and political patronage to the observations of Siki Sakana. The solution Siki Sakana offers in the face of "an uncertain future," leaders who continue to lie, and an impoverished people is to take out "guns" and "attack the rich" ("Deugeubi"). In violent language, the group denounces corruption, traditional prohibitions, and the hypocrisy of the marabouts, advocating a morality of the margins. Nioulte Rapadio, the Medina group, emphasizes the absence of social mobility in the form of a traditional tale: "Once upon a time it happened. It's the pure truth. . . . An old man said that a long time ago, really in the distant past, the country was rich. There was lots of gold. It was prosperous. . . . One day, the king called upon the population for a contribution in gold and in silver. The resources were used for other ends. And the king got the country into debt. The debts could not be paid. That's why the men don't have work, the women can't get married, . . . and there are no more heads of households" ("Rang bi dematoul," *Senerap*, 1997).

The exponential rise in civil wars and the increasingly fatal character of the AIDS epidemic offered a new set of themes to the hip-hop movement in the 1990s, offering it the imaginative resources for creating new forms of African unity and innovative formulas for placing Africa in the global framework. In Senegal, during the presidential election in the year 2000, rap groups burnished their weapons against the ruling classes, participating in a mobilization that resulted in the victory of the "forces of change." Tim

Timol's 1999 title about drugs, "Na fi diok" (to ban, to get rid of) was recontextualized and used as a slogan for a change in power. *Na fi diok* in this sense means "he should leave."

Hip-hop's inscription in global time and sound takes place through a process that moves youth from the rural basis of African identity toward the new formulas of identification that are emerging in the urban context. The city has become the barometer of Africa, the space par excellence in which Africa participates in the reconfiguration of the universal. Young Africans are no longer making their opinions known through a posture of "delinking", as Samir Amin put it, or of indifference toward the world; through their diverse modes of self-expression, they now make their presence felt through a process of strategic self-positioning and adaptations of local conditions.[50] In contrast to the first postcolonial moment, the book and writing are no longer the only signs of a Western modernity that represented the horizon of African nationalism. Youth have endured discourses of African authenticity, the revelation of African difference, the rediscovery of African cultures versus colonial ethnological fabrications, and the capitalist geography of the world that has put Africa in the margins. Today, through civic arts, song, music, plastic arts, and the cinema, they are refashioning precolonial and colonial traditions. Without any complexes or hesitations, youth do their shopping in the global market of sounds, rhythms, colors, fashions, and narratives, imbuing them with African tonalities. They choose neither detachment from the world beat, nor submission to its categorical imperative—liberal, secular, and democratic—but rather a posture that favors compromise and negotiations from which ruse is not necessarily absent. If taking this new position means relying on the legacy of African cultural capital, youth make a rigorous selection from the cultural items of the past, and subject this cultural capital to intense analysis and criticism. In this sense, the contemporary condition of Senegalese rappers inscribes its stories, its dreams, and its project in the world beat. They are attempting to narrate a history to come in mixing composite memories and tales to fill the unstable geography of globalization. It is a history in the making—of dreams, expectations, and pain and suffering—transforming the African youth into cosmopolitan subjects and/or victims.

The foreclosure of the nationalist metanarrative and the new opportunities and fantasies provided by globalization were translated into metaphors, tropes, and iconographic and musical material by the Senegalese youth. Images of sexuality and ornamented and adorned bodies form new figures of family and social relations, constantly reconfigured and refilled with new meanings. They offer new representation of both "traditions" and "modernity." Such operations, whose context and consequences exceed the political and social spheres, seem to be an attempt to reorder history— refracting, distorting, disguising, and displacing precolonial, colonial, and postcolonial, memories.

NOTES

I am grateful to Mara Leichtman for critical suggestions and editorial wisdom.

1. World Bank, *Politique urbaine et développement économique: Un ordre du jour pour les années 90* (Washington, D.C., World Bank, 1991); World Bank, *Management Options for Urban Services* (Washington, D.C., World Bank, 1987); A. Osmont, "La Banque Mondiale et les politiques urbaines nationales," *Politique Africaine* 17 (1985): 58–73; C. Rogerson, "Globalization or Informalization? African Urban Economies in the 1990s," in C. Rakodi, ed., *The Urban Challenge in Africa: Growth and Management of Large Cities* (Tokyo: UN University Press, 1997); and C. Favacque-Vitkovic and L. Godin, *The Future of African Cities: Challenges and Priorities* (Washington, D.C., World Bank, 1998). The tradition of portraying the city in very negative terms is very well represented in colonial and postcolonial novels such as Camara Laye, *L'enfant noir* (Paris: Plon, 1953); C. H. Kane, *L'aventure ambiguë* (Paris: Julliard, 1961); and Eza Boto, *Ville cruelle* (Paris: Présence Africaine, 1953).

2. A. Simone, "Straddling the Divides: Remaking Associational Life in the Informal African City," *International Journal of Urban and Regional Research* 25, no. 1 (March 2001): 102–17; Simone, "Norms of Good Governance and the Urban Realities of Contemporary Africa," unpublished, 2000; Programme de Développement Municipal (PDM), *Pays du Sahel: Communes et développement local dans les pays du Sahel* (Cotonou, Benin Ceda/PDM, 1995); and E. S. Dionne, *Le don et le recours: Ressorts de l'économie urbaine*, Recherches populaires, no. 151/53 (Dakar: ENDA, 1990).

3. See J. D. Hargreaves, "Assimilation in Eighteenth-Century Senegal," *Journal of African History* 6, no. 2 (1965): 177–184; and Raymond F. Betts, *Assimilation and Association in French Colonial Theory, 1890–1914* (1960; Lincoln: University of Nebraska Press, 2004).

4. Raymond F. Betts, "The Establishment of the Medina in Dakar, Senegal," *Africa* 41 (1971): 143–52, quote on 143.

5. J. L. Grabski, "Dakar's Urban Landscapes: Locating Modern Art and Artists in the City," *African Arts* 36, no. 4 (Winter 2003): 28–39, quote on 28.

6. On this subject, see M. Diouf, "Représentations historiques et légitimités politiques au Sénégal 1960–1987," *Revue de la Bibliothèque Nationale* 34 (Winter 1989): 14–24.

7. On the geography of the frescoes, see Enda Tiers Monde, *Set, des murs qui parlent: Nouvelle culture urbaine à Dakar* (Dakar: Enda, 1991); and for an initial

analysis, see J. C. Niane, Vieux Savané, and B. Boris Diop, *Set Setal: La seconde génération des barricades* (Dakar: Sud Éditions, 1991).

8. In particular two songs of the most popular Senegalese World Musician, Youssou Ndour: "Set" and "Xaleey Medina."

9. M. Diouf, "Représentations historiques"; and M. C. Diop and M. Diouf, *Le Sénégal sous Abdou Diouf* (Paris: Karthala, 1990), esp. the chapter, "Le sursaut national contre la négritude."

10. Niane, Savané, and Diop, *Set Setal*, preface.

11. SOADIP stands for Société Africaine de Diffusion et de Promotion. The Société Industrielle d'Aménagement du Sénégal, SIAS, a semiprivate company, took over from SOADIP, a private company, in 1985.

12. Enda Tiers Monde, *Set*, 7–8. Mamadou Dia was the head of the government (président du conseil) after the adoption of a new administrative policy framework called the Loi-Cadre to administer the French colonies. He became prime minister of the independent Republic of Senegal until 1962, when he was removed from power. Union Progressiste Sénégalaise (UPS) is the former name of the Parti Socialiste du Senegal (PS). *Set weec* and *Augias* were voluntarist cleanup operations (e.g, cleaning streets and planting trees) organized by the office of the mayor and the youth branch of the ruling PS party. As such, they were official events, and partisan expressions and were markedly unsuccessful in comparison with the community-organized and controlled Set/Setal operations. *Set weec* is a generic Wolof term expressing the centrality of investments of human energy as opposed to the capital and technological investments that only developed countries can afford. *Augias* derives from Augean stables of Herculean legend, and, thus, French high culture.

13. By "political" (*politicienne*), I mean the search for clientelistic and financial gains in operations that are dependent on the state and the taxpayer, being of supposed public utility. Resources mobilized in this vein are rightly characterized as *"dépenses de légitimation"* (legitimation expenses) by B. El Malki, "L'Afrique et le "système international" in Africa in the 1980s: State and Social Sciences," *Afrique et Développement* 15, no. 3/4 (1990): 13.

14. R. Collignon, "La lutte des pouvoirs publics contre 'les encombrements humains' à Dakar," *Revue Canadienne des Études Africaines* 18 no. 3 (1984): 573–82; and M. C. Diop, "L'administration sénégalaise et la gestion des 'fléaux sociaux,' " *Afrique et Développement* 15, no. 2 (1990), 5–32.

15. *Sopi* means "change in Wolof, the dominant language of Senegal. It was the slogan of the Parti Démocratique Sénégalais (PDS, Senegalese Democratic Party), then the main opposition party, whose leader, Abdoulaye Wade, was the principal rival of the then President Abdou Diouf. *Sopi* was a call to vote out of power the ruling party, the Parti Socialiste (Socialist Party). Wade was elected president of Senegal in 2000 against Diouf, and his party in 2001 became the majority party in the national assembly.

16. For details, cf. Diop and Diouf, *Le Sénégal sous Abdou Diouf*.

17. See S. Wilenz who, in *Rites of Power: Symbolism, Rituals and Politics since the Middle Ages* (Philadelphia: University of Pennsylvania Press, 1985), 4, asserts that all political power is governed by master fictions (great myths) that become incontestable truths.

18. On the cultural and arts policies designed by Senghor, see Tracy Snipe, *Art and Politics in Senegal, 1960–1996* (Trenton, N.J.: Africa World Press, 1998); and Elizabeth Harney, *In Senghor's Shadow: Art, Politics, and the Avant-Garde in Senegal, 1960–1995* (Durham, N.C.: Duke University Press, 2004).

19. As demonstrated by the expositions of the painters, Viye Diba and S. Keita, and the sculptor, Dime, organized by the artists and/or their associations in Dakar in the 1980s (no exhibition catalogues).

20. Refer to the songs of Youssou Ndour and especially his cassette, *Xippi*. In one of his songs, he declares: "I was a country boy, now I am a city man." During an interview with *Cafard Libéré*, in the supplement *Cafard Plus* (December 27, 1991), he is more explicit, defining his music as urban music, which is the case for its thematics as well. The very rapid development of rap as an expression of the difficulties and sorrows of life among youth is part of the same phenomenon.

21. General L. L. Faidherbe was governor of the Senegal colony (1854–61 and 1863–65) and played a crucial role in dismantling the traditional kingdoms of this west African region; he has been considered the founder of modern Senegal and of French African studies. See M. Diouf, *Le Kajoor au 19ème siècle: Pouvoir Ceddo et conquête coloniale* (Paris: Karthala, 1990), chap. 14 and 15; and A. Bathily, "Aux origines de l'africanisme: Le rôle de l'œuvre ethno-historique de Faidherbe dans la conquête française du Sénégal," in *Le mal de voir* (*Cahiers de Jussieu* 10, no. 18) (Paris: Christian Bourgois, 1976), 77–105.

22. On these questions, see M. Diouf, "The French Colonial Policy of Assimilation and the Civility of the *Orininires* of the Four Communes (Sénégal): A Nineteenth-Century Globalization Project," in Birgit Meyer and Peter Geshiere, eds., *Globalization and Identity: Dialectics of Flows and Closure* (London: Blackwell, 1999), 71–96; and Diouf, "Beyond Patronage and 'Technocracy' ?" in M. C. Diop, ed., *Senegal: Essays in Statecraft* (Dakar: Council for the Development of Social Science Research in Africa, 1993).

23. *Ceddo* is the name of the nineteenth-century Wolof warriors.

24. R. Stern and R. White, *African Cities in Crisis* (Boulder, Colo.: Westview Press, 1989).

25. Some refrains of this song are translated in Enda Tiers Monde, *Set*, 6.

26. For more on this topic, read the astute article by S. B. Diagne, justly titled, "L'avenir de la tradition," in Diop, *Senegal*.

27. *Mbalax* is the Senegalese component of World Music, diffused internationally by Youssou Ndour and Ismail Lo, for example.

28. The language of this imaginary is often English, which substantiates it somewhat. See Enda Tiers Monde, *Set*, 13.

29. See ibid., 37–38, 34.

30. Niane, Savané, and Diop, *Set Setal*, put particular emphasis on this associative aspect. See also Enda Tiers Monde, *Set*, 11.

31. I use the term *public space* following J.-L. Amselle, who argues that a group cannot exist socially unless it is accredited, or unless it manages to emerge on the public scene through the mediation of a spokesperson or representatives, thus creating its own public space. See his "Identité et métissages politiques," minutes of the February 20, 1991, session of the Identity and Political Metissage Working Group, working paper no. 16, March 1991.

32. Enda Tiers Monde, *Set*, 26.

33. Ibid. 27. Consult the index of frescoes and paintings, which gives a clear indication of the iconography of Set/Setal.

34. For a comparison, see M. Diouf, "Islam, peinture sous-verre et idéologie populaire," in B. Jewsiewicki, ed., *Art Pictural zaïrois* (Sillery, Que.: Éditions du Septentrion, 1992), 29–40.

35. "Marianne" is the face of the French republic, and "Fatou" is the symbolic name of Senegalese women.

36. Moral themes make up 4.5 percent, according to Enda Tiers Monde, *Set*, p. 27.

37. A *griot*-journalist on Senegalese radio and television, his rise to the position of official *griot* corresponds to the ascent of Abdou Diouf. For further details, see my Représentations historiques," 22, nn. 55 and 59.

38. In order to understand this phenomenon, it is necessary to listen to the songs of Youssou Ndour, in particular the album titled *Xippi*, in which one of the songs proclaims: "I was a country boy, now I am a city man" (J'étais un enfant de la campagne, je suis maintenant un homme de la ville). In an interview with the satirical Sengalese magazine, *Cafard Libéré*, supplément *Cafard Plus*, December 27, 1991, he is more explicit in speaking about his music as an urban music. The extraordinary development of Senegalese rap as the expression of the mal de vivre of youth in Dakar follows the same vein.

39. Niane, Savané, and Diop, *Set Setal*, insist particularly on this associative aspect. See also Enda Tiers Monde, *Set*, 40–41. In *The Anthropology of Anger* (Boulder, Colo.: Lynne Reiner, 1996), Célestin Monga suggests that "Africa must not only be 'seen' but 'heard,' " 99.

40. A *3 Abou* is a traditional three-piece costume for men. A *grand boubou* is a large traditional costume for both men and women. A *camisole* is a long robe for women that is very tight from the breasts to the hips. A *ndöket* is a two-piece costume for women composed of a blouse and a wrap.

41. *Boul Falé* is the title of the musical cassette of the first Senegalese rap group, Positive Black Soul (PBS). As one Senegalese journalist puts it: "*Boul Falé* (*T'occupes!*) is the ras-le-bol expression of a youth in desperate straits and left to itself to face a socio-economic crisis that gets worse ever day." Ibou Tapha Dior, "Positive Black Soul: Vous avez rêvé de l'Amérique. On y a été pour vous brothers," in *Dakar Soir* 9 (August 1–9, 1997): 4.

42. J.-F. Lyotard, "Zone," *Cahiers de Philosophie* 17 (Winter 1993–94): 15–24.

43. J.-F. Werner, *Marges, sexes et drouges à Dakar: Enquête ethnographique* (Paris: Éditions ORSTOM [Office de la Recherche Scientifique et Technique Outre-Mer], 1993).

44. M. Diouf, "Des cultures urbaines entre traditions et mondialisations," in M. C. Diop, ed., *Le Sénégal contemporain* (Paris: Karthala, 2003), 261–94.

45. M. Diagne, "Quand le rap frise la contestation," *Sud Quotidien* (Dakar), August 6, 1997.

46. "C'est américan, africain, européen . . . des rythmes africains et un beat américain." *Dakar Soir,* August 9, 1997.

47. These districts of SICAP (La Société Immobilière du Cap Vert) are the state's housing projects, mainly for middle-class and upper-middle-class civil servants. The names Liberté (freedom) from colonial rule and Amitié (Friendship) with third-world and nonaligned countries are an indication of the beginning of a new era. They were followed by projects called Dieuppeul and Sacré *Coeur.* Thiaroye is a satellite village and suburb of Dakar. Fass and Colobane are working-class districts of Dakar. Rufisque is a city twenty-six kilometers from Dakar.

48. Talibés are the students or followers of a marabout.

49. Thiés is the third-largest city of Senegal, seventy kilometers from Dakar. The city is the crossroad of railroads going to Saint Louis in the north (the border of Mauritania, on the Senegal River) and to the eastern region (Tambacounda) and Bamako (Republic of Mali).

50. Samir Amin, *Itineraire intellectuel* (Paris: L'Harmattau, 1993).

CHAPTER 11

Street Observation Science and the Tokyo Economic Bubble, 1986–1990

JORDAN SAND

This city can be known only by an activity of an ethnographic kind: you must orient yourself in it not by book, by address, but by walking, by sight, by habit, by experience; here every discovery is intense and fragile, it can be repeated or recovered only by memory of the trace it has left in you. . . .

—Roland Barthes, *Empire of Signs* (1970), translated by Richard Howard

INTRODUCTION: NOSTALGIA AS CRITIQUE

The constant social upheaval of capitalism has provoked repeated waves of nostalgic response since at least the early nineteenth century. In a now-common description of postmodern consumer culture, nostalgia itself became big business in the late twentieth century, and the past became no more than a plaything of the culture industries. But we may also see in the huge efflorescence of nostalgia—or rather *nostalgias* plural—in mass society since the 1970s one aspect of a new configuration of social forces, a new arena of struggle even, matched to the structures of capitalism that have emerged. Environmentalist movements, consumer movements, and many local citizens' movements, belong to this new arena of contestation, which can be broadly conceived as a battle over the spaces of everyday life. The problem of historic preservation in cities emerges from this same moment as a battle over both living space and representations of place. It is in this context that nostalgia, as the wellspring of preservationist sensibilities, can function as a mode of critique. Nostalgia in the late twentieth century left the hands of poets, just as architectural commemoration left the sole propriety of the state; both entered the mass market. At the same time, objects and expressions of memory became significant points of conflict.

Compared with New York, London, and Paris, Tokyo lacks the usual trappings of a historic city: preservation districts, large adaptive reuse projects, preservation architects, or suppliers of recycled or replicated period fittings and materials for old buildings. Tokyo was originally built in wood and other perishable materials, and U.S. firebombs leveled most of it in 1945. As one member of a delegation from New York City Hall visiting Tokyo in 1987 remarked to me when I told him of the small preservation movement in the neighborhood where I was living at the time, "I didn't know we'd left anything standing." Without the buildings to display its past, it seems reasonable to suppose, the city cannot expect to attract interest as a historic destination.

Yet in the 1980s, Tokyo did become a historic destination of a kind. Scholars, architects, artists, and popular writers set about recording and preserving the fragments and traces of Tokyo's past, and a mass public responded by searching for the same places or consuming them vicariously through books, magazines, exhibits, and television. Eventually, municipal government began to treat the city's history as one of its greatest assets, entrepreneurs caught on, and the past did indeed become big business. One could tell the story of the rediscovery of Tokyo's history simply in terms of this commodification of the past. It would be a familiar story, drawing on the tropes of a critique of consumer culture and tourism that has itself been a global commodity for as long as historical sites have had market value.[1] To do so, however, would leave basic questions about the nostalgias of particular places and historical moments unanswered. Even after exposing the ineluctable forces of commodification, we must still ask historical questions: what social or political purposes did a particular form of nostalgic expression serve, what did it *do*? And how does the social and economic context of a particular nostalgia shape its mode of expression and the objects it chooses?

This chapter discusses a movement that appeared in Tokyo in this era known as Street Observation Science. As the name indicates, street observation was concerned with observing rather than preserving, but in its unconventional way, it showed that an anonymous mass of Tokyo's residents were themselves preservationists. More explicitly than most nostalgists, too, the inventors of street observation were concerned with the problem of commodification and ironically aware of their complicity in it.

Tokyo's preservationist projects of the 1980s fit poorly in the commercial paradigm that critics have used in talking about preserved historic streetscapes in the United States.[2] The land underneath every building in Tokyo was worth far more than whatever stood on top of it, and the value to the tourist industry of the few surviving buildings that might represent the Tokyo past was uncertain, as none was more than a century old. Nor did these projects lend themselves to a cultural nationalist agenda. Few physi-

374

cal survivals of a proud tradition—the proverbial "heritage" or "patrimony"—were available to be mobilized for conservative purposes. Nostalgia thus counterposed something genuinely in conflict (at least momentarily) with the interests of the state and big business. Instead of latching on to what might easily be memorialized or marketed, Tokyo's nostalgists latched on to what was most vulnerable and ostensibly valueless. Among these projects, street observation went a step further, raising questions about how we define both historical value and contemporary usefulness in the built environment. This made street observation a utopian critique, ambiguous in its political agenda yet radical in its reimagining of the city.

The Bubble City

If straightforward market logic is inadequate to explain the city's historicist rediscovery, the economic context can hardly be ignored. Tokyo nostalgia took shape in a decade when the city was the hub of Japan's global expansion as an economic superpower and the stage for the greatest speculative bubble of the twentieth century.[3] The bubble may be said to have had an inaugural moment: on September 22, 1985, at the Plaza Hotel in New York, Japanese officials gathered with Americans and other representatives of the so-called G5 nations and came to an agreement to push up the value of the yen against the dollar in order to rebalance trade between Japan and the United States, which had colossal deficits at the time. This accord would precipitate a crisis from which Japan's economy is still struggling to recover now more than twenty years later.

Financial markets reacted dramatically to the Plaza accord. The dollar went into a free-fall that would continue until late 1987, when it settled at slightly more than half its 1985 value. Tokyo shops filled with imported luxury goods suddenly rendered cheap by the high yen. Fearing the impact on domestic manufacturers, the Bank of Japan reduced interest rates in 1986 and 1987 until they had reached 2.5 percent, the lowest in the world. Under U.S. pressure, rates were held there for the next two years. Companies and individuals took advantage of the easy credit by going on a speculating spree that sent the stock and property markets soaring.[4]

Few living inside the bubble realized that it was a one. The word itself did not come into use until the early 1990s, after the collapse.[5] Retrospectively, the bubble can be recognized as a local moment of crisis in the expansion of speculative capital under the umbrella of U.S. imperium. Global speculation in financial markets began in the 1970s and took off in the 1980s. Fredric Jameson and others have pointed out the ways that the floating of world currencies after 1971 and the growth of electronic finance were entwined with the social and cultural developments often referred to collectively as postmodernism, because they created a regime of pure representation without reference to a notion of the real (in finance, without reference to gold).[6] Recently, cultural theorist Mark Taylor has gone so far as to call "going off the gold standard" "the economic equivalent of the death of God."[7] At a less metaphysical level, computer networks, new financial instruments, and new methods of calculation were transforming finance into a world-enveloping instantaneous betting machine.[8] The bubble may be seen as Japan's delayed, catastrophic incorporation into this global speculative regime.

In the public rhetoric of the time, however, we find more national triumphalism than anxiety. Japan's affluence was seen as the terminus of a natural process of development. Following a native model of capitalism in response to the challenge of the West, pundits asserted, Japan had now achieved the goals of modernization, in fact surpassing the advanced nations of the West. In Japan, postmodernity was treated as a cause for celebration, even when it was presented in the apocalyptic pronouncements of Jean Baudrillard.[9] A sense of achievement, of *arrival*, rather than any view of the economic condition of the country as aberrant or artificial, dominated self-perceptions within journalism and government at the time.

The high yen and the speculative frenzy that resulted had a wide range of cultural effects outside Japan. It multiplied the prices of impressionist paintings and French wine; raised land values in the Bordeaux region of France; created booms in coastal areas that had potential for resorts and golf courses in California, Hawaii, Australia, and elsewhere around the Pacific; and imported a whole generation of European and American architects to design buildings in Japanese cities, where many of them made themselves rich.[10]

At home in Tokyo, real estate played a special role in the bubble. Central Tokyo land values had been rising by double-digit percentages annually since 1983. They nearly tripled in 1986–87. It was often remarked in the late 1980s that if you sold all of the land in Tokyo you could buy the United States. On the face of it, this was in fact true. As a result of the tremendous price disparity, the largest Japanese firms quickly moved to snap up American real estate "bargains" like New York's Rockefeller Center. Yet it was Tokyo real estate that was the Japanese speculator's dream, for it seemed to be the perfect no-risk investment. With the exception of a brief downturn during the oil crisis of 1975, Japanese urban land values had increased every year since the end of World War II.[11] Now foreign firms were clamoring for office space in the new East Asian financial capital, and the government was moving to eliminate land-use restrictions and height limits under pressure to increase domestic demand. Not far beneath the surface of market calculation, however, lay the most fundamental of many myths of native uniqueness: that the turf of the archipelago itself was somehow different from elsewhere, so beyond rational calculation that it did not obey market rules. Just as imperialist promoters of Manchurian lebensraum in the 1930s had believed that Japan was in crisis because the archipelago could not accommodate its population, Japanese investors in the 1980s believed at heart that land would always appreciate simply because Japan was—to use the common phrase—a "small island nation." An assumption of infinite national expansion, or a repressed wish, was thus the latent content of the joke about selling Tokyo to buy the United States.

Japan's economy had already moved into a new phase in the late 1970s, with conspicuous results for the landscape of the capital region. In the period 1976–80, Japanese manufacturing firms showed a net internal surplus, holding more funds than they had invested, for the first time in postwar history. This encouraged them to invest overseas, spend more on research and development, and speculate in land and stocks. Pressure from the United States to curtail exports provided another push for Japanese manufacturers to move operations offshore. Meanwhile, the weight of manufacturing within Japan was shifting toward microtechnology. By 1982, two Japanese firms were among the top five semiconductor makers in the world. By 1986, Japanese firms held the top three positions.[12] As manufacturers invested in high-tech and began moving production overseas, heavy industry became a less visible part of the domestic urban landscape. More Tokyoites donned suits and "office-lady" uniforms to commute to bright new office blocks, and went out at night in commercial districts like the western Tokyo hubs of Shinjuku and Shibuya, where high-rise buildings housing restaurant and boutique complexes were covered with electronic signage and moving-image billboards. As film and photography spread images of these prosperous and visually overwhelming consumption centers to the rest of the world, Tokyo, whose name had been synonymous with urban industrial pollution in 1970, became many people's archetype of the postindustrial city.[13]

The transformation took place in only part of the city, however. An old downtown of small shopkeepers and artisans persisted. With its blocks of tightly packed rowhouses, this downtown, called *shitamachi*, belonged to a manufacturing city built in the first decades of the century whose remnants were still extensive and decidedly un-postindustrial. In 1986, more

377

than 20 percent of employed Tokyo residents worked in manufacturing. Strikingly, 46 percent of the factories where they worked employed only one to three people.[14]

During the bubble, the gritty, working-class neighborhoods of *shitamachi* became hotbeds of real estate trading, forcing many longtime residents out. A new profession developed, known as the *jiageya* (literally, "land raiser"), a real estate hunter who scoured neighborhoods for vulnerable small properties to buy and assemble into larger lots that could then be sold to development companies. Newspaper reports suggested *jiageya* ties to gangsters and described incidents of violence and intimidation. The usual *jiageya* tactic was to occupy a single house in a row and make it a base from which to create constant public nuisances until neighbors relented and sold. When owners still refused to sell, garbage was hurled into windows, mysterious fires were set, and in a few cases, gangsters backed trucks and earthmoving equipment into occupied houses.[15]

Government and private-sector developers vied to concoct broad solutions to the land crunch. One of the buzzwords in urban policy and in the real estate business at the time was "efficient use" (*yūkō riyō*). The small lots and low-rise wooden structures that had long predominated in the downtown and through much of the city were seen as the first targets for redevelopment to make Tokyo land use "efficient." Prime Minister Nakasone spoke of building a huge ring of high-rises directly over the tracks of the city's thirty-kilometer loop line. Mitsubishi Real Estate proposed converting the central business district into an instant "Manhattan" of sixty new office towers, all forty to fifty stories high, on a one hundred thirteen-hectare site.[16] Several ministries of the national government, city hall offices, and private think tanks announced competing reclamation schemes for vast areas of Tokyo Bay. The site was officially called the "Coastal Auxiliary Capitol Center" (*rinkai fukutoshin*) as if to ensure its realization by declaring it a center. Some even proposed filling in 70 percent of the bay.[17]

The Dilemma of Wealth for Japanese Intellectuals

It was in this climate of rampant speculation, redevelopment, and quasi-utopian master plans that new interest emerged in the city's past, as a site of resistance or refuge, or as a reaffirmation that solid bedrock underlay the giddy heights on which Tokyo's present stood. The 1980s saw a spate of new writing on the city, much of it rooted in walking and street-level observation, which journalists dubbed the "Tokyo boom," the "Edo boom," the "*shitamachi* boom" and, more generally, the "urban writing boom." These "booms" were products of Japan's prolific middle-brow/high-brow print culture, in which academics share space with journalists, television celebrities, and cartoonists.[18]

By the early 1980s, Japan's wealth (the keyword of the time was *yutakasa,* which means something much broader than monetary wealth) had liberated intellectuals from developmentalist paradigms both capitalist and Marxist. In terms of national economic measures, Japan had indeed "arrived," and its wealth was more evenly distributed than in other wealthy societies. Yet intellectually, it was a hollow liberation. Without the surety of either a liberal or a revolutionary master narrative of progress, the theoretical positions of public intellectuals drifted between the poles of cultural essentialism (heavily endorsed by the state),[19] and cosmopolitanism dominated by semiotic theory, a readily commodified exotic import.[20]

For the post-Marxist urbanist in the Tokyo of the 1980s, *yutakasa* thus presented both an opportunity and a challenge. One could now turn to the city's past to find social spaces governed by a logic different from that of the modern state, and from these spaces imagine alternative modernities. Yet only a short step away from any proposed alternative to hegemonic Western modernity waited a nationalist reading that championed Japanese success born of unique native traditions. The popular French theoretical import, on the other hand, treated urban space as a site for the play of signs, diminishing the possibilities of historical or social critique. With the collapse of universal history, and with sweeping theories of Japanese culture in the ascendancy among conservatives, one of the few strategies of escape from the progressive intellectual's quandary was empiricism—extending even to the rejection of theoretical analysis *tout court.*

Empiricism for urbanists meant fieldwork: going out to walk and look and record. The faith in fieldwork, which developed in some instances into an explicit ethos built around walking, led intellectuals and their audiences toward a new attention to the urban environment at the level of everyday life. Among common tropes in this genre were references to how many pairs of shoes one had worn out exploring the city and claims that one's eyes had suddenly awakened to some strange thing that had theretofore gone unnoticed. Some spoke of walking Tokyo as a kind of religious experience, a pilgrimage. All of the efforts to reclaim, remap, and reinvent space by walking shared a reduction of scale, a rejection of the planner's totality, and an emphasis on individual discovery and appropriation that recall Michel de Certeau's notion of walking as an antinomian activity.[21]

STREET OBSERVATION SCIENTISTS

Founded at Tokyo's stodgy University Club in January 1986 (four months after the Plaza accord), the Street Observation Science Society took the outward appearance of a formal academic association, but from the outset, all the academic pomp—from the prepossessing name to the choice of the University Club for a ceremonial announcement to the morning coats that the founders arrived wearing—was tongue-in-cheek. The same tone characterized their "studies," which involved photographing and documenting odd ephemera and grouping them under clever titles, as if they belonged to an as-yet unimagined scheme of Linnaean classifications.

The group embarked on a series of wandering expeditions through Japanese and foreign cities in search of these oddities, which they referred to as "properties" (*bukken*). In magazine articles and books, they published images of these "properties" together with accounts of their discovery and speculations about their significance (fig. 11.1). The project achieved unanticipated popularity, resulting in television appearances for the members and invitations from local government offices around the country to give lectures or training seminars. When spin-offs appeared on television comedy shows and in youth magazines, the threshold had been reached for the trend-watchers to announce a Street Observation Science boom.[22]

Artist Akasegawa Genpei and architecture historian Fujimori Terunobu were the group's main exponents. A central figure in the artistic avant-garde of the 1960s, Akasegawa became a cause célèbre in 1966 when he was prosecuted for using a reproduction of the face of a one thousand-yen note as an art piece. During the four-year trial that followed, he found himself caught between the courts and the art world. The experience left him estranged from the artistic avant-garde, which had its own sanctioning institutions and ideology.[23] From 1970, he began leading students, friends, and fans into the streets of Tokyo to collect ephemera that he termed *hyper-art* (*chō-geijutsu*), and explained as "inexplicable protuberances and concavities connected to buildings and streets in the city, which, while purposeless, have been beautifully preserved."[24] He later named these objects *Tomason*, after an American baseball player (known in the Japanese press only by the transliteration of his last name, Thomason) who had been brought to Japan amid much fanfare and had spent a season on the bench before returning to the United States. *Tomason*-hunting was a communal activity in which the per-

MAZU
TOKYO
O
ARUITE
MIRU

Figure 11.1. Colophon by Harui Yutaka to *A Natural History of the Tokyo Streets* (*Tōkyō rojō hakubutsushi*) by Fujimori Terunobu and Aramata Hiroshi (Tokyo: Kajima Shuppankai, 1987). The caption, in romanized Japanese, reads: "First walk Tokyo and look." © Paper Studio.

sonal expression of the artist was decentered if not erased, offering Akasegawa a mode of aesthetic intervention in the city free of the onus of playing the individual genius and martyr to art (fig. 11.2).[25]

Fujimori had begun walking, also in the early 1970s, out of an interest in undocumented examples of modern architecture. He encountered sharp criticism within his field when he first presented the results of an exhaustive survey of Tokyo buildings he called "signboard architecture" (*kanban kenchiku*). Built along the minor commercial streets of the old downtown in the two decades between the world wars, signboard architecture was an overlooked vernacular of shophouses constructed in wood by native carpenters, but fronted with ornamental facades in brick, tile and copper that made them superficially "Western style" (fig. 11.3). Because they lacked the pedigree of either a Western-trained architect's design or of a native tradition considered pure, they had no place in the national patrimony. Senior scholars questioned whether these false Westernesque buildings were worthy of scholarship and regarded the young Fujimori's coin-

Figure 11.2. *Tomason* no. 1, the "pure staircase" of Yotsuya. Note repair to the bottom railing in the foreground. From *Hyper-art Tomason* (*Chōgeijutsu Tomason*) by Akasegawa Genpei (Tokyo: Byakuya Shobō, 1985). Photo courtesy of Akasegawa Genpei.

age of a catchy term to identify his object of study as impudent. The incident showed how carefully guarded the right to classify and name can be in an academic culture with pretenses to scientific method. In this case, characteristic of Japan's intellectual establishment, naming was seen as a privilege reserved to the older generation. Fujimori survived in the academy, but resolved to reject the hierarchy of expertise and specialization of the human sciences. He also began writing popular essays about his Tokyo explorations, conducted with a group of colleagues he referred to as the Architecture Detective Unit (*kenchiku tanteidan*).[26]

By the time these playful rebels against intellectual institutions joined forces in 1986, the bubble's inaugural moment, they had found a new adversary: "the consumption empire," as Fujimori proclaimed it in a manifesto for the group that bristled with military metaphors. "This empire," he wrote, "has for a long while limited its territory to the inside of shops. . . . But recently it has revealed territorial ambition for the streets we have occupied by custom since the times of our ancestors, and has steadily amassed weapons for an invasion. . . . It has developed strategies to commodify the entire town, and in some places has already successfully forded the rivers."[27] Fujimori raised this alarm not simply against the burgeoning consumerism in the huge shopping areas of western Tokyo, but against the new marketing approach of the Seibu department store chain and its rivals, who were using

382

Figure 11.3. Signboard architecture of the 1920s. Photo by Masuda Akihisa.

their own street observation techniques to penetrate more deeply into the psychology of the consumer masses. Two marketing research offices, one associated with Seibu, the other with the advertising agency Hakuhōdō, had begun charting street fashions and conducting spot interviews in Shibuya in 1981. Drawing on the ideas of urban sociologists, they compiled studies of mental maps and public group behavior, which retailers then used in deciding shop location and displays.[28] To Fujimori and Akasegawa, it seemed that neither the public space of the streets nor the act of walking in them was safe from the manipulation of consumer capitalism.

383

STREET OBSERVATION'S CITY

The Street Observation Science Society thus brought together an artist and a historian who, for different reasons, had both turned toward investigation in the streets of Tokyo. But social and economic conditions in Tokyo at the moment of their meeting gave a new meaning to their investigations. More than a document of buildings or objects of curiosity, the activities of these two and the others who joined them coalesced into a way of walking and seeing that revealed a city different from any proffered by architects, traditional historians, or state and municipal boosterists.

This city might be called the bricolage city, composed of an architecture of making-do. Fujimori's writing on signboard architecture demonstrated that an invisible palimpsest of building practices and policies underlay the visible urban form of the present. Tokyo's streetscape arose first of all from fragmented landholding and small average lot size; frontages of fifteen feet were typical along many commercial streets. These small lots, combined with the tradition of building in wood, universal before 1868 and still predominant in much of the city until the 1960s or 1970s, resulted in a low-rise carpenter-built city, with few examples of rows of buildings unified under an architect's design. Strong landowning rights established at the end of the nineteenth century thwarted attempts at wholesale redevelopment after the city's destruction by earthquake in 1923 and firebombing in 1945. Planners seeking to widen and regularize streets after these calamities were limited by the need to negotiate thousands of small land adjustments. In the process, structures that were supposed to be temporary frequently became permanent.[29] One instance in which regulation did have a significant impact on architecture was in signboard architecture itself, which was the product of a new postearthquake building code that required fireproofing of wood structures. Shop owners and carpenters took the opportunity of fireproofing to put up facades imitating neoclassical, art nouveau, and other styles then fashionable among architects, but in a bricolage manner that Fujimori describes as "fragmentary and haphazard."[30]

The *Tomason*-hunting component of street observation took its cues from the same city of bricolage construction and limited planning interventions. *Tomasons* tended to thrive in places where the street was treated as a commons more than a thoroughfare. Akasegawa searched for signs of care taken to fabricate or preserve objects that would not seem to belong to anyone or serve any practical purpose, as well as accidental juxtapositions caused by the survival of features that planned development would ordinarily eradicate. The anomalies he uncovered extended Fujimori's palimpsest of vernacular building regimes by revealing everywhere a material palimpsest of minute acts of construction.

Most Tokyoites would have readily recognized this bricolage cityscape. In fact, it had a central place in a Tokyo iconography often seen in graphic magazines, as well as in monographic works of some of the country's best-known contemporary photographers, where the city was represented as a chaotic jumble of the ultramodern with fragile relics of the past. Numerous photographers and journalists had recorded the survival of a tiny one-story shack nestled into a triangle-shaped lot on the flank of the 109 Building in Shibuya, one of the most conspicuous icons of the high-tech city of consumption. The shack housed a bar whose owners had set up shop in the black market after the war and refused to give up their land when commercial giant Tōkyū redeveloped the site in 1979.[31] Remnants of the black market district that rose up on the south side of Shinjuku station in the immediate postwar period were documented by photographer Araki Nobuyoshi among others.[32] Many intellectuals haunted another district of tiny bars in one- and two-story shacks elsewhere in Shinjuku known as "Golden Avenue." The appeal of these places lay in large part in the fact that they survived in improbable settings—in this instance, a stone's throw from Shinjuku station, which had become the city's largest commuter rail hub and reportedly the most heavily trafficked spot on earth.[33]

The observationists' work peered underneath the prosaic surfaces of the bricolage city to expose its strangeness. Street observation's "properties" were characterized by what the observationists called their "deviance" (*zure*): deviating from their expected place or scale, they possessed an "expressive excess."[34] Street observation's popular appeal, however, lay equally in the witty way that the names and explanations they gave the objects made them into surreal parodies. *Tomason* classifications included, for example, an "A-bomb type" for the outlines of demolished buildings left on the walls of adjacent buildings, and an "Abe Sada type"—referring to the name of a celebrated murderess who had carried her murdered lover's penis around the city—for the lopped-off and preserved stumps of telephone poles. Pets and potted plants kept out of doors in unusual ways—an old television console converted to a chicken coop; an irrigation system for potted plants using the condensate from an air conditioner—were called "zoos" and "botanical gardens." Fujimori also documented what he called "fossil shops" or "miserable shops" (*mijimeten*): places of business that appeared hardly to be in business, which he described as sites that "throw at the passerby the existential question 'what is trade?' " and "expose the essence of the commodity."[35]

Other members of the group documented handwritten signs, sketched street furniture, photographed and mapped the locations of every type of manhole cover in the city, and collected fragments of ornament from demolished buildings.[36] A street observation expedition involved dividing up a given district and setting out separately with maps and cameras, then assembling again to show one another slides and to brainstorm collectively on how to interpret and classify the objects photographed. These sessions took place amid much laughter.[37] Often the comic effect emerged from anthropomorphizing the object (some "properties" themselves looked like faces) or something related to it. Animal imagery was also common. In this sense, the street observationists were recovering a child's perception of the environment. Freud, citing and elaborating on an idea of Bergson's, proposes that comic enjoyment derives from an unconscious memory of how one experienced the world as a child.[38] Graphic artist and obsessive documentarian Hayashi Jōji, a member of the group whom the others referred to as the "God of Street Observation," was also called their "child prodigy."[39] Because for children the distinction between the animate and inanimate worlds is less sharp, street observation's comic speculations, more than just inspiring laughter, offered a technique for reanimating a physical world rendered inanimate by adulthood. The comedy of street observation treated childlike imagination itself as a faculty to be honed, a weapon against the increasing alienation of urban form from our bodily awareness.[40]

It is important too that most of the objects chosen revealed not only humorous accident, but intention. People had constructed them and preserved them. By organizing them into types—albeit absurd ones—the street observationists conjured the picture of a complete classification, the elements of an imaginary system for city building without planners or architects. The bricolage city composed in this imaginary system retained tangible links to the sensibility of childhood play. Yet those links slipped further and further away the more inorganic the building materials and forms of Tokyo's construction became. Although their position was an ironic one that made no claim of authenticity or autochthony, the humor of the street observationists thus proposed a kind of redemption by bringing the persistent materiality of urban space and the layers of its manufacture back into view.

Earlier urban ephemera collectors come to mind as precursors of Street Observation Science. Walter Benjamin may be called a kindred spirit and perhaps an inspiration.[41] The so-called *derives*—wandering expeditions—of Guy Debord and the Situationist International offer another parallel.[42]

Fujimori and Akasegawa expressed their greatest debt, however, to native forebears. They regarded themselves as the heirs of the urban ethnographers Kon Wajirō and Yoshida Kenkichi, whose studies of public behavior and streetscapes in Tokyo during the 1920s went under the name "modernology" (*kōgengaku*). Modernology offered a precedent for the street observationists' minute empiricism, as well as for their witty visual and verbal style. Working in the streets of a Tokyo rapidly rebuilding after the earthquake of 1923, modernologists Kon and Yoshida had attempted to attune themselves to every new detail of street life that could be recorded, sketched, or enumerated. Modernology treated the social world as an entropic, fluid form on which no overarching schema could be imposed; one could only trace trajectories through it and collect fragments from it.[43]

Whereas modernology had attempted to capture the fleeting present, its 1980s descendants looked back. The fragments they collected spoke of a vanishing past. Yet the street observationists never pointed toward a specific place or time as the lost home of their nostalgic longing. If such a utopian past is to be found anywhere in their worldview, it is in that moment immediately after the city's destruction in September 1923, when surviving Tokyoites were thrown on their own devices and forced to rebuild their lives and shelter themselves with the materials at hand. Kon's own urban explorations had commenced here, as he wandered the devastated city sketching the temporary structures people had built for themselves, musing along the way about the primordial origins of architecture. As Fujimori observed in a 2000 interview, what distinguished the Tokyo of 1923 from the Tokyo of the present was that Tokyoites in 1923 were still self-sufficient; they could provide their own shelter. In Fujimori's eyes, these skills had been all but lost by the 1980s.[44]

STREET OBSERVATION AND SPECULATIVE CAPITAL

Speculation is a kind of seeing with the imagination. When one speculates on a commodity, one tries to look past the commodity as it presently exists in order to see it in the mind of the buyer who will pay more for it. Kon Wajirō's speculations in 1923 on the origins of building and the street observationists' speculations two generations later on the meaning of fragments left from that earlier historical moment return us to the question of whether there is more than a lexical coincidence between speculation on fragments of the past and speculation on the future market value of property. Reflecting on the speculative fever that erupted during Haussmann's redistricting of Paris, Walter Benjamin wrote, "to the phantasmagorias of space to which the flâneur abandons himself, correspond the phantasmagorias of time indulged in by the gambler."[45] The intoxicating character of speculation (as a species of gambling) derives from the unknown time of future prospects, including the prospect that prices may go up at any moment, whereas the intoxicating character of flânerie derives from unknown space, the prospect of new vistas coming into view. Since the observationists themselves did not recognize it, I cannot speak of street observation as a conscious response to the real estate bubble. In their conflicting readings of the cityscape, however, street observation and real estate speculation mirrored one another in ways that suggest more than the structural correspondence Benjamin points to between the flâneur and the gambler. Their mutual reflection expressed a critical tension between two opposing visions of the city in the 1980s. Real estate speculation viewed urban space dematerialized, in the abstract terms of economic calculation; street observation highlighted its materiality by rendering visible and concrete the small acts of producing space. Speculation was predicated on the logic of "efficient use"; street observation cultivated the useless. Even if they did no more than walk and look and record, in their voracious visual consumption of the historical layers of the present, the street observationists offered a plenitude in place of the hollowness of the gaze of the financial speculator, for whom value derives only from projection forward in time.

Yet space and time cannot in actuality be conceived apart from one another.[46] The speculator's phantasmagoria of time constantly reconfigures the physical spaces of the city in which we walk. As the time of financial speculation accelerates toward nanosecond transactions, the future is collapsed into an unstable present, and the spatial phantasmagorias of the urban wanderer are forced deeper into the traces of the past. In a society of ephemeral spectacle, the transformations of the present-day city offer less and less for imagining an alternative urbanism.[47]

The group's preference for "properties" that were low-tech and showed signs of being self-built led them naturally to the old downtown districts, where the layers of history were still visible, along with the material trappings of residents' lives. Here, they found themselves walking the same streets as the *jiageya* land-hunters. The mix of elements that gave a district rich street observation potential tended also to indicate that it was ripe for redevelopment.[48] Yet contrary to other admirers of the architectural past, they never investigated the circumstances that lay behind the sites they photographed and never sought their physical preservation. This refusal to investigate or preserve might at first seem to contradict any reading of street observation as nostalgia, but in fact it reflected a sensibility that was profoundly nostalgic. Choosing preservable objects would have compelled them to define their contemporary relevance at the cost of their aura as inexplicable presences. Research and institutionalized preservation lay on the road to exploitation for other purposes, destroying the capacity of the "property" to speak directly to memory.

Just as they were kept apart from preservable patrimony, the street observationists' "properties" also remained distinct from found art. The observationists set themselves the task of locating objects for an urbanism ungoverned by the commodity form.[49] Found objects transferred into the domain of art, either physically or through the medium of photography, unavoidably acquire commodity value. The transfer also maintains art as a discrete category of activity—something Akasegawa had rejected in the 1970s—by preserving the context of valuation, appreciation, and exchange. Rather than taking found objects and giving them the value of art by placing them in the gallery, street observation sought to do the opposite: to find overlooked, apparently valueless objects outside the gallery that had already been treated *by others* as valuable, which made these objects something artlike (hyperart, in Akasegawa's description) and the people who made or cared for them anonymous masters. Concluding the presentation of a street observation expedition in the journal *Kōkoku hihyō* (Critical Review of Advertising), Akasegawa described street observation's discoveries as "art particles" released into the city following the collapse of Art, like radiation leaked into the environment after an atomic meltdown.[50] Instead of identifying objects as art and thus reinventing them in the present, street observationists speculated on their past, looking beyond their present to the imagined moment when they first emerged as artifacts.

Taking street observation perhaps more seriously than the participants themselves usually intended, we can see this search for the valued yet economically functionless artifact as a pursuit of the real. This was not a naive conception of reality that depended on the ontological authenticity of certain timeless objects posed against the falsehood of modernity, but the proposition of an epistemological reality that could rupture the blasé veneer with which urbanites shielded themselves from overstimulation—a reality that "awakens the eyeballs," as Fujimori described it, or a consciousness of the real as what another member of the group called "an approach to practice."[51] The practice in question, as we have seen, was peripatetic practice, and on the basis of the same ethos, the objects of this practice—street observation's "properties"—were idealized as properties of a nomadic urbanism rather than an organicist conception of stable dwelling. The ghostly presences of the makers of street observation's "properties" hover around them without emerging into view; they have left these marks on the streetscape and moved on. These phantom builders occupy and appropriate territory beyond the purview of the state, rather than fixing themselves within a natural order of property that ultimately, inevitably, is configured by the state. The funny sensation, usually slightly delayed, that comes from discovery of a "property," precipitates a momentary encounter with the real. To physically preserve it, overriding its appropriated character and corralling it back into the managed space of the public, would evacuate it of this reality.

This, in turn, reminds us that the speculator in what in English is called *real estate* gestures, through the language of law, toward some conception of the "real"—and indeed, it is something much closer to the ontological reality of a stable lifeworld that is referenced by the legal term, as the "real" of real estate signifies groundedness and immobility (the Japanese term for real estate, taken from nineteenth-century French civil law, translates literally as "immovable property"). Tokyo's real estate bubble, then, coming as it did in the wake of Japan's entry into the global system of electronic finance, had a schizophrenic character, a consciousness divided between desire generated within the floating, fictional realm of currency arbitrage and desire directed toward the chthonic power of the native soil. To the extent that real estate investment depends on a perceived "realness" in the immovability of land, real estate bubbles are rooted in a shared delusion that something real and external to the plane of speculative exchange grounds and supports the money value of land. Therefore, the bubble economy in one aspect actually represented a reversion to—or the expiring gasp of—a persistent faith in the *real* despite its dislocation by global speculative capital.[52]

The explosion of high-tech and luxury development engendered by the real estate boom around them signified to Fujimori and Akasegawa the final commodification of the urban commons. In response, they sought out objects too place-specific to be abstracted, too plainly useless to be commodified, too absurd to be preserved; and—in an ironic inversion of contemporary values—named these objects with a word borrowed from the real estate profession. But there is also something other than conscious parody here. One can detect a schizophrenia in street observation that inadvertently replicates (rather than challenges) the schizophrenia of bubble-era speculation itself: the desire for the real embodied in their hyperempiricism combined with a mode of speculative suspension that compelled them to place nostalgic investments in a "phantasmagoric" city rather than pursuing a more grounded and conventional preservationism within the frame of the present and practicable. This split desire for the real and the impossible gave street observation a "utopian dimension" characteristic of much avant-gardism, which, in Hal Foster's words, "proposes not what can be so much as what *cannot* be . . . as a critique of what is."[53]

UTOPIANISM AND PLAY IN THE CITY OF THE PAST

The observationists refused any systemization of the street observation process. Their surveys were desultory strings of individual discoveries. The individual observationist's task lay in finding, photographing, and naming objects, not in providing a comprehensive framework for interpreting them. Fujimori's manifesto for the group championed this serial, nonstructuring approach as a return to the age of natural history, before the specialization of the modern sciences.[54] The group rejected institutional consolidation in a similar manner. Members never worked as a team or delegated tasks to others. Despite the prepossessing title, their academic society had no internal structure, no membership list, no journal, and no fees. Outsiders who wanted to join were told they were free to use the name to set up their own societies.[55]

In a rambling conversation about the meaning of street observation and modernology published in the *Street Observation Science Primer*, Akasegawa observed: "Perhaps modernology, to put it paradoxically, is eternal and undying, that is, endlessly reproduced—in short, since it cannot accumulate, there's no way for it to expand [*hidai shiyō ga nai*]." The reference is not explicitly economic, but tempting to read that way, because the rest of Tokyo was engulfed in an orgy of property accumulation at the time. Akasegawa and Fujimori showed no interest in confronting these forces frontally, however. Instead, they wrapped their politics in clever ironies and devoted themselves to the aesthetics of investigation. Picking up Akasegawa's thought, Fujimori replied, "It moves sideways like a crab. It doesn't move toward systematization."[56]

Their anti–system building stance was shared by other post-Marxist intellectuals. Indeed, this was at the heart of the great postmodern turn of the bubble years: the return to Edo, the city before the founding of the Meiji state. Edo served as a utopian antithesis to everything modern, a nostalgic site so freely reimagined that it was almost as much dreamscape as history. Historian Tanaka Yūko's popular and influential book *The Edo Imagination* (*Edo no sōzōryoku*) appeared in 1986, the same year that street observation emerged into the public eye. Tanaka described a cosmopolitan Edo culture that thrived on parody. Edoites, she claimed, gathered information and goods from throughout the world yet rejected any hierarchy of nations or even of knowledge itself.[57] Faced with the 1980s world of international trade wars, grandstanding nationalist politicians causing diplomatic crises and other dilemmas of superpower status, many in the Japanese audience were easily seduced by the utopian appeal in this anarchism of the imagination.

Yet Street Observation Science differed from the utopian invocations of the past in Edo research like Tanaka's because it proposed a mode of practice in the present. Fieldwork, the observationists believed, would counter the bland, somnolent attitude that wealth and homogeneity had engendered by enlarging the possibilities of everyday perception. For ironic effect, Akasegawa organized "*Tomason* Tours," mimicking the Tokyo bus tours in which out-of-towners trailed lemminglike after banner-carrying tour guides. But street observation in the description of its protagonists was anything but passive sightseeing; in fact, it required considerable physical and mental stamina. Akasegawa later recalled feeling so overwhelmed and excited after the group's first expedition that he could not sleep, and the group's publisher, who was also a participant, recalled returning to the office after the expedition exhausted because everything he saw on the habitual route to work had suddenly become new and fascinating, demanding attention.[58] If all this effort seemed to be expended on what was in the end no more than an elaborate game, the street observationists themselves made no apologies, for in their embrace of uselessness, they explicitly sought to create more room for play in the urban environment.

Historically, the irony is that new forms of play were in fact proliferating in Tokyo—often extravagantly expensive play. In the 1960s and 1970s, parody and play could themselves have been conspicuous challenges to bureaucratic capitalism, or what social critics on the Left commonly called the managed society (*kanri shakai*). In the late 1980s, however, they were readily absorbed by it. On the one hand, some people in government, mass media, and marketing—the proverbial apparatchiks of the managed society—were becoming more nonconformist themselves, developing interest in the culturally layered streetscape and questioning large-scale development. On the other hand, aesthetic intervention was ineffectual against the power of accelerated consumer capitalism and the spiraling forces of speculation. Any potential in the observationists' experiments for a larger historical meaning or message about urbanism was compromised by the immediate transformation of the product into another commodity.[59]

The progressive political possibilities of street observation, it must be concluded, were overwhelmed by the power of capital. The street observationists had marched into the field with bold declarations against contemporary capitalism, yet confronting what they themselves judged an undefeatable enemy, chose a variety of absurdism that could easily decline into mere frivolity. Posing the self-built against the planned and "mopped-up" environment, street observation presented in material form the problem of what makes a city livable, or what makes it feel lived-in. At least for those who participated, street observation could have a genuinely transformative effect on the way the contemporary city was perceived. But on the occasions when street observationists speculated about the future rather than the past-in-the-present, their words tended toward fatalism rather than radical utopia.[60] In the neighborhoods where they collected "properties," land prices and inheritance taxes were making it economically impossible for owners to maintain houses for more than a generation, and threats from gangsters were forcing some owners and tenants to abandon them at once. Street observation could offer only very oblique comment on this. In aesthetic terms, the street observationists were champions of the underdog, but if one viewed the rush of speculation and redevelopment as the death of downtown communities—as some of the people who lived in the districts they investigated unquestionably experienced it—then they looked more like jesters dancing at a funeral.

THE CONTEXT AND THE "USEFULNESS" OF STREET OBSERVATION

Let me return to my initial questions. What did street observation as a movement *do*? And how did the socioeconomic context in which it was born shape it?

We could call the street observationists' city a deconstructed vernacular city. They asked: what if the things worth sustaining in our cities, the things that communicate memory and a sense of place, are not just unplanned but accidental, useless, unreplicable, and even microscopic? Small improvisations, fragments of the self-made, and signs of cultivation in an environment that defies the desire for secure settlement were among Tokyo's most remarkable characteristics as a city. Scrap-and-build modernization forced preservationists and historians to pose the fundamental questions underlying all preservation and historicism: what do we seek in the traces of the past, and what *should* we seek? The same questions are now being posed in other East Asian cities, many of which have experienced similarly thorough erasure. There is a danger in commemoration, because every form of commemoration imposes some model of community, not uncommonly a politically conservative one. On the other hand, the model of a less memorializing, flexible historicism popular in U.S. cities today, seen in adaptive reuse projects and design covenants that regulate for harmony of building facades, for example, is a potentially Faustian bargain, accepting development by big capital as a given and, in the same gesture, limiting the terrain of creative thinking about what the city might be. Tokyo exposed the inadequacy of these models and invited a certain radicalism of the nostalgic imagination. Street observation entered in search of a past immune to either statist commemoration or commercial repackaging. It offered a way of seeing the city that reanimates it as a place of habitation, in opposition to the real estate speculator's mode of seeing, which erases the marks of habitation, and a way of remembering that recalls the bodily act of crafting, against the melancholic trap of remembering only through monuments and ruins.

It would be too much of a stretch—and historically inaccurate—to tie Akasegawa's *Tomason* hunting and Fujimori's signboard architecture to Nixon's floating of the dollar in 1971, as they both started prior to the impact of the new currency system. By the time the former avant-gardist and the renegade architecture historian bumped into one another in the streets of Tokyo a decade and a half later, however, the cultural effects of Japan's economic success and of the global speculative regime had come to the fore. The bubble made the meeting of these two streetscape explorers meaningful in a way that was not bounded by issues within avant-garde art or architecture history. Now Akasegawa's absurdist discoveries offered a way of seeing that mirrored and up-ended the hegemonic gaze of speculative capitalism, and Fujimori's vestiges of vernacular construction stood as antitheses to a city whose process of construction was being rendered invisible, together with the mode of production itself.

Although the observationists' explicit critique targeted consumerism, which was hardly new, their activities, images, and writing posed a provocative antithesis to the larger culture of speculation in which they moved in the late 1980s. When this heady moment had passed, the aesthetic sensibility they had cultivated was partly absorbed into more commercial forms. At museums and theme parks in the 1990s, the same vernacular urbanism became something passively consumed, in an atmosphere that combined play and wistful reminiscence.[61] But during the bubble years, when small shopkeepers and housewives were learning to speculate on the future values of stock and real estate, the Street Observation Science Society also taught many Japanese a new way to speculate on the past.

NOTES

1. For a review and countercritique, see John Frow, "Tourism and the Semiotics of Nostalgia," *October* 57 (Summer 1991): 123–51.

2. See, for example, M. Christine Boyer, "Cities for Sale: Merchandising History at South Street Seaport," in Michael Sorkin, ed., *Variations on a Theme Park: The New American City and the End of Public Space* (New York: Noonday Press, 1992), 181–204; and Michael Wallace, "Reflections on the History of Historic Preservation," in Susan Porter Benson, Stephen Brier, and Roy Rosensweig, eds., *Presenting the Past: Essays on History and the Public* (Philadelphia: Temple University Press, 1986), 165–99.

3. Christopher Wood, *The Bubble Economy: The Japanese Economic Collapse* (London: Sidgwick and Jackson, 1992), 11.

4. Yukio Noguchi, "The 'Bubble' and Economic Policies in the 1980s," *Journal of Japanese Studies* 20, no. 2 (Summer 1994): 291–329. See also Pagnamenta Associates, "Setting Sun," videotape, (BBC, 1999), pt. 1.

5. Kathryn Graven and Yumiko Ono, "Japanese Aren't Afraid of Tokyo Market's Rise: Most Investors Believe Good Times Will Continue," *Wall Street Journal*, November 21, 1988, 1; and Michael R. Sesit and Marcus W. Brauchli, "Tokyo's Market: Was It a Bubble Just Waiting to Burst?" *Wall Street Journal*, April 3, 1990, C1. Writing in 1990, even as cautious and perspicacious an economist as Tsuru Shigeto treated the economic indicators of the late 1980s merely as part of the larger pattern of postwar Japanese capitalist growth. Tsuru Shigeto, *Japan's Capitalism: Creative Defeat and Beyond* (Cambridge: Cambridge University Press, 1993).

6. Fredric Jameson, "Culture and Finance Capital," in *The Cultural Turn: Selected Writings on the Postmodern, 1983–1998* (London: Verso, 1998), 136–61; and Jean-Joseph Goux, "Ideality, Symbolicity, and Reality in Postmodern Capitalism," in Stephen Cullenberg, Jack Amariglio, and David F. Ruccio, eds., *Postmodernism, Economics and Knowledge* (London: Routledge, 2001), 166–81.

7. Mark C. Taylor, *Confidence Games: Money and Markets in a World without Redemption* (Chicago: University of Chicago Press, 2004), 6.

8. Widespread application of the Black-Scholes-Merton pricing formula developed in 1973 led to an extraordinary expansion in derivative trading, divorcing investment calculations entirely from material commodities. In an analysis of the significance of this formula, economic historian Donald MacKenzie comments: "Finance theory is a world-making, and not just a world-describing, endeavour." Donald MacKenzie, "Models of Markets: Finance Theory and the Historical Sociology of Arbitrages," *Revue d'Histoire des Sciences* 57 (2004): 409–33.

9. Matsui Takeshi, "Shōhiron būmu: Maaketingu ni okeru 'posutomodan' " [The Consumption Theory Boom: "Postmodernism" in Marketing], *Gendai shisō*, 29, no. 14 (November 2001): 125–26.

10. See Nikkei Bijinesu ed., *Shinsetsu Baburu: Utage wa mada owatte inai* (True Tale of the Bubble: The Feast Is Not Over) (Tokyo: Nikkei Bijinesu, 2000).

11. Noguchi, "The 'Bubble' and Economic Policies in the 1980s," 292, 304.

12. Tsuru, *Japan's Capitalism,* 181–85, 192–99.

13. For descriptions of the transformation of these two western Tokyo hubs in the 1970s, see Roman Cybriwsky, *Tokyo: The Changing Profile of an Urban Giant* (Boston: G. K. Hall, 1991), 156–70.

14. Ibid., 110, 111 (table).

15. Ibid., 139–40.

16. Ibid., 239. For a discussion that shows that densities were already comparable to those in high-rise cities and analyzer the infrastructure problems that would accompany wholesale redevelopment; see Ōno Teruyuki and Reiko Habe Ebaniv, *Toshi kaihatsu o kangaeru: Amerika to Nihon* (Tokyo: Iwanami shoten, 1992).

17. Mike Douglass, "The 'New' Tokyo Story: Restructuring Space and the Struggle for Place in a World City," in Kuniko Fujita and Richard Child Hill, eds., *Japanese Cities in the World Economy* (Philadelphia: Temple University Press, 1993), 99–101. For synopses of all the major plans proposed as of early 1987, see *Gekkan Across henshūshitsu,* ed, *"Tōkyō" no shinryaku* [The Tokyo Invasion] (Tokyo: Parco Shuppan, 1987), 146–61.

18. On the *shitamachi* boom, see Theodore Bestor, "The Shitamachi Revival," *Transactions of the Asiatic Society of Japan,* 4th ser., 5 (1990): 71–86.

19. See H. D. Harootunian, "Visible Discourses, Invisible Ideologies," in Masao Miyoshi and H. D. Harootunian, eds., *Postmodernism and Japan* (Durham, N.C.: Duke University Press, 1989), 63–92.

20. In addition to the profligate use of Baudrillard in popular discourse, the commodification of theory is exemplified by the popularity of the intellectual wunderkind Asada Akira, whose study *Kōzō to chikara* (Structure and Power, 1983) became a bestseller and made the author a household name. Most of the book was a digest of French works in semiology. The majority of readers were said only to read the introduction, which invited Japanese students to treat the acquisition of knowledge as play. For analysis of this and related intellectual phenomena in the 1980s, see Marilyn Ivy, "Critical Texts, Mass Artifacts: The Consumption of Knowledge in Postmodern Japan," in Miyoshi and Harootunian, *Postmodernism and Japan,* 21–46.

21. Michel de Certeau, *The Practice of Everyday Life,* trans. Steven Rendall (Berkeley: University of California Press, 1984), 91–110.

22. Fujimori Terunobu, interview by author, October 22, 2000; New York. References to a street observation boom in the 1980s include Anon., "Tōkyō koko ga ijō da" [These Things in Tokyo Are Abnormal], *Gunkyo* 14 (April 24, 1987): 54; Kashiwagi Hiroshi, "Shōhi shakai no naka no dezain" [Design in the Consumer Society], in Yoshimoto Takaaki, Asada Akira, et al., *Eitiizu: 80 nendai zen kenshō* [Eighties: Complete Inspection of the 1980s] (Tokyo: Kawade Shobō Shinsha, 1990), 179; Iijima Yōichi, "Gitai kenchiku" [Simulation Architecture], in Takaaki et al., *Eitiizu,* 214.

An early "scoop" of the phenomenon, together with quasi-sociological trend analysis can be found in Anon., "Fiirudowaaku no jidai: Toribiaru insein ga fujō suru" [The Age of Fieldwork: Appearance of the Trivial Insane], *Gekkan Akurosu* 142 (January 1986): 38–53. Beginning in the early 1980s, the youth magazine *Takarajima* ran a column called VOW ("Voice of Wonderland") in which readers' discoveries were printed. This column showed pronounced signs of influence from Street Observation Science after 1986.

23. See William A. Marotti, "Simulacra and Subversion in the Everyday: Akasegawa Genpei's 1000-Yen Copy, Critical Art, and the State," *Postcolonial Studies* 4, no. 2 (July 2001): 211–39 and Reiko Tomii, "State v. (Anti-) Art: *Model 1,000-Yen Note Incident* by Akasegawa Genpei and Company," *Positions: East Asia Cultures Critique* no. 10, 1 (Spring 2002): 141–72.

24. Suzuki Takeshi, "Machi ni Tomason o otte" [Hunting *Tomason* in Town], in Akasegawa Genpei, Fujimori Terunobu, and Minami Shinbō, eds., *Rojō kansatsugaku nyūmon* [Street Observation Science Project] (Tokyo: Chikuma Shobō, 1986), 195.

25. Gary Thomason, "father of the *Tomason*," as Akasegawa dubbed him, was recruited by the Tokyo Giants in 1981 and sent home the following year after failing to get any hits. See Akasegawa Genpei, *Chōgeijutsu Tomason* [Hyper-art Tomason] (Byakuya Shobō, 1985), 13–14, 66. Euphony and Akasegawa's peculiar sense of the absurd led to this appellation, which should not be read as intending any comment on either baseball or Americans.

26. Some of these essays are collected in Fujimori Terunobu, *Kenchiku tanteidan no bōken: Tōkyō hen* [Adventures of the Architecture Detective Unit, Tokyo Edition] (Tokyo: Chikuma Shobō, 1986). Fujimori's interest in vernacular urbanism shows broad affinity with the work of Bernard Rudofsky and of Jane Jacobs, both of whom were widely read in Japanese architectural circles, as they were in the United States in the 1960s and 1970s. Rudofsky visited Tokyo's Waseda University in the early 1960s and subsequently offered his praise for aesthetics in Japanese everyday life in *The Kimono Mind: An Informal Guide to Japan and the Japanese* (Garden City, N.Y.: Doubleday, 1965). For analysis of Rudofsky's place in midcentury architectural modernism, see Felicity Scott, "Bernard Rudofsky: Allegories of Nomadism and Dwelling," in Sarah Williams Goldhagen and Réjean Legault, eds., *Anxious Modernisms: Experimentation in Postwar Architectural Culture* (Montreal: Canadian Centre for Architecture; Cambridge, Mass.: MIT Press, 2000), 215–38.

27. Fujimori, "Rojō kansatsu no hata no moto ni" [Under the Banner of Street Observation], in Akasegawa, Fujimori, and Minami, *Rojō kansatsugaku nyūmon*, 9.

28. For the Hakuhōdō office, known as the "Institute for Life and Living," see John L. McCreery, *Japanese Consumer Behavior: From Worker Bees to Wary Shoppers* (Richmond, Surrey: Curzon Press, 2000). The Seibu-based office published the monthly *Gekkan Akurosu* [Monthly Across]. This has now become a Web magazine.

29. André Sorensen, *The Making of Urban Japan: Cities and Planning from Edo to the Twenty-first Century* (London: Routledge, 2002), 125–33; 162–68.

30. Fujimori Terunobu, *Kanban kenchiku* [Signboard Architecture] (Tokyo: Sanseidō, 1988), 171.

31. Nishii Kazuo and Hirashima Akihiro, *Shōwa 20-nen Tōkyō chizu* [A Tokyo Map of Shōwa 20] (Tokyo: Chikuma Shobō, 1986), 300–301.

32. See, for example, Araki Nobuyoshi, *Tōkyō monogatari* [Tokyo Story] (Tokyo: Heibonsha, 1989). Much of Araki's voluminous oeuvre during the 1970s and 1980s documented the layers of occupancy and use in Tokyo streetscapes and buildings. For discussion of Araki's work and the Tokyo streetscape, see Iizawa Kōtarō, *Araki!* (Tokyo: Hakusuisha, 1994), 103–37.

33. Watanabe Hidetsuna, *Shinjuku Gorudengai* [Shinjuku Golden Avenue] (Tokyo: Shōbunsha, 1986).

34. Fujimori, "Rojō kansatsu no hata no moto ni," 17.

35. Fujimori Terunobu, Aramata Hiroshi, and Harui Yutaka, *Tōkyō rojō hakubutsushi* [A Natural History of the Streets of Tokyo] (Tokyo: Kajima Shuppankai, 1987), 297.

36. A group of American women living in Japan later picked up the same interest in the aesthetics of manhole covers and published two volumes of patterns from them: Shirley MacGregor, *Quilting with Manhole Covers: A Treasure Trove of Unique Designs from the Japanese Streets* (Eugene, Ore.: Carriage Trade Press; 1999); and Shirley MacGregor, *Treasures Underfoot: Quilting with Manhole Covers, Round Two* (Eugene, Ore.: Carriage Trade Press, 2001). The former carries an introduction by street observationist Hayashi Jōji.

37. Akasegawa Genpei, Fujmori Terunobu, et al. "Tōkyō rojō meibutsu hyōbanki" [Popular Guide to Famous Things on the Tokyo Streets], *Kōkoku hihyō* 84 (June 1986), 205–35, documents one of these brainstorming sessions. The conversation transcript is punctuated by frequent indications of laughter.

38. Sigmund Freud, *The Joke and Its Relationship to the Unconscious*, trans. by Joyce Crick (London: Penguin Classics, 2002), 214–15.

39. "Jundo 100 percent no kodomo? Iya uchūjin? Soretomo kamisama?" [A 100 percent Pure Child? Man from Space? Or a God?], a conversation between Akasegawa Genpei, Fujimori Terunobu, and Minami Shinbō, in *Hayashi Jōji teki kōgengaku: He to Fujisan* [Hayashi Jōji-Style Modernology: Farts and Mount Fuji] (Tokyo: INAX Shuppan, 2000), 4–12.

40. Elaine Scarry writes of material objects such as furniture as projections of human sentience beyond the body. Many of street observation's properties, whose "madeness" is highlighted by the way they are photographed, remind us that the physical city is itself ultimately a material projection of human sentience. See Elaine Scarry, *The Body in Pain: The Making and Unmaking of the World* (New York: Oxford University Press, 1985).

41. Most particularly the Benjamin of the Arcades project. Early in this project Benjamin saw himself as simply gathering fragments of data. He noted: "Formula; construction from facts. Construction through the complete elimination of theory." Quoted in David Frisby, *Cityscapes of Modernity* (Cambridge: Polity Press, 2001),

41. This empiricism would be harshly criticized by Adorno, who said of the work that it "situated itself at the crossroads of magic and positivism." "Exchange with Theodor W. Adorno on 'The Paris of the Second Empire in Baudelaire,' " in *Walter Benjamin: Selected Writings*, trans. Edward Jephcott et al. (Cambridge, Mass.: Harvard University Press, 2003), 4:102. In the very different intellectual milieu of late-twentieth-century Japan, analogous criticisms were made by urban social theorists who regarded the street observationists as "nihilists."

42. See Greil Marcus, "The Long Walk of the Situationist International," in *Guy Debord and the Situationist International: Texts and Documents*, ed. Tom McDonough (Cambridge, Mass.: MIT Press, 2002); and Tom McDonough, "Situationist Space," in the same volume. In the situationist *derive* the walker is doing the deviating, whereas the observationist treats the object as deviant and takes the position of discoverer. The difference is one of stance, and does not necessarily dictate different practices, because both groups set out to wander without destination, and the character of the deviance as an event and the deviant object as a discovery equally depend on the walker making it so. Still, it reflects a basic contrast in the position of the protagonists, as even their names suggest: the situationists saw themselves as radical agents, reshaping urban space; the observationists saw themselves as bringing to light an urbanism already there, allowing it to work its effects. Akasegawa's work in the group Hi Red Center during the 1960s had been a performance intended to awaken others by puncturing the façade of social order. By 1970, he had abandoned this mode of expression as futile.

43. On modernology, see Miriam Silverberg, "Constructing the Japanese Ethnography of Modernity," *Journal of Asian Studies* 51, no. 1 (1992): 30–54; and H. D. Harootunian, *Overcome by Modernity: History, Culture, and Community in Interwar Japan* (Princeton, N.J.: Princeton University Press, 2000), 178–201.

44. Fujimori, interview, October 22, 2000. See also Fujimori's discussion in his afterword to Kon Wajirō, *Nihon no minka* [Japanese Folkhouses] (Tokyo: Iwanami Bunko, 1989), 350–51. On the ideal of the primitive hut in European modernism, see Joseph Rykwert, *On Adam's House in Paradise: The Idea of the Primitive Hut in Architectural History* (Cambridge, Mass.: MIT Press, 1981).

45. Walter Benjamin, "Haussmann, or the Barricades," in *Reflections: Essays, Aphorisms, Autobiographical Writings*, trans. Edmund Jephcott (New York: Schocken Books, 1978), 159.

46. See discussion of the idea of spatiotemporal utopia in David Harvey, *Spaces of Hope* (Edinburgh: Edinburgh University Press, 2000), 182–96.

47. At least, so it appeared to the observationists. In this view of the present, there is considerable common ground between the nostalgic sensibilities of Fujimori and Guy Debord.

48. Akasegawa Genpei, *Zenmen jikyō!* [Akasegawa Genpei Confesses All!] (Shōbunsha, 2001), 344. Akasegawa notes in this interview that their first work was on the eve of the bubble proper and remarks: "It's good we did it when we did." "It's a precious record," replies his interviewer.

49. They were also aware of the impossibility of this mission. Fujimori's manifesto noted pessimistically that "to date not one concept has not been consumed" by the "consumption empire." "Rojō kansatsu no hata no moto ni," 10.

50. Akasegawa, "Ato kōjō" [Concluding Statement], *Kōkoku hihyō* 84 (June 10, 1986): 234–35.

51. Fujimori, "Rojō kansatsu no hata no moto ni," 15; and Harui, *Tōkyō rojō hakubutsushi*, 297. My thinking here is influenced in part by Hal Foster's discussion of the real in pop art. See *Return of the Real: The Avant-Garde at the End of the Century* (Cambridge, Mass.: MIT Press, 1996), 132–36, 218–20.

52. For related comments on land and cultural representation in 1980s Tokyo, see Uchida Ryūzō and Wakabayashi Mikio, "Tōkyō aruiwa toshi no chisō o sokutei suru" [Tokyo, or Measuring the Strata of the City], *10+1, Tokushū: Tōkyō shinron* [Special issue: New Writing on Tokyo] 12 (1998): 62–79.

53. Foster, *Return of the Real*, 16.

54. Fujimori, "Rojō kansatsu no hata no moto ni," 13–15.

55. This strategy of spontaneous organization found precedents in the political movements against the U.S.-Japan Security Treaty of 1960, which was the high-water mark of political activism in postwar Japan. See Wesley Sasaki-Uemura, *Organizing the Spontaneous: Citizen Protest in Postwar Japan* (Honolulu: University of Hawai'i Press, 2001), 149, 206–11.

56. Akasegawa, Fujimori, and Minami, *Rojō kansatsugaku nyūmon*, 88.

57. Tanaka Yūko, *Edo no sōzōryoku: 18 seiki no media to hyōchō* (Tokyo: Chikuma Shobō, 1986), particularly 230–45.

58. Akasegawa, *Zenmen jikyō!* 341.

59. On the managed society and play, see Marilyn Ivy, "Formations of Mass Culture," in Andrew Gordon, ed., *Postwar Japan as History* (Berkeley: University of California Press, 1993); 239–58. On the engagement of local government with culture, see Jennifer Robertson, *Native and Newcomer: Making and Remaking a Japanese City* (Berkeley: University of California Press, 1991); and Jennifer Robertson, "It Takes a Village: Internationalization and Nostalgia in Postwar Japan," in Stephen Vlastos, ed., *Mirror of Modernity: Invented Traditions in Modern Japan* (Berkeley: University of California Press, 1998), 110–29.

60. At the close of the conversation published in *The Street Observation Science Primer*, for example, Fujimori remarks: "it's the first field with no conclusions," and Minami Shinbō adds: "I guess this will become a book, something fine and proper . . . then it will decline. But that's all right too." (Akasegawa, Fujimori, and Minami, *Rojō kansatsugaku nyūmon*, 116–17) In this important respect the observationists differed sharply from the situationists.

61. The first major example of this new genre of nostalgic commercial leisure sites in the Tokyo area was the Shin-Yokohama Ramen Museum, opened in 1994. See Jordan Sand, "The Ambivalence of the New Breed: Nostalgic Consumerism in 1980s and 1990s Tokyo," in Sheldon Garon and Patricia MacLachlan, eds., *The Ambivalent Consumer* (Ithaca, N.Y.: Cornell University Press, 2006), 104–8.

CHAPTER 12

Spectacle and Death in the City of Bombay Cinema

RANJANI MAZUMDAR

> In contemporary Bombay, the existence of parallel cities is a very
> striking phenomenon. Until a few decades ago, the many worlds in
> the city occupied different spaces, but have now coalesced into a
> singular but multi-faceted entity. Today, the city's image comprises
> of strange yet familiar juxtapositions—a roadside Hindu shrine
> abuts St Thomas' Cathedral, chimney stacks are dwarfed by
> skyscrapers, fishing villages and slums nestle at the foot of luxury
> apartments, and bazaars occupy the Victorian arcades!
> —Mehrotra and Dwivedi, *Bombay: The Cities Within*

Bombay is the quintessentially modern city of India, the country's
commercial display window.[1] Yet the question that constantly begs clarifica-
tion is how we should look at a city where more than half the population
lives in slums or on the streets because they are homeless. The crisis of
housing and the topography of squalor that shapes the landscape of Bombay
has been the topic of much discussion.[2] Academics and poets, journalists and
architects have all written about Bombay's spatial map. The existence of two
worlds is not new to either Bombay or other cities in India. What is different
about the contemporary situation is the new landscape of globalization,
where global mobility and visual signage have introduced an expansive
world of networks and connections, creating new desires and aspirations.
This is a landscape mediated by popular Bombay cinema as it imaginatively
negotiates the two worlds of the city. The traffic between the "real" city and
the imagined cinematic city is a complicated movement driven by a subjective and psychic projection. Journeying through the traffic of visual codes
and signs that move between the physical spaces of Bombay and the topography of its cinematic production, this chapter argues that popular Bombay
cinema is a powerful urban archive.

The context of globalization and its dramatic cultural and spatial effects on
city life provides a vantage point to look at the emergence of two distinctly

different genres. The genre of family films, focusing on family dramas, and the gangster genre, based on the Bombay underworld, have emerged as two of the most powerful cinematic forms of the globalization period. The family films focus on consumer-oriented families, speaking to "tradition" yet geared to global mobility. In these films, the movement into lavish interior spaces relies on a complete erasure of public city spaces. The panoramic interiors of the family films combine design techniques with architectural space to create a "virtual city" where the "global" family can reinvent "Indianness" and modernity. In this scenario, the space of the Bombay street, the *chawl*, the train, and the crowds, which were always central to the narratives of popular cinema, are consistently marginalized.[3] In contrast, the films of the new gangster genre conduct an elaborate exploration of urban space. The dark alleys, the crowded streets, the slums, the peeling walls, and the claustrophobic *chawls* are all on display. Unlike the family films, where public city space is erased, the underworld films negotiate the city through a hyper-real mode that relies on a combination of violence, technology, masculinity, and urban space. Both genres have emerged in the new, charged context of globalization, where migrant imaginaries of travel and mobility have become exemplified in media forms.

Metropolitan India after globalization has been convulsed by a frenzy of chaotic construction—overpasses, shopping malls, multiplexes, hotels and highways, coffee shops, and ATMs—along with a massive automobile boom. Added to this is the transformation of both the home and the outside, where cable television has in a dynamic way affected the eye's optical capacity to wander through diverse locations of the world. The streets and markets are awash with new electronic gadgets, mobile phones, computers, and DVDs, each promoting diverse advertising strategies on walls, on billboards and on lampposts. New forms of lighting have transformed the experience of the night in commercial areas. There is now a rapid profusion of urban consumption, scores of satellite television channels, and a new expanded music culture centered on the film industry. This, then, is the experience of a new delirium of urban life—a complex configuration that exists ubiquitously, drawing on politics, art, celebrity culture, media wars, and fashion. Popular Bombay cinema in India today not only exists within this all-pervasive urban delirium, but is also fundamentally a part of the delirium.

The aestheticization of the streets through the spread of visual signage and surfaces is simultaneously a story of decline. This decline is vividly captured in the prose of Naresh Fernandes who looks at the transformations in the textile mill area of Bombay's Girangaon: "As the city's real estate prices soar ever higher and encourage mill owners to the realization that

402

cotton textiles aren't profitable anymore, glass-and-chrome towers are springing up where factory sheds once stood. Wooden-beamed *chawls*—residential arrangement for mill workers unique to Bombay—are being replaced by new office blocks. Senapati Bapat Marg, dotted with sooty chimneys, is being transformed into the city's Madison Avenue."[4] What then is the fate of the people who occupied the space that is being transformed by the logic of global capital? Surely, this debris of modernity will circulate in some form within the architectural landscape that seeks to erase it through aestheticization? As the expansion of slums, homelessness, and increased migration constantly exert pressure on the built environment, the city of debris overlaps with the city of spectacle in Bombay.

The city of two worlds includes the juxtaposition of lifestyles, habits, and transportation. The proximity of the two worlds makes it virtually impossible to transform the public representation of the city into a thriving, global metropolis, except through excessively authoritarian, politically risky, and unpopular methods. The density and chaotic nature of the city has produced for some of its residents a desire for transcendence from the specificity of space, without abandoning the imaginary space of India. This is articulated most profoundly in the creation of new residential enclaves away from the main city that mimic the built environment of U.S. and European residential areas. The other movement is the transformation of the interiors—of cafes, banks, office spaces, and residences. Despite the coexistence of wealth and poverty cheek by jowl throughout Bombay's physical topography, the redesigning of the interiors provides an escape from the chaotic experience of the street just outside. Capitalist modernity has historically required a regime of spatial aesthetics that can house and generate the magic of the commodity. But public space in a city like Bombay interrupts the aestheticized journey of the commodity. There are but few sanitized public realms that can hide inequality, something that shocks international visitors used to segregated third-world cities. In this situation the *transformation of the interior* provides the fleeting possibility of transcending the physical texture of the cityscape.

In the landscape of cinema, the conflictual experience of globalization has generated two different journeys. Whereas the family film is a retreat from the specificity of urban space through the creation of designed interiors, the gangster genre is an attempt to navigate the Bombay of violence, chaos, crisis, and ruin. Whereas the former articulates an urban desire for transcendence and escape, the latter moves deliberately to articulate loss and despair by excavating the darker side of the city. And although both genres create mythic spaces, one emerges from the delirium of commodity spectacle; the

403

other is shaped by the delirium of crime. Like a dark shadow, the delirium of the underworld follows the delirium of the commodity. The panoramic interior city is a form that seeks to enchant by physically erasing the space of Bombay; the gangster genre seeks to situate Bombay as a city of death and spatial disenchantment.

The Light Space of the Interior City

The visual shock of the two worlds in Bombay can manifest itself during a casual walk. Walking toward a high-rise building surrounded by slums generates a strange experience. Inside the building are elevators that ascend to well-designed apartments with large windows. From high up in the building, the slums down below do not catch the eye. Rather, the expanse of a sprawling city provides a picturesque view. Those who live lower down in the high-rise can see the squalor just outside their apartments.[5] The movement of the eye and the desire to look out can never ensure the perfectly sanitized and ordered vision of the city that many of the city's middle- and upper-class residents desire. As designers gear up to create enclaves of urban interiors, we see the desire for new styles and modern living performed through a transformation of private space. Histories of consumer cultures have shown how a withdrawal of the middle classes into their domestic interiors, electrical kitchens, and private automobiles was required to enhance the experience of consumption. The withdrawal was made possible through the creation of a privatized and depoliticized subjectivity.[6] In India, particularly in Bombay, the visual force of public space has accelerated the stylization of the interior in both literal (redesigning of homes, offices, banks, and cafés) and imaginative terms (through films) after globalization.

The Architecture of "Indianness"

In domestic architecture, the relationship between the indoors and outdoors has been a much debated and complex issue. Space needed to be privatized, but the connections with the outdoors had to be maintained to enhance the experience of visual expanse. Thus "the central design element used to create an illusion of the outside world was the picture window or window wall.[7] This spatial ambiguity where our gaze could move freely between indoor and outdoor space was central to the home and design magazines of the postwar period in the West.[8] The intention was to establish a continuity of interior and exterior worlds. The window backdrop or the ability to connect

404

with the street from the window, offering us a perspective and a distracted gaze at modernity's different offerings, has been central to architectural designs of domestic spaces in the West. The use of the window wall is an indication of how interior space can be made expansive and seamless. This continuity of space found in the elite neighborhoods of Paris, London, and New York cannot be found easily in south Asia. It is not continuity, but the discontinuity between what lies outside in the street and what we imagine to be the space of the interior that pushes the wedge between these two spaces even further as design takes over the space of the interior.

Interior design is central to the space of the familial and the private. Design techniques not only relate the interior to cultural forms, but also mark the space within a hierarchical chain of taste. Interior design also helps to negotiate personal identity, because it is the visible expression of our values and attitudes. Through design techniques the interior becomes a miniature *landscape* where photographs, paintings, artifacts, furniture, and people create both a physical and symbolic world. As Sharon Zukin says, *landscape* is "at once a panorama, a composition, a palimpsest, a microcosm."[9] To understand the semiotics of the interior, it is important to think of this space as a *landscape* that emits a complicated set of cultural and social signs.

The interior extravaganzas of the family films are rooted in landscapes of fear and anxiety. Although fear is not a new phenomena, contemporary transformations linked to globalization, geographic mobility, the virtual takeover of the public realm, the shift to flexible accumulation, the increasing gap between the rich and the poor, and the rise of information technologies have increased the "fear factor." This is evident in the increase in public surveillance, housing security technologies, and car-locking systems. Making a distinction between modern fear and postmodern fear, Nan Ellin suggests that whereas the former led to an understanding of cause and effect in order to ensure a safe future, postmodern fear has "incited a series of closely related and overlapping responses including retribalization, nostalgia, escapism, and spiritual (re)turn."[10] Likewise, the movement of architecture in the new family films is a combination of scenic interiorization through design, combined with neotraditionalist nostalgia for familial values. Inside these projected "dreamhouses," we see the performance of tradition, religious and cultural rituals, romance, and familial devotion. When familial rituals do not play a substantial role, as in films like *Dil To Pagal Hai* (The Heart Is Crazy, 1997) and *Dil Chahata Hai* (The Heart Desires, 2002), we are made to transcend all specificity of place and culture, resulting in a form that seeks to escape both tradition and location. The narratives move seamlessly between national and global locations, while retaining a typically urban feel. Urban spaces are created as spaces of consumption and desire with affluent global families as reference points. The family is the link that binds national and global space and provides access to new notions of lifestyle. The family is also the organizer of a detailed practice of rituals around marriage. In the context of new insecurities and anxieties created by globalization, the family is seen as the marker of cultural stability and ritual, a space where the idea of "Indianness" is constantly played out.[11]

Writer Gita Mehta, commenting on the upheavals unleashed by globalization, says "as the pace of India's exchanges with the outside world accelerates, there is a growing demand both inside India and abroad for some comprehensible definition of what India actually is." This search for "Indianness" and also the desire to be part of the global landscape shapes the production of popular culture in unprecedented ways today. Cultural difference is seen as an essential marker of identity, something that needs to be asserted and "redeemed in a higher global unity." This duality embodies a desire for access to a lifestyle mythology that is seen as global while at the same time also assuaging anxieties about this access through a constant reassertion of "Indianness."[12] The cinematic form mediates this anxiety through a retreat away from the specificity of urban space, particularly Bombay, into an architectural world of design where the "Indianness" of tradition and modernity are played out. Cinema mobilizes the fantasy of a lifestyle unblemished by the chaos and poverty that exists all around. Cinema is perhaps the medium that can best enable the harmony that has historically been possible in some parts of the Western world. Carefully constructed, abiding by international standards of design and fashion, these cinematic interiors become the display window for an urban lifestyle myth that can never fully exist in the physical spaces of the city. Interior design becomes the map for the charting out of a spatial unconscious that desires an urban dreamworld of contemporary consumption.

Art Direction and the New Political Economy of Design

The spectacular retreat into interior spaces as a response to social and economic crisis was first witnessed in the lavish set design strategies of the Hollywood musicals. For spectators who were tired of the hardships of the Depression years, the musical offered an escape route, a journey into fantasyland, where the play of romance, comedy, music, and dancing would inhabit the architectural extravaganza of imaginary worlds. The arresting decors, the geometric organization of dancers on stairs spiralling skyward, moving stages, and fancy costumes and rooms, were all created to dazzle the spectator's eye. The set design for this period became so well known, specialized, and distinctive that it acquired a name—the "Big White Set."[13] Size and whiteness came to symbolize class and wealth. Donald Albrecht notes the importance of dazzling light in the representation of luxury. "While as a visual device, large quantities of lighting added to the beauty of film sets, they also suggested the abundance and the luxurious sheen of the high life. Light heightened virtually every element of décor in movie nightclubs, making objects highly reflective, and stressing smooth surface over texture and mass."[14]

The musical not only reveled in lavish sets but also explored the texture of the sets through dancing bodies that moved, traveled and inhabited space: "Tapping feet, swinging arms, jumping and bending, they inhabit space with greater intensity than mere talkers and walkers. Dancers endow hotel rooms and piazzas with their rhythms and postures; the high style of the hotel rooms and the piazzas is a congenial setting for the high style of dance and the types of narrative it engenders, stories in which identity is a function of dance."[15] This relationship of the body to space as mediated through dance is important for our understanding of spatial exploration. The interior panorama of the Bombay family films is also in many ways explored through song and dance sequences that navigate and explore the spectacular power of architectural splendor and design. Like the "Big White Set" of the Hollywood musicals, the designed interior of the family film genre moves away from built urban space through a mise-en-scène that seeks to enchant.

The production of the panoramic interior is not new to Bombay cinema. The grand staircase or the frontal glance at a large living room was common to many films. Issues of class and power were linked to the use of these spaces. The narratives were also punctuated with spaces representing the less privileged. There is a clear distinction, however, between the panoramic vision of earlier films and the ones that have emerged in the 1990s. Today, the production of the interior has acquired a systematic approach enabled by the coming together of art directors, the advertising world, fashion designers, and the film industry. Although this sort of relationship has been prevalent in Hollywood for years, in India the advertising world was never directly linked to the film industry. Today art directors draw from the work of well-known interior designers to create interior spaces where the mise-en-scène is important for the popularization and marketing of lifestyle cultures. Much of this is also inspired by an expanding magazine culture and print advertising where the predominance of the home and other interior spaces seems to have systematically erased outside space.

One of the major shifts in the whole area of art direction in the Bombay film industry has been the entry of professionally trained interior designers, who are now creating sets for the most expensive films. Sharmishtha Roy, one of the highest-paid art directors in the industry, is a trained interior designer who first worked in the advertising world. Branded as an upmarket art designer because of her lavish sets, Roy is fairly reflexive about her role in the industry. She refers to her sets as "aspirational" because they try to emulate Western culture in terms of both design and lifestyle. In her own work, Roy recognizes that she is recreating a lifestyle that is not "Indian."[16]

Location shooting was actually privileged over studio sets in the early years of cinema. The arrival of sound changed the dynamic, as sets seemed to provide greater quality control over both sound and light. By the 1950s shooting on sets became the norm, even though some outdoor scenes were also incorporated. The arrival of color rekindled the desire for locations, as filmmakers wanted to explore the attractiveness and exotica of real locations in color.[17] From the 1960s to the mid-1980s, locations became the norm as Bombay became a city that was explored by filmmakers. From the railway tracks to the docks, train stations to *chawls,* location shooting helped to bring city spaces alive. The retreat toward carefully designed sets started in the 1990s with the new family films. Roy says this heavy reliance became necessary because of the "virtual" nature of the set, which is impossible to replicate on location. Most films have about six to eight sets, but the big family films can sometimes have almost eighteen sets. Art directors in the past, says Roy, were only asked to prepare a set with certain props that were brought in from specific rental companies that the film industry patronized. Today, Roy insists on a decoration budget, which many of the new art directors see as necessary to create a designer aesthetic that will counter what they perceive to be the flashy aesthetic of the 1960s and 1970s.[18] Instead of regular props, Roy now rents furniture and other accessories, including small decorative items from well-known home furnishing shops.

The emergence of a new global market for Hindi cinema has also played a significant role in the construction of the designed interior. The overseas market of the Indian diaspora is today the largest distribution territory for the film industry.[19] The success of the film *Hum Apke Hain Kaun* (Who Am I to You?, 1994) revealed the importance of the Indian diaspora when a quarter of the total revenue generated by the film was brought in from the overseas market.[20] The narrative place of the diasporic family, both as a reference point for a second-generation south Asian film public in the West and as a new category in Bombay cinema is important. The movement between the diaspora and the industry has reoriented both the spatial and temporal coordinates of the Bombay film through a *transformation of cinema itself*. In fact, the rise of a sanitized aesthetic has become associated with directors who are extremely popular with the Indian diaspora. These directors were born in the industry (sons of film directors and producers), studied abroad, and imbibed a global lifestyle. The release and success of the film *Kuch Kuch Hota Hai* (*KKHH*) (Something Is Happening, 1999), directed by Karan Johar, sharply foregrounded the importance of international travel, lifestyle, and television in the construction of the interior.

Kuch Kuch Hota Hai: Comic Culture and the Performance of Popular Fantasy

KKHH opens with Tina's (Rani Mukherji) funeral, as her husband, Rahul (Shahrukh Khan), stands by the pyre. Memories of his wife, who died soon after childbirth, flash past as he stares at the flames. In one of the flashes, Tina asks Rahul to name their daughter Anjali, the reason for which will soon be revealed in the film. Tina leaves a set of letters with her mother-in-law (Farida Jalal) for her daughter, which she is supposed to read on her eighth birthday. In the letters, Tina describes her college life with Rahul and Anjali (Kajol). The letters reveal that Anjali and Rahul were best friends until the former realizes that she is in love with Rahul. Rahul's involvement with Tina proves to be devastating for Anjali, who suddenly packs her bags one day and leaves to be with her mother. Since that day Rahul and Anjali have never met. Tina is convinced that Rahul and Anjali loved each other and requests her daughter to ensure that the two meet again. The story of college life in the letter is recounted through a long flashback. The subsequent hunt for Anjali and the ensuing romance between Rahul and Anjali forms the second half of the narrative. The movement from college life to the present is mounted through lavish sets—school grounds, classrooms, auditoriums, children's camps, home interiors of all the characters, and hotel lobbies. Barring one shot of the Gateway of India, right at the beginning of the film with a caption saying, "Bombay 8 years later," we have absolutely no reason to believe in the existence of any specific location. Instead, a dazzling display of interiors and natural landscape is deployed to depict teen life, adult romance, and marriage rituals.

Spectators are introduced to Rahul and Anjali's friendship first at a basketball court. The movement of the ball, the energy of the two players, and the rise and fall of the ball through the basket, provides the camera with a range of angles that can help to create the sense of an expansive court. One

Figure 12.1. Publicity image for Karan Johar's *Kuch Kuch Hota Hai* (Something Is Happening), 1999. Photo courtesy of Ramgopal Varma's Factory and Dharma Productions.

side of the court wall has colorful graffiti—very similar to what we see in New York and in many of the productions in the genre of family films. *KKHH* uses the basketball court inventively to create the ambience for the display of teen fashion. All around the indoor stadium are brand names on billboards or cloth banners. Cars, sportswear, shoes, and the like are all advertised through this sequence. Anjali is wearing a DKNY shirt. The court game is quickly followed by a song, which begins outdoors and moves back to the indoor court, to Goa and back. As the two protagonists change costumes, we are provided with a range of teen sports and casualwear attire. The outdoor shots are landscaped in front of buildings that stand out as generic architectural ensembles. Immediately after the song we are introduced to the girls' dorm—a color-coordinated large space with luxury beds, wall paintings, shelves with decorative items, Venetian blinds, and large windows. Several pillars add to the depth in the room with the floor space split into two or three levels.

Rahul's home, navigated several times in the first part of the film, is a largely modern interior. The living room is first introduced with Rahul's mother trying to sing the "Gayatri mantra" with a group of women friends. Suddenly the granddaughter Anjali arrives, and the camera pulls out into a circular tracking shot, capturing the expanse of the room. Black stone pillars and a staircase dissect the middle of the room. What is striking here is the

410

large window in the far corner, which simulates a skyline that is not available in any Indian city, let alone Bombay. The simulated skyline is a slightly faded image of neogothic architecture displayed through the window. Roy said the gothic form was simulated because the characters were supposedly representing people from South Bombay.[21] In a sense, the simulation expressed a nostalgic desire for an upper-class experience of south Bombay that many in the city see as having declined. This desire to simulate the skyline from the window, providing an interior/exterior connection that is not available physically and yet creates imagined possibilities of visual travel, makes the new interior and window an appropriate metaphor for the politics of public erasure. The simulated skyline emerges again but in a slightly different form, a little later in the film. Simulation ensures that the physical topography of public space does not impinge on the design aesthetics of the interior.

The college interior is one of the most striking images of *Kuch Kuch Hota Hai*. We see a corridor that has a sparkling black-and-white floor reminiscent of teen television shows in the United States. One corner of the set has a DJ with his equipment. A bright yellow payphone, a Pepsi machine, and colorful lockers are also placed in the corridor. Karan Johar's own vision of the school space was highly influenced by American popular culture:

> I used to love Archie comics. If you see *Kuch Kuch Hota Hai*, its really that. Its Riverdale High with all the colors for no reason. When I used to see Beverly Hills 90210 and I liked those corridors and those lockers. None of that exists in Indian colleges. Our colleges look like public bathrooms, excuse my saying so. I was twenty five or twenty six and I was influenced by things I saw and things I read about, and basically I was a huge Archie fan. If you see *KKHH*, Shahrukh plays Archie, Rani Mukherji plays Veronica, and Kajol played Bettie. It was exactly that. And the principal looked like Weatherbee, and Mrs. Grundee was Archana Puran Singh.[22]

Roy recalls Johar's brief "give me the classroom of Archie's Riverdale High and the locker room corridor of *Beverly Hills 90210*."[23] In the classroom where all the protagonists meet we are offered a visual array of color, sleek furniture, and teen fashion donned by all the students. The back wall has a huge painting of Shakespeare, and on the left we see what looks like a highly detailed Renaissance painting. The reproduction of the architectural space of comic worlds and television shows immediately draws attention to the role of the film set in the creation of imaginary mental worlds. Cable television's circulation in the past ten years in India, with U.S. shows and MTV programming has only added to the proliferation of international signs.

Kuch Kuch evokes a series of spatial coordinates that link up with representations from comic books, international designer manuals, television advertising, and Hollywood teen films. The public space of the city is completely erased, as in many of the family films where designer wear, brand names, and product placement add to the panoramic interior. In his *Society of the Spectacle*, Guy Debord had defined *spectacle* as "capital accumulated to the point where it becomes an image."[24] Reversing this original thesis, Hal Foster suggests that contemporary spectacle needs to be seen "as an image accumulated to the point where it becomes capital." In the new world of signs, speed, and surface, design forms circulate to entice and affect the urban dwellers' gaze of distraction. The inflation or all-pervasive power of design has increased in the era of digitization and television's expanding presence. Design techniques lie at the heart of both production and consumption. The constant mediation of the commodity through design strategies makes the category and role of design central to our understanding of the signage that defines contemporary urban landscapes. Perhaps as Hal Foster suggests, we now need to speak of a "political economy of design."[25]

In the second half of the film, *Kuch Kuch* creates another order of experience. All the characters are older. They look and dress differently and thus inhabit different kinds of homes and spaces. Whereas Rahul's house displays a semimodernist aesthetic, Anjali's house is constructed as the generic Hindi film set—a palatial house with a grand staircase dissecting the middle of the living room. Chandeliers, carpet on the stairs, traditional costumes, and Rajputana architecture saturate the mise-en-scène when Kajol is introduced in this space. Gold brocades, jewelry, and music add to the opulence of the interior. This part of the film reminds us of *Hum Apke Hain Kaun*, in that *Kuch Kuch* displays the range of architecture that can help the spectator negotiate the complicated experience of tradition and modernity. So while the first half of the film revels in the performance of high consumption and simulated spaces of modernity, the adult romance of the two protagonists in the second half is reinvested with an older narrative of Hindi cinema. Here the freewheeling playfulness of youth is replaced by the play of familial values, tradition, and ritual. Again architectural texture evokes a longing for what is seen as lost.

The romance between Rahul and Anjali, rekindled after many years, is abruptly halted because of Anjali's engagement and impending marriage to Aman (played by Salman Khan). Anjali's withdrawl from Rahul results from a sense of duty; only Aman can really make the decision to withdraw and leave the road open for Rahul and Anjali's marriage. The climax of the film is situated in the palatial interior of Anjali's house. The staircase, the railings, and the columns are used to foreground and add depth to this space. Rahul meets with Anjali in her room, which is reminiscent of a miniature painting, while Rajput architecture expresses nostalgia for an imagined classicism.[26] The only difference here is that Rahul is wearing a suit. Nothing else in the room conveys the texture of the present. This could easily be a historical image. Like a snapshot, the mise-en-scène conveys yearnings and desires that are born out of an anxiety. The imaginary construction of a past through this sequence is a form of architectural withdrawal and nostalgic return to the idea of a "pristine past" that is uncontaminated by the contemporary speed of change.

Aman's final withdrawal and Rahul and Anjali's marriage is saturated in wealth, rituals, traditional lamps, flowers, and marriage costumes. The marriage is the climax of the film, where duty has been restored and romance made possible in the world of familial loyalty and obligations. The fact that Anjali is always dressed in a sari in the second half of the film as opposed to the Western clothes in the first half, only adds to the point I am trying to make. Romance and the incursion into global modernity must necessarily recognize the specificity of the traditional which is performed as a visual marker of "Indianness." This complicated relationship to "Indianness" not only adds to the storytelling strategy of the film, but also enables the spectacular performance of the climax in interiors that express wealth and tradition. Through the exploration of architectural interiors, *Kuch Kuch* expresses both the desire and the anxiety that marks the cultural politics of globalization today. In its virtual spaces, we see the powerful play of the commodity as a simulated sign where both nostalgia for an older order of architecture and the desire for the hypermodern get structured around a tale of love, grief, and final reunion.

The saturation of signs in the form of designer clothing, interior design, and commodities in the family films creates a world that mimics the experience we have in shopping malls. The shopper walking through the mall, moving up and down the escalators is dazzled by the commercial, aesthetic, and architectural splendor of interior spaces. Given the physical topography of urban space in south Asia, particularly Bombay, the desire for a seamless, commodified world can perhaps be made possible *only* through simulation. Television's role in the production of other spaces and worlds creates the desire, but the physical space of cities stands in contradiction to that desire. Like the experience of the shopping mall, cinematic spectatorship relies on a perceptual displacement of external reality, offering instead a "controlled, commodified, and pleasurable substitution."²⁷ Cinema's ability to displace external reality creates the possibility for imaginary worlds, which the new family genre taps into in the current context of urban transformation after globalization. *The panoramic interior expresses a crisis of belonging, fear of the street, and the desire for the good life—all at once.* In this architectural spectacle of light space, the absence of dark space is significant. The shadows of the uncanny, the fear of the street corner, the overwhelming crowd, the chaos of the marketplace, the violence in the street, and the city of strangers remain just outside, threatening to invade but prevented by the new architectural and design aesthetics of the panoramic interior.

THE DARK SPACE OF THE GANGSTER CITY

The city of spectacle can exist only by obliterating the city of *ruin* and darkness. However, the dark shadows of the other city always loom large, threatening to overwhelm the space of spectacle. As the drama of global consumption unfolds in a city where the majority continues to live in very difficult conditions, cinema provides a counternarrative to the designed interior city by drawing on the mythology of the Bombay underworld. These tales of despair and urban degradation embody a significant moment not only in the history of cinema but also in the history of Bombay.

Bombay's underworld history has produced many well-known gangsters, some of whom have been represented as heroic outlaw figures in films. The more current production of gangster films addresses the accelerated activity of the underworld from the mid-1980s onward (Vidhu Vinod Chopra's *Parinda*, 1989; Ramgopal Varma's *Satya*, 1998, *Company*, 2002). Although journalists have written about the underworld, the underworld's linguistic, cultural, and performative styles have been vividly captured in film. There are two reasons for this. First, gang life and the gangster's world have been classic ingredients for a thriller genre and noir cinema. Second, the close connection between the underworld and the film industry has been solidified and consolidated in the past fifteen to twenty years. Journalist Suketu Mehta, for instance, speaks about this symbiotic relationship as a system of signs that moves from the underworld to the film industry and vice versa: "There is a curious symbiosis between the underworld and the movies. The Hindi filmmakers are fascinated by the lives of the gangsters, and draw upon them for material. The gangsters, from the shooter on the ground to the don-in-exile at the top, watch Hindi movies keenly, and model themselves—their dialogue, the way they carry themselves—on their screen equivalents."[28] This mutual fascination and referencing has also found expression in the material connection of finances. The underworld's ties to the film industry functions largely through a culture of secrecy that makes it difficult to determine the extent of its hold over the industry. Throughout the past decade, however, this secret cover has been ripped away by bloody events, controversies, and the arrests of well-known producers and actors in police raids.[29]

What makes the new gangster films significant is their desire to present the main protagonists as people who belong to the underworld. All the films deploy the classic features of the gangster genre to explore issues of masculinity and the idea of a new urban community. Vidhu Vinod Chopra's *Parinda* is an early response to the gangland experience. Ramgopal Varma's *Satya* and *Company* present a distinct shift in the journey of the gangster. Although the films negotiate the city through emotional and spatial registers that mark each one as different, together they provide a glimpse into the hidden recesses of the city. Bombay becomes a gangland marked by violence, terror, claustrophobia, and disenchantment.

THE TOPOGRAPHY OF THE GANGSTER FORM
AND THE BOMBAY UNDERWORLD

Historically, the gangster film as a subgenre of crime films is of particular interest in the context of the urban because these films present us with an alternative topography, an alternative community, and an alternative urban consciousness. Fran Mason sees the gangster as a seminal figure "in the history of twentieth century culture, forming the focus for a range of tensions that have dominated the discourses of industrialized society." These tensions range from an exploration of tradition and modernity to a politics of urban space to the individual's role and struggle in the modern world.[30] The street is usually the primary site of narrative action in gangster films, because it symbolizes freedom from home and enables constant movement and liberation from the claustrophobia of restricted and controlled urban space. The street evokes a sense of power when gangs control it. The control of space is also an expression of masculinity as gangsters fluidly move through space, traversing treacherous parts of the city, often gambling and leisure joints, both at night and in the day. Gangster films are also about transgressing spatial boundaries and social hierarchies.

The "travelogue aspect" of gangster films comes from a number of important features. The underworld is a space of fascination because it gives the outsider access to a world that is felt and seen at the level of the street but whose inner workings are not understood. The performative gestures of the street and a tough demeanor are recognizable and appealing for audiences. The paraphernalia that accompanies the mise-en-scène of a gangster film—guns, cars, spectacular action, city spaces—captures the visible and material seduction of the underworld. Yet these are only surface features of the genre. At a deeper level the genre reveals the contradictions of urban life in ways that go beyond a rational exposition. Jack Shaodian suggests that in the gangster genre

> meanings emerge whether deliberately or not about the nature of the society and the kind of individual it creates. By definition, the genre must shed light on either the society or the outcasts who oppose it, and by definition the gangster is outside, or anti, the legitimate social order. The gangster/crime film is therefore a way of gaining a perspective on society by creating worlds and figures that are outside it. Its basic situation holds that distinction, and the meanings it continues to produce rest on that distinction. (In the thirties, the distinction is clear cut, unquestionable, visible. As the genre evolves, it becomes less so. As a culture becomes more complex, so do its products.)[31]

Despite differences and variations, the core configuration of the gangster genre is easy to see—an urban backdrop, the play of criminality through a community of men, a performative masculinity, the impossibility of romance, the crisis of the family, and the experience of everyday fear and terror. We recognize the visual codes of the gangster film easily given its wide international circulation in the past seventy years.

Organized crime operating through gangs engaged in smuggling, prostitution, extortion, land grabbing, contract killing and corporate crime emerged in Bombay in the 1960s. Bombay, with its commercial enterprises and the prolific film industry, has been the center of underworld operations. Gangs that were initially involved in bootlegging soon expanded their operations to gold smuggling, gambling, extortion, drug peddling, and contract killing. In the 1980s the underworld expanded its base, intensifying its activities with the rise of the gangster Dawood Ibrahim. The extortion racket became a much bigger phenomenon, encompassing all walks of life—from the hawker in the street to businessmen, movie stars, and film producers. Dawood fled to Dubai in the mid 1980s when the police cracked down on the mob after a series of highly publicized killings, but he continued to operate in Bombay through his gang (D Company). Under Dawood, the underworld's connections with the film industry expanded through financial networks and extortion threats. The underworld became a dreaded presence after the Bombay bomb blasts of 1993.[32] Suspected of masterminding the blasts as retaliation for both the demolition of the Babri Mosque by Hindu nationalists and the subsequent pogroms against Muslims in Bombay, Dawood became a household name in the city. The blasts changed Dawood's status from a mob leader to that of an international terrorist because of his suspected connections with both the Persian Gulf and Pakistan.[33]

Access to this culture of the underworld comes to us primarily through cinema. In the gangster films overlapping themes of masculinity and brotherhood, identity and aspiration are played out as a rich performance where excess in every way becomes the driving force of the narratives. The cinematic mise-en-scène and narrative world of these films provide us with clues and myths that link social space with cinematic space. This exchange is not a simple transfer of a "realistic" world but rather a process that expresses *crisis* through a narrative of urban disintegration. It is important therefore to briefly negotiate Bombay's contemporary history, which in the following section is a narrative of urban crisis. Only through this historical contextualization is it possible to make sense of the zones of indeterminacy within which the gangster myth mobilizes its central theme of a Bombay lost in the present performance of violence. As I argue, the genre of gangster films taps into the anxiety, confusion, despair, and fear emerging in city life in the 1980s and 1990s.

BANALITY AND THE CRISIS OF EVERYDAY LIFE

The spatial crisis of Bombay, as I have already indicated, is not new. The acceleration of the crisis linked to criminal activity, however, is more recent. Both journalists and academics have traced the rise in criminal activity to the decline of Bombay's textile mills, which had once provided employment to almost two-thirds of the city's industrial workers.[34] The decline was accelerated by a strike in 1982–83 that lasted for almost eighteen months.[35] The textile strike has been the subject of much debate.[36] Journalistic accounts of the time and rumors about the union leadership's role continue to circulate even twenty years after the strike. Stories of adventurism, backroom deals, and the self-interest of the union leadership abound. There is little dispute, however, that the strike gave rise to an entirely new situation of despair for many workers in the city. In retrospect, the textile strike had all the makings of a "suicidal death wish." Driven by their circumstances but unable to see what they were up against, ordinary workers were caught in a "morass of impotence vis-à-vis the world."[37] While some saw the vast multitude of unemployed men as the reason for an increase in crime, others saw an element of nihilism and self-destruction emerging from workers' inability to sustain the force of the strike. For most workers, in the end, the defeat was a personal tragedy.

The textile strike and its aftermath have functioned as a turning point for describing the transformation of Bombay from a manufacturing city to a global city with an expanding service economy. The dream to change the city into a financial center like Singapore or Hong Kong was often expressed in newspapers even as retrenched workers continued to battle for survival in the city. The despair of the workers has inspired urban poetry, short stories, and even films.[38] The factory sites and the residential areas of the workers in the poststrike period have been depicted as spaces where the pressure of local time, global imaginaries (through television), and spatial claustrophobia collide to create a new urban landscape.[39]

Thomas Blom Hansen provides an exploration of Bombay's heartland in the aftermath of the textile strike. Hansen's vivid exploration of central Bombay reveals how working-class despair became evident in the spatial topography of the neighborhood. Most of its adult population was once employed in the textile mills. Today, central Bombay is known as an area of crime, prostitution, and gang wars. The loss of a cultural and moral fiber is spatially visible, particularly in the Muslim *mohalla* (neighborhood). Extra floors have been added to preexisting buildings, and rooftop workshops have been added to high-rise buildings, creating both noise and air pollution. The presence of hawkers and pavement dwellers have only added to the congested streets. The visible impact of this spatial density is overwhelming. This is the urban landscape of spatial disenchantment where despair shapes architectural texture and density. In addition, large-scale migration to the Persian Gulf from the late 1970s has led to the emergence of many travel agencies and subcontractors for larger agencies that handle employment and visa facilities. Fierce competition to relocate to the Gulf in order to earn more money than was possible at home gave rise to groups of men who took bribes to ensure a trip to the Middle East. Hansen suggests that the gradual proliferation of money through circuits of illegality created an extremely volatile situation, with the Gulf providing an imaginary space for upward mobility and a better life.[40]

Paralleling the spatial decline of the city is the increasing presence of the Hindu nationalist Shiv Sena Party. Responsible for the renaming of Bombay to Mumbai, the Shiv Sena has been active in many political, economic, and cultural zones of the city in the past three decades. Its support base is largely unemployed youth, industrial workers, and office employees, along with some petty gangsters. The organization has long had a habitual relationship to violence, often using emotional themes for its mobilization strategy. Initially presenting a strong regional (Marathi) identity with which the "outsiders" of the city were attacked (particularly south Indians), the party later reinvented itself as a Hindu organization in the mid-1980s.[41] Driven primarily by a culture of brotherhood, self-assertion, and street action, the Shiv Sena has tried to provide a coherent utopian vision to the restlessness and frustrations of unemployed urban youth. It has also been involved in an elaborate extortion racket demanding protection fees from builders, exporters, smugglers, and drug pushers. The organization also promotes a *dada* (hood) culture that is created through its work with neighborhood associations of men (*mitramandals*).

The 1993 bomb blast led to the slaughter of hundreds of Muslims by crowds that included neighbors and former friends. The events of 1992–93 brought into sharp focus the misplaced myth of cosmopolitanism identified with Bombay. As Hindu and Muslim communities became polarized, Muslim isolation, gang wars, and urban decay marked the city after the riots. The Muslim community's negotiation of identity in the aftermath of the riots, says Hansen, has taken two directions—one of internal purification through withdrawal from dependence on the larger society and a second strategy of plebeian assertion through small business, quick-fix jobs, and strongman tactics whereby men can accrue money within a short period of time. He explains that the emergence of the local street *dada* (hood) in these Muslim neighborhoods needs to be understood in this context of plebeian assertion: "The local *dadas* provide effective role models and often material access to signs of the good life displayed in the maze of commercials and TV serials pumped out around the clock by enterprising cable operators here and in other parts of the city. These signifiers range from cellular phones, Maruti gypsy jeeps, air conditioning, visits to bars and the nearby Kamathipura red light district, and, not least, a measure of respect and recognition in the local hierarchies.[42] The combination of cars, cable television, cell phones, and air conditioners points to the new landscape of consumption, a nonrational landscape where the dreams of the "good life" circulate via television within the ruins of modernity. Furthermore, the prevalence of smuggling, drug peddling, and a thriving extortion racket provides a strong identity for many unemployed men.

The rise of gangsters and gangster mythology of the contemporary period needs to be located against this spatial backdrop. Dawood Ibrahim grew up in the central Bombay neighborhood where he became known as a courageous mystical hero. Given the polarization between the two communities, Dawood, even in his absence, is seen as a *dada* who will protect the people during a crisis. The rise of *dada* (hood) culture in the Muslim *mohalla*, according to Hansen, has a striking resemblance to the *dada* culture generated by the Shiv Sena in other neighborhoods. The similarity exists because of the social environment that makes male honor, action, and violence important vehicles for the construction of a radical new urban community.[43]

The brief summary of contemporary events in Bombay that I have traced is not to suggest a simple link between the textile strike and the rise of criminal activity, but to specifically understand the role of spatial density in the construction of new identities. The poststrike city led to an amorphous situation where a self-destructive nihilism became the dominant mood for many who lost their jobs. Sandeep Pendse notes that an "obscure anger" plagued the workers employed in the informal sector after the mills closed down, as they battled shrinking space, accelerated work time, and the constant presence of a crowd. The overcrowding of *chawls* by multiple families saw a gradual destruction of privacy and ordinary conversation, making it difficult to have a personal world. Added to this is the density of construction, which artificially encloses space in the city. "There is a constant, though at most times well hidden and perhaps even unrealized fear that the "closed-up" space may conceal a danger or a death trap."[44] Endless struggle and yet no dream of a better future—this is the ultimate counterpart to the "Bombay dream." Clearly the poststrike city of spatial disenchantment revealed how repetition of existence and loss of control over personal time led to a "banality" of the everyday.

Banality, it has been argued is "time off its hinges—no longer passing through the present in a neat linear succession that places the past behind and the future always out in front."[45] In this inner world of banality, sociological readings are impossible, the past loses its connection to the present, and random events shape the identity of particular sections of the urban crowd. When the banality of everyday life reaches a psychological breaking point, then different kinds of performative drives are unleashed. The emergence of criminality and gang activity needs to be located within a complex spatial map where a series of random events both spectacular and routine have led to the assertion of new identities. The gangland experience needs to be seen as an excessive overflow of the banal that challenges the repetition of daily existence through the construction of a new community.

420

The Underworld in the Urban Delirium

The Bombay underworld today can be understood as a new community of men signified by the use of the term *Bhai* (brother) to refer to members of the gang. The fee paid to assassins for their contract killings is called *Supari* and the language spoken by the gang is Bambayya.[46] Although gang activity includes both Muslims and Hindus, the popular perception is that gangs are overwhelmingly Muslim. This perception is largely due to Dawood Ibrahim's stature as the main figure in the underworld and also because of his connections with the Persian Gulf and Pakistan. Dawood's suspected role in the 1993 bomb blasts linked the underworld to international terrorism, thus furthering the myth of the underworld as predominantly Muslim. After the 1993 explosions, popular urban mythology recounts a split between Chota Rajan (a Hindu gangster) and Dawood, primarily on religious grounds. This split has acquired an enormous mythology in urban retellings of gang activity. Given the culture of fear and secrecy surrounding gangs, particularly after the much-publicized killings of well-known industrialists and film producers, an air of caution is deployed when gang mythology is narrated in film. This caution is evident in the two best-known gangster films (*Satya*, 1998 and *Company*, 2002) where the references are oblique rather than direct, even though popular perception receives the films as narratives based on Dawood Ibrahim's story.

The film industry is responding to Bombay's contemporary urban climate, where criminal activity has erupted as nodes of violence within the city. The sense of a city experiencing disorder and crisis dominates narratives of contemporary Bombay in both journalistic discourse and popular perceptions of the city. There are many variations in this narrative. For instance, one variation portrays the loss of Bombay's so-called cosmopolitan imagination after the riots of 1992–93 when the city of "citizens" turned into a city of strangers. Another narrative deploys the underworld to chart the city's overall decline, degradation, decay, and crisis. A third narrative focuses overwhelmingly on the city's overcrowding and traffic. In the multiplicity of narratives that evoke the decline of India's premier city, it is difficult to trace any single one that can explain the exact nature of the contemporary crisis. *Crisis* is then both an intense experience as well as a metaphor for the contemporary cityscape. For the film industry the experience of crisis can only be rendered to their audiences through narratives of despair. The nature of this expression has to negotiate the idea of a "strategic realism," where a film's relationship to contemporary events is referred to, but never fully explained. The accelerated activity of the Bombay underworld is thus picked up as the thematic concern, which in turn becomes the vehicle through which the idea of disorder and civic crisis can be expressed. Anurag Kashyap, the scriptwriter of *Satya*, claimed that central to his scriptwriting strategy was the exploration of urban space. The events of the underworld were mythologized to create unforgettable characters in *Satya*. Only the underworld could provide the possibility of such brutal depictions of city life. Kashyap's storytelling strategy was based on research on specific events without the trappings of a sociological analysis. Kashyap claimed that he never wants to take a moral position or provide an analytical structure to his stories. On the contrary, inhabiting the experience of Bombay's disorder was more important than charting the causal reasons for it.[47]

As a force, the Bombay underworld provides the city with an urban legend that links parts of the city to gang activity. Because the extortion of money from shopkeepers is a routine affair that plays out the territorial function of gangs on an everyday basis, the culture of the underworld is seen as ubiquitous and all-encompassing. The mythology of the underworld that is reproduced in the cinema is then a combination of "real" events, a contemporary sensibility about Bombay's spatial crisis, and myth making. These connections are crucial to my argument that film is an archive of the city, because crime evades the gaze of the sociologist unless it can be causally explained. The film industry on the other hand, creates an experiential realm of disorder by drawing on what I would call an urban delirium about the underworld. This delirium is a combination of informal knowledge, direct contact, rumor, and journalistic discourse that provides the city with a vibrant mythology of the underworld. The production of contemporary gangster films draws its thematic force from this delirium.

In the hub and movement of traffic, drivers, and passengers circulates an everyday knowledge of crime in the city. Some of this is reported in the press, but much information is transmitted only within the domain of conversations. When people arrive for work from different parts of the city, they bring stories of violence in their neighborhoods. This informally circulated news is combined with the headlines from all the newspapers—a hyperbolic narration of gang violence in the city. Whether by *Midday*, by the *Afternoon Dispatch*, or by the regional press, the reporting on the city has substantial coverage of the underworld.[48] In fact, reports on "encounter killings" and extortions have become a regular news item. Commerce in the city must necessarily reckon with the force of the underworld, either through negotiated space and activity or through monetary payoffs to earn the safety of individuals. Stories of death threats if the money is not provided on time circulate as rumor, providing the city with a hidden but violent narrative. In this daily routine of the city, we see the making of an urban delirium—a sophisticated combination of print, sound, speech, and image.

Director Ramgopal Varma amply demonstrates the transaction between circulating knowledge and film narrative. In an interview, Varma claimed that the making of *Satya* (one of the most successful gangster films of recent times) was "a chance occurrence. I was reading these reports on the underworld, and that started off a train of thoughts in my mind. I wondered about these people—who they were, what they did between killings, whether they suffered from viral flu. They are obviously human beings with a sense of commitment. All these things never occur to you otherwise. You think they are evil people who come from the dark, do their job, and go back into the dark again."[49] Varma wanted to capture the texture of life that formed the gangster's world in between killings. There is a desire here for detail, for an entry into the gangster's psyche. His interest in the lapse between killings is also important because it draws attention to the everyday texture of the gangster's world. Varma's own relationship to the city of Bombay is that of an outsider who sees the deplorable living conditions and claustrophobic overcrowding that are visible everywhere as central to Bombay's spatial identity. In this urban landscape, he wonders about the strategies people adopt to acquire private lives, forms of intimacy, desire, and aspirations. Spatial claustrophobia combined with deprivation creates psychological worlds that are difficult to comprehend. Varma sees the gangster myth as something that emerges from this psychological urban world.[50]

In the gangster films, shooting is done in real locations—alleys, claustrophobic tenements, traffic, hawkers, and the docks are all explored. The gang's places of meeting and operation sometimes look like abandoned factory sites, sometimes like half-constructed buildings. Chase sequences are deployed to navigate the density of the city's public spaces. Instead of the sanitized aesthetics and the bright lights that saturate the mise-en-scène of the domestic interiors of the family films, low-key photography reminiscent of film noir is used in the gangster films to enhance the spatial topography of dread, decay, and death. One of the principal features of noir is its ability to destroy urban spectacle. By using low-key photography to evoke shadowy and mysterious spaces, the texture of the city is given a twist directly in opposition to the phantasmagoria of aerial photography so commonly used in tourism and travelogue films. Urban display is countered by dark shadows, panoramic visions by fragmented shots, and the glitter of daylight by the darkness of the night. There is little doubt that the gangster genre navigates the city of spatial disenchantment like no other existing form in Bombay cinema today. The social space of the city emerges not as an authentic world to be represented "realistically," but through a formal play with mood, mise-en-scène, characterization, and plot.

THE WASTELAND OF SATYA

Ramgopal Varma's *Satya* (Truth), released in 1998, tells the story of Satya, a recent migrant into the city of Bombay who slowly becomes part of an accelerated flow of sporadic and random events that make him join the underworld. *Satya* retains an existential relationship to all the characters: their location within the city is neither causally nor sociologically explained. The city's wasteland and urban detritus saturates the mise-en-scène of the film almost like a space that forms the heart of the city, not its periphery. Within this urban decay and dereliction, gangsters embark on a logic of survival. As Bombay becomes a gangland, the desire for home, domesticity, and peace continues to elude its citizens. The remarkable feature of *Satya* is its play with space and bodies to craft an urban jungle where the "spectacular global city" is completely erased. The iconic imagery of tourism photography is countered through a landscape of claustrophobic spaces, *chawls*, crowded streets, and traffic. We see neither the dance of fashion nor the glint of objects and dramatic architecture. Instead, we embark on a spatial journey that moves from private to public worlds, constructing a city of modern *ruin*.

Shots of the Bombay skyline, the boats, the sea, and the city at night are introduced right at the beginning of the film, followed by shots of cops arresting people. The soundtrack with this visual montage tells us in the "objective" voice of a documentary maker that Bombay is a city that does not sleep; it is a city where the underworld is powerful. The narrator moves from the broader context of the city and its current problems to Satya, a man whose story the film seeks to narrate. This opening suggests a link with current news and the particular relationship of crime to Bombay in recent years. Crime becomes the imaginary reference point from which to tell the story of a city, with Satya emerging as a man who belongs to the crowd of this huge metropolis.

424

Figure 12.2. Manoj Bajpayee and Chakravarthy in Ramgopal Varma's *Satya* (Truth), 1998. Photo courtesy of Ramgopal Varma's Factory.

The underworld in *Satya* is placed as a community of men, operating from different parts of the city. As the emblematic spatial symbol of the city, the street becomes a place of violent crime, with gangs seeking to make their home on the margins of the street. This is why *Satya*'s architectural mise-en-scène is so interesting. At no point in the film are we dazzled by light. The flush of commodities so intrinsic to the family films is crucially absent. We move instead through the bylanes and dark interiors of slums, half-constructed buildings with very little light, dingy rooms, street corners, parking lots, and the prison. Varma uses the steady cam creatively to navigate the decrepit landscape of the city. In one of the major chase sequences early in the film, two members of the gang on a scooter kill a film producer in his Ambassador car at close range. As they run from the police, the camera follows them moving across spaces of Bombay that look horrifyingly shabby. Crossing walls, train tracks, narrow alleys, and open drains, the camera makes sure that the location of the chase takes place in real locations and provides a fairly detailed account of the city's spatial topography (fig. 12.2).

Satya's little one-room apartment is placed next to a darkly lit corridor with clothes hanging against both walls. The shortage of indoor space forces people out into this shared corridor. All the apartments convey cramped quarters, and the camera almost always presents the busy street outside as a backdrop. These are the *chawls* in the most crowded parts of Bombay, and *Satya* attempts to make sure our eye connects the outside to the inside rather than to create a wedge between these spaces. The space from where the gang operates is located inside an empty, half-constructed building with dark alleys, wooden poles, a little table with a few phones, and old chairs strewn around. This is a space that is hidden from the public, but that exists nearly everywhere. Almost like a counterspace to the brightly lit wealthy spaces of the designed city, the ganglands interior space is bereft of all commodities.

The modus operandi of the gang is driven by a logic of survival. In the disenchanted city, it is survival and not a great desire for wealth that constitutes the heart of the gang's operation in *Satya*. This is conveyed throughout the film—from its spaces to its people and to the desires of the gang's members. Even technology is deployed for survival. Cell phones help in the chain of communication that connects all the members of the gang, inevitably playing the crucial role in either planning an assassination or planning some form of intervention. The role of technological debris is also crafted through a very conscious effort to dot the film with second-level technology. Instead of all the new cars that have flooded the market after globalization, we see aging Fiats, Ambassadors (India's eternal Oxford Morris), auto-rickshaws, and a Maruti (Suzuki) van. The car as an emblematic symbol of freedom and fantasy is deliberately undercut. Cars do not glint; their texture is not fetishized—rather, they perform the role of mundane technology and its use value. A music director threatened by the gang is shown with a harmonium instead of the giant music mixer we usually associate with contemporary music production. Satya's hesitancy about his ability to shoot is countered by the gang leader's response: "You don't need to win a competition; all you need to do is place the gun close to the head." The transportation used by the assassins is a motorbike and a rickshaw. This effort to downsize the paraphernalia within which the narrative of crime unfolds in the film becomes part of the larger context of spatial disenchantment. None of the gang members are experts at anything. What binds them together is their will to survive. Their identity and friendship is based on an association within the city. Where and how did these people get together? What is their past? How did they come to the city? The film steers clear of this kind of sociological analysis, moving instead in the direction of a psychological narrative of violence.

When a builder refuses to hand over extortion money to the gang on time, Varma stages an elaborate shootout sequence in an apartment block.

The presence of children in the enclosed playground provides a routine, everyday space of playfulness as the backdrop. The shootout here between two gangs is a speedy combination of dynamic, steady cam movement and stillness, with corridors, stairways, and railings becoming the stage for the action.[51] Like a theatrical performance, the play of bodies in this space presents a violent narrative inside an innocuous building. Instead of the car chases that inform many action films, *Satya*'s action sequences are deliberately played out as "realistic," routine," and "everyday." The action is not spectacularized through technological extravaganza; rather, the brutality of the violence becomes excruciating because of its existence within the banality of everyday routine. The theatricality that marks the ritual act of killing in action films is deliberately undercut. With a decrepit city as the backdrop, devoid of all commodities, and the conscious use of an aesthetics of decay, we are in many ways provided with a metaphor of the city as garbage dump—a metaphor that treats the bodies as unwashed, unruly, and irrational, walking through a space of abundant waste. Instead of mounting the idea of a racy "speed city," *Satya* plays out a spatial topography of slums, *chawls*, and dark alleys invoking the plebian world of violence and vernacular modernity that Hansen so skillfully recounts. Bombay in *Satya* is a disenchanted city where the gang becomes part of an everyday violence that can help them escape the boredom of their existence, the banality of their situation, and the degradation befalling each one of them. In the disenchanted city a narrative that philosophically approaches death as the climactic theatrical performance of urban violence constantly thwarts the desire for a healing touch that can help provide closure. All the protagonists, except one, die at the end of the film.

In many ways the performance of violence operates in *Satya* to draw attention to a crisis of the everyday, where random, unpredictable events challenge the mundane world of repetition. In this space the "death drive" of a community of men comes to signify both the nature of Bombay's everyday and the crisis generated within its routine. If the everyday is the realm of the routine, the mundane, the habitual, then where do we locate the terrain of unpredictability, violence, and spectacular disruption? These are questions whose answers can only be tentatively advanced through forms that can help us journey through the subjectivity and the psychological terrain that forms the core of city life. The landscape of *Satya* provides us insight into a world of despair, degradation, and violence. This is a world that cannot be quantified. It is a world that is fluid, dangerous, and shrouded in mystery. But it is a world that resides in the city both as fact and as fiction.

Notes

This article draws from my book *Bombay Cinema: An Archive of the City* (Minneapolis: University of Minnesota Press, 2007).

1. Rahul Mehrotra and Sharda Dwivedi, *Bombay: The Cities Within* (Bombay: India Book House, 1995), 309.

2. Arjun Appadurai, "Spectral Housing and Urban Cleansing: Notes on Millennial Mumbai," *Public Culture* 12, no 3 (2000): 627–51.

3. *Chawls* are dilapidated buildings with small rooms connected to a shared balcony. A *chawl* of five to seven floors can have almost a thousand people living in it.

4. Naresh Fernandes "Urban Fabric," in Kai Friese, ed., *Elsewhere: Unusual Takes on India* (New Delhi: Penguin Books: 2000), 205.

5. This was my experience when I went to interview a scriptwriter living in Andheri, Bombay.

6. For a vivid account of the middle classes' withdrawal into their comfortable, domestic world of consumption, see Kristen Ross, *Fast Cars, Clean Bodies: Decolonization and the Reordering of French Culture* MIT Press (Cambridge, Mass.: MIT Press, 1996).

7. Lynn Spiegel, "The Suburban Home Companion: Television and the Neighborhood Ideal in Postwar America," in Beatriz Colomina, ed., *Sexuality and Space*, Princeton Papers on Architecture (New York: Princeton Architectural Press, 1992), 187.

8. Ibid. Two of these magazines are *Sunset Homes for Western Living* (San Francisco: Lane Publishing) and San Francisco, *The American House Today* (New York: Reinhold Publishing).

9. Sharon Zukin, *Landscapes of Power: From Detroit to Disney World* (Berkeley: University of California Press, 1991), 16.

10. Nan Ellin, ed., *Architecture of Fear* (New York: Princeton Architectural Press, 1997), 25–26.

11. *Indianness* is being defined here as a conservative and regressive ideology that seeks to construct a national identity through religious and cultural iconography that is largely Hindu. For an interesting account of how the film industry adapts Hollywood films through "Indianization," see Tejaswini Ganti, "And Yet My Heart Is Still Indian: The Bombay Film Industry and the (H)Indianization of Hollywood," in Faye Ginsburg, Lila Abu-Lughod, and Brian Larkin, eds., *Media Worlds: Anthropology on New Terrain* (Berkeley: University of California Press, 2002), 281–300. For an account of the anxiety about the loss of "Indian" values, particularly in regard to the changing representation of women in the media after globalization, see Shohini Ghosh, "The Troubled Existence of Sex and Sexuality: Feminists Engage with Censorship," in Christiane Brosius and Melissa Butcher, eds., *Image Journeys* (Thousand Oaks, Calif.: Sage Publications, 1999, 233–59).

12. The recurring need to assert "Indianness" as a cultural value was first recognized by the advertising world. When foreign brands entered the Indian market in the 1990s, many Indian brands altered their advertising strategy to address the new situation. "Indianness" and globalization both became important to the image of the commodity. The EMW group, for instance, a powerful consumer electronics company in India, briefed its advertising agency to address both the sharp corporate value of their products and the issue of "Indianness." "Indianness" was needed, but it had to be "world class." The crucial question here is a search for an identity, a consumer identity. See William Mazzarella, *Shoveling Smoke: Advertising and Globalization in Contemporary India* (Durham, N.C.: Duke University Press, 2003), 152–59, 184. Gita Mehta is quoted by Mazzarella on 150.

13. Charles Affron and Mirella Jona Affron, *Sets in Motion: Art Direction and Film Narrative* (New Brunswick, N.J.: Rutgers University Press, 1995), 140–41.

14. Donald Albrecht, *Designing Dreams: Modern Architecture and the Movies* (New York: Harper and Row, 1986).

15. Affron and Affron, *Sets in Motion*, 146.

16. Author's interview with Sharmishtha Roy, Bombay, November 2002.

17. For a short history of Bombay's set design strategies, see Rachel Dwyer and Divia Patel, *The Visual Culture of Hindi Film* (London: Reaktion Books, 2002), 42–100.

18. Almost 30 percent of the total production money is allocated for the sets of the family films. Author's interview with Roy, November 2002.

19. India has five major film distribution territories, with Bombay as the largest. Given the scale of diversity and the vast interiors of the country, audiences are often segmented and fragmented according to what the distribution network sees as culturally and socially specific. Therefore, the "A," "B" and "C" centers have come to represent three different streams of audience composition for the distributors. "A" centers constitute the large metropolitan areas like Delhi, Bombay, Calcutta, Bangalore, Chennai, and other big cities. The "B" centers are the smaller towns, also known as the interiors, and the "C" centers are the places where a special group of films, usually low-budget semiporn films, circulate. Among the "A" centers, Bombay was always the biggest territory. But in the 1990s, the overseas market became the single largest territory. This includes the United States, United Kingdom, South Africa, and the Middle East. The Indian diaspora living abroad form the largest chunk of the overseas audience, thus pushing the film industry to respond to their tastes and desires.

20. The film *Taal* (Rhythm, 2000) made $2 million in the overseas market, which is 50 percent more than what the film earned in the domestic market.

21. Author's interview with Roy, Bombay, February 2005. South Bombay is the older part of the city known for its architecture, history and elite apartments.

22. Author's interview with Karan Johar, Bombay, November 2002.

23. Author's interview with Roy, November 2002.

24. Guy Debord, *The Society of the Spectacle* (Brooklyn, N.Y.: Zone Books, 1994), 24.

25. Hal Foster, *Design and Crime and Other Diatribes* (New York: Verso, 2002), 41, 22.

26. The Rajputs were a group of warrior clans who lived in what is now Rajasthan and Madhya Pradesh. As *Kshatriyas* (members of the warrior caste) they saw themselves as people whose divine duty was to fight. There are legendary stories of their courage on the battlefield. Under British rule, they were constituted as one of the principal "martial races." But despite their preoccupation with war, the Rajputs were known as patrons of art and architecture. Some of the finest examples of their craft are forts and palaces. Seen as a fusion architectural form that drew on many traditions, Rajput palaces are compositions built as inner citadels that are surrounded by the city. The inner walls were usually intricately carved and inlaid with mirrors. The form is mimicked and deployed to highlight the exclusivity of many five-star hotels in India.

27. Anne Friedberg, *Window Shopping: Cinema and the Postmodern* (Berkeley: University of California Press, 1993), 122.

28. Mehta is quoted in Quaied Najmi and Dnyanesh Jathar, "Don in Twilight Zone," *New Statesman*, March 12, 2001.

29. The arrest of one of the most powerful film financiers, Bharat Shah, because of his connections with the underworld has clearly established the role of gang money in film production. For information on Dawood's criminal activities, see Rajiv Sharma "D-Company Empire," *Tribune*, December 23, 2002; and Najmi and Jathar, "Don in Twilight Zone."

30. Fran Mason, *American Gangster Cinema: From "Little Caesar" to "Pulp Fiction"* (New York: Palgrave MacMillan, 2002), vii. Although the gangster genre has its antecedents in the Hollywood silent era, the classic cycle takes off with three films made after the coming of sound. In his comprehensive look at the American gangster film, Jonathan Munby suggests that the coming of sound technology and the rise of the gangster genre enabled ethnic minorities to play out their rebelliousness on screen. Clearly, the use of language and accent found their adequate articulation through the arrival of new technologies of the sound film. *Scarface, Public Enemy,* and *Little Caesar* had leading men who played bootleggers of the Prohibition era. All the characters were glorified, leading to many controversies linked to censorship. The coming of the Hollywood production code of the 1930s, which became more active after 1934, put pressure on studios to be careful and explicitly take a moral position on criminals. As many film historians have indicated, the gangster genre was one of the main targets of the production code. See Jonathan Munby, *Public Enemies, Public Heroes: Screening the Gangster from "Little Caesar" to "Touch of Evil"* (Chicago: University of Chicago Press, 1999).

31. *Dreams and Dead Ends: The American Gangster Film* (New York: Oxford University Press, 2003), 5.

32. In 1993, following the demolition of a mosque in Ayodhya, the city of Bombay was torn apart by pogroms against the large Muslim minority, instigated by the Hindu nationalist Shiv Sena party. This was followed by a bomb blast at Bombay's stock exchange, supposedly masterminded by Dawood Ibrahim. S. Hassan Zaidi, a reporter for *Midday*, a Bombay-based newspaper, wrote a book based on his investigation of the blast. The book, *Black Friday*, traces the events and the conspiracy that led up to the blast. The filmmaker Anurag Kashyap adapted the book into a film.

33. For information on Dawood's criminal activities, see Sharma, D-Company Empire"; and Najmi and Jathar, "Don in Twilight Zone."

34. Restructuring and the impact of mechanization led to a crisis in the textile industry from the 1960s onward. Technological backwardness and low capacity utilization made it difficult to run many of the mills efficiently.

35. The strike started over the issue of bonuses. Subsequently, it became the expression for a number of other grievances. The closure of several mills in the aftermath of the strike left many workers unemployed. More than one hundred thousand workers lost their jobs. Some mills were left abandoned, whereas others functioned in dilapidated condition with few workers still on the job. The mill district acquired the look of a ghost town, and workers made their way into the informal sector in a state of desperation.

36. For a critical account of the strike, see Hub Vab Wersch, "Flying a Kite and Losing the String: Communication during the Bombay Textile Strike," in Sujata Patel and Alice Thorner, eds., *Bombay: Metaphor for Modern India* (Bombay: Oxford University Press, 1995), 64–85.

37. Rajni Bakshi, *The Long Haul: The Bombay Textile Workers Strike* (Bombay: BUILD Documentation Centre 1986), 232–33.

38. See Narayan Surve's poem titled "Mumbai" in Sujata Patel and Alice Thorner, eds., *Bombay: Mosaic of Modern Culture* (Bombey: Oxford University Press, 1995), 147–50. Sayed Mirza's film *Salim Langde Pe Mat Ro* dealt with central Bombay in the poststrike period.

39. For a detailed account of the decline of the textile mills see Darryl D. Monte, *Ripping the Fabric: The Decline of Mumbai and Its Mills* (Oxford: Oxford University Press, 2002).

40. Thomas Blom Hansen, *Wages of Violence: Naming and Identity in Postcolonial Bombay* (Princeton, NJ: Princeton University Press, 2001), 164.

41. For a vivid account of the Shiv Sena, see Hansen, *Wages of Violence*. Also see Gerard Heuze, "Cultural Populism: The Appeal of the Shiv Sena," and Jayant Lele, "Saffronization of the Shiv Sena: The Political Economy of the City, State, Nation," in Patel and Thorner, *Bombay: Metaphor for Modern India*.

42. Hansen, *Wages of Violence*, 179–85; quote on 180.

43. Ibid., 180. This *dada* culture lies at the heart of the performance in the gangster films.

44. Sandeep Pendse, "Toil, Sweat and the City," in Patel and Thorner, *Bombay: Metaphor for Modern India*, 19, 14.

45. Gregory J. Seigworth, "Banality for Cultural Studies," *Cultural Studies* 14, no. 2 (2000): 234.

46. The term *Supari* has a long history in the Maratha warrior tradition. *Supari* was a term of honor that acknowledged someone as a great warrior. It is intriguing that gangland Bombay deploys a term of honor to designate the fee for contract killing. Bambayya, is a hybrid language of the street that is inflected with the resonance of multiple tongues. The bulk of the people who use this language belong to the working classes. For a longer discussion on the Bambayya language, see Ranjani Mazumdar, "The Figure of the Bombay *Tapori*: Language, Gesture and the Cinematic City," *Economic and Political Weekly* 36, no. 52. (December 29, 2001): 4872–80.

47. Author's interview with Anurag Kashyap, Bombay, March 2003.

48. Both *Midday* and the *Afternoon Dispatch* are known for their reporting on crime.

49. Varma quoted in an interview in Rediff on the Net, "Movies," October 13, 1999.

50. Author's interview with Varma, Bombay, February 2005.

51. The steady cam is a brace used to fix the camera on the shoulder of the camera person to capture speedy movements without the jerks normally associated with hand-held shots. The steady cam is usually used to film chase sequences. In fact, Ramgopal Varma was the director who first introduced the steady cam in India with his film *Shiva* (1989).

* Contributors *

Sheila Crane is Assistant Professor of the History of Art and Visual Culture at the University of California, Santa Cruz. She is currently completing a book manuscript titled "Mediterranean Crossroads: Marseille and the Remaking of Modern Architecture" and continuing a related project tracing transfers of architectural ideas and translations of built forms and meanings between Algiers and Marseille.

Belinda Davis is Associate Professor of History at Rutgers University. She is the author of *Home Fires Burning: Food, Politics, and Everyday Life in World War I Berlin* (University of North Carolina Press, 2000) and (in preparation) "The Internal Life of Politics: The New Left in West Germany, 1962–1983."

Mamadou Diouf is Charles Moody Professor of History and African American and African Studies at the University of Michigan. His primary research has focused on the colonial and postcolonial political, urban, and cultural history of Senegal and francophone west Africa. He has produced a series of journal articles, book chapters, and books, including *Histoire du Sénégal* (Maisonneuve and Larose, 2001); and *La construction de l'état au Sénégal*, with D. Cruise O'Brien and M. C. Diop (Karthala, 2002).

Philip J. Ethington is Professor of History and Political Science at the University of Southern California, and North American editor of the journal *Urban History* (Cambridge University Press). He is the author of *The Public City: The Political Construction of Urban Life in San Francisco, 1850–1900* (Cambridge University Press, 1994); and "Los Angeles and the Problem of Urban Historical Knowledge" (*American Historical Review*, 2000). He is currently completing the manuscript for a dual print and online book: "Ghost Metropolis, Los Angeles: 1542–2001."

David Frisby is Professor in Sociology and the Cities Programme at the London School of Economics. He is currently completing a major sourcebook with Iain Boyd Whyte, *Metropolis Berlin:1880–1940* (University of California Press); and a monograph, *Otto Wagner's Vienna* (University of Minnesota Press). His recent publications include *Cityscapes of Modernity* (Polity, 2001); *Georg Simmel*, rev. ed. (Routledge, 2002); and (as editor) Georg Simmel, *Philosophy of Money* 3rd enl. ed. (Routledge 2004).

Christina M. Jiménez is Assistant Professor of History at the University of Colorado, Colorado Springs. In her book manuscript "Making an Urban Public: How the City Revolutionized Citizenship in Mexico, 1880–1930," (currently in progress), and articles published in *Urban History* and the *Journal of Urban History*, Jiménez explores the dynamics of popular politics and urban citizenship in Mexico.

Dina Rizk Khoury is Associate Professor of History and International Affairs at George Washington University. She has published a book, *State and Provincial Society in the Ottoman Empire: Mosul, 1540–1834* (Cambridge University Press, 1997) and several articles on Ottoman Iraq. She is currently working on a book on war and memory in modern Iraq.

Ranjani Mazumdar is Associate Professor of Cinema Studies at the School of Arts and Aesthetics, Jawaharlal Nehru University in New Delhi and an independent filmmaker. She is the author of *Bombay Cinema: An Archive of the City* (University of Minnesota Press, 2007). Her documentaries include *Delhi Diary 2001*, on violence, memory, and the city; and *The Power of the Image* (codirected), a television series on Bombay cinema. Her current research focuses on globalization and film culture, film and history, and nonfiction film.

Frank Mort is Professor of Cultural Histories and Director of the Centre for Interdisciplinary Research in the Arts at the University of Manchester. His books include *Dangerous Sexualities: Medico-Moral Politics in England since 1830* (Routledge, 2000); and *Cultures of Consumption* (Routledge, 1996). He is currently completing a cultural history of London in the twentieth century for Yale University Press.

Martin J. Murray is Professor of Sociology at the State University of New York at Binghamton. Among other publications, he is the author of *The Revolution Deferred: The Painful Birth of Post-apartheid South Africa* (Verso, 1994); *Cities in Contemporary Africa* (Palgrave/Macmillan, 2006) (coedited with Garth Myers); *Taming the Disorderly City: Envisioning the Spatial Landscape of Johannesburg after Apartheid* (Cornell University Press, forthcoming 2007); and *City of Extremes: Spatial Politics in Johannesburg after Apartheid* (Duke University Press, forthcoming, 2007). His interests include city planning, architecture, the built environment, and spatial politics.

Jordan Sand is Associate Professor of Japanese History and Culture at Georgetown University. He is the author of *House and Home in Modern Japan: Architecture, Domestic Space, and Bourgeois Culture, 1880–1930* (Harvard University Press, 2003) and of several articles on material culture and urbanism in Japan. He is currently writing a book about Tokyo in the years of the Japanese economic bubble.

Sarah Schrank is Assistant Professor of United States Urban and Cultural History and program director of American Studies at California State University, Long Beach. She has written several articles on art and politics and is the author of *Art and the City: Los Angeles' Civic Imagination and the Politics of Modernism* (University of Pennsylvania Press, forthcoming).

Note: illustrations are indicated by an *f* following the page number.